Perspectives on Free and Open Source Software

Perspectives on Free and Open Source Software

edited by
Joseph Feller, Brian Fitzgerald, Scott A. Hissam, and Karim R. Lakhani

The MIT Press
Cambridge, Massachusetts
London, England

MIT Press books may be purchased at special quantity discounts for business or sales promotional use. For information, please e-mail special_sales@mitpress.mit.edu or write to Special Sales Department, The MIT Press, 5 Cambridge Center, Cambridge, MA 02142.

This book was set in Stone sans and Stone serif by SNP Best-set Typesetter Ltd., Hong Kong. Printed and bound in the United States of America.

Library of Congress Cataloging-in-Publication Data

Perspectives on free and open source software / edited by Joseph Feller . . . [et al.].
  p. cm.
 Includes bibliographical references and index.
 ISBN 0-262-06246-1 (alk. paper)
 1. Shareware (Computer software) 2. Open source software. 3. Computer software—Development. I. Feller, Joseph, 1972–
 QA76.76.S46P47 2005
 005.36—dc22

                                            2004064954

10 9 8 7 6 5 4 3 2 1

My love, thanks and humble apologies go to my very patient and supportive family: Carol, Caelen, Damien, and Dylan.
JF

Arís as Gaeilge: Buíochas mór le mo chlann, Máire, Pól agus Eimear. Is mór agam an iarracht a rinne sibh ar mo shon.
BF

With heartfelt warmth, I dedicate this book to my wife, Jacqueline, and my two sons, Derek and Zachery, who bring meaning to everything I do.
SAH

To Shaheen, Doulat, and Sitarah, your love makes it all possible.
A special note of thanks to Eric von Hippel for being a great mentor and a true chum.
KRL

Contents

Foreword by Michael Cusumano   xi

Acknowledgments   xv

Introduction   xvii
by Joseph Feller, Brian Fitzgerald, Scott Hissam, and Karim R. Lakhani

I │ Motivation in Free/Open Source Software Development   1

1 │ Why Hackers Do What They Do: Understanding Motivation and
Effort in Free/Open Source Software Projects   3
Karim R. Lakhani and Robert G. Wolf

2 │ Understanding Free Software Developers: Findings from the FLOSS
Study   23
Rishab Aiyer Ghosh

3 │ Economic Perspectives on Open Source   47
Josh Lerner and Jean Tirole

II │ The Evaluation of Free/Open Source Software Development   79

4 │ Standing in Front of the Open Source Steamroller   81
Robert L. Glass

5 │ Has Open Source Software a Future?   93
Brian Fitzgerald

6 │ Open Source Software Development: Future or Fad?   107
Srdjan Rusovan, Mark Lawford, and David Lorge Parnas

7 │ Attaining Robust Open Source Software   123
Peter G. Neumann

8 | Open and Closed Systems Are Equivalent (That Is, in an Ideal World)   127
Ross Anderson

9 | Making Lightning Strike Twice   143
Charles B. Weinstock and Scott A. Hissam

III | Free/Open Source Processes and Tools   161

10 | Two Case Studies of Open Source Software Development: Apache and Mozilla   163
Audris Mockus, Roy T. Fielding, and James D. Herbsleb

11 | Software Engineering Practices in the GNOME Project   211
Daniel M. German

12 | Incremental and Decentralized Integration in FreeBSD   227
Niels Jørgensen

13 | Adopting Open Source Software Engineering (OSSE) Practices by Adopting OSSE Tools   245
Jason Robbins

IV | Free/Open Source Software Economic and Business Models   265

14 | Open Source Software Projects as "User Innovation Networks"   267
Eric von Hippel

15 | An Analysis of Open Source Business Models   279
Sandeep Krishnamurthy

16 | The Allocation of Software Development Resources in Open Source Production Mode   297
Jean-Michel Dalle and Paul A. David

17 | Shared Source: The Microsoft Perspective   239
Jason Matusow

V | Law, Community, and Society   247

18 | Open Code and Open Societies   249
Lawrence Lessig

19 | Legal Aspects of Free and Open Source Software   361
David McGowan

20 | **Nonprofit Foundations and Their Role in Community-Firm Software Collaboration   393**
Siobhan O'Mahony

21 | **Free Science   415**
Christopher Kelty

22 | **High Noon at OS Corral: Duels and Shoot-Outs in Open Source Discourse   431**
Anna Maria Szczepanska, Magnus Bergquist, and Jan Ljungberg

23 | **Libre Software Policies at the European Level   447**
Phillipe Aigrain

24 | **The Open Source Paradigm Shift   461**
Tim O'Reilly

Epilogue: Open Source outside the Domain of Software   483
Clay Shirky

References   489
List of Contributors   513
Index   525

Foreword

As with other researchers and authors who study the software business and software engineering, I have had many opportunities to learn about free and open source software (FOSS). There is a lot to know, and I am especially pleased to see this volume of essays from MIT Press because it provides so much information—both quantitative and qualitative—on so many aspects of the open source movement. It will answer many questions as well as continue to inspire more research for years to come.

The research in this book is authoritative and thoughtful and offers something for everyone. For example, economists will want to know the motivations of people and companies (such as IBM or Hewlett Packard), who give freely of their time to create or improve a "public good." Not surprisingly, the research indicates that many FOSS developers are motivated both by the creative challenge as well as self-interest, such as enhancing their reputations as programmers, and then take advantage of this effect when searching for jobs. Because both for-profit and nonprofit organizations pay many programmers to work on open source projects, we find there is also some overlap between the free and open source and commercial software worlds.

Management specialists will want to know if there are business models that enable for-profit firms to take advantage of free or open source software. We learn that there are several seemingly viable commercial opportunities, even though open source, in many ways, is the ultimate commoditization of at least some parts of the software products business. The major business opportunities seem to be the hybrid approaches that make money from selling services (such as for system installation and integration, and technical support) and distributing convenient packages that include both free and open source software as well as some commercial utilities or applications. This is the strategy that Red Hat, the poster child of commercial OSS companies, has followed, and it is finally making money as a distributor and by servicing Linux users.

Social scientists are fascinated by the coordination mechanisms used in open source projects and will learn a lot about how the process works. Computer scientists and software engineers, as well as IT managers, will want to know if open source development methods produce better software than proprietary methods produce. Most of the evidence in this book suggests that the open source methods and tools resemble what we see in the commercial sector and do not themselves result in higher quality. There is good, bad, and average code in *all* software products. Not all open source programmers write neat, elegant interfaces and modules, and then carefully test as well as document their code. Moreover, how many "eyeballs" actually view an average piece of open source code? Not as many as Eric Raymond would have us believe!

After reading the diverse chapters in this book, I remain fascinated but still skeptical about how important open source actually will be in the long run and whether, as a movement, it is raising unwarranted excitement among users as well as entrepreneurs and investors. On the development side, I can sympathize with the frustration of programmers such as Richard Stallman, Linus Torvalds, or Eric Raymond in not being able to improve commercial software and thus determining to write better code that is free and available. Eric Raymond has famously described the open source style of development as similar to a "bazaar," in contrast to top-down, hierarchical design philosophies similar to how the Europeans built cathedrals in the middle ages.

We also know from the history of the mainframe industry, UNIX, and government-sponsored projects that much software has been a free "public good" since the 1950s and that open source-like collaboration has led to many innovations and improvements in software products. But, on the business side, most companies operate to make money and need some guarantee that they can make a return on investment by protecting their intellectual property. To suggest that *all* software should be free and freely available makes no sense. On the other hand, most software requires an iterative style of development, and at least some software is well suited to being written by programmers for other programmers in an open source mode. Increasing numbers of the rest of us can take advantage of this public good when "programmer products" like Linux, Apache, and Send Mail become more widely used or easier to use.

The conclusion I reach from reading this book is that the software world is diverse as well as fascinating in its contrasts. Most likely, software users will continue to see a comingling of free, open source, and proprietary software products for as far as the eye can see. Open source will force some software products companies to drop their prices or drop out of commercial viability, but other products and companies will appear. The business of selling software products will live on, along with free and open source programs. This is most likely how it will be, and it is how it should be.

Michael Cusumano
Groton and Cambridge, Massachusetts
February 2005

Acknowledgments

We would like to express our sincere thanks to Bob Prior and to the whole editorial staff at The MIT Press, for their professionalism and support throughout the process. We would also like to express our appreciation to the many contributors in this volume. This work would not have been possible without their passion for scholarship and research.

Special thanks to Lorraine Morgan and Carol Ryan for their help with preparing the manuscript.

Most of all, we are grateful to the individuals, communities, and firms that constitute the free and open source software movements. Their innovations have challenged our "common knowledge" of software engineering, of organizations and organizing, of the software industry, and of software as a component of contemporary society.

JF, BF, SAH, and KRL

Introduction

Joseph Feller, Brian Fitzgerald, Scott Hissam, and Karim R. Lakhani

What This Book Is About

Briefly stated, the terms "free software" and "open source software" refer to software products distributed under terms that allow users to:

- Use the software
- Modify the software
- Redistribute the software

in any manner they see fit, without requiring that they pay the author(s) of the software a royalty or fee for engaging in the listed activities. In general, such terms of distribution also protect what the publishing world calls the "moral right" of the software's author(s) to be identified as such. Products such as the GNU/Linux operating system, the Apache Web server, the Mozilla Web browser, the PHP programming language, and the OpenOffice productivity suite are all well-known examples of this kind of software.

More detailed, formal definitions for the terms *free* and *open source* are maintained—and vigilantly watch-dogged—by the Free Software Foundation (FSF)[1] and Open Source Initiative (OSI).[2] However, the definitions are substantively identical, and the decision to use one of these terms rather than the other is generally ideological, rather than functional; the FSF prefers the use of a term that explicitly refers to freedom, while the OSI believes that the dual meaning of the English word "free" (*gratis* or *libertas*) is confusing, and instead prefers the emphasis on the availability and modifiability of source code.[3] In Europe the French-English construct *libre software* has been widely adopted to unambiguously capture the connotation intended by the FSF.[4]

Free and open source software (F/OSS), however, is more than a set of terms of distribution. F/OSS is also—or, perhaps, primarily—a collection of tools and processes with which people create, exchange, and exploit software and knowledge in a manner which has been repeatedly called "revolutionary."

Revolutions are a lot like caterpillars—they don't grow old. Either they die young, or they undergo metamorphosis into something quite different. Successful caterpillars become butterflies and successful revolutions replace, or at least transform, the status quo. What is the status of the F/OSS revolution? Has it successfully transformed the software industry? Other industries? Governments and societies? Or, is the revolution still in "chrysalis," with the great change to come tomorrow? Or, has the revolution already died young? Or is it, perhaps, doomed to do so?

In the broadest sense, this book was written to address these questions.

Perspectives on Free and Open Source Software

"In the broadest sense" won't get you very far, though, so we'll be a bit more precise. The earliest research and analysis on F/OSS emerged from within:

• The F/OSS community itself (including the writings of Richard M. Stallman and Eric S. Raymond)
• The technology press (for example *Wired* magazine, O'Reilly and Associates)
• The software engineering research community (for example the ACM and IEEE)

It didn't take long, however, for a substantial and well-rounded literature to emerge—one addressing F/OSS as not only a software engineering phenomenon, but as psychological, philosophical, social, cultural, political, economic, and managerial phenomena as well. The bibliography of this book[5] is testament to the variety and richness of this scholarship.

We wanted this book to bring together, under one roof, provocative and exemplary research and thinking from people within a number of different academic disciplines and industrial contexts. Specifically, we've gathered together work from many of the leading F/OSS researchers and analysts and organized them into five key "perspectives" on the topic. These parts are:

Part I. Motivation in Free/Open Source Software Development
Part II. The Evaluation of Free/Open Source Software Development
Part III. Free/Open Source Software Processes and Tools
Part IV. Free/Open Source Software Economic and Business Models
Part V. Law, Community and Society

Next, we describe each of these parts, offering short summaries of the chapters and suggesting key questions that the reader might bear in mind.

Part I: Motivation in Free/Open Source Software Development

Many first-time observers of the F/OSS phenomenon are startled by the simple fact that large numbers of highly skilled software developers (and users) dedicate tremendous amounts of time and effort to the creation, expansion, and ongoing maintenance of "free" products and services. This *seemingly* irrational behavior has captured the attention of reflective F/OSS community participants and observers.

The three chapters in Part I seek to better describe and understand the motivations of individuals who participate in F/OSS activities.

Lakhani and Wolf (chapter 1) report that the largest and most significant determinant of effort (hours/week) expended on a project was an individual sense of creativity felt by the developer. They surveyed 684 developers in 287 F/OSS projects on SourceForge.net and found that more than 60 percent rated their participation in the projects as the most (or equivalent to the most) creative experience in their lives. Respondents expressed a diverse range of motivations to participate, with 58 percent of them noting user need for software (work and non-work-related) as being important. Intellectual stimulation while coding (having fun), improving programming skills, and an ideological belief that software should be free/open were also important reasons for participating in a F/OSS project. The authors' analysis of the data shows four distinct clusters (approximately equal in size) of response types:

1. Those that expressed enjoyment and learning as primary motivators
2. Those that simply need the code to satisfy non-work-related user needs
3. Those that have work-related needs and career concerns
4. Those that feel an obligation to the community and believe that software should be free/open

These findings indicate an inherent source of strength within the F/OSS community. By allowing individuals with multiple motivation types to coexist and collaborate, the F/OSS community can and does attract a wide range of participants. Individuals can join for their own idiosyncratic reasons, and the F/OSS community does not have to be overly concerned about matching motivations to incentives.

Ghosh (chapter 2) presents a study conducted for the European Union of more than 2,700 F/OSS developers, and reports that more than 53 percent of the respondents indicated "social" motivations to join and continue in the community. The single most important motivation was "to learn and develop new skills." About 31 percent of the respondents noted career and monetary concerns, 13 percent indicated political motivations, and 3 percent had product requirements. Contrary to many altruism-based explanations of participation, Ghosh reports that 55 percent of respondents note "selfish" reasons to participate; that is, they state that they take in more than they contribute. Interestingly, he finds no difference in participation levels in projects between those that are motivated by social concerns and those that are motivated by career/monetary concerns.

Ghosh's study also showed that a majority of the developers are male, and that more than 60 percent are under age 26. Surprisingly (given the nerdish stereotypes prevalent in the mainstream view of F/OSS developers), more than 58 percent of the developers indicated having "significant other" partners with a large fraction (40 percent) living with their partners. About 17 percent of the respondents also indicated having at least one child.

Finally, chapter 3 presents a modified version of Lerner and Tirole's 2002 *Journal of Industrial Economics* paper, "Some Simple Economics of Open Source," one of the most widely cited papers in the F/OSS research literature. Lerner and Tirole employ a simple economic rationale of cost and benefit in explaining why developers choose to participate in F/OSS projects. As long as benefits exceed costs, it makes rational economic sense for a developer to participate in a project. Costs to the developers are defined mainly as opportunity costs in time and effort spent participating in creating a product where they do not get a direct monetary reward for their participation. Additional costs are also borne by organizations where these developers work if they are contributing to F/OSS projects during work hours.

Lerner and Tirole propose that the net benefit of participation consists of immediate and delayed payoffs. Immediate payoffs for F/OSS participation can include meeting user needs for particular software (where working on the project actually improves performance) and the enjoyment obtained by working on a "cool" project. Delayed benefits to participation include career advancement and ego gratification. Participants are able to indicate to potential employers their superior programming skills and talents by contributing code to projects where their performance can be monitored by any interested observer. Developers may also care about their reputation within the software community, and thus contribute code to earn respect. In either case, delayed payoffs are a type of signaling incentive for potential and actual contributors to F/OSS projects.

Part II: The Evaluation of Free/Open Source Software Development

Part I asked "Why do they do it?"; Part II asks "Was it worth it?" In this section, we seek to address a wide range of issues related to evaluating the quality—security, reliability, maintainability, and so on—of both the F/OSS process and its products. Both pro- and anti-F/OSS rhetoric has too often been characterized by grandstanding and FUD[6] flinging. We are confident, then, that the chapters in this section meet some very real needs in both the academic and practitioner communities for objective, empirically grounded assessment.

Glass takes up this theme (the need for objectivity and sobriety) in chapter 4. He positions himself (with great ease and familiarity, it would seem) in front of what he calls the "steamroller" of unexamined hype. Glass raises a wide range of claims about F/OSS, regarding the talent of F/OSS community members, the security and reliability of the software, the sustainability of F/OSS economic and business models, amongst other issues. It is a provocative chapter, and we began Part II with it knowing it would wake you up and sharpen your wits. While you might not agree with all of Glass's arguments, his one overarching claim is irrefutable: if we are to understand and benefit from the F/OSS phenomenon, we cannot do so without robust research and hard evidence.

Fitzgerald (chapter 5), while not quite in front of the steamroller, is at least on the construction site. Drawing on a wide range of research and F/OSS writings, Fitzgerald articulates a number of what he calls "problematic issues," arising from software engineering, business, and sociocultural perspectives. These issues include the scarcity of developer talent (questions of motivation aside), the potentially negative effects of the modularity that characterizes many F/OSS products, the problems with "porting" the F/OSS process into sector-knowledge-intensive vertical software domains, and the churn caused by changing project (or even movement) leadership.

Rusovan, Lawford, and Parnas (chapter 6) change our tack slightly, moving away from the broader and more discursive tone of chapters 4 and 5. Instead, they focus on a single, concrete example, the findings from applying experimental software inspection techniques (Parnas 1994b) to a particular part of the TCP/IP implementation in GNU/Linux. Although they caution against resting an evaluation of the F/OSS process on a single investigation, they do assert that the Linux ARP code was revealed to be "poorly documented," the interfaces "complex," and the module needlessly reliant on "what should be internal details of other modules." Their study points importantly to the need for elegant design and effective documentation in all software, even in the wilds of the "bazaar."

Neumann (chapter 7) in many ways echoes the implied challenges of the previous chapter—arguing that F/OSS is not inherently "better" than proprietary software, but that it has the potential to be. He points to, and briefly summarizes, the dialog that emerged from the 2000 IEEE Symposium on Security and Privacy, and concludes that F/OSS presents us with the opportunity to learn from mistakes which we should have learned from years ago.

Anderson (chapter 8) elaborates considerably on the issues raised by Neumann. Anderson walks the reader through the logic and formulae which demonstrate that releasing a system as F/OSS (thus opening the source code to public scrutiny) enables an attacker to discover vulnerabilities more quickly, but it helps the defenders exactly as much. He goes on to elaborate on the various, specific situations that may cause a break in the potential symmetry between proprietary and F/OSS products. The balance "can be pushed one way or another by many things," he argues, and it is in these practical deviations from the ideal that "the interesting questions lie."

Finally, Weinstock and Hissam (chapter 9) address a wide range of perceptions and "myths" related to the F/OSS phenomenon, and present data gathered in five case studies: the AllCommerce Web store in a box, the Apache HTTP server, the Enhydra application server, NAIS (a NASA-operated Web site that switched from Oracle to MySQL), and Teardrop (a successful Internet attack affecting both F/OSS and proprietary systems). They conclude that F/OSS is a viable source of components from which to build systems, but such components should not be chosen over other sources simply because the software is free/open source. They caution adopters not to embrace F/OSS blindly, but to carefully measure the real costs and benefits involved.

Part III: Free/Open Source Software Processes and Tools

Software engineering (SE) is a very young field of study. The first computer science department (in the United States) was established in just 1962 (Rice and Rosen 2002) and it wasn't until after a NATO conference on the "software crisis" in 1968 that the term "software engineering" came into common use (Naur and Randall 1969; Bauer 1972), and the first degree program for software engineers in the United States wasn't established until 1978 at Texas Christian University.

Software engineering is more than just "coding," it is applying "a systematic, disciplined, quantifiable approach to the development, operation, and maintenance of software" (IEEE 1990); it is also the engineering of software to meet some goal, and to see that the constructed software operates over time and that it is maintained during its expected life.[7]

Such definitions of software engineering have led the way to a plethora of processes, paradigms, techniques, and methodologies, all with the goal of helping to make the process of engineering correct software repeatable and addressing the concerns raised at the 1968 NATO conference on the "software crisis," where it was recognized that software was routinely late, over budget, and simply wrong. To enumerate a list of such processes, paradigms, techniques, and methodologies here would be too arduous, but for the most part it, is generally accepted that the construction or engineering of software involves:

- Need
- Craftsman
- Compensation

In other words, some *individual or group in need* of software obtains that software product from a *programmer or group* for some amount of *compensation*. This is nothing more, really, than the law of supply and demand, which has been tested throughout human civilization. Following such law, if there is no "need," then there is no one to compensate the craftsman for their product, and hence no product. As such, nearly all defined processes for software engineering include some role for the end-user or defining-user in a software engineering process (such as requirements engineering (IEEE 1990) or "use cases" and "actors" in the Rational Unified Process (Jacobson, Booch, and Rumbaugh 1999)). Further, software engineering is concerned with the principles behind effectively organizing the team of engineers that craft the software, and also with how that craftsmanship is accomplished, in relation to:

- Designing the software (its architecture, modules, and interactions)
- Programming, or coding, the designed software
- Testing the software against design and need
- Documenting that which is designed, programmed, and tested
- Managing those that design, program, test, and document

Through the short history of rationalizing the process by which software engineering is, or should be, accomplished, the members of the SE community have reached a fairly common understanding of what software engineering is, and how software engineering should be done. It is the apparent departure of free and open source software (F/OSS) from this understanding (or belief in that understanding), combined with the success (or perceived success) of many F/OSS projects, that has attracted the attention of many in the research community. In this section, a number of authors have been selected to bring to the foreground specific observations from various F/OSS projects.

Mockus, Fielding, and Herbsleb (chapter 10) embarked on an empirical study by examining data from two major F/OSS projects (the Apache HTTP server and Mozilla) to investigate the capacity of F/OSS development practices to compete and/or displace traditional commercial development methods.[8] German (chapter 11) proposes that the actual design of the software (its architecture) is one organizing principle behind the success of the GNOME project, in that it supports open and distributed software engineering practices to be employed by a large number of geographically dispersed code contributors. German then corroborates those practices with empirical evidence from the records available for the project to measure the efficacy of those practices.

Following this, Jørgensen (chapter 12) traces the development cycle of releases of the FreeBSD operating system and presents the results of a survey of FreeBSD software developers, which was conducted to understand the advantages and disadvantages of the software engineering practices used by FreeBSD. The conclusions gleaned from his observations interestingly suggest that a strong project leader is *not* necessarily needed for a F/OSS project (such as FreeBSD) to be successful, although he proposes instead that a well-defined software engineering process is, perhaps, critical.

Finally, Robbins (chapter 13) looks at the common practices used in F/OSS software development projects and at the tools available to support many aspects of the software engineering process. He also points out where the F/OSS community is lacking in tool support for other software engineering processes.

Part IV: Free/Open Source Software Economic and Business Models

Previously, we noted that F/OSS seems to challenge many accepted software engineering norms. It also appears to depart wildly from established software business models, and indeed F/OSS companies, and hybrid proprietary-F/OSS companies have had to create new value offers predicated on software as a service, value of software use rather than value of software purchase, and so on. In this part, we present four chapters examining these new models and the changing relationships between customers and companies, and between companies and competitors.

In chapter 14, von Hippel argues that F/OSS offers extraordinary examples of the power of user innovation, independent of any manufacturing firm. He contends that markets characterized by user innovation "have a great advantage over the manufacturer-centered innovation development systems that have been the mainstay of commerce for hundreds of years" and discusses, convincingly, the parallels between the F/OSS communities and sporting communities also characterized by user innovation.

Krishnamurthy (chapter 15) discusses a series of business models that have emerged in relationship to F/OSS. He articulates the relationships that exist between producers, distributors, third parties, and consumers, and examines the impact of different licensing structures on these relationships. In chapter 16, Dalle and David present a simulation structure used to describe the decentralized, microlevel decisions that allocate programming resources both within and among F/OSS projects. They comment on the impact of reputation and community norms, and on the economic rationale for "early release" policies.

Finally, Matusow (chapter 17) presents the perspective of what has always been the archetypal proprietary software company in the eye of the F/OSS community; namely, Microsoft. In discussing the Shared Source program and related initiatives, this chapter provides interesting insights into the impact that F/OSS has had on the proprietary software industry and, perhaps, vice versa.

Part V: Law, Community, and Society

It has been said that the average Navajo Indian family in 1950s America consisted of a father, mother, two children, and three anthropologists. Many in the F/OSS community no doubt are starting to feel the same way, as what began as a software topic has attracted the efforts of so many researchers from sociology, economics, management, psychology, public policy, law, and many others. The final section of the book presents research focused on legal, cultural and social issues.

Lessig (chapter 18[9]) paints a broad picture and challenges us to think about the social implications of F/OSS and the drivers behind the phenomenon. Starting with the collapse of the Berlin Wall, he considers the move from closed to open societies. He discusses the U.S. model, where the move to having more property that is "perfectly protected" is equated with progress. For Lessig, the issue is not whether the F/OSS development model produces more reliable and efficient software; rather it is about the future of an open society drawing on F/OSS principles. Lessig focuses on the enabling power of combining a "commons" phenomenon with the concept of "property" to stimulate creativity, and also the critical differences between ideas and "real" things. Lessig also identifies the specific threats to ideas posed in cyberspace, a space that is not inherently and perpetually free but can be captured and controlled. Lessig offers a number of compelling examples of double standards where large corporate U.S. interests use the power of copyright law to prevent free communication of ideas, whereas they would presumably decry such curtailments on free communication if they occurred in other parts of the world.

As Niels Bohr once remarked about quantum physics, if it doesn't make you dizzy, then you don't understand it, and the same may hold true for F/OSS licenses. McGowan (chapter 19) deconstructs the legal issues surrounding F/OSS licensing. He presents a primer the structure of F/OSS licenses ("how they are designed to work") and a discussion on copyright, "copyleft," contract law, and other issues that affect the enforceability of licenses ("whether the licenses actually will work this way if tested"). His discussion of the Cyber Patrol hack and the Duke Nukem examples make these complex issues very concrete and accessible.

Moving from licensing to liability, O'Mahony (chapter 20) addresses the fact that as F/OSS moves more into the mainstream, the incorporation of projects as a mechanism to dilute the threat of individual legal liability becomes central. However, incorporation brings its own set of problems, in that it imposes a degree of bureaucracy that is anathema to the hacker spirit of F/OSS. O'Mahony deals directly with this conflict, an issue exacerbated by the many F/OSS developers operating on a voluntary basis with nonstandard systems of rewards and sanctions. O'Mahony identifies a number of dilemmas that have emerged as F/OSS has become more popular and the original hacker ethos and values diluted. She discusses the different incorporation models that have emerged historically and considers why they are inappropriate as organizational models for F/OSS projects. She then compares the foundations created by the Debian, Apache, GNOME, and the Linux Standards Base projects to study how different project "ecologies" approached the task of building a foundation at different points in time.

In chapter 21, Kelty elaborates on the oft-noted parallels between F/OSS and the scientific enterprise. He considers the extent to which they are similar, and also the extent to which F/OSS has (or will) become a necessary enabler of science. He focuses in particular on the social constitution of science—the doing of science, the funding of science, and the valuing of science—and draws parallels between the norms, practices, and artifacts of science and F/OSS. The chapter also considers issues related to law, thus resonating with McGowan's chapter earlier in this section. Likewise, his consideration of the threats facing science (and thus society) are reminiscent of those identified by Lessig.

The chapter by Szczepanska, Bergquist, and Ljungberg (22) illustrates the manner in which researchers can apply an ethnographic perspective to the study of F/OSS. They characterize open source as a social movement, and trace its origins in the literature on the emergence of the network society. They situate F/OSS as a countermovement in opposition to the mainstream IT culture as exemplified by companies such as IBM and Microsoft. Thus, their analysis resonates with the motivation factors identified earlier in the book. The authors use discourse analysis to analyze how the OSS community is molded and to help understand how collective identity is created and communicated. Understanding these discursive practices is especially important because of the decentralized and networked character of the OSS movement. The construction of the hacker is discussed, and the tensions between the Free Software and Open Source movements are analyzed. They further analyze "us" versus "them" constructions in the discourse of the community, and the discursive strategies of the anti-OSS constituencies. Interestingly, the rhetoric of the "American Way" is used by both pro- and anti-F/OSS communities to support their arguments. Finally, the authors consider the power relationships implied by a gift culture, and how these structure the work patterns of the F/OSS community.

Aigrain (chapter 23) who has written much on F/OSS, has drawn on his many years of experience with the European Commission to analyze their policy in relation to F/OSS. (He uses the term *libre software*.) The F/OSS phenomenon is arguably better supported by public bodies in Europe than in the United States, and European Commission support for F/OSS represents a very significant factor in the future success of F/OSS initiatives. Aigrain's analysis identifies choke-points in the EU funding bureaucracy that will deter many F/OSS practitioners, as well as important policy issues of which potential F/OSS researchers in Europe need to be cognizant. Aigrain suggests that, until recently, there was limited awareness of F/OSS issues in the Commission, but that the growing disenchantment with the dissemination and exploitation of software research funded under the traditional proprietary closed model was an important motivating factor. He also identifies as an important motivator the desire to establish an information society based on the open creation and exchange of information and knowledge. Other drivers include concerns about security, privacy, and overreliance on a small number of monopoly suppliers of proprietary software. Aigrain also acknowledges the prompting by advocacy groups such as the Free Software Foundation Europe (FSFE). He insightfully notes need for sensitive support for the F/OSS hacker community in managing the statutory reporting requirements of a funding agency such as the EU. Despite this pragmatism, over the 1999–2002 period, only seven F/OSS projects were approved, with a total budget of €5 million, representing only 0.16 percent of the overall EU IST program funding for research. Aigrain also identifies some challenges for libre software, specifically in the areas of physical computing and network infrastructure, the logical software layer, and information and contents layer.

Finally, in chapter 24, O'Reilly presents a thoughtful and informed essay on F/OSS "as an expression of three deep, long-term trends"; namely, the "commoditization of software," "network-enabled collaboration," and "software customizability (software as a service)." He argues that it is by examining next-generation applications (the killer apps of the Internet, like Google) that "we can begin to understand the true long-term significance of the open source paradigm shift." More to the point, O'Reilly asserts that if we are to benefit from "the revolution," our understanding must penetrate the "foreground elements of the free and open source movements" and instead focus on its causes and consequences.

Rigor and Relevance

We believe that academic research should be both scientifically rigorous and also highly relevant to real-life concerns. We also believe that good research answers questions, but great research creates new questions. Thus we conclude this introduction with some suggested questions for you to keep in mind as you read the book. We've grouped the question into three audience-specific lists for F/OSS project leaders and developers, managers and business professionals, and researchers and analysts. We suspect most of our readers, like most of our authors, wear more than one of these hats.

F/OSS Project Leaders and Developers

- What are the major motivations for the developers in your project?
- Is your project culture such that it can accommodate developers with different motivations to participate? Or does your project risk crowding out developers by having a culture that supports only a single motivation to participate?
- How can you manage both paid and volunteer contributors?
- On what basis do you welcome new members and how can you integrate them into your community?
- How can you best manage the "economy of talent" within your project? How can you settle disagreements and disputes? How can you avoid (destructive) churn?
- How can you manage software complexity? Integration? Testing?
- How can you break the "security symmetry" created by F/OSS?
- How are communication and collaboration facilitated in your project?
- How are changes from the F/OSS community accommodated?
- Can you automate day-to-day activities? What tools do you need to use?
- How can you leverage user innovation? How do you enable your users to contribute to the project?
- Is your project part of a commercial business model/value web? Where does your project fit in?

Managers and Business Professionals

- How can nonfinancial incentives be utilized within your firm's software projects to motivate internal developers?
- How can you spark the essence of creativity among your software developers?
- How do you build an open community of sharing and peer review within your firm?
- How does your firm interact with the wider F/OSS community? What things do you need to be aware of so that you do not drive out F/OSS developers?
- How do you leverage the increasing numbers of F/OSS developers for the benefit of your firm?
- What criteria are important in your evaluation of F/OSS products? How does your procurement process need to change to adjust to F/OSS?
- How do your implementation and change management processes need to change to adjust to F/OSS?

- In what way do your existing processes (or tools) have to adapt to support F/OSS development?
- What criteria do you need to choose a F/OSS license? Or, if you are attempting to emulate the F/OSS process without using F/OSS licensing structures, what challenges do you anticipate?
- What can your firm learn about collaboration and agility from F/OSS project organizations? What can they learn from you? (Remember, you can contribute knowledge, not just code, to the F/OSS community.)
- What business model(s) is your firm engaged in? What role do F/OSS products play in your value offer? F/OSS processes? F/OSS communities?
- How can F/OSS play a role in your firm's "corporate citizenship"?

Researchers and Analysts

- Does the F/OSS phenomenon shed new light on how creativity works in knowledge workers?
- What is it about programming that evokes a creativity response in software developers? Can this be achieved in nonsoftware environments?
- What are noneconomic incentives to innovate in complex product industries?
- How portable are F/OSS motivations and practices to other domains of economic activity and social organizations?
- How can F/OSS processes be utilized in proprietary settings, and vice versa?
- How can F/OSS tools be utilized in proprietary settings, and vice versa?
- What are the weakness of the F/OSS process and toolkit? How can these be addressed?
- What are the strengths of the F/OSS process and toolkit? How can these be leveraged?
- Do the dynamics of F/OSS create new opportunities for research (new methods for data gathering and analysis)? If so, what are the ethics involved?
- Does the F/OSS phenomenon force us to rethink the nature of innovation?
- Does the F/OSS phenomenon force us to rethink the nature of work?
- Does the F/OSS phenomenon force us to rethink the nature of knowledge sharing? Of intangible/intellectual assets?
- Is F/OSS overly reliant on a countercultural identity? How does "success" change the F/OSS process?
- What are the relationships between F/OSS and other forms of creativity and knowledge creation?

• Does F/OSS provide new modes of organizing and collaborating? What are they?

• How does F/OSS actually help address the "digital divide" and the needs of the information society?

Notes

1. http://www.gnu.org/philosophy/free-sw.html.

2. http://www.opensource.org/docs/definition.php.

3. See Feller and Fitzgerald (2002) for a fuller discussion of this. Several of the chapters in this book also address the issue, directly or indirectly.

4. You'll find all three terms (and every possible combination) used by the various authors who wrote the chapters in this book—we let people choose their own labels, rather than normalizing the book with unintentional side effects.

5. Most of the publicly available references in the bibliography of this book can be found in multiple citation management formats (EndNote, Bibtex, and so on) at http://opensource.ucc.ie. Additionally, full-text versions of many of the papers cited are also available in the research repository at http://opensource.mit.edu. We hope that these two resources will be very valuable to our readers.

6. Fear, Uncertainty, and Doubt.

7. Other definitions of software engineering include these same concepts, but go on to include economic aspects (for example, "on time" and "on budget") as well as team management aspects (SEI 2003).

8. Chapter 10 is an edited reprint of Mockus, A., Fielding, R., and Herbsleb, J.D. (2002), "Two Case Studies of Open Source Software Development: Apache and Mozilla," *ACM Transactions on Software Engineering and Methodology*, 11:3, pp. 309–346.

9. The contents of chapter 18 were originally presented by Lawrence Lessig as a keynote address on "Free Software—a Model for Society?" on June 1, 2000, in Tutzing, Germany.

I Motivation in Free/Open Source Software Development

1 Why Hackers Do What They Do: Understanding Motivation and Effort in Free/Open Source Software Projects

Karim R. Lakhani and Robert G. Wolf

"What drives Free/Open Source software (F/OSS) developers to contribute their time and effort to the creation of free software products?" is a question often posed by software industry executives, managers, and academics when they are trying to understand the relative success of the F/OSS movement. Many are puzzled by what appears to be irrational and altruistic behavior by movement participants: giving code away, revealing proprietary information, and helping strangers solve their technical problems. Understanding the motivations of F/OSS developers is an important first step in determining what is behind the success of the F/OSS development model in particular, and other forms of distributed technological innovation and development in general.

In this chapter, we report on the results of a continuing study of the effort and motivations of individuals to contributing to the creation of Free/Open Source software. We used a Web-based survey, administered to 684 software developers in 287 F/OSS projects, to learn what lies behind the effort put into such projects. Academic theorizing on individual motivations for participating in F/OSS projects has posited that external motivational factors in the form of extrinsic benefits (e.g., better jobs, career advancement) are the main drivers of effort. We find, in contrast, that enjoyment-based intrinsic motivation—namely, how creative a person feels when working on the project—is the strongest and most pervasive driver. We also find that user need, intellectual stimulation derived from writing code, and improving programming skills are top motivators for project participation. A majority of our respondents are skilled and experienced professionals working in information technology–related jobs, with approximately 40 percent being paid to participate in the F/OSS project.

The chapter is organized as follows. We review the relevant literature on motivations and then briefly describe our study design and sample characteristics. We then report our findings on payment status and effort in projects, creativity and motivations in projects, and the determinants of effort in projects. We conclude with a discussion of our findings.

Understanding Motivations of F/OSS Developers

The literature on human motivations differentiates between those that are intrinsic (the activity is valued for its own sake) and those that are extrinsic (providing indirect rewards for doing the task at hand) (Amabile 1996; Deci and Ryan 1985; Frey 1997; Ryan and Deci 2000). In this section we review the two different types of motivations and their application to developers in F/OSS projects.

Intrinsic Motivation

Following Ryan and Deci (2000, 56), "Intrinsic motivation is defined as the doing of an activity for its inherent satisfactions rather than for some separable consequence. When intrinsically motivated, a person is moved to act for the fun or challenge entailed rather than because of external prods, pressures, or rewards."[1] Central to the theory of intrinsic motivation is a human need for competence and self-determination, which are directly linked to the emotions of interest and enjoyment (Deci and Ryan 1985, 35). Intrinsic motivation can be separated into two distinct components: enjoyment-based intrinsic motivation and obligation/community-based intrinsic motivation (Lindenberg 2001). We consider each of them in the following sections.

Enjoyment-based Intrinsic Motivation   Having fun or enjoying oneself when taking part in an activity is at the core of the idea of intrinsic motivation (Deci and Ryan 1985). Csikszentmihalyi (1975) was one of the first psychologists to study the enjoyment dimension. He emphasized that some activities were pursued for the sake of the enjoyment derived from doing them. He proposed a state of "flow," in which enjoyment is maximized, characterized by intense and focused concentration; a merging of action and awareness; confidence in one's ability; and the enjoyment of the activity itself regardless of the outcome (Nakamura and Csikszentmihalyi 2003). Flow states occur when a person's skill matches the challenge of a task. There is an optimal zone of activity in which flow is maximized. A task that is beyond the skill of an individual provokes anxiety, and a task that is below the person's skill level induces boredom. Enjoyable activities are found to provide feelings of "creative discovery, a challenge overcome and a difficulty resolved" (Csikszentmihalyi 1975, 181). Popular accounts of programming in general and participation in F/OSS projects (Himanen 2001; Torvalds and Diamond 2001) in particular attest to the flow state achieved by people engaged in writing software. Thus F/OSS participants may be seeking flow states by selecting projects that match their skill levels with task difficulty, a choice that might not be available in their regular jobs.

Closely related to enjoyment-based intrinsic motivation is a sense of creativity in task accomplishment. Amabile (1996) has proposed that intrinsic motivation is a key determining factor in creativity. Amabile's definition of creativity consists of: (1) a task that is heuristic (no identifiable path to a solution) instead of algorithmic (exact solutions are known), and (2) a novel and appropriate (useful) response to the task at hand (Amabile 1996, 35). Creativity research has typically relied on normative or objective assessments of creativity with a product or process output judged creative by expert observers. Amabile (1996, 40), however, also allows for subjective, personal interpretations of creative acts. In particular, she proposes a continuum of creative acts, from low-level to high-level, where individual self-assessment can contribute to an understanding of the social factors responsible for creative output. Thus in our case, a F/OSS project dedicated to the development of a device driver for a computer operating system may not be considered terribly creative by outside observers, but may be rated as a highly creative problem-solving process by some individuals engaged in the project.

Obligation/Community-based Intrinsic Motivations Lindenberg (2001) makes the case that acting on the basis of principle is also a form of intrinsic motivation. He argues that individuals may be socialized into acting appropriately and in a manner consistent with the norms of a group. Thus the goal to act consistently within the norms of a group can trigger a normative frame of action. The obligation/community goal is strongest when private gain-seeking (gaining personal advantage at the expense of other group members) by individuals within the reference community is minimized. He also suggests that multiple motivations, both extrinsic and intrinsic, can be present at the same time. Thus a person who values making money and having fun may choose opportunities that balance economic reward (i.e., less pay) with a sense of having fun (i.e., more fun).

In F/OSS projects, we see a strong sense of community identification and adherence to norms of behavior. Participants in the F/OSS movement exhibit strong collective identities. Canonical texts like *The New Hacker's Dictionary* (Raymond 1996), *The Cathedral and the Bazaar* (Raymond 2001), and the GNU General Public License (GPL) (Stallman 1999a) have created shared meaning about the individual and collective identities of the hacker[2] culture and the responsibilities of membership within it. Indeed, the term *hacker* is a badge of honor within the F/OSS community, as opposed to its pejorative use in popular media. The hacker identity includes solving programming problems, having fun, and sharing code at the same time. Private gain-seeking within the community is minimized by adherence to software licenses like the GPL and its derivatives, which allow for user rights to source code and subsequent modification.

Extrinsic Motivation

Economists have contributed the most to our understanding of how extrinsic motivations drive human behavior. "The economic model of human behavior is based on incentives applied from outside the person considered: people change their actions because they are induced to do so by an external intervention. Economic theory thus takes extrinsic motivation to be relevant for behavior" (Frey 1997, 13).

Lerner and Tirole (2002) posit a rational calculus of cost and benefit in explaining why programmers choose to participate in F/OSS projects. As long as the benefits exceed the costs, the programmer is expected to contribute. They propose that the net benefit of participation consists of immediate and delayed payoffs. Immediate payoffs for F/OSS participation can include being paid to participate and user need for particular software (von Hippel 2001a). Although the popular image of the F/OSS movement portrays an entirely volunteer enterprise, the possibility of paid participation should not be ignored as an obvious first-order explanation of extrinsic motivations. Firms might hire programmers to participate in F/OSS projects because they are either heavy users of F/OSS-based information technology (IT) infrastructure or providers of F/OSS-based IT solutions. In either case, firms make a rational decision to hire programmers to contribute to F/OSS projects.

Another immediate benefit relates to the direct use of the software product. Research on the sources of innovation has shown that users in general and lead users in particular have strong incentives to create solutions to their particular needs (von Hippel 1988). Users have been shown to be the source of innovations in fields as diverse as scientific instruments (Riggs and von Hippel 1994), industrial products (von Hippel 1988), sports equipment (Franke and Shah 2003), and library information systems (Morrison, Roberts, and von Hippel 2000). Thus user need to solve a particular software problem may also drive participation in F/OSS projects.

Delayed benefits to participation include career advancement (job market signaling (Holmström 1999)) and improving programming skills (human capital). Participants indicate to potential employers their superior programming skills and talents by contributing code to projects where their performance can be monitored by any interested observer.[3] Similarly, firms looking for a particular skill in the labor market can easily find qualified programmers by examining code contributions within the F/OSS domain.

Participants also improve their programming skills through the active peer review that is prevalent in F/OSS projects (Moody 2001; Raymond 2001; Wayner 2000). Software code contributions are typically subject to intense peer review both before and after a submission becomes part of the official code base. Source code credit files and public e-mail archives ensure that faulty programming styles, conventions, and logic are communicated back to the original author. Peers in the project community, software users, and interested outsiders readily find faults in programming and often suggest specific changes to improve the performance of the code (von Krogh, Spaeth, and Lakhani 2003). This interactive process improves both the quality of the code submission and the overall programming skills of the participants.

Study Design and Sample Characteristics

Study Design

The sample for our survey was selected from among individuals listed as official developers on F/OSS projects hosted on the SourceForge.net F/OSS community Web site. At the start of our study period (fall 2001), SourceForge.net listed 26,245 active projects. The site requires project administrators to publicly characterize their project's development status (readiness of software code for day-to-day use) as planning, pre-alpha, alpha, beta, production/stable or mature. Projects that are in the planning or pre-alpha stage typically do not contain any source code and were eliminated from the population under study, leaving 9,973 available projects for the sample.

We conducted two separate but identical surveys over two periods. The first was targeted at alpha, beta, and production/stable projects and the second at mature projects. Because of the large number of alpha, beta and production/stable projects and the need to mitigate the effects of self-selection bias, we selected a 10 percent random sample from those projects and extracted individual e-mails from projects that listed more than one developer.[4] Those led to 1,648 specific e-mail addresses and 550 projects. The second survey's sample was selected by obtaining the e-mail addresses of all participants in mature projects that were on multiple-person teams. This procedure identified 103 projects (out of 259) with 573 unique individuals (out of 997).

We collected data through a Web-based survey. We sent personalized e-mails to each individual in our sample, inviting him or her to participate in the survey. Each person was assigned a random personal identification number (PIN) giving access to the survey. Respondents were offered the opportunity to participate in a random drawing for gift certificates upon completion of the survey.

The first survey ran from October 10 to October 30, 2001. During this time, 1,530 e-mails reached their destinations and 118 e-mails bounced back from invalid accounts. The survey generated 526 responses, a response rate of 34.3 percent. The second survey ran from April 8 to April 28, 2002. Of the 573 e-mails sent, all e-mails reached their destinations. The second survey generated 173 responses for a response rate of 30.0 percent. Close examination of the data revealed that 15 respondents had not completed a majority of the survey or had submitted the survey twice (hitting the send button more than once). They were eliminated from the analysis. Overall, the survey had 684 respondents from 287 distinct projects, for an effective response rate of 34.3 percent. The mean number of responses per project was 4.68 (standard deviation (sd) = 4.9, median = 3, range = 1–25).

Who Are the Developers?

Survey respondents were primarily male (97.5 percent) with an average age of 30 years[5] and living primarily in the developed Western world (45 percent of respondents from North America (U.S. and Canada) and 38 percent from Western Europe). Table 1.1 summarizes some of the salient characteristics of the sample and their participation in F/OSS projects.

The majority of respondents had training in IT and/or computer science, with 51 percent indicating formal university-level training in computer science and IT. Another 9 percent had on-the-job or other related IT training. Forty percent of the respondents had no formal IT training and were self taught.

Overall, 58 percent of the respondents were directly involved in the IT industry, with 45 percent of respondents working as professional pro-

Table 1.1
General characteristics of survey respondents

Variable	Obs	Mean	Std. Dev.	Min	Max
Age	677.00	29.80	7.95	14.00	56.00
Years programming	673.00	11.86	7.04	1.00	44.00
Current F/OSS projects	678.00	2.63	2.14	0.00	20.00
All F/OSS projects	652.00	4.95	4.04	1.00	20.00
Years since first contribution to F/OSS community	683.00	5.31	4.34	0.00	21.00

Table 1.2
Location and work relationship for F/OSS contributions

Is supervisor aware of work time spent on the F/OSS project?	Freq.	Percent
Yes aware	254	37.69
No, not aware	113	16.77
Do not spend time at work	307	45.55
Total	674	100.00

grammers and another 13 percent involved as systems administrators or IT managers. Students made up 19.5 percent of the sample and academic researchers 7 percent. The remaining respondents classified their occupation as "other." As indicated by table 1.1, on average the respondents had 11.8 years of computer programming experience.

Payment Status and Effort in Projects

Paid Participants
We found that a significant minority of contributors are paid to participate in F/OSS projects. When asked if they had received direct financial compensation for participation in the project, 87 percent of all respondents reported receiving no direct payments. But, as table 1.2 indicates, 55 percent contributed code during their work time. When asked: "if a work supervisor was aware of their contribution to the project during work hours," 38 percent of the sample indicated supervisor awareness (explicit or tacit consent) and 17 percent indicated shirking their official job while

working on the project. The sum of those who received direct financial compensation and those whose supervisors knew of their work on the project equals approximately 40 percent of the sample, a category we call "paid contributors." This result is consistent with the findings from other surveys targeting the F/OSS community (Hars and Ou 2002; Hertel, Niedner, and Herrmann 2003).

Effort in Projects

We measure effort as the number of hours per week spent on a project. This measure has been used in previous F/OSS studies (Hars and Ou 2002; Hertel, Niedner, and Herrmann 2003) and provides an appropriate proxy for participant contribution and interest in F/OSS projects. Survey respondents were asked how many hours in the past week they had spent working on all their current F/OSS projects in general and "this project" (the focal project about which they were asked motivation questions) in particular. Respondents said that they had, on average, spent 14.1 hours (sd = 15.7, median = 10, range 0–85 hours) on all their F/OSS projects and 7.5 hours (sd = 11.6, median = 3, range 0–75 hours) on the focal project. The distribution of hours spent was skewed, with 11 percent of respondents not reporting any hours spent on their current F/OSS projects and 25 percent reporting zero hours spent on the focal project. Table 1.3 indicates that paid contributors dedicate significantly more time (51 percent) to projects than do volunteers.

Overall, paid contributors are spending more than two working days a week and volunteer contributors are spending more than a day a week on F/OSS projects. The implied financial subsidy to projects is substantial. The

Table 1.3
Hours/week spent on F/OSS projects

	Average (sd)	Paid contributor (sd)	Volunteer (sd)	t statistic (p-value)*
Hours/week on all F/OSS projects	14.3 (15.7)	17.7 (17.9)	11.7 (13.5)	4.8 (0.00)
Hours/week on focal F/OSS project	7.5 (11.6)	10.3 (14.7)	5.7 (8.4)	4.7 (0.00)

* Two-tailed test of means assuming unequal variances
Note: n = 682.

Table 1.4
Creativity in F/OSS projects

Compared to your most creative endeavour, how creative is this project?	Freq.	Percent
Much less	55	8.16
Somewhat less	203	30.12
Equally as creative	333	49.41
Most creative	83	12.31
Total	674	100.00

2001 United States Bureau of Labor Statistics wage data[6] indicated mean hourly pay of \$30.23 for computer programmers. Thus the average weekly financial contribution to F/OSS projects is \$353.69 from volunteers and \$535.07 from paid contributors (via their employers).

Creativity and Motivation in Projects

Creativity and Flow

Respondents noted a very high sense of personal creativity in the focal projects. They were asked: "imagine a time in your life when you felt most productive, creative, or inspired. Comparing your experience on this project with the level of creativity you felt then, this project is. . . ." More than 61 percent of our survey respondents said that their participation in the focal F/OSS project was their most creative experience or was equally as creative as their most creative experience. Table 1.4 describes the response patterns. There was no statistical difference between the responses provided by paid and volunteer developers.

It may seem puzzling to nonprogrammers that software engineers feel creative as they are engaged in writing programming code. As Csikszentmihalyi (1975; 1990; 1996) has shown, however, creative tasks often cause participants to lose track of time and make them willing to devote additional hours to the task, a psychological state he calls "flow." It appears that our respondents may experience flow while engaged in programming. Table 1.5 indicates that 73 percent of the respondents lose track of time "always" or "frequently" when they are programming and more than 60 percent said that they would "always" or "frequently" dedicate one additional hour to programming ("if there were one more hour in the day").

Table 1.5
"Flow" experienced while programming

Ratings on "flow" variables	How likely to lose track of time when programming (%)	How likely to devote extra hour in the day to programming (%)
Always	21.39	12.92
Frequently	51.33	47.14
Sometimes	22.27	34.51
Rarely	4.28	4.11
Never	0.74	1.32
Total	100	100

Note: $n = 682$.

Again, there was no significant statistical difference between the answers provided by volunteers and paid contributors.

Motivations to Contribute

Table 1.6 provides a ratings breakdown of the motivations to contribute to the focal F/OSS project. Respondents were asked to select up to three statements (the table shows the exact wording used in the survey) that best reflected their reasons for participating and contributing to "this" project. As discussed in the literature review, motivations can be put into three major categories: (1) enjoyment-based intrinsic motivations, (2) obligation/community-based intrinsic motivations, and (3) extrinsic motivations. We find evidence for all three types of motivations in F/OSS projects.

User needs for the software, both work- and nonwork-related, together constitute the overwhelming reason for contribution and participation (von Hippel 1988; 2001a; 2002; 2005), with more than 58 percent of participants citing them as important. But, since we asked separate questions about work- and nonwork-related user needs, we also report that 33.8 percent of participants indicated work-related need and 29.7 percent participants indicated nonwork-related need as a motive for participation. Less than 5% of respondents rated both types of user needs as important.[7]

The top single reason to contribute to projects is based on enjoyment-related intrinsic motivation: "Project code is intellectually stimulating to write" (44.9 percent). This result is consistent with our previous findings regarding creativity and flow in projects. Improving programming skills, an extrinsic motivation related to human capital improvement, was a

Table 1.6
Motivations to contribute to F/OSS projects

Motivation	Percentage of respondents indicating up to three statements that best reflect their reasons to contribute	Percentage of volunteer contributors	Percentage of paid contributor	Significant difference (t statistic/p value)
Enjoyment-based intrinsic motivation				
Code for project is intellectually stimulating to write	44.9	46.1	43.1	n.s.
Economic/extrinsic-based motivations				
Improve programming skills	41.3	45.8	33.2	3.56 (p = 0.0004)
Code needed for user need (work and/or nonwork)*	58.7	—	—	—
Work need only	33.8	19.3	55.7	10.53 (p = 0.0000)
Nonwork need	29.7	37.0	18.9	5.16 (p = 0.0000)
Enhance professional status	17.5	13.9	22.8	3.01 (p = 0.0000)
Obligation/community-based intrinsic motivations				
Believe that source code should be open	33.1	34.8	30.6	n.s.
Feel personal obligation to contribute because use F/OSS	28.6	29.6	26.9	n.s.

Table 1.6
(continued)

Like working with this development team	20.3	21.5	18.5	n.s.
Dislike proprietary software and want to defeat them	11.3	11.5	11.1	n.s.
Enhance reputation in F/OSS community	11.0	12.0	9.5	n.s.

Notes: Aggregation of responses that indicated needing software for work and/or nonwork-related need. Not an actual survey question. Overlap in user needs limited to 4.9 percent of sample.

n.s. = not significant, $n = 679$.

close second, with 41.8 percent of participants saying it was an important motivator.

Approximately one-third of our sample indicated that the belief that "source code should be open," an obligation/community motivation, was an important reason for their participation. Nearly as many respondents indicated that they contributed because they felt a sense of obligation to give something back to the F/OSS community in return for the software tools it provides (28.6 percent). Approximately 20 percent of the sample indicated that working with the project team was also a motivate for their contribution. Motivations commonly cited elsewhere, like community reputation, professional status, and defeating proprietary software companies (Raymond 2001; Lerner and Tirole 2002), were ranked relatively low.

Another source of an obligation/community motivation is the level of identification felt with the hacker community. Self-identification with the hacker community and ethic drive participation in projects. Respondents to our survey indicated a strong sense of group identification, with 42 percent indicating that they "strongly agree" and another 41 percent "somewhat agree" that the hacker community is a primary source of their identity.[8] Nine percent of the respondents were neutral and 8 percent were somewhat to strongly negative about the hacker affiliation.[9]

Table 1.6 also indicates significant differences in motivations between paid contributors and volunteers. The differences between the two groups are consistent with the roles and requirements of the two types of F/OSS participants. Paid contributors are strongly motivated by work-related user need (55.7 percent) and value professional status (22.8 percent) more than volunteers. On the other hand, volunteers are more likely to participate because they are trying to improve their skills (45.8 percent) or need the software for nonwork purposes (37%).

To better understand the motives behind participation in the F/OSS community, and the reason that no one motivation, on its own, had more than 50% importance, we decided to do an exploratory cluster analysis to see whether there were any natural groupings of individuals by motivation type. We used k-means cluster analysis, with random seeding. The four-cluster solution provided the best balance of cluster size, motivational aggregation, stability, and consistency and is presented in table 1.7. The motivations that came out highest in each cluster have been highlighted.

Cluster membership can be explained by examining the motivation categories that scored the highest in each cluster. Cluster 3 (29 percent of the

Table 1.7
Cluster results based on motivations and paid status

Motivations	Cluster 1 (%)	Cluster 2 (%)	Cluster 3 (%)	Cluster 4 (%)
Work need	**91**	8	12	28
Nonwork need	11	**100**	0	2
Intellectually stimulating	41	45	**69**	12
Improves skill	20	43	**72**	19
Work with team	17	16	**28**	19
Code should be open	12	22	42	**64**
Beat proprietary software	11	8	9	**19**
Community reputation	**14**	8	11	13
Professional status	**25**	6	22	18
Obligation from use	23	20	6	**83**
Paid for contribution	**86**	18	26	32
Total percentage of sample in each cluster	25	27	29	19

Note: $n = 679$.

sample) consists of individuals who contribute to F/OSS projects to improve their programming skills and for intellectual stimulation. None of the members of this cluster noted nonwork-related need for the project and very few, 12 percent, indicated work-related need for the code. Members of this group indicated an affinity for learning new skills and having fun in the process. The actual end product does not appear to be a large concern; both enjoyment-based intrinsic motivation and career-based extrinsic motivation are important to this group.

All members of cluster 2 (27 percent of the sample) indicate that nonwork-related need for the code is an important motive for their participation. The primary driver for this group is extrinsic user need. Similarly, cluster 1 (25 percent of the sample) represents individuals who are motivated by work-related need with a vast majority (86 percent) paid for their contributions to F/OSS projects. This cluster can also be thought of as composed of people with extrinsic motivations. Cluster 4 (19 percent of the sample) consists of people motivated primarily by obligation/community-based intrinsic motivations. A majority of this cluster report group-identity-centric motivations derived from a sense of obligation to the community and a normative belief that code should be open.

The cluster analysis clearly indicates that the F/OSS community is heterogeneous in motives to participate and contribute. Individuals join for a variety of reasons, and no one reason tends to dominate the community or to cause people to make distinct choices in beliefs. These findings are consistent with collective action research, where group heterogeneity is considered an important trait of successful social movements (Marwell and Oliver 1993).

Determinants of Effort

Our findings so far have confirmed the presence of all three types of motivations, with no clear and obvious determinants of effort. We do note that paid contributors work more hours than volunteers. Given that there were not that many significant differences in motivations between paid and volunteer contributors, though, we are left with an open question regarding the effect the types of motivation (intrinsic vs. extrinsic) on effort in projects. To address the question, we ran an ordinary least squares (OLS) regression on the log of hours/week[10] dedicated to the focal project.

Table 1.8 presents the standardized[11] values of the coefficients of significant variables in the final regression. A personal sense of creativity with a F/OSS project has the largest positive impact on hours per week. Being

Table 1.8
Significant variables in regression of log (project hours/week) and motivations

Variable	Standardized coefficient	t-statistic (p-value)
Creative project experience	1.6	6.00 (0.000)
Paid status	0.88	3.12 (0.002)
Like team	0.84	2.76 (0.004)
Enhance community reputation	0.56	2.00 (0.046)
Differential hours	−1.6	−6.00 (0.000)
IT training	−0.6	−2.28 (0.023)

Note: r-Square = 0.18, n = 630.

paid to write code and liking the team have significant positive effects that are approximately half the weight of a sense of creativity. Caring about reputation in the F/OSS community has about one-third the impact as feeling creative with a project. Number of hours dedicated to other F/OSS projects has a negative impact equal to that of creativity on the current project. We can see that various F/OSS projects compete for time, and that distractions from other projects can reduce the hours spent on the focal project. Having formal IT training also reduces the number of hours spent on a project.

As mentioned in the literature review, proponents of intrinsic motivation theories have assembled an impressive array of experimental evidence to demonstrate that extrinsic rewards have a negative impact on intrinsic motivations. An obvious test in our study is to examine the impact of the interaction between being paid and feeling creative on the number of hours per week dedicated to a project. Regression analysis showed that there was no significant impact on the hours per week dedicated due to the interaction of being paid and feeling creative. Hours per week dedicated to a project did not decline, given that those who are paid to contribute code also feel creative about that project.

Researchers engaged in studying creativity have traditionally used third-party assessments of innovative output as measures of creativity. Thus our finding that a sense of personal creativity is the biggest determinant of effort in F/OSS projects may be due to the inherent innovative nature of the project itself and not to personal feelings of creativity. Since we have multiple responses from many projects, we can test whether the creativity felt is endogenous to the project or to the individual. Results from a fixed-effects regression (Greene 2000) showed that a personal sense of creativity in a project is still positive and significant, indicating that the sense of creativity is endogenous and heterogeneous to the people within projects.

Discussion

The most important findings in our study relate to both the extent and impact of the personal sense of creativity developers feel with regard to their F/OSS projects. A clear majority (more than 61 percent) stated that their focal F/OSS project was at least as creative as anything they had done in their lives (including other F/OSS projects they might have engaged in). This finding is bolstered by the willingness of a majority of survey participants to dedicate additional hours to programming, and, consistent with attaining a state of flow, frequently losing track of time while coding. These observations are reinforced by the similar importance of these creativity-related factors for both volunteer and paid contributors.

The importance of the sense of creativity in projects is underscored by examination of the drivers of effort in F/OSS projects. The only significant determinants of hours per week dedicated to projects were (in order of magnitude of impact):

• Enjoyment-related intrinsic motivations in the form of a sense of creativity
• Extrinsic motivations in form of payment
• Obligation/community-related intrinsic motivations

Furthermore, contrary to experimental findings on the negative impact of extrinsic rewards on intrinsic motivations (Deci, Koestner, and Ryan 1999), we find that being paid and feeling creative about F/OSS projects does not have a significant negative impact on project effort.

Therefore, work on the F/OSS projects can be summarized as a creative exercise leading to useful output, where the creativity is a lead driver of individual effort.

Programming has been regarded as a pure production activity typified as requiring payments and career incentives to induce effort. We believe that this is a limited view. At least as applied to hackers on F/OSS projects, activity should be regarded as a form of joint production–consumption that provides a positive psychological outlet for the participants as well as useful output.

Another central issue in F/OSS research has been the motivations of developers to participate and contribute to the creation of a public good.

The effort expended is substantial. Individuals contribute an average of 14 hours per week. But there is no single dominant explanation for an individual software developer's decision to participate in and contribute to a F/OSS project. Instead, we have observed an interplay between extrinsic and intrinsic motivations: neither dominates or destroys the efficacy of the other. It may be that the autonomy afforded project participants in the choice of projects and roles one might play has "internalized" extrinsic motivations.

Therefore, an individual's motivation containing aspects of both extrinsic and intrinsic is not anomalous. We have observed clusters of individuals motivated by extrinsic, intrinsic, or hybrid extrinsic/intrinsic factors. Dominant motives do not crowd out or spoil others. It is consistent for someone paid to participate in the F/OSS movement to be moved by the political goals of free software and open code.

Other issues merit further investigation. The presence of paid participants—40 percent of our study sample—indicates that both IT-producing and IT-using firms are becoming important resources for the F/OSS community. The contribution of firms to the creation of a public good raises questions about incentives to innovate and share innovations with potential competitors. In addition, the interaction between paid and volunteer participants within a project raises questions about the boundaries of the firm and appropriate collaboration policies.

In conclusion, our study has advanced our understanding of the motivational factors behind the success of the F/OSS community. We note that the F/OSS community does not require any one type of motivation for participation. It is a "big tent." Its contributors are motivated by a combination of intrinsic and extrinsic factors with a personal sense of creativity being an important source of effort.

Notes

We would like to thank the developers on the SourceForge.net F/OSS projects for being so generous with their time while answering our survey. We would also like to thank the following colleagues for their helpful comments and feedback during the early versions of this chapter: Jeff Bates, Jim Bessen, Paul Carlile, Jonathon Cummings, Joao Cunha, Chris DiBona, Jesper Sorensen, and Eric von Hippel. The following colleagues at BCG were extremely helpful during the study: Mark Blaxill, Emily Case, Philip Evans and Kelly Gittlein. Mistakes and errors remain ours.

1. The subject of intrinsic motivation has been well studied in psychology; for reviews see Deci, Koestner, and Ryan (1999) and Lindenberg (2001).

2. *Hacker* as in *The New Hacker's Dictionary* (Raymond 1996): "hacker: n. [originally, someone who makes furniture with an axe] 1. A person who enjoys exploring the details of programmable systems and how to stretch their capabilities, as opposed to most users, who prefer to learn only the minimum necessary. 2. One who programs enthusiastically (even obsessively) or who enjoys programming rather than just theorizing about programming. 3. A person capable of appreciating hack value. 4. A person who is good at programming quickly. 5. An expert at a particular program, or one who frequently does work using it or on it; as in "a Unix hacker." (Definitions 1 through 5 are correlated, and people who fit them congregate.) 6. An expert or enthusiast of any kind. One might be an astronomy hacker, for example. 7. One who enjoys the intellectual challenge of creatively overcoming or circumventing limitations. 8. [deprecated] A malicious meddler who tries to discover sensitive information by poking around. Hence "password hacker," "network hacker." The correct term for this sense is *cracker*.

3. The widespread archiving of all F/OSS project-related materials like e-mail lists and code commits enables a detailed assessment of individual performance.

4. The "greater than one developer" criteria was used to ensure selection of projects that were not "pet" software projects parked on SourceForge.net, but rather projects that involved some level of coordination with other members.

5. At time of study.

6. Available at http://www.bls.gov/oes/2001/oes_15Co.htm, accessed April 2, 2003.

7. A detailed examination of the difference in project types between those that stated work-related needs and those that stated nonwork-related needs showed that there was no technical difference between them. A majority of the projects that were described as nonwork were of sufficient technical scope and applicability that firms also produced similar proprietary versions. We therefore see a blurring of distinction in the software produced for work and nonwork purposes. The general-purpose nature of computing and software creates conditions such that a similar user need can be high in both work and nonwork settings.

8. Respondents were given the definition of "hacker" in note 2 when asked the question about identity.

9. The results were identical when controlled for paid contributor status on a project.

10. We chose to use the log of project hours/week because of the skewness in the reported data. A log transformation allows us to better represent the effects of small changes in the data at the lower values of project hours/week. It is safe to argue that there is a significant difference between 4 versus 8 project hours/week and 25 versus 29 project hours/week. The magnitude of the effort expended is much greater at the

lower values of the measure and the log transformation allows us to capture this shift. Since the log of zero is undefined, all zero values were transformed to 0.00005, giving us the desired impact for a very small and insignificant value.

11. Standardizing the variables to allows us to make comparison across all motivation factors, since the original variables had different underlying values. All variables in the regression were transformed so that the mean = 0 and the variance = 1.

| Understanding Free Software Developers: Findings from the FLOSS Study

Rishab Aiyer Ghosh

This chapter presents an overview of findings from the Survey of Developers from the FLOSS (Free/Libre/Open Source Software) project, involving over 2,700 respondents from among free/open source software developers worldwide. The survey studied several factors influencing developers' participation within the free/open source community, including their perceptions of differences within the community and with the commercial software world; personal, ethical, political, and economic motives for participation; and their degree of interaction within and contribution to the free/open source software community. These results are linked to preliminary findings from a study of developer contribution to the Linux kernel based on an analysis of the source code.

The Need for Empirical Data

The phenomenon of Free/Libre/Open Source Software[1]—the development of software through collaborative, informal networks of professional or amateur programmers, and the networked distribution making it available to developers and end-users free of charge—has been widely and well documented. Editorials and policy papers have been written on the impact of the free software movement on the computer industry, business in general and the economy at large. However, few models have been developed that successfully describe, with supporting data, why or how the system works, or that explain the functioning of collaborative, productive networks without primary dependence on money.

The common speculation regarding the monetary worth of such collaborative development has translated into widely fluctuating share prices for the companies that have devoted much of their business plans to the free software philosophy. But hard data on the monetary value generated by this phenomenon is almost nonexistent. Indeed, hard data on *any* aspect of the FLOSS phenomenon is rare. One reason for this lack of empirical data might be that in a very short period of time, this phenomenon has attracted a lot of research attention. Researchers and practitioners have tended to be quick to state that open source is (or is not) a revolutionary "new" form of something—programming, economic production, or social interaction. These explanations have generally been based on anecdotal evidence or very small sample data, which doesn't make them wrong—just hypothetical.[2]

Given that most models and techniques for economic evaluation and measurement require the use of money, nonmonetary economic activity, such as the creation and distribution free software, is left unmeasured, at least in any usefully quantifiable sense. Although there are studies and models for quantitative analysis of nonpriced goods (e.g., the measurement of knowledge), in an economy they tend to be useful primarily in judging the influence of such goods within organizations, markets, or other socioeconomic structures for which the common forms of measurement are clearly dominated by monetary indicators. Measurement is far more complex and ambiguous in a context where the essential and primary economic activity—the generation of free software through collaborative networks—is unusual in its avoidance of the use of money as mode of exchange.

The lack of empirical data is not surprising, though—it is extremely hard to collect, for several reasons. First, without monetary measures, other indicators of developers' activity have to be used (indeed, defined in order to be used). While there may be some quantitative indicators that are objective in nature,[3] the lack of objective "census-type" sources means that many indicators, quantitative or qualitative, may require the use of surveys.

Who Can We Survey?

This leads to an immediate problem: there is no universal, clearly recognized, objective data on the population to be surveyed. While seemingly obvious, it bears emphasizing that there is no clear definition of a free software developer (other than "someone who writes free software code"); there is no universal list of all developers; there is no accurate information on the number of developers in existence or the growth in this number.[4] There is no census or national accounts database that lists the distribution of developers by country of residence, age, income level, or language.

The lack of a basic data set on the universal population, something that is taken for granted in surveys of many other groups, is unavailable for

FLOSS software developers, with the result that attempts to fill in gaps in empirical factual data through surveys require a choice from among three types of surveys:

1. Survey responses that might be indicative of the general population, but provide reliable data only on the actual respondents.
2. Survey responses that reflect a predefined subset of the general population, providing insights into that subset, but certain responses might be a consequence of the predefinition (preselection) process and thus not reflect the general population.
3. Survey respondents are drawn randomly from the general population; thus, while responses reflect the general population as a whole, they might not be representative of the general population for certain (especially demographic) criteria.

For completeness, the fourth option, which is ideal but unavailable, is also listed:

4. Survey respondents are drawn from the general population in order to be representative of the general population for certain criteria; for example, age or nationality, thus leading to responses that reflect the general population and also follow the distribution (based on the representation criteria) of the general population.

The BCG/OSDN survey (Boston Consulting Group 2002) is an example of the second approach. By prescreening respondents and inviting their response by e-mail, it clearly defined the subset of the general population from which the sample was drawn. As such, responses can be representative of the pre-screened subpopulation, and even weighted in order to truly reflect the defined population subset. However, the results say little about the general population beyond the defined subset, as it was not sampled at all. Indeed, some results, such as nationality, years of experience, or political attitudes might result from the preselection criteria,[5] and though these results provide interesting detail on the sub-population, they cannot be generalized to apply to the universal free software developer.

For the FLOSS developer survey, we chose the third option.

Secondary Sources
Empirical data on FLOSS developers is not only difficult to collect, but once collected might also be somewhat unreliable. This is perhaps a reason to try to find secondary sources to match subjective empirical data, and methods of validating them—it also provides a handy excuse for papers that do not cite empirical data!

Such secondary sources include not just objective data resulting from analysis of source code,[6] but also more conventionally reliable surveys of, for instance, institutions that use free software. Such surveys can be conducted in an orthodox fashion, using industrial databases or public census records to build stratified representative samples, as was done in the FLOSS Survey of User Organisations.[7] Institutional surveys are immensely useful in themselves, to study the large-scale use of free software, but they can also provide data on organizations' relationships with developers that, with some "triangulation," can corroborate the results of developer surveys.

Models and Hypotheses

The FLOSS developer survey aimed to gather data that would support (or refute) the several anecdote-based models of FLOSS development that exist. Broadly, hypothetical models of free software developers attempt to interpret the motives of developers, determine the structure of their interaction, and predict their resulting individual and collective behaviour. (Some models are less concerned about precise motives; Ghosh (1998a) only claims that altruism is not a significant motive, and Benkler (2002) argues that specific modes of organization, rather than motives, are important.)

Our survey was designed to test the assumptions made by many models and to collect a set of data points that could be used to validate or improve such models.

Assumed Motivations

Are developers rational, and if so, are they altruistic, or self-interested? Are they driven by a profit motive, and if so, is it monetary or non-monetary? Do they want to become famous? Are they writing free software to signal their programming proficiency in the job market? Or do they just want to fix a problem for their own use? Are they mainly interested in having fun? Is programming artistic self-expression? Or is it self-development, a distributed university? Or is it a community experience, where the pleasure is in giving to others? Are developers politically driven, wanting to destroy large software companies or the notion of proprietary software and intellectual "property"?

Most models of FLOSS development assume one or another of these motives as the key driver. In fact, it turns out, the truth is all of the above, combined in different proportions for different people. The survey questionnaire had several questions dealing with motivation, some of them with overlapping responses; people don't always think consciously about their motives, and repetition and different phrasing help draw out more data and add perspective.

Assumed Organization

When any group of individuals interacts, the structure of their interaction is a strong determinant of their effectiveness and output. Organizational structure may be a result of the motives of individual participants; it may also prompt or create certain motives. For example, in a strictly hierarchical organization, getting to the top may be an important motive; in a flat organization, being at the top may have fewer benefits and thus be less motivating.

Organizational structure is a predictor of behavior, though, and many models of free software development use an assumed organizational structure in order to predict behavior. Benkler's (2002) "peer production" depends fundamentally on structural assumptions; Lerner and Tirole's "Simple Economics" (chap. 3, this volume) does not directly depend on a certain organizational structure in FLOSS developer communities, but requires that the structure facilitate the spread of reputation (as signaling) within the community and to the employment market (thus also assuming a meta-structure linking the FLOSS community to the priced economy directly via the job market). The "cooking-pot" model and the "bazaar" (Raymond 2001), though, are more tolerant of different organizational structures.

In the context of free software developer communities, one could classify organizational structure on the axes of hierarchy, modularity, and connectivity (see table 2.1). Here, *modular/integrated* refers to the extremes in the integrated nature of the production, while *connectivity* refers to the integrated nature of the interaction (or social links, which might or might not lead to integrated products), so this is not just the organizational structure of a community, but of a *productive* community. Of course the examples given in each box are somewhat arbitrary, as not all boxes can be reasonably filled in and retain relevance to the context of FLOSS development.

Organizational structure can be determined to some extent (and even objectively) by analyzing source code, which allows the measurement of modularity, but also the degree of connectivity and even hierarchy (using concentration of contribution as a proxy) through the identification of authors and clusters of authorship.[8]

Table 2.1
A classification of organizational structures

	Modular, connected	Integrated, connected	Modular, nonconnected	Integrated, nonconnected
Hierarchy	Cabal/inner circle (bazaar), "Simple Economics" (signaling)	Commercial (cathedral)	Benevolent Dictator (bazaar)	Commercial
Flat	"Peer production" with reputation, "Cooking-pot market"	"Hive mind"	"Peer production" (bazaar)	?

Otherwise, determining organizational structure empirically on a large scale is hard.[9] Through a developer survey, it can be estimated by asking about the number of projects a developer participates in, degree of collaboration with other developers, and leadership positions.

Assumed Behavior

Behavior, individual or collected, is what models aim to predict, so empirical data plays a valuable role here in testing the validity of models. Most such data is likely to result from objective studies of developer communities, such as the dynamic study of the developers and components of the Linux kernel in the LICKS project.[10] From developer surveys, especially if conducted repeatedly over time, it would be possible to determine whether certain types of behaviour occur as predicted by models, or indeed as predicted by developers' own responses to other questions.

This is useful in order to validate the strength of reported motivations; for example, it is harder to believe those who claim money is not a motivation if they also report high earnings from their FLOSS software. At the very least, one might expect (from the point of view of consistency) that developer's motives change over time based on the rewards (or lack thereof) they receive through their efforts. Indeed the FLOSS developer survey attempts to measure this dynamic aspect of motivation by asking what motivated developers when they first joined the community, in addition to their motivations for continuing participation. As both questions are asked at the same time, this response relies on developers' memory.

Other measurable aspects of behavior relate to developers' planned future actions (as reported); for instance, with relation to the job market. Later sections elaborate on this topic through the lens of the FLOSS survey.

Conducting the FLOSS Developer Survey

Methodology and Sampling

Early in the design of the FLOSS survey methodology, we faced the question of whether it is possible to survey a representative sample of developers. The question actually has two parts: is it possible to ensure that respondents are developers, and is it possible to identify a sample that is representative of developers based on some filtering criteria? We'll address take the second question first.

Our conclusion, as described previously, was that there is insufficient empirical data on FLOSS software developers to identify the criteria of sampling. However, without empirical data as a basis, it is not possible to demonstrate that a chosen sample of respondents is representative of developers in general: that is, it is impossible to sample developers and know with any confidence that the distribution of nationalities, age, or income levels is representative of the distribution in the total (unsampled) population of developers.

Therefore, we decided that in order to have results with empirical validity for the universal population of developers; we would have to attempt a random sample. The survey was self-distributing that is, it was posted to various developer forums, and then reposted by developers to other forums, many of which are listed in the FLOSS survey report's (http://flossproject.org/) Web site. The survey announcement was translated into various languages in order to correct possible biases inherent in an English-language survey announced only on English-language websites.[11] We can state confidently that the survey was seen by a very large percentage of all developers (it was announced on Slashdot, among other places) and therefore the sample that chose to respond was random, though with some identifiable bias (including, as with any voluntary survey, self-selection).

Having drawn a random sample, we had to ensure that we were indeed drawing a sample of actual developers. We were able to do so through the validation process described in the following section.

Response Rate and Validation

One of the requirements of open, online questionnaires is verifying that the respondents really belong to the group that is under scrutiny. The survey definition of the universal developer population is "everyone who has contributed source code to a free/libre/open source software package." Our respondents belong to this population as follows:[12]

• We asked respondents to provide complete or partial e-mail addresses for validation purposes.
• We matched these e-mail addresses to names or e-mail addresses found in the source code analysis (see Ghosh et al. 2002, part V) or matching them to sources on Internet archives.
• This subsample of 487 respondents individually identified as certain developers were compared to the rest of the respondents by statistically comparing their responses. This process involved a comparison of means and standard deviations of the two groups (known developers and other respondents) with regard to a selection of variables of our data set. The result showed very little statistical difference. In the very few responses where minor differences existed, we found that the group of verified FLOSS developers consisted of slightly more active and professionally experienced persons.

The FLOSS developer survey received 2,774 responses. Due to the page-wise design of the questionnaire, where responses to the first page were recorded even as the next page of questions were presented, this figure represents the respondents who answered the first set of questions, while there were 2,280 responses to the entire questionnaire.

What Do We Know Now?

Demographics: Married with Children?
A presentation of demographics is usually the starting point for an analysis of any survey. For the reasons given earlier, the FLOSS methodology does not provide a sampling that is representative of developer demographics, especially of the geographic distribution of developers. (A comparison of geographical data from different developer surveys, as well as much else that this chapter draws on, is in Ghosh et al. 2003.) It is possible to discuss other features of developer demographics, though, for which the FLOSS survey is likely to be more representative, such as age, gender, and civil status (which we presume have a similar distribution across different nationalities).

Almost all (98.8 percent) of respondents to the FLOSS developer survey are male. This is similar to the 98.6 percent reported as male in the WIDI survey (from a much larger sample size, of nearly 6,000; see Robles-

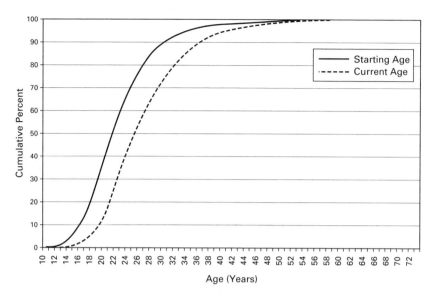

Figure 2.1
Current and starting age of developers (© 2002 International Institute of Infonomics, FLOSS developer survey)

Martínez et al. 2001) and 98 percent reported as male in the BCG survey (chap. 1, this volume). It should be noted that the surveys probably underrepresent female developers. As self-selecting surveys, they are dependent on developers who chose to respond to the survey itself, and to the specific question on gender. However, given the degree of coincidence on this point across three quite different surveys, it would seem unlikely that female participation in the FLOSS developer community is much higher than 5–7 percent.

The FLOSS survey showed developers are quite young, with more than 60 percent between the ages of 16 and 25. Figure 2.1 shows the cumulative percentage for developers' age when they first started free software development, compared with developers' current age. Because we asked when respondents first started development and their age at that time, we were able to calculate two age points for each developer as well as identify the peak year for the start of development—2000 (the survey was carried out in early 2002).

Despite the apparent youth of developers, as figure 2.2 shows, single developers are in a minority (albeit a large one, 41.4 percent) and about the same as the surprisingly large fraction (39.9 percent) who live together

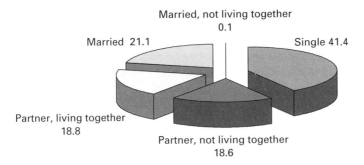

Figure 2.2
Civil status of developers

with a partner or spouse. Again, going against the nerdish stereotype, 17 percent of developers reported having children. Half of those have one child. There is a correlation between having children (or even being married) and having a stronger career-oriented participation in development. Most children were reported to be under two years of age at the time of the survey. One might thus wonder whether as the free software baby boom coincided with the dot-com peak, developers saw their earning possibilities soar and took on financial and familial responsibilities.

Motivation

The FLOSS survey addressed the complex issue of what motivates developers to contribute to the community in a series of multidimensional questions. This aspect in particular is elaborated in much detail in Ghosh et al. 2003, so only brief summary is presented here.

When I started writing about free software—and "non-monetary economic"[13]—phenomena in the mid-1990s, there was widespread suspicion among traditional economists and others that this was a domain either for hobbyists or for irrational groups of people mainly driven by warm fuzzy feelings of communal sharing and gifts. Since the idea of a gift is usually associated with knowing the recipient, and the politics of developers in particular tend towards the libertarian rather than the communitarian, the notion of "gift economy"[14] might seem unjustified. As open source became a hot topic for investigation in the social sciences, recent hypotheses usually supposed largely rational, self-interested motives, among the most extreme being that open source is explained by the "simple economics" of signaling for better career prospects and hence monetary returns.[15]

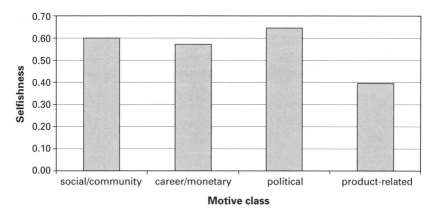

Figure 2.3
"Selfishness" or "profit-seeking measure" of developers

In the absence of clear monetary transactions, the interplay of contri-bution and return can be described in the form of "balanced value flow"[16] where one assumes rational self-interest but allows that self-interest can include a range of different types of reward, not just monetary compen-sation. While the FLOSS survey attempts to measure some of these possi-ble rewards, a simple question is to ask whether individual developers value their own contribution more or less than their perceived rewards; that is, "I give more than/less than/the same as I take" in relation to the devel-oper community at large.

We asked exactly this, and the resulting "selfishness measure" or "altru-ism measure" is shown in figure 2.3, for respondents falling into four moti-vation categories (as described later in this section). This measure ranges from –1 (purely altruistic) and +1 (purely selfish) and is calculated as the difference between the "selfish" responses ("I take more than give ") and the "altruistic" responses ("I give more than I take"), as a fraction of total responses.[17]

What we see is that more respondents are selfish than altruistic from all motive classes. Indeed, 55.7 percent of all developers classified their rela-tionship with the community as "I take more than I give" and a further 14.6 percent felt their contribution and reward was balanced; only 9 percent could be classed as consciously altruistic in that they reported that they give more than take. It should be noted that this measure does not reflect selfishness or altruism as *intent*—which is what would be correct—but as an *outcome*, in which case the words don't fit as accurately. Thus,

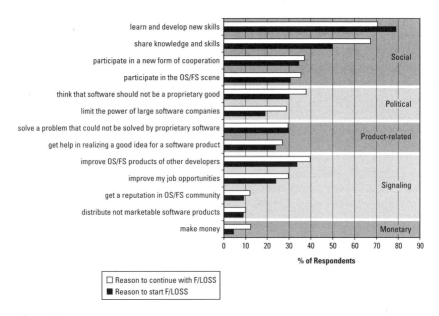

Figure 2.4
Initial and current motivations for FLOSS development (© 2002 International Institute of Infonomics)

the responses are consistent with self-interested participation and indicate that developers perceive a net positive value flow.

Figure 2.4 shows responses to the two main questions on motivation, asking developers for their reasons to first start developing free software and their reasons for continuing in the free software community. The chart groups the reported reasons into broad headings. Most notable is that the most important, reason to join and continue in the community is "to learn and develop new skills," highlighting the importance of free software as a voluntary training environment.

As a preliminary attempt to integrate the multiple, simultaneous reasons provided, respondents have been organized into four motivation classes (figure 2.5): social/community motives; career or monetary concerns; political motives; purely product-related motives. This is further explained in Ghosh et al. 2003, but in summary, while many developers express social or community-related motives, only those who also express career concerns were included in the second category, while only those who also express political views were placed in the third category. The last category is necessarily small, because it comprises those who expressed *only* product-

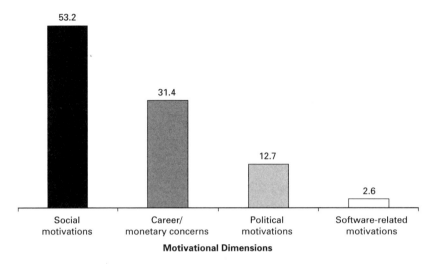

Figure 2.5
Developers by motive class, as percentage of total developers (© 2002 International Institute of Infonomics, FLOSS Developer Survey)

related motives (participating in the developer community to improve a software product, for instance). Of course, there are many ways of forming these categories and how one forms them changes how they correlate to other variables.

Organization

The FLOSS community shows simultaneously signs of both extreme concentration and widespread distribution. Measures of source code authorship show that a few individuals are responsible for disproportionately large fractions of the total code base and this concentration is increasing over time (the Gini coefficient for the Linux kernel[18] is 0.79). Several previous studies using a variety of objective metrics have shown that large fractions of code are developed by a small minority of contributors.[19]

However, the same studies and methods show that the majority of developers contribute relatively small amounts of code, and participate in a single or very few projects. Arguably, in the spirit of Raymond's (2001) view that "given enough eyeballs, all bugs are shallow" we can assume that the small high-contribution minority would not be as productive, and would be unable on their own to complete projects, without the support of vast armies of low-contribution participants. Moreover, the same objective metrics show that the majority of projects (or packages, or even modules in the Linux kernel) have a single author or very few contributors.

Put together, these results suggest that the community is organized into not a single core with a vast periphery, but a collection of cores each with their own smaller, overlapping peripheries. This organization is fractal in nature, in that the shape of concentration curves[20] remains the same no matter what level of detail is used; that is, the distribution of high- and low-contribution developers is more or less the same whether one looks at "all projects on Sourceforge" or at "modules in the Linux kernel."

The fractal nature of this would suggest an organizational mechanism that is universal within the community, involving the development of strong leadership structures in a highly modularized environment. This is consistent with the FLOSS developer survey, where for the first time individuals were asked to measure their leadership role.

As figure 2.6 shows, only 35 percent of respondents claim to *not* be leaders of any project, while 32 percent report they lead a single project. Meanwhile, only 2 percent claim to lead more than five projects.

Figure 2.7 corroborates objective and other data sources showing that most people have been involved in a small number of projects (a similar

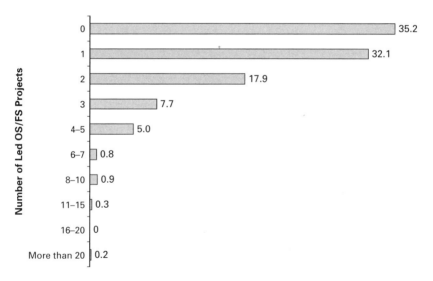

Figure 2.6
Leadership: number of projects involved in, percentage of respondents

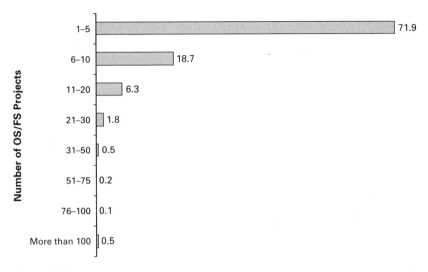

Figure 2.7
Number of projects involved in so far, percentage of respondents

but slightly different picture was reported when asked about current involvement in projects, which probably says more about a developer's ability to manage time than his degree of involvement as such).

Finally, most models assume that there is considerable collaboration and, more importantly, communication between developers in order to make this highly modularized, distributed form of production work. Figure 2.8 shows what people reported when asked for the number of other members of the developer community with whom they are in regular contact. The terms *contact* and *regular* were deliberately left undefined by us for two reasons: any definition we chose would be arbitrary, and we wanted to see whether developers believe they are in regular contact, which is an important insight into their own perception of the community's organizational structure. Surprisingly, as many as 17 percent reported being in regular contact with *no one*, thus indicating that significant development does take place in isolation (structural, if not necessarily social), at least between points of code release.

What is perhaps predictable, and consistent with the other findings, is that the vast majority of developers maintain regular contact with a small number of other developers—indeed, more than 50 percent are in contact with one to five others.

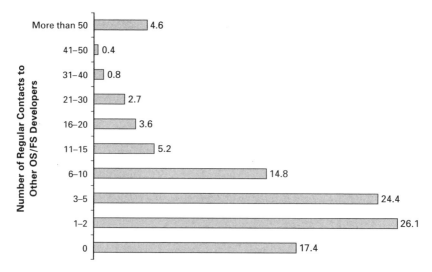

Figure 2.8
Regular contact with other developers, percentage of respondents

Subjective Responses, Objective Data?

Responses to any survey such as this one are necessarily subjective. Naturally, this is so even for the several questions that would have objective answers, such as the number of projects to which a developer has contributed, or monthly income, or whether such income is a direct result of involvement in free software development.

Some of these objective data can be checked against secondary sources, which may be more reliable or less subjective than survey responses. Some objective data, and even subjective data, can be checked against responses to other survey questions—although this doesn't make the responses any less subjective, one can at least know whether the subjectivity is internally consistent or self-contradictory.

Do Reported Motives Match Reported Rewards?
One of the most interesting things that can be checked for consistency is the relationship between reported motives and reported rewards. When asking people for their motives behind any action, one has to be aware that answers are not necessarily accurate, for several reasons:

• People are not conscious of their motives all the time.
• People might suppress some motives in preference for others, either unconsciously or deliberately, because of what they believe are the "correct" motives—this effect may be less striking in an anonymous Web survey than in a face-to-face interview, but probably still exists.
• People might report some motives but not others—especially when there are multiple motives, some that are "necessary but not sufficient" might be ignored.

This is certainly true for respondents to the FLOSS developer survey. But it is possible to get a truer understanding of respondents' motives by comparing reported motives to reported rewards. We assume that people who develop free software for a given motive (for example, to earn money) also report an above-average incidence of related rewards (above-average income). Not all motives have rewards that can be directly measured—most don't. Certainly, rewards generally result after a considerable time lapse, and such rewards would become apparent only through repeated panel surveys. But there is some degree of consistency control that can be performed within a single survey.

The first thing that comes to mind is whether there is any difference in reported income levels across motivation categories (as described previously), and whether motive category is reflected in earnings from participation in free software development. Figure 2.9 shows whether respondents from different motive classes earned income directly from FLOSS, indirectly only, or not at all. Figure 2.10 shows the mean income levels for motive classes (respondents were not asked for their level of income from FLOSS, so this reflects income from all sources).

Clearly, there is a strong indication that those who report career and monetary motives get what they want; that is, they report a low level of not earning income from FLOSS and high level of earning directly from FLOSS, as compared with other motive classes. In contrast, the politically motivated are least likely to earn any income, direct or indirect, from FLOSS. It is interesting to note that although those with purely product-related motives (such as distributing software that they could not market in a proprietary way, or looking at FLOSS as a method of implementing an idea) are less likely to earn money from FLOSS than other groups, they earn the most, on average (see figure 2.10). This is consistent with, as an example, a picture of software professionals with proprietary software as a (large) income source who turn to this development mode to solve a technical or product-related problem.

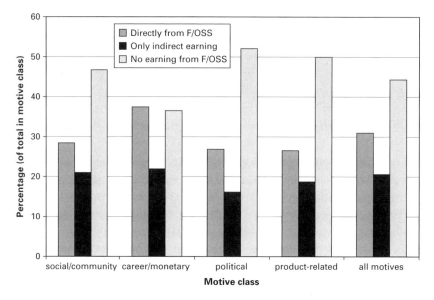

Figure 2.9
Earning from FLOSS by motive class

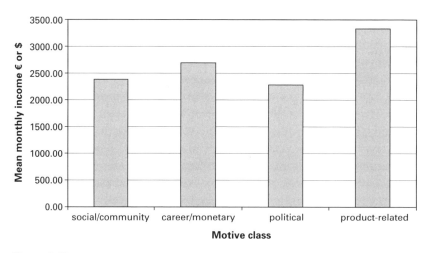

Figure 2.10
Income by motive class

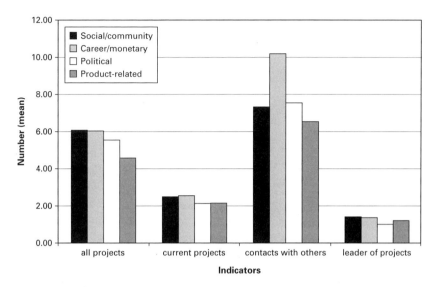

Figure 2.11
Social activity rewards by motive class

Figure 2.11 compares other possible reward indicators by motive class. These could possibly be treated as proxies for social or community-type rewards. While it seems clear that those motivated by career or monetary concerns get above-average levels of the appropriate sort of reward, the picture is blurred for the social/community and political motive class (at least from this set of indicators; there are many other candidates from the FLOSS survey). From this figure, it is apparent that social/community-driven and career/monetary-driven developers have similar levels of involvement in past and current projects as well as leadership of projects. (It should be emphasized that the career/monetary class includes those who did not explicitly state they wanted to earn money—those who were only interested in, for instance, reputation and possible job prospects form the largest share of this group.) What is striking is that the career/monetary group has a much higher level of regular contact with other developers than other groups do, possibly indicating that they are successful in developing the reputation that they value.

One "reward" indicator, in the sense that it sheds light on developers' perception of the sort of community to which they belong, is the Hobbes measure shown in figure 2.12. The Hobbes measure ranges from −1 (all others are altruistic) to +1 (all others are selfish). This indicator was

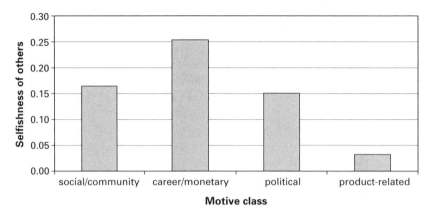

Figure 2.12
Others' selfishness—"Hobbes measure"—by motive class

calculated using a similar method to the "selfishness measure," in the form of the statement about other developers that "they give less than/more than/the same as they take" in relationship to the developer community. By and large, respondents were more likely to see other developers as altruistic and themselves as selfish. Unsurprisingly, the chart shows that a majority thought other developers in general are not altruistic, and notably more from the career/monetary group assumed that other developers are selfish than from any other group.

Developers motivated purely for product reasons have the most utopian view of the community, possibly because they feel for others, as they do for themselves (as the least "selfish" group, as seen previously), that there is more being put into the community than taken out of it.

Other Data Sources

It has already been shown for some variables that more objective data sources can corroborate the subjective data provided by respondents to the FLOSS developer survey. While a comparison of these data is beyond the scope of this text, the FLOSS source code scan (Ghosh et al. 2002, part V), the Orbiten Survey (Ghosh and Ved Prakash 2000) and the LICKS project (Ghosh and David 2003) provide extensive presentations of data on an aggregate level, especially on developer participation in and leadership of projects, that can be compared with subjective survey responses.

Conclusion

This chapter has presented some of the most interesting findings from the FLOSS developer survey. These findings highlight the crucial role that empirical data must play in the formation of models and hypotheses regarding the creation, organization, and activity of the free software developer community. The study also shows the utility of empirical data even when it is not possible to fully provide high levels of statistical accuracy, due to the unavailability of accurate data sources and census-type information on the universal population of developers.

Hopefully, this chapter provides the impetus for the process of using multiple sources of subjective and objective inputs on developer activity to better understand the motivations—and assess the rewards—behind the participation of individuals in this fascinating form of value production and exchange.

Notes

The FLOSS project was funded by the European Union's 5th Framework Programme (IST). The FLOSS consortium comprised the International Institute of Infonomics/University of Maastricht and Berlecon Research, Berlin. In addition to this author, Ruediger Glott, Bernhard Krieger, and Gregorio Robles were members of the Infonomics FLOSS team. Detailed results, the full questionnaire and analysis are in the FLOSS report (Ghosh et al. 2002, part IV).

1. This paper uses the terms *free software, open source software,* and *libre software* interchangeably, except where a specific distinction is made clear in the text. Most often the term *FLOSS* is used (Free/Libre/Open Source Software). Although it was originally a project title rather than a generic neutral term for the class of software, many commentators and writers have adopted FLOSS as such a term since the publication of the final FLOSS project report in July 2002. It should be noted that despite the media and policy focus on "Open Source" (in English, at least), *free software* is a more popular term among developers themselves—see http://flossproject.org/floss1/stats_1.htm.

2. Models and hypotheses are legion: "cooking-pot market" (Ghosh 1998a); "bazaar" (Raymond 2001); "gift exchange" (Barbrook 1998); "users turning producer" (von Hippel 2001a); "rational—signalling" (Lerner and Tirole 2002); "peer production" (Benkler 2002).

3. Such indicators may objectively answer at least part of the question about defining transactions: "who is doing how much of what with whom" seems to fall apart when the "how much" is no longer monetary, apparently eliminating the need for

actors to record their transactions. Nonmonetary indicators are described in more detail in Ghosh 2005 and a methodology for extracting them in an objective form from free software source code is detailed in Ghosh 2002.

4. A study of the distribution of code productivity among developers was first performed in the Orbiten survey (Ghosh and Ved Prakash 2000) by studying a sample of source code, and also using a different method based on annotations provided by developers in a large software archive (see Dempsey et al. 2002). Since then, statistics from developer portals such as Sourceforge.net provide at least the order of magnitude of the total developer population, if not accurate population size or demographic estimates.

5. In comparison to broader surveys (FLOSS; Robles-Martínez et al. 2001, which includes more than 5,000 respondents; Dempsey et al. 2002), the BCG survey (chap. 1, this volume) showed a higher degree of U.S. participants, more developers with several years of experience, and less animosity towards proprietary software companies. This may be related to the preselection criteria, which specifically included developers in mature projects on Sourceforge.net, a U.S.-based, open source portal. A sample that included, say, low-contribution developers on Savannah—a Free Software Foundation portal and hence more politically conscious—could have led to fairly different results.

6. See note 4.

7. Ghosh et al. 2002, part I. This survey of 1,452 industrial and public sector organizations in Europe on their use of open source software is beyond the scope of this paper. However, the FLOSS user survey did query organizations on their motivations for use, and also their support of developers, corroborating some of the results of the FLOSS developer survey.

8. Ghosh and Ved Prakash 2000; Ghosh 2002; Ghosh et al. 2002, part V; Ghosh and David 2003.

9. There have been small-scale studies of the organizational structure of the Apache, Jabber, Mozilla and other projects.

10. Ghosh and David 2003.

11. We assumed that developers can answer the survey in English, though—we didn't have the budget for a multilingual survey. As a result, we expect that we have an underrepresentation of east Asian and possibly Latin American developers.

12. See the FLOSS report, "Part IVa: Survey of Developers—Annexure on validation and methodology."

13. Ghosh 1994; Ghosh 1995; Ghosh 1998a.

14. Barbrook 1998.

15. Lerner and Tirole 2002.

16. Ghosh 2005.

17. Another way of looking at this is: if the selfish response is +1 and the altruistic response is −1 (the balanced response "I give as much as I take" is 0), then the "selfishness measure" is the mean of all responses.

18. In this context, the Gini coefficient measures the concentration of distribution: 0.0 represents uniform distribution (equal contribution from all participants), and 1.0 indicates full concentration (one participant contributes everything). The value here is for Linux kernel version 2.5.25, taken from the LICKS study of three versions of the kernel; see Ghosh and David 2003 for details.

19. The Orbiten survey (Ghosh and Ved Prakash 2000) and the FLOSS source code survey (Ghosh et al. 2002, part V) measured authorship of source code; Dempsey et al. 2002 analysed data from the Linux Software Map.

20. Lorenz curves, which plot authors' cumulative share of contribution and are the basis for Gini coefficients; for an example of their use in analyzing concentration of contribution in the Linux kernel, see Ghosh and David 2003.

3 | Economic Perspectives on Open Source

Josh Lerner and Jean Tirole

Introduction

In recent years, there has been a surge of interest in open source software development. Interest in this process, which involves software developers at many different locations and organizations sharing code to develop and refine software programs, has been spurred by three factors:

• *The rapid diffusion of open source software.* A number of open source products, such as the Apache web server, dominate product categories. In the personal computer operating system market, International Data Corporation estimates that the open source program Linux has from seven to twenty-one million users worldwide, with a 200 percent annual growth rate. Many observers believe it represents a leading challenger to Microsoft Windows in this important market segment.

• *The significant capital investments in open source projects.* Over the past two years, numerous major corporations, including Hewlett-Packard, IBM, and Sun Microsystems, have launched projects to develop and use open source software. Meanwhile, a number of companies specializing in commercializing Linux, such as Red Hat, have completed initial public offerings, and other open source companies such as Cobalt Networks, Collab.Net, Scriptics, and Sendmail have received venture capital financing.

• *The new organization structure.* The collaborative nature of open source software development has been hailed in the business and technical press as an important organizational innovation.

To an economist, the behavior of individual programmers and commercial companies engaged in open source processes is startling. Consider these quotations by two leaders of the free software and open source communities:

The idea that the proprietary software social system—the system that says you are not allowed to share or change software—is unsocial, that it is unethical, that it is simply wrong may come as a surprise to some people. But what else can we say about a system based on dividing the public and keeping users helpless? (Stallman 1999a, 54)

The "utility function" Linux hackers are maximizing is not classically economic, but is the intangible of their own ego satisfaction and reputation among other hackers. [Parenthetical comment deleted.] Voluntary cultures that work this way are actually not uncommon; one other in which I have long participated is science fiction fandom, which unlike hackerdom explicitly recognizes "egoboo" (the enhancement of one's reputation among other fans). (Raymond 2001, 564–565)

It is not initially clear how these claims relate to the traditional view of the innovative process in the economics literature. Why should thousands of top-notch programmers contribute freely to the provision of a public good? Any explanation based on altruism[1] only goes so far. While users in less developed countries undoubtedly benefit from access to free software, many beneficiaries are well-to-do individuals or Fortune 500 companies. Furthermore, altruism has not played a major role in other industries, so it remains to be explained why individuals in the software industry are more altruistic than others.

This chapter seeks to make a preliminary exploration of the economics of open source software. Reflecting the early stage of the field's development, we do not seek to develop new theoretical frameworks or to statistically analyze large samples. Rather, we seek to draw some initial conclusions about the key economic patterns that underlie the open source development of software. (See table 3.1 for the projects we studied.) We find that much can be explained by reference to economic frameworks. We highlight the extent to which labor economics—in particular, the literature on "career concerns"—and industrial organization theory can explain many of the features of open source projects.

At the same time, we acknowledge that aspects of the future of open source development process remain somewhat difficult to predict with "off-the-shelf" economic models. In the final section of this chapter, we highlight a number of puzzles that the movement poses. It is our hope that this chapter will itself have an "open source" nature: that it will stimulate research by other economic researchers as well.

Finally, it is important to acknowledge the relationship with the earlier literature on technological innovation and scientific discovery. The open source development process is somewhat reminiscent of "user-driven innovation" seen in many other industries. Among other examples, Rosenberg's

Table 3.1
The open source programs studied

Program	Apache	Perl	Sendmail
Nature of program	World Wide Web (HTTP) server	System administration and programming language	Internet mail transfer agent
Year of introduction	1994	1987	1979 (predecessor program)
Governing body	Apache Software Foundation	Selected programmers (among the "perl-5-porters") (formerly the Perl Institute)	Sendmail Consortium
Competitors	Internet Information Server (Microsoft); various servers (Netscape)	Java (Sun); Python (open source program); Visual Basic, ActiveX (Microsoft)	Exchange (Microsoft) IMail (Ipswitch); Post.Office (Software.com)
Market penetration	55% (September 1999) (of publicly observable sites only)	Estimated to have one million users	Handles ~80 percent of Internet e-mail traffic
Web site:	http://www.apache.org	http://www.perl.org	http://www.sendmail.com

(1976b) studies of the machine tool industry and von Hippel's (1988) studies of scientific instruments have highlighted the role that sophisticated users can play in accelerating technological progress. In many instances, solutions developed by particular users for individual problems have become more general solutions for wide classes of users. Similarly, user groups have played an important role in stimulating innovation in other settings; certainly, this has been the case since the earliest days in the computer industry (e.g., Caminer et al. 1996).

A second strand of related literature examines the adoption of the scientific institutions ("open science," in Dasgupta and David's (1994) terminology) within for-profit organizations. Henderson and Cockburn (1994) and Gambardella (1995) have highlighted that the explosion of knowledge in biology and biochemistry in the 1970s triggered changes in the management of research and development in major pharmaceutical firms. In particular, a number of firms encouraged researchers to pursue basic research, in addition to the applied projects that typically characterized these organizations. These firms that did so enjoyed substantially higher research and development productivity than their peers, apparently because the research scientists allowed them to more accurately identify promising scientific developments (in other words, their "absorptive capacity" was enhanced) and because the interaction with cutting-edge research made these firms more attractive to top scientists. At the same time, the encouragement of "open science" processes has not been painless. Cockburn, Henderson, and Stern (1999) highlight the extent to which encouraging employees to pursue both basic and applied research led to substantial challenges in designing incentive schemes, because of the very different outputs of each activity and means through which performance is measured.[2]

But as we shall argue, certain aspects of the open source process—especially the extent to which contributors' work is recognized and rewarded—are quite distinct from earlier settings. This study focuses on understanding this contemporaneous phenomenon rather than making a general evaluation of the various cooperative schemes employed over time.

The Nature of Open Source Software

While media attention to the phenomenon of open source software has been only recent, the basic behaviors are much older in origin. There has long been a tradition of sharing and cooperation in software development. But in recent years, both the scale and formalization of the activity have expanded dramatically with the widespread diffusion of the Internet.[3] In the following discussion, we highlight three distinct eras of cooperative software development.

The First Era: The Early 1960s to the Early 1980s

Many of the key aspects of the computer operating systems and the Internet were developed in academic settings such as Berkeley and MIT during the 1960s and 1970s, as well as in central corporate research facilities where researchers had a great deal of autonomy (such as Bell Labs and Xerox's Palo Alto Research Center). In these years, programmers from different organizations commonly shared basic operating code of computer programs—source code.[4]

Many of the cooperative development efforts in the 1970s focused on the development of an operating system that could run on multiple computer platforms. The most successful examples, such as Unix and the C language used for developing Unix applications, were originally developed at AT&T's Bell Laboratories. The software was then installed across institutions, either for free or for a nominal charge. Further innovations were made at many of the sites where the software was installed, and were in turn shared with others. The process of sharing code was greatly accelerated with the diffusion of Usenet, a computer network begun in 1979 to link together the Unix programming community. As the number of sites grew rapidly, the ability of programmers in university and corporate settings to rapidly share technologies was considerably enhanced.

These cooperative software development projects were undertaken on a highly informal basis. Typically no effort to delineate property rights or to restrict reuse of the software were made. This informality proved to be problematic in the early 1980s, when AT&T began enforcing its (purported) intellectual property rights related to Unix.

The Second Era: The Early 1980s to the Early 1990s

In response to these threats of litigation, the first efforts to formalize the ground rules behind the cooperative software development process emerged. This movement ushered in the second era of cooperative software development. The critical institution during this period was the Free Software Foundation, begun by Richard Stallman of the MIT Artificial Intelligence Laboratory in 1983. The foundation sought to develop and disseminate a wide variety of software without cost.

One important innovation introduced by the Free Software Foundation was a formal licensing procedure that aimed to preclude the assertion of patent rights concerning cooperatively developed software (as many believed that AT&T had done in the case of Unix). In exchange for being able to modify and distribute the GNU (a "recursive acronym" standing for "GNU's not Unix"), software, software developers had to agree to make the source code freely available (or at a nominal cost). As part of the General Public License (GPL, also known as "copylefting"), the user also had to agree not to impose licensing restrictions on others. Furthermore, all enhancements to the code—and even code that intermingled the cooperatively developed software with separately created software—had to be licensed on the same terms. It is these contractual terms that distinguish open source software from shareware (where the binary files but not the underlying source code are made freely available, possibly for a trial period only) and public-domain software (where no restrictions are placed on subsequent users of the source code).[5]

This project, as well as contemporaneous efforts, also developed a number of important organizational features. In particular, these projects employed a model where contributions from many developers were accepted (and frequently publicly disseminated or posted). The official version of the program, however, was managed or controlled by a smaller subset of individuals closely involved with the project, or in some cases, by an individual leader. In some cases, the project's founder (or a designated successor) served as the leader; in others, leadership rotated between various key contributors.

The Third Era: The Early 1990s to Today
The widespread expansion of Internet access in the early 1990s led to a dramatic acceleration of open source activity. The volume of contributions and diversity of contributors expanded sharply, and numerous new open source projects emerged, most notably Linux (an operating system developed by Linus Torvalds in 1991). As discussed in detail next, interactions between commercial companies and the open source community also became commonplace in the 1990s.

Another innovation during this period was the proliferation of alternative approaches to licensing cooperatively developed software. During the 1980s, the GPL was the dominant licensing arrangement for cooperatively developed software. This situation changed considerably during the 1990s. In particular, Debian, an organization set up to disseminate Linux, developed the "Debian Free Software Guidelines" in 1995. These guidelines allowed licensees greater flexibility in using the program, including the right to bundle the cooperatively developed software with proprietary code. These provisions were adopted in early 1997 by a number of individuals involved in cooperative software development, and were subsequently dubbed the "Open Source Definition." As the authors explained:

License Must Not Contaminate Other Software

The license must not place restrictions on other software that is distributed along with the licensed software. For example, the license must not insist that all other programs distributed on the same medium must be open-source software. Rationale: Distributors of open-source software have the right to make their own choices about their own software (Open Source Initiative 1999).

These new guidelines did not require open source projects to be "viral": they need not "infect" all code that was compiled with the software with the requirement that it be covered under the license agreement as well. At the same time, they also accommodated more restrictive licenses, such as the GPL.

The past few years have seen unprecedented growth of open source software. At the same time, the movement has faced a number of challenges. We highlight two of these here: the "forking" of projects (the development of competing variations) and the development of products for high-end users.

The first of these two issues has emerged in a number of open source projects: the potential for programs to splinter into a number of variants. In some cases, passionate disputes over product design have led to such splintering of open source projects. Examples of such splintering occurred with the Berkeley Unix program and Sendmail during the late 1980s.

Another challenge has been the apparently lesser emphasis on documentation and support, user interfaces,[6] and backward compatibility in at least some open source projects. The relative technological features of software developed in open source and traditional environments are a matter of passionate discussion. Some members of the community believe that this production method dominates traditional software development in all respects. But many open source advocates argue that open source software tends to be geared to the more sophisticated users.[7] This point is made colorfully by one open source developer:

[I]n every release cycle Microsoft always listens to its *most ignorant customers*. This is the key to dumbing down each release cycle of software for further assaulting the non-personal-computing population. Linux and OS/2 developers, on the other hand, tend to listen to their *smartest* customers. . . . The good that Microsoft does in bringing computers to non-users is outdone by the curse that they bring on experienced users (Nadeau 1999).

Certainly, the greatest diffusion of open source projects appears to be in settings where the end users are sophisticated, such as the Apache server installed by systems administrators. In these cases, users are apparently more willing to tolerate the lack of detailed documentation or easy-to-understand user interfaces in exchange for the cost savings and the permission to modify the source code themselves. In several projects, such as Sendmail, project administrators chose to abandon backward compatibility in the interests of preserving program simplicity.[8] One of the rationales for this decision was that administrators using the Sendmail system were responsive to announcements that these changes would be taking place, and rapidly upgraded their systems. In a number of commercial software projects, it has been noted, these types of rapid responses are not as common. Once again, this reflects the greater sophistication and awareness of the users of open source software.

The debate about the ability of open source software to accommodate high-end users' needs has direct implications for the choice of license. The recent popularity of more liberal licenses and the concomitant decline of the GNU license are related to the rise in the "pragmatist" influence. These individuals believe that allowing proprietary code and for-profit activities in segments that would otherwise be poorly served by the open source community will provide the movement with its best chance for success.

Who Contributes?

Computer system administrators, database administrators, computer programmers, and other computer scientists and engineers occupied about 2.1 million jobs in the United States in 1998. (Unless otherwise noted, the information in this paragraph is from U.S. Department of Labor 2000.) A large number of these workers—estimated at between five and ten percent—are either self-employed or retained on a project-by-project basis by employers. Computer-related positions are projected by the federal government to be among the fastest-growing professions in the next decade.

The distribution of contributors to open source projects appears to be quite skewed. This is highlighted by an analysis of 25 million lines of open source code, constituting 3,149 distinct projects (Ghosh and Ved Prakash 2000). The distribution of contributions is shown in figure 3.1. More than three-quarters of the nearly 13,000 contributors made only one contribution; only one in twenty-five had more than five contributions. Yet the top decile of contributors accounted for fully 72 percent of the code contributed to the open source projects, and the top two deciles for 81 percent (see figure 3.2). This distribution would be even more skewed if those who simply reported errors, or "bugs," were considered: for every individual who contributes code, five will simply report errors (Valloppillil, 1998). To what extent this distribution is unique to open source software is unclear: the same skewness of output is also observed among programmers employed in commercial software development facilities (e.g., see Brooks 1995 and Cusumano 1991), but it is unclear whether these distributions are similar in their properties.

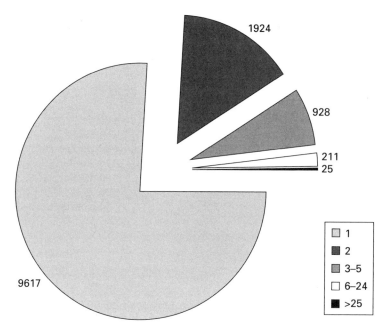

Figure 3.1
Distribution of contributions by participant (Ghosh and Prakash 2000)

The overall picture that we drew from our interviews and from the responses we received in reaction to the first draft of the paper is that the open source process is quite elitist. Important contributors are few and ascend to the "core group" status, the ultimate recognition by one's peers. The elitist view is also supported by Mockus, Fielding, and Herbsleb's (2000) study of contributions to Apache. For Apache, the (core) "developers mailing list" is considered as the key list of problems to be solved, while other lists play a smaller role. The top 15 developers contribute 83 percent to 91 percent of changes (problem reports by way of contrast offer a much less elitist pattern).

Some evidence consistent with the suggestion that contributions to open source projects are being driven by signaling concerns can be found in the analysis of contributors to a long-standing archive of Linux postings maintained at the University of North Carolina by Dempsey et al. 1999. These authors examine the suffix of the contributors' e-mail addresses. While the location of many contributors cannot be precisely identified (for instance, contributors at ".com" entities may be located anywhere in the world), the

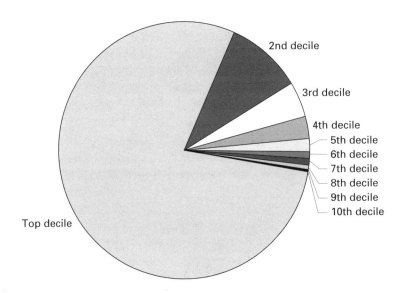

Does not include 9% of code, where contrbutor could not be identified.

Figure 3.2
Distribution of code contributed by decile: Does not include 9 percent of code where contributor could not be identified. (Ghosh and Prakash 2000)

results are nonetheless suggestive. As figure 3.3 depicts, 12 percent of the contributors are from entities with an ".edu" suffix (typically, U.S. educational institutions), 7 percent from ".org" domains (traditionally reserved from U.S. nonprofits), 37 percent are from Europe (with suffixes such as ".de" and ".uk"), and 11 percent have other suffixes, many of which represent other foreign countries. This suggests that many of the contributions are coming from individuals outside the major software centers.

What Does Economic Theory Tell Us about Open Source?

This section and the next use economic theory to shed light on three key questions: Why do people participate?[9] Why are there open source projects in the first place? And how do commercial vendors react to the open source movement?

What Motivates Programmers?

A programmer participates in a project, whether commercial or open source, only if he or she derives a net benefit from engaging in the activ-

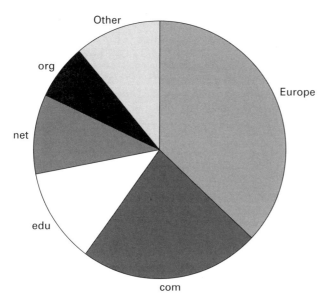

Figure 3.3
Suffix of Linux contributors' e-mail (Dempsey et al. 1999)

ity. The net benefit is equal to the immediate payoff (current benefit minus current cost) plus the delayed payoff (delayed benefit minus delayed cost).

A programmer working on an open source software development project incurs a variety of benefits and costs. The programmer incurs an opportunity cost of time. While is working on this project, a programmer is unable to engage in another programming activity. This opportunity cost exists at the extensive and intensive margins. First, programmers who would work as independents on open source projects would forgo the monetary compensation they would receive working for a commercial firm or a university. Second, and more to the point, for a programmer with an affiliation with a commercial company, a university or research lab, the opportunity cost is the cost of not focusing on the primary mission. For example, the academic's research output might sag, and the student's progress towards a degree slow down; these examples typify delayed costs. The size of this opportunity cost of not focusing on the primary mission of course depends on the extent of monitoring by the employer and, more generally, the pressure on the job.

Two immediate benefits might counter this cost. First, programmers, when fixing a bug or customizing an open source program, might actually improve rather than reduce their performance in the mission endowed upon them by their employer. This is particularly relevant for system administrators looking for specific solutions for their company. Second, the programmer compares the enjoyability of the mission set by the employer and the open source alternative. A "cool" open source project might be more fun than a routine task.

The delayed reward covers two distinct, although hard-to-distinguish, incentives. The *career concern incentive* refers to future job offers, shares in commercial open source-based companies,[10] or future access to the venture capital market.[11] The *ego gratification incentive* stems from a desire for peer recognition. Probably most programmers respond to both incentives. There are some differences between the two. The programmer mainly pre-occupied by peer recognition may shun future monetary rewards, and may also want to signal his or her talent to a slightly different audience than a programmer motivated by career concerns. From an economic perspective, however, the incentives are similar in most respects. We group the career concern incentive and the ego gratification incentive under a single heading: the *signaling incentive*.

Economic theory (e.g., Holmström 1999) suggests that this signaling incentive is stronger,

1. the more visible the performance to the relevant audience (peers, labor market, venture capital community)
2. the higher the impact of effort on performance
3. the more informative the performance about talent

The first condition gives rise to what economists call "strategic complementarities." To have an "audience," programmers will want to work on software projects that will attract a large number of other programmers. This suggests the possibility of multiple equilibria. The same project might attract few programmers because programmers expect that others will not be interested; or it may flourish as programmers (rationally) have faith in the project.

The same point applies to forking in a given open source project. Open source processes are in this respect quite similar to academic research. The latter is well known to exhibit fads: see the many historical examples of simultaneous discoveries discussed by Merton (1973). Fields are completely neglected for years, while others with apparently no superior intrinsic interest attract large numbers of researchers. Fads in academia are frowned upon for their inefficient impact on the allocation of research. It should not be ignored, however, that fads also have benefits. A fad can create a strong signaling incentive: researchers working in a popular area may be highly motivated to produce a high-quality work, since they can be confident that a large audience will examine their work.[12]

Turning to the leadership more specifically, it might still be a puzzle that the leader initially releases valuable code to the community.[13] Despite the substantial status and career benefits of being a leader of an important open source project, it would seem that most would not resist the large monetary gains from taking a promising technology private. We can only conjecture as to why this is not the case. One possibility is that taking the technology private might meet layers of resistance within the leader's corporation. To the extent that the innovation was made while working in-house, the programmer must secure a license from the employer;[14] and the company, which does not want to lose a key programmer, might not be supportive of the request. Another possibility is that the open source process may be a more credible way of harnessing energies when fighting against a dominant player in the industry.

Comparison between Open Source and Closed Source Programming Incentives

To compare programmers' incentives in the open source and proprietary settings, we need to examine how the fundamental features of the two environments shape the incentives just reviewed. We first consider the relative short-term rewards, and then turn to the deferred compensation.

Commercial projects have an edge on the current compensation dimension because the proprietary nature of the code generates income, which makes it worthwhile for private companies to offer salaries.[15] This contention is the old argument in economics that the prospect of profit encourages investment, which is used, for instance, to justify the awarding of patents to encourage invention.

By way of contrast, an open source project might well lower the cost for the programmer, for two reasons:

1. *"Alumni effect":* Because the code is freely available to all, it can be used in schools and universities for learning purposes; so it is already familiar to programmers. This reduces their cost of programming for Unix, for example.[16]

2. *Customization and bug-fixing benefits:* The cost of contributing to an open source project can be offset if the activity brings about a private benefit (bug fixing, customization) for the programmer and his or her firm. Note again that this factor of cost reduction is directly linked to the openness of the source code.[17]

Let us now turn to the delayed reward (signaling incentive) component. In this respect too, the open source process has some benefits over the closed source approach. As we noted, signaling incentives are stronger, the more visible the performance and the more attributable the performance to a given individual. Signaling incentives therefore may be stronger in the open source mode for three reasons:

1. *Better performance measurement:* Outsiders can observe only inexactly the functionality and/or quality of individual elements of a typical commercially developed program, as they are unable to observe the proprietary source code. By way of contrast, in an open source project, the outsiders are able to see not only what the contribution of each individual was and whether that component "worked," but also whether the task was hard, whether the problem was addressed in a clever way, whether the code can be useful for other programming tasks in the future, and so forth.

2. *Full initiative:* The open source programmer is his or her own boss and takes full responsibility for the success of a subproject. In a hierarchical commercial firm, though, the programmer's performance depends on a supervisor's interference, advice, and so on. Economic theory predicts that the programmer's performance is more precisely measured in the former case.[18]

3. *Greater fluidity:* It may be argued that the labor market is more fluid in an open source environment. Programmers are likely to have less idiosyncratic, or firm-specific, human capital that limits shifting one's efforts to a new program or work environment. (Since many elements of the source code are shared across open source projects, more of the knowledge they have accumulated can be transferred to the new environment.)

These theoretical arguments also provide insights as to *who* is more likely to contribute and *what tasks* are best suited to open source projects. Sophisticated users derive direct benefits when they customize or fix a bug in open source software.[19] A second category of potential contributors consists of individuals with strong signaling incentives; these contributors might use open source software as a port of entry. For instance, open source processes may give a talented system administrator at a small academic institution (who is also a user!) a unique opportunity to signal talent to peers, prospective employers, and the venture capital community.[20]

As to the tasks that may appeal to the open source community, one would expect that tasks such as those related to the operating systems and programming languages, whose natural audience is the community of programmers, would give rise to strong signaling incentives. (For instance, the use of Perl is largely restricted to system administrators.) By way of contrast, tasks aiming at helping the much less sophisticated end user—design of easy-to-use interfaces, technical support, and ensuring backward compatibility—usually provide lower signaling incentives.[21]

Evidence on Individual Incentives

A considerable amount of evidence is consistent with an economic perspective. First, user benefits are key to a number of open source projects. One of the origins of the free software movement was Richard Stallman's inability to improve a printer program because Xerox refused to release the source code. Many open source project founders were motivated by information technology problems that they had encountered in their day-to-day work. For instance, in the case of Apache, the initial set of contributors was almost entirely system administrators who were struggling with the same types of problems as Brian Behlendorf. In each case, the initial release was "runnable and testable": it provided a potential, if imperfect, solution to a problem that was vexing data processing professionals.

Second, it is clear that giving credit to authors is essential in the open source movement. This principle is included as part of the nine key requirements in the "Open Source Definition" (Open Source Initiative 1999). This point is also emphasized by Raymond 2001, who points out "surreptitiously filing someone's name off a project is, in cultural context, one of the ultimate crimes."

More generally, the reputational benefits that accrue from successful contributions to open source projects appear to have real effects on the developers. This is acknowledged within the open source community itself. For instance, according to Raymond 2001, the primary benefits that accrue to successful contributors of open source projects are "good reputation among one's peers, attention and cooperation from others . . . [and] higher status [in the] . . . exchange economy." Thus, while some of benefits conferred from participation in open source projects may be less concrete in nature, there also appear be quite tangible—if delayed—rewards.

The Apache project provides a good illustration of these observations. The project makes a point of recognizing all contributors on its web site—even those who simply identify a problem without proposing a solution. Similarly, the organization highlights its most committed contributors, who have the ultimate control over the project's evolution. Moreover, it appears that many of the skilled Apache programmers have benefited materially from their association with the organization. Numerous contributors have been hired into Apache development groups within companies such

Table 3.2
Commercial roles played by selected individuals active in open source movement

Individual	Role and company
Eric Allman	Chief Technical Officer, Sendmail, Inc. (support for open source software product)
Brian Behlendorf	Founder, President, and Chief Technical Officer, Collab.Net (management of open source projects)
Keith Bostic	Founder and President, Sleepycat Software
L. Peter Deutsch	Founder, Aladdin Enterprises (support for open source software product)
William Joy	Founder and Chief Scientist, Sun Microsystems (workstation and software manufacturer)
Michael Tiemann	Founder, Cygnus Solutions (open source support)
Linus Torvalds	Employee, Transmeta Corporation (chip design company)
Paul Vixie	President, Vixie Enterprises (engineering and consulting services)
Larry Wall	Employee, O'Reilly Media (software documentation publisher)

as IBM, become involved in process-oriented companies such as Collab.Net that seek to make open source projects more feasible (see following discussion), or else moved into other Internet tools companies in ways that were facilitated by their expertise and relationships built up during their involvement in the open source movement. Meanwhile, many of the new contributors are already employed by corporations and working on Apache development as part of their regular assignments.

There is also substantial evidence that open source work may be a good stepping stone for securing access to venture capital. For example, the founders of Sun, Netscape, and Red Hat had signaled their talent in the open source world. In table 3.2, we summarize some of the subsequent commercial roles played by individuals active in the open source movement.

Organization and Governance
Favorable characteristics for open source production are (a) its modularity (the overall project is divided into much smaller and well-defined tasks ("modules") that individuals can tackle independently from other tasks) and (b) the existence of fun challenges to pursue.[22] A successful open source

project also requires a credible leader or leadership, and an organization consistent with the nature of the process. Although the leader is often at the origin a user who attempts to solve a particular program, the leader over time performs less and less programming. The leader must provide a "vision," attract other programmers, and, last but not least, "keep the project together" (prevent it from forking or being abandoned).

Initial Characteristics   The success of an open source project is dependent on the ability to break the project into distinct components. Without parcelling out work in different areas to programming teams who need little contact with one another, the effort is likely to be unmanageable. Some observers argue that the underlying Unix architecture lent itself well to the ability to break development tasks into distinct components. It may be that as new open source projects move beyond their Unix origins and encounter new programming challenges, the ability to break projects into distinct units will be less possible. But recent developments in computer science and programming languages (for example the development of object-oriented programming) have encouraged further modularization, and may facilitate future open source projects.

The initial leader must also assemble a critical mass of code to which the programming community can react. Enough work must be done to show that the project is possible and has merit. At the same time, to attract additional programmers, it may be important that the leader does not perform too much of the job on his own and leaves challenging programming problems to others.[23] Indeed, programmers will initially be reluctant to join a project unless they identify an exciting challenge. Another reason why programmers are easier to attract at an early stage is that, if successful, the project will keep attracting a large number of programmers in the future, making early contributions very visible.

Consistent with this argument, it is interesting to note that each of the four cases described previously appeared to pose challenging programming problems.[24] At the initial release of each of these open source programs, considerable programming problems were unresolved. The promise that the project was not near a "dead end," but rather would continue to attract ongoing participation from programmers in the years to come, appears to be an important aspect of its appeal.

In this respect, Linux is perhaps the quintessential example. The initial Linux operating system was quite minimal, on the order of a few tens of thousands of lines of code. In Torvalds' initial postings, in which he sought to generate interest in Linux, he explicitly highlighted the extent to which the version would require creative programming in order to achieve full functionality. Similarly, Larry Wall attributes the much of the success of Perl to the fact that it "put the focus on the creativity of the programmer." Because it has a very limited number of rules, the program has evolved in a variety of directions that were largely unanticipated when Wall initiated the project.

Leadership

Another important determinant of project success appears to be the nature of its leadership. In some respects, the governance structures of open source projects are quite different. In a number of instances, including Linux, there is an undisputed leader. While certain aspects are delegated to others, a strong centralization of authority characterizes these projects. In other cases, such as Apache, a committee resolves the disputes by voting or a consensus process.

At the same time, leaders of open source projects share some common features. Most leaders are the programmers who developed the initial code for the project (or made another important contribution early in the project's development). While many make fewer programming contributions, having moved on to broader project management tasks, the individuals that we talked to believed that the initial experience was important in establishing credibility to manage the project. The splintering of the Berkeley-derived Unix development programs has been attributed in part to the absence of a single credible leader.

But what does the leadership of an open source project do? It might appear at first sight that the unconstrained, quasi-anarchistic nature of the open source process leaves little scope for a leadership. This perception is incorrect. While the leader has no "formal authority" (is unable to instruct anyone to do anything), he or she has substantial "real authority" in successful open source projects.[25] That is, a leader's "recommendations," broadly viewed, tend to be followed by the vast majority of programmers working on the project. These recommendations include the initial "vision" (agenda for work, milestones), the subsequent updating of goals as the project evolves, the appointment of key leaders, the cajoling of programmers so as to avoid attrition or forking, and the overall assessment of what has been and should be achieved. (Even though participants are free to take the project where they want as long as they release the modified code, acceptance by the leadership of a modification or addition provides some certification as to its quality and its integration/compatibility with the overall project. The certification of quality is quite crucial to the open source project, because the absence of liability raises concerns among users that are stronger than for commercial software, for which the vendor is liable).

The key to a successful leadership is the programmers' trust in the leadership: that is, they must believe that the leader's objectives are sufficiently congruent with theirs and not polluted by ego-driven, commercial, or political biases. In the end, the leader's recommendations are only meant to convey information to the community of participants. The recommendations receive support from the community only if they are likely to benefit the programmers; that is, only if the leadership's goals are believed to be aligned with the programmers' interests.

For instance, the leadership must be willing to accept meritorious improvements, even though they might not fit within the leader's original blueprint. Trust in the leadership is also key to the prevention of forking. While there are natural forces against forking (the loss of economies of scale due to the creation of smaller communities, the hesitations of programmers in complementary segments to port to multiple versions, and the stigma attached to the existence of a conflict), other factors may encourage forking. User-developers may have conflicting interests as to the evolution of the technology. Ego (signaling) concerns may also prevent a faction from admitting that another approach is more promising, or simply from accepting that it may socially be preferable to have one group join the other's efforts, even if no clear winner has emerged. The presence of a charismatic (trusted) leader is likely to substantially reduce the probability of forking in two ways. First, indecisive programmers are likely to rally behind the leader's preferred alternative. Second, the dissenting faction might not have an obvious leader of its own.

A good leader should also clearly communicate its goals and evaluation procedures. Indeed, the open source organizations go to considerable efforts to make the nature of their decision making process transparent: the process by which the operating committee reviews new software proposals is frequently posted and all postings archived. For instance, on the Apache web site, it is explained how proposed changes to the program are reviewed by the program's governing body, whose membership is largely based on contributions to the project. (Any significant change requires at least three "yes" votes—and no vetoes—by these key decision-makers.)

Commercial Software Companies' Reactions to the Open Source Movement

This section examines the interface between open and closed source software development. Challenged by the successes of the open source movement, the commercial software corporations may employ one of two strategies. The first is to emulate some incentive features of open source processes in a distinctively closed source environment. Another is to try to mix open and closed source processes to get the best of both worlds.

Why Don't Corporations Duplicate the Open Source Incentives?
As we already noted, owners of proprietary code are not able to enjoy the benefits of getting free programming training in schools and universities (the alumni effect); nor can they easily allow users to modify their code and customize it without jeopardizing intellectual property rights.

Similarly, and for the reasons developed earlier, commercial companies will never be able to fully duplicate the visibility of performance reached in the open source world. At most, they can duplicate to some extent some of the signaling incentives of the open source world. Indeed, a number of commercial software companies (for example, video game companies, and Qualcomm, creators of the Eudora email program) list people who have developed the software. It is an interesting question why others do not. To be certain, commercial companies do not like their key employees to become highly visible, lest they be hired away by competitors.[26] But, to a large extent, firms also realize that this very visibility enables them to attract talented individuals and provides a powerful incentive to existing employees.[27]

To be certain, team leaders in commercial software build reputations and get identified with proprietary software just as they can on open source projects; but the ability of reputations to spread beyond the leaders is more limited, due to the nonverifiability of claims about who did what.[28]

Another area in which software companies might try to emulate open source development is the promotion of widespread code sharing within the company. This may enable them to reduce code duplication and to broaden a programmer's audience. Interestingly, existing organizational forms may preclude the adoption of open source systems within commercial software firms. An internal Microsoft document on open source (Valloppillil 1998) describes a number of pressures that limit the implementation of features of open source development within Microsoft. Most importantly, each software development group appears to be largely autonomous. Software routines developed by one group are not shared with others. In some instances, the groups seek to avoid being broken up by not documenting a large number of program features. These organizational attributes, the document suggests, lead to very complex and interdependent programs that do not lend themselves to development in a "compartmentalized" manner nor to widespread sharing of source code.[29]

The Commercial Software Companies' Open Source Strategies
As should be expected, many commercial companies have undertaken strategies (discussed in this section) to capitalize on the open source movement. In a nutshell, they expect to benefit from their expertise in some segment whose demand is boosted by the success of a complementary open source program. While improvements in the open source software are not appropriable, commercial companies can benefit indirectly in a complementary proprietary segment.[30]

Living Symbiotically Off an Open Source Project   One such strategy is straightforward. It consists of commercially providing complementary services and products that are not supplied efficiently by the open source community. Red Hat for example, exemplifies this "reactive" strategy.[31]

In principle, a "reactive" commercial company may want to encourage and subsidize the open source movement; for example, by allocating a few programmers to the open source project.[32] Red Hat will make more money on support if Linux is successful. Similarly, if logic semiconductors and operating systems for personal computers are complements, one can show by a revealed preference argument that Intel's profits will increase if Linux (which, unlike Windows, is free) takes over the PC operating system market. Sun may benefit if Microsofts' position is weakened; Oracle might wish to port its database products to a Linux environment in order to lessen its dependence on Sun's Solaris operating system, and so forth. Because firms do not capture all the benefits of the investments, though, the free-rider problem often discussed in the economics of innovation should apply here as well. Subsidies by commercial companies for open source projects should remain limited unless the potential beneficiaries succeed in organizing a consortium (which will limit the free-riding problem).

Code Release   A second strategy is to take a more proactive role in the development of open source software. Companies can release existing proprietary code and create some governance structure for the resulting open source process. For example, Hewlett-Packard recently released its Spectrum Object Model linker to the open source community in order to help the Linux community port Linux to Hewlett-Packard's RISC architecture.[33] This is similar to the strategy of giving away the razor (the released code) to sell more razor blades (the related consulting services that HP will provide).

When can it be advantageous for a commercial company to release proprietary code under an open source license? The first situation is, as we have noted, when the company expects to thereby boost its profit on a complementary segment. A second is when the increase in profit in the proprietary complementary segment offsets any profit that would have been made in the primary segment, had it not been converted to open source. Thus, the temptation to go open source is particularly strong when the company is too small to compete commercially in the primary segment or when it is lagging behind the leader and about to become extinct in that segment.[34,35]

Various efforts by corporations selling proprietary software products to develop additional products through an open source approach have been undertaken. One of the most visible of these efforts was Netscape's 1998 decision to make Mozilla, a portion of its browser source code, freely available. This effort encountered severe difficulties in its first year, receiving only approximately two dozen postings by outside developers. Much of the problems appeared to stem from the insufficiently "modular" nature of the software: as a reflection of its origins as a proprietary commercial product, the different portions of the program were highly interdependent and interwoven. Netscape eventually realized it needed to undertake a major restructuring of the program, in order to enhance the ability of open source programmers to contribute to individual sections. It is also likely that Netscape raised some suspicions by not initially adopting the right governance structure. Leadership by a commercial entity may not internalize enough of the objectives of the open source community. In particular, a corporation may not be able to credibly commit to keeping all source code in the public domain and to adequately highlighting important contributions.[36]

For instance, in the Mozilla project, Netscape's unwillingness to make large amounts of browser code public was seen as an indication of its questionable commitment to the open source process. In addition, Netscape's initial insistence on the licensing terms that allowed the corporation to relicense the software developed in the open source project on a proprietary basis was viewed as problematic (Hamerly, Paquin, and Walton 1999).

(The argument is here the mirror image of the standard argument in industrial economics that a firm may want to license its technology to several licensees in order to commit not to expropriate producers of complementary goods and services in the future: see Shepard (1987) and Farrell and Gallini (1988).) Netscape initially proposed the "Netscape Public License," a cousin to the BSD license that allowed Netscape to take pieces of the open source code and turn them back into a proprietary project again. The licensing terms, though, may not have been the hindering factor, since the terms of the final license are even stricter than those of the GPL. Under this new license (the "Mozilla Public License"), Netscape cannot relicense the modifications to the code.

Intermediaries   Hewlett-Packard's management of the open source process seems consistent with Dessein (1999). Dessein shows that a principal with formal control rights over an agent's activity in general gains by delegating his control rights to an intermediary with preferences or incentives that fall between or combine between his and the agent's. The partial alignment of the intermediary's preferences with the agent's fosters trust and boosts the agent's initiative, ultimately offsetting the partial loss of control for the principal. In the case of Collab.Net's early activities, the congruence with the open source developers was obtained through the employment of visible open source developers (for example, the president and chief technical officer is Brian Behlendorf, one of the cofounders of the Apache project) and the involvement of O'Reilly, a technical book publisher with strong ties to the open source community.

Four Open Economic Questions about Open Source

There are many other issues posed by open source development that require further thought. This section highlights a number of these as suggestions for future work.

Which Technological Characteristics Are Conducive to a Smooth Open Source Development?
This chapter has identified a number of attributes that make a project a good or poor candidate for open source development. But it has stopped short of providing a comprehensive picture of determinants of a smooth open source development. Let us mention a few topics that are worth further investigation:

• *Role of applications and related programs.* Open source projects differ in the functionalities they offer and in the number of add-ons that are required to make them attractive. As the open source movement comes to maturity, it will confront some of the same problems as commercial software does; namely, the synchronization of upgrades and the efficient level of backward compatibility. A user who upgrades a program (which is very cheap in the open source model) will want either the new program to be backward compatible or applications to have themselves been upgraded to the new version.[37] We know from commercial software that both approaches to compatibility are costly; for example, Windows programmers devote a lot of time to backward compatibility issues, and encouraging application development requires fixing applications programming interfaces about three years before the commercial release of the operating system. A reasonable conjecture could be that open source programming would be appropriate when there are fewer applications or when IT professionals can easily adjust the code so as to ensure compatibility themselves.

• *Influence of competitive environment.* Based on very casual observation, it seems that open source projects sometimes gain momentum when facing a battle against a dominant firm, although our examples show open source projects can do well even in the absence of competition.[38] To understand why this might be the case (assuming this is an empirical fact, which remains to be established!), it would be useful to go back to the economics of cooperative joint ventures. These projects are known to work better when the members have similar objectives.[39] The existence of a dominant competitor in this respect tends to align the goals of the members, and the best way to fight an uphill battle against the dominant player is to remain united. To be certain, open source software development works differently from joint venture production, but it also relies on cooperation within a heterogeneous group; the analogy is well worth pursuing.

• *Project lifespan.* One of the arguments offered by open source advocates is that because their source code is publicly available, and at least some contributions will continue to be made, its software will have a longer duration. (Many software products by commercial vendors are abandoned or no longer upgraded after the developer is acquired or liquidated, or even when the company develops a new product to replace the old program.) But another argument is that the nature of incentives being offered open source developers—which, as discussed earlier, lead them to work on highly visible projects—might bring about a "too early" abandonment of projects that experience a relative loss in popularity. An example is the

XEmacs project, an open source project to create a graphical environment with multiple "windows" that originated at Stanford. Once this development effort encountered an initial decline in popularity, many of the open source developers appeared to move onto alternative projects.

Optimal Licensing

Our discussion of open source licensing has been unsatisfactory. Some licenses (e.g., BSD and its close cousin the Apache license) are relatively permissive, while others (e.g., GPL) force the user to distribute any changes or improvements (share them) if they distribute the software at all.

Little is known about the trade-off between encouraging add-ons that would not be properly supplied by the open source movement and preventing commercial vendors (including open source participants) from free riding on the movement or even "hijacking" it. An open source project may be hijacked by a participant who builds a valuable module and then offers proprietary APIs to which application developers start writing. The innovator has then built a platform that appropriates some of the benefits of the project. To be certain, open source participants might then be outraged, but it is unclear whether this would suffice to prevent the hijacking. The open source community would then be as powerless as the commercial owner of a platform upon which a "middleware" producer superimposes a new platform.[40]

The exact meaning of the "viral" provisions in the GPL license, say, or more generally the implications of open source licenses, have not yet been tested in court. Several issues may arise in such litigation: for instance, determining who has standing for representing the project if the community is fragmented, and how a remedy would be implemented (for example, the awarding of damages for breach of copyright agreement might require incorporating the beneficiaries).

Coexistence of Commercial and Open Source Software

On a related note, the existence of commercial entities living symbiotically off the efforts of open source programmers as well as participating in open source projects raises new questions.

The flexible open source licenses allow for the coexistence of open and closed source code. While it represents in our view (and in that of many open source participants) a reasonable compromise, it is not without hazards.

The coexistence of commercial activities may alter the programmers' incentives. Programmers working on an open source project might be tempted to stop interacting and contributing freely if they think they have an idea for a module that might yield a huge commercial payoff. Too many programmers might start focusing on the commercial side, making the open source process less exciting. Although they refer to a different environment, the concerns that arise about academics' involvement in start-up firms, consulting projects, and patenting could be relevant here as well. While it is too early to tell, some of these same issues may appear in the open source world.[41]

Can the Open Source Process Be Transposed to Other Industries?

An interesting final question is whether the open source model can be transposed to other industries. Could automobile components be developed in an open source mode, with GM and Toyota performing an assembler function similar to that of Red Hat for Linux? Many industries involve forms of cooperation between commercial entities in the form of for-profit or not-for-profit joint ventures. Others exhibit user-driven innovation or open science cultures. Thus a number of ingredients of open source software are not specific to the software industry. Yet no other industry has yet produced anything quite like open source development. An important research question is whether other industries ever will.

Although some aspects of open source software collaboration (such as electronic information exchange across the world) could easily be duplicated, other aspects would be harder to emulate. Consider, for example, the case of biotechnology. It might be impossible to break up large projects into small manageable and independent modules and there might not be sufficient sophisticated users who can customize the molecules to their own needs. The tasks that are involved in making the product available to the end user involve much more than consumer support and even friendlier user interfaces. Finally, the costs of designing, testing, and seeking regulatory approval for a new drug are enormous.

More generally, in many industries the development of individual components require large-team work and substantial capital costs, as opposed to (for some software programs) individual contributions and no capital investment (besides the computer the programmer already has). Another obstacle is that in mass-market industries, users are numerous and rather unsophisticated, and so deliver few services of peer recognition and ego gratification. This suggests that the open source model may not easily be transposed to other industries, but further investigation is warranted.

Our ability to answer confidently these and related questions is likely to increase as the open source movement itself grows and evolves. At the same time, it is heartening to us how much of open source activities can be understood within existing economic frameworks, despite the presence of claims to the contrary. The literatures on "career concerns" and on competitive strategies provide lenses through which the structure of open source projects, the role of contributors, and the movement's ongoing evolution can be viewed.

Notes

The assistance of the Harvard Business School's California Research Center, and Chris Darwall in particular, is gratefully acknowledged. We also thank a number of practitioners—especially Eric Allman, Mike Balma, Brian Behlendorf, Keith Bostic, Tim O'Reilly, and Ben Passarelli—for their willingness to generously spend time discussing the open source movement. George Baker, Jacques Crémer, Rob Merges, Bernie Reddy, Pierre Régibeau, Bernard Salanié, many open source participants, seminar participants at the American Economics Association annual meetings, European Economic Association Bolzano meetings, Harvard, and three anonymous referees provided helpful comments. Harvard Business School's Division of Research provided financial support. The Institut D'Economie Industrielle receives research grants from a number of corporate sponsors, including French Telecom and the Microsoft Corporation. This chapter is a modified version of Lerner and Tirole 2002, for which Blackwell Publishing holds the copyright and has granted permission for this use. All opinions and errors remain our own.

1. The media like to portray the open source community as wanting to help mankind, as it makes a good story. Many open source advocates put limited emphasis on this explanation.

2. It should be noted that these changes are far from universal. In particular, many information technology and manufacturing firms appear to be moving to less of an emphasis on basic science in their research facilities (for a discussion, see Rosenbloom and Spencer 1996).

3. This history is of necessity highly abbreviated and we do not offer a complete explanation of the origins of open source software. For more detailed treatments, see Browne 1999; DiBona, Ockman, and Stone 1999; Gomulkiewicz 1999; Levy 1994; Raymond 2001; and Wayner 2000.

4. Programmers write source code using languages such as Basic, C, and Java. By way of contrast, most commercial software vendors provide users with only object, or binary, code. This is the sequence of 0s and 1s that directly communicates with the computer, but which is difficult for programmers to interpret or modify. When the source code is made available to other firms by commercial developers, it is typically licensed under very restrictive conditions.

5. It should be noted, however, that some projects, such as the Berkeley Software Distribution (BSD) effort, did take alternative approaches during the 1980s. The BSD license also allows anyone to freely copy and modify the source code (as long as credit was given to the University of California at Berkeley for the software developed there, a requirement no longer in place). It is much less constraining than the GPL: anyone can modify the program and redistribute it for a fee without making the source code freely available. In this way, it is a continuation of the university-based tradition of the 1960s and 1970s.

6. Two main open source projects (GNOME and KDE) are meant to remedy Linux's limitations on desktop computers (by developing mouse and windows interfaces).

7. For example, Torvalds (interview by Ghosh 1998b) argues that the Linux model works best with developer-type software. Ghosh (1998) views the open source process as a large repeated game process of give-and-take among developer-users (the "cooking pot" model).

8. To be certain, backward compatibility efforts can sometimes be exerted by status-seeking open source programmers. For example, Linux has been made to run on Atari machines—a pure bravado effort, since no one uses Ataris anymore.

9. We focus primarily on programmers' contributions to code. A related field of study concerns field support, which is usually also provided free of charge in the open source community. Lakhani and von Hippel 2003 provide empirical evidence for field support in the Apache project. They show that providers of help often gain learning for themselves, and that the cost of delivering help is therefore usually low.

10. Linus Torvalds and others have been awarded shares in Linux-based companies that went public. Most certainly, these rewards were unexpected and did not affect the motivation of open source programmers. If this practice becomes "institutionalized," such rewards will in the future be expected and therefore impact the motivation of open source leaders. More generally, leaders of open source movements may initially not have been motivated by ego gratification and career concerns. Like Behlendorf, Wall, and Allman, the "bug fixing" motivation may have originally been paramount. The private benefits of leadership may have grown in importance as the sector matured.

11. Success at a commercial software firm is likely to be a function of many attributes. Some of these (for example, programming talent) can be signaled through participation in open source projects. Other important attributes, however, are not readily signaled through these projects. For instance, commercial projects employing a top-down architecture require that programmers work effectively in teams, while many open source projects are initiated by relatively modest pieces of code, small enough to be written by a single individual.

12. Dasgupta and David (1994) suggest an alternative explanation for these patterns: the need to impress less-informed patrons who are likely to be impressed by

the academic's undertaking research in a "hot" area. These patterns probably are driven by academic career concerns. New fields tend to be relatively more attractive to younger researchers, since older researchers have already invested in established fields and therefore have lower marginal costs of continuing in these fields. At the same time, younger researchers need to impress senior colleagues who will evaluate them for promotion. Thus, they need the presence of some of their seniors in the new fields.

13. Later in this chapter we will discuss *companies'* incentives to release code.

14. Open source projects might be seen as imposing less of a competitive threat to the firm. As a result, the firm could be less inclined to enforce its property rights on innovations turned open source. Alternatively, the firm may be unaware that the open source project is progressing.

15. To be certain, commercial firms (e.g., Netscape, Sun, O'Reilly, Transmeta) supporting open source projects are also able to compensate programmers, because they indirectly benefit financially from these projects. Similarly, the government and non-profit corporations have done some subsidizing of open source projects. Still, there should be an edge for commercial companies.

16. While we are here interested in private incentives to participate, note that this complementarity between apprenticeship and projects is socially beneficial. The social benefits might not increase linearly with open source market share, though, since the competing open source projects could end up competing for attention in the same common pool of students.

17. To be certain, commercial companies leave APIs (application programming interfaces) for other people to provide add-ons, but this is still quite different from opening the source code.

18. On the relationship between empowerment and career concerns, see Ortega 2000. In Cassiman's (1998) analysis of research corporations (for-profit centers bringing together firms with similar research goals), free riding by parent companies boosts the researchers' autonomy and helps attract better talents. Cassiman argues that it is difficult to sustain a reputation for respecting the autonomy of researchers within firms. Cassiman's analysis looks at real control, while our argument here results from the absence of formal control over the OS programmer's activity.

19. A standard argument in favor of open source processes is their massive parallel debugging. Typically, commercial software firms can ask users only to point at problems: beta testers do not fix the bugs, they just report them. It is also interesting to note that many commercial companies do not discourage their employees from working on open source projects. In many cases where companies encourage such involvement, programmers use open source tools to fix problems. Johnson (1999) builds a model of open source production by a community of user-developers. There

is one software program or module to be developed, which is a public good for the potential developers. Each of the potential developers has a private cost of working on the project and a private value of using it; both of which are private information. Johnson shows that the probability that the innovation is made need not increase with the number of developers, as free-riding is stronger when the number of potential developers increases.

20. An argument often heard in the open source community is that people participate in open source projects because programming is fun and because they want to be "part of a team." While this argument may contain a grain of truth, it is somewhat puzzling as it stands, for it is not clear why programmers who are part of a commercial team could not enjoy the same intellectual challenges and the same team interaction as those engaged in open source development. (To be sure, it may be challenging for programmers to readily switch employers if their peers in the commercial entity are not congenial.) The argument may reflect the ability of programmers to use participation in open source projects to overcome the barriers that make signaling in other ways problematic.

21. Valloppillil (1998) further argues that reaching commercial grade quality often involves unglamorous work on power management, management infrastructure, wizards, and so forth, that makes it unlikely to attract open source developers. Valloppillil's argument seems a fair description of past developments in open source software. Some open source proponents do not confer much predictive power on his argument, though; they predict, for example, that open source user interfaces such as GNOME and KDE will achieve commercial grade quality.

22. Open source projects have trouble attracting people initially unless they leave fun challenges "up for grabs." On the other hand, the more programmers an open source project attracts, the more quickly the fun activities are completed. The reason why the projects need not burn out once they grow in ranks is that the "fixed cost" that individual programmers incur when they first contribute to the project is sunk, and so the marginal cost of continuing to contribute is smaller than the initial cost of contributing.

23. E.g., Valloppillil's (1998) discussion of the Mozilla release.

24. It should be cautioned that these observations are based on a small sample of successful projects. Observing which projects succeed or fail and the reasons for these divergent outcomes in an informal setting such as this one is quite challenging.

25. The terminology and the conceptual framework are here borrowed from Aghion-Tirole 1997.

26. For instance, concerns about the "poaching" of key employees was one of the reasons cited for Steve Jobs's recent decision to cease giving credit to key programmers in Apple products (Claymon 1999).

27. For the economic analysis of employee visibility, see Gibbons 1997 and Gibbons and Waldman's (1999) review essays. Ronde 1999 models the firms' incentives to "hide" their workers from the competition in order to preserve their trade secrets.

28. Commercial vendors try to address this problem in various ways. For example, Microsoft developers now have the right to present their work to their users. Promotions to "distinguished engineer" or to a higher rank more generally, as well as the granting of stock options as a recognition of contributions, also make the individual performance more visible to the outside world.

29. Cusamano and Selby (1995), though, document a number of management institutions at Microsoft that attempt to limit these pressures.

30. Another motivation for commercial companies to interface with the open source world might be public relations. Furthermore, firms may temporarily encourage programmers to participate in open source projects to learn about the strengths and weaknesses of this development approach.

31. Red Hat provides support for Linux-based products, while VA Linux provided hardware products optimized for the Linux environment. In December 1999, their market capitalizations were $17 and $10 billion respectively, though they have subsequently declined significantly.

32. Of course, these programmers also increase the company's ability to learn from scientific and technical discoveries elsewhere and help the company with the development of the proprietary segment.

33. Companies could even (though probably less likely) encourage ex nihilo development of new pieces of open source software.

34. See, for example, the discussion of SGI's open source strategy in Taschek (1999).

35. It should also be noted that many small developers are uncomfortable doing business with leading software firms, feeling them to be exploitative, and that these barriers may be overcome by the adoption of open source practices by the large firms. A rationalization of this story is that, along the lines of Farrell and Katz (2000), the commercial platform owner has an incentive to introduce substitutes in a complementary segment, in order to force prices down in that segment and to raise the demand for licenses to the software platform. When, however, the platform is available through, for instance, a BSD-style license, the platform owner has no such incentives, as he or she cannot raise the platform's price. Vertical relationships between small and large firms in the software industry are not fully understood, and would reward further study.

36. An interesting question is why corporations do not replicate the modular structure of open source software in commercial products more generally. One possibility may be that modular code, whatever its virtues for a team of programmers

working independently, is not necessarily better for a team of programmers and managers working together.

37. The former solution may be particularly desirable if the user has customized last generation's applications.

38. Wayner (2000) argues that the open source movement is not about battling Microsoft or other leviathans and notes that in the early days of computing (say, until the late seventies) code sharing was the only way to go as "the computers were new, complicated, and temperamental. Cooperation was the only way that anyone could accomplish anything." This argument is consistent with the hypothesis stated later, according to which the key factor behind cooperation is the alignment of objectives, and this alignment may come from the need to get a new technology off the ground, from the presence of a dominant firm, or from other causes.

39. See, for example, Hansmann 1996.

40. The increasing number of software patents being granted by the U.S. Patent and Trademark Office provide another avenue through which such a hijacking might occur. In a number of cases, industry observers have alleged that patent examiners—not being very familiar with the unpatented "prior art" of earlier software code—have granted unreasonably broad patents, in some cases giving the applicant rights to software that was originally developed through open source processes.

41. A related phenomenon that would reward academic scrutiny is "shareware." Many of packages employed by researchers (including several used by economists, such as MATLAB, SAS, and SPSS) have grown by accepting modules contributed by users. The commercial vendors coexist with the academic user community in a positive symbiotic relationship. These patterns provide a useful parallel to open source.

II The Evaluation of Free/Open Source Software Development

4 | Standing in Front of the Open Source Steamroller

I am a contrarian by nature. I have a certificate pronouncing me the "premier curmudgeon of software practice." I am the author of a regular column in *IEEE Software* magazine called "The Loyal Opposition." I have been standing up in front of advancing software steamrollers throughout my career:

• Attempting to diminish the communication chasm between academe in industry, beginning as far back as the early 1960s (and, I would add, continuing to this day)

• Opposing the apparent inevitability of IBM hardware and software in the 1960s (I participated on a team that put a complete homegrown software system—including, for example, a homegrown operating system—on its IBM hardware in order to allow us to more easily transition to other vendors later on)

• Questioning the insistent academic push for formal methods in software, beginning in the 1970s (I questioned them then, and I fault the academic community for advocating without evaluating them now)

• Looking objectively at each new software fad and fancy, from the structured approaches to object orientation to the agile methods, to find out whether there is any research support for the hyped claims of conceptual zealots (there almost never is)

All of that marks me, of course, as someone you might want to listen to, but not necessarily believe in!

Here in this book on open source and free software, I want to take that same contrarian position. To date, much of the writing on open source software has been overwhelmingly supportive of the idea. That overwhelming support is the steamroller that I intend to stand up in front of here.

Before I get to the primary content of this chapter, disaggregating and questioning the primary tenets of open source, let me present to you here some of the qualifications that have resulted in my feeling confident enough to take such an outrageous position:

- I am a 45+-year veteran of the software profession.
- I have deliberately remained a software technologist throughout my career, carefully avoiding any management responsibilities.
- As a technologist, I have made the most of what I call the "Power of Peonage"—the notion that a skilled and successful technologist has political powers that no one further up the management hierarchy has, because they are not vulnerable to loss of position if someone chooses to punish them for their actions; one of my favorite sayings is "you can't fall off the floor" (I once wrote a book of anecdotes, now out of print, about that "Power of Peonage")
- Two of my proudest moments in the software field involved building software products for which I received no compensation by my employer:
· A Fortran-to-Neliac programming language translator, back in those anti-IBM days I mentioned previously, which I built in my spare time at home just to see if I could do it (I called my translator "Jolly Roger," because its goal was to make it possible to transition IBM-dependent Fortran programs to the vendor-independent Neliac language my team had chosen to support).
· A generalization of a chemical composition scientific program whose goal was to calculate/simulate the thrust that mixing/igniting certain chemicals in a rocket engine would produce. When I began my Thanksgiving Day work at home, the product would handle only combinations of five chemical elements. When I finished, the program could handle any additional sixth element for which the users could supply the needed data. (This addition allowed my users to determine that boron, being touted in the newsmagazines of that time as the chemical element of rocketry's future, was worthless as an additive.)

So, am I in favor of programmers doing their own programming thing on their own time? Of course. It is the claims and political activities that go along with all of that that form the steamroller I want to stand in front of. Let me tell you some of what I dislike about the open source movement.

Hype

Hype is not unknown in the software field in general. The advocates of every new software idea exaggerate the benefits of using that idea. Those exaggerated claims generally have no basis in reality (see, for example, Glass 1999). Unfortunately, and perhaps surprisingly, the advocates of open source are no better in this regard than their callous proprietary colleagues. Claims are made for the use and future of open source software that simply boggle the rational mind, as described in the following sections.

Best People

The claim is frequently made that open source programmers are the best programmers around. One author, apparently acting on input from open source zealots, said things like "Linux is the darling of talented programmers," and opined that the open source movement was "a fast-forward environment in which programming's best and brightest . . . contribute the most innovative solutions" (Sanders 1998).

Is there any evidence to support these claims? My answer is "No," for several reasons:

- There is little data on who the best programmers are. Attempts to define Programmer Aptitude Tests, for example, which evaluate the capabilities of subjects to become good programmers, have historically been largely failures. In an early study, the correlation between computer science grades and practitioner achievement was found to be negative. Although some programmers are hugely better than others—factors up to 30:1 have been cited—nothing in the field's research suggests that we have found an objective way of determining who those best people are.
- Since we can't identify who the best people are, there is no way to study the likelihood of their being open source programmers. Thus those who claim that open source people are software's "best and brightest" cannot possibly back up those claims with any factual evidence.
- It is an interesting characteristic of programmers that most of them tend to believe that they are the best in the field. Certainly, I know that few programmers are better than I am! It used to be a standard joke in the software field that, if a roomful of programmers were asked to rate themselves, none of them would end up in the second tier. Therefore, I suspect that if you took any group of programmers—including open source programmers—and asked them if they were the field's best and brightest, they would answer in the affirmative. That, of course, does not make it so.

Most Reliable

The claim is also frequently made that open source software is the most reliable software available. In this case, there are some studies—and some interesting data—to shed light on this claim.

The first thing that should be said about open source reliability is that its advocates claim that a study identified as the "Fuzz Papers" (Miller, Fredriksen, and So 1990; Miller et al. 1995; Forrester and Miller 2000) produced results that showed that their software was, indeed, more reliable than its proprietary alternatives.

As a student of software claims, I have followed up on the Fuzz Papers. I obtained the papers, read and analyzed them, and contacted their primary author to investigate the matter even further. The bottom line of all that effort is that the Fuzz Papers have virtually nothing to say about open source software, one way or the other, and their author agrees with that assessment (he does say, though, that he personally believes that open source may well be more reliable). Thus it is truly bizarre that anyone would claim that these studies (they are peculiar studies of software reliability, and to understand why I say "peculiar," you should read them yourself!) support the notion that open source code is more reliable.

Since then at least one academic researcher has done further, real studies of open source code reliability. In that work, we find that open source programmers do not tend to use any special reliability techniques—for example, fully 80% of them do not produce any test plans, and only 40% use any test tools. The author surmises that "open source people tend to rely on other people to look for defects in their products" (Zhao and Elbaum 2000).

That latter point deserves more discussion. One popular saying in the open source world is "Given enough eyeballs, all bugs are shallow" (Raymond 2001, 41). What this means is that the open source culture, which involves people reading and critiquing the code of others, will tend to find and eventually eliminate all software bugs. But there is a problem with this belief. It is based on the assumption that all open source code will be thoroughly reviewed by its readers. However, the review of open source code is likely to be very spotty. We will see later in this chapter that open source people tend to review heavily code that particularly interests them, and spend little or no time on code that does not. Therefore, there is no guarantee that any piece of open source code will be thoroughly reviewed by members of the community. To make matters worse, there is no data regarding how much of any open source code is in fact reviewed. As a result, the belief that all open source code will be subjected to "many eyeballs" is naive and, in the end, unprovable.

Most Secure

Just as the claims are rampant that open source software is more reliable than its proprietary alternatives, there are analogous claims that it is more secure. The more the drumbeat of concern for secure software accelerates, the louder those claims become.

Unlike the software reliability issue, there is very little evidence on either side of the ledger regarding software security. Certainly security holes have been found in proprietary software. Certainly also, holes have been found in open source code (see, for example, Glass 2002a). And both sides have made strong claims that their software is either secure, or that they are making it so.

Probably the most accurate thing anyone can say about software security is that (a) it is all too easy for programmers to leave holes, independent of how the code is being written (for a list of the top five security-related software defects, see Glass 2003a); (b) the perversity of "crackers" tends to mean that wherever they seek security holes, they are likely to find them, and they tend to seek wherever the loudest claims are that the software is secure! (For example, in the book *Know Your Enemy* (Honeypot Project 2002), a study of cracker techniques by using "honeypot" systems to trap them, one "black hat" was specifically going after Linux-based .edu systems because of their claims of invulnerability, a chilling thought for both open source advocates and academics who use their wares).

And with respect to the open source claims, there is plenty of anecdotal evidence (e.g., Glass 2003b) to back both the security claims of the open source advocates and their proprietary counterparts, but there is really no definitive evidence to cause either side to be seen as victorious.

Economic Model

Probably the most fascinating thing about the open source movement is its economic model. Here are people often willing to work for no recompense whatsoever, except the joy of a job well done and the accolades of their peers! It all seems terribly noble, and in fact that nobility is undoubtedly part of the appeal of the open source movement.

It also seems faintly Utopian. There have been lots of Utopian movements in the past, where workers banded together to work for that joy of a job well done and for the common good (and, once again, for the accolades of their peers). There are two interesting things about Utopian movements. They begin in enormous enthusiasm. And they end, usually a few decades later, in failure. What are the most common causes of Utopian failure?

• The impractical nature of the economic model (I will discuss that in following sections).

• Political splintering, as discussed in a following section (note that some Utopian religious societies, such as the Harmonists, also failed because they decided to practice celibacy, but that fact seems totally unrelated to the open source movement!).

So, regarding that practicality issue, just how impractical is the open source movement? To date, the answer would appear to be that there is no sign of the movement's collapse because it is impractical.

There is little evidence one way or the other as to the size of the movement, but the frequency of its mention in the computing popular press would tend to suggest that it is growing. Its advocates are also increasingly outspoken. And companies have sprung up that, while not making money on open source products, are making money on servicing those products (e.g., Red Hat).

Then there is the issue of Communism, an issue that is usually present in discussions about the problems of open source, although it has rarely surfaced. There is a faint whiff of Communism about the concept of working for no financial gain. Open source is certainly not about "from each according to his ability, to each according to his need," so that whiff is indeed faint. But the sense of nobility that open source proponents feel, in working for no financial gain, resonates with some of the other basic Communist philosophies. And the open source proponents themselves can sometimes sound just like Communists. One columnist (Taschek 2002) recently spoke of anti-Linux forces as "capitalist interests," and later on as "capitalist forces." He also claimed that some anti-Linux people are behaving as "Microsoft lackeys." While opposing capitalism and using the word "lackeys" is not proof that the author of that column is Communist, the rhetoric he chose to use certainly reminds one of Communist rhetoric. Whether Communism is a good thing or not is, of course, up to the reader. But in this discussion of the practicality of the open source economic model, it is worth noting that the Communist system is in considerable decline and disfavor in today's world.

It is particularly interesting that advocates of open source refer to "the cathedral and the bazaar" in their discussions of the movement and its alternatives (Raymond 2001). In that view, open source represents the bazaar, a place where people freely trade their wares and skills, and the proprietary movement is represented by the cathedral, a bricks-and-mortar institution with little flexibility for change. I find that particularly interesting, because, when I first saw this particular analogy, I assumed that open source would be the cathedral, a pristine and worshipful place, and proprietary software would be the bazaar, where products and money change hands, and there is a strong tendency toward working for profit! I suppose that those who invent analogies are entitled to make them work in any way they wish. But my own thinking about this pair of analogies is that the open source way of viewing it is fairly bizarre!

Does the open source economic model show promise of working in the long term? There is no evidence at present that it will not, but on the other hand it is worth noting that the analogies we can draw between it and other relevant economic models is primarily about models that eventually failed.

Political/Sociological Model

It is common in open source circles to see the participants in the open source movement as willing, independent enthusiasts. But, on deeper analysis, it is evident that there is a strange kind of hierarchy in the movement.

First of all, there are the methodology gurus. A very few outspoken participants articulate the movement and its advantages, through their writings and speakings, spreading the gospel of open source.

More significantly, there are also product gurus. Because of the large number of people reading, critiquing, and offering changes to open source products, there is a need for someone to adjudicate among those proposed changes and configure the final agreed-upon version of the product. Linux, for example, has its Linus Torvalds, and it would be difficult to imagine the success of the Linux operating system without Linus. I will discuss a bit later why a product guru is needed.

Then there are the contributors of open source products. These are the programmers who develop products and release them into the open source product inventory. Some of these contributors, if their product is especially successful, may become product gurus.

And finally, there is that great mass of open source code readers. Readers analyze and critique code, find its faults, and propose changes and enhancements. As in many hierarchies, the success of the open source movement is really dependent on these readers at the bottom of the hierarchy. Its claims of reliability and security, for example, are in the end entirely dependent on the rigor and energy and skill which the readers place in their work.

To understand this hierarchy better, it is necessary to contemplate how it functions when a change or an error fix for a product is proposed. The change moves up the hierarchy to the product guru, who then makes a decision as to whether the change is worthy of inclusion in the product. If it is, the change is made and becomes a permanent part of the product.

It is when the change is rejected for inclusion that things can get interesting. Now the reader who identified the change has a dilemma to deal with. Either he/she must forget about the change, or make that change in a special and different version of the product. This latter is actually considered an option in the open source movement, and there is a verb—*forking*—that covers this possibility. The reader who wants his change made in a special version is said to have *forked* the product, and the further development of the product may take place on both of these forks.

But forking is an extremely uncommon thing to do in the open source movement, with good reason. First of all, there is the possibility of loss of commonality. The Unix operating system, for example, is roundly criticized because there are multiple versions of that product, each with its own advocate (often a vendor), and as a result there is really no such thing as *the* Unix system any more. That is a serious enough problem that it warrants strict attention to whether forking a product is really a good thing.

There is an even stronger reason, though, why forking is uncommon. It has been well known in the software field for more than 30 years that making modifications to a standard product is a bad idea. It is a bad idea because, as the product inevitably progresses through many versions—each of which usually includes desirable changes and modifications—the forked version(s) are left out of that progress. Or, worse yet, the new changes are constantly being added to the forked version (or the forking changes are being added to the new standard version) by the person who created the fork, both of which are terribly labor-intensive and error-prone activities.

Now, let's step back and look at the impact of this forking problem on the field of open source. The claim is frequently made by open source advocates that programmers who find fault with a product are free to make their own fixes to it, and are capable of doing so because they have access to the product's source code. That's all well and good if those changes are eventually accepted into the product, but if they are not, then the very serious problem of forking arises. Thus the notion of the average user feeling free to change the open source product is a highly mixed blessing, and one unlikely to be frequently exercised.

There is another interesting sociological problem with open source. Again, the claim is frequently made that users can read their code and find and fix its problems. This is all well and good if the users are programmers, but if they are not this is simply a technical impossibility. Code reading is a difficult exercise even for the trained programmer, and it is simply not possible, to any meaningful degree, for the non-programmer user. What this means is that only code where programmers are the users is likely to receive the benefits of open source code reading, such as the "many eyeballs" reliability advantages mentioned previously. And how much code is used by programmers? This is an important question, one for which fortunately there are answers. The largest category of code, according to numerous censuses of programs, is for business applications—payroll, general ledger, and so on. The next largest category is for scientific/engineering applications. In neither of these cases are the users, in general, programmers. It is only for the category "systems programs" (e.g., operating systems, compilers, programmer support tools) where, commonly, the users are in fact programmers. Thus the percentage of software that is likely to be subject to open source reading is at best pretty minuscule.

All of these open source hierarchic sociological conditions are a bit ironic, in the context of some of the claims made for open source. For example, one zealot, in the midst of reciting the benefits of open source and urging people to switch to its use, said "Abandon your corporate hierarchies," implying that hierarchies didn't exist in the open source movement. As we have seen, that claim is extremely specious.

Remember that we spoke earlier about Utopian societies eventually dying because of political splintering? So far, the open source movement has nicely avoided many of those kinds of hazards, especially since forking (which might be the source of such splintering) turns out to be such a bad idea (for nonpolitical reasons). There is one serious fracture in the open source movement, between those who believe in "free" software and those who believe in "open source" software (an explanation of the differences is vitally important to those on both sides of the fracture, but of little importance to anyone else studying the movement from a software engineering perspective), but so far, except for public spats in the literature, these differences seem to have had little effect on the field.

However, there are some interesting political considerations afoot here. Both the open source and proprietary supporters have begun trying to enlist political support to ensure and enhance the future of their approaches (Glass 2002b). For example, one South American country (Peru) is considering a law that would require "free software in public administration," on the grounds that free software is the only way to guarantee local control of the software product (as we have seen earlier, that is a dangerously naive argument). And the U.S. Department of Defense is said to have been inundated by requests from proprietary companies like Microsoft to oppose the use of open source code in DoD systems. This kind of thing, ugly at best, may well get uglier as time goes on.

All of that brings us to another fascinating question. What is the future of open source . . . and how is it related to the past of the software field?

The Future . . . and the Past

First, let's look back at the past of open source software. Raymond (2001) dates open source back to "the beginnings of the Internet, 30 years ago."

That doesn't begin to cover open source's beginnings. It is important to realize that free and open software dates back to the origins of the computing field, as far back as the 1950s, fifty-odd years ago. Back then, all software was available for free, and most of it was open.

Software was available for free because it hadn't really occurred to anyone that it had value. The feeling back then was that computer hardware and software were inextricably intertwined, and so you bought the hardware and got the software thrown in for free. And software was open because there was little reason for closing it—since it had no value in the marketplace, it didn't occur to most people in the field that viewing source code should be restricted. There were, in fact, thriving software bazaars, where software was available for the taking from user organizations like SHARE, and the highest accolade any programmer could receive was to have his or her software accepted for distribution in the SHARE library, from which it was available to anyone in the field.

Freely available, open software remained the rule into the mid-1960s, when antitrust action against IBM by the U.S. Department of Justice first raised the issue of whether the so-called "bundling" of software with hardware constituted a restriction of trade. Eventually, IBM "unbundled" hardware and software, and—for the first time—it was possible to sell software in the open marketplace. However, IBM (it was widely believed at the time) deliberately underpriced its software to inhibit a marketplace for software, which might enable computer users to move beyond IBM products into those of other hardware vendors (who had historically not offered as much bundled software as IBM). Thus, even when software was no longer free and open, there was still not much of a marketplace for it.

It was a matter of another decade or so before the marketplace for software became significant. Until that happened, there was a plethora of small software companies not making much money, and nothing like today's Microsoft and Computer Associates.

Whether all of that was a good thing or a bad thing can, of course, be considered an open question. But for those of us who lived through the era of software that was free and open because there were no alternatives, a return to the notion of free and open software (and the loss of the capability to profit from products in which we feel pride) feels like a huge regressive step. However, there aren't many of us old-timers around anymore, so I suppose this argument is of little interest to the issue of the future of open source as seen from the twenty-first century.

Because of all of that, let's return to a discussion of the future of open source. Advocates tend to make it sound like open source is without question the future of the software field, saying things like "the open-source age is inevitable," while chiding Microsoft (the primary putative enemy of open source, as we have already seen above) for sticking to the "buggy whip" proprietary approach (Pavlicek 2002).

Raymond (2001) goes even further. He says things like "Windows 2000 will be either canceled or dead on arrival," "the proprietary Unix sector will almost completely collapse," "Linux will be in effective control of servers, data centers, ISPs, and the Internet," and ultimately, "I expect the open source movement to have essentially won its point about software within the next three to five years." And then he proposes a blueprint for fighting the war that he sees necessary to make it so, with things like "co-opting the prestige media that serves the Fortune 500" (he names, for example, the *New York Times* and the *Wall Street Journal*), "educating hackers in guerrilla marketing techniques," and "enforcing purity with an open source certification mark." It is important to realize, of course, that we are well into his predicted three-to-five-year future, and none of those things have happened. Clearly, open source zealots are going to have to readjust their timetable for the future, if not give up on it entirely.

There are other views of software's future, of course. Some of those views I have expressed in the preceding material, which suggest that open source, far from being software's future, may be a passing fad, a Utopian-like dream. Others simply go on about their business ignoring open source, for the most part, participating in the proprietary software market place with only an occasional uneasy glance over their shoulders. Still others, looking for a safety play, are betting on both open source and proprietary software, developing products consistent with both approaches (ironically, IBM is one of those companies). But perhaps my most favorite view of the future of the software field comes from Derek Burney, CEO (at the time of this pronouncement) of Corel, a company which had elected to host its future tools development work on the open source Linux operating system. Responding to a question about developing open source versions of Corel's WordPerfect software suite, he said "We have no plans to do so." Then he added "In my opinion, open source makes sense for operating systems and nothing more."

The future of open source? It could range anywhere from "the inevitable future of the software field" to "it's only good for operating systems, nothing more" to "it's in all probability a passing fad."

No matter how you slice it—inevitable future or passing fad—the notion of open source software has certainly livened up the software scene, circa 2005!

5   Has Open Source Software a Future?

Brian Fitzgerald

Open Source Software (OSS) has attracted enormous media and research attention since the term was coined in February 1998. From an intellectual perspective, the concept abounds with paradoxes, which makes it a very interesting topic of study. One example is the basic premise that software source code—the "crown jewels" for many proprietary software companies—should be provided freely to anyone who wishes to see it or modify it. Also, there is a tension between the altruism of a collectivist gift-culture community—an "impossible public good" as Smith and Kollock (1999) have characterized it—and the inherent individualism that a reputation-based culture also implies. Furthermore, its advocates suggest that OSS represents a paradigm shift in software development that can solve what has been somewhat controversially termed the "software crisis" (i.e., systems taking too long to develop, costing too much, and not working very well when eventually delivered). These advocates point to the quality and reliability of OSS software, its rapid release schedule, and its availability at very little or no cost. Other supporters of OSS believe that it is an initiative that has implications well beyond the software field and suggest that it will become the dominant mode of work for knowledge-workers in the information society. These themes feature in the chapters in this volume by Kelty (chapter 21) and Lessig (chapter 18) earlier, and have also been reported by many others (Bollier 1999; Himanen 2001; Markus, Manville, and Agres 2000; O'Reilly 2000).

However, despite these claims, a closer analysis of the OSS phenomenon suggests that there are a complex range of problematic issues from the triple perspectives of software engineering, general business factors, and socio-cultural issues that serve to question the extent to which the OSS phenomenon will even survive, let alone prosper. This chapter identifies and discusses these challenges. This strategy of identifying these potential

Table 5.1
Problematic issues for OSS from software engineering, business, and sociocultural perspectives

---

Problematic issues from a software engineering perspective

- OSS is not really a revolutionary paradigm shift in software engineering
- Not enough developer talent to support increased interest in OSS
- Code quality concerns
- Difficulties of initiating an OSS development project and community
- Negative implications of excessive modularity
- Insufficient interest in mundane tasks of software development
- Version proliferation and standardization problems

Problematic issues from a business perspective

- Insufficient focus on strategy in OSS development community
- "Free beer" rather than "free speech" more important to OSS mass market
- Insufficient transfer to vertical software domains
- OSS a victim of its own success

Problematic issues from a sociocultural perspective

- OSS becomes part of the establishment
- Burnout of leading OSS pioneers
- Unstable equilibrium between modesty and supreme ability required of OSS project leaders
- "Alpha-male" territorial squabbles in scarce reputation cultures

---

"failure factors" in advance is deliberate, in that the OSS movement can address these issues if deemed necessary.

The chapter is laid out as follows. In the next section the specific challenges from the software engineering perspective are outlined. Following this, the potential pitfalls from the overall business perspective are discussed. Finally, the problematic issues in relation to the sociocultural perspective are addressed. These challenges are summarized in table 5.1.

Problematic Issues from a Software Engineering Perspective

OSS is often depicted as a revolution or paradigm shift in software engineering. This may be largely due to Raymond's distinction between the cathedral and the bazaar. Raymond chose the "cathedral" as a metaphor for the conventional software engineering approach, generally characterized by tightly coordinated, centralized teams following a rigorous development process. By contrast, the "bazaar" metaphor was chosen to reflect the babbling, apparent confusion of a mid-Eastern marketplace. In terms of software development, the bazaar style does not mandate any particular development approach—all developers are free to develop in their own way and to follow their own agenda. There is no formal procedure to ensure that developers are not duplicating effort by working on the same problem. In conventional software development, such duplication of effort would be seen as wasteful, but in the open source bazaar model, it leads to a greater exploration of the problem space, and is consistent with an evolutionary principle of mutation and survival of the fittest, in so far as the best solution is likely to be incorporated into the evolving software product. This duplication of effort reveals a further aspect of OSS that seems to set it apart from conventional software development—namely, the replacing of the classic Brooks Law ("adding manpower to a late software product makes it later" (Brooks 1995)) with the more colloquial so-called Linus's Law ("given enough eyeballs, every bug is shallow"). Brooks had based his law on empirical evidence from the development of the IBM 360 operating system (reckoned then to be the most complex thing mankind had ever created). Thus, according to Brooks, merely increasing the number of developers should exacerbate the problem rather than be a benefit in software development. However, as already mentioned previously, proponents of the OSS model have argued that it does indeed scale to address the elements of the so-called "software crisis."

OSS is Not Really a Revolutionary Paradigm Shift in Software Engineering

If all the positive claims about OSS were true, then we might expect that OSS could be categorized as a revolutionary paradigm shift for the better in software engineering. At first glance, OSS appears to be completely alien to the fundamental tenets and conventional wisdom of software engineering. For example, in the bazaar development style, there is no real formal design process, there is no risk assessment nor measurable goals, no direct monetary incentives for most developers, informal co-ordination and control, much duplication and parallel effort. All of these are anathema to conventional software engineering. However, upon closer analysis, certain well-established principles of software engineering can be seen to be at the heart of OSS. For example, code modularity is critically important (and also an Achilles heel, as will be discussed later). Modules must be loosely coupled, thereby allowing distributed development in the first place. Likewise, concepts such as peer review, configuration management and release management are taken to extreme levels in OSS, but these are well-understood topics in traditional software engineering. In summary, the code in OSS products is often very structured and modular in the first place, contributions are carefully vetted and incorporated in a very disciplined fashion in accordance with good configuration management, independent peer review and testing. Similarly, Linux benefited a great deal (probably too well, as the threat from the SCO Group in May 2003 to take legal action over breach of its Unix patents would suggest) from the evolution of Unix as problems in Unix were addressed over time (McConnell 1999). Overall then, the extent to which OSS represents a radical "silver bullet" in software development does not really measure up to scrutiny.

Not Enough Developer Talent to Support Increased Interest in OSS

The main contributors of the OSS community are acknowledged to be superbly talented "code gods," suggested by some to be among the top five percent of programmers in terms of their skills. Also, as they are self-selected, they are highly motivated to contribute. The remarkable potential of gifted individuals has long been recognized in the software field. Brooks (1987) suggests that good programmers may be a hundred times more productive than mediocre ones. Thus, given the widely recognized talent of the OSS leaders, the success of OSS products may not be such a complete surprise. Indeed, it is more critical in the case of OSS, as the absence of face-to-face interaction or other organizational cues makes it vital that there be an ultimate arbiter whose authority and ability is pretty much above question, and who can inspire others, resolve disputes and prevent forking (more on this later).

However, just as OSS is not actually a paradigm shift in software engineering, it is in fact somewhat reminiscent of the Chief Programmer Team (CPT) of the 1970s (Baker 1972). While the CPT appeared to show early promise, there just were not enough high quality programmers around to fuel it. Similarly, the explosion of interest in OSS and the identification of "itches to be scratched" may not be supported by the pool of development talent available. To some extent one could argue, that this is already the case. For example, the SourceXchange service provided by the major OSS player, Collab.Net, which sought to create a brokering service where companies could solicit OSS developers to work on their projects, actually ceased operations in April 2001. Likewise, a study by Capiluppi et al. (2003) of over 400 Freshmeat.net projects revealed that the majority were solo works with two or fewer developers, and also with little apparent vitality, as in a follow-up study six months later, 97 percent showed no change in version number or code size.

Code Quality Concerns

The corollary of the previous discussion is obvious. While the early OSS pioneers may have been "best-of-breed" programmers, the eventual programming ability of the programmers who participate in OSS could become a problem. It is well-known that some programmers are net-negative producers (NNP). That is, the project actually suffers from their involvement as their contributions introduce problems into the code base in the longer term. Unfortunately, due to the popularity of OSS, a lot of these NNP programmers may get involved and succeed in getting their poor quality code included, with disastrous consequences. One could argue that OSS is more likely to be vulnerable to this phenomenon, as the formal interviewing and recruitment procedures that precede involvement in commercial software development are not generally part of the OSS process, although the long probationary period served on the high-profile OSS projects clearly serves a useful filtering purpose. However, it is by no means certain that this process could scale to deal with increased popularity of the OSS development mode. Indeed, some studies have now questioned the quality of OSS code in Linux, for example, the chapter in this volume by Rusovan and Lawford and Parnas (chapter 6), and also an earlier study by Stamelos et al. (2001). Other influential figures such as Ken Thompson (1999), creator of Unix, have put the case very bluntly:

I view Linux as something that's not Microsoft—a backlash against Microsoft, no more and no less. I don't think it will be very successful in the long run. I've looked at the source and there are pieces that are good and pieces that are not. A whole bunch of random people have contributed to this source, and the quality varies drastically. (p. 69)

Tellingly, all these negative opinions are based on analysis of the actual source code, rather than anecdotal opinion. Of course, one could argue that open source is vulnerable to such criticism since the code is open, and that the proprietary code in closed commercial systems might be no better.

Difficulties of Initiating an OSS Development Project and Community

Increasingly, organizations might choose to release their code in an open source fashion. However, simply making large tracts of source code available to the general development community is unlikely to be successful, since there is then no organizational memory or persistent trace of the design decisions through which the code base evolved to that state. Thus, making the source code of Netscape available in the Mozilla project was not sufficient in itself to immediately instantiate a vibrant OSS project (although some very good OSS development tools have emerged as by-products). In most OSS projects, changelogs and mailing lists provide a mechanism whereby new developers can read themselves into the design ethos of the project, in itself perhaps not the most efficient mechanism to achieve this. Gorman (2003) describes the phenomenon in the Linux virtual memory (VM) management subproject whereby new developers may complain about the use of the buddy allocator algorithm, which dates from the 1970s, for physical page allocation, as they feel the slab allocator algorithm might be better, for example. However, they fail to appreciate the design rationale in the evolution of the project which led to that choice.

Furthermore, the principle of "having a taillight to follow," which often guides OSS development as developers incrementally grow an initial project, may perhaps not be robust enough for development if OSS products are to be produced in vertical domains where domain knowledge is critical (an issue discussed in the next section). Linus Torvalds's apparent inability to successfully manage a small development team at Transmeta (Torvalds and Diamond 2001) suggests that the concept may be too ephemeral and individualistic to provide any continuities to general software project management.

Negative Implications of Excessive Modularity

Modularity is necessary in OSS for a number of reasons. Firstly, as previously mentioned, it allows work to be partitioned among the global pool of developers. Also, as projects progress, the learning curve of the rationale behind requirements, design decisions, and so on becomes extremely steep. Thus, to facilitate the recruitment of new contributors, developers need to be able to reduce their learning focus below the level of the overall project. Modularity helps achieve this; thus, it is a *sine qua non* for OSS. Indeed, many OSS projects were rewritten to be more modular before they could be successfully developed in an OSS mode, including Sendmail, Samba, and even Linux itself (Feller and Fitzgerald 2002; Narduzzo and Rossi 2003). However, the cognitive challenge in designing a highly modular architecture of autonomous modules with minimal interdependencies is certainly not trivial (Narduzzo and Rossi 2003).

Also, the increase in modularity increases the risk of one of the well-known and insidious problems in software engineering: that of common coupling between modules, where modules make references to variables and structures in other modules which are not absolutely necessary. Thus, changes to data structures and variables in seemingly unrelated modules can have major follow-on implications. In this way, OSS systems evolve to become very difficult, if not impossible, to maintain in the long run. Some evidence of such a phenomenon being potentially imminent in the case of Linux may be inferred from Rusovan, Lawford, and Parnas (chapter 6 in this volume), and also in a study of the modularity of Linux (Schach, Jin, and Wright 2002).

Insufficient Interest in Mundane Tasks of Software Development
Many software tasks are of the mundane variety—documentation, testing, internationalization/localization, field support. Although tedious and mundane, these are vital, particularly as projects mature and need to be maintained and updated by new cohorts of developers. The exciting development tasks could be cherry-picked by OSS developers. Despite the hope that nontechnical OSS contributors and users will undertake some of the documentation and testing tasks, this has not really happened; certainly, there is no parallel to the enthusiasm with which code is contributed. However, this is perhaps understandable in a reputation-based culture, where the concept of a "code god" exists, but that of "documentation god" does not. The more rigorous studies of OSS developers that have been conducted recently for example, those reported in earlier chapters in this volume by Ghosh (chapter 2) and Lakhani and Wolf (chapter 1), reveal that altruistic motives do not loom large for OSS developers, certainly if the main beneficiaries of such effort would be outside their immediate community. Furthermore, an earlier study by Lakhani and von Hippel (2003) which analyzed the provision of field support for Apache suggests that the actual cost of providing this service is much lower for developers than one might expect, while it also provides substantial benefits to their own work, which is a significant motivation.

Version Proliferation and Standardization Problems
The many different commercial versions of Linux already pose a substantial problem for software providers developing for the Linux platform, as they have to write and test applications developed for these various versions. Also, in the larger OSS picture, as products have been developed more or less independently, interoperability and compatibility problems

among different product versions pose very time-consuming problems. Smith (2003) reports an exchange with an IT manager in a large Silicon Valley firm who lamented, "Right now, developing Linux software is a nightmare, because of testing and QA—how can you test for 30 different versions of Linux?"

One could argue that standards are of even more critical importance to the OSS community than to traditional proprietary development, since the developers do not meet face-to-face, and any mechanism that can facilitate collective action, such as the development of common standards for integration, must be a welcome one. Indeed, Smith (2003) has written a very compelling argument for the open source and standardization communities to collaborate. The primary reason for the successful dissemination of the Internet and World Wide Web technologies has been adherence to open standards. It is no coincidence that the key components of the Web and Internet are open source software: the BIND domain name server, Sendmail, the Apache web server, and so on. Standards are key to interoperable platforms. However, the outlook on standards in OSS at present is not altogether encouraging. There are a variety of initiatives which are moving broadly in this direction—for example, the Free Standards Group (http://www.freestandards.org), the Linux Standard Base and United Linux (http://www.unitedlinux.com), the Linux Desktop Consortium (http://desktoplinuxconsortium.org), and the Free Desktop group (http://www.freedesktop.org). However, these initiatives are overlapping in some cases, and are not well integrated. Also, the agenda in some cases is arguably not entirely to do with the establishment of open standards.

Problematic Issues from a Business Perspective

Just as there are challenges from a software engineering perspective, there are also fundamental challenges to OSS from the overall business perspective. This is not altogether surprising, perhaps, when one considers that the open source concept was quite literally a phenomenal overnight success in concept marketing that forced its way onto the Wall Street agenda. However, its origins are largely in a voluntary hacker community, and it is unlikely that such a community would be skilled in the cutthroat strategic maneuvering of big business.

Insufficient Focus on Strategy in OSS Development Community

OSS represents a varied mix of participants, who have very different agenda and motivations for participation—see chapters in this volume by Ghosh (chapter 2), and Lakhani and Wolf (chapter 1). Also, being loosely connected and pan-globally distributed, there is not really the possibility for the detailed strategic business planning that conventional organizations can achieve. Indeed, there is evidence of some possibly inappropriate strategic choices. For example, despite the high profile, one could argue that competing with Microsoft on desktop applications—where they possess the "category killer" application suite—is an unwise strategic use of resources in the long term. In contrast, Microsoft has abstracted some of the better ideas from OSS and may have muddied the water sufficiently with its "shared source" strategy to confuse the issue as to what OSS actually represents. Recognizing the power of the social and community identification aspects of OSS, Microsoft has introduced the Most Valued Professionals (MVP) initiative, and will extend source code access to this select group. Also, their new Open Value policy extends discretion to sales representatives to offer extreme discounts and zero percent financing to small businesses who may be likely to switch to OSS (Roy 2003). These strategies are clever, especially when allied to studies that appear to show that the total cost of ownership (TCO) of Linux is cheaper than Windows over a five-year period. It is difficult for the OSS community to emulate this kind of nimble strategic action. Also, the dispute between the open source and free software communities over the definitional issues and the relative importance of access to source code has not helped to present a unified front.

"Free Beer" Rather than "Free Speech" More Important to OSS Mass Market

By and large, many software customers may not really care about the ideology of free as in "unfettered" software rather than free as in "zero cost." This is especially salient given the downturn in the economy, and also now that many IT budgets are being drastically reduced in the aftermath of their increased budget allocation in the runup to 2000. For these organizations, zero cost or almost zero cost is the critical condition. Thus, access to the source code is not really an issue—many organizations would have neither the competence nor even the desire to inspect or modify the source code, a phenomenon labeled as the Berkeley Conundrum (Feller and Fitzgerald 2002). Indeed, these organizations are actually unlikely to distinguish between open source software, shareware, public domain software, and very cheap proprietary software (see Fitzgerald and Kenny 2003). Not having any experience with soliciting customer or market opinion, OSS developers are unlikely to perceive these market subtleties, and many OSS developers may not wish to cater for the mass market anyway.

Insufficient Transfer to Vertical Software Domains

The early examples of OSS products were in horizontal domains—infra-structure software and the like. These back-office systems were deployed by tech-savvy IT personnel who were not deterred by FUD tactics or the lack of installation wizards to streamline the process. Also, since these were back-office systems and didn't require major budgetary approval, they were generally deployed without explicit management permission. Indeed, management might well have been very concerned at the departure from the traditional contractual support model with the perceived benefit of recourse to legal action in the event of failure (the legal issue is one which we will return to later).

In these initial OSS domains, requirements and design issues were largely part of the established wisdom. This facilitated a global developer base as students or developers in almost any domain with programming ability could contribute, since the overall requirements of horizontal infrastructure systems are readily apparent. Indeed, Morisio et al. 2003 suggests that the majority of OSS projects on SourceForge are in horizontal domains, developing software that produces other software. However, in vertical domains, where most business software exists, the real problems are effective requirements analysis and design, and these are not well catered for in open source. The importance of business domain expertise has long been known (Davis and Olson 1985; Vitalari and Dickson 1983). Students and developers without any experience in the particular domain simply do not have the necessary knowledge of the application area to derive the necessary requirements which are a precursor to successful development. While much has been made of the number of OSS projects aimed at producing ERP systems, the success of such initiatives is perhaps an open question. The GNUe project which has been in existence for about four years (http://www.gnuenterprise.org) has the worthy goal of developing an OSS ERP system together with tools to implement it, and a community of resources to support it (Elliott 2003), but whether a project that appears (at the time of writing) to comprise 6 core developers, 18 active contributors, and 18 inactive ones can fulfill its goal of producing a fully fledged ERP system is an open question. Certainly, it seems unlikely that a large pool of OSS hackers would perceive this as an "itch worth scratching."

OSS a Victim of Its Own Success

Ironically, the success of the OSS phenomenon is also a source of threat to its survival. The moral of Icarus melting his wings by flying too near the sun comes to mind. While OSS was a fringe phenomenon, there was a certain safety in its relative obscurity. However, once it entered the mainstream and threatened the livelihood of the established players, the stakes shifted. O'Mahony (chapter 20 in this volume) identifies the incorporation of several OSS projects as resulting from a fear of legal liability. In a litigious culture, this fear appears to be well grounded, as at the time of writing, the SCO Group had sent a letter to 1,500 Fortune 1,000 companies and 500 global corporations advising them that Linux might have breached Unix patents owned by SCO, a potentially serious setback for Linux and open source software in general, as it could cause organizations to postpone deployment of open source software through fear of litigation. However, the extra overhead of incorporation has drawbacks. O'Mahony's study of the GNOME project supports the view expressed by Raymond (2001) that extra constraints are not welcome to the OSS community, as they go against the overall hacker ethos. She reports a tension within the GNOME development community over the fact that the GNOME Foundation control the release coordination.

General Resistance from the Business Community

There have been analyses of OSS which have likened it to Mauss's Gift Culture (for example, chapter 22 in this volume). However, in a gift economy, the recipient generally welcomes and accepts the gift. However, there is some evidence that users may not welcome the gift of OSS software. Users may fear being deskilled if they are forced to switch from popular commercial software to OSS alternatives (Fitzgerald and Kenny 2003). Also, IT staff may also have similar concerns about potential damage to their career prospects by switching from popular commercial products to OSS offerings.

There are a number of possible impediments to switching to OSS alternatives, including the cost of transition and training, reduced productivity in the interim, and general interoperability and integration problems. Also, the process may be more time-consuming than the average business user is prepared to tolerate. Personally, this author is aware of an MIT-trained engineer who worked for many years at the extremely high-tech Xerox PARC, and despite this impeccable technological pedigree, admits to spending about 17 hours installing a complete OSS solution of Linux and desktop applications, a process that required much low-level intervention, and he was still left with niggling interaction bugs between the components at the end of the process. Although the user-friendliness of

OSS installation is growing daily, these obscure difficulties will frustrate users for whom time is their most precious commodity.

Problematic Issues from a Sociocultural Perspective

Finally, there is a set of challenges to OSS from the sociocultural perspective. These are possibly the most serious challenges, as they are probably the most difficult to detect and counter in that they get to the heart of human nature and social interaction.

OSS Becomes Part of the Establishment

Undoubtedly, OSS has been attractive for many because of its antiestablishment image, and the brightest and most creative young minds have been naturally attracted to it. Iacono and Kling (1996) identify traits, such as being counter-cultural and challenging the status quo, as important for technology movements. However, as OSS has become more popular and mainstream, these bright young anarchists are likely to be far less interested. Also, as the skill level of the contributors diminishes, the badge of pride associated with being part of the community is greatly diminished. While the studies in this volume by Lakhani and Wolf (chapter 1) and Ghosh (chapter 2) do reinforce the notion of young participants in OSS projects, Ghosh's study reveals a more conformist family orientation as a significant component of OSS development now. History provides several examples of radical movements which became subsumed into the mainstream quite quickly—French Impressionism in the nineteenth century, for example.

Also, as money enters the equation in the context of record-breaking IPOs and huge investment by large corporations, the desire for financial reward could further upset the equilibrium. Red Hat, trumpeted as the patron of the open source software movement in the early days, could become the dominant monopoly in the market-place, which would raise its own problems. Moreover, the prices for the high-level packages and proprietary add-ons, together with increasingly restrictive conditions that some OSS providers are imposing, is increasingly bringing them in line with commercial software (Roy 2003). This may result in an Orwellian *Animal Farm* scenario, a story that began with a clear separation between the "good" animals and the "bad" humans, but that eventually progressed to a point where it became impossible to distinguish between the animals and the humans. Likewise, it may become increasingly difficult to distinguish the notional OSS "good guys" from the notional "evil empires" of commercial proprietary software.

Burnout of Leading OSS Pioneers

There is an obvious danger that the leading pioneers will burn out. Not just from the excessive workload—Linus Torvalds is estimated to receive at least 250 emails per day concerning the Linux kernel, for example—but as family commitments arise for a greater proportion of developers, it will be harder to commit the time necessary to lead projects. Also, if these pioneers are primarily in it for the passion, challenge, freedom, and fun, then as the phenomenon becomes more popular, these characteristics get downplayed far more. The threat of legal action has become much more of a reality now, making OSS development a far more stressful affair than in the past.

Unstable Equilibrium Between Modesty and Supreme Ability Required of OSS Project Leaders

OSS pioneer developers need to be modest to ensure that others will contribute. Indeed, Torvalds's initial email posting in 1991 inviting others to help develop Linux is a model of modesty and humility. If other potential OSS developers think their contribution is unnecessary or would not be welcome, they would not be motivated to help, and the project would never get off the ground. However, in addition to modesty and self-deprecation, OSS leaders need to be superbly talented and charismatic. The greater the perceived talent of OSS project leaders, the less likely that their authority will be questioned when they arbitrate on disputes, choose between competing contributions, set the direction for the project, and generally prevent forking. In the absence of rewards and incentives that apply in traditional software development, the supreme authority of a "code god" leader is important, especially given that developers may be distributed across different cultures and countries. However, this mix of social skills, modesty, charisma, and superb talent are not ones that are in common supply in any area of human endeavor, let alone the software arena.

Alpha-Male Territorial Squabbles in Scarce Reputation Culture

OSS is fundamentally a reputation-based economy, and the initiator of an OSS project potentially attracts the greatest reputation, so egoism is very much part of the mix. Unfortunately, as already mentioned, OSS is a male-dominated preserve. While at some levels it is presented as a collectivist Utopia, analysis of the mailing lists reveal a good deal of heated and robust dissension (chap. 22 this volume). Also, Michlmayr and Hill (2003) reveal that on the Debian project there is some resentment about the use of nonmaintainer uploads, as these are generally interpreted as a sign of the primary maintainer not performing the task adequately. Michlmayr and Hill report that this stigma was not a part of Debian in the past, and suggest that it may be due to the growth of Debian from 200 to 1,000 developers. This possibility is in keeping with the general argument here that increased popularity and growth in OSS projects will contribute to the onset of such problems. The potential for discord is great. Already, there have been some complaints by OSS contributors about rejection of their code contributions on some projects (Feller and Fitzgerald 2002).

At a higher level, the internal dispute in the OSS community itself, with the well-publicized disagreement between the founders, does not augur well for the successful future of the movement, especially when added to the wrangling between the open source and free software communities over the intricacies and fine detail of definitional issues, which are increasingly less relevant as the OSS phenomenon continues to evolve.

Also, reputation may be a scarcer resource that may scale far less than first anticipated, in that only a small handful of people may actually achieve widespread name recognition. One of the findings of the FLOSS study (chap. 2, this volume) was that respondents were as likely to report knowing fictional developers (made up for the study) as much as actual developers when it got beyond the first few well-known names. This is likely to further stoke the flames of competition.

Conclusion

The OSS phenomenon is an interesting one with such enormous potential, not solely from the software perspectives, but also in its role as a catalyst for the new organizational model in the networked economy, and as an essential facilitator in creating the open information society and bridging the "Digital Divide." Other chapters in this book have addressed these issues eloquently, and it is this author's fervent hope that the OSS phenomenon survives, prospers, and delivers to its complete potential. This chapter has been written in the spirit of promoting more critical discussion of OSS and identifying the challenges that may need to be overcome.

6 | Open Source Software Development: Future or Fad?

Srdjan Rusovan, Mark Lawford, and David Lorge Parnas

This chapter discusses the quality of Open Source Software (OSS). Questions about the quality of OSS were raised during our effort to apply experimental software inspection techniques (Parnas 1994b) to the ARP (Address Resolution Protocol) module in the Linux implementation of TCP/IP. It (1) reviews OSS development, (2) discusses that approach in the light of earlier observations about software development, (3) explains the role of ARP, (4) discusses problems that we observed in the Linux implementation of ARP, and (5) concludes with some tentative observations about OSS.

Ultimately, It's the Product that Counts

In recent decades, there have been so many problem software projects—projects that did not produce products, produced inadequate products, or produced products that were late or over budget—that researchers have become very concerned about the process by which organizations develop software. Many processes have been proposed—often with claims that they are a kind of panacea that will greatly reduce the number of problem projects. Process researchers are generally concerned with the "people side" of software development, looking at issues such as the organization of teams and project management.

We sometimes seem to lose sight of the fact that a software development process is just a means of producing a product and we should not ignore the quality of the product. We expect more from a real software product than that the current version "works." We expect it to have an "architecture"[1] that makes it practical to correct or update the product when changes are required.

This chapter reports on our look at one very well-known OSS product, the Linux operating system. What we learned by studying one component of Linux raises some important issues about the process by which it was developed.

A Brief History of Linux

Linux was initially developed by Linus Torvalds in 1991. Linux has been revised many times since then. The work is done by a group of volunteers who communicate through the linux-kernel mailing list on the Internet. Torvalds has acted as the main kernel developer and exercised some control over the development. Commercial companies have added value by packaging the code and distributing it with documentation.

Linux is a Unix-like operating system. Most of the common Unix tools and programs can run under Linux and it includes most modern Unix features. Linux was initially developed for the Intel 80386 microprocessor. Over the years, developers have made Linux available on other architectures. Most of the platform-dependent code was moved into platform-specific modules that support a common interface.

Linux is a kernel; it does not include all the applications such as file system utilities, graphical desktops (including windowing systems), system administrator commands, text editors, compilers, and so forth. However, most of these programs are freely available under the GNU General Public License and can be installed in a file system supported by Linux (Bovet and Cesati 2000).

Introduction to Open Source Software (OSS)

Linux is one of the most widely available pieces of "open source" software; some people believe Linux and open source are synonymous. However, the "open source" concept has been applied to many other software products.

What Is Open Source Software?

In traditional commercial software development, software is treated as valuable intellectual property; the source code is not distributed and is protected by copyright and license agreements. Developers have gone to court to deny government agencies the right to inspect their software, and there have been lawsuits because a developer believed that source code had been stolen and used without permission.

In contrast, OSS is distributed with complete source code and recipients are encouraged to read the code and even to modify it to meet their individual needs. Moreover, recipients are encouraged to make their changes available to other users, and many of their changes are incorporated into the source code that is distributed to all users. There are many varieties of OSS approaches, and many subtle issues about how to make them work, but the essence is to reject the assumption that source is private property that must be protected from outsiders.

The success of Linux and other open source products have demonstrated that OSS distribution is workable. Some products that were once proprietary have become open source and some products are available in both open source and proprietary versions.

"Brooks's Law" and Open Source Software

In his classic work *The Mythical Man Month*, Fred Brooks (1995) describes one of the fundamental facts about software development: adding more programmers to a project doesn't necessarily reduce time to completion; in fact, it can delay completion.

Intuitively, it might seem that adding programmers would increase the amount of programming that gets done (because two programmers can write more code than one programmer), but that does not mean that the goals of the project will necessarily be achieved sooner. A number of factors may contribute to the phenomenon that Brooks describes:

• Unless the coding assignments have been carefully chosen, the total amount of code written may increase as several programmers solve shared problems with code that is not shared.

• It is not often the case that two programmers can work without communicating with each other. Adding programmers often increases the number of interfaces between coding assignments (modules). Whether or not the interfaces are defined and documented, the interfaces exist and programmers must spend time studying them. If the interfaces are not accurately and completely documented, programmers will spend time consulting with other programmers or reading their code.

• Programmers must spend time implementing methods of communicating between modules.

• Often, some programmers duplicate some function already provided by others.

• It is often necessary to change interfaces, and when this happens, the programmers who are affected by the change must negotiate[2] a new interface. This process can seriously reduce the rate of progress. When two programmers are discussing their code, neither is writing more.

Brooks's observations should make us ask how open source software development could possibly succeed. One advantage of the open source approach is its ability to bring the effort of a worldwide legion of programmers to bear on a software development project, but Brooks's observations suggest that increasing the number of programmers might be counterproductive.

Two factors should be noted when considering Brooks's observations:

• Brooks's observations were about the development of new code, not the analysis or revision of existing code. We see no reason not to have several programmers review a program simultaneously. Of course, two people may agree that the code is wrong but identify different causes and propose different, perhaps inconsistent, changes. As soon as we start to consider changes, we are back in a code development situation and Brooks's observations are relevant.

• Brooks's observations are most relevant when the code structure does not have well-documented module interfaces. Since the original publication of Brooks's observations, many programmers, (not just open source programmers) have accepted the fact that software should be modular. If the code is organized as a set of modules with precisely documented stable interfaces, programmers can work independently of each other; this can ameliorate some of the problems that Brooks observed.

Open Source Software Is Not the Same as Free Software
One of the main advantages of Linux is the fact that it is "free software." It is important to understand that "free" means much more than "zero price."[3] "Free" is being used as in "free spirit," "free thought," and perhaps even "free love." The software is unfettered by traditional intellectual property restrictions.

More precisely, "free software" refers to the users' freedom to run, copy, distribute, study, change, and improve the software. In addition to the permission to download the source code without paying a fee, the literature identifies four freedoms, for the recipients of the software (Raymond 2001):

• The freedom to run the program, for any purpose.
• The freedom to study how the program works, and adapt it to one's own needs.
• The freedom to redistribute copies to others.
• The freedom to improve the program, and release improvements to the public, in the expectation that the whole community benefits from the changes.

A program is considered "free" software if users have all of these freedoms. These freedoms result (among other things) in one not having to request, or pay for, permission to use or alter the software. Users of such software are free to make modifications and use them privately in their own work; they need not even mention that such modifications exist.

It is important to see that the four freedoms are independent. Source code can be made available with limits on how it is used, restrictions on changes, or without the right to redistribute copies. One could even make the source available to everyone but demand payment each time that it is used (just as radio stations pay for playing a recording).

It is also important to note that "open source" does not mean "noncommercial." Many who develop and distribute Linux do so for commercial purposes. Even software that has the four freedoms may be made available by authors who earn money by giving courses, selling books or selling extended versions.

Open Source Development of Linux
The fact that all recipients are permitted to revise code does not mean that the project needs no organization. There is a clear structure for the Linux development process.

A significant part of the Linux kernel development is devoted to diagnosing bugs. At any given time, only one version (the "stable kernel") is considered debugged. There is another version of the kernel called the *development kernel*; it undergoes months of debugging after a feature freeze. This doesn't mean that the kernel is inherently buggy. On the contrary, the Linux kernel is a relatively mature and stable body of code. However, Linux is both complex and important. The complexity means that bugs in new code are to be expected; the importance means that a new version should not be released before finding and correcting those bugs.

The Linux development community has a hierarchical structure; small "clans" work on individual projects under the direction of a team leader who takes responsibility for integrating that clan's work with that of the rest of the Linux developers "tribe."

If one understands the Linux development process, the power of open source software development becomes apparent. Open source projects can attract a larger body of talented programmers than any one commercial project. However, the effective use of so many programmers requires that projects follow good coding practices, producing a modular design with well-defined interfaces, and allowing ample time for review, testing, and debugging.

By some standards, the Linux kernel is highly modular. The division into stable and development versions is intended to minimize interference between teams. At a lower level, the kernel has followed a strictly modular design, particularly with respect to the development of device drivers. Programmers working on USB support for version 2.4 of the Linux kernel have been able to work independently of those programmers who are working to support the latest networking cards for the same version. However, as we illustrate later, the interfaces between these modules are complex and poorly documented; the "separation of concerns" is not what it could be.

In the next section, we discuss the part of Linux that implements a part of the TCP/IP protocol to see how well the process really worked in that one case. We begin with a short tutorial on the protocol. It is included so that readers can appreciate the complexity of the task and understand how critical it is that the code be correct. The following description is only a sketch. It has been extracted from more detailed descriptions (Steven 1994; Comer 2000) for the convenience of the reader.

Communication Across the Internet

Programs that use physical communications networks to communicate over the internet must use TCP/IP (Transmission Control Protocol/Internet Protocol). Only if they adhere to this protocol are Internet applications interoperable. (Details on the conventions that constitute TCP/IP can be found in Steven 1994 and Comer 2000.)

The Internet is actually a collection of smaller networks. A subnetwork on the Internet can be a local area network like an Ethernet LAN, a wide area network, or a point-to-point link between two machines. TCP/IP must deal with any type of subnetwork.

Each host on the Internet is assigned a unique 32-bit Internet Protocol (IP) address. IP addresses do not actually denote a computer; they denote a connection path through the network. A computer may be removed and replaced by another without changing the IP address. However, if a host computer is moved from one subnetwork to another, its IP address must change.

Local network hardware uses physical addresses to communicate with an individual computer. The local network hardware functions without reference to the IP address and can usually function even if the subnetwork is not connected to the internet. Changes within a local network may result in a change in the physical address but not require a change in the IP address.

Address Resolution Protocol (ARP)

The Address Resolution Protocol (ARP) converts between physical addresses and IP addresses. ARP is a low-level protocol that hides the underlying physical addressing, permitting Internet applications to be written without any knowledge of the physical structure. ARP requires messages that travel across the network conveying address translation information, so that data is delivered to the right physical computer even though it was addressed using an IP address.

When ARP messages travel from one machine to another, they are carried in physical frames. The frame is made up of data link layer "packets." These packets contain address information that is required by the physical network software.

The ARP Cache To keep the number of ARP frames broadcast to a minimum, many TCP/IP protocol implementations incorporate an *ARP cache*, a table of recently resolved IP addresses and their corresponding physical addresses. The ARP cache is checked before sending an ARP request frame.

The sender's IP-to-physical address binding is included in every ARP broadcast: receivers update the IP-to-physical address binding information in their cache before producing an ARP packet.

The software that implements the ARP is divided into two parts: the first part maps an IP address to a physical address (this is done by the `arp_map` function in the Linux ARP module) when sending a packet, and the second part answers ARP requests from other machines.

Processing of ARP Messages ARP messages travel enclosed in a frame of a physical network, such as an Ethernet frame. Inside the frame, the packet is in the data portion. The sender places a code in the header of the frame to allow receiving machines to identify the frame as carrying an ARP message.

When the ARP software receives a destination IP address, it consults its ARP cache to see if it knows the mapping from the IP address to physical address. If it does, the ARP software extracts the physical address, places the data in frame using that address, and sends the frame (this is done by the `arp_send` function in the Linux ARP module). If it does not know the mapping, the software must broadcast an ARP request and wait for reply (this is done by `arp_set`, a predefined function in the Linux ARP module).

During a broadcast, the target machine may be temporarily malfunctioning or may be too busy to accept the request. If so, the sender might not receive a reply or the reply might be delayed. During this time, the host must store the original outgoing packet so it can be sent once the address has been resolved. The host must decide whether to allow other application programs to proceed while it processes an ARP request (most do). If so, the ARP software must handle the case where an application generates an additional ARP request for the same address.

For example, if machine A has obtained a binding for machine B and subsequently B's hardware fails and is replaced, A may use a nonexistent hardware address. Therefore it is important to have ARP cache entries removed after some period.

When an ARP packet is received, the ARP software first extracts the sender's IP and hardware addresses. A check is made to determine whether a cache entry already exists for the sender. Should such a cache entry be found for the given IP address, the handler updates that entry by rewriting the physical address as obtained from the packet. The rest of the packet is than processed (this is done by the `arp_rcv` function in the Linux ARP module).

When an ARP request is received, the ARP software examines the target address to ascertain whether it is the intended recipient of the packet. If the packet is about a mapping to some other machine, it is ignored. Otherwise, the ARP software sends a reply to the sender by supplying its physical hardware address, and adds the sender's address pair to its cache (if it's not already present). This is done by the `arp_req_get` and `arp_req_set` functions in the Linux ARP module.

During the period between when a machine broadcasts its ARP request and when it receives a reply, additional requests for the same address may be generated. The ARP software must remember that a request has already been sent and not issue more.

Once a reply has been received and the address binding is known, the relevant packets are placed into a frame, using the address binding to fill the physical destination address. If the machine did not issue a request for an IP address in any reply received, the ARP software updates the sender's entry in its cache (this is done by the `arp_req_set` function in the Linux ARP module), then stops processing the packet.

ARP Packet Format   ARP packets do not have a fixed format header. To make ARP useful for a variety of network technologies, the length of fields that contain addresses is dependent upon the type of network being used. To make it possible to interpret an arbitrary ARP message, the header includes fixed fields near the beginning that specify the lengths of the addresses found in subsequent fields of the packet. The ARP message format is general enough to allow it to be used with a broad variety of physical addresses and all conceivable protocol addresses.

Proxy ARP   Sometimes it is useful to have a device respond to ARP broadcasts on behalf of another device. This is particularly useful on networks with dial-in servers that connect remote users to the local network. A remote user might have an IP address that appears to be on the local network, but the user's system would not be reachable when a message is received, because it is actually connected intermittently through a dial-in server.

Systems that were trying to communicate with this node would not know whether the device was local, and would use ARP to try and find the associated hardware address. Since the system is remote, it does not respond to the ARP lookups; instead, a request is handled through Proxy ARP, which allows a dial-in server to respond to ARP broadcasts on behalf of any remote devices that it services.

Concurrency and Timing

In reading the previous sketch of the implementation of ARP, it must be remembered that this protocol is used for communication between computers on a network, and that many processes are active at the same time. There is concurrent activity on each computer and the computers involved are communicating concurrently. Opportunities for deadlocks and "race conditions" abound. Certain processes will time-out if the communication is too slow. Moreover, rapid completion of this communication is essential for acceptable performance in many applications.

Linux ARP Kernel Module

The Linux ARP kernel protocol module implements the Address Resolution Protocol. We have seen that this is a very complex task. The responsible module must perform the task precisely as specified, because it will be interacting with other computers that may be running different operating systems. One would expect this module to be especially well written and documented. This section reports on our review of this code.

Analysis of the ARP Module

Linux implements ARP in the source file *net/ipv4/arp.c*, which contains nineteen functions. They are `arp_mc_map`, `arp_constructor`, `arp_error_report`, `arp_solicit`, `arp_set_predefined`, `arp_find`, arp_bind_neighbour, arp_send, parp_redo, arp_rcv, arp_req_set, arp_state_to_flags, arp_req_get, arp_req_delete, arp_ioctl, arp_get_info, arp_ifdown, initfunc, and ax2asc.

Linux ARP as a Module

We wanted to evaluate the ARP module[4] because it is a critical component of the operating system for most users, because it is inherently complex, and because it has to be correct. We expected to find a structure that allows modules to be designed, tested, and changed independently; that is, a structure in which you can modify the implementation of one module without looking at the internal design of others. This condition requires that the modules' interfaces[5] be well documented, easily understood, and designed so that it need not change if there are changes in its implementation or internal interfaces with hardware and other modules. Every well defined module should have an interface that provides the only means to access the services provided by the module.

We found the Linux networking code difficult to read. One problem was the use of function pointers. To understand the code and the dereferencing of a function pointer, it is necessary to determine when, where, and why the pointer was set. A few lines of comment directing people in this regard would have been incredibly helpful. Without them, one is required to search the full code in order to be able to understand portions of it. Such situations have negative implications for both reliability and security. Unless they have already become familiar with it, Linux TCP/IP code is difficult for even the most experienced programmers.

We found nothing that we could identify as a precise specification of the module and nothing that we consider to be good design documentation.[6] This is a serious fault. Even if one has read all the code and understands what it does, it is impossible to deduce from the code what the expected semantics of an interface are. We cannot deduce the requirements unless we assume that the code is 100% correct, will never change, and all of the properties of the code are not required by programs that interact with it. The inability to distinguish between required properties and incidental properties of the present code will make it difficult to write new versions of the kernel.

With properly documented interfaces, it would be possible to find bugs by confirming that the code on both sides of an interface obeys the documented semantics; a programmer would not need gness what each component was intended to do.

The Linux ARP module includes 31 different header files; most of them are long, ranging from a few hundred to a few thousand lines. It was very difficult to investigate all of them and find connections between every function in the ARP module and other functions inside and outside the module. Functions from the ARP module call functions from other modules. It is not a problem to find the functions that are directly invoked, but often those functions call some other functions in some other module. There are many indirect invocations resulting in many potential cycles. Some of those functions return values, most of which are not explained. We are not told what the returned values represent, and cannot even find some reasonable comment about them. We can only guess what they represent.

Many of the header files are implemented in other source modules. Since all calls to functions are interpreted using header files, it is impossible to understand and check the ARP source module without looking at the internals of other modules.

Design and Documentation Problems in the Linux ARP Module

Concrete Examples

The source file `neighbour.c`, in `net/core/neighbour.c`, includes 40 functions. Only ten of them are called by arp functions from the `arp.c` module. Those ten functions call many other functions. It is unreasonably hard to determine how those ten functions interact with the other thirty. These functions are:

- `neigh_if down` (this function is called by `arp_ifdown`)
- `neigh_lookup` (this function is called by `arp_find`)
- `pneigh_lookup` (this function is called by `arp_rcv`)
- `pneigh_delete` (this function is called by `arp_req_delete`)
- `neigh_update` (this function is called by `arp_rcv`)
- `neigh_event_ns` (this function is called by `arp_rcv`)
- `pneigh_enqueue` (this function is called by `arp_rcv`)
- `neigh_table_init` (this function is called by `init_func`)
- `neigh_app_ns` (this function is called by `arp_rcv`)
- `neigh_sysctl_register` (this function is called by `init_func`)

Just one `neighbour.c` function is called from the `arp.c` module: `neigh_ifdown` (struct neigh_table *tbl, struct device*dev) then calls the next functions: atomic read (andtbl → lock), start_bh_atomic (), atomic_read (andn → refcnt), deltimer (andn → timer), neigh_destroy (n), deltimer (andtbl → proxy_queue).

None of these functions are explained or documented. All of them continue to call other functions without any kind of guidance to people who are trying to understand code. We found several books and papers about this code (for instance, Bovet and Cesati 2000), but none of them answer questions in detail.

The source file neighbour.c also includes 11 different header files but 7 of them (linux/config.h, linux/types.h, linux/kernel.h, linux/socket.h, linux/sched.h, linux/netdevice.h, and net/sock.h) are the same ones that are included in the arp.c source file. That makes the interface unnecessarily big and complex. The arp.c module (that is, Linux C networking code) is also complex; 19 ARP functions call 114 different functions outside of the module arp.c.

Some of arp.c functions—arp_set_predefined (13 different calls), arp_rcv (16 different calls), arp_ioctl (9 different calls), arp_get info (10 different calls)—are especially difficult for handling and understanding.

The file arp.h should declare the interface for the ARP module. It appears to declare eight access functions. However, it also includes two other header files, which then in turn include additional header files. A simplified version of the *includes hierarchy* resulting from arp.h is represented in figure 6.1. The actual *includes hierarchy* is more complicated, as 22 files that are included only from the file sched.h have been summarized as a single node in the graph in order to improve the figure's readability. Once the transitive closure of the includes is taken into account, file arp.h includes an additional 51 header files!

One of the two "includes" that appear explicitly in file arp.h declares the interface for the file net/neighbour.h, which contains the interface declarations and data structure from the net/core/neighbour.c code used by the ARP module. That one file contains approximately 36 function prototypes.[7] Many of the other header files not explicitly included in arp.h also contain additional function prototypes. In our view, this file illustrates a thoroughly unprofessional style of programming and documentation, violating the principles of information hiding by making all of the access functions and many of the data structures from lower-level modules implicitly available to any module using the ARP module.

Impressions

Our impression is that the whole hierarchy and relation between source modules (*.c) could be simpler. Lots of functions and header files are

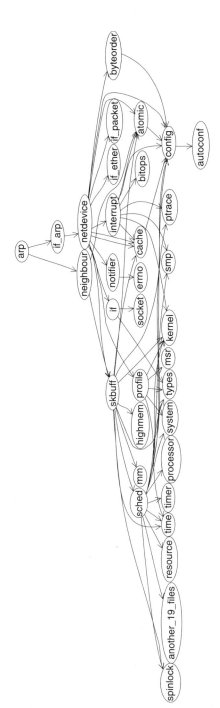

Figure 6.1
Includes hierarchy for arp.h file

redundant and too repetitive. However, in code of this sort, without help of documentation, anyone would be afraid to make the changes.

Analyzing the ARP module felt like walking through a dark forest without a map. There were no directions explaining what given functions are really doing or clear explanations about their connections to another modules. It was not possible to understand most of the written code and it was not possible to define ARP as a module in the sense that we described at the beginning of this section.

Conclusions

Nobody should draw conclusions about a software development method by looking at one example. However, one example should raise questions and act as a warning.

The ARP is a critical module in any modern operating system and must conform precisely to a set of complex rules. Because it serves as an interface with other computers, it is likely that it will have to be changed when network standards are improved. It is reasonable to expect this module to be of the highest quality, well structured, well documented and as "lean" as possible.

Our examination of the Linux ARP code has revealed quite the opposite. The code is poorly documented, the interfaces are complex, and the module cannot be understood without first understanding, what should be internal details of other modules. Even the inline comments suggest that changes have been made without adequate testing and control. A cursory examination of the same module in operating systems that were developed by conventional (strictly controlled source code) methods did not show the same problems.

Nothing that we found in examining this code would suggest that the process that produced it should be used as a model for other projects. What we did find in this case is exactly what Fred Brooks's more than three-decades-old observations would lead us to expect. The attraction of OSS development is its ability to get lots of people to work on a project, but that is also a weakness. In the absence of firm design and documentation standards, and the ability to enforce those standards, the quality of the code is likely to suffer. If Linus Torvalds and the core developers were no longer participating in the Linux kernel project, we would expect that the Linux kernel could be reliably enhanced and modified only if an accurate, precise, and up-to-date description of its architecture and interfaces were always available. Without this, the changes are not likely to maintain the conceptual integrity needed to prevent deterioration of the software (Parnas 1994b).

Notes

1. For the purpose of this chapter, we will consider the "architecture" to be (1) the division of the software into modules, (2) the interfaces between those modules, and (3) the *uses relation* between the externally accessible programs of those modules (Parnas 1979; Parnas, Clements, and Weiss, 1985).

2. In some cases, revised interfaces are dictated by the most powerful party, not negotiated.

3. In fact, many who acquire Linux pay a (relatively small) price for a "distribution" and some pay additional amounts for support such as documentation and advice about that version of Linux.

4. We use the word *module* to refer to a work assignment for a programmer or team (Parnas 1979).

5. The *interface* between two modules comprises all of the information about one module that would be needed to verify that the other was correct. Information about a module that is not included in the interface is considered to be *internal* implementation information.

6. The protocol itself is, of course, the subject of specification documents. However, even correct implementations of the protocol can differ internally. We were looking for specific documents of the Linux code components.

7. 1/3 of them are simple inline access functions.

7 Attaining Robust Open Source Software

Peter G. Neumann

"Is open source software inherently better than closed-source proprietary software?" This is a question that is frequently heard, with various intended meanings of "better." As a particularly demanding case, let us consider critical applications with stringent requirements for certain attributes such as security, reliability, fault tolerance, human safety, and survivability, all in the face of a wide range of realistic adversities—including hardware malfunctions, software glitches, inadvertent human actions, massive coordinated attacks, and acts of God. In addition, let's toss in operational requirements for extensive interoperability, evolvability, maintainability, and clean interface design of those systems, while still satisfying the critical requirements. In this context, we are interested in developing, operating, and using computer systems that are robust and easily administered.

To cut to the chase, the answer to the simple question posed in the first sentence is simple in concept, but decidedly not so simple in execution: Open source software is not intrinsically better than closed-source proprietary software. However, it has the potential for being better if its development process addresses many factors that are not normally experienced in mass-market proprietary software, such as the following:

• Well-defined and thoroughly evaluated requirements for system and application behavior, including functional requirements, behavioral requirements, operational requirements, and—above all—a realistic range of security and reliability requirements.

• System and network architectures that explicitly address these requirements. Sound architectures can lead to significant cost and quality benefits throughout the development and later system evolution.

• A system development approach that explicitly addresses these requirements, pervasively and consistently throughout the development.

- Use of programming languages that are inherently able to avoid many of the characteristic flaws (such as buffer overflows, type mismatches, wild transfers, concurrency flaws, and distributed-system glitches) that typically arise in unstructured, untyped, and error-prone languages and that seem to prevail over decades, through new system releases and new systems.
- Intelligent use of compilers and other development tools that help in identifying and eliminating additional flaws. However, sloppy programming can subvert the intent of these tools, and thus good programming practice is still invaluable.
- Extensive discipline on the part of designers, implementers, and managers throughout the entire software development process. This ultimately requires better integration of architecture, security, reliability, sound programming techniques, and software engineering into the mainstream of our educational and training programs.
- Pervasive attention to maintaining consistency with the stated requirements throughout operation, administration, and maintenance, despite ongoing system iterations. Some combination of formal and informal approaches can be very helpful in this regard.

Conceptually, many problems can be avoided through suitably chosen requirements, architectures, programming languages, compilers, and other analysis tools—although ultimately, the abilities of designers and programmers are a limiting factor.

The answer to the initially posed question should not be surprising to anyone who has had considerable experience in developing software that must satisfy stringent requirements. However, note that although the same discipline could be used by the developers of closed-source software, marketplace forces tend to make this much more difficult than in the open-source world. In particular, there seems to be an increasing tendency among the mass-market proprietary software developers to rush to market, whether the product is ready or not—in essence, letting the customers be the beta testers. Furthermore, efforts to reduce costs often seem to result in lowest-common-denominator products. Indeed, satisfying stringent requirements for security and reliability (for example) is generally not a goal that yields maximum profits. Thus, for practical reasons, I conclude that the open-source paradigm has significant potential that is much more difficult to attain in closed-source proprietary systems.

The potential benefits of nonproprietary nonclosed-source software also include the ability to more easily carry out open peer reviews, add new functionality either locally or to the mainline products, identify flaws, and fix them rapidly—for example, through collaborative efforts involving people irrespective of their geographical locations and corporate allegiances. Of course, the risks include increased opportunities for evil-doers to discover flaws that can be exploited, and to insert trap doors and Trojan horses into the code. Thus a sensible environment must have mechanisms for ensuring reliable and secure software distribution and local system integrity. It must also make good use of good system architectures, public-key authentication, cryptographic integrity seals, good cryptography, and trustworthy descriptions of the provenance of individual components and who has modified them. Further research is needed on systems that can be predictably composed out of evaluated components or that can surmount some of the vulnerabilities of the components. We still need to avoid design flaws and implementation bugs, and to design systems that are resistant to Trojan horses. We need providers who give real support; warranties on systems today are mostly very weak. We still lack serious market incentives. However, despite all the challenges, the potential benefits of robust open-source software are worthy of considerable collaborative effort.

For a further fairly balanced discussion of the relative advantages and disadvantages with respect to improving security, see five papers (Lipner 2000; McGraw 2000; Neumann 2000; Schneider 2000; and Witten et al. 2000) presented at the 2000 IEEE Symposium on Security and Privacy. The session was organized and chaired by Lee Badger. These contributions all essentially amplify the pros and/or cons outlined here. Lipner explores some real benefits and some significant drawbacks. McGraw states flatly that "openish" software will not really improve security. Schneider notes that "the lion's share of the vulnerabilities caused by software bugs is easily dealt with by means other than source code inspections." He also considers inhospitability with business models. The Witten paper explores economics, metrics, and models. In addition, Neumann's Web site includes various papers and reports that can be helpful in achieving the goals of system development for critical requirements, with particular attention to the requirements, system and network architectures, and development practices. In particular, see Neumann 2004 for a report for DARPA (summarized briefly in Neumann 2003a) on the importance of architectures in attaining principled assuredly trustworthy composable systems and networks, with particular emphasis on open source but with general applicability as well. That report is part of the DARPA CHATS program on composable high-assurance trusted systems, which is seriously addressing many of the promising aspects of making open-source software much more robust. Furthermore, see the archives of the ACM Risks Forum (http://www.risks.org), a summary index (Neumann 2003b) to countless cases of systems that failed to live up to their requirements, and an analysis of many of these risks cases and what needs to be done to minimize the risks (Neumann 1995). It is an obvious truism that we should be learning not to make the same mistakes so consistently. It is an equally obvious truism that these lessons are not being learned—most specifically with respect to security, reliability, survivability, interoperability, and many other "-ilities."

8 Open and Closed Systems Are Equivalent (That Is, in an Ideal World)

Ross Anderson

People in the open source and free software community often argue that making source code available to all is good for security. Users and experts can pore over the code and find vulnerabilities: "to many eyes, all bugs are shallow," as Eric Raymond (2001, 41) puts it. This idea is not entirely new. In the world of cryptography, it has been standard practice since the nineteenth century to assume that the opponent knows the design of your system, so the only way you can keep him out is by denying him knowledge of a temporary variable, the key (Kerckhoffs 1883).

However, open design is not an idea that everyone accepts, even now. Opponents of free software argue that "if the software is in the public domain, then potential hackers have also had the opportunity to study the software closely to determine its vulnerabilities" (Brown 2002). This issue is now assuming economic and political importance, as the antitrust settlement between Microsoft and the Department of Justice compels Microsoft to make a lot of information about interfaces available to its competitors—but with the provision that data whose disclosure might prejudice security may be withheld (Collar-Kotelly 2002). Unsurprisingly, Microsoft is now discovering that many more aspects of its systems are security-relevant than had previously been thought.

There is a related issue: whether information about discovered vulnerabilities may be published. In February 2003, Citibank obtained an injunction prohibiting any reporting of security vulnerabilities of automatic teller machine systems disclosed by myself and two colleagues at a trial which we were attending as expert witnesses. This was counterproductive for the bank, as it compelled us to publish our attacks in an invited talk and a technical report in the days just before the gagging hearing. We were slashdotted and the technical report was downloaded over 110,000 times (Anderson and Bond 2003; Bond and Zielinski 2003). But this is unlikely to be the last time that gagging orders are used against security vulnerabilities; if anything, the Digital Millennium Copyright Act and the proposed European Union Directive on the enforcement of intellectual property rights (http://europa.eu.int/comm/internal_market/en/indprop/piracy/index.htm) will make them even more common.

So there is growing public interest in the question of whether openness is of more value to the attacker or the defender. This question is much more general than whether software source code should be available to users. A wide range of systems and components can be either easier or more difficult to test, inspect, and repair, depending on the available tools and access. Hardware devices can often be reverse engineered with surprisingly little effort—although the capital resources needed to fabricate a compatible clone might be scarce. The difference between "open" and "closed" may also be legal rather than technical; if laws prohibit the reporting of defects, or the manufacture of compatible products, this can have much the same effect as logical or physical tamper-resistance. So in what follows I will consider "open systems" versus "closed systems," which differ simply in the difficulty in finding and fixing a security vulnerability.

In May 2002, I proved a controversial theorem (Anderson 2002): under the standard assumptions of reliability growth theory, it does not matter whether the system is open or closed. Opening a system enables the attacker to discover vulnerabilities more quickly, but it helps the defenders exactly as much.

This caused consternation in some circles, as it was interpreted as a general claim that open systems are no better than closed ones. But that is not what the theorem implies. Most real systems will deviate in important ways from the standard reliability growth model, and it will often be the case that open systems (or closed systems) will be better in some particular application. My theorem lets people concentrate on the differences between open and closed systems that matter in a particular case.

An Illustration: Auction Equivalence

Computer scientists are familiar with some kinds of equivalence theorem. For example, Turing's work teaches us that in some sense, all computers are equal. A machine that is Turing-powerful can be used to simulate any other such machine; a TRS-80 can in theory emulate an Ultrasparc CPU. But no computerist would interpret that to mean that any old toy computer can take over the hosting of our university's research grant database.

The equivalence of open and closed systems is a different kind of result, more like the equivalence results one finds in economics. To illustrate how such results tend to work, let's consider the revenue equivalence theorem in auction theory.

Auctions have been around for thousands of years, and have long been a standard way of selling things as diverse as livestock, fine art, mineral rights, and government bonds. How to run them has recently become a hot topic among both technologists and economists. Huge amounts have been raised in many countries from spectrum auctions, and eBay has become one of the most successful Internet companies. Auctions are also proposed as a means of allocating scarce resources in distributed systems. However, it's not always obvious how to design the most appropriate type of auction. Consider the following three schemes.

1. In the *sealed-bid* auction, everyone submits a sealed envelope containing their bid. The auctioneer opens them and awards the contract to the highest bidder.
2. In the *English* auction, the auctioneer starts out the bidding at some reserve price, and keeps on raising it until one bidder remains, who is the winner. The effect of this is that the bidder who places the highest valuation on the contract wins, but at the valuation of the next-highest bidder (plus the bid increment).
3. The *all-pay* auction is similar to the English auction, except that at each round all the bidders have to pay the current price. Eventually, there is only one bidder left, who gets the contract—but the losers don't get a refund. (This scheme models what happens in litigation, or in a symmetric war of attrition.)

The fundamental result about auctions is the *revenue equivalence theorem*, which says that under ideal conditions, you get the same revenue from any well-behaved auction (Klemperer 1999). The bidders will adjust their strategies to the rules set by the auctioneer, and the auctioneer will end up with the same amount of money on average.

Yet, in practice, the design of auctions matters enormously. During the recent spectrum auctions, for example, very small changes in the rules imposed by different governments led to huge differences in outcomes. The UK and Danish governments raised large amounts of money, while the Dutch and the Austrians got peanuts. How can this be squared with theory?

The simple answer is that auctions are often not well behaved, and conditions are rarely ideal. For example, revenue equivalence assumes that bidders are risk-neutral—they are indifferent between a certain profit of $1 billion and a 50 percent chance of a profit of $2 billion. But established phone companies may be risk-averse, seeing a failure to secure bandwidth for 3 G mobiles as a strategic threat to their company's existence, and may therefore be ready to pay more at a sealed-bid auction out of defensiveness. Another problem is that bidders were often able to abuse the auction process to signal their intentions to each other (Klemperer 2002). Yet another is entry deterrence; incumbents in an industry may be able to scare away new entrants by a variety of tactics. Yet another is that if the private information of the bidders is correlated rather than independent, the English auction should raise more money than the sealed-bid auction (Milgrom and Weber 1982). Yet another is that if some of the bidders have budgetary constraints, the all-pay auction may raise more money (a nice explanation from economic theory of why litigation consumes such a large share of America's GDP).

So the revenue equivalence theorem is important for auction designers. It should not be seen as establishing the conditions under which auction rules don't matter, so much as identifying those conditions that do matter.

With this insight, let's return to the equivalence of open and closed systems. First, we'll take a look at the standard assumptions and results of reliability growth theory.

Security Reliability Growth

Safety-critical software engineers have known for years that for a large, complex system to have a mean time to failure (MTTF) of 100,000 hours, it must be subject to at least that many hours of testing (Butler and Finelli 1991). This was first observed by Adams (1984) in a study of the bug history of IBM mainframe operating systems, and has been confirmed by extensive empirical investigations since. The first theoretical model explaining it was published by Bishop and Bloomfield (1996), who proved that under standard assumptions this would be the worst-case behavior. Brady, Anderson, and Ball (1999) tightened this result by showing that, up to a constant factor, it was also the expected behavior.

Such reliability growth models were developed for software reliability in general, but they can be applied to bugs of any particular type, such as defects that might cause loss of life, or loss of mission, or the breach of a security policy. They require only that there are enough bugs for statistical arguments to work, and that a consistent definition of "bug" is used throughout.

When we test software, we first find the most obvious bugs—that is, the bugs with the lowest mean time to failure. After about ten minutes, we might find a bug with a ten-minute MTTF. Then after half an hour we might get lucky and find a bug with an MTTF of forty-two minutes, and so on. In a large system, luck cancels out and we can use statistics. A hand-waving argument would go as follows: after a million hours of testing, we'd have found all the bugs with an MTTF of less than a million hours, and we'd hope that the software's overall reliability would be proportional to the effort invested.

Reliability growth models seek to make this more precise. Suppose that the probability that the ith bug remains undetected after t random tests is $e^{-E_i t}$. The Brady-Anderson-Ball model cited above shows that, after a long period of testing and bug removal, the net effect of the remaining bugs will under certain assumptions converge to a polynomial rather than exponential distribution. In particular, the probability E of a security failure at time t, at which time n bugs have been removed, is

$$E = \sum_{i=n+1}^{\infty} e^{-E_i t} \approx K/t \tag{1}$$

over a wide range of values of t. In the appendix to this chapter, I sketch the proof of why this is the case. For present purposes, note that this explains the slow reliability growth observed in practice. The failure time observed by a tester depends only on the initial quality of the code (the constant of integration K) and the time spent testing it thus far.

Does this theory apply to security vulnerabilities? Recently, Rescorla (2004) has studied the available bug databases and concluded that the rate at which vulnerabilities are depleted by discovery is very low. The visual trends one can see for bugs introduced in any particular year and then discovered in subsequent years show a slow decline; and in fact, once one allows for possible sampling bias, it is even possible that the rate of vulnerability discovery is constant. The available data support the assumption that vulnerabilities can be considered independent, and are consistent with the model's prediction of very slow reliability growth as a result of vulnerability discovery and removal. The numbers of vulnerabilities per product (dozens to low hundreds) are also sufficient for statistical assumptions to hold.

Equivalence of Open and Closed Systems

Consider now what happens if we make the tester's job harder. Suppose that after the initial alpha testing of the product, all subsequent testing is done by beta testers who have no access to the source code, but can only try out various combinations of inputs in an attempt to cause a failure. If this makes the tester's job on average λ times harder—the bugs are λ times more difficult to find—then the probability that the ith bug remains undetected becomes $e^{-E_i t/\lambda}$, and the probability that the system will fail the next test is

$$E = \sum_{i=n}^{\infty} e^{-E_i t/\lambda} \approx K/\lambda t \tag{2}$$

In other words, the system's failure rate has just dropped by a factor of λ, just as we would expect.

However, what if all the testing to date had been carried out under the more difficult regime? In that case, only $1/\lambda$ the amount of effective testing would have been carried out, and the λ factors would cancel out. Thus the failure probability E would be unchanged.

Going back to our intuitive argument, making bugs five times more difficult to find will mean that we now work almost an hour to find the bug whose MTTF was previously 10 minutes, and over three hours for the 42-minute bug (Fenton and Neil (1999) suggest that λ lies between 3 and 5 for mature systems). But the reliability of software still grows as the time spent testing, so if we needed 10,000 hours of testing to get a 10,000-hour-MTTF product before, that should still hold now. We will have removed a smaller set of bugs, but the rate at which we discover them will be the same as before.

Consider what happens when proprietary software is first tested by insiders with access to source code, then by outsiders with no such access. With a large commercial product, dozens of testers may work for months on the code, after which it will go out for beta testing by outsiders with access to object code only. There might be tens of thousands of beta testers, so even if λ were as large as 100, the effect of the initial, open, alpha-testing phase will be quickly swamped by the very much greater overall effort of the beta testers.

Then a straightforward economic analysis can in principle tell us the right time to roll out a product for beta testing. Alpha testers are more expensive, being paid a salary; as time goes on, they discover fewer bugs and so the cost per bug discovered climbs steadily. At some threshold, perhaps once bug removal starts to cost more than the damage that bugs could do in a beta release product, alpha testing stops. Beta testing is much cheaper; testers are not paid (but may get discounted software, and still incur support costs). Eventually—in fact, fairly quickly—the beta test effort comes to dominate reliability growth.

So, other things being equal, we expect that open and closed systems will exhibit similar growth in reliability and in security assurance. This assumes that there are enough bugs to do statistics, that they are independent and identically distributed, that they are discovered at random, and that they are fixed as soon as they are found.

Symmetry Breaking

This analysis does not of course mean that, in a given specific situation, proprietary and open source are evenly matched. A vendor of proprietary software may have exogenous reasons for not making source code available. Microsoft managers once argued that they feared an avalanche of lawsuits by people holding software patents with little or no merit, but who hoped to extract a settlement by threatening expensive litigation. The technical assumptions of reliability growth theory could also fail to hold for many reasons, some of which I'll discuss below. If the analogy with the revenue equivalence theorem is sound, then this is where we expect the interesting economic and social effects to be found.

Even though open and closed systems are equally secure in an ideal world, the world is not ideal, and is often adversarial. Attackers are likely to search for, find, and exploit phenomena that break the symmetry between open and closed models. This is also similar to the auction theory case; phone companies spent considerable sums of money on hiring economists to find ways in which spectrum auctions could be gamed (Klemperer 2002).

Transients

Transient effects may matter, as K/t holds only at equilibrium. Suppose that a new type of abstract attack is found by an academic researcher and published. It may be simple to browse the GNU/Linux source code to see whether it can be applied, but much more complex to construct test cases, write debugging macros, and so on to see whether an exploit can be made for Windows. So there may be time-to-market issues for the attacker.

According to Adams (1984), IBM fixed mainframe operating system bugs the eighth time they were reported, while Leung (2002) studied the optimal frequency of security updates from the customer perspective. Because of the risk that applying a service pack may cause critical systems to stop working, it may be quite rational for many customers to delay application. Vendors also delay fixing bugs, because it costs money to test fixes, bundle them up into a service pack, and ship them to millions of customers. So there may be time-to-market issues for the defenders, too, and at several levels.

Transient effects may be the dominant factor in network security at present, as most network exploits use vulnerabilities that have already been published and for which patches are already available. If all patches were applied to all machines as soon as they were shipped, then the pattern of attacks would change radically. This is now rightly an area of active research, with engineers developing better patching mechanisms and security economists engaging in controversy. For example, Rescorla argues that, in order to optimize social welfare, vulnerability disclosure should be delayed (Rescorla 2004), while Arora, Telang, and Xu (2004) argue that either disclosure should be accelerated, or vendor liability increased.

Transaction Costs

These time-to-market issues largely depend on the effects of a more general problem, namely transaction costs. Transaction costs may persuade some vendors to remain closed. For example, if source code were made available to beta testers too, then the initial reliability of beta releases would be worse, as the testers would be more efficient. Fairly soon, the reliability would stabilize at the status quo ante, but a much larger number of bugs would have had to be fixed by the vendor's staff. Avoiding this cost might sometimes be a strong argument against open systems.

Complexity Growth

Software becomes steadily more complex, and reliability growth theory leads us to expect that the overall dependability will be dominated by newly added code (Brady, Anderson, and Ball 1999). Thus, while we may never get systems that are in equilibrium in the sense of the simple model, there may be a rough second-order equilibrium in which the amount of new code being added in each cycle is enough to offset the reliability gains from bug-fixing activities since the last cycle. Then the software will be less dependable in equilibrium if new code is added at a faster rate.

So commercial featuritis can significantly undermine code quality. But software vendors tend to make their code just as complex as they can get away with, while collaborative developers are more likely to be "scratching an itch" than trying to please as many prospective customers as possible (Raymond 2001). Certainly products such as OpenOffice appear to lag the commercial products they compete with by several years in terms of feature complexity.

Correlated Bugs

Just as correlated private information can break the equivalence of different types of auction, so also can correlations between security vulnerabilities cause the equivalence of attack and defense to fail.

Recently, most reported vulnerabilities in operating systems and middleware have related to stack overflow attacks. This may have helped the attackers in the beginning; an attacker could write a test harness to bombard a target system with unsuitable inputs and observe the results. More recently, technological changes may have tilted the playing field in favor of the defenders: the typical information security conference now has a number of papers on canaries, static code analysis tools, and compiler extensions to foil this type of attack, while Microsoft's programmers have been trained in their own way of doing things (Howard and LeBlanc 2002).

In extreme cases, such effects can lead to security systems becoming brittle. The cryptographic processors used by banks to protect cash machine PINs, for example, have been around for some twenty years. Their design was relatively obscure; some products had manuals available online, but few people outside the payment industry paid them any attention. After the first attacks were published in late 2000, this changed. Many further attacks were soon found and the technology has been rendered largely ineffective (Anderson and Bond 2003; Anderson 2001a).

Code Quality

In the ideal case, system dependability is a function only of the initial code quality K and the amount of testing t. However, it is not clear that code quality is a constant. Many people believe that open systems tend to have higher quality code to begin with, that is, a lower value of K.

Knowing that one's code may be read and commented on widely can motivate people to code carefully, while there may also be selection effects: for example, programmers with greater skill and motivation may end up working on open systems. A lot of labor is donated to open system projects by graduate students, who are typically drawn from the top quartile of computer science and engineering graduates. Meanwhile, commercial deadlines can impose pressures as deadlines approach that cause even good coders to work less carefully. Open systems may therefore start out with a constant-factor advantage.

Effectiveness of Testing

Just as K can vary, so can t. It is quite conceivable that the users of open products such as GNU/Linux and Apache are more motivated to report system problems effectively, and it may be easier to do so, compared with Windows users, who respond to a crash by rebooting and would not know how to report a bug if they wanted to.

An issue that may push in the other direction is that security testing is much more effective if the testers are hostile (Anderson and Beduidenhoudt 1996). Evaluators paid by the vendor are often nowhere near as good at finding flaws as the people who attack a system once it's released—from competitors to research students motivated by glory. In many cases, this effect may simply tweak the value of λ. However, there have been occasional step-changes in the number and hostility of attackers. For example, after Sky-TV enciphered the channel broadcasting *Star Trek* in the early 1990s, students in Germany could no longer get legal access to the program, so they spent considerable energy breaking its conditional access system (Anderson 2001a). In the case of Windows versus GNU/Linux, people may be more hostile to Windows both for ideological reasons and because an exploit against Windows allows an attacker to break into more systems.

What is the net effect on t (and K)? Recently, both Windows and GNU/Linux have been suffering about fifty reported security vulnerabilities a year (for precise figures by product and release, see Rescorla 2004). Given that Windows has perhaps ten to twenty times as many users, one would expect t to be larger and thus K/t to be smaller by this amount; in other words, we would expect Windows to be ten to twenty times more reliable. As it clearly isn't, one can surmise that different values of K and of testing effectiveness (in effect, a multiplier of t) help GNU/Linux to make back the gap.

Policy Incentives on the Vendor
In addition to the code and testing quality effects, which work through individual programmers and testers, there are also incentive issues at the corporate level.

The motivation of the vendor to implement fixes for reported bugs can be affected in practice by many factors. The U.S. government prefers vulnerabilities in some products to be reported to authority first, so that they can be exploited by law enforcement or intelligence agencies for a while. Vendors are only encouraged to ship patches once outsiders start exploiting the hole too.

Time-to-Market Incentives on the Vendor
There are also the issues discussed previously (Anderson 2001b): the economics of the software industry (high fixed costs, low variable costs,

network effects, lock-in) lead to dominant-firm markets with strong incentives to ship products quickly while establishing a leading position. Firms will therefore tend to ship a product as soon as it's good enough; similarly, given that fixing bugs takes time, they might fix only enough bugs for their product to keep up with the perceived competition. For example, Microsoft takes the perfectly pragmatic approach of prioritizing bugs by severity, and as the ship date approaches, the bug categories are allowed to slip. So more severe bugs are allowed through into the product if they are discovered at the last minute and if fixing them is nontrivial (Myrhvold, N., personal communication).

Industry Structure Issues for the Vendor

The size of the vendor and the nature of sectoral competition can be the source of a number of interesting effects. Gal-Or and Ghose show that larger firms are more likely to benefit from information sharing than smaller ones, as are firms in larger industries; and that information sharing is more valuable in more competitive industries (Gal-Or and Ghose 2003). The critical observation is that openness saves costs—so the biggest spenders save the most.

The extent to which industries are vertically integrated could also matter. Many vulnerabilities affecting Windows PCs can be blamed on Microsoft as the supplier of the most common operating system and the dominant productivity application, as well as Web server and database products. On the other hand, smart cards are typically designed by one firm, fabricated by a second using components licensed from multiple specialists, then loaded with an operating system from a third firm, a JVM from a fourth, and a crypto library from a fifth—with power analysis countermeasures bought in from yet another specialist. On top of this, an OEM will write some applications, and the customer still more.

The security of the resulting product against a given attack—say, fault induction—may depend on the interaction between hardware and software components from many different sources. Needless to say, many of the component vendors try to dump liability either upstream or downstream. In such an environment, obscure proprietary designs can undermine security as they facilitate such behavior. Laws such as the EU electronic signature directive, which make the cardholder liable for security failures, may compound the perverse incentive by leading all the other players to favor closed design and obscure mechanisms (Bohm, Brown, and Gladman 2000).

PR Incentives on the Vendor

Firms care about their image, especially when under pressure from regulators or antitrust authorities. Our team has long experience of security hardware and software vendors preferring to keep quiet about bugs, and shipping patches only when their hand is forced (e.g., by TV publicity). They may feel that shipping a patch undermines previous claims of absolute protection. Even if "unbreakable security" is not company policy, managers might not want to undermine assurances previously given to their bosses. So there may be information asymmetries and principal-agent effects galore.

The argument is now swinging in favor of policies of vulnerability disclosure after a fixed notice period; without the threat of eventual disclosure, little may get done (Rain Forest Puppy 2003; Fisher 2003). This is not going to be a panacea, though; on at least one occasion, a grace period that we gave a vendor before publication was consumed entirely by internal wrangling about which department was to blame for the flaw. In another case, vendors reassured their customers that attacks colleagues and I had published were "not important," so the customers had done nothing about them.

Operational Profile

Another set of issues has to do with the operational profile, which is how the reliability community refers to test focus. The models discussed above assume that testing is random; yet in practice, a tester is likely to focus on a particular subset of test cases that are of interest to her or are easy to perform with her equipment.

However, the individual preferences and skills of testers still vary. It is well known that software may be tested extensively by one person, until it appears to be very reliable, only to show a number of bugs quickly when passed to a second tester (Bishop 2001). This provides an economic argument for parallelism in testing (Brady, Anderson, and Ball 1999). It is also a strong argument for extensive beta testing; a large set of testers is more likely to be representative of the ultimate user community.

Experienced testers know that most bugs are to be found in recently added code, and will focus on this. In fact, one real advantage that source code access gives to an attacker is that it makes it easier to identify new code. In theory, this does not affect our argument, as the effects are subsumed into the value of λ. In practice, with systems that depart from the ideal in other ways, it could be important.

Adverse Selection

Operational profile issues can combine with adverse selection in an interesting way. Security failures often happen in the boring bits of a product, such as device drivers and exception handling. The tempting explanation is that low-status programmers in a development team—who may be the least experienced, the least motivated, the least able (or all of the above)—are most likely to get saddled with such work.

Coase's Penguin and the Wild West

A related argument for closed systems is as follows. Think of the Wild West; the bandits can concentrate their forces to attack any bank on the frontier, while the sheriff's men have to defend everywhere. Now, the level of assurance of a given component is a function of the amount of scrutiny that it actually gets, not of what it might get in theory. As testing is boring, and volunteers generally only want to fix failures that irritate them, the amount of concentrated attention paid by random community members to (say) the smartcard device drivers for GNU/Linux is unlikely to match what an enemy government might invest (Schaefer 2001).

A counterargument can be drawn from Benkler's (2002) model, that large communities can include individuals with arbitrarily low reservation prices for all sorts of work. A different one arises in the context of reliability growth theory. Efficacy of focus appears to assume that the attacker is more efficient than the defender at selecting a subset of the code to study for vulnerabilities; if they were randomly distributed, then no one area of focus should be more productive for the attacker than any other.

The more relevant consideration for security assurance is, I believe, the one in Benkler (2002)—that a large number of low-probability bugs structurally favors attack over defense. In an extreme case, a system with 10^6 bugs each with an MTTF of 10^9 hours will have an MTBF of 1,000 hours, so it will take about that much time to find an attack. But a defender who spends even a million hours has very little chance of finding that particular bug before the enemy exploits it. This problem was known in generic terms in the 1970s; the model described here makes it more precise. (It also leads to Rescorla's (2004) disturbing argument that if vulnerabilities truly are uncorrelated, then the net benefit of disclosing and fixing them may be negative—patched software doesn't get much harder to attack, while software that's not patched yet becomes trivial to attack.)

Do Defenders Cooperate or Free-Ride?

I mentioned that the users of open systems might be better at reporting bugs. Such factors are not restricted to the demand side of the bug-fixing business, but can affect the supply side too. The maintainers of open systems might take more pride in their work, and be more disposed to listen to complaints, while maintainers working for a company might be less well motivated. They might see bug reports as extra work and devise mechanisms—even subconsciously—to limit the rate of reporting. On the other hand, a corps of paid maintainers may be much easier to coordinate and manage, so it might get better results in the long term once the excitement of working on a new software project has paled. How might we analyze this?

I mentioned industries, such as the smartcard industry, where many defenders have to cooperate for best results. Varian presents an interesting analysis of how defenders are likely to react when the effectiveness of their defense depends on the sum total of all their efforts, the efforts of the most energetic and efficient defender, or the efforts of the least energetic and efficient defender (Varian 2002). In the total-efforts case, there is always too little effort exerted at the Nash equilibrium as opposed to the optimum, but at least reliability continues to increase with the total number of participants.

Conclusion

The debate about open versus closed systems started out in the nineteenth century when Auguste Kerckhoffs (1883) pointed out the wisdom of assuming that the enemy knew one's cipher system, so that security could reside only in the key. It has developed into a debate about whether access to the source code of a software product is of more help to the defense, because they can find and fix bugs more easily, or to attackers, because they can develop exploits with less effort.

This chapter gives a partial answer to that question. In a perfect world, and for systems large and complex enough for statistical methods to apply, the attack and the defense are helped equally. Whether systems are open or closed makes no difference in the long run.

The interesting questions lie in the circumstances in which this symmetry can be broken in practice. There are enough deviations from the ideal for the choice between open and closed to be an important one, and a suitable subject for researchers in the economics of information security. The balance can be pushed one way or another by many things: transient

effects, transaction costs, featuritis, interdependent or correlated vulnerabilities, selection effects, incentives for coders and testers, agency issues,
policy and market pressures, changing operational profiles and the effects
of defenders who cheat rather than collaborating. (This list is almost
certainly not complete.)

Although some of these effects can be modeled theoretically, empirical
data are needed to determine which effects matter more. It might be
particularly interesting, for example, to have studies of reliability growth
for code that has bifurcated, and now has an open and a closed version.

In conclusion, I have not proved that open and closed systems are always
equivalent. They are in an ideal world, but our world is not ideal. The significance of this result is, I hope, to have made a start towards a better
understanding of the circumstances in which open systems (or closed
systems) are best, and to help us focus on the factors that actually matter.

Appendix

The following exposition is taken from Brady, Anderson, and Ball (1999),
and uses an argument familiar to students of statistical mechanics. If there
are $N(t)$ bugs left after t tests, let the probability that a test fails be $E(t)$,
where a test failure counts double if it is caused by two separate bugs.
Assume that no bugs are reintroduced, so that bugs are removed as fast as
they are discovered. That is:

$$dN = -Edt \tag{3}$$

By analogy with theormodynamics, define a temperature $T = 1/t$ and
entropy $S = \int dE/T$. Thus $S = \int t dE = Et - \int E dt$. This can be solved by substi-
tuting equation 3, giving $S = N + Et$. The entropy S is a decreasing function of t (since $dS/dt = t dE/dt$ and $dE/dt < 0$). So both S and N are bounded
by their initial value N_0 (the number of bugs initially present) and the
quantity $S - N = Et$ is bounded by a constant k (with $k < N_0$), that is:

$$E \leq k/t \tag{4}$$

Et vanishes at $t = 0$ and $t = W_0$, where W_0 is the number of input states
the program can process. It has a maximum value $Et = k$. I now wish to
show that this maximum is attained over a wide range of values of t, and
indeed that $Et \approx k$ for $N_0 \ll t \ll W_0$. This will be the region of interest in
most real-world systems.

We can write equation (4) as $Et = k - g(t)$ where $0 \leq g(t) \leq k$. Since $g(t)$
is bounded, we cannot have $g(t) \sim t^x$ for $x > 0$. On the other hand, if

$g(t) = At^{-1}$, then this makes a contribution to N of $-\int g(t)dt/t = A/t$, which is reduced to only one bug after A tests, and this can be ignored as $A < k$. Indeed, we can ignore $g(t) = At^{-x}$ unless x is very small. Finally, if $g(t)$ varies slowly with t, such as $g(t) = At^{-x}$ for small x, then it can be treated as a constant in the region of interest, namely $N_0 \ll t \ll W_0$. In this region, we can subsume the constant and near-constant terms of $g(t)$ into k and disregard the rest, giving:

$$E \approx k/t \tag{5}$$

Thus the mean time to failure is $1/E \approx t/k$ in units where each test takes one unit of time.

More precisely, we can consider the distribution of defects. Let there be $\rho(\varepsilon)d\varepsilon$ bugs initially with failure rates in ε to $\varepsilon + d\varepsilon$. Their number will decay exponentially with characteristic time $1/\varepsilon$, so that $E = \int \varepsilon \rho(\varepsilon)e^{-\varepsilon t}d\varepsilon \approx k/t$. The solution to this equation in the region of interest is:

$$\rho(\varepsilon) \approx k/\varepsilon \tag{6}$$

This solution is valid for $N_0 \ll 1/\varepsilon \ll W_0$, and is the distribution that will be measured by experiment. It differs from the ab initio distribution because some defects will already have been eliminated from a well-tested program (those in energy bands with $\rho(\varepsilon) \sim \varepsilon^x$ for $x > -1$) and other defects are of such low energy that they will almost never come to light in practical situations (those in energy bands with $\rho(\varepsilon) \sim \varepsilon^x$ for $x < -1$).

Note

I got useful comments from Rob Brady, Hal Varian, Jacques Crémer, Peter Bishop, Richard Clayton, Paul Leach, Peter Wayner, Fabien Petitcolas, Brian Behlendorf, Seth Arnold, Jonathan Smith, Tim Harris, Andrei Serjantov, and Mike Roe; from attendees at the Toulouse conference on Open Source Software Economics where I first presented these ideas; and from attendees talks I gave on the subject at City University, London, and Edinburgh University.

Charles B. Weinstock and Scott A. Hissam

The Software Engineering Institute (SEI) is a federally funded research and development center (FFRDC) that is operated by Carnegie Mellon University and sponsored by the U.S. Department of Defense (DoD). One of our many activities is to advise the DoD on software-related issues. Several years ago, a new silver bullet arrived with the words "open-source software" (OSS) emblazoned on its side. As OSS became more prevalent, we were asked to determine its applicability to DoD systems—was it really a silver bullet? To answer these questions, we undertook a study of what OSS is, how it is developed, and how it is contributing to the way we develop software. In particular, we wanted to learn where and how OSS fit into the general practice of software engineering. The study attempted to identify OSS from a practical perspective, with the goal of differentiating between hype and reality. To this end, we conducted interviews, participated in open-source development activities, workshops, and conferences, and studied available literature on the subject. Through these activities, we have been able to support and sometimes refute common perceptions about OSS.

Perceptions of OSS

It is not surprising, given the attention that OSS has received, that there are myths about OSS—both positive and negative. In this section, we'll look at some of the myths.

Myth: OSS, being under constant peer review by developers around the world and around the clock, must therefore be of higher quality; that is, it must be more reliable, robust, and secure than other software.

Raymond (2001) argues that OSS developers write the best code they can possibly write because others will see the code. He also asserts Linus's Law:

"Given enough eyeballs, all bugs are shallow (p. 41)." Because there are thousands of developers reviewing OSS code, a flaw in the code will be obvious to someone.

In fact there *is* open-source software that is good software and, by many measures, high-quality software (Linux and Apache, to name but two). Does all OSS shares this status?

Myth: Having the source code for OSS gives more control because of the ability to read and modify the source code at will.

This myth is viewed as the main advantage that OSS has over closed-source software (CSS), where one is at the mercy of the vendor. If the vendor should go out of business (or otherwise stop supporting the software), the user has no recourse. With OSS, there is no vendor to go out of business. We'll explore the relationship of OSS to CSS further in a later section.

Myth: OSS has poor documentation and little support.

The assumption is that hackers are off coding wildly and have neither the time nor the motivation to document what they produce. The concern that there is little support comes from the sense that there is no one to phone when there is a problem. O'Reilly (1999) discusses this myth briefly. There is a trend towards gaps in support and/or documentation being filled by support companies (e.g., Red Hat). Does this apply to all OSS?

Myth: There are armies of programmers sitting around waiting and eager to work on an OSS project free of charge, making it possible to forego the traditional development costs associated with traditional software-development activities.

The old adage "You can lead a horse to water, but you can't make him drink" best describes the OSS community—that is, "You can put the code out in the community, but you can't make a hacker code." The likelihood that an OSS product will be successful (or that the hackers will help you) is based on the characteristics of that product.

Myth: OSS hackers are a group of mavericks working in an unorganized, haphazard, ad hoc fashion.

Given the global reach of the Internet and the therefore distributed nature of hacker-based development, this might seem to be an obvious conclusion. For some, this is the allure of the OSS development process—that there is no "process-monger" or program manager hanging over the progress of the development effort (hence the process is unpredictable and progress is immeasurable). We refute this myth in the following Apache case study.

Case Studies

One of the ways in which we attempted to understand the OSS phenomenon was to get involved in or research several efforts/events. There were five such studies, each giving us a different perspective of OSS, in terms of software development, the products themselves, and users:

- AllCommerce—an e-commerce storefront solution
- Apache—an open-source Web server
- Enhydra—a Java-based application server
- NAIS—a NASA-operated Web site that switched from Oracle to MySQL
- Teardrop—a successful Internet attack affecting OSS and CSS

The purpose in selecting these specific OSS projects was to take varying perspectives of OSS, in terms of software development, the products themselves, and users.

The AllCommerce case study focused on software development in the OSS paradigm. A member of the SEI technical staff got involved in the process of hacking the product to discover bugs and add new features to the product. The express purpose of this case study was to obtain firsthand experience in working on an OSS product from the inside; that is, to learn the process by which changes are actually proposed, tracked, selected/ voted on, and accepted. We learned that while it is fairly easy to have an impact on OSS, the OSS project needs a critical mass to stay alive. This can happen because there are many people interested in the project (for whatever reason) or because of the existence of a serious sponsor. In the case of AllCommerce, development progressed only when it had a sponsor that provided support in terms of employee time and other resources. When that sponsor folded, AllCommerce for all intents and purposes went dormant, and as of this writing remains so.

The Apache case study took an academic, research perspective (actually the result of a doctoral thesis) of the OSS-development process. This case study looked at the individual contributions made to the Apache Web server over the past five years and examined whether that contributor was from core or noncore Apache developers. From this study we learned that the core developers hold on to control of what goes into Apache and what does not. As a result the development process for Apache ends up being very similar to the development process of a good commercial software vendor (Hissam et al. 2001).

From a purely product-centric perspective, the Enhydra case study focused on the qualitative aspects of an OSS product and looked at coding problems found in the product by conducting a critical code review. We learned that claims to the contrary notwithstanding, the Enhydra source code is no better than commercial source code we have reviewed in the past. The code as a whole is not outstanding, but it is not terrible, either; it is simply average. It appears in this case that the many eyes code-review assertion has not been completely effective, given that our review was casual and tended to look for common coding errors and poor programming practices.

The NAIS case study, which focused on the end user, looked at a real application developer who switched from a commercially acquired software product to an OSS product. Specifically, this case study examined how and why that particular OSS product was selected, the degree to which the application developer was engaged with the OSS development community, and the level of satisfaction that the NAIS had with the selected OSS product. They chose MySQL to replace an Oracle database that they could no longer afford and have been quite happy with the results.

Finally, the Teardrop case study looked into one of the predominant assertions about OSS: that OSS is more secure than software developed under more traditional means. This case study takes apart one of the most successful distributed denial-of-service (DDoS) attacks and looks at the role that OSS played in the propagation of that attack on CSS and the response by the OSS community. The code that was exploited to conduct this attack had a problem that was easily fixed in the source code. At the same time another problem, which had not yet been exploited was also fixed. This was fine for the Unix systems this code ran on. It turns out, though, that Microsoft Windows shared the same flaws and only the first of them was fixed on the initial go around. Attackers noted the fix in the Unix code that tipped them off to a problem that they were ultimately able to use against Windows—until it too was fixed (Hissam, Plakosh, and Weinstock 2002).

From this study we learn that OSS is not only a viable source of components from which to build systems, but also that the source code enables the integrator to discover other properties of the component that are not typically available when using CSS components. Unfortunately there is a cost to this benefit, as cyber terrorists also gain additional information about those components and discover vulnerabilities at a rate comparable to those looking to squash bugs.

This is not to say that security through obscurity is the answer. There is no doubt that sunshine kills bacteria. That is, the openness of OSS development can lead to better designs, better implementations, and eventually better software. However, until a steady state in any software release can be achieved, the influx of changes, rapid release of software (perhaps before its time), and introduction of new features and invariably flaws will continue to feed the vicious cyclic nature of attack and countermeasure.

What It Takes for a Successful OSS Project

The success of an open-source project is determined by several things that can be placed loosely into two groups: people and software. For instance, the development of an OSS accounting system is less likely to be successful than that of a graphics system. The potential developer pool for the former is much smaller than that for the latter—just because of interest. Paraphrasing Raymond (2001), "The best OSS projects are those that scratch the itch of those who know how to code." This says that a large potential user community is not by itself enough to make an open-source project successful. It also requires a large, or at least dedicated, developer community. Such communities are difficult to come by, and the successful project is likely to be one that meets some need of the developer community.

The success stories in OSS all seem to scratch an itch. Linux, for instance, attracts legions of developers who have a direct interest in improving an operating system for their own use. However, it scratches another important itch for some of these folks: it is creating a viable alternative to Microsoft's products. Throughout our discussions with groups and individuals, this anti-Microsoft Corporation sentiment was a recurring theme.

Another successful open-source project is the Apache Web server. Although a core group is responsible for most of its development, it is the Web master community that actually contributes to its development.

On the other hand, as we saw in the AllCommerce case study, without serious corporate sponsorship AllCommerce was unable to sustain itself as a viable open-source project. Without being paid, there weren't enough developers who cared deeply enough to sustain it.

Although people issues play a large part in the success of an open-source project, there are software issues as well. These issues can be divided into two groups as well: design and tools.

The poorly thought out initial design of an open-source project is a difficult impediment to overcome. For instance, huge, monolithic software does not lend itself very well to the open-source model. Such software requires too much upfront intellectual investment to learn the software's architecture, which can be daunting to many potential contributors. A well-modularized system, on the other hand, allows contributors to carve off chunks on which they can work.

At the time we conducted our study, an example of an open-source project that appeared to work poorly because of the structure of the software was Mozilla (the open-source Web browser). In order to release Mozilla, Netscape apparently ripped apart Netscape Communicator, and the result, according to some, was a "tangled mess." Perhaps it is not coincidental that until recently, Mozilla had trouble releasing a product that people actually used.

To its credit, Netscape realized that there was a problem with Mozilla and, in an attempt to help the situation, created a world-class set of open-source tools. These tools, such as Bonsai, Bugzilla, and Tinderbox, support distributed development and management and helped developers gain insight into Mozilla. While perhaps not true several years ago, the adoption of a reasonable tool base is required for an open-source project to have a significant chance of success (if only to aid in the distributed-development paradigm and information dissemination). Tools such as revision-control software and bug-reporting databases are keys to success. Fortunately for the community, organizations like SourceForge (http://www.sourceforge.net) are making such tool sets easily available; this goes a long way towards solving that aspect of the problem.

A final factor in the success of an open-source project is time. Corporate software development can be hampered by unrealistically short time horizons. OSS development can be as well. However in the former case, projects are all too often cancelled before they have a chance to mature, while in the latter case an effort can continue (perhaps with reduced numbers of people involved). The result may be that an apparent failed open-source project becomes a success. Because of this it is difficult to say that a particular project has failed. Examples of OSS projects that appeared to have failed yet now seem to be succeeding include GIMP (Photoshop-like software) and the aforementioned Mozilla. "It hasn't failed; it just hasn't succeeded—yet."

The OSS Development Model

It might not be surprising that the development process for OSS differs from traditional software development. What might be surprising to some is how ultimately similar they are.

Traditional software development starts with a detailed requirements document that is used by the system architect to specify the system. Next comes detailed system design, implementation, validation, verification, and ultimately, maintenance/upgrade. Iteration is possible at any of these steps. Successful OSS projects, while not conducted as traditional (e.g., commercial) developments, go through all of these steps as well.

But the OSS development model differs from its traditional perhaps not-so-distant cousin. For instance, requirements analysis may be very ad hoc. Successful projects seem to start with a vision and often an artifact (e.g., prototype) that embodies that vision—at least in spirit. This seems to be the preferred way of communicating top-level requirements to the community for an OSS project. As the community grows, the list of possible requirements will grow as well. Additional requirements or new features for an OSS project can come from anyone with a good (or bad) idea. Furthermore, these new requirements actually may be presented to the community as a full-fledged implementation. That is, someone has what he thinks is a good idea, goes off and implements it, and then presents it to the community. Usually this is not the case in a traditional project.

In a traditional project, the system architect will weigh conflicting requirements and decide which ones to incorporate and which to ignore or postpone. This is not done as easily in an OSS development effort, where the developer community can vote with its feet. However successful projects seem to rely on a core group of respected developers to make these choices. The Apache Web server is one example of such a project. This core group is taking on the role of a system architect. If the core group is strong and respected by the community, the group can have the same effect (virtually identical) as determining requirements for a traditional development effort.

Implementation and testing happens in OSS development efforts much as it does for traditional software–development efforts. The main difference is that these activities are often going on in parallel with the actual system specification. Individual developers (core or otherwise) carve out little niches for themselves and are free to design, implement, and test as they see fit. Often there will be competing designs and implementations, at most one of which will be selected for inclusion in the OSS system. It is the core group (for systems so organized) that makes the selections and keeps this whole process from getting out of control.

Finally, to conduct maintenance activities, upgrade, re-release, or port to new platforms, the open-source community relies on sophisticated tools for activities such as version control, bug tracking, documentation maintenance, and distributed development. The OSS project that does not have or use a robust tool set (usually open source itself) either has too small a community to bother with such baggage or is doomed to failure. This is also the case for traditional development.

The Relationship of OSS to CSS

Judging from the press it receives, OSS is something new in the world of software development. To the limited extent that the press itself is sensitive to the term, there is truth to that statement. It would be fair to acknowledge that more people (and not just software engineers) are now sensitive to the term *open source* than ever before—for which we can also thank the press. But what makes OSS new to the general, software systems engineering community is that we are faced with more choices for viable software components than ever before. But you may ask yourself, before what?

The World Before OSS
Before OSS became a popular term, software engineers had three generalized choices for software components:

• The component could be built from the ground up.
• The component could be acquired from another software project or initiative.
• The component could be purchased from the commercial marketplace.

If the component were to be built from the ground up, there were basically two approaches: to actually undertake the development of the component from within the development organization (i.e., inhouse), or to negotiate a contract to develop the component via an external software-development organization. Essentially the component was custom-built. As such, the software sources were available for the component acquired in this fashion.

Another approach was to locate components of similar functionality from other (potentially similar) software projects. The term often used in this context was *reuse* or *domain-specific reuse*. If a component could be located, it could then be adapted for the specific needs of the using software-development activity. In U.S. government vernacular, this was also referred to as government off-the-shelf (GOTS) software. Typically, reuse libraries and GOTS software came in binary and source-code form.

Finally, software engineers had the option of looking to the commercial marketplace for software components. Software-development organizations would undergo market surveys trying to locate the components that best fit their needs. Evaluations would commence to determine which of the commercial offerings most closely matched and a selection would be made. In many instances, the source code was not delivered as part of the component's packaging. In some cases, the source code may have been available for an additional cost (if at all). And in the event that the source code could be bought, there were (and still are) very restrictive limitations placed on what could and could not be done to those sources.

The World after OSS

With the advent of OSS, the community has an additional source of components, which is actually a combination of all three of the choices listed earlier. OSS and reusable components are very much alike in that they are both developed by others and often come in binary and source-code form. But like reusable components, it can be challenging to understand what the OSS component does (Shaw 1996).

Because it comes with the source, OSS is similar to custom-built software. However, it lacks the design, architectural, and behavioral knowledge inherent to custom-built software. This is also a problem with commercially purchased software. This lack of knowledge allows us to draw a strong analogy between OSS and COTS software in spite of the source code being available for the former and not for the latter.

The SEI has been studying COTS-based systems for a number of years and has learned some important lessons about them, many of which apply directly to OSS.[1]

Organizations adopting an OSS component have access to the source, but are not required to do anything with it. If they choose not to look at the source, they are treating it as a black box. Otherwise they are treating it as a white box. We discuss both of these perspectives in the following sections.

OSS as a Black Box

Treating OSS as a black box is essentially treating it as a COTS component; the same benefits and problems will apply. For instance, an organization adopting COTS products should know something about the vendor (e.g., its stability and responsiveness to problems), and an organization adopting OSS should know something about its community.

If the community is large and active, the organization can expect that the software will be updated frequently, that there will be reasonable quality assurance, that problems are likely to be fixed, and that there will be people to turn to for help. If the community is small and stagnant, it is less likely that the software will evolve, that it will be well tested, or that there will be available support.

Organizations that adopt COTS solutions are often too small to have much influence over the direction in which the vendor evolves the product (Hissam, Carney, and Plakosh 1998). Black-box OSS is probably worse in this regard. A COTS component will change due to market pressure, time-to-market considerations, the need for upgrade revenue, and so forth. OSS components can change for similar market reasons, but can also change for political or social reasons (factions within the community), or because someone has a good idea—though not necessarily one that heads in a direction suitable to the organization.

Organizations that adopt COTS products can suffer from the vendor-driven upgrade problem: the vendor dictates the rate of change in the component, and the organization must either upgrade or find that the version it is using is no longer supported. This same problem exists with OSS. The software will change, and eventually the organization will be forced to upgrade or be unable to benefit from bug fixes and enhancements. The rate of change for an eagerly supported OSS component can be staggering.

Organizations that adopt COTS solutions often find that they have to either adapt to the business model assumed by the component or pay to have the component changed to fit their business model (Oberndorf and Foreman 1999). We have found that adapting the business model usually works out better than changing the component, as once you change a component you *own* the solution. If the vendor does not accept your changes, you'll be faced with making them to all future versions of the software yourself.

For black-box OSS, it may be easier for a change to make its way back into the standard distribution. However, the decision is still out of the organization's control. If the community does not accept the change, the only recourse is to reincorporate the change into all future versions of the component.

Because of a lack of design and architectural specifications, undocumented functionality, unknown pre- or post-conditions, deviations from supported protocols, and environmental differences, it is difficult to krfow how a COTS component is constructed without access to the source code. As a consequence, it can be difficult to integrate the component. With OSS, the source is available, but consulting it means that the component is no longer being treated as a black box.

OSS as a White Box

Because the source is available, it is possible to treat OSS as a white box. It therefore becomes possible to discover platform-specific differences, uncover pre- and post-conditions, and expose hidden features and undocumented functionality. With this visibility comes the ability to change the components as necessary to integrate them into the system.

However sometimes the source is the only documentation that is provided. Some consider this to be enough. Linus Torvalds, the creator of Linux, has been quoted as saying, "Show me the source" (Cox 1998). Yet if this were the case, there would be no need for Unified Modeling Language (UML), use cases, sequence diagrams, and other sorts of design documentation. Gaining competency in the OSS component without these additional aids can be difficult.

An organization that treats OSS as a white box has a few key advantages over one that treats it as a black box. One advantage is the ability to test the system knowing exactly what goes on inside the software. Another advantage is the ability to fix bugs without waiting for the community to catch up. A seeming advantage is the ability to adapt the system to the organization's needs. But as already discussed, the rejection of your change by the community means that you own the change and have given up many of the benefits of OSS.

Acquisition Issues

According to the President's Information Technology Advisory Committee (PITAC): "Existing federal procurement rules do not explicitly authorize competition between open-source alternatives and proprietary software. This ambiguity often leads to a de facto prohibition of open-source alternatives within agencies" (PITAC 00, 6).

The PITAC recommends that the federal government allow open-source development efforts to "compete on a level playing field with proprietary solutions in government procurement of high-end computing software." We wholeheartedly endorse that recommendation.

In the presence of such a level playing field, acquiring OSS would not be fundamentally very different from acquiring COTS software. The benefits and risks would be similar and both must be judged on their merits.

We've already discussed issues such as security in the open-source context, so we won't consider them here. Those sorts of issues aside, there are two risks that an organization acquiring OSS faces:

- That the software won't exactly fit the needs of the organization
- That ultimately there will be no real support for the software

We'll address each of these in turn.

A key benefit of OSS is that the sources are available, allowing them to be modified as necessary to meet the needs of the acquiring organization. While this is indeed a benefit, it also introduces several significant risks. Once the OSS is modified, many open-source licenses require the organization to give the changes back to the community. For some systems this might not be a problem, but for others, there might be proprietary or sensitive information involved. Thus it is very important to understand the open-source license being used.

As discussed in the preceding section on CSS, just because a modification is given back to the community does not mean that the community will embrace it. If the community doesn't embrace it, the organization faces a serious choice. It can either stay with the current version of the software (incorporating the modifications) or move on to updated versions—in which case, the modifications have to be made all over again. Staying with the current version is the easy thing to do, but in doing so, you give up some of the advantages of OSS.

With COTS software there is always the risk of the vendor going out of business, leaving the organization with software but no support. This can be mitigated somewhat by contract clauses that require the escrowing of the source code as a contingency. No such escrow is needed for OSS. However, in both cases, unless the organization has personnel capable of understanding and working with the software's source code, the advantage of having it available is not clear. Certainly there would be tremendous overhead should there be a need to actually use the source code; by taking it over, you are now essentially in the business of producing that product.

Most government software is acquired through contracts with contractors. A contractor proposing an open-source solution in a government contract needs to present risk-mitigation plans for supporting the software, just as it would have to do if it were proposing a COTS product. In the case of a COTS product, this might include statements regarding the stability of the vendors involved. No such statement is valid regarding OSS. The community surrounding an open-source product is not guaranteed to be there when needed, nor is it guaranteed to care about the support needs of the government. Furthermore, if the proposing contractor is relying on the OSS community to either add or enhance a product feature or accept a contactor-provided enhancement in the performance of the government-funded software-development contract, the government should expect a mitigation if the OSS community does not provide such an enhancement or rejects the enhancement outright. Thus the ultimate support of the software will fall on the proposing contractor.

Security Issues

There are, of course, unique benefits of OSS—many of which have been discussed elsewhere in this book. From an acquisition point of view, the initial cost of OSS is low. Also, at least for significant open-source products, it is likely (but by no means guaranteed) that the quality of the software will be on a par with many COTS solutions. Finally, when modifications are needed, it is guaranteed that they can be made in OSS. For COTS software, there is always the possibility that the vendor will refuse. (But, as we've seen, the ability to modify is also a source of risk.)

Trust in the software components that are in use in our systems is vital, regardless of whether the software comes from the bazaar or the cathedral. As integrators, we need to know that software emanating from either realm has been reviewed and tested and does what it claims to do. This means that we need eyes that look beyond the source code and look to the bigger picture. That is the holistic and system view of the software—the architecture and the design.

Others are beginning to look at the overall OSS development process (Feller and Fitzgerald 2000; Nakakoji and Yamamoto 2001; Hissam et al. 2001). More specifically, from the Apache case study (discussed earlier), we observed what type of contributions have been made to the Apache system and whether those who made them were from core or noncore Apache developers. We learned that a majority (90 percent) of changes to the system (implementation, patches, feature enhancements, and documentation) were carried out by the core-group developers, while many of the difficult and critical architectural and design modifications came from even fewer core developers. Noncore developers contributed to a small fraction of the changes. What is interesting is that the Apache core developers are a relatively small group compared to the noncore developers—in fact, the size of the core developers is on a par with the typical size of development teams found in CSS products.

This is not intended to imply that OSS lacks architectural and design expertise. Actually, the Apache modular architecture is likely central to its success. However, even with the existence of a large community of developers participating actively in an OSS project, the extent that many eyes are really critiquing the holistic view of the system's architecture and design, looking for vulnerabilities is questionable.

This is an issue not just for OSS: it is a problem for CSS as well. That is, in CSS we have to trust and believe that the vendor has conducted such a holistic review of its commercial software offerings. We have to trust the vendor, because there is little likelihood that any third party can attest to a vendor's approach to ridding its software of vulnerabilities. This specific point has been a thunderous charge of the OSS community, and we do not contest that assertion. But we caution that just because the software is open to review, it should not automatically follow that such a review has actually been performed (but of course you are more than welcome to conduct that review yourself—welcome to the bazaar).

Making Lightning Strike Twice

Instances of successful OSS products such as Linux, Apache, Perl, sendmail, and much of the software that makes up the backbone of today's Web are clear indications that successful OSS activities can strike often. But like with lightning, we can ask, "Is it possible to predict where the next strike will be?" or "Is it possible to make the next strike happen?"

Continuing with this analogy, we can answer these questions to the extent that science will permit. Like lightning, meteorologists can predict the likelihood of severe weather in a metro region given atmospheric conditions. For OSS, it may be harder to predict the likelihood of success for an OSS product or activity, but certain conditions appear to be key, specifically:

• It is a working product. Looking back at many of the products, especially Apache and Linux, none started in the community as a blank slate. Apache's genesis began with the end of the National Center for Supercomputing Applications (NCSA) Web server. Linus Torvalds released Linux version 0.01 to the community in September 1991. Just a product concept and design in the open-source community has a far less likely chance of success. A prototype, early conceptual product, or even a toy is needed to bootstrap the community's imagination and fervor.

• It has committed leaders. Likewise as important is a visionary or champion of the product to chart the direction of the development in a (relatively) forward-moving direction. Although innovation and product evolution are apt to come from any one of the hackers in the development community, at least one person is needed to be the arbiter of good taste with respect to the product's progress. This is seen easily in the Apache project (the Apache Foundation).

• It provides a general community service. This is perhaps the closest condition to the business model for commercial software. It is unlikely that a commercial firm will bring a product to market if there is no one in the marketplace who will want to purchase that product. In the open-source community, the same is also true. Raymond (2001) points out a couple of valuable lessons:

· "Every good work of software starts by scratching a developer's personal itch." (p. 32)

· "Release early, release often. And listen to your customers." (p. 39)

· "To solve an interesting problem, start by finding a problem that is interesting to you." (p. 61).

From these lessons, there is a theme that talks to the needs of the developers themselves (personal itch) and a community need (customers or consumers who need the product or service).

• It is technically cool. You are more likely to find an OSS device driver for a graphics card than an accounting package. Feller and Fitzgerald (2002) categorized many of the open-source projects in operation, noting that a high percentage of those were Internet applications (browsers, clients, servers), system and system-development applications (device drivers, code generators, compilers, and operating systems/kernels), and game and entertainment applications.

• Its developers are also its users. Perhaps the characteristic that is most indicative of a successful OSS project is that the developers themselves are also the users. Typically, this is a large difference between OSS and commercial software. In commercial software, users tend to convey their needs (i.e., requirements) to engineers who address those needs in the code and then send the software back to the users to use. A cycle ensues, with users conveying problems and the engineers fixing and returning the code. However in OSS, it is more typical that a skilled engineer would rather repair the problem in the software and report the problem along with the repair back to the community. The fact that OSS products are technically cool explains why many of the most popular ones are used typically by the developer community on a day-to-day basis. (Not many software developers we know use accounting packages!)

This is not to say that any product or activity exhibiting these conditions will, in fact, be successful. But those products that are considered to be successful meet all of them.

This leads us to the next question: "Is it possible to make the next strike happen?" In lightning research, scientists use a technique called *rocket-and-wire technique* to coax lightning from the skies to the ground for research purposes. In that technique and under the optimum atmospheric conditions, a small rocket is launched trailing a ground wire to trigger lightning discharges (Uman 1997). For OSS, a comparable technique might involve creating conditions that are favorable to OSS development but may fail to instigate a discharge from the OSS community.

At this point, we abandon our lightning analogy and observe (and dare predict) that there will be other successful OSS products and activities in the coming years. Furthermore, we surmise that such products will exhibit the conditions discussed previously. Whether they happen by chance or by design is difficult to tell.

In Closing

We view OSS as a viable source of components from which to build systems. However, we are not saying that OSS should be chosen over other sources simply because the software is open source. Rather like COTS and CSS, OSS should be selected and evaluated on its merits. To that end, the SEI supports the recommendations of the PITAC subpanel on OSS to remove barriers and educate program managers and acquisition executives and allow OSS to compete on a level playing field with proprietary solutions (such as COTS or CSS) in government systems.

Adopters of OSS should not enter into the open-source realm blindly and should know the real benefits and pitfalls that come with OSS. Open source means that everyone can know the business logic encoded in the software that runs those systems, meaning that anyone is free to point out and potentially exploit the vulnerabilities with that logic—anyone could be the altruistic OSS developer or the cyber terrorist. Furthermore, having the source code is not necessarily the solution to all problems: without the wherewithal to analyze or perhaps even to modify the software, it makes no difference to have it in the first place.

It should not follow that OSS is high-quality software. Just as in the commercial marketplace, the bazaar contains very good software and very poor software. In this report, we have noted at least one commercial software vendor that has used its role in the OSS community as a marketing leverage point touting the "highest-quality software," when in fact it is no better (or worse) than commercial-grade counterparts. Caveat emptor (let the buyer beware); the product should be chosen based on the mission needs of the system and the needs of the users who will be the ultimate recipients.

Note

1. See the COTS-Based Systems (CBS) Initiative Web site at http://www.sei.cmu.edu/cbs.

III Free/Open Source Processes and Tools

10 Two Case Studies of Open Source Software Development: Apache and Mozilla

Audris Mockus, Roy T. Fielding, and James D. Herbsleb

The open source software (OSS) "movement" has received enormous attention in the last several years. It is often characterized as a fundamentally new way to develop software (Di Bona et al. 1999; Raymond 2001) that poses a serious challenge (Vixie 1999) to the commercial software businesses that dominate most software markets today. The challenge is not the sort posed by a new competitor that operates according to the same rules but threatens to do it faster, better, and cheaper. The OSS challenge is often described as much more fundamental, and goes to the basic motivations, economics, market structure, and philosophy of the institutions that develop, market, and use software.

The basic tenets of OSS development are clear enough, although the details can certainly be difficult to pin down precisely (see Perens 1999). OSS, most people would agree, has as its underpinning certain legal and pragmatic arrangements that ensure that the source code for an OSS development will be generally available. Open source developments typically have a central person or body that selects some subset of the developed code for the "official" releases and makes it widely available for distribution.

These basic arrangements to ensure freely available source code have led to a development process that is, according to OSS proponents, radically different from the usual industrial style of development. The main differences most often mentioned are the following:

- OSS systems are frequently built by large numbers (i.e., hundreds or even thousands) of volunteers. It is worth noting, though, that currently a number of OSS projects are supported by companies and some participants are not volunteers.
- Work is not assigned; people undertake the work they choose to undertake.

- There is no explicit system-level design, or even detailed design (Vixie 1999).
- There is no project plan, schedule, or list of deliverables.

Taken together, these differences suggest an extreme case of geographically distributed development, where developers work in arbitrary locations, rarely or never meet face to face, and coordinate their activity almost exclusively by means of e-mail and bulletin boards. What is perhaps most surprising about the process is that it lacks many of the traditional mechanisms used to coordinate software development, such as plans, system-level design, schedules, and defined processes. These "coordination mechanisms" are generally considered to be even more important for geographically distributed development than for colocated development (Herbsleb and Grinter 1999), yet OSS represents an extreme case of distributed development that appears to eschew them all.

Despite the very substantial weakening of traditional ways of coordinating work, the results from OSS development are often claimed to be equivalent or even superior to software developed more traditionally. It is claimed, for example, that defects are found and fixed very quickly because there are "many eyeballs" looking for the problems—Raymond (2001) calls this "Linus's Law." Code is written with more care and creativity, because developers are working only on things for which they have a real passion (Raymond 2001).

It can no longer be doubted that OSS development has produced software of high quality and functionality. The Linux operating system has recently enjoyed major commercial success, and is regarded by many as a serious competitor to commercial operating systems such as Windows (Krochmal 1999). Much of the software for the infrastructure of the Internet, including the well-known BIND, Apache, and sendmail programs, were also developed in this fashion.

The Apache server (one of the OSS software projects under consideration in this case study) is, according to the Netcraft survey, the most widely deployed Web server at the time of this writing. It accounts for nearly 70% of the 54 million Web sites queried in the Netcraft data collection. In fact, the Apache server has led in "market share" each year since it first appeared in the survey in 1996. By any standard, Apache is very successful.

Although this existence proof means that OSS processes can, beyond a doubt, produce high-quality and widely deployed software, the exact means by which this has happened, and the prospects for repeating OSS successes, are frequently debated (see, for example, Bollinger et al. 1999 and McConnell 1999). Proponents claim that OSS software stacks up well against commercially developed software both in quality and in the level of support that users receive, although we are not aware of any convincing empirical studies that bear on such claims. If OSS really does pose a major challenge to the economics and the methods of commercial development, it is vital to understand it and to evaluate it.

Introduction

This chapter presents two case studies of the development and maintenance of major OSS projects: the Apache server and Mozilla. We address key questions about their development processes, and about the software that is the result of those processes. We first studied the Apache project, and based on our results, framed a number of hypotheses that we conjectured would be true generally of open source developments. In our second study, which we began after the analyses and hypothesis formation were completed, we examined comparable data from the Mozilla project. The data provide support for several of our original hypotheses.

Our research questions focus on two key sets of properties of OSS development. It is remarkable that large numbers of people manage to work together successfully to create high-quality, widely used products. Our first set of questions (Q1 to Q4) is aimed at understanding basic parameters of the process by which Apache and Mozilla came to exist.

Q1: What were the processes used to develop Apache and Mozilla?
In answer to this question, we construct brief qualitative descriptions of the Apache and Mozilla development processes.

Q2: How many people wrote code for new functionality? How many people reported problems? How many people repaired defects?
We want to see how large the development communities were, and identify how many people actually occupied each of these traditional development and support roles.

Q3: Were these functions carried out by distinct groups of people? That is, did people primarily assume a single role? Did large numbers of people participate somewhat equally in these activities, or did a small number of people do most of the work?
Within each development community, what division of labor resulted from the OSS "people choose the work they do" policy? We want to construct a profile of participation in the ongoing work.

Q4: Where did the code contributors work in the code? Was strict code ownership enforced on a file or module level?

One worry regarding the "chaotic" OSS style of development is that people will make uncoordinated changes, particularly to the same file or module, that interfere with one another. How does the development community avoid this?

Our second set of questions (Q5 to Q6) concerns the outcomes of these processes. We examine the software from a customer's point of view, with respect to the defect density of the released code, and the time to repair defects, especially those likely to significantly affect many customers.

Q5: What is the defect density of Apache and Mozilla code?

We compute defects per thousand lines of code, and defects per delta in order to compare different operationalizations of the defect density measure.

Q6: How long did it take to resolve problems? Were high-priority problems resolved faster than low-priority problems? Has resolution interval decreased over time?

We measured this interval because it is very important from a customer perspective to have problems resolved quickly.

In the following section, we describe our research methodology for both the Apache and Mozilla projects. This is followed in the third section by the results from the study of the Apache project, and hypotheses derived from those results. The fourth section presents our results from the study of the Mozilla project, and a discussion of those results in light of our previous hypotheses.

Methodology and Data Sources

In order to produce an accurate description of the open source development processes, we wrote a draft of description of each process, then had it reviewed by members of the core OSS development teams. For the Apache project, one of the authors (RTF), who has been a member of the core development team from the beginning of the Apache project, wrote the draft description. We then circulated it among all other core members and incorporated the comments of one member who provided feedback. For Mozilla, we wrote a draft based on many published accounts of the Mozilla process.[1] We sent this draft to the Chief Lizard Wrangler, who checked the draft for accuracy and provided comments. The descriptions in the next section are the final product of this process. The commercial development process is well known to two of the authors (AM and JDH) from years of experience in the organization, in addition to scores of interviews with developers. We present a brief description of the commercial process at the end of this section.

In order to address our quantitative research questions, we obtained key measures of project evolution from several sources of archival data that had been preserved throughout the history of the Apache project. The development and testing teams in OSS projects consist of individuals who rarely, if ever, meet face to face, or even via transitory media such as the telephone. One consequence is that virtually all information on the OSS project is recorded in electronic form. Many other OSS projects archive similar data, so the techniques used here can be replicated on any such project. (To facilitate future studies, the scripts used to extract the data are available for download at http://mockus.org/oss.)

Apache Data Sources

Developer E-mail List (EMAIL)   Anyone with an interest in working on Apache development could join the developer mailing list, which was archived monthly. It contains many different sorts of messages, including technical discussions, proposed changes, and automatic notification messages about changes in the code and problem reports. There were nearly 50,000 messages posted to the list during the period starting in February 1995. Our analysis is based on all e-mail archives retrieved on May 20, 1999.

We wrote Perl scripts to extract the date, the sender identity, the message subject, and the message body, which was further processed to obtain details on code changes and problem reports (see later discussion). Manual inspection resolved such things as multiple e-mail addresses in cases where all automated techniques failed.

Concurrent Version Control Archive (CVS)   The CVS commit transaction represents a basic change similar to the Modification Request (MR) in a commercial development environment. Every MR automatically generates an e-mail message stored in the *apache-cvs* archive that we used to reconstruct the CVS data. (The first recorded change was made on February 22, 1996. The version 1.0 of Apache released in January 1996 had a separate CVS database.) The message body in the CVS mail archive corresponds to one MR and contains the following information: date and time of the change, developer login, files touched, numbers of lines added and deleted for each file, and a short abstract describing the change. We further processed the abstract to identify people who submitted and/or reviewed the change.

Some changes were made in response to problems that were reported. For each MR that was generated as a result of a problem report (PR), we obtained the PR number. We refer to changes made as a result of a PR as "fixes," and changes made without a problem report as "code submissions." According to a core participant of Apache, the information on contributors and PRs was entered at least 90 percent of the time. All changes to the code and documentation were used in the subsequent analysis.

Problem Reporting Database (BUGDB)   As in CVS, each BUGDB transaction generates a message to BUGDB stored in a separate BUGDB archive. We used this archive to reconstruct BUGDB. For each message, we extracted the PR number, affected module, status (open, suspended, analyzed, feedback, closed), name of the submitter, date, and comment.

We used the data elements extracted from these archival sources to construct a number of measures on each change to the code, and on each problem report. We used the process description as a basis to interpret those measures. Where possible, we then further validated the measures by comparing several operational definitions and by checking our interpretations with project participants. Each measure is defined in the following sections within the text of the analysis where it is used.

Mozilla Data Sources

The quantitative data were obtained from CVS archives for Mozilla and from the Bugzilla problem tracking system.

Deltas were extracted from the CVS archive running the CVS log on every file in the repository. MRs were constructed by gathering all deltas that share login and comment and are recorded within a single three-minute interval. The comment acknowledges people who submitted the code and contains relevant PR numbers (if any). As before, we refer to MRs containing PRs as "fixes," and the remaining MRs as "code submissions."

The product is broken down into directories /layout, /mailnews, and so on. Files required to build a browser and mail reader are distributed among them. We have selected several directories that correspond to modules in Mozilla (so that each one has an owner) and that are similar in size to the Apache project (that is, that generate between 3 thousand and 12 thousand delta per year). Abbreviated descriptions of directories taken from Mozilla documentation (Howard 2000) follow:

- /*js* contains code for tokenizing, parsing, interpreting, and executing JavaScript scripts.
- /*layout* contains code for the layout engine that decides how to divide up the "window real estate" among all the pieces of content.
- /*editor* contains code used for the HTML editor (i.e., Composer in Mozilla Classic), for plain-text and HTML mail composition and for text fields and text areas throughout the product.
- /*intl* contains code for supporting localization.
- /*rdf* contains code for accessing various data and organizing their relationships according to Resource Description Framework (RDF), which is an open standard.
- /*netwerk* contains code for low-level access to the network (using sockets and file and memory caches) as well as higher-level access (using various protocols such as http, ftp, gopher, and castanet).
- /*xpinstall* contains the code for implementing the SmartUpdate feature from Mozilla Classic.

We refer to developers with e-mail domains *netscape.com* and *mozilla.org* as *internal developers*, and all others we call *external developers*. It is worth noting that some of the 12 people with the *mozilla.org* e-mail address are not affiliated with Netscape. We attempted to match email to full names to eliminate cases where people changed e-mail addresses over the considered period or used several different e-mail addresses, or when there was a spelling mistake.

To retrieve problem report data, we used scripts that would first retrieve all problem report numbers from Bugzilla, and then retrieve the details and the status changes of each problem report. In the analysis, we consider only three status changes for a problem report. A report is first CREATED, then it is RESOLVED, either by a fix or other action. (There are multiple reasons possibly; however, we discriminated only between FIXED and the rest in the following analysis.) After inspection, the report reaches the state of VERIFIED if it passes, or is reopened again if it does not pass. Only reports including code changes are inspected. Each report has a priority associated with it, with values P1 through P5. PRs also include the field "Product," with "Browser" being the most frequent value, occurring in 80 percent of PRs.

Data for Commercial Projects

The change history of the files in the five commercial projects was maintained using the Extended Change Management System (ECMS) (Midha 1997) for initiating and tracking changes, and the Source Code

Control System (SCCS) (Rochkind 1975) for managing different versions of the files.

We present a simplified description of the data collected by ECMS and SCCS that are relevant to our study. SCCS, like most version control systems, operates over a set of source code files. An atomic change, or *delta*, to the program text consists of the lines that were deleted and those that were added in order to make the change. Deltas are usually computed by a file-differencing algorithm (such as UNIX *diff*), invoked by SCCS, which compares an older version of a file with the current version.

SCCS records the following attributes for each change: the file with which it is associated, the date and time the change was "checked in," and the name and login of the developer who made it. Additionally, the SCCS database records each delta as a tuple including the actual source code that was changed (lines deleted and lines added), the login of the developer, the MR number (discussed later), and the date and time of the change.

In order to make a change to a software system, a developer might have to modify many files. ECMS groups atomic changes to the source code recorded by SCCS (over potentially many files) into logical changes referred to as Modification Requests (MRs). There is typically one developer per MR. An MR may have an English-language abstract associated with it, provided by the developer, describing the purpose of the change. The open time of the MR is recorded in ECMS. We use the time of the last delta of an MR as the MR close time. Some projects contain information about the project phase in which the MR is opened. We use it to identify MRs that fix post-feature test and postrelease defects.

Commercial Development Process

Here we describe the commercial development process used in the five comparison projects. We chose these projects because they had the time span and size of the same order of magnitude as Apache, and we have studied them previously, so we were intimately familiar with the processes involved and had access to their change data. In all projects, the changes to the source code follow a well-defined process. New software features that enhance the functionality of the product are the fundamental design unit by which the systems are extended. Changes that implement a feature or solve a problem are sent to the development organization and go through a rigorous design process. At the end of the design process, the work is assigned to developers in the form of Modification Requests, which list the work to be done to each module. To perform the changes, a developer makes the required modifications to the code, checks whether the changes are satisfactory (within a limited context; that is, without a full system build), and then submits the MR. Code inspections, feature tests, integration, system tests, and release to customer follow. Each of these stages may generate fix MRs, which are assigned to a developer by a supervisor who assigns work according to developer availability and the type of expertise required. In all of the considered projects, the developers had ownership of the code modules.

The five considered projects were related to various aspects of telecommunications. Project A involved software for a network element in an optical backbone network such as SONET or SDH. Project B involved call handling software for a wireless network. The product was written in C and C++ languages. The changes used in the analysis pertain to two years of mostly porting work to make legacy software run on a new real-time operating system. Projects C, D, and E represent operations administration and maintenance support software for telecommunications products. These projects were smaller in scale than projects A and B.

Study 1: The Apache Project

The Apache Development Process

Q1: What was the process used to develop Apache?
Apache began in February 1995 as a combined effort to coordinate existing fixes to the NCSA httpd program developed by Rob McCool. After several months of adding features and small fixes, Apache developers replaced the old server code base in July 1995 with a new architecture designed by Robert Thau. Then all existing features, and many new ones, were ported to the new architecture and it was made available for beta test sites, eventually leading to the formal release of Apache httpd 1.0 in January 1996.

The Apache software development process is a result of both the nature of the project and the backgrounds of the project leaders, as described by Fielding (1999). Apache began with a conscious attempt to solve the process issues first, before development even started, because it was clear from the very beginning that a geographically distributed set of volunteers, without any traditional organizational ties, would require a unique development process in order to make decisions.

Roles and Responsibilities   The Apache Group (AG), the informal organization of people responsible for guiding the development of the Apache

HTTP Server Project, consisted entirely of volunteers, each having at least one other "real" job that competed for their time. For this reason, none of the developers could devote large blocks of time to the project in a consistent or planned manner, therefore requiring a development and decision-making process that emphasized decentralized workspaces and asynchronous communication. AG used e-mail lists exclusively to communicate with each other, and a minimal quorum voting system for resolving conflicts.

The selection and roles of core developers are described in Fielding 1999. AG members are people who have contributed for an extended period of time, usually more than six months, and are nominated for membership and then voted on by the existing members. AG started with 8 members (the founders), had 12 through most of the period covered, and now has 25. What we refer to as the set of "core developers" is not identical to the set of AG members; core developers at any point in time include the subset of AG that is active in development (usually 4 to 6 in any given week) and the developers who are on the cusp of being nominated to AG membership (usually 2 to 3).

Each AG member can vote on the inclusion of any code change, and has commit access to CVS (if he or she desires it). Each AG member is expected to use his or her judgment about committing code to the base, but there is no rule prohibiting any AG member from committing code to any part of the server. Votes are generally reserved for major changes that would affect other developers who are adding or changing functionality.

Although there is no single development process, each Apache core developer iterates through a common series of actions while working on the software source. These actions include discovering that a problem exists or new functionality is needed, determining whether a volunteer will work on the issue, identifying a solution, developing and testing the code within their local copy of the source, presenting the code changes to the AG for review, and committing the code and documentation to the repository. Depending on the scope of the change, this process might involve many iterations before reaching a conclusion, although it is generally preferred that the entire set of changes needed to solve a particular problem or add a particular enhancement be applied in a single commit.

Identifying Work to Be Done   There are many avenues through which the Apache community can report problems and propose enhancements. Change requests are reported on the developer mailing list, the problem reporting system (BUGDB), and the Usenet newsgroups associated with the

Apache products. The developer discussion list is where new features and patches for bugs are discussed and BUGDB is where bugs are reported (usually with no patch). Change requests on the mailing list are given the highest priority. Since the reporter is likely to be a member of the development community, the report is more likely to contain sufficient information to analyze the request or contain a patch to solve the problem. These messages receive the attention of all active developers. Common mechanical problems, such as compilation or build problems, are typically found first by one of the core developers and either fixed immediately or reported and handled on the mailing list. In order to keep track of the project status, an agenda file (*STATUS*) is stored in each product's repository, containing a list of high-priority problems, open issues among the developers, and release plans.

The second area for reporting problems or requesting enhancements is in the project's BUGDB, which allows anyone with Web or e-mail access to enter and categorize requests by severity and topic area. Once entered, the request is posted to a separate mailing list and can be appended to via e-mail replies or edited directly by the core developers. Unfortunately, due to some annoying characteristics of the BUGDB technology, very few developers keep an active eye on the BUGDB. The project relies on one or two interested developers to perform periodic triage of the new requests: removing mistaken or misdirected problem reports, answering requests that can be answered quickly, and forwarding items to the developer mailing list if they are considered critical. When a problem from any source is repaired, the BUGDB is searched for reports associated with that problem so that they can be included in the change report and closed.

Another avenue for reporting problems and requesting enhancements is the discussion on Apache-related Usenet newsgroups. However, the perceived noise level on those groups is so high that only a few Apache developers ever have time to read the news. In general, the Apache Group relies on interested volunteers and the community at large to recognize promising enhancements and real problems, and to take the time to report them to the BUGDB or forward them directly to the developer mailing list. In general, only problems reported on released versions of the server are recorded in BUGDB.

In order for a proposed change actually to be made, an AG member must ultimately be persuaded it is needed or desirable. "Showstoppers"—that is, problems that are sufficiently serious (in the view of a majority of AG members) that a release cannot go forward until they are solved—are always addressed. Other proposed changes are discussed on the developer mailing list, and if an AG member is convinced that it is important, an effort is made to get the work done.

Assigning and Performing Development Work   Once a problem or enhancement has found favor with the AG, the next step is to find a volunteer who will work on that problem. Core developers tend to work on problems that are identified with areas of the code with which they are most familiar. Some work on the product's core services, and others work on particular features that they developed. The Apache software architecture is designed to separate the core functionality of the server, which every site needs, from the features, which are located in modules that can be selectively compiled and configured. The core developers obtain an implicit "code ownership" of parts of the server that they are known to have created or to have maintained consistently. Although code ownership doesn't give them any special rights over change control, the other core developers have greater respect for the opinions of those with experience in the area being changed. As a result, new core developers tend to focus on areas where the former maintainer is no longer interested in working, or in the development of new architectures and features that have no preexisting claims.

After deciding to work on a problem, the next step is attempting to identify a solution. In many cases, the primary difficulty at this stage is not finding a solution, but in deciding which of various possibilities is the most appropriate solution. Even when the user provides a solution that works, it might have characteristics that are undesirable as a general solution or might not be portable to other platforms. When several alternative solutions exist, the core developer usually forwards the alternatives to the mailing list in order to get feedback from the rest of the group before developing a solution.

Prerelease Testing   Once a solution has been identified, the developer makes changes to a local copy of the source code and tests the changes on his or her own server. This level of testing is more or less comparable to unit test, and perhaps feature test in a commercial development, although the thoroughness of the test depends on the judgment and expertise of the developer. There is no additional testing (e.g., regression, system test) required prior to release, although review is required before or after committing the change (see next section).

Inspections   After unit testing, the core developer either commits the changes directly (if the Apache guidelines under revision with Apache

Group 2004 call for a commit-then-review process) or produces a "patch" and posts it to the developer mailing list for review. In general, changes to a stable release require review before being committed, whereas changes to development releases are reviewed after the change is committed. If approved, the patch can be committed to the source by any of the developers, although in most cases it is preferred that the originator of the change also perform the commit.

As described previously, each CVS commit results in a summary of the changes being automatically posted to the apache-cvs mailing list, including the commit log and a patch demonstrating the changes. All of the core developers are responsible for reviewing the apache-cvs mailing list to ensure that the changes are appropriate. Most core developers do in fact review all changes. In addition, since anyone can subscribe to the mailing list, the changes are reviewed by many people outside the core development community, which often results in useful feedback before the software is formally released as a package.

Managing Releases   When the project nears a product release, one of the core developers volunteers to be the release manager, responsible for identifying the critical problems (if any) that prevent the release, determining when those problems have been repaired and the software has reached a stable point, and controlling access to the repository so that developers don't inadvertently change things that should not be changed just prior to the release. The release manager creates a forcing effect in which many of the outstanding problem reports are identified and closed, changes suggested from outside the core developers are applied, and most loose ends are tied up. In essence, this amounts to "shaking the tree before raking up the leaves." The role of release manager is rotated among the core developers with the most experience with the project.

In summary, this description helps to address some of the questions about how Apache development was organized and provides essential background for understanding our quantitative results. In the next section, we take a closer look at the distribution of development, defect repair, and testing work in the Apache project, as well as the code and process from the point of view of customer concerns.

Quantitative Results

In this section, we present results from several quantitative analyses of the archival data from the Apache project. The measures we derive from these data are well suited to address our research questions (Basili and Weiss 1984). However, they might be unfamiliar to many readers since the software metrics are not in wide use—see, for example, Carleton et al. 1992 and Fenton 1994. For this reason and to give the reader some sense of what kinds of results might be expected, we provide data from several commercial projects. Although we picked several commercial projects that are reasonably close to Apache, none is a perfect match, and the reader should not infer that the variation between these commercial projects and Apache is due entirely to differences between commercial and OSS development processes.

It is important to note that the server is designed so that new functionality need not be distributed along with the core server. There are well over 100 feature-filled modules that are distributed by third parties and thus not included in our study. Many of these modules include more lines of code than the core server.

The Size of the Apache Development Community

Q2: How many people wrote code for new Apache functionality? How many people reported problems? How many people repaired defects?

The participation in Apache development overall was quite wide, with almost 400 individuals contributing code that was incorporated into a comparatively small product. In order to see how many people contributed new functionality and how many were involved in repairing defects, we distinguished between changes that were made as a result of a problem report (fixes) and those that were not (code submissions). We found that 182 people contributed to 695 fixes, and 249 people contributed to 6,092 code submissions.

We examined the BUGDB to determine the number of people who submitted problem reports. The problem reports come from a much wider group of participants. In fact, around 3,060 different people submitted 3,975 problem reports, whereas 458 individuals submitted 591 reports that subsequently caused a change to the Apache code or documentation. The remaining reports did not lead to a change because they did not contain sufficient detail to reproduce the defect, the defect was already fixed or raised, the issue was related to incorrect configuration of the product, or the defect was deemed to be not sufficiently important to be fixed. Many of the reports were in regard to operating system faults that were fixed by the system vendor, and a few others were simply invalid reports due to spam directed at the bug reporting system's e-mail interface. There were 2,654 individuals who submitted 3,384 reports that we could not trace to a code change.

How Was Work Distributed within the Development Community?

Q3: Were these functions carried out by distinct groups of people? That is, did people primarily assume a single role? Did large numbers of people participate somewhat equally in these activities, or did a small number of people do most of the work?

First, we examine participation in generating code. Figure 10.1 plots the cumulative proportion of code changes (vertical axis) versus the top N contributors to the code base (horizontal axis).

The contributors are ordered by the number of MRs from largest to smallest. The solid line in figure 10.1 shows the cumulative proportion of changes against the number of contributors. The dotted and dashed lines show the cumulative proportion of added and deleted lines and the proportion of delta (an MR generates one delta for each of the files it changes). These measures capture various aspects of code contribution.

Figure 10.1 shows that the top 15 developers contributed more than 83 percent of the MRs and deltas, 88 percent of added lines, and 91 percent of deleted lines. Very little code and, presumably, correspondingly small effort is spent by noncore developers (for simplicity, in this section we

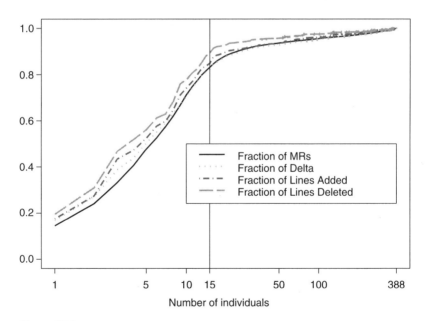

Figure 10.1
Cumulative distribution of contributions to the code base

refer to all the developers outside the top 15 group as *noncore*). The MRs done by core developers are substantially larger, as measured by lines of code added, than those done by the noncore group. This difference is statistically significant. The distribution of the MR fraction is significantly (p-value < 0.01) smaller (high values of the distribution function are achieved for smaller values of the argument) than the distribution of added lines using the Kolmogorov-Smirnov test. The Kolmogorov-Smirnov test is a nonparametric test that uses empirical distribution functions (such as shown in figure 10.1). We used a one-sided test with a null hypothesis that the distribution of the fraction of MRs is not less than the distribution of the fraction of added lines. Each of the two samples under comparison contained 388 observations representing the fraction of MRs and the fraction of lines added by each developer.

Next, we looked separately at fixes only. There was a large (p-value < 0.01) difference between distributions of fixes and code submissions. (We used a two-sample test with samples of the fraction of MRs for fixes and code submissions. There were 182 observations in the fix sample and 249 observations in the code submission sample.) Fixes are shown in figure 10.2. The scales and developer order are the same as in figure 10.1.

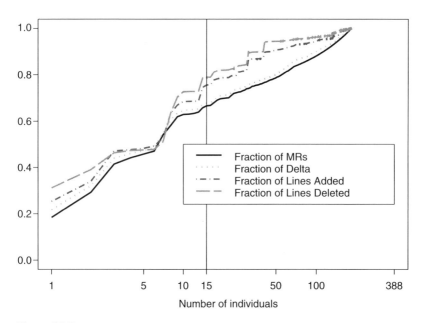

Figure 10.2
Cumulative distribution of fixes

Figure 10.2 shows that participation of the wider development community is more significant in defect repair than in the development of new functionality. The core of 15 developers produced only 66 percent of the fixes. The participation rate was 26 developers per 100 fixes and 4 developers per 100 code submissions, that is, more than six times lower for fixes. These results indicate that despite broad overall participation in the project, almost all new functionality is implemented and maintained by the core group.

We inspected the regularity of developer participation by considering two time intervals: before and after January 1, 1998. Forty-nine distinct developers contributed more than one fix in the first period, and the same number again in the second period. Only 20 of them contributed at least two changes in both the first and second periods. One hundred and forty developers contributed at least one code submission in the first period, and 120 in the second period. Of those, only 25 contributed during both periods. This indicates that only a few developers beyond the core group submit changes with any regularity.

Although developer contributions vary significantly in a commercial project, our experience has been that the variations are not as large as in the Apache project. Since the cumulative fraction of contribution is not commonly available in the programmer productivity literature, we present examples of several commercial projects that had a number of deltas within an order of magnitude of the number Apache had, and were developed over a similar period. Table 10.1 presents basic data about this comparison group. All projects come from the telecommunications domain (see earlier sections). The first two projects were written mostly in the C language, and the last three mostly in C++.

Table 10.1

Statistics on Apache and five commercial projects

	MRs (K)	Delta (K)	Lines added (K)	Years	Developers
Apache	6	18	220	3	388
A	3.3	129	5,000	3	101
B	2.5	18	1,000	1.5	91
C	1.1	2.8	81	1.3	17
D	0.2	0.7	21	1.7	8
E	0.7	2.4	90	1.5	16

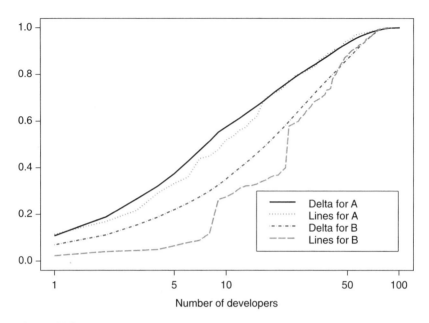

Figure 10.3
Cumulative distribution of the contributions in two commercial projects

Figure 10.3 shows the cumulative fraction of changes for commercial projects A and B. (To avoid clutter, and because they do not give additional insights, we do not show the curves for projects C, D, or E.)

The top 15 developers in project B contributed 77 percent of the delta (compared to 83 percent for Apache) and 68 percent of the code (compared to 88 percent). Even more extreme differences emerge in porting of a legacy product done by project A. Here, only 46 and 33 percent of the delta and added lines are contributed by the top 15 developers.

We defined "top" developers in the commercial projects as groups of the most productive developers that contributed 83 percent of MRs and 88 percent of lines added. We chose these proportions because they were the proportions we observed empirically for the summed contributions of the 15 core Apache developers.

If we look at the amount of code produced by the top Apache developers versus the top developers in the commercial projects, the Apache core developers appear to be very productive, given that Apache is a voluntary, part-time activity and the relatively "lean" code of Apache (see table 10.2). Measured in thousands of lines of code (KLOC) per year, they achieve a level of production that is within a factor of 1.5 of the top full-time devel-

Table 10.2

Comparison of code productivity of top Apache developers and top developers in several commercial projects

	Apache	A	B	C	D	E
KMR/developer/year	.11	.03	.03	.09	.02	.06
KLOC/developer/year	4.3	38.6	11.7	6.1	5.4	10

opers in projects C and D. Moreover, the Apache core developers handle more MRs per year than the core developers on any of the commercial projects. (For reasons we do not fully understand, MRs in Apache are much smaller, in lines of code added, than in the commercial projects we examined.)

Given the many differences among these projects, we do not want to make strong claims about how productive the Apache core has been. Nevertheless, one is tempted to say that the data suggest rates of production that are at least in the same ballpark as commercial developments, especially considering the part-time nature of the undertaking.

Who Reports Problems?   Problem reporting is an essential part of any software project. In commercial projects, the problems are mainly reported by build, test, and customer support teams. Who is performing these tasks in an OSS project?

The BUGDB had 3,975 distinct problem reports. The top 15 problem reporters submitted only 213 or 5 percent of PRs. Almost 2,600 developers submitted one report, 306 submitted 2, 85 submitted 3, and the maximum number of PRs submitted by one person was 32.

Of the top 15 problem reporters only 3 are also core developers. It shows that the significant role of system tester is reserved almost exclusively for the wide community of Apache users.

Code Ownership

Q4: Where did the code contributors work in the code? Was strict code ownership enforced on a file or module level?

Given the informal distributed way in which Apache has been built, we wanted to investigate whether some form of "code ownership" has evolved. We thought it likely, for example, that for most of the Apache modules, a single person would write the vast majority of the code, with perhaps a few minor contributions from others. The large proportion of code written by the core group contributed to our expectation that these 15 developers most likely arranged something approximating a partition of the code, in order to keep from making conflicting changes.

An examination of persons making changes to the code failed to support this expectation. Out of 42 *.c* files with more than 30 changes, 40 had at least 2 (and 20 had at least 4) developers making more than 10 percent of the changes. This pattern strongly suggests some other mechanism for coordinating contributions. It seems that rather than any single individual writing all the code for a given module, those in the core group have a sufficient level of mutual trust that they contribute code to various modules as needed.

This finding verifies the previous qualitative description of code "ownership" to be more a matter of recognition of expertise than one of strictly enforced ability to make commits to partitions of the code base.

Defects

Q5: What is the defect density of Apache code?
First we discuss issues related to measuring defect density in an OSS project and then present the results, including comparison with four commercial projects.

How to Measure Defect Density   One frequently used measure is postrelease defects per thousand lines of delivered code. This measure has several major problems, though. First, "bloaty" code is generally regarded as bad code, but it will have an artificially low defect rate. Second, many incremental deliveries contain most of the code from previous releases, with only a small fraction of the code being changed. If all the code is counted, this will artificially lower the defect rate. Third, it fails to take into account how thoroughly the code is exercised. If there are only a few instances of the application actually installed, or if it is exercised very infrequently, this will dramatically reduce the defect rate, which again produces an anomalous result.

We know of no general solution to this problem, but we strive to present a well-rounded picture by calculating two different measures and comparing Apache to several commercial projects on each of them. To take into account the incremental nature of deliveries, we emulate the traditional measure with defects per thousand lines of code added (KLOCA) (instead of delivered code). To deal with the "bloaty" code issue, we also compute defects per thousand deltas.

To a large degree, the second measure ameliorates the "bloaty" code problem, because even if changes are unnecessarily verbose, this is less likely to affect the number of deltas (independent of size of delta). We do not have usage intensity data, but it is reasonable to assume that usage intensity was much lower for all the commercial applications. Hence we expect that our presented defect density numbers for Apache are somewhat higher than they would have been if the usage intensity of Apache were more similar to that of commercial projects. Defects, in all cases, are reported problems that resulted in actual changes to the code.

If we take a customer's point of view, we should be concerned primarily with defects visible to customers; that is, postrelease defects, and not build and testing problems. The Apache PRs are very similar in this respect to counts of postrelease defects, in that they were raised only against official stable releases of Apache, not against interim development "releases."

However, if we are looking at defects as a measure of how well the development process functions, a slightly different comparison is in order. There is no provision for systematic system test in OSS generally, and for the Apache project in particular. So the appropriate comparison would be to presystem-test commercial software. Thus, the defect count would include all defects found during the system test stage or after (all defects found after "feature test complete," in the jargon of the quality gate system).

Defect Density Results Table 10.3 compares Apache to the previous commercial projects. Project B did not have enough time in the field to accumulate customer-reported problems and we do not have presystem test defects for project A. The defect data for Apache was obtained from BUGDB, and for commercial projects from ECMS as described previously. Only defects resulting in a code change are presented in table 10.3.

The defect density in commercial projects A, C, D, and E varies substantially. Although the user-perceived defect density of the Apache

Table 10.3
Comparison of Defect Density Measures

Measure	Apache	A	C	D	E
Postrelease Defects/KLOCA	2.64	0.11	0.1	0.7	0.1
Postrelease Defects/KDelta	40.8	4.3	14	28	10
Postfeature test Defects/KLOCA	2.64	*	5.7	6.0	6.9
Postfeature test Defects/KDelta	40.8	*	164	196	256

product is inferior to that of the commercial products, the defect density of the code before system test is much lower. This latter comparison may indicate that fewer defects are injected into the code, or that other defect-finding activities such as inspections are conducted more frequently or more effectively.

Time to Resolve Problem Reports

Q6: How long did it take to resolve problems? Were high-priority problems resolved faster than low-priority problems? Has resolution interval decreased over time?

The distribution of Apache PR resolution interval is approximated by its empirical distribution function that maps the interval in days to proportion of PRs resolved within that interval. Fifty percent of PRs are resolved within a day, 75 percent within 42 days, and 90 percent within 140 days. Further investigation showed that these numbers depend on priority, time period, and whether the PR causes a change to the code.

Priority We operationalized priority in two ways. First, we used the priority field reported in the BUGDB database. Priority defined in this way has no effect on interval. This lack of impact is very different from commercial development, where priority is usually strongly related to interval. In Apache BUGDB, the priority field is entered by a person reporting the problem and often does not correspond to the priority as perceived by the core developer team.

In our second approach for operationalizing priority, we categorized the modules into groups according to how many users depended on them. PRs were then categorized by the module to which they pertained. Such categories tend to reflect priorities, since they reflect number of users (and developers) affected. Figure 10.4 shows comparisons among such groups of modules. The horizontal axis shows the interval in days and the vertical axis shows the proportion of MRs resolved within that interval. "Core" represents the kernel, protocol, and other essential parts of the server that must be present in every installation. "Most sites" represents widely deployed features that most sites will choose to include. PRs affecting either "Core" or "Most sites" should be given higher priority, because they potentially involve many (or all) customers and could potentially cause major failures. On the other hand, "OS" includes problems specific to certain operating systems, and "Major optional" includes features that are not as widely deployed. From a customer's point of view, "Core" and "Most

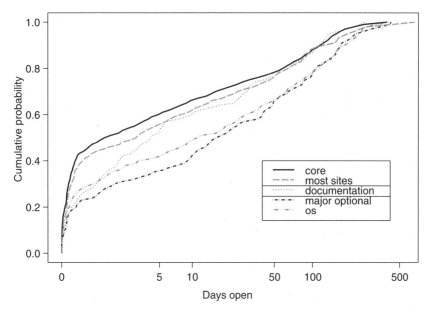

Figure 10.4

Proportion of changes closed within given number of days

sites" PRs should be solved as quickly as possible, and the "OS" and "Major optional" should generally receive lower priority.

The data (figure 10.4) show exactly this pattern, with much faster close times for the higher-priority problems. The differences between the trends in the two different groups are significant (p-value < 0.01 using the Kolmogorov-Smirnov test), whereas the trends within groups do not differ significantly. The documentation PRs show mixed behavior, with "low-priority" behavior for intervals under five days and "high-priority" behavior otherwise. This may be explained by a lack of urgency for documentation problems (the product still operates), despite being very important.

Reduction in Resolution Interval To investigate whether the problem resolution interval improves over time, we broke the problems into two groups according to the time they were posted (before or after January 1, 1997). The interval was significantly shorter in the second period (p-value < 0.01). This change indicates that this important aspect of customer support improved over time, despite the dramatic increase in the number of users.

Hypotheses

In this case study, we reported results relevant to each of our research questions. Specifically, we reported on:

- The basic structure of the development process
- The number of participants filling each of the major roles
- The distinctiveness of the roles, and the importance of the core developers
- Suggestive, but not conclusive, comparisons of defect density and productivity with commercial projects
- Customer support in OSS

Case studies such as this provide excellent fodder for hypothesis development. It is generally inappropriate to generalize from a single case, but the analysis of a single case can provide important insights that lead to testable hypotheses. In this section, we cast some of our case study findings as hypotheses, and suggest explanations of why each hypothesis might be true of OSS in general. In the following section, we present results from Study 2, another case study, which allows us to test several of these hypotheses. All the hypotheses can be tested by replicating these studies using archival data from other OSS developments.

Hypothesis 1:   Open source developments will have a core of developers who control the code base. This core will be no larger than 10 to 15 people, and will create approximately 80 percent or more of the new functionality.

We base this hypothesis both on our empirical findings in this case and on observations and common wisdom about maximum team size. The core developers must work closely together, each with fairly detailed knowledge of what other core members are doing. Without such knowledge, they would frequently make incompatible changes to the code. Since they form essentially a single team, they can be overwhelmed by communication and coordination overhead issues that typically limit the size of effective teams to 10 to 15 people.

Hypothesis 2:   For projects that are so large that 10 to 15 developers cannot write 80 percent of the code in a reasonable time frame, a strict code ownership policy will have to be adopted to separate the work of additional groups, creating, in effect, several related OSS projects.

The fixed maximum core team size obviously limits the output of features per unit time. To cope with this problem, a number of satellite projects, such as Apache-SSL, were started by interested parties. Some of these projects produced as much or more functionality than Apache itself. It seems likely that this pattern of core group and satellite groups that add unique functionality targeted to a particular group of users will frequently be adopted in such cases.

In other OSS projects, such as Linux, the kernel functionality is also small compared to application and user interface functionalities. The nature of relationships between the core and satellite projects remains to be investigated; yet it might serve as an example of how to break large monolithic commercial projects into smaller, more manageable pieces. We can see the examples where the integration of these related OSS products is performed by a commercial organization; for example, Red Hat for Linux, ActivePerl for Perl, and CYGWIN for GNU tools.

Hypothesis 3: In successful open source developments, a group larger by an order of magnitude than the core will repair defects, and a yet larger group (by another order of magnitude) will report problems.

Hypothesis 4: Open source developments that have a strong core of developers, but never achieve large numbers of contributors beyond that core will be able to create new functionality, but will fail because of a lack of resources devoted to finding and repairing defects.

Many defect repairs can be performed with only a limited risk of interacting with other changes. Problem reporting can be done with no risk of harmful interaction at all. Since these types of work typically have fewer dependencies among participants than does the development of new functionality, potentially much larger groups can work on them. In successful development, these activities will be performed by larger communities, freeing up time for the core developers to develop new functionality. Where an OSS development fails to stimulate wide participation, either the core will become overburdened with finding and repairing defects, or the code will never reach an acceptable level of quality.

Hypothesis 5: Defect density in open source releases will generally be lower than commercial code that has only been feature-tested; that is, received a comparable level of testing.

Hypothesis 6: In successful open source developments, the developers will also be users of the software.

In general, open source developers are experienced users of the software they write. They are intimately familiar with the features they need, and the correct and desirable behavior. Since the lack of domain knowledge is one of the chief problems in large software projects (Curtis, Krasner, and Iscoe 1988), one of the main sources of error is eliminated when domain experts write the software. It remains to be seen whether this advantage can completely compensate for the absence of system testing. In any event, where the developers are not also experienced users of the software, they are highly unlikely to have the necessary level of domain expertise or the necessary motivation to succeed as an OSS project.

Hypothesis 7: OSS developments exhibit very rapid responses to customer problems.

This observation stems both from the "many eyeballs implies shallow bugs" observation cited earlier (Raymond 2001), and the way that fixes are distributed. In the "free" world of OSS, patches can be made available to all customers nearly as soon as they are made. In commercial developments, by contrast, patches are generally bundled into new releases, and made available according to some predetermined schedule.

Taken together, these hypotheses, if confirmed with further research on OSS projects, suggest that OSS is a truly unique type of development process. It is tempting to suggest that commercial and OSS practices might be fruitfully hybridized, a thought which led us to collect and analyze the data reported in Study 2.

Subsequent to our formulation of these hypotheses, we decided to replicate this analysis on another open source project. We wanted to test these hypotheses, where possible, and we particularly wanted to look at a hybrid commercial/OSS project in order to improve our understanding of how they could be combined, and what the results of such a combination would be. Recent developments in the marketplace brought forth several such hybrid projects, most notably the Mozilla browser, based on the commercial Netscape browser source code.

In the next section, we use the methodology described earlier to characterize Mozilla development, to answer the same basic questions about the development process, and insofar as possible, test the hypotheses we developed in Study 1.

Study 2: The Mozilla Project

Mozilla has a process with commercial roots. In the face of stiff competition, Netscape announced in January, 1998 that their Communicator product would be available free of charge, and that the source code would also be free of charge. Their stated hope was to emulate the successful development approach of projects such as Linux. The group mozilla.org was chartered to act as a central point of contact and "benevolent dictator" for the open source effort. Compared to the Apache project, the work in the Mozilla project is much more diverse: it supports many technologies including development tools (CVS, Bugzilla, Bonsai, Tinderbox) that are not part of the Web browser. It also builds toolkit-type applications, some of which are used to build a variety of products, such as Komodo from ActiveState. At the time of writing, it is unclear how well Netscape's open source strategy has succeeded.

There are many ways in which characteristics of open source and commercial development might be combined, and Mozilla represents only a single point in a rather large space of possibilities. It must be kept in mind, therefore, that very different results might be obtained from different hybridization strategies. In our conclusions, we describe what we see as the strengths and weaknesses of the Mozilla approach, and suggest other strategies that seem promising.

We base our description of the Mozilla development process on references[2] with a view from the inside (Baker 2000; Paquin and Tabb 1998), from the outside (Oeschger and Boswell 2000), and from a historic perspective (Hecker 1999; Zawinski 1999).

The Mozilla Development Process

Q1: What was the process used to develop Mozilla?
Mozilla initially had difficulty attracting the level of outside contributions that was expected. Mitchell Baker, "Chief Lizard Wrangler" of mozilla.org, expressed the view that "the public expectations for the Mozilla project were set astoundingly high. The number of volunteers participating in the Mozilla project did not meet those expectations. But there has been an important group of volunteers providing critical contributions to the project since long before the code was ready to use." After one year, one of the project leaders quit, citing lack of outside interest because of the large size, cumbersome architecture, absence of a working product, and lack of adequate support from Netscape.

However, after the documentation was improved, tutorials were written, and the development tools and processes refined, participation started slowly to increase. Some documents now available address the entire range of outsider problems (such as Oeschger and Boswell 2000). Also, the fact that the development tools were exported to be used in commercial software projects at Hewlett-Packard, Oracle, Red Hat, and Sun Microsystems

(Williams 2000), is evidence of their high quality and scalability. At the time of this writing, Mozilla is approaching its first release—1.0.

Mozilla has substantial documentation on the architecture and the technologies used, and has instructions for building and testing. It also has Web tools to provide code cross-reference (LXR) and change presentation (Bonsai) systems. A brief point-by-point comparison of the Apache and Mozilla processes is presented in table 10.8 in the appendix to this chapter. Next, we describe the necessary details.

Roles and Responsibilities   Mozilla is currently operated by the mozilla.org staff (12 members at the time of this writing) who coordinate and guide the project, provide process, and engage in some coding. Only about four of the core members spend a significant part of their time writing code for the browser application. Others have roles dedicated to such things as community QA, milestone releases, Web site tools and maintenance, and tools such as Bugzilla that assist developers. Although the external participation (beyond Netscape) has increased over the years, even some external people (from Sun Microsystems, for example) are working full-time, for pay, on the project.

Decision-making authority for various modules is delegated to individuals in the development community who are close to that particular code. People with an established record of good quality code can attempt to obtain commit access to the CVS repository. Directories and files within a particular module can be added or changed by getting the permission of the module owner. Adding a new module requires the permission of mozilla.org. Much responsibility is delegated by means of distributed commit access and module ownership; however, mozilla.org has the ultimate decision-making authority, and retains the right to designate and remove module owners, and to resolve all conflicts that arise.

Identifying Work to Be Done   Mozilla.org maintains a roadmap document (Eich 2001) that specifies what will be included in future releases, as well as dates for which releases are scheduled. Mozilla.org determines content and timing, but goes to considerable lengths to ensure that the development community is able to comment on and participate in these decisions.

Anyone can report bugs or request enhancements. The process and hints are presented in Mozilla Project. The bug reporting and enhancement request process uses the Bugzilla problem-reporting tool, and requires requesters to set up an account on the system. Bugzilla also has tools that allow the bug reporter to see the most recent bugs, and if desired, to search the entire database of problem reports. Potential bug reporters are urged to use these tools to avoid duplicate bug reports. In addition, bug reporters are urged to come up with the simplest Web page that would reproduce the bug, in order to expedite and simplify the bug's resolution. Bugzilla provides a detailed form to report problems or describe the desired enhancement.

Assigning and Performing Development Work   The mozilla.org members who write browser code appear to focus on areas where they have expertise and where work is most needed to support upcoming releases. The development community can browse Bugzilla to identify bugs or enhancements on which they would like to work. Fixes are often submitted as attachments to Bugzilla problem reports. Developers can mark Bugzilla items with a "helpwanted" keyword if they think an item is worth doing but don't themselves have the resources or all the required expertise. Discussions can also be found in Mozilla news groups, which may give development community members ideas about where to contribute. Mozilla.org members may use the Mozilla Web pages to note particular areas where help is needed. When working on a particular Bugzilla item, developers are encouraged to record that fact in Bugzilla in order to avoid duplication of effort.

Prerelease Testing   Mozilla.org performs a daily build, and runs a daily minimal "smoke test" on the build for several major platforms, in order to ensure the build is sufficiently stable to allow development work on it to proceed. If the build fails, "people get hassled until they fix the bits they broke." If the smoke test identifies bugs, they are posted daily so that developers are aware of any serious problems in the build.

Mozilla currently has six product area test teams that take responsibility for testing various parts or aspects of the product, such as standards compliance, the mail/news client, and internationalization. Netscape personnel are heavily represented among the test teams, but the teams also include mozilla.org personnel and many others. The test teams maintain test cases and test plans, as well as other materials such as guidelines for verifying bugs and troubleshooting guides.

Inspections   Mozilla uses two stages of code inspections: module owners review a patch in the context of the module and a smaller designated group (referred to as *superreviewers*, who are technically highly accomplished) review a patch for its interaction with the code base as a whole before it is checked in.

Managing Releases Mozilla runs a continuous build process (Tinderbox) that shows what parts of the code have issues for certain builds and under certain platforms. It highlights the changes and their authors. It also produces binaries nightly and issues "Milestones" approximately monthly. As Baker (2000) points out:

[T]he Milestone releases involve more than Tinderbox. They involve project management decisions, usually a code freeze for a few days, a milestone branch, eliminating "stop-ship" bugs on the branch and a bit of polishing. The decision when a branch is ready to be released as a Milestone is a human one, not an automated Tinderbox process. These Milestone decisions are made by a designated group, known as "drivers@mozilla.org," with input from the community.

Quantitative Results

In this section, we report results that address the same six basic questions we answered with respect to Apache in the previous section. There are some differences between the projects that must be understood in order to compare Mozilla to Apache in ways that make sense.

First, Mozilla is a *much* bigger project. As shown in table 10.4, Apache had about 6,000 MRs, 18,000 delta, and 220,000 lines of code added. In contrast, Mozilla consists of 78 modules (according to the Mozilla Project at the time of this writing), some of which are much larger than the entire Apache project. The following analyses are based on seven of the Mozilla modules.

The Size of the Mozilla Development Community

Q2: How many people wrote code for new functionality? How many people reported problems? How many people repaired defects?

By examining all change login and comment records in CVS, we found 486 people who contributed code and 412 who contributed code to PR fixes that were incorporated. Numbers of contributors to individual modules are presented in table 10.5.

Table 10.5 presents numbers of people who contributed code submissions, problem fixes, and who reported problems. Because some problem reports do not correspond to a module in cases when the fix was not created or committed, we provide numbers for people who reported problems resulting in a fix and estimate of the total number using the overall

Table 10.4
Sizes of Apache, five commercial projects, and seven Mozilla modules

	MRs (K)	Delta (K)	Lines added (K)	Years	Developers
Apache	6	18	220	3	388
A	3.3	129	5,000	3	101
B	2.5	18	1,000	1.5	91
C	1.1	2.8	81	1.3	17
D	0.2	0.7	21	1.7	8
E	0.7	2.4	90	1.5	16
/layout	12.7	42	800	2.6	174
/js	4.6	14	308	2.6	127
/rdf	4.1	12	274	2	123
/netwerk	3.2	10	221	1.6	106
/editor	2.9	8	203	2	118
/intl	2	5	118	1.8	87
/xpinstall	1.9	5	113	1.7	102

Table 10.5
Population of contributors to seven Mozilla modules

	Number of people whose code submissions were included in the code base	Number of people whose fixes were added to code base	Number of people who reported bugs that resulted in code changes	Number of people who reported problems (estimated)
/layout	174	129	623	3035
/js	127	51	147	716
/rdf	123	79	196	955
/netwerk	106	74	252	1228
/editor	118	85	176	857
/intl	87	47	119	579
/xpinstall	102	64	141	687

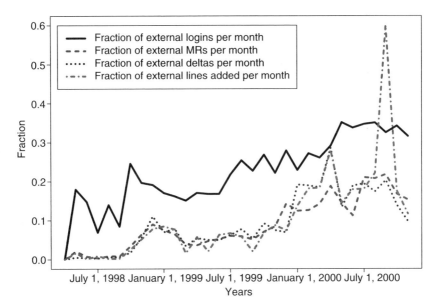

Figure 10.5
Trends of external participation in Mozilla project

ratio in Mozilla of the total number of people who reported PRs divided by the number of people who reported PRs that resulted in code changes. Based on the Bugzilla database, 6,837 people reported about 58,000 PRs, and 1,403 people reported 11,616 PRs that can be traced to changes to the code. To estimate the total number of people reporting PRs for a module (rightmost column), we multiplied the preceding column by 6,837/1,403.

External Participation   Because Mozilla began as a commercial project and only later adopted an open source approach; in order to understand the impact of this change, it is essential to understand the scope and nature of external participation. To this end, we examined the extent and the impact of external participation in code contributions, fix contributions, and defect reporting.

Figure 10.5 plots external participation over time. The measures include the fraction of external developers and the fraction of MRs, delta, and number of added lines contributed monthly by external developers.

Figure 10.5 shows gradually increasing participation over time, leveling off in the second half of 2000. It is worth noting that outside participants tend, on average, to contribute fewer changes and less code relative to

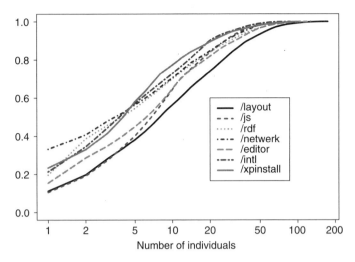

Figure 10.6
The cumulative distribution of contributions to the code base for five Mozilla modules

internal participants. It might reflect the part-time nature of the external participation.

Much larger external participation may be found in problem reporting. About 95 percent of the 6,873 people who created PRs were external, and they reported 53 percent of the 58,000 PRs.

Q3: Were these functions carried out by distinct groups of people; that is, did people primarily assume a single role? Did large numbers of people participate somewhat equally in these activities, or did a small number of people do most of the work?

Figure 10.6 shows cumulative distribution contributions (as for Apache in figure 10.1). The developer participation does not appear to vary as much as in the Apache project. In particular, Mozilla development had much larger core groups relative to the total number of participants. The participation curve for Mozilla is more similar to the curves of commercial projects presented in figure 10.3.

The problem reporting participation was very uniform in Apache, but contributions vary substantially in Mozilla, with 50 percent of PRs reported by just 113 people, with the top person reporting over 1,000 PRs (compared to Apache, where the top reporter submitted only 32 PRs). Forty-six of these 113 PR submitters did not contribute any code, and only 25 of the 113 were external. Unlike Apache, where testing was conducted almost

Table 10.6
Comparison of productivity of the "top" developers in selected Mozilla modules

Module	KMR/dev/year	KLOCA/dev/year	Size of core team
/layout	0.17	11	35
/js	0.13	16	24
/rdf	0.11	11	26
/netwerk	0.13	8.4	24
/editor	0.09	8	25
/intl	0.08	7	22
/xpinstall	0.07	6	22

exclusively by the larger community, and not the core developers, there is very substantial internal problem reporting in Mozilla, with a significant group of dedicated testers. Nevertheless, external participants also contribute substantially to problem reporting.

Given that most of the core developers work full-time on the project, we might expect the productivity figures to be similar to commercial projects (which, when measured in deltas or lines added, were considerably higher than for Apache). In fact, the productivity of Netscape developers does appear to be quite high, and even exceeds the productivity of the commercial projects that we consider (see table 10.6).

As before, we defined core or "top" developers in each module as groups of the most productive developers that contributed 83 percent of MRs and 88 percent of lines added. There was one person in the "core" teams of all seven selected modules and 38 developers in at least two "core" teams. Almost two-thirds (64 out of 102) of the developers were in only a single core team of the selected modules.

Although the productivity numbers might be different due to numerous differences between projects, the data certainly appear to suggest that productivity in this particular hybrid project is comparable to or better than the commercial projects we examined.

Code Ownership

Q4: Where did the code contributors work in the code? Was strict code ownership enforced on a file or module level?

For the Apache project, we noted that the process did not include any "official" code ownership; that is, there was no rule that required an owner to sign off in order to commit code to an owned file or module. We looked at who actually committed code to various modules in order to try to determine whether a sort of de facto code ownership had arisen in which one person actually committed all or nearly all the code for a given module. As we reported, we did not find a clear ownership pattern.

In Mozilla, on the other hand, code ownership is enforced. According to Howard 2000 and the Mozilla Project, the module owner is responsible for fielding bug reports, enhancement requests, and patch submissions in order to facilitate good development. Also, before code is checked in, it must be reviewed by the appropriate module owner and possibly others. To manage check in privileges, Mozilla uses a Web-based tool called *despot*.

Because of this pattern of "enforced ownership," we did not believe that we would gain much by looking at who actually contributed code to which module, since those contributions all had to be reviewed and approved by the module owner. Where there is deliberate, planned code ownership, there seemed to be no purpose to seeing if de facto ownership had arisen.

Defects

Q5: What is the defect density of Mozilla code?

Because Mozilla has yet to have a nonbeta release, all PRs may be considered to be post-feature-test (i.e., prerelease). The defect density appears to be similar to, or even slightly lower than Apache (see table 10.7). The

Table 10.7
Comparison of post-feature-test defect density measures

Module	#PR/KDelta	#PR/KLOC added
Apache	40.8	2.6
C	164	5.7
D	196	6.0
E	256	6.9
/layout	51	2.8
/js	19	0.7
/rdf	27	1.4
/netwerk	42	3.1
/editor	44	2.5
/intl	20	1.6
/xpinstall	56	4.0

defect density, whether measured per delta or per thousand lines of code, is much smaller than the commercial projects, if one counts all defects found after the feature test. The highest defect density module has substantially lower defect density than any of the commercial projects, post-feature-test. Compared to the postrelease defect densities of the commercial products, on the other hand, Mozilla has much higher defect densities (see table 10.3).

Since the Mozilla project has yet to issue its first nonbeta release, we cannot assess postrelease defect density at the time of this writing. Although these Mozilla results are encouraging, they are difficult to interpret definitively. Without data on postrelease defects, it is difficult to know whether the post-feature-test densities are low because there really are relatively few defects in the code, or because the code has not been exercised thoroughly enough. As we reported earlier, though, more than 6,000 people have reported at least one problem with Mozilla, so we are inclined to believe that the low defect densities probably reflect relatively low defect code, rather than code that has not been exercised.

Time to Resolve Problem Reports

Q6: How long did it take to resolve problems? Were high-priority problems resolved faster than low-priority problems? Has resolution interval decreased over time?

Out of all 57,966 PRs entered in the Bugzilla database, 99 percent have a valid creation date and status change date; 85 percent of these have passed through the state RESOLVED and 46 percent of these have resolution FIXED, indicating that a fix was checked into the codebase; 83 percent FIXED bugs have passed through the state VERIFIED, indicating that inspectors agreed with the fix.

Figure 10.7 plots the cumulative distribution of the interval for all resolved PRs broken down by whether the PR resolution is FIXED, by priority, by the module, and by date (made before or after January 1, 2000). All four figures show that the median resolution interval is much longer than for Apache. We should note that half of the FIXED PRs had 43 percent or more of their resolution interval spent after the stage RESOLVED and before the stage VERIFIED. It means that mandatory inspection of changes in Mozilla almost doubles the PR resolution interval. But this increase does not completely account for the difference between Apache and Mozilla intervals; half of the observed Mozilla interval is still significantly longer than the Apache interval.

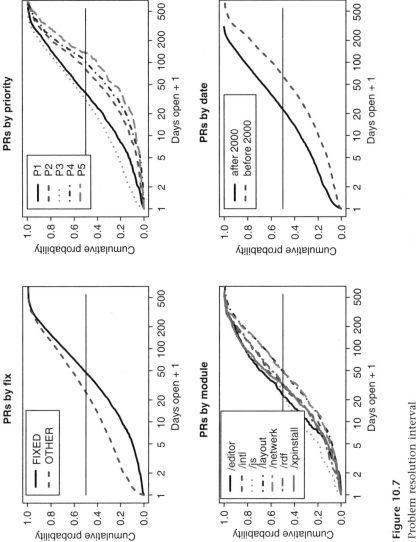

Figure 10.7
Problem resolution interval

Half of the PRs that result in fixes or changes are resolved in less than 30 days, and half of the PRs that do not result in fixes are resolved in less than 15 days. This roughly corresponds to the inspection overhead (inspections are only done for FIXED PRs).

There is a significant relationship between interval and priority. Half of the PRs with priority P1 and P3 are resolved in 30 days or less, and half of priority P2 PRs are resolved in 80 days or less, whereas the median interval of P4 and P5 PRs exceeds 100 days. The recorded priority of PRs did not matter in the Apache context, but the "priority" implicitly determined by affected functionality had an effect on the interval. These results appear to indicate that Mozilla participants were generally sensitive to PR priority, although it is not clear why priority P3 PRs were resolved so quickly.

There is substantial variation in the PR resolution interval by module. The PRs have a median interval of 20 days for /editor and /js modules and 50 days for /layout and /netwerk modules. This is in contrast to Apache, where modules could be grouped by the number of users they affect. Furthermore, /editor affects fewer users than /layout (2-D graphics), yet resolution of the latter's problems is slower, unlike in Apache, where the resolution time decreased when the number affected users increased.

The resolution interval decreases drastically between the two periods, possibly because of the increasing involvement of external developers or maturity of the project. We observed a similar effect in Apache.

Hypotheses Revisited

Hypothesis 1: Open source developments will have a core of developers who control the code base. This core will be no larger than 10 to 15 people, and will create approximately 80 percent or more of the new functionality.

Hypothesis 2: For projects that are so large that 10 to 15 developers cannot write 80 percent of the code in a reasonable time frame, a strict code ownership policy will have to be adopted to separate the work of additional groups, creating, in effect, several related OSS projects.

These hypotheses are supported by the Mozilla data. The essential insight that led to these hypotheses is that when several people work on the same code, there are many potential dependencies among their work items. Managing these dependencies can be accomplished informally by small groups of people who know and trust each other, and communicate frequently enough so that each is generally aware of what the others are doing.

At some point—perhaps around an upper limit of 10 to 15 people—this method of coordinating the work becomes inadequate. There are too many people involved for each to be sufficiently aware of the others. The core groups for the various modules in Mozilla (with module size comparable to Apache in the range of 3 to 12 thousand delta per year and of duration longer than one year) range from 22 to 36 people and so are clearly larger than we contemplated in these hypotheses. And, much as we predicted, a form of code ownership was adopted by the various Mozilla teams.

There are at least two ways, though, that the Mozilla findings cause us to modify these hypotheses. Although the size of the project caused the creation of multiple separated project "teams" as we had anticipated (e.g., Chatzilla and other projects that contribute code to an /extensions directory), we observe code ownership on a module-by-module basis, so that the code owner must approve any submission to the owned files. This process uses ownership to create a mechanism whereby a single individual has sufficient knowledge and responsibility to guard against conflicts within the owned part of the code. There is no "core" group as in the Apache sense, where everyone in the privileged group is permitted to commit code anywhere.

This leads to a further point that not only did the Mozilla group use ownership in ways we did not quite expect, they used other mechanisms to coordinate the work that are independent of ownership. Specifically, they had a more concretely defined process, and they had a much stricter policy regarding inspections. Both of these mechanisms serve also to maintain coordination among different work items. Based on these additional findings, we would rephrase Hypotheses 1 and 2 as follows:

Hypothesis 1a: Open source developments will have a core of developers who control the code base, and will create approximately 80 percent or more of the new functionality. If this core group uses only informal ad hoc means of coordinating their work, the group will be no larger than 10 to 15 people.

Hypothesis 2a: If a project is so large that more than 10 to 15 people are required to complete 80 percent of the code in the desired time frame, then other mechanisms, rather than just informal ad hoc arrangements, will be required to coordinate the work. These mechanisms may include one or more of the following: explicit development processes, individual or group code ownership, and required inspections.

Hypothesis 3:   In successful open source developments, a group larger by an order of magnitude than the core will repair defects, and a yet larger group (by another order of magnitude) will report problems.

For the modules that we report on in Mozilla, we observed large differences between the size of core team (22 to 35), the size of the communities that submit bug fixes that are incorporated into the code (47 to 129) and that find and report bugs that are fixed (119 to 623), and the estimated total population of people that report defects (600 to 3,000). These differences are substantial and in the direction of the hypothesis, but are not as large as in Apache. In particular, the group that adds new functionality is larger than we would have expected. This is likely due to the hybrid nature of the project, where the core developers are operating in a more industrial mode, and have been assigned to work full-time on the project. Since Mozilla does not deviate radically from the prediction, and since the prediction was meant to apply only to pure open source projects, we don't believe that it requires modification at this time.

Hypothesis 4:   Open source developments that have a strong core of developers but never achieve large numbers of contributors beyond that core will be able to create new functionality, but will fail because of a lack of resources devoted to finding and repairing defects.

We were not able to test this hypothesis with the Mozilla data, since it did in fact achieve large numbers of contributors.

Hypothesis 5:   Defect density in open source releases will generally be lower than commercial code that has only been feature-tested; that is, received a comparable level of testing.

The defect density of the Mozilla code was comparable to the Apache code; hence we may tentatively regard this hypothesis as supported. In Mozilla, there appears to be a sizable group of people who specialize in reporting defects—an activity corresponding to testing activity in commercial projects. Additionally, as we mentioned previously, Mozilla has a half-dozen test teams that maintain test cases, test plans, and the like. The project also uses a sophisticated problem-reporting tool, Bugzilla, that keeps track of top problems to speed problem reporting and reduce duplicate reports, and maintains continuous multiplatform builds. Inspections, testing, and better tools to support defect reporting apparently compensate for larger and more complex code. We must be very cautious in interpreting these results, because it is possible that large numbers of defects will be found when the product is released.

Hypothesis 6:   In successful open source developments, the developers will also be users of the software.

The reasoning behind this hypothesis was that low defect densities are achieved because developers are users of the software and hence have considerable domain expertise. This puts them at a substantial advantage relative to many commercial developers who vary greatly in their domain expertise. This certainly appears to be true in the Mozilla case. Although we did not have data on Mozilla use by Mozilla developers, it is wildly implausible to suggest that the developers were not experienced browser users, and thus "domain experts" in the sense of this hypothesis.

Hypothesis 7: OSS developments exhibit very rapid responses to customer problems.

In the hybrid Mozilla case, response times are much longer than in the case of Apache. This may be due to the more commercial-like aspects of development; that is, the need to inspect, to submit the code through the owner, and so on. It also uses a 30-day release (milestone) cycle that more closely resembles commercial processes than the somewhat more rapid Apache process. Furthermore, the Mozilla product is still in the beta stage, and that might partly explain slower response times. Hence, it is not clear that the Mozilla data bear on this hypothesis, as long as it is taken to apply only to OSS, not to hybrid projects.

It should be noted that rapid responses to customer problems together with low defect density may significantly increase the availability of OSS software by minimizing the number and shortening the duration of downtime of customer's systems.

Conclusion: Hybrid Hypotheses

As we pointed out in the introduction, there are many ways in which elements of commercial and open source processes could be combined, and Mozilla represents only a single point in that space. The essential differences have to do with coordination, selection, and assignment of the work.

Commercial development typically uses a number of coordination mechanisms to fit the work of each individual into the project as a whole (see for example Grinter, Herbsleb, and Perry 1999 and Herbsleb and Grinter 1999). Explicit mechanisms include such things as interface specifications, processes, plans, staffing profiles, and reviews. Implicit mechanisms include knowledge of who has expertise in what area, customs, and habits regarding how things are done. In addition, of course, it is possible to substitute communication for these mechanisms. So, for example, two people could develop interacting modules with no interface specification, merely by staying in constant communication with each other. The "communication-only" approach does not scale, of course, as size and complexity quickly overwhelm communication channels. It is always necessary, though, as the default means of overcoming coordination problems, as a way to recover if unexpected events break down the existing coordination mechanisms, and to handle details that need to be worked out in real time.

Apache adopts an approach to coordination that seems to work extremely well for a small project. The server itself is kept small. Any functionality beyond the basic server is added by means of various ancillary projects that interact with Apache only through Apache's well-defined interface. That interface serves to coordinate the efforts of the Apache developers with anyone building external functionality, and does so with minimal ongoing effort by the Apache core group. In fact, control over the interface is asymmetric, in that the external projects must generally be designed to what Apache provides. The coordination concerns of Apache are thus sharply limited by the stable asymmetrically controlled interface.

The coordination necessary *within* this sphere is such that it can be successfully handled by a small core team using primarily implicit mechanisms; for example, a knowledge of who has expertise in what area, and general communication about what is going on and who is doing what, when. When such mechanisms are sufficient to prevent coordination breakdowns, they are extremely efficient. Many people can contribute code simultaneously, and there is no waiting for approvals, permission, and so forth, from a single individual. The core people just do what needs to be done. The Apache results show the benefits in speed, productivity, and quality.

The benefit of the larger open source community for Apache is primarily in those areas where coordination is much less of an issue. Bug fixes occasionally become entangled in interdependencies; however, most of the effort in bug fixing is generally in tracking down the source of the problem. Investigation, of course, cannot cause coordination problems. The tasks of finding and reporting bugs are completely free of interdependencies, in the sense that they do not involve changing the code.

The Mozilla approach has some, but not all, of the Apache-style OSS benefits. The open source community has taken over a significant portion of the bug finding and fixing, as in Apache, helping with these low-interdependency tasks. However, the Mozilla modules are not as independent from one another as the Apache server is from its ancillary projects. Because of the interdependence among modules, considerable effort (i.e., inspections) needs to be spent in order to ensure that the interdependencies do not cause problems. In addition, the modules are too large for a team of 10 to 15 to do 80 percent of the work in the desired time. Therefore, the relatively free-wheeling Apache style of communication and implicit coordination is likely not feasible. The larger Mozilla core teams must have more formal means of coordinating their work, which in their case means a single module owner who must approve all changes to the module. These characteristics produce high productivity and low defect density, much like Apache, but at relatively long development intervals.

The relatively high level of module interdependence may be a result of many factors. For example, the commercial legacy distinguishes Mozilla from Apache and many other purely open source projects. One might speculate that in commercial development, feature content is driven by market demands, and for many applications (such as browsers) the market generates great pressure for feature richness. When combined with extreme schedule pressure, it is not unreasonable to expect that the code complexity will be high and that modularity may suffer. This sort of legacy may well contribute to the difficulty of coordinating Mozilla and other commercial-legacy hybrid projects.

It may be possible to avoid this problem under various circumstances, such as:

- New hybrid projects that are set up like OSS projects, with small teams owning well-separated modules
- Projects with OSS legacy code
- Projects with a commercial legacy, but where modules are parsed in a way that minimizes module-spanning changes (see Mockus and Weiss 2001 for a technique that accomplishes this)

Given this discussion, one might speculate that overall, in OSS projects, low postrelease defect density and high productivity stem from effective use of the open source community for the low-interdependence bug finding and fixing tasks. Mozilla's apparent ability to achieve defect density levels like Apache's argues that even when an open source effort maintains much of the machinery of commercial development (including elements of planning, documenting the process and the product, explicit code ownership, inspections, and testing), there is substantial potential benefit. In particular, defect density and productivity both seem to benefit from recruiting an open source community of testers and bug fixers. Speed, on the other hand, seems to require highly modularized software and small highly capable core teams and the informal style of coordination this permits.

Interestingly, the particular way that the core team in Apache (and, we assume, many other OSS projects) is formed might be another of the keys to their success. Core members must be persistent and very capable to achieve core status. They are also free, while they are earning their core status, to work on any task they choose. Presumably they will try to choose something that is both badly needed and where they have some specific interest. While working in this area, they must demonstrate a high level of capability, and they must also convince the existing core team that they would make a responsible, productive colleague. This setup is in contrast to that of most commercial development, where assignments are given out that may or may not correspond to a developer's interests or perceptions of what is needed.

We believe that for some kinds of software—in particular, those where developers are also highly knowledgeable users—it would be worth experimenting, in a commercial environment, with OSS-style "open" work assignments. This approach implicitly allows new features to be chosen by the developers/users rather than a marketing or product management organization.

We expect that time and future research will further test our hypotheses and will demonstrate new approaches that would elegantly combine the best technologies from all types of software development environments. Eventually, we expect such work to blur distinctions between the commercial and OSS processes reported in this article.

Appendix

Table 10.8
Comparison of Apache and Mozilla processes

	Apache	Mozilla
Scope	The Apache project we examined includes only the Apache server.	The Mozilla project includes the browser, as well as a number of development tools and a toolkit. Some of these projects are as large or larger than the Apache server.
Roles and responsibilities	The Apache Group (AG) currently has about 25 members, all of whom are volunteers. They can commit code anywhere in the server. The core development group includes the currently active AG members as well as others who are very active and under consideration for membership in AG.	Mozilla.org has 12 members, who are assigned to this work full-time. Several spend considerable time coding, but most play support and coordination roles. Many others have substantial responsibility— for example, as owners of the approximately 78 modules, and leaders of the 6 test teams. Many of the non-mozilla.org participants are also paid to spend time on Mozilla development.
Identifying work to be done	Since only the AG has commit access to the code, they control all changes. The process is an open one, however, in the sense that others can propose fixes and changes, comment on proposed changes, and advocate them to the AG.	Anyone can submit a problem report or request an enhancement, but mozilla.org controls the direction of the project. Much of this authority is delegated to module owners and test teams, but mozilla.org reserves the right to determine module ownership and to resolve conflicts.

Table 10.8
(continued)

	Apache	Mozilla
Assigning and performing development work	Anyone can submit patches, choosing to work on his or her own enhancements or fixes, or responding to the developer mailing list, news group, or BUGDB. Core developers have "unofficial" areas of expertise where they tend to do much of the work. Other core developers tend to defer to experts in each area.	Developers make heavy use of the Bugzilla change management tool to find problems or enhancements on which to work. They are asked to mark changes they choose to work on in order to avoid duplication of effort. Developers can use Bugzilla to request help on a particular change, and to submit their code.
Prerelease testing	Developers perform something like commercial unit and feature testing on a local copy.	Minimal "smoke screen" tests are performed on daily builds. There are six test teams assigned to parts of the product. They maintain test cases, guidelines, training materials, and so on, on the mozilla.org Web site.
Inspections	All AG members generally review all changes. They are also distributed to the entire, development community, who also frequently submit comments. In general, inspections are done before commits on stable releases, and after commits on development releases.	All changes undergo two stages of inspections, one at the module level, and one by a member of the highly qualified "super reviewer" group. Module owners must approve all changes in their modules.
Managing releases	The job of release manager rotates through experienced members of AG. Critical problems are identified; access to code is restricted. When the release manager determines that critical problems are resolved and code is stable, the code is released.	Mozilla has daily builds and "Milestone" releases approximately monthly. The code is frozen for a few days prior to a Milestone releases; critical problems are resolved. A designated group at mozilla.org is responsible for Milestone decisions.

Acknowledgments

We thank Mitchell Baker for reviewing the Mozilla process description and Manoj Kasichainula for reviewing the Apache process description. We also thank all the reviewers for their insightful comments.

This work was done while A. Mockus and J. D. Herbsleb were members of software Production Research Department at Lucent Technologies' Bell Laboratories. This article is a significant extension to the authors' paper "A case study of open source software development: the Apache server" that appeared in the Proceedings of the 22nd International Conference on Software Engineering, Limerick, Ireland, June 2000 (ICSE 2000), pp. 263–272.

Notes

1. Please see Ang and Eich 2000; Baker 2000; Eich 2001; Hecker 1999; Howard 2000; Mozilla Project; Oeschger and Boswell 2000; Paquin and Tabb 1998; Williams 2000; Yeh 1999; and Zawinski 1999.

2. Ang and Eich 2000; Baker 2000; Eich 2001; Hecker 1999; Howard 2000; Mozilla Project; Oeschger and Boswell 2000; Paquin and Tabb 1998; Williams 2000; Yeh 1999; and Zawinski 1999.

11 Software Engineering Practices in the GNOME Project

One of the main goals of empirical studies in software engineering is to help us understand the current practice of software development. Good empirical studies allow us to identify and exploit important practical ideas that can potentially benefit many other similar software projects. Unfortunately, most software companies consider their source code and development practices to be a trade secret. If they allow researchers to investigate these practices, it is commonly under a nondisclosure agreement. This practice poses a significant problem: how can other researchers verify the validity of a study if they have no access to the original source code and other data that was used in the project? As a consequence, it is common to find studies in which the reader is asked to trust the authors, unable to ever reproduce their results. This situation seems to contradict the main principle of empirical science, which invites challenge and different interpretations of the data, and it is through those challenges that a study strengthens its validity.

Bruce Perens describes open source software (OSS) as software that provides the following minimal rights to their users: (1) the right to make copies of the program and distribute those copies; (2) the right to have access to the software's source code; and (3) the right to make improvements to the program (Perens 1999). These rights provide empirical software engineering researchers with the ability to inspect the source code and share it without a nondisclosure agreement. Furthermore, many of these projects have an "open source approach" to the historical data of the project (email, bug tracking systems, version control). Finally, researchers can participate actively or passively in the project in a type of anthropological study.

The economic model on which closed source software (CSS) projects are based is fundamentally different than that of OSS projects, and it is necessary to understand that not all *good* OSS practices might be transferable to the realm of CSS projects. It is, however, important to identify these practices, which at the very least will benefit other OSS projects, and at best, will benefit any software project.

As of March 2003, SourceForge.net lists more than 58,000 projects and more than 590,000 users. Even though most of these projects might be small, immature, and composed by only a handful of developers (Krishnamurthy 2002), the number of projects suggests that the study of practices in OSS software development is an important area of research with the potential to benefit a significant audience.

One free software (FS) project (and therefore OSS) of particular interest is (http://www.gnome.org) the GNU Network Object Model Environment (GNOME). GNOME is an attempt to create a free (as defined by the General Public License, or GPL) desktop environment for Unix systems. It is composed of three main components: an easy-to-use graphical user interface (GUI) environment; a collection of tools, libraries, and components to develop this environment; and an "office suite" (Gwynne 2003). There are several features of GNOME that make it attractive from the point of view of a researcher:

1. GNOME is a widely used product. It is included in almost every major Linux distribution: Sun offers GNOME for Solaris, IBM offers it for AIX, and it is also available for Apple's OS X.
2. Its latest version (2.2) is composed of more than 2 million lines of code divided into more than 60 libraries and applications.
3. More than 500 individuals have contributed to the project (those who have write-access to the CVS repository) and contributors are distributed around the world.
4. GNOME contributors maintain a large collection of information relevant to the project that traces its history: several dozens of mailings lists (including their archives), a developers, Web site with a large amount of documentation, a bug tracking system, and a CVS repository with the entire history of the project dating to 1997.
5. Several commercial companies, such as Red Hat, Sun Microsystems, and Ximian contribute a significant amount of resources to the project, including full-time employees, who are core contributors to the project. In some cases, these companies are almost completely responsible for the development of a library or an application (for an example see "Case Study: Evolution" later in this chapter). Given that most of the contributors of these projects belong to the same organization, it could be argued that they resemble CSS projects.

6. From the economic and management point of view, it provides an interesting playground in which the interests of the companies involved (who want to make money) have to be balanced with the interests of the individuals who contribute to the project (who are interested in the openness and freedom of the project).

Architecture

GNOME targets two different types of audiences. On one hand, it is intended for the final user, who is interested on having a cohesive set of applications for the desktop, including an office suite. On the other hand, it contains a collection of APIs and development tools that assist programmers in the creation of GUI applications.

The deliverables of GNOME are therefore divided into three main groups:

1. *Libraries.* One of the first goals of the project was to provide a library of GUI widgets for X11[1]. It currently contains libraries for many other purposes: printing, XML processing, audio, spell-checking, SVG and HTML rendering, among others. Any function that is expected to be used by more than one application tends to be moved into a library.

2. *Applications.* The official distribution of GNOME contains a minimal set of applications that includes a "task bar" (called a "panel" in GNOME), applets to include in the task bar, a text editor, a windows manager, a file manager, and helper applications to display a variety of file types. GNOME also includes a set of optional applications for end users, such as a mail client, a word processor, a spreadsheet, and an accounting package; and some for developers, such as an IDE (Integrated Development Environment).

3. *Documentation.* Documentation comes in two types: one for developers and one for final users. The former includes a description of the APIs provided by the libraries, while the latter describes how to use the different GNOME applications.

Figure 11.1 depicts the interaction between libraries, applications, and the rest of the operating system. Libraries provide common functionality to the applications and they interact with X11, with the operating system, and with non-GNOME libraries. GNOME applications are expected to use these libraries in order to be isolated from the running environment. The window manager (which is required to be GNOME-aware) serves also as an intermediary between GNOME applications and X11. ORBit is the

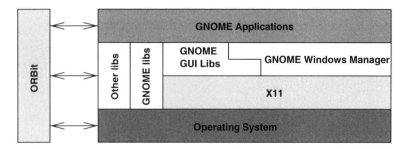

Figure 11.1
GNOME is composed of a collection of libraries and applications. The libraries are responsible for interacting between the user and X11 or the operating system. ORBit is a CORBA implementation that is responsible for interprocess communication.

GNOME implementation of CORBA and it is responsible for the communication between applications.

Project Organization

The success of an OSS project depends on the ability of its maintainers to divide it into small parts on which contributors can work with minimal communication between each other and with minimal impact to the work of others (Lerner and Triole 2000). The division of GNOME into a collection of libraries and applications provides a natural way to split the project into subprojects that are as independent as possible from each other. These subprojects are usually called *modules* (*module* is the name used by CVS to refer to a directory in the repository). The core distribution of GNOME 2.2 is composed of approximately 60 different modules.

And as a project grows bigger, it tends to be split into further submodules, which minimize the interaction between contributors. Using softChange to analyze the historical data from the CVS repository (German and Mockus 2003) has resulted some interesting facts about the division of work in GNOME. Because CVS does not have a notion of "transaction" (identifying an atomic operation to the repository), one of the tasks of softChange is to try to reconstruct these transactions (which softChange calls a Modification Request, or MR). The CVS data of a total of 62 modules was analyzed. In order to account for contributors that are no longer active, it was decided to narrow the analysis to 2002. An MR can be started only by a contributor who has a CVS account. Sometimes a patch is submitted, by someone who does not have a CVS account, to one of the core contributors of the corresponding module, who then proceeds to evaluate it, accept it, and commit it if appropriate. This analysis does not take these sporadic contributors into account.

In 2002, a total of 280 people contributed to these 62 modules. It was decided to further narrow the analysis and consider only contributors to the code base (who will be referred as *programmers*) and consider only MRs involving C files (C is the most widely used language in GNOME, and the number of C files in these modules outnumber the files in the next language—bash—by approximately 50 times).

A total of 185 programmers were identified. Ninety-eight programmers contributed 10 or fewer MRs, accounting for slightly less than 3 percent of the total MRs. The most active programmer (in terms of MRs) accounted for 7 percent of the total. The top 10 programmers accounted for 46 percent of the total MRs. Even though these numbers need to be correlated with the actual number of lines of code (LOCS) or defects (bugs) removed per MR, they indicate that a small number of developers are responsible for most of the coding of the project. Zawinsky, at one time one of the core Mozilla contributors, commented on this phenomenon: "If you have a project that has 5 people who write 80 percent of the code, and 100 people who have contributed bug fixes or a few hundred lines of code here and there, is that a 105-programmer project?" (as cited in Jones 2002). When taking into account the division of the project into modules, this effect seemed more pronounced. Table 11.1 shows the top five programmers for some of the most actively modified modules of GNOME.

Module Maintainers

Module maintainers serve as leaders for their module. Lerner and Triole (2000) identified the main roles of a leader in an OSS project as:

• Providing a vision
• Dividing the project into parts in which individuals can tackle independent tasks
• Attracting developers to the project
• Keeping the project together and preventing forking[2]

GNOME has been able to attract and maintain good, trustworthy maintainers in its most important modules. Many of these maintainers are employees paid by different companies to work on GNOME.

As it was described in German 2002, several companies have been subsidizing the development of GNOME. Red Hat, Sun Microsystems, and Ximian are a few of the companies who pay full-time employees to work

Table 11.1
Top five programmers of some the most active modules during 2002

Module	Total number of programmers	Programmer	Proportion of MRs
glib	24	owen	31%
		matthiasc	18%
		wilhelmi	10%
		timj	10%
		tml	9%
gtk+	48	owen	37%
		matthiasc	12%
		tml	9%
		kristian	8%
		jrb	4%
gnome-panel	49	mmclouglin	42%
		jirka	12%
		padraigo	6%
		markmc	6%
		gman	6%
ORBit2	11	michael	51%
		mmclouglin	28%
		murrayc	9%
		cactus	5%
		scouter	3%
gnumeric	19	jody	34%
		mortenw	23%
		guelzow	17%
		jpekka	12%
		jhellan	9%

The first column shows the name of the module, the second shows the total number of programmers who contributed in that year, and the third shows the userid of the top five programmers and the proportion of their MRs with respect to the total during the year. In this table, only MRs that included C files are considered.

on GNOME. Paid employees are usually responsible for the following tasks: project design and coordination, testing, documentation, and bug fixing. These tasks are usually less attractive to volunteers. By taking care of them, the paid employees make sure that the development of GNOME continues at a steady pace. Some paid employees also take responsibility (as module maintainers) for some of the critical parts of the project, such as gtk+ and ORBit (Red Hat), the file manager Nautilus (Eazel, now bankrupt), and Evolution (Ximian). Paid employees contribute more than just code; one of the most visible contributions of Sun employees is the proposal of the GNOME Accessibility Framework a set of guidelines and APIs intended to make GNOME usable by a vast variety of users, including persons with disabilities. For example, in Evolution, the top 10 contributors (who account for almost 70% of its MRs) are all Ximian employees.

Volunteers still play a very important role in the project, and their contributions are everywhere: as maintainers and contributors to modules, as bug hunters, as documenters, as beta testers, and so on. In particular, there is one area of GNOME development that continues to be performed mainly by volunteers: internationalization. The translation of GNOME is done by small teams of volunteers (who usually speak the language in question and who are interested in support for their language in GNOME).

As with any other open source project, GNOME is a meritocracy, where people are valued by the quality (and quantity) of their contributions. Most of the paid contributors in GNOME were at some point volunteers. Their commitment to the project got them a job to continue to do what they did before as a hobby.

Requirement Analysis

Most OSS projects have a requirement's engineering phase that is very different from the one that takes place in traditional software projects (Scacchi 2002). At the beginning of GNOME the only stakeholders were the developers, who acted as users, investors, coders, testers, and documenters, among other roles. While they had little interest in the commercial success of the project, they wanted to achieve respect from their peers for their development capabilities and wanted to produce software that was used by the associated community. In particular, the following sources of requirements in GNOME can be identified (German 2003):

• *Vision.* One or several leaders provide a list of requirements that the system should satisfy. In GNOME, this is epitomized by the following nonfunctional requirement: "GNOME should be completely free software" (*free* as defined by the Free Software Foundation; free software gives the following rights to its users: to run the software for any endeavor; to inspect its source code, modify it; and to redistribute the original product or the modified version).

• *Reference applications.* Many of its components are created with the goal of replacing similar applications. The GNOME components should have most of the same, if not the exact same, functionality as these reference applications. For example, gnumeric uses Microsoft Excel as its reference, ggv uses gv and kghostview, and Evolution uses Microsoft Outlook and Lotus Notes.

• *Asserted requirements.* In a few cases, the requirements for a module or component are born from a discussion in a mailing list. In some cases, a requirement emerges from a discussion whose original intention was not requirement analysis. In other instances (as in the case of Evolution), a person posts a clear question instigating discussion on the potential requirements that a tool or library should have. Evolution was born after several hundred messages were created describing the requirements (functional and nonfunctional) that a good mailer should have before coding started. More recently, companies such as Sun and IBM have started to create requirements documents in areas that have been overlooked in the past. One of them is the GNOME Accessibility Framework.

• *A prototype.* Many projects start with an artifact as a way to clearly state some of the requirements needed in the final application. Frequently a developer proposes a feature, implements it, and presents it to the rest of the team, which then decides on its value and chooses to accept the prototype or scrap the idea (Hissam et al. 2001). GNOME, for example, started with a prototype (version 0.1) created by Miguel de Icaza as the starting point of the project.

• *Post hoc requirements.* In this case, a feature in the final project is added to a module because a developer wants that feature and he or she is willing to do most of the work, from requirements to implementation and testing. This feature might be unknown to the rest of the development team until the author provides them with a patch, and a request to add the feature to the module.

Regardless of the method used, requirements are usually gathered and prioritize by the maintainer or maintainers of a given module and potentially the Foundation (see next section, "The GNOME Foundation"). A maintainer has the power to decide which requirements are to be implemented and in which order. The rest of the contributors could provide input and apply pressure on the maintainers to shape their decisions (as in post hoc requirements). A subset of the contributors might not agree with the maintainer's view, and might appeal to the Foundation for a decision on the issue. These differences in opinion could potentially jeopardize the project and create a fork. So far this has not happened within GNOME. On the other hand, some contributors have left the project after irreconcilable differences with the rest of the team. For example, Carsten Haitzler Rasterman, creator of Enlightenment, left GNOME partially due to differences in opinion with the rest of the project (Haitzler 1999).

The GNOME Foundation

Until 2000, GNOME was run by a "legislature," in which each of its contributors had a voice and a vote and the developer's mailing list was the floor where the issues were discussed. Miguel de Icaza served as the constitutional monarch and supreme court of the project, and had the final say on any unsolvable disputes. This model did not scale well, and was complicated when Miguel de Icaza created Helixcode (now Ximian), a commercial venture aimed at continuing the development of GNOME, planning to generate income by selling services around it.

In August 2000, the GNOME Foundation was instituted. The mandate of the Foundation is "to further the goal of the GNOME Project: to create a computing platform for use by the general public that is completely free software" (The GNOME Foundation 2000). The Foundation fulfills the following four roles (Mueth and Pennington 2002): (1) it provides a democratic process in which the entire GNOME development community can have a voice; (2) it is responsible for communicating information about GNOME to the media and corporations; (3) it will guarantee that the decisions on the future of GNOME are done in an open and transparent way; (4) it acts as a legal entity that can accept donations and make purchases to benefit GNOME.

The Foundation comprises four entities: its members (any contributor to the project can apply for membership); the board of directors (composed of 11 democratically elected contributors, with at most 4 with the same corporate affiliation); the advisory board (composed of companies and not-for-profit organizations); and the executive director. As defined by the Foundation's charter, the board of directors is the primary decision-making body of the GNOME Foundation. The members of the board are supposed to serve in a personal capacity and not as representatives of their employers. The Board meets regularly (usually every two weeks, via telephone call) to discuss the current issues and take decisions in behalf of the entire community. The minutes of each meeting are then published in one of the GNOME mailing lists (foundation-announce).

Committees

Given the lack of a single organization driving the development according to its business goals, OSS projects tend to rely on volunteers to do most of the administrative tasks associated with that project. In GNOME, committees are created around tasks that the Foundation identifies as important. Contributors then volunteer to be members of these committees. Examples of committees are the GUADEC team (responsible for the organization of the GNOME conference), the Web team (responsible for keeping the Web site up to date), the sysadmin team (responsible for system administration of the GNOME machines), the release team (responsible for planning and releasing the official GNOME releases), the Foundation membership team (responsible for maintaining the membership list of the foundation), and several others.

The Release Team

In an OSS project that involves people from different organizations and with different time commitments to the project, it is not clear how to best organize and keep track of a release schedule. GNOME faced the same difficulty. Each individual module might have its own development timeline and objectives. Planning and coordination of the overall project is done by the release team. They are responsible for developing, in coordination with the module maintainers, release schedules for the different modules and the schedule of the overall project. They also keep track of the development of the project and its modules, making sure that everything stays within schedule. Jeff Waugh, a GNOME Foundation member, summarized the accomplishment of the team and the skills required in his message of candidacy to the Board of Directors in 2002:

[The release team] has earned the trust of the GNOME developer community, madly hand-waved the GNOME 2.0 project back on track, and brought strong cooperation and "the love" back to the project after a short hiatus. It has required an interesting combination of skills, from cheerleading and Maciej-style police brutality to subtle diplomacy and "networking."

Case Study: Evolution

Ximian Evolution evolved within the GNOME project as its groupware suite based around a mail client. The project started in the beginning of

1998. At the end of 2000, Ximian (previously called Helixcode, after its creating company founded by Miguel de Icaza) started operations and decided to take over the development of Evolution. By the end of 2002, Evolution was composed of approximately 185,000 lines of code, written mostly in C. Evolution recently received the 2003 LinuxWorld Open Source Product Excellence Award in the category of Best Front Office Solution. One of the objectives of Evolution is to provide a FS product with functionality similar to Microsoft Outlook or Lotus Notes (Perazzoli 2001).

As with most of the GNOME modules, the development environment includes CVS (used for version control of the files of the project), Bugzilla (used to track defects), one mailing list for developers and one for users, and a collection of documentation pages hosted at the Ximian and GNOME developers' Web sites.

As is required by the GNOME guidelines, when a contributor commits a MR, he or she modifies the relevant changelog file to add a description of the current change. The commit triggers an e-mail message to the GNOME cvs-commits mailing list, which will include all the details of the transaction: who made it, when, the files modified, and the log message. Usually, the changelog and the CVS log messages indicate the nature of the change, list defect numbers from Bugzilla, and often include a URL pointing to the change and/or to the defect.

Figure 11.2 displays the number of MRs for each month of the project. Before Ximian was born, the level of activity was very low. It is also interesting how the number of MRs correlates to the number of releases, peaking just before version 1.0, at the same time that the frequency of small releases increased.

Figure 11.3 shows the net number lines of code added to the project (this number includes comments and empty lines) as a function of time. It also shows the number of new files added to the project (removed files are not taken into account) and correlates this information with the release dates. Some interesting observations can be made. There seems to be a correlation of added LOCS and new files, and the number of added LOCS and new files is flat in the month previous to release 1.0, suggesting a period in which debugging took precedence over new features. After release 1.0, the development was relatively flat compared to the previous period. From the evolutionary point of view, it is particularly interesting to see that during April 2002, more than 5,000 LOCS were removed from the project. Thanks to the changelog, it was possible to learn that the LOCS removed were automatically generated, and no longer needed. Being able to discover the reasons behind changes to a project emphasizes the

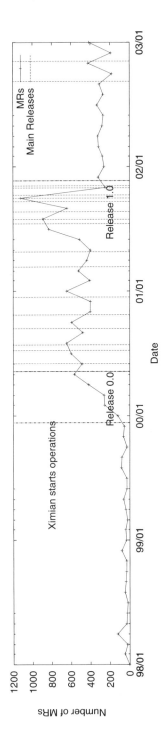

Figure 11.2
Number of MRs per month in Evolution. There is a significant increase in activity after Ximian starts operations, and the largest activity coincides with the release of version 1.0.

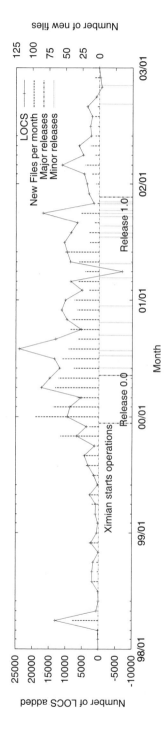

Figure 11.3

Growth of the source code of Evolution. The left axis shows the number of lines added to the project (sum of deltas equals lines added minus lines removed), while the right axis shows the number of files added each month.

importance of the changelogs in the development process. Readers are invited to read German and Mockus 2003 for a more in-depth analysis of Evolution.

Conclusions and Future Work

GNOME is a successful and mature FS project with a large number of contributors. It has been able to evolve from a purely volunteer effort into one that is mainly driven by the industry, while still allowing active participation by volunteers. Like many other OSS projects, a relatively small number of core contributors are responsible for most of the project. The source code is divided into modules, in which the interaction between contributors is minimized.

GNOME's development process is open. A large amount of data is available, tracing its history to the beginning. This data encompasses mailing lists, version control records, and bug tracking, giving the researcher the ability to inspect the code at a given moment in the past, and correlate it to its then-current defects and e-mail messages from its contributors. Some examples are shown on how this data can be used. Further and more in-depth empirical studies are needed to understand the interactions of its contributors, its architectural evolution, and its quality, for example. A comparative analysis of GNOME and KDE (GNOME's main competitor for the Unix desktop) will provide insight on how different (or similar) these two projects are in their development processes and architectures.

GNOME, like many other large OSS projects, provides a gold mine of data ready to be exploited. The resulting studies have the potential to provide a better understanding of how OSS evolves, identifying some good practices that could benefit many other OSS projects and, to a lesser extent, closed source projects too.

Acknowledgments and Disclaimer

This research has been supported by the National Sciences and Engineering Research Council of Canada and the British Columbia Advanced Systems Institute. The author would like to thank Joe Feller, Scott Hissam, and Dan Hoffman for their invaluable comments during the preparation of this document. Any opinions, findings and conclusions expressed in this document are those of the author and do not necessarily reflect the views of the GNOME project or the GNOME Foundation.

Notes

1. The beginning of the project can be traced back to a license war between the advocates of FS and those using Qt, at that time a proprietary GUI library for X11, (a windowing system for the UNIX operating system) which was eventually released under the GPL and is the basis of the KDE project; it is similar in scope to GNOME. See Perens 1998 for a discussion of this issue.

2. Sometimes when some of the developers of an open source application disagree, they decide to create an alternative version of the project that continues its life independently from the original project. This new application is known as a *fork* of the original one.

12 | Incremental and Decentralized Integration in FreeBSD

Niels Jørgensen

There is a tremendous sense of satisfaction to the "see bug, fix bug, see bug fix get incorporated so that the fix helps others" cycle.
—FreeBSD developer

The activity of integration in a software development project may be defined as an assembly of parts. The activity is crucial, because when fragments produced by different programmers are integrated into larger parts, many errors that were previously not visible might emerge. Steve McConnell, in his book *Rapid Development* (McConnell 1996, 406) writes that one of the advantages of doing a daily build of the entire product is that it helps debugging.

You bring the system to a good known state, and then you keep it there.... When the product is built and tested every day, it's much easier to pinpoint why the product is broken on any given day. If the product worked on Day 17 and is broken on Day 18, something that happened between the builds on Days 17 and 18 broke the product.

The FreeBSD project's approach to software integration is highly incremental and decentralized. A stream of bug fixes and new features are integrated into the project's development branch, typically numbering several dozens each day. Integration of a change is the responsibility of the developer working on the change, in two ways. First, the developer has the authority to actually add the change on his own decision, without having to ask someone for approval. Second, the developer is responsible for conducting integration test of his change, including a trial building of the full system and correcting the errors this trial reveals. There is freedom and accountability—changes not properly integrated can be backed out again, and developers risk having their repository privileges revoked.

FreeBSD's delegation of commit authority distinguishes it from projects where only an individual is in control of the repository, such as Linux, and this delegation is, in my view, more in the spirit of open source.

An analysis of the pros and cons of FreeBSD's approach to integration, as attempted in this chapter, may shed light on a wide range of projects that in some way follow Raymond's "release early, release often," since integration is a prerequisite of release—that is, at least if there's anything new in the release! FreeBSD is also interesting as a case of geographically distributed software development. In such projects, integration is generally acknowledged to be an extremely difficult coordination problem; see, for example, Herbsleb and Grinter 1999.

The remainder of the chapter is organized as follows. The first two sections introduce FreeBSD and discuss the notions of integration and coordination in software projects. The remainder of the chapter traces the lifecycle of a change, from work initialization to production release. The conclusion discusses the impact on coordination that may be attributed to FreeBSD's approach to integration.

FreeBSD's Software and Organization

FreeBSD's processes for integration and other activities must support development of extremely complex software by an organization of distributed individuals.

The FreeBSD operating system is a descendant of the Unix variant developed at U.C. Berkeley, dating back to 1977. FreeBSD and its siblings, which include NetBSD and OpenBSD, were found to run 15 percent of the approximately 1.3 million Internet servers covered in a 1999 survey (Zoebelein 1999).

The project's source code repository is publicly available at a Web site (www.freebsd.org), so that any change committed creates a new release immediately. The repository's development branch (or trunk) contains approximately 30,000 files with 5 million lines of code. Approximately 2,000 changes were made to the trunk in October 2002, each typically modifying only a few lines, in one or a few files.

The project participants are the approximately 300 committers; that is, developers having repository write access, plus external contributors whose changes are inserted via committers. More than 1,200 external contributors have contributed to the project's own base of sources, and several thousand users have submitted bug reports. Project leadership is a so-called "core team" with nine members elected by the committers.

In addition to organizing the development of the operating system kernel, the project assumes a role analogous to a Linux distributor such as Red Hat. FreeBSD's release 5.0 of January 2003 included more than *8,000* ported open source programs for server or workstation use with FreeBSD. The project writes comprehensive documentation—for example, the January 2003 release notes for release 5.0 describe several hundred new, mostly minor, features. Various free services to FreeBSD's users are provided—including, most notably, monitoring security—as a basis for issuing warnings and releases of corrected software.

Part of the data underlying this chapter was collected during a survey in November 2000 among FreeBSD's committers (then numbering approximately 200) that received 72 responses. Subsequently, 10 respondents were interviewed via mail. The survey questions were typically directed at the committers' most recent work. For example, the question "When was the last time the committer had caused a broken build?" Results were 8 percent within the last month, 30 percent within the last three months. (Quotations are from the survey and interviews when no other reference is provided.)

Given the absence of hired developers and a corporate building with managers on the top floor, in what sense is FreeBSD an organization, if at all? Within the fields of systems development and organization theory, the concept of organization is quite broad. FreeBSD's informal organization has similarities with Baskerville's and others' notion of a postmodern organization. "In an era of organizational globalization and competitive information systems, we begin to recognize that undue regularity in an organization and its information system may inhibit adaptation and survival. . . . The post-modern business organization is . . . fluid, flexible, adaptive, open. . . ." (Baskerville, Travies, and Truex 1992, 242–243).

FreeBSD's organization is in some ways also similar to Mintzberg's "adhocracy" archetype: a flat organization of specialists forming small project groups from task to task. Mintzberg considered the adhocracy to be the most appropriate form for postwar corporate organizations depending increasingly on employees' creative work (Mintzberg 1979).

There is, though, also a strong element of continuity in FreeBSD's organization. The technological infrastructure has remained essentially the same from the project's inception in the beginning of the 1990s; for example, e-mail for communication, CVS for version control, the C language for programming, and the make program for building. The operating system's basic design has remained the same for more than a decade. "FreeBSD's distinguished roots derive from the latest BSD software releases from . . . Berkeley. The book *The Design and Implementation of the 4.4BSD*

Operating System . . . thus describes much of FreeBSD's core functionality in detail" (McKusick et al. 1996) [4.4BSD was released in 1993].

Although many new features have been incorporated into FreeBSD, there is a further element of stability in that FreeBSD's usage as an Internet server or workstation has been the source of most of the demand for new features, then and now.

Mintzberg's archetypes for organizations that are more traditional than the adhocracy can be characterized on the basis of how central control is established: standardization of work processes, worker skills, or work output, respectively. FreeBSD bears resemblance with Mintzberg's divisionalized archetype, being split into relatively independent divisions to whom the organization as a whole says "We don't care how you work or what your formal education is, as long as the software you contribute does not break the build."

Integration = Assembly of Parts

In this context, *integration* is assumed to mean all the activities required to assemble the full system from its parts, as in (Herbsleb and Grinter 1999).

In software engineering textbooks, integration and testing are frequently viewed as constituting a phase involving a series of steps, from unit testing to module and subsystem testing to final system testing. Approaches presented include strategies for selecting the order in which to integrate parts, such as top-down or bottom-up, referring to the subroutine call structure among parts. (For example, see Sommerville 2001 and Pressman 2000.) The notion of integration is viewed in the sequel as independent of lifecycle context, but with testing as the major activity as in the classical context. Integration is by no means the act of merely "adding" parts together. This statement is analogous to coding being more than generation of arbitrary character sequences. Integration-related activity is viewed as completed simply when the project or individual *considers* it completed; for example, precommit testing is completed when the developer commits.

The canonical error detected during integration is an interdependency (with another part) error. This type of error ranges from subroutine interfaces (for example, syntax of function calls) to execution semantics (for example, modification of data structures shared with other parts). Some errors are easily detected—for example, syntax errors caught by the C compiler during building, or a crash of a newly built kernel. Other errors are unveiled only by careful analysis, if found at all prior to production release.

Malone and Crowston define coordination as "management of dependencies," and suggest dependency analysis as the key to further insight into coordination-related phenomena. Producer/consumer relationships and shared resources are among the generic dependencies discussed in Malone and Crowston 1994.

Producer/consumer dependencies may be of interest for analyses of integration: If part A defines a subroutine called by part B, there is a producer/consumer relationship between the developers of A and B. Notably, these coordination dependencies involve *developers*, not software. A developer might find himself depending on another developer's *knowledge* of specific parts; for instance, to correct (technical) dependency errors. At an underlying level, developer time is a limited resource, so there may be a high cost associated with A's developer having to dive deep into part B to overcome a given distribution of knowledge.

Also, a shared resource dependency can be identified in FreeBSD involving the project's development version. At times, the trunk is overloaded with premature changes, leading to build breakage. In the spirit of Malone and Crowston's interdisciplinary approach, one may compare the human activity revolving around the trunk with a computer network: both are limited, shared resources. Network traffic in excess of capacity leads to congestion. Build breakage disrupts work, not just on the "guilty" change, but numerous other changes occurring in various lifecycle phases that rely on a well-functioning trunk.

Division of Organization, Division of Work

Work on a change in FreeBSD can be divided into the following types of activities:

• Pre-integration activities, such as coding and reviewing, where the project's "divisions," the individual developers, have a high degree of freedom to choose whatever approach they prefer; for example, there is no requirement that a change is described in a design document.

• Integration activities, such as precommit testing and parallel debugging, which are controlled more tightly by project rules—for example, the rule that prior to committing a change, a committer must ensure that the change does not break the build.

Parnas's characterization of a module as "a responsibility assignment rather than a subprogram" (Parnas 1972) pinpoints the tendency that organizational rather than software architectural criteria determine the way tasks are decomposed in FreeBSD; namely, into entities small enough to be worked on by an individual. Sixty-five percent of the respondents said that their last task had been worked on largely by themselves only, with teams consisting of two and three developers each representing 14 percent.

The basic unit in FreeBSD's organization is the maintainer. Most source files are associated with a maintainer, who "owns and is responsible for that code. This means that he is responsible for fixing bugs and answering problem reports" (FreeBSD 2003b).

The project strongly encourages users of FreeBSD to submit problem reports (PRs) to a PR database, which in March 2003 contained more than 3,000 open reports, and is probably the project's main source of new tasks to be worked on.

Maintainers are involved in maintenance in the broadest sense: thirty-eight percent said their last contribution was perfective (a new feature), 29 percent corrective (bug fixing), 14 percent preventive (cleanup), and 10 percent adaptive (a new driver). Typical comments were, "I do all of the above [the four types of changes]; my last commit just happened to be a bugfix" and "But if you had asked a different day, I would answer differently."

Work on code by nonowners may be initialized for a number of reasons. First, regardless of the owner's general obligation to fix bugs, bugs are in fact frequently fixed by others. Nearly half the developers said that within the last month there had been a bugfix to "their" code contributed by someone else. Second, changes may be needed due to dependencies with files owned by others.

To resolve coordination issues arising from someone wanting to change code they do not own, the first step is to determine the identity of the maintainer. Not all source files have a formal maintainer; that is, a person listed in the makefile for the directory. "In cases where the 'maintainer-ship' of something isn't clear, you can also look at the CVS logs for the file(s) in question and see if someone has been working recently or predominantly in that area" (FreeBSD, 2003a). And then, "Changes . . . shall be sent to the maintainer for review before being committed" (FreeBSD 2003b).

The approach recommended for settling disputes is to seek consensus: "[A commit should happen] only once something resembling consensus has been reached" (FreeBSD 2003a).

Motivation

Enthusiasm jumps when there is a running system.

—Brooks 1987

For work on a change to commence, a maintainer or other developer must be motivated to work on it, and for the project in the first place.

In FreeBSD, not only is the development version of the system usually in a working state, but also, the committers have the authority to commit changes to it directly. This delegation of the authority to integrate appears to be very important for motivation. As many as 81 percent of the committers said that they were encouraged a lot by this procedure: "I don't feel I am under the whim of a single person," and "I have submitted code fixes to other projects and been ignored. That was no fun at all."

This may supplement motivating factors found in surveys to be important for open source developers in general, where improvement of technical skills and some kind of altruism are among the top (Hars and Ou 2002 and Ghosh et al. 2002).

In describing why they like FreeBSD's decentralized approach, several committers pointed to the mere practical issue of reducing work. One said, "It is frequently easier to make a change to the code base directly than to explain the change so someone else can do it," and another commented, "Big changes I would have probably done anyway. Small changes . . . I would not have done without commit access."

A large part of the work committers do for FreeBSD is paid for, although of course not by the project as such. Twenty-one percent of the FreeBSD committers said that work on their latest contribution had been fully paid for, and another 22 percent partially paid for. Consistently, Lakhani and Wolf (chap. 1, this volume) found that 40 percent of OSS developers are paid for their work with open source. It is interesting that the decentralized approach to integration is appealing also from the perspective of FreeBSD's paid contributors: "I use FreeBSD at work. It is annoying to take a FreeBSD release and then apply local changes every time. When . . . my changes . . . are in the main release . . . I can install a standard FreeBSD release . . . at work and use it right away."

A complementary advantage of the delegation of commit responsibility is that the project is relieved from having to establish a central integration team. McConnell recommends in his analysis of projects that use daily building that a separate team is set up dedicated to building and integration. "On most projects, tending the daily build and keeping the smoke test up to date becomes a big enough task to be an explicit part of someone's job. On large projects, it can become a full-time job for more than one person (McConnell 1996, 408)."

FreeBSD's core team appoints people to various so-called "coordinator" tasks, on a voluntary basis of course. A subset of the coordinator assignments can be viewed as falling within tasks of configuration management: management of the repository, bug reporting system, and release management. Another subset deals with communication: coordination of the mailing lists, the Web site, the documentation effort, the internationalization effort, as well as coordinating public relations in general. However, there is no build coordinator, team, or the like. Indeed, integrating other people's changes may be viewed as less rewarding, and assignment to the task is used in some projects as a penalty (McConnell 1996, 410).

Planning for Incremental Integration

We are completely standing the kernel on its head, and the amount of code changes is the largest of any FreeBSD kernel project taken thus far.
—FreeBSD's project manager for SMP

While most changes in FreeBSD are implemented by a single developer, some changes are implemented by larger "divisions." An example is FreeBSD's subproject for Symmetric Multiprocessing (SMP), to which approximately 10 developers contributed. SMP is crucial for the exploitation of new cost-effective PCs with multiple processors. An operating system kernel with SMP is able to allocate different threads to execute simultaneously on the various processors of such a PC. Specifically, release 5.0 (March 2003) enables SMP for threads running in kernel mode. The 4.x releases enable SMP only for user-mode threads.

A crucial decision facing large subprojects such as SMP is whether to add changes incrementally to the development branch, or to insulate development on a separate branch and then integrate all at once. In either case, the subproject is responsible for integration. The latter approach may give rise to "big bang integration" problems, causing severe delays and sometimes project failure (McConnell 1996, 406).

The FreeBSD decision in favor of the more incremental approach was influenced by a recent experience in BSD/OS, a sibling operating system: "They [BSD/OS] went the route of doing the SMP development on a branch, and the divergence between the trunk and the branch quickly became unmanageable.... To have done this much development on a branch would have been infeasible" (SMP project manager).

The incremental approach implied that the existing kernel was divided gradually into two, three, or more distinct areas in which a separate thread was allowed to run. The SMP project used a classical approach, with a written plan that defined work breakdown and schedule, some design documentation, and a project manager, and was launched at a large face-to-face meeting. This planned approach may have been necessary to maintain the development version in a working state during such deep kernel surgery.

Code

Parnas was right, and I was wrong.
—Brooks 1995

Brooks, in the original 1975 version of *The Mythical Man-Month*, recommended a process of public coding as a means of quality control via peer pressure and getting to know the detailed semantics of interfaces. In his twentieth anniversary edition, he concluded to the contrary, in favor of Parnas' concept of information hiding in modules.

Coding in FreeBSD is indeed public: the repository is easily browsable via the Web, and an automatic message is sent to a public mailing list summarizing every commit.

From a quality assurance point of view, FreeBSD's public coding enables monitoring of compliance with the project's guidelines for coding, which includes a style guide for the use of the C language and a security guide, for instance, with rules intended to avoid buffer overflows. It also encourages peer pressure to produce high quality code in general. In response to the survey statement "Knowing that my contributions may be read by highly competent developers has encouraged me to improve my coding skills," 57 percent answered "Yes, significantly," and 29 percent said "Yes, somewhat." A committer summarized: "Embarrassment is a powerful thing."

From the point of view of software integration, the public nature of the coding process might compensate to some degree for the lack of design documents; in particular, specifications of interfaces. This compensation is important, because the division of work among FreeBSD's developers appears to reflect the distributed organization (as discussed in the section "Division of Organization, Division of Work"), rather than a division of the product into relatively independent modules. Thirty-two percent said that their last task had required changing related code on which there was concurrent work (most characterized them as minor changes, though). According to the SMP project manager, "One of the things that worried me . . . was that we wouldn't have enough manpower on the SMP project to keep up with the changes other developers were making. . . . [T]he SMP changes touch huge amounts of code, so having others working on the code at the same time is somewhat disruptive."

To resolve interdependencies with concurrent work, developers watch the project mailing lists. Typical comments are: "By monitoring the mailing lists, I can usually stay on top of these things [related code work]" and "Normally I know who else is in the area," and "I usually follow the lists closely and have a good idea of what is going on."

In response to the statement "Knowing and understanding more about related, ongoing code work would help me integrate my code into the system," 26 percent agreed "Significantly" and 46 percent said "Somewhat". Interdependency with related coding is a central issue that has not been fully resolved in FreeBSD's model.

Review

The project strongly suggests that any change is reviewed before commit. This is the first occasion where the developer will receive feedback on his code. Also, all the subsequent phases in the lifecycle of a change as defined in this chapter might give rise to feedback, and a new lifecycle iteration beginning with coding.

The Committers' Guide rule 2 is "Discuss any significant change *before* committing" (in web page). "This doesn't mean that you ask permission before correcting every obvious syntax error. . . . The very best way of making sure you're on the right track is to have your code reviewed by one or more other committers. . . . When in doubt, ask for review!" (FreeBSD 2003a).

The data indicate that there are frequent reviews in FreeBSD. Code reviewing is the most widespread. Fifty-seven percent had distributed code for reviewing (typically via email) within the last month, and a total of 85 percent within the last three months. Almost everybody (86 percent) said they had actually received feedback the last time they had asked for it, although this may have required some effort. Some responses were, "I have to aggressively solicit feedback if I want comments," and, "If I don't get enough feedback, I can resort to directly mailing those committers who have shown an interest in the area."

Design reviewing is less frequent: within the last three months, only 26 percent had distributed a design proposal, which was defined in a broad sense as a description that was not a source file. Although as many as 93 percent said they actually received feedback, a major obstacle to an increase in review activity appears to be that it is difficult to enlist reviewers. All in

all, there is indication that it would be difficult for the project to introduce mandatory design documents, for instance, describing interfaces or
modifications to interfaces, to aide integration: "I did get feedback . . . of
the type 'This looks good' . . . but very little useful feedback," and, "Getting
solid, constructive comments on design is something like pulling teeth."

Precommit Testing: Don't Break the Build

Can people please check things before they commit them? I like a working compile
at least *once* a week.

—mail message to the developer's list

In the lifecycle of a change, the committer's activities to test the change
prior to committing it to the development branch can be viewed as the
first activity contributing directly to the integration of the change.

At the heart of FreeBSD's approach to integration is the requirement that
committers conduct thorough enough precommit testing so as to ensure,
at a minimum, that the change does not break the build of the project's
development version. The build is the transformation of source files to executable program, which is an automated process. Breaking it means that
the compilation process is aborted, so that an executable program is not
produced. There is an ongoing effort to persuade developers to try to
comply to this requirement, but at the same time the rule requires pragmatic interpretation.

The main purpose of keeping the build healthy is, in my understanding
of FreeBSD's process, that the trunk is vital for debugging; boosting morale
is secondary. At one extreme, the debugging purpose would be defeated by
a demand that changes are completely free of errors. The other extreme is
when the build is overloaded with error-prone changes—then it becomes
difficult to identify which newly added changes have caused an error.
Moreover, when the trunk can not be built, other testing than the build-
test itself is halted.

The don't-break-the-build requirement is stated as rule number 10: "Test
your changes before committing them" in the Committers' Guide, where
it is explained as follows: "If your changes are to the kernel, make sure you
can still compile [the kernel]. If your changes are anywhere else, make sure
you can still [compile everything but the kernel]" (FreeBSD 2003a).

A major challenge is for the project to strike a balance between two ends:
avoiding broken builds on the development branch (which disrupts the
work of many developers downloading and using it), and limiting to a

reasonable level the precommit effort required by the individual developer. It appears that there is indeed room for relevant exceptions: "I can remember one instance where I broke the build every 2–3 days for a period of time; that was necessary [due to the nature of the work]. That was tolerated—I didn't get a single complaint" (interview with FreeBSD committer, November 2000).

The committer obtains software for precommit testing by checking out a copy of the most recent version of the project's development version, and adding the proposed change. The hardware used is (normally) an Intel-based PC at the developer's home or work.

Pragmatic interpretation seems to be particularly called for with respect to the number of different platforms on which a developer should verify the build. Due to platform differences, a build may succeed on one and fail on another. FreeBSD supports a wide range of processor platforms, four of which (i386, sparc64, PC98, alpha) are so-called tier 1 architectures; that is, architectures that the project is fully committed to support. Rule number 10 continues: "If you have a change which also may break another architecture, be sure and test on all supported architectures" (FreeBSD 2003a).

The project has made a cluster of central build machines available, including all tier 1 architectures, to which sources can be uploaded and subjected to a trial build prior to commit. However, uploading to and building on remote machines is tedious, which can be seen as a cost of the delegated approach to integration. There are frequent complaints that committers omit this step.

Developers' learning about the system as a whole, and their acquisition of debugging skills, may be a result of the delegated approach to building, as opposed to the traditional approach of creating a team dedicated to building and integration.

Correcting a broken build can be highly challenging. This is partly because the activity is integration-related: a build failure may be due to dependencies with files not directly involved in the change and so possibly outside of the area of the developer's primary expertise. Debugging an operating system kernel is particularly difficult, because when running it has control of the machine.

Typical comments were: "Debugging build failures . . . has forced me to learn skills of analysis, makefile construction . . . etc. that I would never be exposed to otherwise," and, "I have improved my knowledge about other parts of the system."

In response to the statement "I have improved my technical skills by debugging build failures," 43 percent chose "Yes, significantly" and 29 percent "Yes, somewhat."

It is difficult to assess the actual technical competencies of a development team, and even more difficult to judge whether they are enhanced by FreeBSD's approach to integration. A number of developers indicated that they were competent before joining FreeBSD. One reported, "The way you get granted commit privileges is by first making enough code contributions or bug fixes that everyone agrees you should be given direct write access to the source tree. . . . By and large, most of the committers are better programmers than people I interview and hire in Silicon Valley."

Development Release (Commit)

I can develop/commit under my own authority, and possibly be overridden by a general consensus (although this is rare).
—FreeBSD developer

Development release of a change consists of checking it in to the repository by the committer, upon which it becomes available to the other committers, as well as anyone else who downloads the most recent version of the "trunk." It is up to the committer to decide when a change has matured to an appropriate level, and there is no requirement that he or she provide proof that the change has been submitted to review.

The repository is revision controlled by the CVS tool. A single command suffices for uploading the change from the developer's private machine to the central repository. Revision control also enables a change to be backed out.

There is a well-defined process for the case in which, upon a commit, it turns out that an appropriate consensus had not been reached in advance. "Any disputed change must be backed out . . . if requested by a maintainer. . . . This may be hard to swallow in times of conflict. . . . If the change turns out to be the best after all, it can easily be brought back" (FreeBSD 2003a).

Moreover, a consensus between committers working in some area can be overridden for security reasons: "Security related changes may override a maintainer's wishes at the Security Officer's discretion."

McConnell recommends that projects using daily builds create a *holding area*; that is, a copy of the development version through which all changes must pass on their way to the (proper) development version, to filter away changes not properly tested. The purpose is to preserve the development version in a sound state, because developers rely on it for testing their own code (McConnell 1996, 409). FreeBSD has no such filtering of the stream of changes flowing into the trunk, and so depends strongly on the committee's willingness and ability to release only reasonably tested changes.

Parallel Debugging

We . . . don't have a formal test phase. Testing tends to be done in the "real world." This sounds weird, but it seems to work out okay.
—FreeBSD Developer

Upon commit to the trunk, a change is tested; in a sense, this is consistent with Raymond's notion of parallel debugging (Raymond 2001). The trunk is frequently downloaded—for example, 25 percent of the commitments said they had downloaded and built the development version on five or more days in the preceding week. There may be in principle two different reasons for FreeBSD developers to be working with the most recent changes, other than for the direct purpose of testing them. First, for precommit testing to be useful, they must use the most recent version. Second, to benefit from the newest features and bugfixes, advanced users may wish to use the most recent version for purposes not related to FreeBSD development at all.

The first test of a newly committed change is the build test. Regardless of the rules set up to prevent broken builds on the trunk, the project's members are painfully aware that there is a risk for this to happen. Broken builds will normally be detected by developers, but to ensure detection, the project runs automated builds twice a day on the four tier 1 architectures—so-called "Tinderbox builds," the result of which are shown on a Web page (http://www.freebsd.org/~des).

FreeBSD has no organized effort for systematic testing, such as with predefined testcases. There is also no regression test to which all new versions of the trunk are subjected. McConnell suggests that checking the daily build should include a "smoke test" that should be "thorough enough that if the build passes, you can assume that it is stable enough to be tested more thoroughly" (McConnell 1996).

It should be noted, though, that there is an element of a smoke test involved in booting the newly built operating system, and launching standard programs such as editors and compilers, as carried out on a regular basis by FreeBSD's committers.

The community's use of the development version—once it is in a working state—produces a significant amount of feedback: some respondents indicated that they receive a constant flow of problem reports; nearly half the respondents said that, within the last month, someone else had reported a problem related to "their" code. (Also there is feedback in terms of actual bugfixes, as mentioned in the earlier section "Division of Organization, Division of Work.") Thus there is indication that keeping the build healthy is valuable for debugging, in addition to the importance for precommit testing as such. However, there is also indication that the feedback generated by parallel debugging mostly pinpoints simple errors: "In actuality, the bug reports we've gotten from people have been of limited use. The problem is that obvious problems are quickly fixed, usually before anyone else notices them, and the subtle problems are too 'unusual' for other developers to diagnose." (FreeBSD project manager)

Production Release

We were spinning our thumbs. . . . It was a really boring month.
— FreeBSD developer, referring to the month preceding the 4.0 release

Production release is the final step in integrating all changed work. A production release is a snapshot of a branch in the repository, at a point where the project considers it to be of sufficiently high quality, following a period of so-called "stabilization". This section discusses the process leading to major production releases (such as version 5.0) that are released at intervals of 18 months or more. In addition, the project creates minor production releases (5.1) at intervals of three to four months. Radical changes such as kernel-enabled SMP are released only as part of major production releases.

During stabilization prior to a major production release, the trunk is subjected to community testing in the same manner as during ordinary development. The difference is that new commits are restricted: only bugfixes are allowed. The committers retain their write access, but the release engineering team is vested with the authority to reject all changes considered to be not bugfixes of existing features, and the team's approval is needed prior to commit.

Stabilization is also a more controlled phase in the sense that a schedule is published: the code-freeze start date tells committers the latest date at which they may commit new features, and the un-freeze date when they can resume new development on the trunk. The stabilization period for

5.0 lasted for two months, the first month being less strict with new features being accepted on a case-by-case basis. Indeed, while change initialization is somewhat anarchistic, work during the final steps towards production release is managed rather tightly. For example, the release engineering team defined a set of targets for the release, involving for example the performance of the new SMP feature (FreeBSD Release Engineering Team 2003).

The ability to create production releases merely by means of the process of stabilization is a major advantage of FreeBSD's approach to integration. The process is relatively painless—there is no need for a separate phase dedicated to the integration of distinct parts or branches, because the software has already been assembled and is in a working state.

A major disadvantage of "release by stabilization" is the halting of new development. When the potential represented by developers with an "itch" to write new features is not used, they may even feel discouraged. To accommodate, the release engineering team may terminate stabilization prematurely. This implies branching off at an earlier point of time a new production branch, where the stabilization effort is insulated from new development on the trunk. Then commits of new features (to the trunk) do not risk being released to production prematurely, or introducing errors that disrupt stabilization. Indeed, production release 5.0 was branched away from the trunk before it was considered stable. However, there is a trade-off, because splitting up into branches has a cost. First, bugfixes found during stabilization must be merged to the development branch. Second, and more importantly, the project wants everybody to focus on making an upcoming production release as stable as possible. Splitting up into branches is splitting the community's debugging effort, which is the crucial shared resource, rather than the trunk as such.

Conclusion

Respect other committers. . . . Being able to work together long-term is this project's greatest asset, one far more important than any set of changes to the code.
—FreeBSD 2003a, the Committer Guide's description of rule 1

FreeBSD accomplishes coordination across a project that is geographically widely distributed. FreeBSD's incremental and decentralized approach to integration may be a key factor underlying this achievement: it may enhance developer motivation and enable a relatively painless process for creating production releases by maturing the project's development version. The project avoids allocation of scarce developer resources to dedicated build or integration teams, with the perhaps not-so-interesting task of integrating other people's changes or drifted-apart branches.

The project's development branch is something of a melting pot. There is no coffee machine at which FreeBSD's developers can meet, but the development branch is the place where work output becomes visible and gets integrated, and where the key project rule—don't break the build—is applied and redefined.

A disadvantage of FreeBSD's approach to integration is the risk of overloading the trunk with interdependent changes, when too many changes are committed too early. In a sense there is a limited capacity to the trunk, and one that can not be overcome simply by branching, since the underlying scarce resource is the community effort of parallel debugging.

FreeBSD's decentralized approach seems to contradict hypotheses that hierarchy is a precondition to success in open source development. For example, Raymond stressed the need for a strong project leader, albeit one who treats contributors with respect (Raymond 2001). Healy and Schussman studied a number of apparently unsuccessful open source projects, and asserted that the importance of hierarchical organization is systematically underplayed in analyses of open source (Healy and Schussman 2003). The author of this chapter would stress the need for mature processes rather than hierarchy. FreeBSD is a promising example of a decentralized organization held together by a project culture of discussion and reinterpretation of rules and guidelines.

13   Adopting Open Source Software Engineering (OSSE) Practices by Adopting OSSE Tools

Jason Robbins

The open source movement created a set of software engineering tools with features that fit the characteristics of open source development processes. To a large extent, the open source culture and methodology are conveyed to new developers via the toolset itself and the demonstrated usage of these tools on existing projects. The rapid and wide adoption of open source tools stands in stark contrast to the difficulties encountered in adopting traditional Computer-Aided Software Engineering (CASE) tools. This chapter explores the characteristics that make these tools adoptable and discusses how adopting them may influence software development processes.

One ongoing challenge facing the software engineering profession is the need for average practitioners to adopt powerful software engineering tools and methods. Starting with the emergence of software engineering as a field of research, increasingly advanced tools have been developed to address the difficulties of software development. Often these tools addressed accidental difficulties of development, but some have been aimed at essential difficulties such as management of complexity, communication, visibility, and changeability (Brooks 1987). Later, in the 1990's, the emphasis shifted from individual tools toward the development process in which the tools were used. The software process movement produced good results for several leading organizations, but it did not have much impact on average practitioners.

Why has adoption of CASE tools been limited? Often the reason has been that they did not fit the day-to-day needs of the developers who were expected to use them: they were difficult to use, expensive, and special purpose. The fact that they were expensive and licensed on a per-seat basis caused many organizations to only buy a few seats, thus preventing other members of the development team from accessing the tools and artifacts only available through these tools. One study of CASE tool adoption found that adoption correlates negatively with end user choice, and concludes that successful introduction of CASE tools must be a top-down decision from upper management (Iivari 1996). The result of this approach has repeatedly been "shelfware": software tools that are purchased but not used.

Why have advanced methodologies not been widely adopted? Software process improvement efforts built around capability maturity model (CMM) or ISO-9000 requirements have required resources normally only found in larger organizations: a software process improvement group, time for training, outside consultants, and the willingness to add overhead to the development process in exchange for risk management. Top-down process improvement initiatives have often resulted in a different kind of shelfware, where thick binders describing the organization's software development method (SDM) go unused. Developers who attempt to follow the SDM may find that it does not match the process assumptions embedded in current tools. Smaller organizations and projects on shorter development cycles have often opted to continue with their current processes or adopt a few practices of lightweight methods such as extreme programming in a bottom-up manner (Beck 2000).

In contrast, open source projects are rapidly adopting common expectations for software engineering tool support, and those expectations are increasing. Just four years ago, the normal set of tools for an open source project consisted of a mailing list, a *bugs* text file, an *install* text file, and a CVS server. Now, open source projects are commonly using tools for issue tracking, code generation, automated testing, documentation generation, and packaging. Some open source projects have also adopted object-oriented design and static analysis tools. The feature sets of these tools are aimed at some key practices of the open source methodology, and in adopting the tools, software developers are predisposed to also adopt those open source practices.

Exploring and encouraging development and adoption of open source software engineering tools has been the goal of the http://tigris.org Web site for the past three years. The site hosts open source projects that are developing software engineering tools and content of professional interest to practicing software engineers. Tigris.org also hosts student projects on any topic, and a reading group for software engineering research papers. The name "Tigris" can be interpreted as a reference to the Fertile Crescent between the Tigris and Euphrates rivers. The reference is based on the hypothesis that an agrarian civilization would and did arise first in the location best suited for it. In other words, the environment helps define the society, and more specifically, the tools help define the method. This is similar to McLuhan's proposition that "the medium is the message" (McLuhan 1994).

Some Practices of OSS and OSSE

The open source movement is broad and diverse. Though it is difficult to make generalizations, there are several common practices that can be found in many open source software projects. These practices leave their mark on the software produced. In particular, the most widely adopted open source software engineering tools are the result of these practices, and they embody support for the practices, which further reinforces the practices.

Tools and Community

Provide Universal, Immediate access to All Project Artifacts   The heart of the open source method is the accessibility of the program source code to all project participants. Beyond the source code itself, open source projects tend to allow direct access to all software development artifacts such as requirements, design, open issues, rationale, development team responsibilities, and schedules. Tools to effectively access this information form the centerpiece of the open source development infrastructure: projects routinely make all artifacts available in real time to all participants worldwide over the Internet. Both clients and server components of these tools are available on a wide range of platforms at zero cost. This means that all participants can base their work on up-to-date information. The availability of development information is also part of how open source projects attract participants and encourage them to contribute.

In contrast, traditional software engineering efforts have certainly made progress in this area, but it is still common to find projects that rely on printed binders of requirements that rapidly become outdated, use LAN-based collaboration tools that do not scale well to multisite projects, purchase tool licenses for only a subset of the overall product team, and build silos of intellectual property that limit access by other members of the same organization who could contribute. While e-mail and other electronic communications are widely used in closed source projects, the information in these systems is incomplete because some communication happens face-to-face or via documents that are never placed in a shared repository.

Staff Projects with Motivated Volunteers   Open source projects typically have no dedicated staff. Instead, work is done by self-selected developers who volunteer their contributions. Self-selection is most likely to occur when the developers are already familiar with the application domain and development technologies. Developers allocate their own time to tasks that they select. This means that every feature is validated by at least one person who strongly desired it. Motivation for open source development comes in many forms, including one's own need for particular software, the joy of construction and expression, altruism, the need for external validation of one's own ideas and abilities, the ideology of free software as a form of freedom, and even social and financial rewards. The other side of joy as a motivation is that unlikable jobs tend to go undone, unless they are automated. While some high-profile open source projects have ample potential contributors, a much larger number of average open source projects rely on the part-time efforts of only a few core members.

In contrast, traditional software engineering projects are staffed and funded. Often organizations emphasize continuity and stability as ways to keep costs down over the life of a product line. Achieving staff continuity in a changing business and technology environment demands that training be part of the critical path for many projects. Traditional software engineers are motivated by many of the same factors found in open source, as well as professionalism and direct financial incentives. Resources are always limited, even in well-funded commercial projects, and it is up to management to determine how those resources are allocated.

Work in Communities that Accumulate Software Assets and Standardize Practices   Collaborative development environments (CDEs) such as SourceForge[1] and SourceCast[2] now host large development communities that would have previously been fragmented across isolated projects hosted on custom infrastructure. This is one of the most important shifts in open source development. It was partly inspired by the Mozilla.org toolset, which itself descended from a more traditional software engineering environment. These large development communities reduce the effort needed to start a new project by providing a complete, standard toolset. They warehouse reusable components, provide access to the developers that support them, and make existing projects in the communities accessible as demonstrations of how to use those tools and components. Preference for standards and conventions is particularly strong in the selection of tools in open source projects. Increasingly, it is the development community as a whole that has made decisions about the set of tools in the

CDE, and individual projects accept the expectation of using what is provided. In particular, a great increase in the reliance on issue-tracking tools by open source projects has resulted from the availability and demonstrated usage of issue trackers in CDEs.

Many larger commercial software development organizations do have organization-wide standards and site licenses for fundamental tools such as version control. However, it is still common for projects to acquire licenses for specific tools using a project-specific budget with little standardization across projects. Software process improvement (SPI) teams have attempted to standardize practices through training, mandates, and audits. However, they have rarely been able to leverage the visibility of best practices across projects. Peer visibility is an important key to making a methodology become ingrained in a development culture. Likewise, providing a repository of reusable components is not, in itself, enough to drive reuse: developers look for evidence that others are successfully reusing a given component.

Open Systems Design

Follow Standards to Validate the Project, Scope Decision Making, and Enable Reuse A preference for following standards is deeply ingrained in the open source culture. The need for pre-1.0 validation of the project and the lack of formal requirements generation in open source projects tends to encourage reliance on externally defined standards and conventions. Deviation from standards is discouraged because of the difficulty of specifying an alternative with the same level of formality and agreement among contributors. Standards also define interfaces that give choice to users and support diversity of usage.

Standards and open systems are also emphasized in traditional development projects. The current move to web services is one important example of that. However, the marketplace often demands that new products differentiate themselves from existing offerings by going beyond current standards. At the same time, pressure to maximize returns may justify a decision to implement only part of a standard and then move on to other revenue-generating functionality.

Practice Reuse and Reusability to Manage Project Scope Open source projects generally start with very limited resources, often only one or two part-time developers. Projects that start with significant reuse tend to be more successful, because they can demonstrate results sooner, they focus discussions on the project's value-added, and they resonate with the cultural preference for reuse. Even if a project had implemented its own code for a given function, peer review often favors the elimination of that code, if a reusable component can replace it. Reusable components can come from projects that explicitly seek to create components for use by developers, or they can spin out of other projects that seek to produce end user products. In fact, spinning out a reusable component is encouraged, because it fits the cultural preference for reuse, and often gives a mid-level developer the social reward of becoming a project leader.

The return on building reusable components can be hard to estimate in advance. So the justification for reusable components in traditional software development may be unclear, even in organizations with reuse initiatives. In contrast, the motivations for open source participation apply to the development of components as much or more than they do to the development of end user products. Traditional development teams are responsible for maximizing returns on their current project; the cost of providing ongoing support for reusable components can be at odds with that goal. In contrast, open source components can achieve a broad population of users that can support one another.

Support Diversity of Usage and Encourage Plurality of Authorship Open source products are often cross-platform and internationalized from the start. They usually offer a wide range of configuration options that address diverse use cases. Any contributor is welcome to submit a new feature to "scratch an itch" (Raymond 2001). Such willingness to add functionality can lead to feature creep and a loss of conceptual integrity. This sort of occurrence can make it harder to meet predefined deadlines, but it broadens the appeal of the product, because more potential users get their own win conditions satisfied. Since users are responsible for supporting each other, the increase in the user population can provide the increased effort needed to support the new features. Peer review, standards, and limited resources can help limit undirected feature creep.

While traditional development tools may have great depth of functionality, they tend to have fewer options and more platform restrictions than their open source counterparts, making it harder for large organizations to select a single tool for all development efforts across the enterprise. Commercial development projects manage a set of product features in an effort to maximize returns while keeping support costs under control. Likewise, management assigns specific tasks to specific developers and holds them accountable for those tasks, usually to the exclusion of serendipitous contributions. Even if an outside contributor submitted a new piece of functionality, the cost of providing technical support for that functionality may still prevent its integration.

Planning and Execution

Release Early, Release Often   Open source projects are not subject to the economic concerns or contractual agreements that turn releases into major events in traditional development. For example, there are usually no CDs to burn and no paid advertising campaigns. That reduced overhead allows them to release as early and often as the developers can manage. A hierarchy of release types is used to set user expectations: "stable" releases may happen at about the same rate as releases in traditional development, but "nightly" releases are commonly made available, and public "development" releases may happen very soon after the project kickoff and every few weeks thereafter. In fact, open source projects need to release pre-1.0 versions in order to attract the volunteer staff needed to reach 1.0. But, a rush toward the first release often means that traditional upstream activities such as requirements writing must be done later, usually incrementally. Reacting to the feedback provided on early releases is key to requirement-gathering and risk-management practices in open source.

In contrast, a traditional waterfall development model invests heavily in upstream activities at the start of the project in an attempt to tightly coordinate work and minimize the number of releases. Many organizations have adopted iterative development methodologies, for example, extreme programming (Beck 2000) or "synch and stabilize" (Cusumano and Selby 1995). However, they still must achieve enough functionality to have a marketable 1.0 release. And concerns about exposing competitive information and the overhead of integration, training, marketing, and support create a tendency toward fewer, more significant releases.

Place Peer Review in the Critical Path   Feedback from users and developers is one of the practices most central to the open source method. In many open source projects, only a core group of developers can commit changes to the version control system; other contributors must submit a patch that can be applied only after review and discussion by the core developers. Also, it is common for open source projects to use automated email notifications to prompt broad peer review of each CVS commit. Peer review has also been shown to be one of the most effective ways to eliminate defects in code, regardless of methodology (Wiegers 2002). The claim that "given enough eyeballs, all bugs are shallow" (Raymond 2001, 41) under-scores the value of peer review, and it has proven effective on some high profile open source projects. However, unaided peer review by a few average developers, who are for the most part the same developers who wrote the code in the first place, is not a very reliable or efficient practice for achieving high quality.

Although the value of peer reviews is widely acknowledged in traditional software engineering, it is unlikely to be placed in the critical path unless the project is developing a safety-critical system. Traditional peer reviews require time for individual study of the code followed by a face-to-face review meeting. These activities must be planned and scheduled, in con-trast to the continuous and serendipitous nature of open source peer review.

Some Common OSSE Tools

This section reviews several open source software engineering tools with respect to the practices defined previously. Editors, compilers, and debug-gers have not been included; instead, the focus is on tools that have more impact on collaborative development. Most of these tools are already widely used, while a few are not yet widely used but are set to rapidly expand in usage.

Version Control

CVS, WinCVS, MacCVS, TortoiseCVS, CVSWeb, and ViewCVS   The Con-current Versions System (CVS) is the most widely used version control system in open source projects. Its features include a central server that always contains the latest versions and makes them accessible to users over the Internet; support for disconnected use (i.e., users can do some work while not connected to the Internet); conflict resolution via merging rather than locking to reduce the need for centralized coordination among devel-opers; simple commands for checking in and out that lower barriers to casual usage; cross-platform clients and servers; and, a vast array of options for power users. It is common for CVS to be configured to send e-mail noti-fications of commits to project members to prompt peer review. WinCVS, MacCVS, and TortoiseCVS are just three of many free clients that give users a choice of platform and user interface style. CVS clients are also built into many IDEs and design tools. CVSWeb and ViewCVS are Web-based tools for browsing a CVS repository.

Adoption of CVS among open source projects is near total, and the concepts embodied in CVS have clearly influenced the open source methodology. CVS can easily provide universal access to users of many platforms and many native languages at locations around the globe. The practice of volunteer staffing takes advantage of CVS's straightforward interface for basic functions, support for anonymous and read-only access, patch creation for later submission, and avoidance of file locking. CVS has been demonstrated to scale up to large communities, despite some shortcomings in that regard. The protocol used between client and server is not a standard; however, CVS clients have followed the user interface standards of each platform. In fact, the command-line syntax of CVS follows conventions established by the earlier RCS system. A separation of policy from capability allows a range of branching and release strategies that fit the needs of diverse projects. Frequent releases and hierarchies of release quality expectations are facilitated by CVS's ability to maintain multiple branches of development. Peer review is enabled by easy access to the repository, and is encouraged by email notifications of changes.

Subversion, RapidSVN, TortoiseSVN, and ViewCVS Subversion is the leading successor to CVS. Its features include essentially all of CVS's features, with several significant enhancements: it has a cleaner, more reliable, and more scalable implementation; it is based on the existing WebDAV standard; it replaces CVS's concepts of branches and tags with simple naming conventions; and, it has stronger support for disconnected use. RapidSVN and TortoiseSVN are two of several available Subversion clients. ViewCVS can browse Subversion repositories as well as CVS repositories. Also, Subversion repositories can be browsed with any standard Web browser and many other applications, due to the use of the standard WebDAV protocol.

It will take time for Subversion to be widely adopted by open source projects, but interest has already been very high and many early uses have been documented. Subversion improves on CVS's support for universal access by following standards that increase scalability and ease integration. Diverse users already have a choice of several Subversion clients; however, there are fewer than those of CVS. Subversion's simplification of branching lowers the learning curve for potential volunteers and supports a diversity of usage. Support for frequent releases and peer review in Subversion is similar to that of CVS.

Issue Tracking and Technical Support

Bugzilla Bugzilla was developed to fit the needs of the Mozilla open source project. Its features include: an "unconfirmed" defect report state needed for casual reporters who are more likely to enter invalid issues; a "whine" feature to remind developers of issues assigned to them; and a Web-based interface that makes the tool cross-platform, universally accessible, and that lowers barriers to casual use.

Bugzilla has been widely adopted and deeply integrated into the open source community over the past few years. The Bugzilla database on Mozilla.org has grown past 200,000 issues, and a dozen other large open source projects each host tens of thousands of issues. The whine feature helps address the lack of traditional management incentives when projects are staffed by volunteers. Bugzilla has been demonstrated to scale up to large communities, and the organized history of issues contained in a community's issue database serve to demonstrate the methodology practiced by that community. When developers evaluate the reusability of a component, they often check some of the issues in the project issue tracker and look for signs of activity. Conversely, when developers feel that they have no recourse when defects are found in a reusable component, they are likely to cease reusing it. There is a remarkable diversity of usage demonstrated in the issues of large projects: developers track defects, users request support, coding tasks are assigned to resources, patches are submitted for review, and some enhancements are debated at length. Frequent releases and peer review of project status are enabled by Bugzilla' clear reporting of the number of pending issues for an upcoming release.

Scarab The Scarab project seeks to establish a new foundation for issue-tracking systems that can gracefully evolve to fit many needs over time. Scarab covers the same basic features as does Bugzilla, but adds support for issue de-duplication on entry to defend against duplicates entered by casual participants; an XML issue exchange format; internationalization; and highly customizable issue types, attributes, and reports.

Interest and participation in the Scarab project has been strong, and the tool is rapidly becoming ready for broader adoption. Scarab's support for internationalization and XML match the open source practices of universal access and preference for standards and interoperability. Scarab's biggest win comes from its customizability, which allows the definition of new issue types to address diverse user needs.

Technical Discussions and Rationale

Mailing Lists Mailing lists provide a key advantage over direct e-mail, in that they typically capture messages in Web-accessible archives that serve as a repository for design and implementation rationale, as well as end user support information. Some of the most common usages of mailing lists include: question and answer sessions among both end users and developers, proposals for changes and enhancements, announcements of new releases, and voting on key decisions. Voting is often done using the convention that a message starting with the text "+1" is a vote in favor of a proposal, a message with "+0" or "–0" is an abstention with a comment, and a message with "–1" is a veto, which must include a thoughtful justification. While English is the most commonly used natural language for open source development, mailing lists in other languages are also used.

Open source developers adopted mailing lists early, and now they are used on very nearly every project. Since mailing lists use e-mail, they are standards-based, cross-platform, and accessible to casual users. Also, since the e-mail messages are free-format text, this single tool can serve a very diverse range of use cases. It is interesting to note that the preference is for plain-text messages: HTML-formatted e-mail messages and integration of e-mail with other collaboration features have not been widely adopted. Project mailing list archives do help set the tone of development communities, but the flexibility of mailing lists allows so many uses that new potential developers might not recognize many of the patterns. Peer review usually happens via mailing lists, because CVS's change notifications use e-mail, and because e-mail is the normal medium for discussions that do not relate to specific issues in the issue database.

Project Web Sites Open source predates the Web, so early open source projects relied mainly on mailing lists, file transfer protocol (FTP), and later, CVS. Open source projects started building and using Web sites soon after the introduction of the Web. In fact, several key open source projects such as Apache are responsible for significant portions of today's Web infrastructure. A typical open source Web site includes a description of the project, a users' guide, developer documentation, the names of the founding members and core developers, the license being used, and guidelines for participation. Open source Web sites also host the collaborative development tools used on the project. Users can find related projects by following links from one individual project to another, but increasingly, projects are hosted at larger community sites that categorize related projects.

Project Web sites have been universally adopted by recent open source projects. Web sites provide universal access to even the most casual users. Web page design can adjust to suit a wide range of diverse uses and preferences. The temptation to build an unusual Web site for a particular project is sometimes in conflict with the goals of the larger community site. Community-wide style sheets and page design guidelines reduce this conflict, as do tools like Maven and SourceCast that define elements of a standard appearance for each project's Web content. Internet search engines enable users to find open source products or reusable components. The Web supports the practice of issuing frequent releases simply because the project's home page defines a stable location where users can return to look for updates. Also, Internet downloads support frequent reuse by eliminating the need for printed manuals, CDs, packaging, and shipping.

HOWTOs, FAQs, and FAQ-O-Matic   HOWTO documents are goal-oriented articles that guide users through the steps needed to accomplish a specific task. Lists of frequently asked questions (FAQs) help to mitigate two of the main problems of mailing lists: the difficulty of summarizing the discussion that has gone before, and the wasted effort of periodically revisiting the same topics as new participants join the project. FAQ-O-Matic and similar tools aim to reduce the unlikable effort of maintaining the FAQ.

FAQs and HOWTOs are widely used, while FAQ-O-Matic is not nearly so widely used. This may be the case because simple HTML documents serve the purpose and allow more flexibility. FAQs and HOWTOs are universally accessible over the Internet, and tend to be understandable by casual users because of their simple, goal-oriented format. Developer FAQs and HOWTOs can help potential volunteers come up to speed on the procedures needed to make specific enhancements. When FAQ-O-Matic is used, it helps reduce the tedious task of maintaining a FAQ, and makes it easier for users to suggest that new items be added. Many HOWTO documents conform to a standard SGML document type and are transformed into viewable formats by using DocBook or other tools.

Wiki, TWiki, and SubWiki   A *wiki* is a collaborative page-editing tool in which users may add or edit pages directly through their web browser. Wikis use a simple and secure markup language instead of HTML. For example, a word written like "NameOfPage" would automatically link to another page in the wiki system. Wikis can be more secure than systems that allow entry of HTML, because there is no way for users to enter potentially dangerous JavaScript or to enter invalid HTML markup that could prevent the overall page from rendering in a browser. TWiki is a popular wiki-engine with support for page histories and access controls. SubWiki is a new wiki-engine that stores page content in Subversion.

Wiki-engines are used in many open source projects, but by no means in a large fraction of all open source projects. Wiki content is universally accessible over the Web. Furthermore, volunteers are able to make changes to the content without the need for any client-side software, and they are sometimes even free to do so without any explicit permission. Wiki sites do have a sense of community, but Wiki content tends to serve as an example of how to loosely organize pages of documentation, rather than a demonstration of any particular development practice.

Build Systems

Make, Automake, and Autoconf   The Unix "make" command is a standard tool to automate the compilation of source code trees. It is one example of using automation to reduce barriers to casual contributors. And there are several conventions that make it easier for casual contributors to deal with different projects. Automake and Autoconf support portability by automatically generating makefiles for a particular Unix environment.

These tools are widely used; in fact, if it were not for Ant (see the following section) the use of make would still be universal. While makefiles are not particularly easy to write or maintain, they are easy for users and volunteer developers to quickly learn to run. Makefiles are based on a loose standard that dates back to the early days of Unix. Developers who intend to reuse a component can safely assume that it has a makefile that includes conventional make targets like "make clean" and "make install." Makefiles are essentially programs themselves, so they can be made arbitrarily complex to support various diverse use cases. For example, in addition to compiling code, makefiles can be used to run regression tests. Running regression tests frequently is one key to the practice of frequent releases.

Ant   Ant is a Java replacement for make that uses XML build files instead of makefiles. Each build file describes the steps to be carried out to build each target. Each step invokes a predefined task. Ant tasks each perform a larger amount of work than would a single command in a makefile. This process can reduce the tedium of managing complex makefiles, increase consistency across projects, and ease peer review. In fact, many projects seem to use build files that borrow heavily from other projects or examples in the Ant documentation. Many popular IDEs now include support for Ant.

Ant is being adopted rapidly by both open source and traditional software development projects that use Java. Ant is accessible to developers on all platforms, regardless of whether they prefer the command-line or an IDE. Ant build files tend to be more standard, simpler, and thus more accessible to potential volunteers. Since Ant build files are written in XML, developers are already familiar with the syntax, and tools to edit or otherwise process those files can reuse standard XML libraries. As Ant adoption increases, developers evaluating a reusable Java component can increasingly assume that Ant will be used and that conventional targets will be included. As with make, Ant can be used for regression testing to support the practice of delivering frequent releases.

Tinderbox, Gump, CruiseControl, XenoFarm, and Maven   Nightly build tools automatically compile a project's source code and produce a report of any errors. In addition to finding compilation errors, these tools can build any make or Ant target to accomplish other tasks, such as regression tests, documentation generation, or static source code analysis. These tools can quickly catch errors that might not have been noticed by individual developers working on their own changes. Some nightly build tools automatically identify and notify the developer or developers who are responsible for breaking the build, so that corrections can be made quickly. Tinderbox and XenoFarm can also be used as "build farms" that test the building and running of the product on an array of different machines and operating systems.

Nightly build tools have been used within large organized communities such as Mozilla.org and Jakarta.apache.org, as well as by independent projects. These tools help provide universal access to certain important aspects of the project's current status: that is, does the source code compile and pass unit tests? Volunteers may be more attracted to projects with clear indications of progress than they would otherwise. And the limited efforts of volunteers need not be spent on manually regenerating API documentation or running tests. Component reuse is encouraged when developers can easily evaluate the status of development. Organized open source development communities use nightly build tools to help manage dependencies between interdependent projects. Frequent releases are facilitated by nightly build automation that quickly detects regressions and notifies the responsible developers.

Design and Code Generation

ArgoUML and Dia ArgoUML is a pure-Java UML design tool. ArgoUML closely follows the UML standard, and associated standards for model interchange and diagram representation. In addition to being cross-platform and standards based, it emphasizes ease of use and actively helps train casual users in UML usage. ArgoUML's design critics catch design errors in much the same way that static analysis tools catch errors in source code. ArgoUML is one of very few tools to support the Object Constraint Language (OCL), which allows designers to add logical constraints that refine the meaning of their design models. Dia is a more generic drawing tool, but it has a UML mode that can also generate source code.

UML modeling tools have experienced only limited adoption among open source projects, possibly because of the emphasis on source code as the central development artifact. Tools such as ArgoUML that are themselves open source and cross-platform provide universal access to design models, because any potential volunteer is able to view and edit the model. Emphasis on standards in ArgoUML has allowed for model interchange with other tools and the development of several plug-ins that address diverse use cases. If design tools were more widely used in open source projects, UML models would provide substantial support for understanding components prior to reuse, for peer reviews at the design level, and for the sharing of design patterns and guidelines within development communities.

Torque, Castor, and Hibernate Torque is a Java tool that generates SQL and Java code to build and access a database defined by an XML specification of a data model. It is cross-platform, customizable, and standards-based. Torque's code generation is customizable because it is template-based. Also, a library of templates has been developed to address incompatibilities between SQL databases. Castor addresses the same goals, but adds support for persistence to XML files and parallels relevant Java data access standards. Hibernate emphasizes ease of use and rapid development cycles by using reflection rather than code generation.

Open source developers have adopted database code generation tools at about the same rate that traditional developers have. Projects that have adopted them are able to produce products that are themselves portable to various databases. Code generation tools can increase the effectiveness of volunteer developers and enable more frequent releases by reducing the unlikable tasks of writing repetitive code by hand, and debugging code that is not part of the project's value-add. Code generation is itself a form of reuse in which knowledge about a particular aspect of implementation is discussed by community members and then codified in the rules and templates of the generator. Individual developers may then customize these rules and templates to fit any unusual needs. Peer review of schema specifications can be easier than reviewing database access code.

XDoclet, vDoclet, JUnitDoclet, and Doxygen   These code generation tools build on the code commenting conventions used by Javadoc to generate API documentation. Doxygen works with C, C++, IDL, PHP, and C#, in addition to Java. XDoclet, vDoclet, and JUnitDoclet can be used to generate additional code rather than documentation. For example, a developer could easily generate stubs for unit tests of every public method of a class. Another use is the generation of configuration files for Web services, application servers, or persistence libraries. The advantage of using comments in code rather than an independent specification file is that the existing structure of the code is leveraged to provide a context for code generation parameters.

Like the code generators listed previously, doclet-style generators are a form of reuse that reduces the need to work on unlikable tasks, and output templates can be changed to fit the needs of diverse users. The doclet approach differs from other code generation approaches in that no new specification files are needed. Instead, the normal source code contains additional attributes used in code generation. This is a good match for the open source tendency to emphasize the source code over other artifacts.

Quality Assurance Tools

JUnit, PHPUnit, PyUnit, and NUnit   JUnit supports Java unit testing. It is a simple framework that uses naming conventions to identify test classes and test methods. A test executive executes all tests and produces a report. The JUnit concepts and framework have been ported to nearly every programming language, including PHPUnit for PHP, PyUnit for Python, and NUnit for C#.

JUnit has been widely adopted in open source and traditional development. It has two key features that address the practices of the open source methodology: test automation, which helps to reduce the unlikable task of manual testing that might not be done by volunteers; and unit test reports, which provide universally accessible, objective indications of project status. Frequent testing and constant assessment of product quality support the practice of frequent releases. Visible test cases and test results can also help emphasize quality as a goal for all projects in the community.

Lint, LCLint, Splint, Checkstyle, JCSC, JDepend, PyCheck, RATS, and Flawfinder The classic Unix command "lint" analyzes C source code for common errors such as unreachable statements, uninitialized variables, or incorrect calls to library functions. More recently designed programming languages have tighter semantics, and modern compilers perform many of these checks during every compilation. LCLint and splint go substantially further than "lint" by analyzing the meaning of the code at a much deeper level. Checkstyle, JCSC, and PyCheck look for stylistic errors in Java and Python code. RATS and flawfinder look specifically for potential security holes.

Adoption and use of these tools is limited, but several projects seem to have started using Checkstyle and JDepend as part of Maven. Analysis tools can also be viewed as a form of reuse where community knowledge is encoded in rules. Relying on standard rules can help open source developers avoid discussions about coding conventions and focus on the added value of the project. Static analysis can prompt peer review and help address weaknesses in the knowledge of individual developers.

Codestriker Codestriker is a tool for remote code reviews. Developers can create review topics, each of which consists of a set source file changes and a list of reviewers. Reviewers then browse the source code and enter comments that are related to specific lines of code. In the end, the review comments are better organized, better contextualized, and more useful than an unstructured e-mail discussion would have been.

Codestriker seems well matched to the open source development practices, but its usage does not seem to be widespread yet. It is accessible to all project members, because it is Web-based and conceptually straightforward. If it were widely used, its model of inviting reviewers would give an important tool to project leaders who seek to turn consumers into volunteers by giving them tasks that demand involvement and prepare them to make further contributions.

Collaborative Development Environments

SourceCast and SourceForge   CDEs, such as SourceCast and SourceForge, allow users to easily create new project workspaces. These workspaces provide access to a standard toolset consisting of a web server for project content, mailing lists with archives, an issue tracker, and a revision control system. Access control mechanisms determine the information that each user can see and the operations that he or she can perform. CDEs also define development communities where the same tools and practices are used on every project, and where users can browse and search projects to find reusable components. Both SourceCast and SourceForge include roughly the same basic features. However, SourceCast has been used for many public and private mid-sized communities with an emphasis on security. And SourceForge has demonstrated enormous scalability on the public http://sourceforge.net site and is also available for use on closed networks.

CDEs have been widely adopted by open source projects. In particular, a good fraction of all open source projects are now hosted on http://source-forge.net. CDEs provide the infrastructure needed for universal access to project information: they are Web-based, and both SourceCast and Source-Forge have been internationalized. The use of a standardized toolset helps projects avoid debating tool selection and focus on their particular added value. SourceCast offers a customizable and fine-grained permission system that supports diverse usage in both open source and corporate environments. SourceForge provides specific support for managing the deliverables produced by frequent releases.

Missing Tools
Although there is a wide range of open source software engineering tools available to support many software engineering activities, there are also many traditional development activities that are not well supported. These activities include requirements management, project management, metrics, estimation, scheduling, and test suite design. The lack of tools in some of these areas is understandable, because open source projects do not need to meet deadlines or balance budgets. However, better requirements management and testing tools would certainly seem just as useful in open source work as they are in traditional development.

The Impact of Adopting OSSE Tools

Drawing conclusions about exactly how usage of these tools would affect development inside a particular organization would require specific knowledge about that organization. However, the previous descriptions can suggest changes to look for after adoption:

• Because the tools are free and support casual use, more members of the development team will be able to access and contribute to artifacts in all phases of development. Stronger involvement can lead to better technical understanding, which can increase productivity, improve quality, and smooth hand-offs at key points in the development process.

• Because the "source" to all artifacts is available and up-to-date, there is less wasted effort due to decisions based on outdated information. Working with up-to-date information can reduce rework on downstream artifacts.

• Because casual contributors are supported in the development process, nondeveloper stakeholders, such as management, sales, marketing, and support, should be more able to constructively participate in the project. Stronger involvement by more stakeholders can help quickly refine requirements and better align expectations, which can increase the satisfaction of internal customers.

• Because many of the tools support incremental releases, teams using them should be better able to produce releases early and more often. Early releases help manage project risk and set expectations. Frequent internal releases can have the additional benefit of allowing rapid reaction to changing market demands.

• Because many of the tools aim to reduce unlikable work, more development effort should be freed for forward progress. Productivity increases, faster time-to-market, and increased developer satisfaction are some potential benefits.

• Because peer review is addressed by many of the tools, projects may be able to catch more defects in review or conduct more frequent small reviews in reaction to changes. Peer reviews are generally accepted as an effective complement to testing that can increase product quality, reduce rework, and aid the professional development of team members.

• Because project Web sites, accessible issue trackers, and CDEs provide access to the status and technical details of reusable components, other projects may more readily evaluate and select these components for reuse. Also, HOWTOs, FAQs, mailing lists, and issue trackers help to cost-effectively support reused components. Expected benefits of increased reuse include faster time-to-market, lower maintenance costs, and improved quality.

• Because CDEs help establish communities, they offer both short- and long-term benefits. In the short term, development communities can reduce the administrative and training cost of using powerful tools, and make secure access to diverse development artifacts practical. CDEs can reinforce and compound the effects of individual tools, leading to long-term benefits including accumulation of development knowledge in a durable and accessible form, increased quality and reuse, and more consistent adoption of the organization's chosen methodology.

Notes

1. SourceForge is a trademark of VA Software Corporation.

2. SourceCast is a trademark of CollabNet, Inc.

IV Free/Open Source Software Economic and Business Models

14 Open Source Software Projects as User Innovation Networks

Eric von Hippel

Free and open source software projects are exciting examples of user innovation networks that can be run by and for users—no manufacturer required.[1] Such networks have a great advantage over the manufacturer-centered innovation development systems that have been the mainstay of commerce for hundreds of years: they enable each user, whether an individual or a corporation, to develop exactly what it wants rather than relying on a manufacturer to act as its (often very imperfect) agent. Moreover, individual users do not have to develop everything they need on their own: they can benefit from innovations developed by others and freely shared within the user community.

User innovation networks existed long before and extend far beyond free and open source software projects. Such networks can be found developing physical products as well. Consider and compare the following examples of early-stage user innovation networks—one in software, the other in sports.

Apache Web Server Software

The Apache Web Server (which is free and open source software) is used on server computers that host Web pages and provide appropriate content as requested by Web browsers. Such computers are the backbone of the Internet-based World Wide Web infrastructure.

The server software that evolved into Apache was developed by University of Illinois undergraduate Rob McCool for, and while working at, the National Center for Supercomputing Applications (NCSA). The source code as developed and periodically modified by McCool was posted on the Web so that users at other sites could download, use, modify, and further develop it.

When McCool departed NCSA in mid-1994, a small group of webmasters who had adopted his server software for their own sites decided to take on the task of continued development. A core group of eight users gathered all documentation and bug fixes and issued a consolidated patch. This "patchy" Web server software evolved over time into Apache. Extensive user feedback and modification yielded Apache 1.0, released on December 1, 1995.

In the space of four years and after many modifications and improvements contributed by many users, Apache has become the most popular Web server software on the Internet, garnering many industry awards for excellence. Despite strong competition from commercial software developers such as Microsoft and Netscape, it is currently in use by more than 62 percent of the millions of Web sites worldwide.[2]

High-Performance Windsurfing

High-performance windsurfing, the evolution of which was documented by Shah (2000), involves acrobatics such as midair jumps and turns. Previously, the sport tended to focus on traditional sailing techniques, using windsurfing boards essentially as small, agile sailboats.

The fundamentals of high-performance windsurfing were developed in 1978 in Hawaii by a group of like-minded users. The development of a major innovation in technique and equipment was described to Shah by high-performance windsurfing pioneer Larry Stanley.

In 1978, Jurgen Honscheid came over from West Germany for the first Hawaiian World Cup and discovered jumping, which was new to him, although Mike Horgan and I were jumping in 1974 and 1975. There was a new enthusiasm for jumping, and we were all trying to outdo each other by jumping higher and higher. The problem was that the riders flew off in midair because there was no way to keep the board with you—and as a result you hurt your feet, your legs, and the board.

Then I remembered the "Chip," a small experimental board we had built with footstraps, and thought "It's dumb not to use this for jumping." That's when I first started jumping with footstraps and discovering controlled flight. I could go so much faster than I ever thought, and when you hit a wave it was like a motorcycle rider hitting a ramp; you just flew into the air. All of a sudden, not only could you fly into the air, but you could land the thing—and not only that, but you could change direction in the air!

The whole sport of high-performance windsurfing really started from that. As soon as I did it, there were about 10 of us who sailed all the time together and within one or two days there were various boards out there that had footstraps of various kinds on them and we were all going fast and jumping waves and stuff. It just kind of snowballed from there.

By 1998, more than a million people were engaged in windsurfing, and a large fraction of the boards sold incorporated the user-developed innovations for the high-performance sport.

Over time, both of these user innovation networks have evolved and become more complex. Today, although they look different on the surface, they are in fact very similar in fundamental ways. Both have evolved to include many thousands of volunteer participants. Participants in free and open source software projects interact primarily via the Internet using various specialized Web sites volunteer users have set up for their use. Participants in innovation sports networks tend to interact by physically traveling to favorite sports sites and to types of contests that innovative users have designed for their sport. Most users of free and open source software simply "use the code," relying on interested volunteers to write new code, debug others' code, answer requests for help posted on Internet help sites, and help coordinate the project. Similarly, most participants in an evolving sport simply "play the game," relying on those so inclined to develop new techniques and equipment, try out and improve innovations developed by others, voluntarily provide coaching, and help to coordinate group activities such as leagues, and meets (Franke and Shah 2003).

User Innovation Networks "Shouldn't Exist," But They Do

Manufacturers, not users, have traditionally been considered the most logical developers of the innovative products they sell. There are two major reasons for this. First, financial incentives to innovate seem on the face of it to be higher for manufacturers than for individual or corporate users of a product or service. After all, a manufacturer has the opportunity to sell what it develops to an entire marketplace of users. Individual user-innovators, on the other hand, are seen as typically benefiting primarily from their own internal use of their innovations. Benefiting from diffusion of an innovation to the other users in a marketplace has been assumed to require some form of intellectual property protection followed by licensing. Both are costly to attempt, with very uncertain outcomes.

The second reason is that for an innovation to achieve widespread diffusion invention and development must be followed by production, distribution, and field support. Because these tasks involve large economies of scale for physical products, it has generally been assumed that manufacturers have major cost advantages over individual users and networks of users. How could users possibly accomplish these tasks as cost-effectively as manufacturers?

Yet, implausible or not, user innovation development and consumption networks clearly do exist. Moreover, when products they develop compete head-to-head against products developed by manufacturers—Apache against Microsoft's and Netscape's server software, for example—the former seem capable of beating the latter handily in the marketplace. Not only do these networks exist, they even triumph! As Galileo is said to have murmured after officially recanting his statement that the earth moves around the sun: "And yet it moves!" What is going on here?

Conditions that Favor User Innovation Networks

We argue that complete fully functional innovation networks can be built up horizontally—with actors consisting only of innovation users (more precisely, "user/self-manufacturers"). Of course, nonuser enterprises can also attach to or assume valuable roles in user innovation networks. Red Hat and IBM provide well-known examples of nonuser involvement in the free and open source software context; professional sports leagues and commercial producers of sports equipment are examples in the case of user sports networks. It is only our contention that nonusers are not essential, and that "horizontal" innovation networks consisting only of users can develop, diffuse, maintain, and consume innovations.

Horizontal user innovation networks can flourish when (1) at least some users have sufficient incentive to innovate and do so, (2) at least some users have an incentive to voluntarily reveal their innovations and the means to do so, and (3) diffusion of innovations by users can compete with commercial production and distribution. When only the first two conditions hold, a pattern of user innovation and trial will occur, followed by commercial manufacture and distribution of innovations that prove to be of general interest.

Innovation by Users

Users have sufficient incentive to innovate when they expect their benefits to exceed their costs. Clearly, many innovators have a use-incentive for innovating in free and open source software projects. Thus, Niedner, Hertel, and Hermann (2000) report that contributors of code to open source projects asked to agree or disagree with statements regarding their possible motivations for this ranked gain from "facilitating my work due to better software" as the highest-ranked benefit (average level of respondent agreement with that statement was 4.7 on a scale of 5). Similarly, 59 percent of contributors to open source projects sampled by Lakhani and Wolf (chap. 1, this volume) report that use of the output they create is one of the three most important incentives inducing them to innovate. Empirical research also documents the presence of user innovation in many additional fields. Thus, Enos (1962); Knight (1963); Freeman (1968); Rosenberg (1976a); von Hippel (1988); Shaw (1985); and Shah (2000) are among those finding that users, rather than manufacturers, are often the initial developers of what later become commercially significant new products and processes.

Innovation also has been found to be a relatively frequent activity among users that have a strong interest in a product or process area, and it tends to be concentrated in the "lead user" segment of user populations (see Table 14.1).[3]

Research on innovation-related incentives and capabilities provides a theoretical basis for all of these findings. Conditions under which users will—and will not—have incentives to innovate have been explored (von Hippel 1988). In addition, low-cost access to "sticky"[4]—costly to transfer—information has been found to be an important enabling factor for user innovation (von Hippel 1994; Ogawa 1997). Thus, information important to successful innovation, such as need and context of use information is *generated* at user sites and is naturally accessible there, but it can be very costly to move from users' sites to outside developers. For example, the conditions that cause software—and jumping windsurfers—to fail are available "for free" at the site of a user with the problem, but can be very costly to reproduce elsewhere. Also, information about user needs and the context of use is not static. Rather, it evolves at the user site through "learning by doing" as the user experiments with prototype innovations. (Recall from the windsurfing example that users *discovered* that they could and wanted to control the direction of a board when it was in the air only *after* they began experimenting with the prototype footstraps they had developed.)

The concentration of innovation activity among the "lead users" in a user population can also be understood from an economic perspective. Given that innovation is an economically motivated activity, users expecting significantly higher economic or personal benefit from developing an innovation—one of the two characteristics of lead users—will have a

Table 14.1
User innovation tends to be frequent and concentrated among "lead users"

Innovation area	Number of users sampled	Percentage developing and building innovation for own use	Were the innovating users "lead users"?
Industrial products			
Printed circuit CAD software (a)	136 user/firm attendees at PC-CAD conference	24.3%	Yes
Pipe hanger hardware (b)	74 pipe hanger installation firms	36%	NA
Library information systems (c)	102 Australian libraries using computerized library information systems	26%	Yes
Apache OS server software security features (d)	131 Apache users	19.1%	Yes
Consumer products			
Outdoor consumer products (e)	153 outdoor-specialty mail-order catalog recipients	9.8%	Yes
"Extreme" sporting equipment (f)	197 expert users	37.8%	Yes
Mountain biking equipment (g)	291 expert users	19.2%	Yes

Sources: (a) Urban and von Hippel 1988; (b) Herstatt and von Hippel 1992; (c) Morrison, Roberts, and von Hippel 2000; (d) Franke and von Hippel 2002; (e) Luthje 2003; (f) Franke and Shah 2003; (g) Luthje, Herstatt, and von Hippel 2002.

higher incentive to innovate and are therefore more likely to do so. Also, given that lead users experience needs in advance of the bulk of a target market, the nature, risks, and eventual size of that target market are often not clear to manufacturers. This lack of clarity can reduce manufacturers' incentives to innovate, and increase the likelihood that lead users will be the first to develop their own innovative solutions for needs that later prove to represent mainstream market demand.

User Incentives to Freely Reveal Their Innovations

Progress and success in user innovation networks is contingent on at least some users "freely revealing" their innovations.[5] Without free revealing, each user would have to redevelop the same innovation in order to use it, resulting in a huge system-level cost, or resort to protecting and licensing their innovations and collecting revenues from other users, which would burden the networks with tremendous overhead.

Research has shown that users in a number of fields do freely reveal details of their innovations to other users and even to manufacturers (von Hippel and Finkelstein 1979; Allen 1983; Lim 2000; Morrison, Roberts, and von Hippel 2000; Franke and Shah 2003). Of course, free revealing is clearly visible in free and open source software networks, and is also clearly present in the sports innovation example; innovating users gather on the beach, inspect one another's creations, and imitate or develop additional modifications that they, in turn, freely reveal.

To economists, free revealing is surprising, because it violates a central tenant of the economic theory of innovation. In this classical view, appropriating returns to innovation requires innovators to keep the knowledge underlying an innovation secret or to protect it by patents or other means. After all, noncompensated spillovers of innovation-related information should represent a loss that innovators would seek to avoid if at all possible, even at some cost. Why then do we observe that some innovation-related information is voluntarily freely revealed?

The answer to this puzzle has several components. First, note that software code (and other public goods) have aspects that remain private to the innovator even after the code has been freely revealed as a public good. This thinking has been codified in a "private-collective" model of innovation incentives (von Hippel and von Krogh 2003). As illustration, consider some of the private benefits retained by users who write and then freely reveal their code. Code may be written precisely to suit the private needs of the code writer—and may serve the needs of free riders less well (Harhoff et al. 2003). Also, the learning and enjoyment gained from actually writing the code—benefits that have been shown to be highly valued by contributors to open source software projects (Lakhani and Wolf, chap. 1, this volume)—cannot be shared by free riders who only adopt the completed product. Nor can the private reputation of an innovator be shared by a free-riding adopter of that innovation (Lerner and Tirole 2002). Finally, when free riders do adopt and use code that has been freely revealed, that action in itself leads to significant private benefits for the code creator: others will help debug the code; it may be integrated into the authorized OS code, leading others to help update and maintain it; higher use (greater "market share") will yield "network effect" advantages; and so on.

A second point important to explaining the practice of free revealing is that profitably creating and serving a market for software you may develop is often not a trivial undertaking. And when benefits from free revealing such as those just described exceed the benefits that are *practically* obtainable from other courses of action such as licensing or selling, then free revealing should be the preferred course of action for a profit-seeking firm.

Finally, we note that the costs associated with free revealing may be low—or in any case, unavoidable—because others who know the same thing will reveal even if you do not. And when the costs of freely revealing an innovation are low, even a low level of benefit can be adequate reward. Competitive losses from free revealing of intellectual property depend upon the degree of rivalry between the software developer and those who may adopt that software as free riders. Thus, users who write and freely reveal software code will expect low losses if they have only low or no rivalry with potential adopters. (For example, there is low rivalry among town libraries: they serve different populations and do not seek to gain market share from each other.) Also, if more than one person or firm has developed a particular piece of software, everyone's decision to freely reveal can be determined by the action of the innovator with the *least* to lose. That is, even those who would prefer to hide their software to keep it from rivals may nonetheless freely reveal if they expect that others will do this if they do not (Lakhani and von Hippel 2003).

Innovation Diffusion by Users

"Full-function" user innovation and production networks—no manufacturer required—are possible only when self-manufacturing and/or distribution of innovative products directly by users can compete with commercial production and distribution. In the case of free and open source software, this is possible because innovations can be "produced"

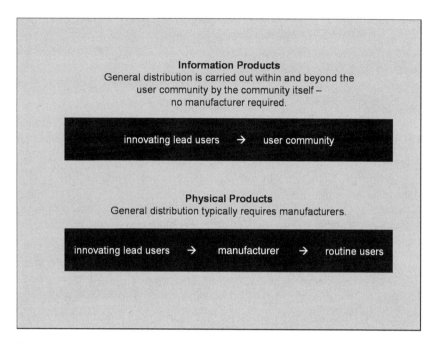

Figure 14.1
How lead user innovations are distributed

and distributed essentially for free on the Web, software being an information rather than a physical product (Kollock 1999). In the case of the sports innovation example, though, equipment (but not technique) innovations are embodied in a physical product that, to achieve general diffusion, must be produced and physically distributed; activities that, as mentioned earlier, involve significant economies of scale. The result, in the case of the windsurfing example and for physical products generally, is that while innovation can be carried out by users and within user innovation networks, production and diffusion of products incorporating those innovations is usually carried out by manufacturing firms (figure 14.1).

Ongoing Exploration of User Innovation Networks

The advent of the Web and consequent public proliferation of free and open source software development projects has focused intense academic attention on the phenomenon of user innovation networks in general, and free and open source software in particular. The thousands of extant free and open source software projects represent natural experiments that academics and others can study to better understand this phenomenon. Among the issues being explored now are conditions under which free and open source software projects can be expected to succeed, how they can be most successfully managed, and what attracts the interest of volunteers. We can expect rapid progress on these fronts.

What is very exciting, it seems to us, is that innovation networks exclusively by and for users, networks that by any yardstick of traditional economics shouldn't exist, can create, diffuse and maintain complex innovation products without *any* manufacturer involvement. This means that in at least some, and probably many, important fields users can build, consume, and support innovations on their own independent of manufacturer incentives to participate and manufacturer-related "agency costs."[6]

Direct development and diffusion of innovations by and for users via horizontal user innovation networks can improve individual user's abilities to get what they really want—because they have an increasingly practical and economical pathway to "do it themselves." As we learn to understand these networks better, we will be in a position to improve such networks where they now exist and may be able to extend their reach and attendant advantages as well.[7]

Notes

1. In the "functional" sources of innovation lexicon, economic actors are defined in terms of the way in which they expect to derive benefit from a given innovation. Thus, firms or individuals that expect to profit from an innovation by in-house use are innovation "users." Innovation "manufacturers," in contrast, are firms or individuals that expect to profit from an innovation by selling it in the marketplace (von Hippel 1988). By user "network," I mean user nodes interconnected by information transfer links that may involve face-to-face, electronic, or any other form of communication. User networks can exist within the boundaries of a membership group but need not. User innovation networks also may, but need not, incorporate the qualities of user "communities" for participants, where these are defined as "networks of interpersonal ties that provide sociability, support, information, a sense of belonging, and social identity" (Wellman, Boase, and Chen 2002, 4).

2. Netcraft April 2003 Web Server Survey, http://news.netcraft.com/archives/2003/04/13/april_2003_web_server_survey.html.

3. Lead users are defined as users of a given product or service type that combine two characteristics: (1) lead users expect attractive innovation-related benefits from a solution to their needs and are therefore motivated to innovate, and (2) lead users

experience needs that will become general in a marketplace, but experience them months or years earlier than the majority of the target market (von Hippel 1986). Note that lead users are not the same as early adopters of an innovation. They are typically ahead of the entire adoption curve in that they experience needs before *any* responsive commercial products exist—and therefore often develop their own solutions.

4. The stickiness of a given unit of information in a given instance is defined as the incremental expenditure required to transfer that unit of information to a specified locus in a form useable by a given information seeker. When this cost is low, information stickiness is low; when it is high, stickiness is high. A number of researchers have both argued and shown that information required by technical problem-solvers is indeed often costly to transfer for a range of reasons (von Hippel 1994). The requirement to transfer information from its point of origin to a specified problem-solving site will not affect the locus of problem-solving activity when that information can be shifted at no or little cost. However, when it is costly to transfer from one site to another in useable form—in my term, sticky—the distribution of problem-solving activities can be significantly affected.

5. When we say that an innovator "freely reveals" proprietary information, we mean that all existing and potential intellectual property rights to that information are voluntarily given up by that innovator and all interested parties are given access to it—the information becomes a public good. Thus, free revealing of information by a possessor is defined as the granting of access to all interested agents without imposition of any direct payment. For example, placement of nonpatented information in a publicly accessible site such as a journal or public Web site would be free revealing under this definition. Note that free revealing as so defined does not mean that recipients necessarily acquire and utilize the revealed information at no cost to themselves. Recipients might, for example, have to pay for a journal subscription or an Internet connection or a field trip to acquire the information being freely revealed. Also, some may have to obtain complementary information or other assets in order to fully understand that information or put it to use. However, if the information possessor does not profit from any such expenditures made by information adopters, the information itself is still freely revealed, according to our definition (Harhoff et al. 2003).

6. *Manufacturers* are the agents of users with respect to new products and services. It is their job to develop and build what users want and need; they do not want the products for themselves. The trouble is that, when manufacturers' incentives don't match those of users—and they often do not—users end up paying an agency cost when they delegate design to manufacturers. A major part of this agency cost takes the form of being offered products that are not the best possible fit with users' needs, even assuming that manufacturers know precisely what those needs are. Manufacturers want to spread their development costs over as many users as possible, which

leads them to want to design products that are a close enough fit to induce purchase from many users rather than to design precisely what any particular user really wants.

7. Recent working papers on free and open source software and user innovation by many researchers can be downloaded from the Web sites http://opensource.mit.edu and http://userinnovation.mit.edu. These sites are intended for those interested in keeping up-to-date on, and perhaps contributing to, our understanding of these phenomena.

An Analysis of Open Source Business Models

Sandeep Krishnamurthy

Open source software products provide access to the source code (or basic instructions) in addition to executable programs, and allow for this source code to be modified and redistributed. This freedom is a rarity in an industry where software makers zealously guard the source code as intellectual property.

In making the source code freely available, a large number of developers are able to work on the product. The result is a community of developers spread around the world working to better a product. This approach has led to the popular operating system Linux, which has emerged as a credible threat to Microsoft's products—especially on the server side. Other famous open-source products include Apache (a program used to run Web sites), OpenOffice (an alternative to Microsoft Office), and Sendmail (the program that facilitates the delivery of approximately 80 percent of the world's e-mail).

Open source is typically viewed as a cooperative approach to product development, and hence more of a technology model. It is typically not viewed as a business approach. However, increasingly we find that entire companies are being formed around the open source concept. In a short period of time, these companies have amassed considerable revenues (although it is fair to say that most of these firms are not yet profitable).

Consider two companies in particular: Red Hat and Caledera/SCO.[1] In its last full year of operations (12 months ending February 28, 2002), Red Hat's revenues were almost $79 million. In its last full year of operations (12 months ending October 31, 2002) Caledera/SCO's revenues were about $64 million. The growth figures are even more impressive—Caledera/SCO grew its revenue from $1 million in 1998 to $64 million in 2002 and Red Hat grew from $42 million in 2000 to $79 million in 2002.

All software companies exist to make maximum profits. Therefore, it is common for these corporations to seek out new ways of generating revenues and reducing costs. Increasingly, companies are using open source as a business strategy to achieve both these objectives.

On the cost reduction side, software producers are now able to incorporate the source code from an open source product into an existing code base. This allows them to reduce the cost of production by reusing existing code. For example, Microsoft, the world's largest software maker, has used source code from a leading open source operating system (Berkeley System Distribution or BSD) in its Windows 2000 and XP products and has acknowledged this on a public web site.[2] It is becoming more common for companies to forge strategic alliances with communities of open source software developers. The community develops the product and thus reduces the cost burden on the company. A prime example of this is the strategic alliance between Ximian and Microsoft in building a connection between the Net initiative and Linux.[3]

On the revenue side, some open source products are now in such great demand that there is a strong need for support services for enterprise customers. These support services includes installation, training/certification, and ongoing technical assistance. Service contracts for these products have become a strong revenue source for companies such as Red Hat Linux.

From the consumer perspective, open source products are attractive due to their reduced cost and comparable performance. Governments, for example, are increasingly motivated to adopt open source products to reduce the expenditure of scarce taxpayer money. Some governments (such as Argentina and Peru) have experimented with moving entirely to an open-source model.

Even for individual consumers, open source products are becoming accessible. Wal-Mart has started to carry PCs that run Linux. Many free applications are now available for PCs. For example, OpenOffice and KOffice are free, open source products that directly compete with Microsoft's Office suite.

In this chapter, my focus is on explicating the different business models that we see in the open-source arena.

Producers of Open Source Products—The Community

The producers of open source products (figure 15.1) are typically a diverse group of developers with a shared passion for a product. They do not seek a profit and do not distinguish between corporate and individual users.

Therefore, they make (a) the product and (b) the source code available for free to any interested user. There is usually support available through

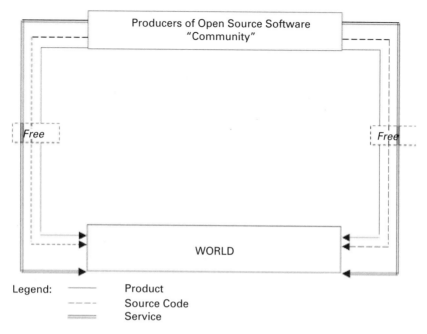

Figure 15.1
Producers of open source products

electronic mailing lists and Usenet groups. Members participate to learn more about the product and believe that others will help them if they have a need (Lakhani and von Hippel 2003). Surprisingly, the customer support provided by communities surrounding products such as Apache and Linux have won awards for excellence.

The community of producers is frequently portrayed as being inimical to corporate profits. However, I submit that the community is simply *indifferent* to its own profits as well as profits that any corporation can make from its products. Open source developer communities are frequently interested in adoption of the product by the intended target audience. Importantly, they want any interested developer to have access to the entire code so that the person can tinker with it to make improvements.

There is no sense of direct competition with companies. A company that views a community as its competitor is welcome to look at its entire source code, whereas the opposite is never true. Communities do not distinguish between users across countries. When the product is available for free, it is amazingly easy to make a product global. There is no issue of taxation or piracy.

The community controls what happens with the product by making one crucial choice—the license. The original developers control the copyright for the intellectual property at all times. However, there is considerable variation between licenses with regard to how derived works may be distributed.

There are a number of licenses from which communities can choose. However, they can be broadly classified as the GNU General Public License (GPL) versus everything else. The GPL is the most famous license and products such as Linux are distributed using it. The key feature of the GPL is that it restricts the terms of distribution of derived works. If a company incorporates GPLed source code in its products, it must make the source code for any product it sells in the marketplace available to any interested party under the terms of the GPL. This provision frightens corporations interested in selling open source products. However, it is important to note that there is a whole host of other licenses that do not have this stipulation.

In my view, the derived works clause is so powerful that it affects how business models are constructed. The discussion about business models is therefore broken down into the GPL and the non-GPL model. Generally speaking, use of GPL reduces the profit potential of companies.

It is very important to note that the open source community does not set a price on a software product. Even in the case when the product is available for free, anybody can incorporate the product and sell it for a price. Even with a GPL license this is possible. Obviously, in the case of GPL, there is the attendant duty of making the source code for derived works freely available.

Business Models

In this section, I discuss the main business models built around the open source philosophy. It is certainly true that some companies benefit from the sale of hardware that runs open source products. Similarly, the market for embedded products can be great. However, for the purposes of this chapter, I focus on the software and service-oriented business.

The Distributor

The distributor provides access to the source code and the software. In the case of Linux, leading distributors include Red Hat, Caldera, and SUSE. Distributors make money in these ways:

1. Providing the product on CD rather than as an online download—most people are not comfortable with downloading the product from a Web site. One survey of 113,794 Linux users indicated that 37 percent of respondents preferred to obtain Linux in CD form.[4] Therefore, there is money to be made selling the product in CD form. According to one source (http://www.distrowatch.com), as of February 2003, the highest price that was being charged for a Linux CD was $129 (Lindows) and the lowest price for a CD was zero (for instance, Debian and Gentoo).

2. Providing support services to enterprise customers—enterprises are willing to pay for accountability. When they have a problem, they do not want to send a message to a mailing list and wait for support that may or may not be of the highest quality. They have no interest in sifting through technical FAQs to find the answer. Therefore, there is money to be made in services such as support for installation, answering technical questions and training employees to use the product.

3. Upgrade services—in which enterprises can now enter into long-term agreements with distributors to ensure that they get the latest upgrade. By acting as application service providers, distributors can help their clients get the latest version of the product seamlessly.

The business model of distributors is shown in figure 15.2.

The Software Producer (Non-GPL Model)

Software producers can benefit from the open source software community in two ways. First, they can incorporate the source code of an existing product in a larger code base and create a new product. Second, they can also take an entire open source product and bundle it with existing products. (I am using the term *derived product* in a very general sense here to include both these cases.) The source code for the derived product does not need to be disclosed, because the license is not GPL.

As mentioned earlier, Microsoft has incorporated the code from BSD in its products and has not released the source code to any interested party. All Microsoft had to do was to acknowledge that it benefited from BSD's code.

The software producer benefits from lowered cost of production and hence increased margin, in this case. There is a service revenue stream in place here as well. The business model itself is shown in figure 15.3.

Interestingly, the source code for the original product is still available to the end users from the community. In the cases where the derived product is a small adaptation of the original product, this may be very useful to the end users. This is the cost the for-profit software producer pays to get the source code for free.

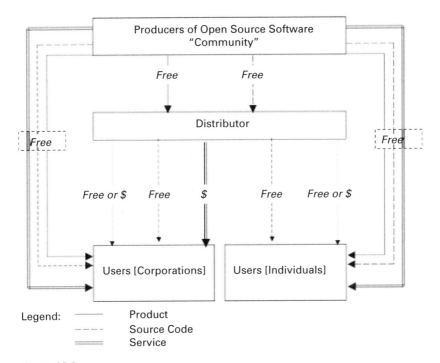

Figure 15.2
The distributor business model

The Software Producer (GPL Model)

The key difference between figures 15.3 and 15.4 is that in the latter, which shows the business model for this case, the software producer is forced to make the source code for the derived product available to the end user.

Let us compare the GPL and non-GPL models. The release of the source code in the GPL model accelerates innovation, due to more rapid feedback and input. Greater inclusion of users builds relationships, and hence loyalty. Also, if the user builds a new version of the product for commercial use, the company gets to see it along with the source code. However, it does expose the inner workings of the company's product to the users.

Ultimately, the difference between the GPL and non-GPL models is in terms of what the seller expects from the user. The GPL software producer expects an empowered user who is eager to engage in a two-way conversation. The non-GPL software producer wants the recipient of the software to simply use it and do nothing else.

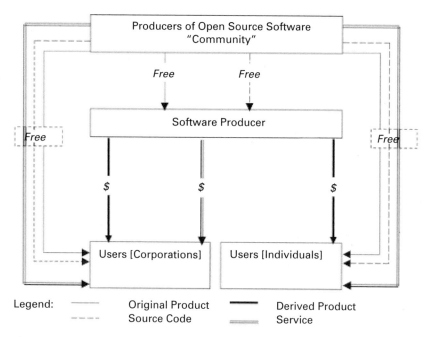

Figure 15.3
The software producer—non-GPL model

The Third-Party Service Provider

The mission of third-party service providers is simple. They don't care where you got the code or where you got the product. If the product you are using meets a broad set of criteria, they will fully support it. They have one single revenue stream—service. Their business model is shown in figure 15.5.

Why should users—especially corporations—use these providers? The bottom line is that paid service generally equates to higher-quality service. Moreover, in many cases, third-party service providers are local and may therefore be able to provide onsite assistance that is typically impossible in the case of free service on mailing lists and user groups. It is important to keep in mind that these service providers are competing with the community to provide customer service.

I have presented two types of models here—one in which the company sells software and service and one in which a company simply offers a service. It is interesting to speculate on whether a company can survive on the sale of software alone.

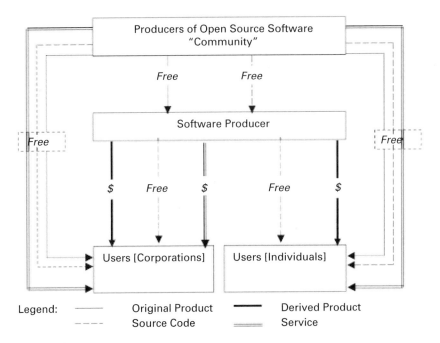

Figure 15.4
The software producer—GPL model

Surviving on the sale of software alone is not easy to achieve. Remember that the community is already making a free version of the product available. The company must be able to add considerable value to the product to generate sufficient margins.

How can a company add value? First, it can choose a version of the product that is stable and that is most suited to its users' needs. Second, it can create a suite of products that are well integrated. These products may come from different sources—some open source, some commercial. The value addition is in creating one package that works well together.

In general, we find that sale of software alone is insufficient to sustain a business. What is needed is software and service. For many software sellers, they already have a relationship with enterprise customers. They can benefit most by up-selling—that is, selling more to existing corporate customers. Selling service then becomes a logical conclusion. Even with commercial software, all software sellers use service as a strong secondary revenue stream.

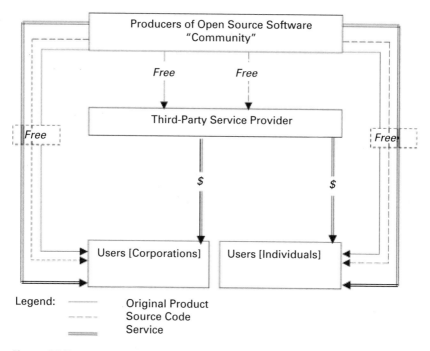

Figure 15.5
Third-party service provider

Advantages and Disadvantages of Open Source

Let us now take a close look at the potential advantages and disadvantages of using open-source technology to develop new products.

Advantages

Robustness Traditionally, a company hires a set number of developers to craft the software. Next, a group of testers work with the product to make sure the number of bugs is minimized. After that point, the product is launched to the market. In direct contrast with the open source method, a much larger number of developers and testers can work on the product and test it under a variety of conditions.

The open source method could potentially lead to a more robust product. The term *robust* here is used in Neumann's sense—that is, an intentionally inclusive term embracing meaningful security, reliability, availability, and system survivability in the face of a wide and realistic range of potential adversities (Neumann 1999). Open source leaders have long maintained that this methodology leads to greater reliability (Ghosh 1998b).

Several studies corroborate this. A study by Bloor Research clearly demonstrated the superior robustness of Linux over Windows NT (Godden 2000). A study conducted by Netcraft in August 2001 found that 92 percent of the top 50 often-requested sites with the longest uptimes ran Apache (http://uptime.netcraft.com).

Flexibility to User   One of the problems with regular software programs is that unless you work with all the software from one company, you do not have the flexibility of "mixing and matching." In the words of Linus Torvalds (Ghosh 1998b), "In fact, one of the whole ideas with free software is not so much the price thing and not having to pay cash for it, but the fact that with free software you aren't tied to any one commercial vendor. You might use some commercial software on top of Linux, but you aren't forced to do that or even to run the standard Linux kernel at all if you don't want to. You can mix the different software you have to suit yourself."

Support from a Community   Traditionally, if a user has a problem, he or she has to contact the technical support division of the company. In many cases, the level of support is poor (especially in the case of free service) or the user may have to pay a fee to get high-quality service. Moreover, after a point, users are asked to pay for this support. With open source software, one has a highly motivated community willing to answer questions (Lakhani and von Hippel 2003). In the case of Linux, Linux User Groups (or LUGs) are numerous and do an excellent job providing service.

Disadvantages

Even though open source product development has a lot of positives, it also comes with its share of negatives.

Version Proliferation   Consider the data in table 15.1. This is based on the survey of 3568 machines. The count is the number of machines and the percentage is of machines running a particular version. As shown in the table, there are at least 62 versions of the software running at this time.

The reason for this multiplicity of versions is due to a complicated version release structure employed by Linux. Releases can be either even-numbered or odd-numbered. The former represent relatively stable software that can be used by enterprise customers. In particular, version 2.0

and 2.2 were major releases that were a long time in the making. On the other hand, odd-numbered releases are developmental versions of the product with new product features. This complicated structure was employed to satisfy two audiences—developers and enterprise customers (Moon and Sproull 2000).

This version proliferation makes it very difficult for the end-user to identify the best version of the product. Companies such as Red Hat play an important role here by selecting one version to support.

Usability Some open source products suffer from poor usability (Nichols and Twidale 2003). This problem may stem from the way projects are structured, the nature of the audience, and the level of resources available to open source projects. However, for major products (such as Stars), this is an opportunity for a new business.

Analyzing the Profit Potential of Open Source Products

Not all open source products have a high profit potential. To analyze the profit potential of an open-source product, I use two dimensions—customer applicability and relative product importance. The classification scheme that results from this is shown in figure 15.6.

Customer applicability refers to the proportion of the market that can benefit from the software. For example, if a product is being designed for a rarely used operating system, only a small proportion of consumers will be able to benefit from it. This will make the level of customer applicability small. On the other extreme, some products are designed for a large number of computing environments or the computing environment that is most commonly found. This makes it high on customer applicability.

Relative product importance refers to how important a program is to the functioning of the user's computer. An operating system is clearly the most important. Without it, the computer will not be able to function. On the other extreme, a screensaver program will add some value to the user—but it is something that the user can do without.

The products with the highest profit potential have high relative product importance and high customer applicability (Quadrant II in figure 15.6). These are the stars that we hear most about. Companies are started around these products. They have large developer communities supporting them. These products have the greatest direct and indirect marketing support. These products have the highest profit potential. An example of

Table 15.1
Survey of Linux kernel versions

Number	Kernel	Count	%	Number	Kernel	Count	%
1	2.0.28	3	0.10%	58	2	33	0.90%
2	2.0.32	2	0.10%	59	2.2	488	13.70%
3	2.0.33	2	0.10%	60	2.4	3,019	84.60%
4	2.0.34	2	0.10%	61	2.5	25	0.70%
5	2.0.34C52 SK	2	0.10%	62	Others		0.10%
6	2.0.36	6	0.20%				
7	2.0.37	4	0.10%				
8	2.0.38	5	0.10%				
9	2.0.39	3	0.10%				
10	2.2.10	2	0.10%				
11	2.2.12	10	0.30%				
12	2.2.13	15	0.40%				
13	2.2.14	34	1.00%				
14	2.2.15	2	0.10%				
15	2.2.16	62	1.70%				
16	2.2.17	23	0.60%				
17	2.2.18	23	0.60%				
18	2.2.18pre21	4	0.10%				
19	2.2.19	126	3.50%				
20	2.2.19ext3	5	0.10%				
21	2.2.19pre17	11	0.30%				
22	2.2.20	69	1.90%				
23	2.2.20RAID	2	0.10%				
24	2.2.21	11	0.30%				
25	2.2.22	29	0.80%				
26	2.2.23	10	0.30%				
27	2.2.24	8	0.20%				
28	2.2.25	24	0.70%				
29	2.2.5	9	0.30%				
30	2.4.0	6	0.20%				
31	2.4.10	42	1.20%				
32	2.4.12	10	0.30%				
33	2.4.13	9	0.30%				

Table 15.1
(continued)

Number	Kernel	Count	%
34	2.4.14	12	0.30%
35	2.4.16	48	1.30%
36	2.4.17	63	1.80%
37	2.4.18	1056	29.60%
38	2.4.19	391	11.00%
39	2.4.2	44	1.20%
40	2.4.20	942	26.40%
41	2.4.20.1	2	0.10%
42	2.4.21	178	5.00%
43	2.4.3	13	0.40%
44	2.4.4	28	0.80%
45	2.4.5	9	0.30%
46	2.4.6	7	0.20%
47	2.4.7	54	1.50%
48	2.4.8	18	0.50%
49	2.4.9	46	1.30%
50	2.4.x	2	0.10%
51	2.5.63	2	0.10%
52	2.5.65	2	0.10%
53	2.5.66	2	0.10%
54	2.5.67	4	0.10%
55	2.5.68	4	0.10%
56	2.5.69	6	0.20%
57	Others		1.70%

Source: Alvestrand, Harald, "The Linux Counter Project," http://www.linuxcounter.org, accessed May 14, 2003)

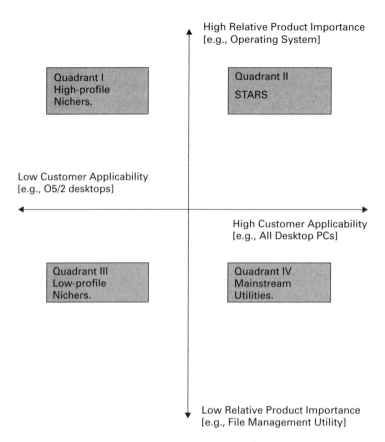

Figure 15.6
Classification of open source products

such a product is Linux. Its relative importance is high because it is an operating system and its customer applicability is high because it can be installed on every desktop PC.

On the other extreme, products that have low relative product importance and low customer applicability are the *low-profile nichers* (Quadrant III in figure 15.6). These products serve a specific niche and itch a small scratch (Raymond 2001). They are never going to be dominant products that will run on a large proportion of desktops. But that is not the goal of the creators of these products. The creators know they are filling a small niche and their goal is to fill it effectively. These products have the lowest profit potential. A good example of such a product is Wings3D, which is a very powerful polygon mesh modeler. This is perhaps a program that students of advanced mathematics might find useful.

The products with low relative product importance and high customer applicability are the *mainstream utilities* (Quadrant IV in figure 15.6). These are products that everybody can benefit from. However, they are not critical to the functionality of the computer. For instance, TouchGraph's Google Browser converts the search results within result into a graphical map. This makes for an interesting map of the results. However, it may not be something, by itself, that is commercially feasible. Another great example of a mainstream utility is Agnostos—a Web-based tool for managing to-do lists. Such products could make excellent promotional items for companies.

Finally, the products with high relative product importance and low customer applicability are the *high-profile nichers* (Quadrant I in figure 15.6). These products are regarded very highly within the specific niche that they serve. However, beyond that, they are not well known. If marketed well, they can lead to a profitable operation. A great example of this is SquirrelMail. This is a program that can be used to run an Internet Service Provider's (ISP) mail operation. It is very well regarded within its niche.

Why Should Corporate Users Switch to Open Source Products?

There are three responses to this question.

The first issue is product performance. Large companies will not adopt a product just because it is built using a certain product development style. They care about performance. Open source products have been making inroads into large companies because they are good—it is just that simple. In many cases, open-source products have been evaluated for their technical merits and their ability to meet stringent requirements. They have been adopted because they met and exceeded these requirements. Examples of notable adoptions include Amazon and Yahoo's use of Perl, Orbitz's use of Linux and Apache, and Google's usage of Linux.

Second, since open source products are usually available for free as an online download, corporations can treat it as a low product risk. They can download the product and play with it in a back office for a while. Even if they decide not to implement it, they will have not paid anything. Of course, this only covers the upfront cost of purchasing the product (see next point about total cost of ownership).

Third, corporations must evaluate the total cost of ownership (i.e., the cost of purchasing, installing, and maintaining the product) of corporate alternatives with open source products and see what that tells them. If the total cost of ownership is in fact lower with open source products, there may be a case. The total cost of ownership is sensitive to the nature of the organization and should be evaluated by each organization as such.

Key Factors that Affect Profits

Support from Primary Developer Community

The key engine for innovation within the open source ecosystem is the primary developer community (Shankland 2002). If this community is focused on innovation, everybody benefits. Distributors can use the latest version in their next release. Software producers can add the latest code. Customers get the product with the best performance that is most stable.

The success of a developer community crucially depends on its leadership structure. However, a variety of leadership styles and structures are observed. For instance, Linus Torvalds is generally considered to be a strong leader in all senses of the word. On the other hand, a committee runs Apache. At this time, it seems like the issue is clarity of the direction for the project. This may be provided by one leader or a group of people working closely together.

Presence of Dominant Competitive OSS Products

OSS products compete with each other fiercely. Open source products compete for developers, distributors, and customers. Developers want to be associated with products that are likely to have a major impact. Distributors would like to devote resources only to products that are likely to become very successful. Customers want to use products that they can rely on.

There are two levels of competition: the product category level (BSD and Linux are competing open source operating systems) and the distribution level (the distributors of Linux are in aggressive competition with each other).

The competition among Linux distributors is especially interesting. Red Hat has established a dominant position—especially in the American market. One source puts its market share in the 50 percent range.[5] However, many other distributors are vying for share. Recently, four Linux distributors—Caldera, Conectiva, SuSE, and TurboLinux—have decided that instead of competing with one another, they must compete with the market leader, Red Hat. To this end, they have formed a group called UnitedLinux. This company will release one product that all four will support. However, each individual company retains its identity and will strive to differentiate on the service side.

While some competition may be necessary for product innovation, excessive competition can hamper long-term profitability.

Presence of Dominant Competitive Closed Source Products

Perhaps the greatest threat to profits from an OSS product is the presence of competitive non-OSS products. Linux competes with Microsoft's Windows products. OpenOffice competes with Microsoft Office. Products such as OpenCourse and Moodle compete with commercial products such as WebCT and Blackboard in the course design arena.

In all these cases, the commercial competitor has a resource advantage that can be used to gain market power through advertising, salesperson interaction with large corporations, and public relations. Sometimes the presence of such competition creates an underdog mentality that can help the open-source product to some degree. On the other hand, it is very hard to compete with major corporations on a regular basis.

Relative Competitive Position

In the final analysis, what really matters is the competitiveness of the product. If the product is truly innovative, it will have a strong chance. If it is does not stack up well against competitive products, it will not. The hope is that making the source code available for free will lead to greater innovation. However, this may fail to materialize if a software product does not attract too many developers.

Need for Marketing

Building awareness for open source products is a challenge. Consider the case of Linux. There is a two-level challenge here. On the first level, one must build awareness for Linux itself (product category awareness). On the second level, one must create awareness for a specific distribution, such as Red Hat (brand awareness). Distributors will be interested in boosting only brand awareness. Red Hat wants to be closely associated with Linux and wants people to equate Linux with their brand name.

If there are no companies in the market, the community will have to take on this challenge. In that case, awareness is built using techniques such as word of mouth that are not resource-intensive.

Of course, building awareness alone is insufficient. What is needed is greater product knowledge followed by trial of the product.

Conclusion

We now know that it is possible to build a business around the open source strategy. We are increasingly finding that open source software communities are awesome competitors. They are able to compete with large companies on an equal footing and even defeat them. They are, therefore, not to taken lightly or dismissed offhand.

Open source software is not for hobbyists any more. Instead, it is a business strategy with broad applicability. Businesses can be built around this idea. When reading this paper, I want the reader to grapple with the specifics of how to build and grow such a business.

To this end, I have proposed three fundamental business models: distributor, software producer (GPL and non-GPL), and the third-party service provider. These are sustainable models that can lead to robust revenue streams. The business models provided here can be enhanced by the addition of further revenue streams. For instance, we now know that certification of developers on an open source product can lead to strong revenues.

Not all products have the same profit potential. Therefore, not all open source software products have the same profit potential. I have classified open source software products into four categories: Stars, High-profile nichers, Low-profile nichers, and Mainstream utilities. Businesses can be built around Stars. High-profile nichers can lead to robust revenue streams if properly marketed. The other two categories may not lead to high profits. Because many open source software products are freely available, managers must scan public repositories to find out which products will be suitable for their business.

The future of open source software is bright. Increasingly, we will find that these products will take a central role in the realm of software and will find a larger place in all our lives.

Notes

1. SCO has been in the news recently for its contentious lawsuit with IBM. The lawsuit claims that IBM inappropriately used portions of source code copyrighted by SCO. Details of the legal battle are available at http://www.groklaw.net.

2. See http://support.microsoft.com. Knowledge Base article 306819.

3. Ximian is now owned by Novell.

4. http://counter.li.org/reports/machines.html, accessed on February 9, 2002.

5. http://www.newsfactor.com/perl/story/20036.html

16 Allocation of Software Development Resources in Open Source Production Mode

Jean-Michel Dalle and Paul A. David

I find that teams can grow much more complex entities in four months than they can build.

—Frederick P. Brooks, Jr.; *The Mythical Man-Month*

We aim in this chapter to develop a stochastic simulation structure capable of describing the decentralized, microlevel decisions that allocate programming resources both within and among free/libre and open source software (FLOSS) projects, and that thereby generate an array of FLOSS system products, each of which possesses particular qualitative attributes.[1] Agent-based modeling of this kind offers a framework for integrating microlevel empirical data about the extent and distribution of participation in "open source" program development, with mesolevel observations concerning the social norms and organizational rules governing those activities. It thus takes a step beyond the preoccupation of much of the recent economics literature with the nature of the current and prospective rewards—whether psychic or material—that motivate individuals to develop and freely distribute open source software. Moreover, by facilitating investigation of the "general equilibrium" implications of the microbehaviors among the participants in FLOSS communities, this modeling approach provides a powerful tool for identifying critical structural relationships and parameters that affect the emergent properties of the macro system.

The core or behavioral kernel of the stochastic simulation model of open source and free software production presented here represents the effects of the reputational reward structure of FLOSS communities (as characterized by Raymond 2001) to be the key mechanism governing the probabilistic allocation of agents' individual contributions among the constituent components of an evolving software system. In this regard, our approach follows the institutional analysis approach associated with studies of academic researchers in "open science" communities. For the purposes of this first step, the focus of the analysis is confined to showing the ways in which the specific norms of the reward system and organizational rules can shape emergent properties of successive releases of code for a given project, such as its range of functions and reliability. The global performance of the FLOSS mode, in matching the functional and other characteristics of the variety of software systems that are produced with the needs of users in various sectors of the economy and polity, obviously, is a matter of considerable importance that will bear upon the long-term viability and growth of this mode of organizing production and distribution. Our larger objective, therefore, is to arrive at a parsimonious characterization of the workings of FLOSS communities engaged across a number of projects, and their collective productive performance in dimensions that are amenable to "social welfare" evaluation. Seeking that goal will pose further new and interesting problems for study, a number of which are identified in the essay's conclusion. We contend that that these too will be found to be tractable within the framework provided by refining and elaborating on the core ("proof of concept") model that is presented in this paper.

A New/Old Direction for Economic Research on the Phenomenon of FLOSS

The initial contributions to the social science literature addressing the FLOSS phenomenon have been directed primarily to identifying the motivations underlying the sustained and often intensive engagement of many highly skilled individuals in this noncontractual and unremunerated mode of production.[2] That focus reflects a view that widespread voluntary participation in the creation and free distribution of economically valuable goods is something of an anomaly, at least from the viewpoint of mainstream microeconomic analysis. A second problem that has occupied observers, and especially economists, is to uncover the explanation for the evident success of products of the FLOSS mode in market competition against proprietary software—significantly on the basis not only of their lower cost, but their reputedly superior quality.[3] This quest resembles the first, in reflecting a state of surprise and puzzlement about the apparently greater efficiency that these voluntary, distributed production organizations have been able to attain vis-à-vis centrally managed, profit-driven firms that are experienced in creating "closed," software products.

Anomalies are intrinsically captivating for intellectuals of a scientific or just a puzzle-solving bent. Yet the research attention that has been stimulated by the rapid rise of an FLOSS segment of the world's software-producing activities during the 1990s owes something also to the belief that this phenomenon and its relationship to the free and open software movements could turn out to be of considerably broader social and economic significance. There is, indeed, much about these developments that remains far from transparent, and we are sympathetic to the view that a deeper understanding of them may carry implications of a more general nature concerning the organization of economic activities in networked digital technology environments. Of course, the same might well be said about other aspects of the workings of modern economies that are no less likely to turn out to be important for human well-being.

Were the intense research interest that FLOSS software production currently attracts to be justified on other grounds, especially as a response to the novelty and mysteriousness of the phenomena, one would need to point out that this too is a less-than-compelling rationale; the emergence of FLOSS activities at their present scale is hardly so puzzling or aberrant a development as to warrant such attention. Cooperative production of information and knowledge among members of distributed epistemic communities who do not expect direct remuneration for their efforts simply cannot qualify as a new departure. There are numerous historical precursors and precedents for FLOSS, perhaps most notably in the "invisible colleges" that appeared among the practitioners of the new experimental and mathematically approaches to scientific inquiry in western Europe in the course of the seventeenth century.[4] The professionalization of scientific research, as is well known, was a comparatively late development, and, as rapidly as it has proceeded, it has not entirely eliminated the contributions of nonprofessionals in some fields (optical astronomy being especially notable in this regard); communities of "amateur" comet-watchers persist, and their members continue to score—and to verify—the occasional observational coup.

"Open science," the mode of inquiry that became fully elaborated and institutionalized under systems of public and private patronage during the latter part of the nineteenth and the twentieth centuries, thus offers an obvious cultural and organizational point of reference for observers of contemporary communities of programmers engaged in developing free software and open source software.[5] The "communal" ethos and norms of "the Republic of Science" emphasize the cooperative character of the larger purpose in which individual researchers are engaged, stressing that the accumulation of reliable knowledge is an essentially social process. The force of its universalist norm is to render entry into scientific work and discourse open to all persons of "competence," while a second key aspect of "openness" is promoted by norms concerning the sharing of knowledge in regard to new findings and the methods whereby they were obtained.

Moreover, a substantial body of analysis by philosophers of science and epistemologists, as well as theoretical and empirical studies in the economics of knowledge, points to the superior efficiency of cooperative knowledge-sharing among peers as a mode of generating additions to the stock of scientifically reliable propositions.[6] In brief, the norm of openness is incentive compatible with a collegiate reputational reward system based upon accepted claims to priority; it also is conducive to individual strategy choices whose collective outcome reduces excess duplication of research efforts, and enlarges the domain of informational complementaries. This brings socially beneficial spillovers among research programs and abets rapid replication and swift validation of novel discoveries. The advantages of treating new findings as public goods in order to promote the faster growth of the stock of knowledge are thus contrasted with the requirement of restricting informational access in order to enlarge the flow of privately appropriable rents from knowledge stocks.

The foregoing functional juxtaposition suggests a logical basis for the existence and perpetuation of institutional and cultural separations between two normatively differentiated communities of research practice. The open "Republic of Science" and the proprietary "Realm of Technology" on this view, constitute distinctive organizational regimes, each of which serves a different (and potentially complementary) societal purpose. One might venture farther to point out that the effective fulfilling of their distinctive and mutually supporting purposes was for some time abetted by the ideological reinforcement of a normative separation between the two communities; by the emergence of a distinctive ethos of "independence" and personal disinterestedness ("purity") that sought to keep scientific inquiry free to the fullest extent possible from the constraints and distorting influences to which commercially oriented research was held to be subject.

Therefore, if we are seeing something really new and different in the FLOSS phenomenon, that quality hardly can inhere in attributes shared with long-existing open science communities. Rather, it must be found elsewhere; perhaps, in the sheer scale on which these activities are being conducted, in the global dispersion and heterogeneous backgrounds of the participants, in the rapidity of their transactions, and in the pace at which their collective efforts reach fruition. This shift in conceptualization has the effect of turning attention to a constellation of technical conditions whose coalescence has especially affected this field of endeavor. Consider just these three: the distinctive immateriality of "code," the great scope for design modularity in the construction of software systems, and the enabling effects of advances in digital (computer-mediated) telecommunications during the past several decades. Although it might be thought that the intention here is merely to portray the historically unprecedented features of the FLOSS movements as primarily an "Internet phenomenon," we have something less glib than that in mind.

It is true that resulting technical characteristics of both the work-product and the work-process alone cannot be held to radically distinguish the creation of software from other fields of intellectual and cultural production in the modern world. Nevertheless, they do suggest several respects in which it is misleading to interpret the FLOSS phenomenon simply as another subspecies of "open science." The knowledge incorporated in software differs in at least two significant respects from the codified knowledge typically produced by scientific work groups. Computer software is "technology" (with a small "t"), which is to say that it becomes effective as a tool immediately, without requiring further expenditures of effort upon development. This immediacy has significant implications not only at the microlevel of individual motivation, but for the dynamics of collective knowledge-production. Indeed, because software code is "a machine implemented as text," its functionality is peculiarly self-exemplifying. Thus, "running code" serves to short-circuit many issues of "authority" and "legitimation" that traditionally have absorbed much of the time and attention of scientific communities, and to radically compress the processes of validating and interpreting new contributions to the stock knowledge.[7]

In our view, FLOSS warrants systematic investigation in view of a particular historical conjuncture; indeed, a portentous constellation of trends in the modern economy. The first trend is that information-goods that share these technical properties are moving increasingly to the center of the stage as drivers of economic growth. The second is that the enabling of peer-to-peer organizations for information distribution and utilization is an increasingly obtrusive consequence of the direction in which digital technologies are advancing. Third, the "open" (and cooperative) mode of organizing the generation of new knowledge has long been recognized to have efficiency properties that are much superior to institutional solutions to the public goods problem, which entail the restriction of access to information through secrecy or property rights enforcement. Finally, and of practical significance for those who seek to study it systematically, the FLOSS mode of production itself is generating a wealth of quantitative information about this instantiation of "open epistemic communities." This last development makes FLOSS activities a valuable window through which to study the more generic and fundamental processes that are responsible for its power, as well as the factors that are likely to limit its domain of viability in competition with other modes of organizing economic activities.

Consequently, proceeding from this reframing of the phenomenon, we are led to a conceptual approach that highlights a broader, ultimately more policy-oriented set of issues than those which hitherto have dominated the emerging economics literature concerning FLOSS. A correspondingly reoriented research agenda is needed. Its analytical elements are in no way novel, though, but merely newly adapted to suit the subject at hand. It is directed to answering a fundamental and interrelated pair of questions: First, by what mechanisms do FLOSS projects mobilize the human resources, allocate the participants' diverse expertise, coordinate the contributions, and retain the commitment of their members? Second, how fully do the products of these essentially self-directed efforts meet the long-term needs of software users in the larger society, and not simply provide satisfactions of various kinds for the developers? These will be recognized immediately by economists to be utterly familiar and straightforward—save for not yet having been explicitly posed or systematically pursued in this context.

Pursuing these questions in more concrete terms brings one immediately to inquire into the workings of the system that actually allocates software development resources among various software systems and applications when the production of code takes place in a distributed community of volunteers, as it does in the FLOSS regime. How does the ensemble of developers collectively "select" among the observed array of projects that are launched, and what processes govern the mobilization of sufficient resource inputs to enable some among those to attain the stage of functionality and reliability that permits their being diffused into wider use—that is to say, use beyond the circle of programmers immediately engaged in the continuing development and debugging of the code itself?

Indeed, it seems only natural to expect that economists would provide an answer to the question of how, in the absence of directly discernible market links between the producing entities and "customers," the output mix of the open source sector of the software industry is determined. Yet, to date, the question does not appear to have attracted any significant research attention. This curious lacuna, moreover, is not a deficiency peculiar to the economics literature, for it is notable also in the writings of some of the FLOSS movement's pioneering participants and popular exponents.[8] Although enthusiasts have made numerous claims regarding the qualitative superiority of products of the open source mode, when these are compared with software systems tools and applications packages developed by managed commercial projects, scarcely any attention is directed to the issue of whether the array of completed OS/FS projects also is "better" or "just as good" in responding to the varied demands of software users.

It is emblematic of this gap that the metaphor of "the bazaar" was chosen by Eric S. Raymond (2001) to convey the distinctively unmanaged, decentralized mode of organization that characterizes open source software development projects—despite the fact that the bazaar describes a mode of distribution, not of production. Indeed, the bazaar remains a peculiar metaphor for a system of production: the stalls of actual bazaars typically are retail outlets, passive channels of distribution rather than agencies with direct responsibility for the assortment of commodities that others have made available for them to sell. Given the extensive discussion of the virtues and deficiencies of the bazaar metaphor that was stimulated by Raymond, it is rather remarkable that the latter's rhetorical finesse of the problem of aligning the activities of producers with the wants of users managed to pass with scarcely any comment.

In contrast, the tasks we have set for ourselves in regard to FLOSS represent an explicit return to the challenge of providing nonmetaphorical answers to the classic economic questions of whether and how this instance of a decentralized decision resource allocation process could achieve coherent and socially efficient outcomes. What makes this an especially interesting problem, of course, is the possibility of assessing the extent to which institutions of the kind that have emerged in the free software and open source movements are enabling them to accomplish that outcome—without help either from the "invisible hand" of the market mechanism driven by price signals, or the "visible hands" of centralized managerial hierarchies.[9] Responding to this challenge requires that the analysis be directed towards ultimately providing a means of assessing the social optimality properties of the way "open science," "open source," and kindred cooperative communities organize the production and regulate the quality of the information tools and goods—outputs that will be used not only for their own, internal purposes, but also by others with quite different purposes in the society at large.

The General Conceptual Approach: Modeling FLOSS Communities at Work

The parallels that exist between the phenomena of "open source" and "open science," to which reference already has been made, suggests a modeling approach that builds on the generic features of nonmarket social interaction mechanisms. These processes involve feedback from the cumulative results of individual actions, and thereby are capable of achieving substantial coordination and coherence in the collective performance of the ensemble of distributed agents. This approach points in particular to the potential significance of the actors' consciousness of being "embedded" in peer reference groups, and therefore to the to role of collegiate recognition and reputational status considerations as a source of systematic influence directing individual efforts of discovery and invention.

Consequently, our agent-based modeling framework has been structured with a view to its suitability for subsequent refinement and use in integrating and assessing the significance of empirical findings—including those derived from studies of the microlevel incentives and social norms that structure the allocation of software developers' efforts within particular projects and that govern the release and promotion of software code. While it does not attempt to mimic the specific features of collegiate reputational reward systems such as are found in the Republic of Science, it is clear that provision eventually should be made to incorporate functional equivalents of the conventions and institutions governing recognized claims to scientific "priority" (being first), as well as the symbolic and other practices that signify peer approbation of exemplary individual performance.

The systems analysis approach familiar in general equilibrium economics tells us that within such a framework we also should be capable of asking how the norms and signals available to microlevel decision-makers in the population of potential participants will shape the distribution of resources among different concurrent projects, and direct the attention of individual and groups to successive projects. Their decisions in that regard will, in turn, affect the growth and distribution of programmers' experience with the code of specific projects, as well as the capabilities of those who are familiar with the norms and institutions (for example, software licensing practices) of the FLOSS regime. Obviously, some of those capabilities are generic and thus would provide potential "spillovers" to other areas of endeavour—including the production of software goods and services by commercial suppliers. From this point it follows that to fully understand the dynamics of the FLOSS mode and its interactions with the rest of the information technology sector, one cannot treat the expertise of the software development community as a given and exogenously determined resource.

It should be evident from the foregoing discussion that the task upon which we are embarked is no trivial undertaking, and that to bring it to completion we must hope that others can be drawn into contributing to this effort. We report here on a start towards that goal: the formulation of a highly stylized dynamic model of decentralized, microlevel decisions that shape the allocation of FLOSS programming resources among project tasks and across distinct projects, thereby generating an evolving array of FLOSS system products, each with its associated qualitative attributes. In such work, it is hardly possible to eschew taking account of what has been discovered about the variety prospective rewards—both material and psychic—that may be motivating individuals to write free and open source software. For, it is only reasonable to suppose that these may influence how they allocate their personal efforts in this sphere.

At this stage, it is not necessary to go into great detail on this matter, but among the many motives enumerated, it is relevant to separate out those involving what might be described as "independent user-implemented innovation."[10] Indeed, this term may well apply to the great mass of identifiably discrete projects, because a major consideration driving many individuals who engage in the production of open source would appear to be the direct utility or satisfaction they expect to derive by using their creative outputs.[11] The power of this motivating force obviously derives from the property of immediate efficacy, which has been noticed as a distinctive feature of computer programs. But, no less obviously, this force will be most potent where the utilitarian objective does not require developing a large and complex body of code, and so can be achieved quite readily by the exertion of the individual programmer's independent efforts. "Independent" is the operative word here, for it is unlikely that someone writing an obscure driver for a newly marketed printer that he wishes to use will be at all concerned about the value that would be attached to this achievement by "the FLOSS community." The individuals engaging in this sort of software development might use open source tools and regard themselves as belonging in every way to the free software and open source movements. Nevertheless, it is significant that the question of whether their products are to be contributed to the corpus of nonproprietary software, rather than being copyright-protected for purposes of commercial exploitation, really is one that they need not address ex ante. Being essentially isolated from active collaboration in production, the issue of the disposition of authorship rights can be deferred until the code is written.

That is an option that typically is not available for projects that contemplate enlisting the contributions of numerous developers, and for which there are compelling reasons to announce a licensing policy at the outset. For all intents and purposes, "independent", or I-mode software production activity stands apart from the efforts that entail participation in collective developmental process, involving successive releases of code and the cumulative formation of a more complex, multifunction system. We will refer to the latter as FLOSS production in *community-mode* or, for convenience *C-mode*, contrasting it with software production in *I-mode*. Since I-mode products and producers almost by definition tend to remain restricted in their individual scope and do not provide as direct an experience of social participation, the empirical bases for generalizations about them is still very thin; too thin, at this point, to support interesting model-building. Consequently, our attention here focuses exclusively upon creating a suitable model to simulate the actions and outcomes of populations of FLOSS agents that are working in C-mode.

It would be a mistake, however, to completely conflate the issue of the sources of motivation for human behavior with the separable question of how individuals' awareness of community sentiment and their receptivity to signals transmitted in social interactions serve to guide and even constrain their private and public actions; indeed, even to modify their manifest goals. Our stylized representation of the production decisions made by FLOSS developers' therefore does not presuppose that career considerations of "ability signaling," "reputation-building," and the expectations of various material rewards attached thereto, are dominant or even sufficient motivations for individuals who participate in C-mode projects. Instead, it embraces the weaker hypothesis that awareness of peer-group norms significantly influences (without completely determining) microlevel choices about the individuals' allocation of their code-writing inputs, whatever assortment of considerations may be motivating their willingness to contribute those efforts.[12]

Our model-building activity aims eventually to provide more specific insights not only into the workings of FLOSS communities, but also into their interaction with organizations engaged in proprietary and "closed mode" software production. It seeks to articulate the interdependences among distinct subcomponents of the resource allocation system, and to absorb and integrate empirical findings about microlevel mobilization and allocation of individual developer efforts both among projects and within projects. Stochastic simulation of such social interaction systems is a powerful tool for identifying critical structural relationships and parameters that affect the emergent properties of the macro system. Among the latter properties, the global performance of the FLOSS mode in matching the functional distribution and characteristics of the software systems produced to the evolving needs of users in the economy at large, obviously is an issue of importance for our analysis to tackle.

It is our expectation that in this way, it will be feasible to analyze some among the problematic tensions that may arise been the performance of a mode of production guided primarily by the internal value systems of the participating producers, and that of a system in which the reward structure is tightly coupled by managerial direction to external signals deriving from the satisfaction of end-users' wants. Where the producers are the end-users, of course, the scope for conflicts of that kind will be greatly circumscribed, as enthusiasts for "user-directed innovation" have pointed out.[13] But the latter solution is likely to serve the goal of customization only by sacrificing some of the efficiencies that derive from producer specialization and division of labor. The analysis developed in this paper is intended to permit investigations of this classic trade-off in the sphere of software production.

Behavioral Foundations for C-Mode Production of Software

An important point of departure for our work is provided by a penetrating discussion of the operative norms of knowledge production within FLOSS communities that appears in Eric Raymond's less widely cited essay "Homesteading the Noosphere" (Raymond 2001, 65–111).[14] Within the "noosphere"—the "space" of ideas, according to Raymond—software developers allocate their efforts according to the relative intensity of the reputation rewards that the community attaches to different code-writing "tasks." The core of Raymond's insights is a variant of the collegiate reputational reward system articulated by sociological studies of open science communities: the greater the significance that peers would attach to the project, to the agent's role, and the greater is the extent or technical criticality of his or her contribution, the greater is the "reward" that can be anticipated.

Caricaturing Raymond's more nuanced discussion, we stipulate that (a) launching a new project is usually more rewarding than contributing to an existing one, especially when several contributions have already been made; (b) early releases typically are more rewarding than later versions of project code; (c) there are some rewarding projects within a large software system that are systematically accorded more "importance" than others. One way to express this is to say that there is a hierarchy "peer regard," or reputational significance, attached to the constituents elements of a family of projects, such that contributing to the Linux kernel is deemed a (potentially) more rewarding activity than providing Linux implementation of an existing and widely used applications program, and the latter dominates writing an obscure driver for a newly marketed printer.

To this list we would append another hypothesized "rule": (d) within each discrete project, analogously, there is hierarchy of peer-regard that corresponds with (and possibly reflects) differences in the structure of mesolevel technical dependences among the "modules" or integral "packages" that constitute that project. In other words, we postulate that there is lexicographic ordering of rewards based upon a discrete, technically based "treelike" structure formed by the successive addition of project components. Lastly, for present purposes, it can be assumed that (e) new projects are created in relation to existing ones, so that it always is possible to add a new module in relation to an existing one, to which it adds a new functionality. The contribution made by initiating this new module (being located one level higher in the tree) will be accorded less significance than its counterparts on the structure's lower branches.

Thus, our model postulates that the effort-allocation decisions of agent's working in C-mode are influenced (inter alia) by their perceptions concerning the positioning of the project's packages in a hierarchy of peer regard; and further stipulates that the latter hierarchy is related to the structure of the technical interdependences among the modules.

For present purposes, it is not really necessary to specify whether dependent or supporting relationships receive the relatively greater weight in this "calculus of regard." Still, we will proceed on the supposition that modules that are more intensely implicated by links with other packages that include "supportive" connections reasonably are regarded as "germinal" or "stem" subroutines[15] and therefore may be depicted as occupying positions towards the base of the treelike architecture of the software project. Assuming that files contributed to the code of the more generic among the modules, such as the kernel or the memory manager of an operating system (e.g., Linux), would be called relatively more frequently by other modules might accord them greater "criticality"; or it might convey greater notice to the individual contributor that which would apply in the case of contributions made to modules having more specialized functions, and whose files were "called" by relatively few other packages.

For the present purposes, Raymond's rules can be restated as holding that: (1) there is more "peer regard" to be gained by a contribution made to a new package than by the improvement of existing packages; (2) in any given package, early and radically innovative contributions are more rewarded than later and incremental ones; (3) the lower level and the more generic a package, the more easily a contribution will be noticed, and therefore the more attractive a target it will be for developers. Inasmuch as "contributions" also are acknowledged by Raymond as correcting "bugs of omission," each such contribution—or "fix"—is a patch for a "bug," be it a simple bug, an improvement, or even a seminal contribution to a new package. Therefore every contribution is associated with a variable expected payoff that depends on its nature and "location."[16]

The decision problem for developers is then to choose which "bug" or "problem" will occupy their attention during any finite work interval. We find here another instance of the classic "problem of problem choice" in science, which the philosopher Charles S. Pierce (1879) was the first to formalise as a microeconomic decision problem. But we need not go back to the static utility calculus of Pierce. Instead, we can draw upon the graph-theoretic model that more has recently been suggested by Carayol and Dalle's (2000) analysis of the way that the successive choices of research agendas by individual scientists can aggregate into collective dynamic patterns of knowledge accumulation. The latter modelling approach is a quite suitable point of departure, precisely because of the resemblance between the reputation game that Raymond (2001) suggests is played by open source software developers and behavior of open science researchers in response to collegiate reputational reward systems, as described by Dasgupta and David (1994). Although we treat agents' "problem choices" as being made independently in a decentralised process, they are nonetheless influenced by the context that has been formed by the previous effort-allocating decision of the ensemble of researchers. That context can be represented as the state of the knowledge structure accumulated, in a geological manner, by the "deposition" of past research efforts among a variety of "sites" in the evolving research space—the "noosphere" of Raymond's metaphor of a "settlement" or "homesteading" process.

A Simulation Model of OS/FS C-Mode Production

Our approach conceptualizes the macrolevel outcomes of the software production process carried on by an FLOSS community as being qualitatively oriented by the interplay of successive individual effort-allocating decisions taken members of a population of developers whose expected behaviors are governed by "norms" or "rules" of the sort described by Raymond.[17] The allocation mechanism, however, is probabilistic rather than deterministic—thereby allowing for the intervention of other influences affecting individual behavior. So far as we are aware, there exist no simple analytical solutions characterizing limiting distributions for the knowledge structures that will result from dynamic nonmarket processes of this kind. That is why we propose to study software production in the open source mode by numerical methods, using a dynamic stochastic (random-graph) model.

In this initial exploratory model, briefly described, at any given moment a particular FLOSS development "agent" must choose how to allocate a fixed level of development effort—typically contributing new functionalities, correcting bugs, and so on—to one or another among the alternative "packages" or modular subsystems of a particular project. The alternative actions available at every such choice-point also include launching a new module within the project.[18] Agents' actions are probabilistic and conditioned on comparisons of the expected nonpecuniary or other rewards associated with each project, given specifications about the distribution of their potential effort endowments.[19]

We consider that open source developers have different effort endowments, evaluated in thousands of lines of code (KLOC), and normalized according to individual productivities. The shape of the distribution of effort endowments, strictly speaking, cannot be inferred immediately from the (skewed) empirical distribution of the identified contributions measured in lines of code, but one can surmise that the former distribution also is left-skewed—on the basis of the relative sizes of the "high-activity" and "low-activity" segments of the developer population found by various surveys, and notably the FLOSS survey (Ghosh et al. 2002). This feature is in line with the most recent surveys, which have stressed that most open source contributors engage in this activity on a part-time, unpaid basis.[20] The effort endowment of individuals at each moment in time is therefore given here by an exponential distribution; that is, smaller efforts will be available for allocation with higher probability. Namely, efforts, denoted by α, are generated according to the following inverted cumulative density function:

$$\alpha = -\frac{1}{\delta}\ln(1-p) \qquad (1.1)$$

where $p \in [0;1]$ and δ is a constant.

Effort endowments measure how many KLOC a given hacker can either add or delete in the existing code, as a common measure of changes of source code in computer science is indeed not only with lines added, but also with lines deleted to account better for the reality of development work, bug correction, and code improvement: therefore it is a question of spending developer time (writing lines of code) on a given project (module).

Then, as we have argued (previously) we consider that all the modules, taken together, are organized as in a tree that grows as new contributions are added, and that can grow in various ways depending on which part of it (low or high level modules, notably) developers select. To simulate the growth of this tree and the creation of new modules, we attach a virtual (potential) new node (module, package) to each existing one at a lower level and starting with version number 0: each virtual module represents an opportunity to launch a new project that can be selected by a developer, and become a real module with a nonzero version number. Figure 16.1 gives a symbolic representation of the growth process (represented bottom-up) and of the creation of new modules where dashed lines and circles stand for virtual nodes (potential new software packages). Figure 16.2 presents an example of a software tree whose growth (again represented bottom-up) was generated by the stochastic simulation model, where numbers associated with each module precisely account for versions: indeed, we further consider that, for each module, its version number, denoted by v and indexed here by its distance to the root module d, is a good proxy to account for its performance, and that this version number increases nonlinearly with the sum of total KLOC added and deleted, here denoted by x, according to:

$$v_d(x) = \log(1 + xd^\mu) \tag{1.2}$$

where μ is a characteristic exponent and d is the distance of the module to the germinal or stem module of the project tree. Further, without loss of generality, we choose the normalization that sets the distance of the stem module itself to be 1. As $d \geq 1$, the specification given by equation 1.2 further implies that it is easier to improve versions for low-level modules than for those at higher levels.[21]

Then developers allocate their individual effort endowments at every (random) moment in order to maximise the expected reputation-benefit that it will bring, considering each possible bug that is available to be corrected—or each new project to be founded ("bug of omission").[22] We suppose that the cumulative expected[23] reward (private value) for each

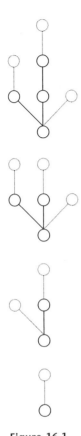

Figure 16.1
The upwards-evolving tree; a figurative representation of a software system's growth process

existing and potential new project, denoted by r and also indexed by distance d to the root module, is a function of the version number, and therefore an increasing function of the cumulative efforts measured in KLOC, but also that initial contributions are evaluated as rewarding as long as they are above a given threshold.

$$r_d(x) = v_d(x)d^{-\lambda} \tag{1.3}$$

$$r_d(x) = 0 \; whenever \; v_d(x) \leq v_\theta. \tag{1.4}$$

Here v_θ stands as a release "threshold" below which no reward is therefore gained by developers: this threshold accounts for the existence of a norm according to which releasing early is more or less encouraged in

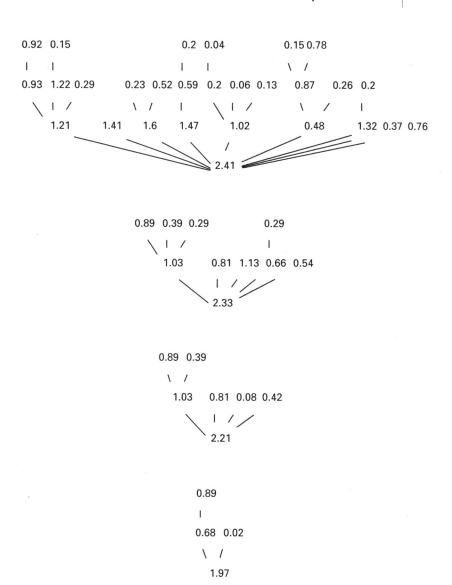

Figure 16.2
Typical simulation of a software project growth process

FLOSS communities.[22] Namely, it can be rewarding to release projects before they are functioning—developers can get "credits" for quite early releases—as it is assumed to be socially efficient because it is a way to attract other developers: an assumption that we will analyze later in this chapter, and to which we will in fact try to give a better analytical ground.

Note also that in equation 1.3 the reward depends on the height of the project in the software tree—the lower the package, the higher the expected reward, according to a power law of characteristic exponent $\lambda \geq 0$,[25] according to the behavioral foundations of FLOSS community norms as we have abstracted them.

Each existing and potential project is thus associated with an expected payoff depending on its location in the software tree, on its current level of improvement (possibly 0), and on individual efforts. More precisely, the expected payoff, denoted by ρ, which corresponds for any given developer to spending its (entire) effort endowment α working on (existing) module m, located at distance d from the root, and whose current level of improvement is x, is:

$$\rho(m) = r_d(x+\alpha) - r_d(x) \qquad (1.5)$$

We suppose that each developer computes the expected rewards associated with each of the nodes according to this last formula and his/her own effort endowment, but also taking into account the rewards associated with the launching of new projects. According to the growth algorithm described earlier, there is simply one possible new activity—which would correspond to the creation of a new module—for each existing package in the global project tree. Numerically, this is strictly analogous to computing the expected reward of "virtual" nodes located as a "son" of each existing node, whose distance to the root module is therefore the distance of the "parent" node plus 1, and whose version and total KLOC are initially 0. Then the expected reward, denoted by ρ', and associated with launching a new project as a "son" of node m with effort α is given by:

$$\rho'(m) = r_{d+1}(\alpha) \qquad (1.6)$$

We translate these payoffs into a stochastic "discrete choice" function, considering further that there are nonobservable levels of heterogeneity among developers, but that their choice will on average be driven by these expected payoffs. Then:

$$P(chosen\ module = module\ m) = \frac{\rho(m)}{\sum_{i=1(root\ module)}^{number\ of\ modules} \rho(i) + \sum_{i=1(virtual\ son\ to\ the\ root\ module)}^{number\ of\ modules} \rho'(i)} \qquad (1.7)$$

Our goal then is to examine what pattern of code generation emerges from this system, and how sensitive its morphology (software-tree forms) is to parameter variation; that is, to variations of the rewards given by the value system of the FLOSS-hacker's ethos, and simply to the demography of the population of hackers. The obvious trade-offs of interest are those between intensive effort being allocated to the elaboration of a few "leaves" (modules) which may be supposed to be highly reliable and fully elaborated software systems whose functions in each case are nonetheless quite specific, and the formation of an "dense canopy" containing a number and diversity of "leaves" that typically will be less fully developed and less thoroughly "debugged."

We therefore focus on social utility measurements according to the following basic ideas:

1. Low-level modules are more valuable than high-level ones simply because of the range of other modules and applications that eventually can be built upon them.

2. A greater diversity of functionalities (breadth of the tree at the lower layers) is more immediately valuable because it provides software solutions to fit a wider array of user needs.

3. Users value greater reliability, or the absence of bugs, which is likely to increase as more work is done on the code, leading to a higher number of releases. Releases that carry higher version numbers are likely to be regarded as "better" in this respect.[26]

We capture these ideas according to the following simple[27] "social utility" function:

$$u = \sum_{m}^{(modules)} \left[(1 + v_d(m))^v - 1 \right] d^{-\xi} \tag{1.8}$$

where $v \in [0; 1]$ and $\varphi \geq 0$ are characteristic exponents; that is, both can vary independently to allow for various comparative weights of improvement, measured by version numbers, and specialization of modules, measured by distance to the root module, in social utility.

Emergent Properties

Preliminary results[28] tend to stress the social utility of developer community "norms" that accord significantly greater reputational rewards for adding, and contributing to the releases of low level modules. Figure 16.3 presents the typical evolution of social utility with various values of λ

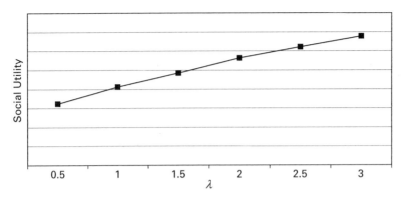

Figure 16.3
Typical evolution of social utility with various values of λ

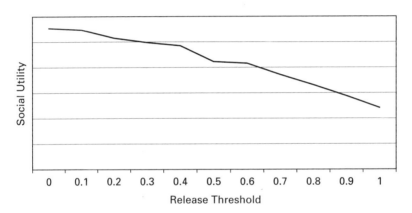

Figure 16.4
The evolution of social utility depending on v_θ

(efficiencies are averaged over 10 simulation runs, while other parameters remain similar—$\delta = 3$ $\mu = 0.5$ $v = 0.5$ $\xi = 2$).[29] According to these results, the social utility of software produced increases with λ—i.e., with stronger community norms—because lower modules are associated with higher rewards, compared to higher ones when λ increases according to the previous equations.

Further, our preliminary explorations of the model suggest that policies of releasing code early tend to generate tree-shapes that have higher social utility scores. Then figure 16.4 gives the evolution of social utility depending on v_θ (here, utilities are averaged over simply five simulation runs, while $\delta = 3$ $\mu = 0.5$ $v = 0.5$ $\xi = 2$ $\lambda = 2$).[30]

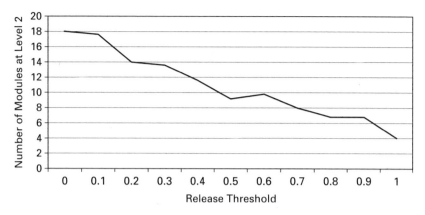

Figure 16.5
The number of modules at "level 2"

The intuitively plausible interpretation of this last finding is that early releases create bases for further development, and are especially important in the case of low-level modules, as they add larger increments to social utility. The reputational reward structure posited in the model encourages this roundabout process of development by inducing individual efforts to share the recognition for contributing to code, and notably to low level code. Figure 16.5 brings some rather conclusive evidence in favor of this explanation by displaying the number of modules at "level 2,"; that is, at distance 1 from the kernel ("germinal" or "stem") module.

When developers get rewarded for very early releases of modules (lower release threshold), the number of lower modules (here at level 2, or at distance 1 from the root module) increases significantly; lower-level modules get created. Indeed, and to go one step further, we suggest that early releases of low-level modules could be considered *seminal*, according to an expression often used to characterize important and initial scientific contributions (articles), meaning that these contributions, however limited, create subsequent and sufficient opportunities for other developers to earn reward by building on them. That is specially true at lower levels, because expected rewards for subsequent contributions are sufficiently high to attract further developers.

This points to the functional significance of one of the strategic rules—"release early" and "treat your users as co-developers"—that Raymond has put forward for open source development, in the classic exposition, *The Cathedral and the Bazaar* (2001). As Raymond himself puts it:

[Treating your users[31] as co-developers] The power of this effect is easy to underestimate. . . . In fact, I think Linus [Torvalds]'s cleverest and most consequential hack was not the construction of the Linux kernel itself, but rather his invention of the Linux development model. When I expressed this opinion in his presence once, he smiled and quietly repeated something he has often said: "I'm basically a very lazy person who likes to get credit for things other people actually do." (Raymond 2001, 27)

By this, we can understand the mechanism for eliciting seminal contributions—that is, of early release and attraction of codevelopers—to operate in the following way: rewarding early release, and allowing others to build upon it, does not simply create a sufficiently rewarding opportunity for potential codevelopers to be attracted, but also brings extra reward to the individual who has disclosed a seminal work. Here, at least for low-level modules, interdependent expected rewards are such that they create incentives for what Raymond (2001, 27) calls "loosely-coupled collaborations enabled by the Internet"—that is to say, for cooperation in a positive-sum game, positive both for the players and for social efficiency. In a sense, and at a metalevel, Linus Torvalds's seminal contribution was not only the kernel, but a new method of software development, which was indeed new and different from the more classical methods that had previously been supported by the FSF for most GNU tools (Raymond 2001, 27 and 29). Once again:

Linus (Torvalds) is not (or at least, not yet) an innovative genius of design in the way that, say, Richard Stallman or James Gosling (of NeWS and Java) are. Rather, Linus seems to me to be a genius of engineering and implementation, with . . . a true knack for finding the minimum-effort path from point A to point B. . . . Linus was keeping his hackers/users constantly stimulated and rewarded—stimulated by the prospect of having an ego-satisfying piece of the action, rewarded by the sight of constant (even *daily*) improvement in their work. (Raymond 2001, 29–30)

The price to be paid for implementing such an early release scheme is, of course, that the higher number of modules being created come at the sacrifice of lower-level versions that might have been produced with equivalent levels of efforts. Figure 16.6 presents the evolution of the version of the kernel, of the average version of level 2 modules, and of the average version of the modules over the entire software tree depending on the release threshold v_θ (same parameter values, still averaged over five simulation runs).

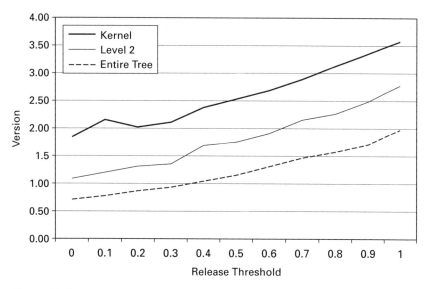

Figure 16.6
The evolution of the version of the kernel

Conclusion and To-Do List

Although there are clearly many things to be improved in this very preliminary attempt to model the workings of FLOSS communities, we hope that we might have brought some preliminary indications about the kind of insights such a tool might provide to observers and practitioners of FLOSS. We have notably suggested that strong reputational community norms foster a greater social utility of software produced, and also suggested some preliminary evidence in favor of the empirical "release early" rule, and tried to provide a more general rationale for early release policies—although there can be some drawbacks in terms of code robustness, for instance.

As a consequence of these findings, we have opted for an early release of our work on this topic: in a sense, one should look at all the footnotes in the former sections not only as disclaimers about the preliminary nature of our attempts, but also as opportunities for improvement and for codevelopment of our model. Although we certainly "commit" to do part of this job, we are also convinced that, considering the complexity of FLOSS communities, we need to harness significant effort to develop a proper model of FLOSS communities.

In this respect, and standing as a temporary conclusion, let us briefly summarize for now at least part of the to-do list of features that should be added to the model:

Microbehaviors Clearly, the behavior of developers (contributors) thus far is caricatured as myopic and, more seriously, still lacks several important dynamic dimensions. First, learning is missing: as a matter of fact, acquiring the skills to debug a particular module, or to add new functionalities to it, is not costless. But the model does not make allowance for these "start-up" costs, which would affect decisions to shift attention to a new package of code in the project. Secondly, instead of choosing how to apply their currently available "flow" development inputs (code-writing time, in efficiency units) among alternative "modules," developers might consider aggregating their efforts by working offline over a longer interval. Intertemporal investment strategies of this sort would permit individuals to make a larger, and possibly more significant, contribution to a module and thereby garner greater peer-recognition and rewards.[32] Thirdly, and perhaps most obviously, the model in its presently simplified form abstracts entirely from behavioral heterogeneities. The latter could derive from the variety of motivations affecting the effort that developers are willing to devote to the community project, or to differences in preferences for writing code, as distinct from engaging in newsgroup discussions with other contributors. But, as we have modelled effort in efficiency units (KLOCs per period), differences in innate or acquired skill among contributors also would contribute to generating a (changing) distribution of input capacities in the developer population. The convolution of that distribution with the distribution of motivational intensities would then have to be considered by the simulation model when a "potential developer" is drawn at random from the population, for interindividual differences in the extent of the (effective) "endowment" would influence the (simulated) pattern of microbehaviors.

Release Policies Release policies can be viewed as reflecting the governance structure of a project and therefore treated as a "predetermined" variable, or "fixed effect" that potentially distinguishes one project from another.[33] Such policies can be viewed as a factor influencing the distribution of developer efforts among different FLOSS projects, and thereby affecting their relative advance toward maturity. But, as differences among the operating rules followed by maintainers of different modules within a complex project would create de facto local policy variations release rules, this too can be incorporated by the model among the set of conditions affected the internal allocation of developers' contributions. Global release policies, affected by how accessible the project's code is to users through one or more for-profit and nonprofit "distributions" of its code, constitutes yet another important aspect of performance. This may affect both perceived reliability, market adoption, and so feed back to influence the project's success in mobilizing supporting resources both within the developer community and from external sources.

Willingness to Contribute to Different Projects As has been noted, developers might have variable effort endowments, depending, for instance, on the global shape of a project, or on other variables such as its market share, release policies, licensing schemes, and so on. The varying profiles formed by the latter characteristics of projects, together with their effects in eliciting developers' individual inputs, will affect the allocation of development resources among the different software projects that coexist and the new ones that are being launched. That represents a key "supply side" determinant of the evolving population of projects. But the positioning the of projects in the "software systems product space," and in particular their relationship to current projects that are intended as product substitutes, is another aspect of the dynamics of resource allocation in the developer community at large. It will therefore be important to extend the model in this direction, by defining the dimensions of the "product space"; only when "categories can be represented" will it become possible to simulate the effects of what Raymond (2001) describes as "category killers"— project trees, in our metaphor, that block the sunlight and absorb the nutrients in the area around them, preventing other project trees from establishing themselves there.

Users End-users have not really been implemented yet in the model, save for the fact that developers are assumed to be also users, in that they know what the bugs (actual ones, and bugs of omission) are! Users are likely, as a group, to have different preferences from developers; for instance, being disposed to grant more weight to reliability rather than to the range of functionalities embedded in a single program. Furthermore, some developers (some communities?) may be more strongly motivated than others to work on "popular" projects—that is, by projects that are able to attract users from the general, inexpert population by fulfilling their working requirement, affording network compatibilities with coworkers, being properly distributed.[34] Again, it would be appropriate for the model to represent such considerations and, by allowing for alternative distributions of developer attitudes, to investigate their potential impacts upon the pattern of FLOSS project development.

Sponsorship Sponsorship, and more generally, symbiotic relationships with commercial entities of various kinds (ancillary service companies, editors of complementary commercial application packages, even proprietary software vendors), can influence FLOSS development by adding and directing efforts. This influence can take a variety of forms, ranging from commercial distribution of FLOSS-based products to hiring prominent developers and letting them contribute freely to selected open-source projects. The interaction with complementary enterprises in the software systems and services sector, therefore, will have to be modelled along with the direct competition between the underlying FLOSS code and the products of commercial vendors of proprietary software and bundled services.

Authority and Hierarchies In a sense, the reputation rewards associated with contributing to the development of a project are obtained only if the developers' submitted "patches" are accepted by the module or project maintainer. Rather than treating the latter's decisions as following simple "gate-keeping" (and "bit-keeping") rules that are neutral in regard to the identities and characteristics of the individual contributors, it may be important to model the acceptance rate as variable and "discriminating" on the basis of the contributing individuals' experience or track records. This approach would enable the model to capture some features of the process of "legitimate peripheral participation" through which developers are recruited. Modules towards the upper levels in the tree, having fewer modules calling them, might be represented as requiring less experience for a given likelihood of acceptance. Comparative neophytes to the FLOSS community (newbies) thus would have incentives to start new modules or contribute to existing ones at those levels, but over time, with the accumulation of a track record of successful submissions, would tend to migrate to lower branches of new trees.[35]

All of the foregoing complicating features of the resource allocation within and among FLOSS development projects are more or less interdependent, and this list is not exhaustive. There is therefore a great deal of challenging model-building work still to be done, and additional empirical research must be devoted to obtaining sensible parameterizations of the simulation structure. But we maintain that this effort is worth undertaking because we are convinced that FLOSS research activity, be it in computer science, economics, or other social sciences, is now proliferating rapidly in empirical and theoretical directions, and some integrative tools are needed to better assess the findings and their implications. Empirical research of several kinds, about the nature of the involvement of developers in projects and their motivations, about the ecology of FLOSS projects as typically observed in SourceForge-like environments, about the commercial ecology and economy that now accompany all successful FLOSS projects, should not only be confronted with the model and its findings, but should also orient further modelling advances.

As it is essential for theorists to engage in a continuing dialog with empirical researchers, agent-based simulation modeling would appear to provide at least part of the necessary language for conducting such exchanges. It is therefore to be hoped that by exploring this approach, it will prove possible eventually to bring social science research on the free and open source model of software development to bear in a reliably informative way upon issues of public and private policy for a sector of the global economy that manifestly is rapidly growing in importance.

Notes

We gratefully acknowledge the informative comments and suggestions of Matthijs den Besten, Rishab Ghosh, Karim R. Lakhani, and an anonymous reviewer on previous drafts of this paper, as well as Nicolas Carayol's participation in our initial discussions of the modeling approach. Andrew Waterman contributed capable research assistance on a number of critical points in the literature. According to the conclusions suggested precisely in this chapter, we have found ourselves inclined to provide an early release of our on-going project to open-source development: however, certainly none of those who have helped can be held responsible for defects that have remained, or for the views expressed here.

This research has drawn support from the Project on the Economic Organization and Viability of Open Source Software, funded under National Science Foundation Grant NSF IIS-0112962 to the Stanford Institute for Economic Policy Research. See *http://siepr.stanford.edu/programs/OpenSoftware_David/OS_Project_Funded_Announcmt.htm*.

1. Although the focus of this paper is with the open source mode of production, rather than with the terms on which the resulting software is licensed, the two aspects are not unrelated in the organization of the class of large "community-mode" projects that will be seen to be of particular interest here. Hence the term "free/libre and open source software" is used in referring to both the projects and their output. We follow the growing practice of using "libre" to emphasize that the

intended meaning of "free" in "free software" relates to the "liberal" access conditions, rather than its pecuniary costs.

2. See, among the salient early contributions to the "economics of open source software," Ghosh 1998a; Harhoff, Henkel and von Hippel 2000; Lakhani and von Hippel 2003; Lerner and Tirole 2000; Weber 2000; Kogut and Metiu 2001.

3. In this particular vein, see for example Dalle and Jullien 2000, 2003; Bessen 2001; Kuan 2001; Benkler 2002.

4. See for example David 1998a, 1998b, 2001b, and references to the history of science literature supplied therein.

5. This point has not gone unrecognized by observers of the free and open software movements. In "The Magic Cauldron," Raymond (2001) explicitly notices the connection between the information-sharing behavior of academic researchers and the practices of participants in FLOSS projects. Further, Raymond's (2001) illuminating discussion of the norms and reward systems (which motivate and guide developers selections of projects on which to work) quite clearly parallels the classic approach of Robert K. Merton (1973) and his followers in the sociology of science. This is underscored by Raymond's (1999a) rejoinder to N. Berzoukov's allegations on the point. See also DiBona et al. 1999 for another early discussion; Kelty 2001 and David, Arora, and Steinmueller 2001 expand the comparison with the norms and institutions of open/academic science.

6. See Dasgupta and David 1994 and David 1998c, 2001b on the cognitive performance of open science networks in comparison with that of proprietary research organizations.

7. Therefore, it might well be said that in regard to the sociology and politics of the open source software communities, "the medium is the message."

8. See for example Raymond 2001; Stallman 1999a; and Dibona, Ockman, and Stone 1999 and the statements of contributors collected therein.

9. Benkler 2002 has formulated this problem as one that appears in the organizational space between the hierarchically managed firm and the decentralized competitive market, focuses attention primarily on the efficiency of software project organizations, rather than considering the regime as a whole.

10. The term evidently derives from von Hippel's (2001b, 2002) emphasis on the respects in which open source software exemplifies the larger phenomenon of "user-innovations."

11. See the work of von Hippel (1998) on user innovation, and the view that the use-utility of the software to FLOSS developers provided a powerful incentive for their contributions to its production. Raymond (2001, 23–24) declares that "every good work of software starts by scratching a developer's personal itch" and refers to

the well-known phrase about necessity being the mother of invention. But whether the "developers' itches" are caused only by the need for particular software, rather than intrinsic interest in programming problems, or other aspects of the development and debugging process, or the acquisition of particular skills, was left open by Raymond. He contrasts Linux developers with commercial software developers whose days are spent "grinding away for pay at programs they neither need *nor love*" [emphasis added]. For further discussion, and survey evidence regarding motivations, see Lakhani and Wolf, chap. 1 and Ghosh, chap. 2, this volume.

12. It will be seen that the probabilistic allocational rules derive from a set of distinct community norms, and it will be quite straightforward within the structure of the model to allow for heterogeneity in the responsiveness to peer influence in this respect, by providing for interindividual differences in weighting within the rule-set. This may be done either probabilistically, or by creating a variety of distinct types of agents and specifying their relative frequencies in the population from which contributions are drawn. For the purposes of the basic model presented here, we have made a bold simplification by specifying that all potential contributors respond uniformly to a common set of allocational rules.

13. See von Hippel 2001b and Franke and von Hippel 2002, on the development of "user toolkits for innovation," which are specific to a given production system and product or service type, but within those constraints, enable producers to transfer user need–related aspects of product or service design to the users themselves.

14. Although Raymond is an astute participant-observer of these FLOSS communities, and his sociological generalizations have the virtue of inherent plausibility, it should be noted that these propositions have yet to be validated by independent empirical tests. See for example Hars and Ou 2002; Hertel, Niedner, and Herrmann 2003; Lakhani et al. 2003; and the systematic survey or interviews with representative samples of OS/FS community participants done by the FLOSS survey (Ghosh et al. 2002) and its U.S. counterpart—"FLOSS-US"—at Stanford University.

15. Caution is needed when using the word "root" to designate the germinal modules, because importing that term from the arboral metaphor may be confusing for programmers: we are told by one informant that in "Unix-speak," the system administrator is called "root," and the top of the file structure, likewise, is "root." Indeed, our hypothesized "dependency tree" might also be in some extent related to the more familiar directory tree structure, but this correlation is likely to very imperfect.

16. Note that here we neglect, for the moment, the possibility that bugs can become more attractive "targets" because they've existed for long and have thus drawn the attention of the community of developers, and also more specific peer assessments of the "quality" of patches.

17. We are fully aware of the limits of modeling exercises such as this one. Clearly, it cannot not replicate the world, nor should it attempt to do so. Rather, it may clarify and give insights about the phenomena under examination. Abstracting from the complexity of the actual processes proceeds abductively—working back and forth interactively between analytical deductions informed by empirical findings, and empirical tests of theoretical propositions. Eliciting comments for participant observations in FLOSS projects, especially empirical evidence and criticisms of particular abstractions embedded in the simulation structure, is therefore a vital part of our procedure. It is both a means of improving the usefulness of the simulation experiments performed with the model, and a means of enriching the body of systematic information about processes and structural features of FLOSS organization that experts regard as being especially important. We have made several conscious simplifications in the "reduced-form" formulation presented next, which we flag in the notes, and comment upon in the conclusion. But we may also have unknowingly suppressed or distorted other relevant features, and therefore strongly encourage comments on the specifications of the model.

18. And, in later elaborations of the basic model, launching an entirely different project.

19. In the simplest formulations of the model, agents' endowments are treated as "fixed effects" and are obtained as random draws from a stationary distribution. More complex schemes envisage endogenously determined and serially correlated coding capacities, with allowance for experience-based learning effects at the agent level.

20. We allow that there may be a small number of participants who are supported, in some cases by commercial employers, to participate in open source projects on a full-time basis: indeed, recent works (Hertel, Niedner, and Herrmann 2003; Lakhani et al. 2003) have provided more detailed results in this respect, which will clearly need to be addressed in later versions of the model.

21. We consider here more or less continuous "release policies"—that is, any improvement in any given module is released as soon as it is contributed. No contribution gets rejected, and accepted contributions are not piled up waiting for a later release: this is indeed a strong assumption of this reduced-form model, as we know from Linux and other projects that many pataches get rejected and that there is always several pending patches. Furthermore, modules are released independently—there is no coordination between the release of several modules, as it is more or less the case when they are grouped into a distribution that gets released regularly, at release dates decided by whomever is in charge of maintaining it. In this first step of our modeling exercise, continuous release stands as an abstraction of Raymond's and others' "release frequently" rule.

22. To simplify the allocation problem for the purposes of modeling, we consider that a randomly drawn developer, with an associated endowment of effort, makes

a commitment to work on a particular bug exclusively until that endowment is exhausted.

23. This reward is of course actually conditioned by the fact that the project will attract subsequent developers.

24. This parameter characterizes another aspect of "release policy" norms within the community, as for the "release frequently" rule.

25. This expected cumulative reward function could also vary depending on the quality of the code; that is, of its ability to attract early developers or late debuggers, or to grant more reward to all of them.

26. This formulation treats all bugs symmetrically, regardless of where they occur in the code. This is so because the version number of a module that is close to the root is counted the same way as the version of a module that is far from the root. Yet bugs in low-level modules are likely to cause problems for users of many applications than is the case for high-level modules that are bug-ridden. This complication could readily be handled by reformulating the social utility measure.

27. In the future, we might be willing to implement a better differentiation between functionality and reliability, with the idea also that users might typically value both aspects differently from developers.

28. This is based upon a static ex post evaluation of the resulting tree form, and it is evident that the results may be altered by considering the dynamics and applying social time discount rates to applications that become available for end users only at considerably later dates. In other words, the social efficiency of the reward structure that allocates developers' efforts will depend upon the temporal distribution, as well as relative extent to which FLOSS-generated code meets the needs of final users rather than the needs/goals of the agents who choose to work on these projects.

29. This result holds for various other values of these parameters, although more complete simulations are needed to assess the range of its validity. To exclude a potential artifact, note that this result also holds if new nodes are created at the same distance from the root as their parent node (instead of their parent node's distance plus one).

30. This result holds for various other values of these parameters, although more complete simulations are needed to fully assess the range of its validity.

31. The fact that these codevelopers are users essentially guarantees that they provide solutions to existing and relevant problems: this effect is related to von Hippel's analysis of FLOSS as "user-innovation," but also to another of Raymond's observations, according to which only contributions are useful in open source development, as opposed to people showing up and proposing to "do something." Furthermore, this is close to the "given enough eyeballs, all bugs are shallow" rule, and

from one of the key reasons why open source development (Linus's Law) appears to violate Brooks's Law—although the citation we have put in front of this paper tends to prove that Fred Brooks had the intuition that software productivity could actually be improved if software was grown instead of built. Here, the "release early" and "attract user-codevelopers" rules stand as necessary conditions for this property to hold, because they make the set of existing problems explicit to all those who might be able not only to encounter them, as users, but still more importantly to solve them, as codevelopers, while be rewarded in doing so and increasing also the author of the seminal contribution's final reward.

32. What makes this an interesting strategic decision to model is the risk that while working offline, so to speak, for an extended period, and not submitting increments of code in more continuous flow, someone else might submit a discrete contribution that would have the same functional attributes, thereby preempting the investment's chance of being accepted. The perceived hazard rates for "credit losses" of that sort might be modeled as a rise as more developers gain familiarity with a given module, or others technically related to it.

33. Such policies can be treated as applying uniformly across all the modules of a project, or as defining a prespecified range of release intervals defined either in temporal terms or in terms of incremental code.

34. Indeed, there may we some developers who would be quite insensible to those motivations, even shun projects of that kind, believing that commercial software vendors would cater to those needs, and that they would serve the needs of "minority" users. Survey information may be used to reach some inferences about the distribution of such FLOSS community attitude regarding different categories of software, which in turn could be introduced as a dimension of interproject diversity.

35. The complex interplay of factors of learning and trust, and the ways that they might shape path-dependent career trajectories of members of the FLOSS developer communities, have been carefully discussed in recent work by Mateos-Garcia and Steinmueller (2003).

17 | Shared Source: The Microsoft Perspective

Jason Matusow

Within the software industry, the debate continues about the roles of open source, free, commercial, and noncommercial software. The reality is that there are far more commonalities than differences. Where differences do exist, though, it is helpful to examine their implications for businesses, individuals, academic institutions, and government organizations.

The dialogue surrounding the different approaches to software development and distribution covers a vast array of issues, including consumer flexibility, cost versus value, economic opportunity, intellectual property (IP) rights associated with software, industry standards, security, privacy, business and licensing models, and more. These broad themes are woven with source code as a common thread. On the surface, source code has always been the exclusive domain of the programmer. But underlying the engineering aspects of source code generation and modification are some fundamental questions regarding the future of software innovation. Therefore, the debate goes on.

The odd thing about source code is that many speak about it, but few are able or willing to work with it. In 2002, with the goal of establishing clarity and context, Microsoft undertook private research regarding source code access for the software being used by businesses and governments.[1] Conventional wisdom might have predicted that we would find corporate IT professionals scouring source code in their daily work. Instead, we found that approximately 95 percent of organizations do not look at the source code of the operating systems serving as the core of their technology infrastructure. In addition, we found that while approximately 5 percent do look at the source code, less than 1 percent will modify it. As one looks at increasingly smaller organizations, the practice of accessing and modifying source code further drops.

The barrier to entry for understanding complex source code is significant. Although there are millions of software developers in the world today, they still represent a small fraction of the total population of those using computers. Furthermore, there is an uneven distribution of development skills among programmers, so the community looking at highly complex code is smaller still. For most organizations, the cost and relative benefit of employing highly skilled developers is prohibitive, especially considering the abundance of quality packaged software.[2]

Even so, organizations stated that the opportunity to access operating system source code is important to them.[3] The majority of companies and governments supported the option of seeing source code. Simply put, transparency increases trust.

This suggests that to most people having the *option* of doing something is of far greater importance than actually doing it. For example, look at the idea behind government-mandated full disclosure of the financial information of publicly traded companies. Even though these statements are public, they are extremely complicated and require a thorough understanding of finance to truly gain insight into the health of a given firm. The vast majority of private investors are dependent on a relatively small community of professionals to interpret the numbers and provide guidance. The option of viewing the numbers is broadly available, and trust is therefore established through the availability of transparency. For most, though, it is an option that will never be exercised.

Transfer the private investor scenario to the typical users of today's operating systems and the situation looks much the same. Most organizations or individuals have no intention of going under the hood of their operating system to tinker with source code.[4] Organizations and average consumers depend heavily on commercial vendors to provide the expected levels of quality and support. This is where commercial software providers deliver value in the products they build and sell.[5]

Over the past few years, I have been running the Microsoft Shared Source Initiative. Through this initiative, we are making various types of Microsoft source code available to customers, governments, partners, and competitors worldwide. Some of our source code, such as that for Windows, permits reference use only (meaning that no modifications can be made), while our other programs, covering technologies such as Windows CE.NET, allow for modifications and redistribution of that source code.[6]

Through my work on Shared Source, I have had countless conversations with individuals and organizations about the role of source code in meeting their particular needs. Even though we have delivered source code to more than a million engineers, it is a tiny percentage of the total developer population working with Microsoft technologies. Our practical experience on a global scale confirms the relationship between the operational and peace-of-mind needs described earlier. Again, the factors of transparency, choice, trust, and need all play a role in our approach to the licensing of our source code.

Our approach to this issue is based on three simple ideas. First, our customers want source access both for its technical benefits, and because transparency increases trust. Second, there is no uniform way for Microsoft to provide source access that covers all business and licensing needs across all product offerings. Third, customers will be more successful with the source code if solid tools and information are provided along with the technology. Under these basic assumptions, Microsoft has been developing the Shared Source approach. Shared Source is not open source; rather, it is the means for a company that directly commercializes software to provide source code access without weakening its competitive differentiators or business model. Microsoft recognizes the benefits of the open source model, yet also understands that it is not necessarily a model that will work for everyone.

The goals of this chapter are twofold. First, to place the Shared Source Initiative and commercial software into the broader context of the ongoing source licensing debate. Second, to provide insight into how Microsoft has approached the licensing of its core intellectual property assets.

A Natural Move to the Middle

In 2000 and 2001, there appeared to be clear delineation among those involved in the source licensing debate. Microsoft was seen to be a polarizing factor as a continuum of positions was established, with the traditional intellectual property holders at one end and those opposed to software as commercial property at the other. Individuals and organizations advocating open source software deliberately positioned themselves as an alternative to Microsoft's practices or as active opponents of Microsoft. Now in 2004, as everyone deals with the aftershocks of the dot-com era, a wave of practicality has washed over businesses and individuals alike.

Open source software (OSS) itself, as a classification of software, has bifurcated into commercial and noncommercial segments. For many, the most interesting OSS work going on today falls into the fully commercial category, since significant dollars, resources, and technology are coming from those seeking to use OSS as the basis for strategic business purposes (see table 17.1).

Careful observation of the commercial software community shows a consolidation of source licensing practices by a majority of the most significant players. In today's marketplace, software development, licensing, and business strategies fall under a blend of community and commercial models. Few software companies are left that can properly call themselves either purely OSS (in the sense of OSS as a community-driven, not-for-profit exercise) or purely commercial.

For the sake of this discussion, let's draw a line of distinction between noncommercial and commercial software. The merits of both may be observed in the software ecosystem that has developed over the past 30 years, as discussed later in this chapter.

Noncommercial software may be roughly grouped into three categories:

• *Research:* Government and academic researchers who produce technologies designed to move the general state of the art forward.
• *Teaching and learning:* Professors, students, and self-educators who work with, and learn from, software that is available free of charge and have no intention of commercializing the software generated in the learning process.
• *Community development and problem solving:* Hobbyists and professional developers who produce software with no intention of commercialization; this software may be meant to replace existing commercial options or to solve problems vendors have not addressed.

Commercial software may be roughly grouped into two categories:

• *Direct commercialization:* Those who use the product of community and/or corporate development as a mechanism for generating a direct revenue stream.
• *Indirect commercialization:* Those who use the product of community and/or corporate development to facilitate the success of another product or service for the generation of revenue.

It is worth noting here that the concepts of noncommercial and commercial software have nothing to do with the availability of source code. If a long-standing commercial software vendor provides source code of a given product, this does not change the fact that the software is commercial in nature. At the same time, if a piece of software is produced and maintained as communal, noncommercial software, there is no reason a commercial entity may not make use of it without altering its standing as noncommercial software.

Table 17.1
Software development strategies

Direct commercialization	Community development	Red Hat Inc.'s distribution of Linux is a combination of community-built software through the Free and Open Source models and corporate-funded professional development contributions. The pricing of its Premium Editions, its certification practices for hardware and applications, and its support policies are all mechanisms to directly commercialize the operating system.
		Apple Computer Inc. has combined community software with commercial software to create the OS X operating system. The company is directly commercializing the software while utilizing community-developed code.
	Corporate development	Microsoft has built the Windows product using corporate development resources. The product is directly commercialized through the licensing of the binary version of the product. The source code is now available to a limited community through the Shared Source Initiative.
		CollabNet Inc. has built a proprietary tool that is directly commercialized through the licensing of the binary version of the product and through associated services. The product facilitates the use of the OSS development model, which could be used to create noncommercial software.
Indirect commercialization	Community development	IBM Corp. has heavily participated in the community-based development of the Apache Web server. While IBM is not directly commercializing the Apache server, it is driving the return on investment revenue stream through the sale of the WebSphere product. RealNetworks Inc. released significant

Table 17.1
(continued)

		segments of its Helix product source code, which was originally commercially developed. The goal of community development around the Helix product set is to generate a larger market for other revenue-generating products.
	Corporate development	Adobe Systems Inc.'s Acrobat Reader is a product of corporate development and of closely held intellectual property. Reader is downloadable at no cost to drive the sale of the full Acrobat product. (Adobe Systems Inc. does provide the file format specification for .pdf files, but they are not releasing the source code to their implementation. More information may be found at http://www.adobe.com.)
		Driver development kits (DDKs) and software development kits (SDKs) are provided by all commercial operating system vendors (examples include Novell Inc.'s NDK and Microsoft's DDK). These developer tools often contain sample source code that can be modified and redistributed, yet the kits themselves are provided at no cost to developers. There is no direct commercial value to the DDKs or SDKs themselves; rather, they create opportunity for others to build software and hardware for that platform.

Table 17.1 maps the commercial categories listed previously to examples from the software industry. Many of the companies in the table closely associate themselves with the OSS movement, yet they are clearly commercial enterprises. Some of those listed have no direct affiliation with the concepts of OSS, yet their behavior can be instructive, specifically, their approach to the distribution of software.

A common misperception about software developed under the open source model is that a random group of distributed developers is creating the software being adopted by businesses. Although this is true for some smaller projects, the reality is that professional corporate teams or highly structured not-for-profit organizations are driving the production, testing, distribution, and support of the majority of the key OSS technologies. The concepts behind source code access are not the determining factors as to whether the software is commercial. Source code access plays a role in both commercial and noncommercial environments.

Source code access issues unquestionably affect the future of innovation in the industry. The move to the middle outlined earlier is a result of the influence of these issues on the industry to date.

The Software Ecosystem

At the core of software evolution is the interaction among government, academic, and private research. These relationships represent an integrated, natural ecosystem. Though these organisms exist independently and conduct independent "development," there are clear areas of interdependency that yield dramatically greater results for the whole.

This ecosystem has been at the heart of the ongoing cycle of sustained innovation that has made information technology one of the most dynamic industries in the economy.[7] The blending of differing development, licensing, and business models has been the central factor for success.

Governments and universities undertake basic research and share this knowledge with the public.[8] In turn, companies in the private sector use some of these technologies in combination with their even greater ongoing investment in research and development[9] to create commercial products, while also contributing to the work of common standards bodies. Their success leads to greater employment and tax revenues, as well as additional funding for academic research projects.[10]

The concepts associated with the software ecosystem are not unique to discussions of source code access. Take aviation, for example. Although the vast majority of us have little everyday use for an F-15 Eagle jet fighter, government and academic research and development behind the fighter for everything from metallurgy to heads-up displays have benefited the production and operation of commercial airplanes.

For a more IT-centric example, consider TCP/IP. Born as a government research project, it matured in academia under the OSS development model and evolved into an open industry standard. After that, it was further refined and brought into the computing mainstream via proprietary implementations by commercial software companies such as Novell, Apple, IBM, and Microsoft.

Microsoft's Windows operating system, on the other hand, was developed privately and for profit. But the product includes many components born of government and academically funded work and contains implementations of dozens of open industry standards. Furthermore, the publication of thousands of application programming interfaces created business opportunities for tens of thousands of software businesses and has resulted in innumerable custom applications that address individual needs.

So where will this line of reasoning take us? If the past is any indication, the future of software will not be the result of the dominance of a single development, licensing, or business model. Future innovation will not come solely from government, private industry, or a loose coalition of individuals acting in the best interests of society at large. The continued health of the cycle of sustained innovation—the fruits of which we have enjoyed for three decades—will depend entirely on the continued melding of approaches and technologies. In the end, the consumers of software, both custom and packaged, will be the beneficiaries, particularly as natural market forces continue to shape the actions and results of corporations and individuals alike.

Striking a Balance

Given the ongoing move to the middle of software vendors and the effects of the software ecosystem, the question for Microsoft has been how to find the proper balance between greater transparency, sustainable business, and innovation investment.

OSS is clearly having an effect on how software companies think about and treat their intellectual property assets.[11] The sharing of source code, while beneficial in many ways, also presents challenges to the accepted concepts of the commercialization of software and competitive differentiation. The modus operandi for most software companies has been to closely protect IP assets in software products to maintain uniqueness and competitiveness in the market. Trade secret law, which covers many aspects of software that are obscured by the compilation process, has played a pivotal role in the IP protection strategy of most commercial software companies. Historically, this protection has been maintained through either binary-only distribution or source code distribution under nondisclosure agreements. Yet OSS and other source-sharing models are moving organizations to seek a balance between IP protection (particularly with respect to protection of trade secrets) and customer/partner benefit.

Arguably, intellectual property rights have become more important as the desirability and functionality of transparency increases. The creative use and combination of all four forms of IP protection are paving the way for further source code sharing by allowing companies to selectively ratchet back trade secret protection.[12]

This is not to say that it always makes sense for companies to provide the source code to their software products, thereby limiting or destroying their trade secrets. Commercial software companies balance perceived customer needs and desires with a host of other business concerns. For instance, many investors demand that companies protect their assets through all means possible so as to protect the future returns on investment and ensure a healthy revenue stream. Anyone who has ever gone through the process of attempting to raise capital for a software business can attest to this. In some situations, it may be that trade secrets in a software product are essential to preserving the market advantage of that product. Accordingly, a company would be unwilling to make the source code to that product available.

Most successful software businesses reinvest material amounts of their gross incomes into research and development. Microsoft is now investing approximately $5 billion annually, or approximately 15 percent of gross revenues, in our future.[13] So where does this leave us? How do you balance the obvious benefits of source code transparency and flexibility for developers against the software business reality of protection of assets and the need for healthy sources of revenue?

Each software company must decide for itself which path to take. For Microsoft, it was clear that customers, partners, and governments were eager for us to move toward transparency and flexibility. At the same time, we had to take that step with an eye to the other side of the equation as well. Through this process, we created the Shared Source Initiative.

The Shared Source Initiative

Microsoft is sharing source code with customers, partners, and governments globally. We have released source programs delivering well over 100 million lines of source code. The Shared Source Initiative evolved as we sought to both address customer and partner requests to have greater access to source code and look carefully at the benefits and potential pitfalls of the OSS and Free Software approaches. We then selectively applied lessons learned from those approaches and our existing business model to better meet customers' needs.

Shared Source is a framework, not a license.[14] Any commercial software company needs to analyze the interplay among the elements of development models, licensing, and business models to establish a successful strategy whereby source code may be shared or opened in a way that benefits customers without jeopardizing the company's ability to remain in business. Microsoft's licensing approach ranges from reference-only grants (where licensees may review Microsoft source code for the purposes of reference and debugging, but are not granted modification or redistribution rights) to broad grants that allow licensees to review, modify, redistribute, and sell works with no royalties paid to Microsoft.

There are now hundreds of thousands of developers with Microsoft source code. We have taken what is arguably the most commercially valuable intellectual property in the software industry and made it available to thousands of organizations in more than 60 countries.[15] Shared Source programs now deliver source code for Windows, Windows CE.NET, Visual Studio.NET, C#/CLI, ASP.NET, and Passport technologies. Over time, we will continue to evaluate source code as a feature of our products and also how our customers and partners may best use the source code.

One of the most common misperceptions of the Shared Source model is that it is limited to "look but don't touch" and a single license. In fact, Shared Source covers four key concepts:

• *Support existing customers:* Provide source access for existing customers to facilitate product support, deployments, security testing, and custom application development.
• *Generate new development:* Provide instructional source code through samples and core components for the facilitation of new development projects.
• *Augment teaching and research:* Provide source code and documentation for use in classrooms and textbook publishing and as a basis for advanced research.

• *Promote partner opportunity:* Provide licensing structure and source code to encourage mutually advantageous new business opportunities for partners.

At the time of the writing of this chapter, seven Microsoft product groups are providing source code with some ability to create derivative works of the source code.[16] Three of the groups are placing source code in the community's hands with rights to create derivative works and distribute them commercially, meaning that a programmer can get the code, modify it, and redistribute it under a traditional commercial binary license for profit—never paying Microsoft a dime. All the current source code programs from Microsoft are provided at no cost.[17]

Building a Shared Source Program

Microsoft has applied significant resources to establish the various Shared Source programs. Every source release depends on a series of decisions made to deliver the proper balance between customer and business benefits. We have also invested in engineering resources to deliver augmented tools and documentation that increase the value of source code access.

Table 17.2 provides a small sample of the questions and process Microsoft works through when establishing a source release. This is by no means a complete analysis tool, but rather a sample of the decision-making process for a commercial software provider considering a source-sharing program.

A well-designed source release should accomplish a few key goals:

• Provide educational insight into the product or project being shared. Value is derived for many simply through availability and analysis rather than modification of source code.
• Deliver related tools, documentation, and support to increase the value to the individual working with the source code, particularly in programs with derivative rights associated with them.
• Establish clear feedback mechanisms to facilitate the improvement of the code base.
• Identify the community that most benefits from access to the source code.
• Define a set of rights that protects the creator of the source code and those working with the source code.

Table 17.2
Shared source consideration

	Questions	Considerations
Determining objectives	What community are you planning to serve with this source code?	Not all source releases have to be global and available to the general public. Working with gated communities, large customers, key partners, or particular government agencies might be more appropriate for some situations.
	What is the benefit of this source code to these organizations and individuals?	Source code does not address all IT concerns. Understanding how the source will be beneficial is a critical factor in determining granted rights and delivery mechanisms.
	How many people will have the source code and how will you interact with them?	Broad-reach programs may have significant resource requirements for source delivery and/or community participation. This goes beyond logistical concerns such as download capacity. The amount of engineering participation, feedback processing, and continued investment, among other elements, must be considered.
	What geographies will be eligible for source access?	Aside from the more obvious concerns about the localization of documentation, there are significant legal differences to be considered from country to country. The treatment of IP issues varies greatly and you should seek legal counsel on this issue. (This concern is universal for any source model—OSS, Shared Source, or otherwise. For example, many of the most popular OSS licenses are based on assumptions of the U.S. copyright system. Because code is used globally, the legal standards applied to licenses vary greatly.)

Table 17.2
(continued)

	Questions	Considerations
Source management	What source are you planning to share?	Just as the community you plan to share source code with is not necessarily 100 percent of the population, the source code you share does not have to represent 100 percent of a product. Certain components of a product are extremely valuable, are licensed to you by a third party under terms that prohibit disclosure of source code, or are subject to government export restrictions.
	Do you have rights to share the targeted source base?	Commercial software often contains components that originated elsewhere and are being reused or licensed within a larger product. The greater the number of copyright holders there are for a given piece of software, the greater the complexity involved in source-sharing of commercial products.
	Have you cleaned the code for public consumption and thought about the quality of comments?	Within source code, developers place comments to provide insight into their thought processes. There can be significant value in augmenting comments within particularly complex code segments. Unfortunately, there is often colorful language in source code, and public consumption should be taken into account.
	Do you have a source management strategy in place for bug fixes and future releases related to the public source program?	Most successful software engineering projects have mature source management processes in place. If you are taking a previously nonshared code base and moving it out to a broader set of developers, you need to establish a process for delivering

Table 17.2
(continued)

	Questions	Considerations
		ongoing inhouse engineering work to the community that now has the source code.
	How will you handle incoming suggestions or code fixes?	Along the same lines as new inhouse code delivery, you need to establish a process for receiving suggestions, bug fixes, and new features from the community that has access to the code. You might also want to consider the legal ramifications and risks associated with incorporating incoming suggestions or code fixes into your code base.
Licensing	What rights do you plan to give for viewing, debugging, modifying, and distributing?	Although the input of attorneys is important in establishing licensing rights for source code, the far more important voice is that of your customers and partners. The driving factor must be how they will benefit most from the source code. Fiduciary responsibility to investors regarding the protection of IP is critical as well, but that thinking should be applied secondarily. A successful source license program establishes a balance between these factors to the benefit of all involved.
	If you grant derivative rights, can the redistribution be commercial?	Microsoft has opted to implement two types of derivative work license approaches to differentiate business goals within our source licensing programs. The commercialization of derivative works is a key focal point for commercial software vendors releasing source code.

Table 17.2
(continued)

	Questions	Considerations
Fulfillment	What is the delivery mechanism for the source code? Will it simply be a package of source code or will there be added value through a delivery tool?	There is a wide range of source delivery options. The OSS community has a number of sites such as VA Software Corp.'s SourceForge for the delivery of source code and the management of projects. You may choose to host your own environment, as Microsoft has done with its GotDotNet WorkSpaces project. Microsoft also built a secure Web infrastructure for the delivery of Windows source code: MSDN Code Center Premium. Other groups within Microsoft have opted for simple Web downloads of source files, leaving the choice of toolset and engineering environment up to the individual developer. Determining the size of the community to be involved and the amount of source code included in the release is an important factor in choosing a delivery mechanism.
	How will you engage the community of individuals and organizations who have the source code?	Although a community of developers may spontaneously form around a given source base, successful programs will likely include involvement from the engineers who built the code. Furthermore, strong project management helps keep community involvement productive.
	Have you produced additional support documentation for the source base?	The creation of good software documentation has proven to be one of the most expensive and difficult problems in the industry. The more information provided to developers working with a given source base, the better. Although this is not mandatory, it will certainly improve the quality of the source-sharing program as a whole.

Lessons Learned and a Look Ahead

The most fundamental lesson we have learned through the Shared Source process is that source code is a product feature. For many, it is a feature that will never be used, but an option that is good to have. Our customers and partners who have source code, and who are actively using it, tell us that it is invaluable to the way they use our products. Yet this number represents a minute fraction of the total number of individuals and organizations using our products.

Microsoft's Shared Source Initiative is only two years old, but we have been providing source code to academic institutions and OEMs for more than 12 years. Before 2001, our source sharing reached a limited audience and was less formal than it is today. We have been listening to our customers and are learning from OSS—that is the blend to which we aspire with this initiative. In many ways, Shared Source is still in its version 1.0 phase. The success of the programs to date has shown us the importance of expanding this initiative into other code bases.

Licensing of source code will continue to be a hot button for the industry for the foreseeable future. There are some basic questions about the role of IP in future innovation. At the heart of Shared Source is a belief that intellectual property, and the protection of that property, is behind the fundamental success of an ongoing cycle of sustained innovation. The dissemination of source code is exceedingly beneficial, but not to the exclusion of a successful software industry. Nor is it the panacea for all information technology concerns; multiple models will continue to coexist. It is one part of a much larger puzzle, and I for one am glad to be sitting at the table working on a few small pieces.

Notes

1. This private research involved more than 1,100 individuals in five countries representing business decision makers, IT professionals, and developers. The study was completed in April 2003.

2. This premise is based on an extremely simplified view of Ronald Coase's concept of transaction costs and how they influence organizational behavior. Coase was awarded the Nobel Prize in Economic Sciences in 1991 for his work regarding the significance of transaction costs and property rights for the institutional structure and functioning of the economy (http://coase.org, accessed May 20, 2003).

3. The same research in note 1 revealed that approximately 60 percent of respondents felt that having the option to view source code was critical to running software in a business setting.

4. This is equally true for Windows, Linux, Mac OS, Netware, OS/400, and other major commercial operating systems. The smallest of these represents millions of lines of source code (an operating system is more than just a kernel), and as they mature, complexity increases rather than decreases.

5. Clearly, the capability of community support cannot be underestimated. For years, there have been newsgroups and mailing lists where the community has provided support for commercial, open, free, and shareware software. When organizations are dealing with their mission-critical systems, however, they primarily seek professional support with service-level agreements to mitigate risk.

6. As of May 2003, Microsoft has programs in place for Windows, Windows CE.NET, Visual Studio.NET, C#/CLI, ASP.NET, and Passport. Under the Windows programs, only academic researchers are given rights to modify the source code. For all other source programs, modification and redistribution rights are granted. Please see http://www.microsoft.com/sharedsource/ for further details.

7. In the latter half of the 1990s alone, information-related industries, representing 8.3 percent of the U.S. economy, fueled approximately 30 percent of overall economic growth and at least half the acceleration in productivity rates (U.S. Department of Commerce, U.S. Government Working Group on Electronic Commerce, "Leadership for the New Millennium: Delivering on Digital Progress and Prosperity," Jan. 16, 2001).

8. In fact, U.S. federal agencies are required by law to encourage certain grant recipients and public contractors to patent the results of government-sponsored research, and universities are active in asserting research-related intellectual property rights. Since at least 1980, the U.S. government has pursued a vigorous policy of transferring the results of federally funded technology research to industry to promote innovation and commercialization. See the Bayh-Dole Act of 1980, the Stevenson-Wydler Technology Innovation Act of 1980, the Federal Technology Transfer Act of 1986, Executive Order 12591 of 1987, the National Technology Transfer and Advancement Act of 1995, and the Technology Transfer Commercialization Act of 2000.

9. From 1969 through 1994, U.S. high-tech R&D investment was $77.6 billion from the government and $262 billion from private industry (the National Science Foundation's Industrial Research and Development Information System (IRIS); accessed Oct. 11, 2002, at http://www.nsf.gov/sbe/srs/iris/start.htm.)

10. A good example of this is Google, Inc. Google was federally funded as one of 15 Stanford University Digital Libraries Initiative Phase 1 Projects. In 1996, the technology was disclosed to Stanford's Office of Technology Licensing (OTL). In 1998,

the OTL gave permission to Sergey Brin and Larry Page to establish a commercial entity based on the technology. Today, Google, Inc. is a successful firm generating revenue for both the company and Stanford University.

11. Within the source licensing industry debate, there are some who argue about the use of the term *intellectual property*. The use of it here covers the holistic concept of copyright, patent, trade secret, and trademark.

12. Recent cases involving both SuSE Linux and Red Hat have highlighted the importance of trademark in the open source business model.

13. It is not uncommon for software firms to reinvest between 15 and 30 percent of gross revenues in R&D.

14. http://www.opensource.org, visited Sept 8, 2004. There are 54 licenses that the Open Source Initiative has stated meet its criteria for being an "open source" license. As commercialization of OSS continues to expand, and as commercial software companies continue to push the limits of source sharing, there is likely to be a continued proliferation of source licenses as each organization and individual determines what terms it is most comfortable with for the distribution of its IP.

15. At this time, there is no comparable sharing of source code for flagship products in the software industry. Although many vendors provide top customers with sources upon request, few have put broad-reach programs in place. It is likely that this status will change over time as the positive effects of OSS, Shared Source, and other source delivery programs continue to be recognized.

16. The Windows Academic Shared Source and OEM licenses allow researchers to create temporary modifications of the Windows source code for research and testing purposes. All other constituency groups with Windows source access (enterprise customers, system integrators, and government agencies) have reference-only rights—meaning that they may view and debug, but may not create derivative works of the source code.

17. Due to the delay between writing and publishing of this document, specific details of the programs have been left out. If you would like further information on source availability from Microsoft, please visit http://www.microsoft.com/sharedsource/.

V   Law, Community, and Society

18 | Open Code and Open Societies

Lawrence Lessig

It has been more than a decade since the wall fell; more than a decade since the closed society was declared dead; more than a decade since the ideals of the open society were said to have prevailed; more than a decade since the struggle between open and closed was all but at an end.

We stand here in an odd relationship to those who saw that closed society pass. For we celebrate its passing, while a more pervasive closed culture grows up around us. We are confident in our victory, and yet our victory is being undone. If there was an open society, if we have known it, then that open society is dying. In the most significant sense that idea could embrace, it is passing away.

In the United States, we believe we understand the passing of the closed society. We believe we understand its source—that society collapsed because it was weak; it was weak because its economy was dead; its economy was dead because it had no free market, no strong system of property, no support for the exchange and freedom that a property based free market might produce.

We believe we understand property equals progress; and more property equals more progress; and more perfectly protected property equals more perfectly protected progress.

Now in this view, we are not terribly naive. Property historically has been a key to progress; it has been an important check on arbitrary state power; it has been a balance to concentrations of power that otherwise pervert. Property is no doubt central and important to a free society and free culture. And so to question property, to question my countrymen, is not to doubt its importance.

It is instead to put its importance in context. To let us see something about what the progress that property produces depend upon. To let us understand the mix of resources that produce progress. And to force us to account for that mix.

Now I know you are beginning to wonder: what exactly does this have to do with open source, or free software? How does this topic contribute to the discussion of this book?

But I confess to no such mistakes. I insist that we begin here, because it is extremely important to place the issues of open source, and free software, in their full context. It is important, in other words, to understand their significance—for their significance is much more than most allow.

Most think about these issues of free software, or open source software, as if they were simply questions about the efficiency of coding. Most think about them as if the only issue that this code might raise is whether it is faster, or more robust, or more reliable than closed code. Most think that this is simply a question of efficiency.

Most think this, and most are wrong. The issues of open source or free software are not simply the issues of efficiency. If that were all this issue was about, there would be little reason for anyone to pay any more attention to this subject than to the question of whether an upgrade to Office really is faster than the version it replaced.

I think the issues of open source and free software are fundamental in a free society. I think they are at the core of what we mean by an open society. But to see their relation to this core, we must see the context.

Pierre de Fermat was a lawyer, and an amateur mathematician. He published one paper in his life—an anonymous article written as an appendix to a colleague's book. But while he published little, he thought lots about the open questions of mathematics of his time. And in 1630, in the margin of his father's copy of Diophantus's *Arithmetica*, he scribbled next to an obscure theorem (namely, $Xn + Yn = Zn$ has no non-zero integer solutions for $N > 2$) "I have discovered a truly remarkable proof which this margin is too small to contain."

It's not clear that Fermat had a proof at all. Indeed, in all his mathematical papers, there was but one formal proof. But whether a genius mathematician or not, Fermat was clearly a genius self-promoter, for it is this puzzle that has made Fermat famous. For close to 400 hundred years, the very best mathematicians in the world have tried to pen the proof that Fermat forgot.

In the early 1990s, after puzzling on and off about the problem since he was a child, Andrew Wiles believed that he had solved Fermat's last theorem. He published his results—on the Internet, as well as other places—but very soon afterwards, a glitch was discovered. The proof was flawed. So he withdrew his claim to have solved Fermat's theorem.

But he could not withdraw the proof. It was out there, in the ether of an Internet, and could not be erased. It was in the hands of many people, some of whom continued to work on the proof, even though flawed. And after extensive and engaged exchange on the net, the glitch was undone. The problem in Wiles's proof was fixed. Fermat's last theorem was solved.

Where was Wiles's flawed proof before it was solved?

Probably no reader of this chapter is homeless; we all have a place where we sleep that is not the street. That place may be a house; it may be an apartment; it may be a dorm; it may be with friends. But that place, and the stuff in it, is probably property—the property of someone, giving that someone the right to exclude.

But what about the road leading up to that place? What about the highway leading to that road? To whom does that belong? Who has the right to exclude others from the roads? Or from the sidewalks? Or from the parks? Whose property is the sidewalks or the parks?

There is a concept called *copyright*. It is a species of something called *intellectual property*. This term, intellectual property, is a recent creation. Before the late nineteenth century in America, the concept did not exist. Before then, copyright was a kind of monopoly. It was a state-granted right to control how someone used a particular form of text. But by the late nineteenth century, so familiar was this monopoly that it was common, and unremarkable, to call it property.

In the Anglo-American tradition, the origin of this concept of copyright was contested. At its birth, there were those who said that an author's copyright was his property. His right, perpetually, to control the duplication and use of what he had produced. And there were others who were wildly opposed to such an idea—who believed any control the author had was simply the bad consequences of a state-imposed monopoly.

But in the classic style of the English, and in the early style of the Americans, a compromise was chosen. A copyright was a monopoly granted to an author for a limited time, after which, the copyrighted material fell into the public domain. As the American Supreme Court Justice Joseph Story put it, copyright on this conception "is beneficial . . . to authors and inventors, . . . [and beneficial] to the public, as it will promote the progress of science and the useful arts, and admit the people at large, *after a short interval*, to the full possession and enjoyment of all writings and inventions without restraint" (emphasis added).

It is hard to imagine how significant the early decision was to make copyright a limited right in England. The House of Lords finally decided that copyright was limited by the Statute of Anne in the 1770s. Until that time, publishers claimed a perpetual copyright. But when the right passed to the public, an extraordinary amount of work fell into the public domain. The works of Shakespeare, for example, for the first time were free of the control of monopolistic publishers.

So, where is a copyright-protected work once it falls out of copyright protection? What is the place where it sits? What exactly is a copy of Romeo and Juliet after the copyright passes?

Andrew Wiles's flawed proof; the streets, or sidewalks, or parks; *Romeo and Juliet* after the copyright passes: all of these things exist in a place modern political culture has forgotten. All of these things exist in the commons—in a public domain, from which anyone can draw. Anyone can draw from the commons—and here is the crucial idea—without the permission of anyone else. These resources exist in a place where anyone in society is free to draw upon them, where anyone can take and use without the permission of anyone else.

Now of course, strictly speaking, stuff in the commons is not necessarily free. The streets can be closed; or you might be required to get a permit to hold a protest before city hall. The parks might ban people in the evening. Public beaches get full.

But the critical feature of a resource in the commons is not that the resource is free, as Richard Stallman describes it, in the sense of free beer. There may well be restrictions on access to a resource in the commons. But whatever restrictions there are, these restrictions are, as we lawyers say, content-neutral. A park might be closed in the evening, but it is not closed to liberals and open to conservatives. The restrictions that are imposed on a resource in the commons are restrictions that are neutral and general.

Thus, the first idea to see is how important the commons is—not against property, but with property. How important the commons is to the production and creation of other property. How important it is to the flourishing of other property. The point in emphasizing the importance of a commons is not to deny the significance of property. It is instead to show how property depends upon a rich commons. How creativity depends upon a rich commons. How one feeds on the other. The issue is therefore never *whether* property or a commons, but *how* the two might mix.

We need the streets to move goods to market: the streets, a commons; goods, private property. We need a marketplace within which to sell our goods: a market place, a commons; goods, private property.

Now among commons, among public domains, we might distinguish two categories. We might think about the public domain of real things, and the public domain of intellectual things. The public domain, for example, of streets and parks, and the public domain of ideas, or created works. These commons serve similar functions, but they are importantly different. They are different because while the use of a real thing—like a park, or a road—consumes a park or a road, the use of an idea restricts nothing. If I sing a song that you have written, then you still have as much of the song as you had before. My using your song does not diminish your possession of it.

The realm of ideas, then, in the words of economists, is not rivalrous in the way that the realm of real things is. This difference is crucial in the digital age. But it is a point that has been understood since the beginning of my country. America's greatest philosopher of freedom, Thomas Jefferson, understood it. And the following is perhaps the most powerful passage from his writing that in my view defines the dilemma of our age:

If nature has made any one thing less susceptible than all others of exclusive property, it is the action of the thinking power called an idea, which an individual may exclusively possess as long as he keeps it to himself; but the moment it is divulged, it forces itself into the possession of everyone, and the receiver cannot dispossess himself of it. Its peculiar character, too, is that no one possesses the less, because every other possess the whole of it. He who receives an idea from me, receives instruction himself without lessening mine; as he who lites his taper at mine, receives light without darkening me. That ideas should freely spread from one to another over the globe, for the moral and mutual instruction of man, and improvement of his condition, seems to have been peculiarly and benevolently designed by nature, when she made them, like fire, expansible over all space, without lessening their density at any point, and like the air in which we breathe, move, and have our physical being, incapable of confinement, or exclusive appropriation. Inventions then cannot, in nature, be a subject of property. (Letter form Thomas Jefferson to Isaac McPherson [13 August 1813] in *The Writings of Thomas Jefferson*, vol. 6, Andrew A. Lipscomb and Albert Ellery Bergh, eds., 1903, 330, 333–334.)

Notice the crucial steps in Jefferson's story: "Its peculiar character . . . is that no one possess the less because every other possess the whole. . . . He who receives an idea from me receives instruction himself without lessening mine; as he who lites his taper at mine receives light without darkening me."

Ideas function differently. Their nature, in Jefferson's words, is different. It is in their nature to be inexhaustible; uncontrollable; necessarily free. Nature has made it so; and we can enjoy, as we enjoy the beauty of sunset, this extraordinary value that nature has given us.

Jefferson was brilliant; but arguably Jefferson was wrong. He identified a crucial fact about ideas and things intellectual; he defended the world that ideal created; he promoted it—the ideal of the Enlightenment. But he was wrong to believe that Nature would protect it. He was wrong to believe that Nature would conspire always to keep ideas free. He was wrong to believe that he knew enough about what Nature could do to understand what Nature would always defend.

For the critical fact about the world we know—cyberspace—is that cyberspace changes Jefferson's Nature. What Jefferson thought couldn't be captured, can in cyberspace be captured. What Jefferson thought could not in nature be controlled, can in cyberspace be controlled. What Jefferson thought essentially and perpetually free is free only if we choose to leave it open; free only if we code the space to keep it free; free only if we make it so. What Jefferson thought Nature guaranteed, turns out to be a good idea that we must defend.

How is this control made possible? When cyberspace was born, a gaggle of well-paid Chicken Littles raced about the legislatures of major world democracies and said copyright would be killed by cyberspace; intellectual property was dead in cyberspace, and, they squawked, Congress must do something in response. Chicken Littles—people convinced the sky was falling, well-paid Chicken Littles—paid by Hollywood.

At the same time these Chicken Littles were racing about Congresses and Parliaments, they were also racing about the West Coast in America, signing up coders—software and hardware producers—to help them build something called *trusted systems* to better protect their content. Trusted systems—code meant to counter a feature of the then-dominant code of cyberspace, that content could be copied for free and perfectly; that it could distributed for free and without limit; that content might for once be outside of the control of Hollywood.

These features of the original Net Hollywood considered to be bugs. And so they scampered about trying to find coders who could build a system that would make content safe on the Net—which means to make it safe to distribute without losing control.

These Chicken Littles then were smart—they turned to code from both coasts in America. From the East Coast, they got good East Coast code—laws that radically increased the protection content received; from the West Coast, they got great West Coast code—software and hardware that would make it possible to encrypt and protect content. And these two projects find their ultimate genius in a statute passed by Congress in 1998—the Digital Millennium Copyright Act, with its anticircumvention provision.

I've made something of a career telling the world that code is law. That rules built into software and hardware functions as a kind of law. That we should understand code as kind of law, because code can restrict or enable freedoms in just the way law should. And that if we are really concerned about liberty first, then we should protect liberty regardless of the threats.

I meant that originally as a metaphor. Code is not literally law; code, I argued, was like law. But in the anticircumvention provision of the DMCA, Congress has turned my metaphor into reality. For what the anticircumvention provision says is that building software tools to circumvent code that is designed to protect content is a felony. If you build code to crack code, then you have violated the U.S. code. Even if the purpose for which you are cracking this code is a completely legitimate use of the underlying content. Even if it would be considered fair use, that doesn't matter. Cracking code is breaking the law. Code is law.

Let's take an example. DVD movies are protected by a very poor encryption algorithm called CSS. To play a DVD movie on a computer requires unlocking CSS. Programs for unlocking CSS were licensed to manufacturers of Mac and Windows machines. Owners of those machines could therefore buy DVD movies, and play those movies on their computers.

People running the GNU/Linux operating system could not. There was no code to enable CSS to be unlocked under the GNU/Linux operating system. The owners of CSS had not licensed it to Linux. So a group of GNU/Linux programmers cracked CSS, and built a routine, deCSS, that would enable DVD movies to be played on GNU/Linux systems.

Under the anticircumvention provision of the DMCA, that was a crime. They had built code that cracked a technological protection measure; building such code violated the law; even though the only behavior enabled by this code—made more simple by this code than it was before this code—was the playing of a presumptively legally purchased DVD. No pirating was enabled; no illegal copying was made any easier; simply enabling the playing of this movie on a different machine—that's all deCSS did; but cracking CSS to enable that legitimate use was a crime.

Now notice what this event represents. Content providers build code that gives them more control than the law of copyright does over their content. Any effect to disable that control is a crime. Thus the law backs up the contents holders' power to control their content more firmly than copyright does. Copyright law gets privatized in code; the law backs this privatized law up; and the result is a radical increase in the control that the content holder has over his content.

Control: for this is the essence of the power that code creates here. The power to control the use of content. The power to control how it is played, where, on what machines, by whom, how often, with what advertising, etc. The power to control all this is given to the content holders by the code that West Coast coders build; and that power gets ratified by the product of East Coast coders—law.

Now this radical increase in control gets justified in the United States under the label of "property"; under the label of protecting property against theft. The idea has emerged that any use of copyrighted material contrary to the will of content controller is now theft; that perfect property is the ideal of intellectual property; that perfect control is its objective.

But that was not Jefferson's conception; that was not the conception of the early founders of the balanced package of intellectual property and an intellectual commons. That was never the idea originally. For the idea about control over content has always been that we give content providers enough control to give them the incentive to produce; but what they produce then falls into the public domain. We given an incentive to produce new work, but that new work then becomes part of an intellectual commons, for others to draw upon and use as they wish—without the permission of anyone else—free of the control of an another.

Hollywood has corrupted this vision. It has replaced it with a vision of perfect control. And it has enforced that vision of perfect control on the Net, and on laws that regulate the Net. And it is slowly turning the Net into its space of control.

Consider an example: You all know the meme about the free nature of the Internet; about how ideas flow freely, about the Net as Jefferson's dream. That was its past. Consider a picture of its future.

iCraveTV was an Internet broadcaster in Canada. Under Canadian law, they were permitted to capture the broadcasts from Canadian television, and rebroadcast that in any medium they wanted. iCraveTV decided to rebroadcast that TV across the Internet.

Now free TV is not allowed in the United States. Under U.S. law, the rebroadcaster must negotiate with the original broadcaster. So iCraveTV used technologies to block Americans from getting access to iCraveTV. Canadians were to get access to free TV; Americans were not.

But it is in the nature of the existing architecture of the Net that it is hard perfectly to control who gets access to what. So there were a number of Americans who were able to get access to iCraveTV, despite the company's efforts to block foreigners.

Hollywood didn't like this much. So as quickly as you could say "cut," it had filed a lawsuit in a Pittsburgh federal court, asking that court to shut down the Canadian site. The argument was this: whether or not free TV is legal in Canada, it is not legal in the United States. And so since some in the United States might, God forbid, get access to free TV, the United States Court should shut down free TV. Copyright laws in the United States were being violated; massive and quick response by the federal courts was called for.

Now step back for a moment and think about the equivalent claim being made elsewhere. Imagine, for example, a German court entering a judgment against Amazon.com, ordering Amazon.com to stop selling *Mein Kampf* anywhere because someone in Germany had succeeded in accessing *Mein Kampf* from Amazon. Or imagine a court in China ordering an American ISP to shut down its dissidents' site, because the speech at issue was illegal in China. It would take just a second for an American to say that those suits violate the concept of free speech on the Net; that they undermine the free flow of information; that they are an improper extension of state power into the world of cyberspace.

But free speech didn't register in this Pittsburgh court. The idea of the rights of Canadians to their free TV didn't matter. The court ordered the site shut down, until the site could prove that it could keep non-Canadians out.

The pattern here should be clear. Though nations like the United States will sing about the importance of free speech in cyberspace, and about keeping cyberspace free, when it comes to issues of national security—as all things copyright are—values fall away. The push will be to zone the space, to allow rules to be imposed that are local. And the technologies for zoning and controlling will quickly develop. Technologies of control, justified under the ideal of property, backed up by law. Technologies of perfect control, justified under the ideal of property backed up by law.

This is our future. It is the story of how an open space gets closed. It is the structure under which the closed society reemerges. Where the few control access for the many; where the few control content. Where to use, or play, or criticize, or share content you need the permission of someone else. Where the commons has been shrunk to nothing. Where everything to which you have access, you have access because you have asked permission of someone else.

Now software is a kind of content. Like stories, or plays, or poems, or film, it is content that others use, and others build upon. It is content that defines the nature of life in cyberspace. It is code that determines how free speech is there; how much privacy is protected; how fully access is guaranteed. Code legislates all this; code builds this control into its content.

This content, like any content, can exist in the commons, or it can exist privately, as property. It can exist in a form that guarantees that anyone can take and use the resource; or can exist in a form that makes it impossible for others to take and use this resource.

Open source or free software is software that lives in a commons. It is a resource that others can take, and use, without the permission of someone else; that, like the works of Shakespeare, is there for anyone to use as they wish without the permission of an owner—take, and use, and build upon to make something better, or better fitted to the particular needs of a particular context.

Two things make open code open. First, architecturally, it is open, in the sense that its source code is available for anyone to take. And second, law makes it open. In its core sense, open code is required to be kept open; closing it, or taking it out of the public hands is a violation of the terms on which it was acquired.

Closed code is different. Closed code—Microsoft's applications—this code does not exist in the commons. It is private property. One gets access only as another permits; one is permitted only as another allows.

Here again, *closed* is defined along two dimensions. First, architecturally —the source is not available; second, legally—one is not permitted to crack and steal the code.

These differences are significant, both for the life of code coded open or closed. But also for the life of life within the open or closed code. If code is law, if it functions as law, if it regulates and controls as law, then a critical difference between open and closed code is the difference of public or secret law. Who knows the control built into a closed system; who knows the data that is collected; who know how technology regulates or interferes; who knows what freedom are preserved?

But open code makes these questions transparent. We know the regulations, because the regulator is open. We know the protections, because coders can see how it works. We know its security, because we can watch how it protects. We know its trustworthiness, because we can see with whom it talks.

We know all this because this regulation is transparent. Like the requirement of public laws, it assures that the public knows how it is being regulated. Knows, so it can resist; or knows, so it can change.

I've built an architecture in this chapter that has left room for the place of open and closed code. I have tried to get you to see how our tradition supports balance—a symbiotic balance between property and a commons, and especially between intellectual property and an intellectual property; I've tried to describe how all current trends are counter to this balance; that the push now is to maximize control in the hands of content controlled; perfect control, perpetually assured; and I've tried to suggest that software—code—is content, just as music or Shakespeare is. And that it too needs to live in this balance between open and closed.

Our challenge—those of us who see this importance in balance, and see the importance in maintaining balance—is to resist this closing of the Internet's mind—to resist this power and control built into content. Our challenge is to find ways to get people to see the value in the commons as well as in property.

And open code is the only strong idealism that will get people to see. Open code is the only place where these ideals live. It is the only place where we can prove that balance and the commons does something good—for innovation, for creativity for growth.

Because here is the central blind spot of my culture, and my country. While we parade around in our certainty that perfect property is perfect progress—while we insist the East died because it didn't protect property, right in our midst is a phenomenon that is inconsistent with this story— the Internet. A space built on a commons, where because most early code governing the Net was open code, and where because of the architectural principle of end-to-end, the network owner could not control how the Net would be used—the resource of the Net was left open for innovation; all could draw upon its riches; no one could close another out.

Upon this architecture of openness; upon this ecology where practically all was within a commons, the greatest innovation and growth we have seen was built.

People will see the importance of the commons when we speak about code. They will see it as we speak about content as code. When we describe the innovation that gets built on top of open systems like GNU/Linux; when we point to the past which has proven the value.

But this open content as code will be resisted by those who would close content: resisted by Hollywood. And the battles that we are just beginning are battles about whether and how content is kept free. For the model for content that captures Hollywood's eye is a model of a closed system, of closed content, of maximal control.

An open society must resist this extreme. It must resist a world where to use and build upon resources from our culture you need the permission of Hollywood—of someone else.

History has a way of finding irony. It seems to revel in its irony. So, here is the irony of our time. The ideal that seemed so central to killing the closed society of yesterday—property—that ideal is now closing the open society of today. The same tool of freedom of yesterday is becoming a tool of control today. Not the same control, or the same control to as evil an end. But, nonetheless, a control on creativity and innovation; a shifting of that control from individuals to corporations; from anyone to the few.

Only the ideals of the open source and free software movement can resist this change. Only the values expressed here can show something different. Oddly only we—as universities—resist the temptations of large revenues from patents, as science gets corralled by the restrictions of patents, as culture continues to be captured by property that locks it up.

Only this movement will resist this closing. But to resist it, we must speak beyond the efficiencies of software, or beyond the significance of those efficiencies. To resist it, we must show how its values, the values of this movement, are the values of free society generally.

Note

The contents of this chapter were presented by Lawrence Lessig (at the time, the Jack N. and Lillian R. Berkman Professor for Entrepreneurial Legal Studies, Harvard Law School) as a keynote address for "Free Software—a Model for Society?" on June 1, 2000, in Tutzing, Germany.

19 | Legal Aspects of Free and Open Source Software

David McGowan

This chapter is about how the law affects free and open source software (F/OSS) development. It discusses the basic principles of copyright and contract law relevant to F/OSS development, and the way these legal principles constitute an environment that sustains the social practices of the F/OSS communities. It also discusses open legal questions and challenges they may present for the future.

Section I in this chapter discusses the structure of F/OSS licenses—how they are designed to work. Section II discusses some issues and questions regarding this design—whether the licenses actually will work this way if tested. If you are already familiar with copyright and licensing law, you might want to skip Section I and go straight to Section II. Section III discusses two criticisms an influential private firm has leveled at the GNU General Public License (GPL).

Section I

Whether a program qualifies as F/OSS is in one sense a legal question. When developers write code and fix it in a tangible medium, copyright law gives them the exclusive right to reproduce the code, distribute it, and make works derived from their original work. Subject to some important exceptions such as fair use, persons who would like to do these things with code need the author's permission.[1]

Authors grant such permission through licenses. The terms "free" software or "open source" software refer to software distributed under licenses with particular sorts of terms. A common reference guide to such licenses is the "Open Source Definition," which was originally written by Bruce Perens and is now maintained by the Open Source Initiative. It sets out several conditions a license must satisfy if code subject to the license is to qualify as "open source software."[2]

Some aspects of this definition pertain to distribution of code. Programs distributed under a F/OSS license "must include source code, and must allow distribution in source code as well as compiled form." (Posting the source code on the Internet satisfies this requirement.) Such a license "shall not restrict any party from selling or giving away the software as a component of an aggregate software distribution containing programs from several different sources," nor may the license "require a royalty or other fee for such sale." An F/OSS license "must allow modifications and derived works, and must allow them to be distributed under the same terms as the license of the original software."[3]

Much of the attention given to F/OSS development focuses on the GPL's requirement that authors who copy and distribute programs based on GPL'd code (derivative works) must distribute those programs under the GPL. This requirement is specified in Section 2(b) of the GPL, which is the *copyleft* term. I will discuss that term in a moment. In the terminology of the Free Software Foundation (FSF), licenses that require derivative works to be Free Software are copyleft licenses. Source-code licenses that allow free copying but do not contain such a requirement are "Free Software" licenses but not copyleft licenses.

The Open Source Definition has some more detailed requirements as well. F/OSS licenses may not discriminate among persons, groups, or fields of endeavor. Other requirements ensure that programmers get credit (or blame) for their work. For example, while a license must allow users to modify the code and make derivative works, it may require them to distribute modified source code in two parts: the original code as written by the licensor and, under a separate name or version number, the licensee's modifications. The definition also states that F/OSS license terms must not extend to other software that is merely distributed alongside code subject to the license. This provision does not pertain to programs that interact with F/OSS code when executed, rather than merely being distributed with them.[4]

Several well-known licenses satisfy the Open Source Definition. I will start with the most famous, the GNU GPL. The GPL sets out a two-pronged strategy designed to enforce the norms of F/OSS development. The first is to have the original author retain the copyright in the author's code or assign it to an entity, such as the FSF, that will enforce these norms. The second is to allow developers to copy, modify, and redistribute the code only as long as they agree to comply with the GPL's terms, which embody at least some of the norms of the F/OSS communities. If a licensee violates the terms, the authors or their assignees may enforce the norms through a copyright infringement action. Courts routinely enjoin the unlicensed use of copyrighted works, so the threat of an infringement action is a powerful enforcement tool.[5]

The GPL helps developers establish and maintain social practices and understandings that perform a nifty bit of legal jujitsu.[6] The GPL employs copyright to suspend the usual operation of copyright within the domain of F/OSS development. This effect of the GPL gets most of the press, and rightly so. Even from a purely legal point of view, in its brevity, its clarity, and its creative use of rights, the GPL is an elegant piece of work. Better still, its elegance does not detract from its effectiveness. The GPL is a working document, too. Here's how it is designed to work.

The GPL defines two important terms: "the Program" means a work subject to the license, and "work based on the Program" refers either to the program "or any derivative work under copyright law: that is to say, a work containing the Program or a portion of it either verbatim or with modifications and/or translated into another language." The basic license term provides that licensees "may copy and distribute verbatim copies of the Program's source code as you receive it . . . provided that you conspicuously and appropriately publish on each copy an appropriate copyright notice and disclaimer of warranty; keep intact all the notices that refer to this License and to the absence of any warranty, and give any other recipients of the Program a copy of this License along with the Program."[7]

Licensees may "modify [their] copy or copies of the Program or any portion of it, thus forming a work based on the Program, and copy and distribute such modifications or work" so long as, among other things, they "cause any work that [they] distribute or publish . . . to be licensed as a whole at no charge to all third parties under the terms of this License."[8] The license also states that these terms apply to "the modified work as a whole" but not to "identifiable sections of that work [that] are not derived from the Program, and can be reasonably considered independent and separate works in themselves" when such independent works are distributed on their own. When independent works are distributed "as part of a whole which is a work based on the Program," though, they are subject to the license as it applies to the whole.[9] Under this model, "each time you redistribute the Program (or any work based on the Program), the recipient automatically receives a license from the original licensor to copy, distribute or modify the Program subject to these terms and conditions."

The GPL further provides that a licensee "may not copy, modify, sublicense, or distribute the Program except as expressly provided under" the GPL. "Any attempt otherwise to copy, modify, sublicense or distribute the

Program is void, and will automatically terminate your rights under this License." In that event, however, "parties who have received copies, or rights, from you under this License will not have their licenses terminated so long as such parties" comply with the GPL's terms.[10] As to how the license binds users in the first place, the GPL says that "by modifying or distributing the Program (or any work based on the Program), you indicate your acceptance of this License to do so, and all its terms and conditions for copying, distributing or modifying the Program or works based on it."[11]

An illustration may help explain how these terms are designed to work in practice. Imagine three parties: A, B, and C. Suppose A writes a program and distributes it to B under the GPL. A either does or does not give B notice of the GPL terms. If he does, then let us assume that B is bound.[12] If A does not give B enough notice to form a binding agreement, then B might argue that she is not bound, but then she has no license—meaning no permission–to copy, modify, or distribute A's code. If B does any of these things without a license, A may sue her for infringement and ask a court to enjoin B's use.

The thing to notice about this part of the structure is that whether B is "bound" by the GPL is really beside the point. Absent a private deal with the author, the GPL is the only thing that gives B the right to copy, modify, or distribute A's code. If the GPL does not apply to B then, if B does any of these things, B infringes A's copyright. It is in B's interest that the GPL apply to B, so there is no logical reason for her to fight it.

Suppose B is bound by the GPL and would like to produce and distribute a work based on A's program. There are two cases to consider here. (I will just identify them now; I discuss them in more detail in Section II.) The first case would arise if B wrote a program in which she copied some of A's code and combined it with some new code of her own to form a single work. Conventional derivative work analysis deals easily with this case.

The second case would arise if B wrote a program consisting entirely of her own code but that interacted with A's code when it was executed. Derivative work analysis is more complex and controversial in this case. A might argue that if executing B's program caused A's program to be copied and to interact with B's program, then the combination of the two programs amounted to a work based on A's program, and therefore to a derivative work under the GPL. (Technically speaking, this claim would be best analyzed as one where the user infringed A's right to make derivative works and B contributed to this infringement by distributing her code.)[13] The FSF has taken this position with regard to at least some programs that interact with GPL'd code.[14] Others disagree.[15] I discuss this disagreement in Section II.

For simplicity, I will stick with the first case for now. The GPL gives B the right to copy A's code and to modify it to create a derivative work. B's copying and modification of the code are therefore lawful.[16] B therefore owns the rights to her contribution to the derivative work—the original code she wrote herself—and A owns the rights to his code, subject to B's GPL rights.[17]

Suppose B sends her work, containing both A's original code and B's new code, to C. B either does or does not give C enough notice of the GPL terms to bind C. If she does, C is bound by the GPL. If she does not, A might assert that B's failure to give notice to C violated Section One of the GPL. Whether on that ground or some other, suppose B has violated the GPL. Her violation terminates her rights from A. B could no longer copy, modify, or distribute A's code, including any of A's code that B copied into B's derivative work.

If B tried to do any of these things after her GPL rights terminated, A could sue B for both breach of the GPL and for infringement. The most likely result of such a suit would be an injunction preventing B from copying, modifying, or distributing A's code. B would still hold the rights in the code she wrote, which she received by default when she wrote it. As a practical matter, however, this fact might not mean much to B, whose code might be worth little or nothing without A's code.

As to C, if C uses A's code (whether she received it from B or some other source) in a manner inconsistent with the GPL, then A may sue C for infringement. If C adheres to the GPL terms, however, even if she received it from B, whose GPL rights had terminated, then the GPL grants her a continuing right to use A's code.

Section 2(b) of the GPL does not apply to A, who owns all the exclusive rights in the original code. Indeed, some developers run parallel versions of a program, with one version being F/OSS and the other being "private." As discussed more fully in Section II, this fact presents some risk that A might release F/OSS code to the community and then attempt to revoke the GPL rights of his licensees so he could distribute his code solely in binary form for a profit.

Though A could do this with respect to his own code, he could not commercialize the contributions of developers who improved that code, unless those developers agreed. As noted previously, if B had A's permission to write code forming a derivative work, then B owns the rights to the code she wrote. Subsequent termination of her GPL rights to A's code does not change that fact. B is bound by the GPL to release her derivative work under the GPL, so we may presume as a default matter that A receives the derivative program as a licensee under the GPL.[18] If A chooses to incorporate B's code into the original program and take advantage of the improved derivative work then, as to that code, A is a licensee and is bound by Section 2(b).

Under the F/OSS model, programs can easily become (indeed, are designed to be) quilts of code from many different authors, each of whom owns rights as to which the others are licensees. As a practical matter, for projects in which more than one developer contributes important work, at least each major contributor would have to agree to "privatize" the code if the project were to be taken private in its most current and complete form. Past a fairly small scale, the web of intersecting and blocking copyrights the GPL creates would make it very hard for any developer to use the code for strategic or anticompetitive purposes.

The GNU project also has created the GNU Lesser General Public License (LGPL), which is designed for certain software libraries "in order to permit linking those libraries into non-free programs." A commercial developer wishing to write programs that interact with GPL'd code might balk at the risk that a court would accept the FSF's interpretation of the GPL and, in at least some cases, treat the developer's program as an infringement of the GPL author's right to make derivative works. Some programs are more valuable if a large number of complementary programs work with them. Some developers therefore might wish to enhance the popularity of their programs by giving commercial firms the option of using F/OSS programs without subjecting the firms' conventionally licensed code to F/OSS treatment.[19]

To achieve this goal, the LGPL distinguishes between programs that contain library material or are derived from library material (a "work based on the library") and those designed to be compiled or linked with the library (a "work that uses the library"). The LGPL provides that works based on a library may be distributed only subject to restrictions similar to those of the GPL.[20]

As to a work that uses a library, the LGPL says that "in isolation," such a work "is not a derivative work of the Library, and therefore falls outside the scope of this License." It also says, however, that "linking a 'work that uses the Library' with the Library creates an executable that is a derivative of the Library (because it contains portions of the Library), rather than a 'work that uses the library.'" Nevertheless, the LGPL allows a developer to "combine or link a 'work that uses the Library' with the Library to produce a work containing portions of the Library, and distribute that work under terms of [the developer's] choice, provided that the terms permit modification of the work for the customer's own use and reverse engineering for debugging such modifications." A developer who pursues this course must comply with additional conditions.[21]

As I mentioned earlier, many licenses besides the GPL comply with the Open Source Definition. (As of this writing, the definition lists more than 40 compliant licenses.) The other licenses tend to get less press, though, because many of them impose few obligations on licensees, so no one has anything to complain about. The BSD and MIT licenses are examples here. These licenses allow unlimited use of the programs they cover, subject only to obligations to include a copyright notice when distributing the program, a disclaimer of warranties, and for the BSD license, a requirement that the rightsholder's permission be given before the author's name can be used in advertising a work derived from code subject to the license. In this regard, the Apache license is similar to the BSD license.

The important general points are that these are nonexclusive licenses, which means that the original author may grant particular users greater rights than are contained in the standard form license, and that without the licenses the legal default rule is that users cannot copy, modify, or distribute code. That means the licenses make users better off than they would be with only the default copyright rule, and the original author has the power to negotiate private transactions that make users better off than they would be with the standard F/OSS license.

Section II

This section discusses whether in practice F/OSS licenses will work as designed. I divide the issues between contract questions and intellectual property questions.

Contract Law

The key to F/OSS production is the way copyrights are deployed by the various licenses. The legal status of those licenses is therefore an important question, which I explore here using the GPL as an example.

Are F/OSS Licenses Really Contracts? Contract analysis must begin with the copyright default rule. Absent the author's permission, or a defense such as fair use, users have no legal right to copy, modify, or distribute code. That is true regardless how a user acquires the code; the copyright gives the author rights against the world. That is why, as noted earlier, a downstream user would *want* the GPL to be enforceable, to give the user a defense against an infringement action. At this level, there is really no question whether the GPL works. The code to which it applies is subject to the author's default legal rights, just like any other copyrighted work.

For this reason, the term "contract" fits somewhat awkwardly with F/OSS practices. Contracts involve bargains, which require that the contracting parties exchange something. What do users give authors of GPL'd code? The GPL itself does not seem to obligate users to give the author anything. Indeed, with the exception of the warranty disclaimer, the license does not cover the act of running the code. Only copying, distribution, and modification are subject to its conditions. In this sense, the GPL is just a permission to use code.[22] Because it demands no bargain, one could argue that the GPL cannot form a "real" contract.

The difference between granting someone the permission to use code and striking a bargain for its use might seem unimportant, and in most cases it probably is. The difference might be important, though, if a user tried to sue an author on the ground that GPL'd code caused the user harm. A user might try to draw an analogy to real property cases, where property owners owe licensees a duty not to harm them through gross negligence and to warn them of defects in the property, or of dangerous activities on the property, of which the owner is aware but the licensee is not.[23] Or a user might try to rely on laws imposing general duties of care, or to draw an analogy to cases extending duties to anyone who uses property with permission.[24]

Like F/OSS licenses generally, the GPL ends with a disclaimer of warranties. It makes clear that the author does not vouch for the code and will not pay damages if the code causes harm; users use the code at their own risk.[25] F/OSS code is relatively transparent, and persons who use it are likely well enough informed to fall within the class of persons who know or should know of any dangers in the code, so the risk of liability probably is low. The warranty disclaimer in the GPL might avoid litigation over such matters, though, or at least limit damages in the unlikely event someone files suit.

To the extent a court might otherwise find that authors of GPL'd code owe users a duty, one might find a "bargain" in the users' agreement to relinquish rights in their favor, which a duty might create, in exchange for the rights to use the code. If the requirements of contract formation are met, such disclaimers would work to protect authors against claims for economic harm.[26] There are other situations in which the GPL's status as a contract might be relevant. A small group of developers who actually agreed to share work on a joint project might use the GPL to memorialize their agreement. Or an author might try to terminate the license she granted, and a user might want to use contract or contractlike theories to fight back. In each case, the user would be better off if the court treated the license as a contract. It is therefore worth taking a moment to consider how the GPL fares under traditional contract formation principles.

Can a Contract Really Be Formed This Way? As long as authors follow its terms, the GPL fares quite well under conventional contract formation principles. No unusual doctrines or new laws are needed to accommodate it.

The default rule of formation is that a contract may be formed "in any manner sufficient to show agreement, including conduct by the parties which recognizes the existence of such a contract."[27] A licensor may form a contract by giving users upfront notice that their use will be subject to certain license terms, and then allowing users to accept these terms by clicking through dialogue boxes or breaking a shrinkwrap seal.[28] There is no reason why using the software could not count as acceptance of the license terms so long as the user had notice of the terms and the chance to read them before using the code. (Whether particular terms may be enforced in particular cases is, and should be, a separate question.)

The key is to adopt a sensible approach to notice. We do this in physical space all the time. Persons who receive printed forms and do not read them understand that they are agreeing to the substance of the transaction—parking or renting a car, flying on a plane, obtaining a credit card, and so on—plus some contract terms of unknown content. They know that they do not know all the relevant terms, and they willingly proceed on that basis.[29] Persons in such circumstances are protected from opportunism and abuse by doctrines such as unconscionability and unfair surprise.[30]

As long as authors do what it says, the GPL works well within the existing model of contract formation. Section 1 of the GPL requires licensees to publish "conspicuously and appropriately . . . on each copy" of code they distribute "an appropriate copyright notice and disclaimer of warranty" and to "give any other recipients of the Program a copy of" the GPL. Those distributing modified code must comply with this term as well and, if the code works interactively, must cause the modified code to display a copyright notice when it is run and tell users how to view a copy of the

GPL.[31] If authors comply with these terms, downstream users should be aware of the GPL's conditions when they use GPL'd code.

If everyone is doing what the GPL says they are supposed to do, and the terms of the GPL are placed on distributed code, the formation question resembles a standard form contract situation. The GPL does not require a user to click through a dialogue box, of course, but there is nothing talismanic about that method. It is just one way of making sure that users have notice of license terms and, as importantly, of helping authors demonstrate to a court that they did. The key is to give users notice of the GPL terms in a way that they cannot help but see them, or make a conscious choice to skip over them, before they begin using the code.

A developer who released code with a reference to the GPL and a link to its terms would not comply with the GPL's notice requirement, and would run a greater risk of formation problems. (The link might go dead, for example.) Some developers might follow such an approach, however, and there is still a chance it would be effective as between the original author (who is not bound by the notice requirement of the GPL) and that author's licensees.[32] Though a recent case found that a link at the bottom of a screen did not provide users enough notice that the code they downloaded was subject to a license,[33] when GPL'd code is circulated among developers who are familiar with F/OSS norms and practices, a reference to the GPL combined with a link to a Web page posting its full terms might be sufficiently well understood to justify an inference of assent, even if the full terms of the GPL were not included on each copy of the code.

Does It Matter If You Don't Deal with the Author? A related issue is privity of contract. The basic idea is that only a person who has rights can grant them. If I do not have the author's rights in the original code, but only that the GPL's grant of conditional permission to use the code, then how can I give you rights to the code? You can't give what you don't have. Because of this concern, Professor Robert Merges has suggested that the GPL may not bind downstream users who take code from someone other than the rightsholder.[34]

I do not think this is a significant worry for GPL users, however. The GPL is a nonexclusive, transferable license. It grants licensees the power to distribute code so long as they include the GPL's terms with the distribution. It makes sense to view redistribution of GPL'd code as simply a transfer within the terms of the original license. An analogy might be drawn to a licensee who holds the rights to distribute a movie in North America, who contracts with regional distributors, who may then contract with individual venues to show the work. In addition, one may view authors of derivative works as the licensors of at least their improvements to a program, and perhaps of the derivative work as a whole (though this latter point is less clear). A court holding this view of matters would probably not view a lack of privity as a barrier to an enforceable agreement.

Are the Rights Irrevocable?   No. The GPL states no term for the rights it grants. Two courts of appeal have held that a license that states no term is terminable according to whatever state law governs the contract.[35] In one case that meant the license was terminable at the licensor's will.[36] Another court, the Ninth Circuit Court of Appeals, which covers the West Coast, concluded that a license that states no term has an implicit term of 35 years.[37] That court based this odd holding on a provision in the Copyright Act that gives authors a five-year window (beginning in the 35th year) to terminate a license agreement regardless of the license terms or state contract law.[38] The court's statutory interpretation was poor, however. Other courts have declined to follow it on this point, and they are right. Outside the Ninth Circuit, it is best to presume that rights holders may terminate the rights of GPL licensees pursuant to applicable state law, which may mean termination at will in many cases.[39]

At least in theory, the ability to terminate at will poses a risk of opportunistic behavior by rights holders. Termination might or might not present a very great practical risk, depending on the code in question. An initial author could terminate the GPL rights she had granted to use and modify her code, but not the rights licensees had in the code they wrote to form a derivative work.[40]

So, to return to our earlier example, if B wrote a derivative work that used A's code, and if A may terminate the GPL rights he grants, then A may prevent B from distributing A's original code in B's derivative work. Termination presumably would be effective as against persons receiving B's work under the GPL, for B could not give them greater rights to A's code than B had herself. B could, though, continue to distribute her own code, as to which she holds the rights. Whether A's termination was a large blow to the project as a whole would depend on how important his original code was. Whether B's code would be worth anything without A's would depend on the same thing.

Whether A would be likely to terminate would depend at least in part on whether he needed to use B's code, because a termination by A could invite reciprocal termination by B. Projects that incorporate code from many authors, therefore, seem unlikely candidates for unilateral termination. And for projects to which the community has chosen not to contribute its efforts, privatization might do little to disrupt community norms.

So far as I know, the risk of GPL termination is almost completely theoretical. (I discuss in the next section the only case in which it was even slightly tangible.) There is no reason for panic. Future iterations of the GPL and other licenses may well address this question.

Can the Rights Holder Assign the Rights? What Implications Do Assignments Have?   Authors of F/OSS code may assign their rights. An author might want to assign the rights to an organization willing to police license violations, for example. The organization could then monitor use of the code and take enforcement action where necessary. The FSF serves this role for some projects.[41]

Assignments also might be relevant if developers were sued for distributing code. This issue came up in a suit prompted by a hack of "CyberPatrol," an Internet filter marketed by Microsystems, Inc.[42] In early 2000, Eddy L.O. Jansson, working from Sweden, and Matthew Skala, working from Canada, decided to take CyberPatrol apart to see how it worked. They were particularly interested in what sites it blocked.

Their efforts produced four things, which they released as package entitled *cp4break*. The first was an essay called *The Breaking of CyberPatrol® 4*.[43] This essay described in some detail the process by which Jansson and Skala were able to discover the encryption and decryption code protecting the filter's database of blocked sites, and how they were able to break the encryption. In addition to the essay, Jansson and Skala released three programs. One of these programs, called *cphack.exe*, was released in both source and binary code form, and was written to run on Windows. One source file in that program stated: "CPHack v0.1.0 by Eddy L O Jansson/Released under the GPL." Jansson added this message on his own; he meant to tell Skala he had done so, but he forgot.

Microsystems responded to the distribution of the cp4break package with a suit against Jansson and Skala for copyright infringement, breach of contract, and interference with prospective economic advantage. A trial court in Boston issued a temporary restraining order against the defendants.[44] Jansson and Skala did not want to litigate; Microsystems wanted the strongest legal tools possible to prevent distribution of the code. The parties agreed on a settlement with several terms, one of which was that Jansson and Skala assign their rights in the code to Microsystems, which could then (at least in theory) attempt to terminate any rights created by the GPL and proceed on a copyright infringement theory against anyone posting the code.

When news of the settlement broke, media reports questioned whether Jansson and Skala could assign exclusive rights in *cphack.exe* to Microsystems after having placed a reference to the GPL on the code. Some accounts reported statements that rights transferred by the GPL are irrevocable.[45] As noted earlier, that is an overstatement. The common law contract rule might allow termination of rights at the will of either party.

Either a prior assignment of exclusive rights or a fixed license term might make it hard for developers like Jansson and Skala to settle such cases. Suppose Jansson and Skala had assigned the rights to *cphack.exe* to an entity formed to administer GPL rights in the interests of the F/OSS communities. What would have happened then? Microsystems no doubt would have sued the two hackers anyway. But Jansson and Skala would not have been able to assign the rights in *cphack.exe* to Microsystems, because they would not have had the rights. Microsystems might have settled for an agreement that Jansson and Skala leave their products alone. If Microsystems really cared about an assignment, however, then Jansson and Skala might not have been able to settle the case as quickly and easily as they did. They would have had to rely on their assignee to assign the rights to the plaintiff to settle the suit.

Similar problems might arise if Jansson and Skala's rights were subject to a fixed term. In that case, their assignment to Microsystems might be subject to that term, which might make the assignment less attractive to Microsystems and make the case harder to settle.[46] For these reasons, the questions of assignment and the ability of authors to terminate GPL rights represent areas of potential tension between the interests of individual authors and the interests of the F/OSS communities.

Intellectual Property Rights

F/OSS production is based on copyright. Even the GPL could not enforce its conditions on copying, modification, and distribution of code without the right to exclude that authors obtain when they fix their work in a tangible medium. Without copyright, there is no copyleft. Even more permissive licenses, such as the BSD or MIT licenses, require the right to exclude to enforce the few conditions those licenses impose.

There is no reason to expect F/OSS development to free itself from copyright.[47] If we assume there will always be opportunistic persons or firms who might try to appropriate a base of F/OSS code for use in a proprietary program, then F/OSS production will always have to rely on the right to exclude being vested in a person or entity willing to wield that right to enforce community norms and thwart appropriation of the community's work. Otherwise developers might find themselves underwriting someone else's profit margins. Developers might do quite a lot of work simply for the joy of it, but their views might change if someone else were free-riding to profit from their labor.

The F/OSS model creates some copyright issues, however. Perhaps the thorniest issue comes up when a developer writes a program that works with GPL'd code but the developer does not want to release that program under the GPL. This question falls under the more general topic of the way the GPL relates to derivative works.

Three portions of the GPL are relevant to the derivative works issue. The GPL defines the phrase "work based on the program," which includes "either the [GPL'd] Program or any derivative work under copyright law: that is to say, a work containing the Program or a portion of it, either verbatim or with modifications and/or translated into another language." Section 2 of the GPL states that a licensee "may modify your copy . . . of the Program or any portion of it, thus forming a work based on the Program, and copy and distribute such modifications" if the licensee causes "any work that you distribute or publish, that in whole or in part contains or is derived from the Program or any part thereof, to be licensed as a whole at no charge to all third parties under the terms of this License." In substance, these terms express the view that any program that qualifies under copyright standards as a work derived from a GPL'd work must itself be released under the GPL.

The Copyright Act defines a derivative work as one "based upon one or more preexisting works. . . ." The concept includes some specified categories not relevant here and a catch-all provision encompassing "any . . . form in which a work may be recast, transformed, or adapted."[48] A work "is not derivative unless it has been substantially copied from the prior work."[49] The right to make derivative works therefore overlaps the right to make copies; substantial copying exists at least where an author could maintain an infringement action based on the derivative author's copying.[50] The right to make derivative works is different, though, because it may be infringed even by adaptations or transformations that are not fixed in a tangible medium. The right to copy is not violated unless the copy is fixed.[51]

As noted earlier, there are two ways a program might constitute a work based on a GPL'd program, and thus be treated as a derivative work. The first is uncontroversial. If in writing her program B copies substantially from A's GPL'd program, then B has met the copying requirement and her program will be a work derived from A's program. If B does not have either A's permission to copy A's code or a defense for her copying (such as fair use), then B's production of her program violates A's right to produce derivative works. B may be enjoined from distributing her program, even if she transforms or adapts to new purposes the code she has copied from A.[52]

What if B does not copy A's code but writes a program that, when executed, invokes A's code and combines with it to perform some function? This question is harder than the first, and the answer to it is the subject of some controversy within the F/OSS communities.

The FSF has taken the position that, in at least some cases, a program is subject to the GPL if it combines with GPL'd code when it is executed. The argument is that the combination of the two programs constitutes a derivative work based on the GPL'd program.[53] The quotations in Part I from the LGPL reflect this reasoning. In the only reported case in which this issue arose, the court enjoined on trademark grounds the distribution of a program that worked with GPL'd code. The court said the "[a]ffidavits submitted by the parties' experts raise a factual dispute concerning whether the . . . program is a derivative or an independent and separate work under GPL ¶ 2."[54] The case settled without judicial resolution of this issue.

I am sympathetic to the FSF's position on this issue. In simplest terms, the FSF defends the proposition that authors should not have to share the product of their labor with people who will not share with them. The key concept here is the consent of the author (who is free to negotiate a deal under different terms if he chooses), so one could generalize this proposition to say that authors should not be forced to allow others to use their code in cases where authors do not consent to the use.

That proposition in turn could be justified by Locke's theory of property, which holds that persons have property rights in themselves, thus in their labor, and thus in the products of their labor, at least so long as their production does not diminish the quality or quantity of inputs in the common, and thus available to others.[55] One could even add that in *Eldred v. Ashcroft*, Justice Ginsburg cited as one basis for upholding the Copyright Term Extension Act a congressional history of taking into account concerns of "justice" and "equity" for authors.[56]

I suspect many free software advocates would object to this line of argument, however, and it does have its problems. Copyright is more often described as a utilitarian reward system than the embodiment of Lockean theory,[57] and there are utilitarian objections to this approach. There are also significant doctrinal problems. Nevertheless, there is some doctrinal support for the FSF's position, which I will discuss before discussing the problems.

The key to analyzing this question is to identify the original work and the alleged derivative work so the relationship between the two can be examined in relation to the author's rights. *Micro Star v. FormGen, Inc.*, demonstrates the type of analysis needed. That case dealt with the "Duke Nukem" video game. As sold in stores, the game included 29 levels and a utility that allowed players to create their own levels. Players did this by writing files that worked with the Duke Nukem game engine and art library. When executed, player files would instruct the game engine what to retrieve from the art library and how to deploy those images to create the new level. The product of these interactions was a new, player-created, Duke Nukem game level.[58]

FormGen encouraged players to post their levels on the Internet. Micro Star downloaded 300 of these player files, burned them onto a CD, and sold the CD commercially. It then filed suit seeking a judicial declaration that its activities did not infringe FormGen's rights; FormGen counterclaimed for infringement, asking the court to enjoin distribution of Micro Star's CD. FormGen claimed the derivative works at issue were "the audiovisual displays generated when" its Duke Nukem code was "run in conjunction with" the player-generated files Micro Star distributed.[59]

Micro Star tried to place FormGen between Scylla and Charybdis by advancing two arguments relevant here. An earlier case had held that a work could not be a derivative work unless it was distributed "in a concrete or permanent form."[60] If the derivative work in question was the audiovisual display generated when a player file was executed, Micro Star said, then it did not distribute that work at all, much less in a concrete or permanent form. Micro Star only copied and distributed player files that, when executed in conjunction with FormGen's own code, helped generate the infringing display.

The court rejected this argument on the ground that the infringing audiovisual displays were "in the [player] files themselves," and Micro Star had fixed those files to its CDs. The court understood that the files did not preserve the infringing displays as such, but it thought the displays were "in" the files because "the audiovisual display that appears on the computer monitor when a [player-written] level is played is described—in exact detail—by" a file fixed on Micro Star's CD. The court later said that "[b]ecause the audiovisual displays assume a concrete or permanent form in the . . . files," the precedent in question "stands as no bar to finding that *they* are derivative works."[61] The italicized language treats the code and the output as one and the same, an approach congenial to the FSF's view.

Having avoided Scylla, however, the opinion was dangerously close to being swallowed by Charybdis, in the form of the rule that a work is not derivative unless it copies from the original. Micro Star's CDs included only the players' code, which FormGen had not written. The player's code invoked FormGen's art library but did not include any material copied from that library. Micro Star pointed out that "[a] work will be considered a derivative work only if it would be considered an infringing work if the material which it has derived from a prior work had been taken without the consent of a copyright proprietor of such prior work," and argued that because the player files did not copy FormGen's code they could not be derivative works.[62]

The court rejected this argument on the ground that the original work at issue was the Duke Nukem "story," which Micro Star infringed by distributing code that, when executed with FormGen's code, generated what were in effect sequels to that story. The court noted that the player-written files at issue would work only with FormGen's code, and said in passing that if these files could be used by some other program to generate some other story, there would in that case be no infringement of FormGen's rights.[63]

This qualification suggests that the opinion is best understood as applying a contributory infringement theory of liability, though the court did not decide the case on that ground. If it is the display that infringes, then the infringer is the person who creates the display. In *Micro Star*, that would be the player who runs Micro Star's player-developed files in conjunction with the Duke Nukem game. Micro Star might be liable for contributing to this infringement by distributing the files, but then its liability would depend on whether the files had substantial noninfringing uses.[64] Because the player files could not work with any other program, that issue would have been decided in FormGen's favor, meaning the court reached a sensible result on the facts before it, even if one might debate its doctrinal analysis.

Micro Star offers some support for treating works that interact with GPL'd code as derivative works subject to the GPL. The court did find that a program not copied from an author's code could be enjoined as infringing the author's right to create derivative works because the program produced an infringing audiovisual display when executed in conjunction with the author's code. To that extent, it supports the proposition that a work may infringe the right to create derivative works by interacting with an existing program. In addition, the earlier case that held a derivative work must assume a concrete or relatively permanent form, a rule that presents a problem for the idea that interoperation creates a derivative work, was probably wrong on that point.[65] *Micro Star* undercut the earlier holding, thus strengthening the case for the FSF's position.

If one takes seriously the notion that the derivative work at issue was the audiovisual display of a "sequel" to the Duke Nukem "story," however, then the point of the case is the output and its relation to a protected story, not the interaction of code. On this reading, the case does not imply anything about the interaction of code that does not produce infringing output.

One could of course try to extend this holding to cases where code interacted but did not produce infringing output. There is some authority for that extension. In *Dun and Bradstreet Software Services, Inc. v. Grace Consulting, Inc.*,[66] the Third Circuit found infringement as a matter of law where a consultant both copied and modified code and wrote programs that invoked the rightsholders' code when executed.[67] Because the case involved literal copying and license violations as well as the writing of programs that interacted with the plaintiff's code, and because the defendant's programs appeared to function as substitutes for upgrades to the plaintiff's original programs, rather than as complements, it is hard to determine the opinion's reach on the derivative works issue. Nevertheless, in *Dun and Bradstreet* there was no infringing output similar to the audiovisual display at issue in *Micro Star* (the output most clearly at issue was a W-2), so it fits better with the FSF's position than does *Micro Star*.

Notwithstanding this authority, there are problems with the proposition that one creates a work derivative of a program just by writing another program that interacts with it. At the simplest level, neither the statutory language nor the language of the GPL supports the argument very well. It is a stretch to say that a program that interacts with GPL'd code "recast[s], transform[s], or adapt[s]" that code, as the statutory language requires.[68] It is more natural to say the program simply runs the code, causing it to do no more than it was designed to do in the way it was designed to do it. And, as the general counsel of the Open Source Initiative has pointed out, the GPL does not refer to "combining" one work with another.[69] The definition of a "work based on a program" piggybacks on the legal definition of derivative works, and the copyleft provision itself refers to a work that "contains or is derived from the Program."[70]

Piggybacking on that legal definition creates problems, because programs that work with GPL'd code but do not copy from it do not, standing alone, satisfy the requirement that a derivative work copy from the original. That means the programs are not in and of themselves derivative works, which is indeed the position taken in the LGPL. But if it is only the combination of the programs that is the infringing work, then the person who combines them is the infringer. On the FSF's account it is the individual user who infringes; the author of the program that works with GPL'd code is at worst a contributory infringer.

Because the derivative works argument in this context is a contributory infringement argument, it is subject to two defenses. Both these defenses rest on the facts of particular cases, so they cut against general statements that invoking GPL'd code creates a derivative work. They do not mean interoperation cannot create a derivative work, but they call into question the proposition that it always does.

First, if users who create the combined work by executing the programs have a defense, such as fair use, then there is no infringement. In that case, the author of the program that works with GPL'd code would not be liable; one cannot be liable for contributing to something that did not happen.[71]

Second, the author would not be liable for contributory infringement if the program in question had substantial noninfringing uses. For example, suppose the program at issue combines both with GPL'd code written by an author who claims the combination is a derivative work and with other programs not subject to the GPL, or with other GPL'd programs whose authors do not object to interoperation. Assume these facts mean that, in those applications, the program does not infringe anything. In that case, the program would not be subject to liability for contributory infringement on the ground that some infringing uses should not stifle development and distribution of devices that do more than break the law.[72]

Perhaps more fundamentally, the economic justification for the derivative right weakens when it is extended to a program that does no more than cause another program to run as it was intended to run. Actual transformations or adaptations of a program satisfy demand in different ways than does the original. As the *Micro Star* court's analogy to movie sequels pointed out, players who purchased the original 29 levels of Duke Nukem got added value from the additional levels written by other players, which amounted to "new" stories. A utility that sped up or slowed down play by altering data generated by the game might add that kind of value, too.

In those cases, the derivative right allows the author to capture revenues from the value added by transforming their original work. Authors could not capture that revenue in their original sale, because they did not sell the transformed work. When a program is not adapted to do anything other than what it is originally distributed to do, though, there is no adaptation or transformation value added for the original author to capture. The author presumably charged in the original sale the profit-maximizing price for ordinary uses of his program, so there is at best a weak case for treating as derivative works programs that do no more than invoke the ordinary operations of his original program.[73]

Against this point, one might say such concerns are irrelevant to F/OSS development. Unlike conventional commercial development, F/OSS development is not about capturing all the monetary value of one's work, but about the principle of share and share alike. This difference is real and it is important. It is a difference in the way different developers use copyright law, however. It is not a difference embodied in the law itself. For a court to treat programs that combine with a GPL'd program as derivative works of that program, the court would either have to extend the derivative works concept as a whole beyond the economic rationale that justifies it in ordinary cases or create a special rule for F/OSS programs. The Copyright Act provides one definition for all derivative works, though. Neither that definition nor the cases interpreting it supply a premise that might justify such a distinction.

A significant strength of the GPL with regard to other issues is that it requires no such special treatment. It implements the principle of "share and share alike" using doctrines and arguments no conventional developer could protest. In such cases, developers using the GPL can do quite well asking judges to do just what they normally do in copyright cases. That would not be true if the developer had to ask the judge—a busy generalist who probably is not familiar with software development—to distinguish F/OSS cases from other cases.

Lastly, there is a utilitarian concern. A rule that one program may form a derivative work of another by interacting with it would make it harder for developers to write interoperable programs. Cases have recognized a fair use defense to infringement where transformative users copied code in the process of reverse engineering to gain access to uncopyrightable interfaces, to which they then wrote programs. The defense extends to copying needed to test such programs to make sure they would work with hardware such as a game console.[74]

The copying of copyrighted material at issue in these cases was ancillary to the development of programs that worked with unprotected interfaces, so the letter of these holdings does not extend to routine copying of protected code, which is the problem raised by a program that interacts with another program. Still, the leading case said the increase in computer games compatible with a particular console—an increase attributable to reverse engineering and the copying it entailed—was a "public benefit." The court also said "it is precisely this growth in creative expression, based on the dissemination of other creative works and the unprotected ideas contained in those works, that the Copyright Act was intended to promote."[75] It is possible that these cases undervalue competition between platforms and de facto standards and overvalue competition within them.[76] Regardless of whether that is true, the concerns these cases express are legitimate and, in any event, are reflected in current copyright doctrine.

The position that works that combine with GPL'd code are derivative works of that code is in tension with the values these courts cited in holding that reverse engineering to achieve interoperability is a fair use of copyrighted works. It is true that developers who write programs that work with GPL'd code are free to release their programs under the GPL, thus eliminating the concern, but it is often true that an independent developer could achieve interoperability by taking a license. From the perspective of copyright policy, the question is how far the author's rights should extend into the space surrounding their work.

No court has actually decided this question, so it would be a mistake to suggest there is a clear-cut answer. Nevertheless, current doctrine and utilitarian considerations suggest that courts are not likely to extend the derivative works concept to programs that interact with a GPL'd program but that are neither created by copying code from it nor transform it into something analogous to a sequel. There might be unusual cases in which it makes sense to treat interoperation as the creation of a derivative work. Whether there are and what they might be will have to be worked out by judges in the context of the facts of particular cases.

Section III

Debates over F/OSS development practices and licenses have become common as the GNU/Linux operating system has become more popular, and conventional firms such as Microsoft have come to see the F/OSS communities as more of a threat to their business models. Much of this debate concerns general matters of social ethics or economics, which are addressed elsewhere in this volume. Some of it concerns legal issues, a couple of which warrant brief comment here. The main point is that the most prominent legal criticisms of the GPL are actually criticisms of copyright; they do not establish any difference between code distributed under conventional licenses and code distributed under the GPL.

The first criticism is that the GPL is a "viral" license that might "infect" proprietary programs. Microsoft at one time posted a FAQ that said the GPL "attempts to subject independently created code (and associated intellectual property) to the terms of the GPL if it is used in certain ways together with GPL code." On this view, "a business that combines and distributes GPL code with its own proprietary code may be obligated to share with the rest of the world valuable intellectual property (including patent) rights in *both* code bases on a royalty-free basis." Variations on this theme run throughout the FAQ and statements by Microsoft executives.[77]

There is no reason to believe the GPL could somehow force into the F/OSS worlds code a private firm wanted to treat as a commercial product. At worst, whoever held the rights to a GPL'd program could try to enjoin the firm from distributing commercially a program that combined with the GPL'd code to form a derivative work, and to recover damages for infringement.[78] In cases where a program actually copied code from a GPL'd program, such a suit would be a perfectly ordinary assertion of copyright, which most private firms would defend if the shoe were on the other foot. A commercial firm producing a program that created a derivative work because it copied a GPL'd program could avoid such litigation by writing its own code instead of copying someone else's.

The criticism is really directed at the second type of derivative work argument, based on interoperation, which I discussed in Section II. If courts adopted a special definition of derivative works that applied only to F/OSS code, then the "viral" criticism might make a legitimate point against the GPL that would not apply equally to conventionally licensed code. There is little if any chance that courts will do that, though. If courts reject the general idea that interoperation alone creates a derivative work, the "viral" criticism is moot. If courts adopt that general view, then the resulting doctrine of derivative works would apply equally to both F/OSS and conventionally licensed code.

Even in that case, however, so long as a firm did not infringe any rights when it was writing a program that created a derivative work when executed (as opposed to a program that constituted a derivative work because it contained copied code), the firm would still hold the rights in its work. The program itself would not be a derivative work; at worst, it would be a tool that contributed to the infringing creation of a derivative work by the user who executed the program in conjunction with GPL'd code.

If the program at issue worked with programs other than the GPL'd program written by our hypothetical plaintiff, then the firm might be able to establish that the program had substantial noninfringing uses, which would defeat the contributory infringement claim.[79] Even if the firm were found liable for contributory infringement, in this type of case there is no reason to believe such a finding would deprive the firm of its rights in its work, rather than subjecting it to an injunction against distribution and to damages.[80]

Microsoft's FAQ also suggests that the GPL's disclaimer of warranties leaves users vulnerable in the event a GPL distribution infringes a third party's rights. This point is partly sound.[81] The true author would not be bound by the GPL, which would therefore provide users no defense if she asserted her rights. And it is possible that the disclaimers in the GPL might prevent users from seeking recourse against whomever gave them the code under the GPL. Commercial vendors commonly disclaim warranties, too, though, including warranties of noninfringement.[82] This risk is therefore properly attributable to copyright licensing practices generally, rather than to the GPL in particular.

Conclusion

As a legal matter, F/OSS production confirms the wonderful versatility of a system that creates general property rights and allows individuals to deploy them in the ways that best suit their needs. F/OSS production rests ultimately on the right to exclude, but the point of the right in F/OSS communities is that it is not used. Like the sword of Damocles, the point is not that it falls, but that it hangs.

The main point of F/OSS licenses and practices is the social structure they support—the opportunities they create, the practices they enable, and the practices they forbid. The achievements of the F/OSS communities are, of course, mostly a testament to the community members who have taken advantage of the opportunities these licenses have created. But the licenses are an elegant use of legal rules in a social context, and should be appreciated on those terms.

Notes

Professor of Law, University of Minnesota Law School. My thanks to Dan Burk and Mark Lemley for discussing these subjects with me. Mistakes that remain are my fault. This essay is adapted from David McGowan, Legal Implications of Open Source Software, 2001 Univ. Ill. L. Rev. 241.

1. 17 U.S.C. §§201(a); 102; 106.

2. See the Open Source Definition version 1.9, available at http://www. opensource.org/docs/definition_plain.html. All references in this chapter to the Open Source Definition are to version 1.9.

3. Open Source Definition, §§1–3.

4. Open Source Definition, §§4–6; 9.

5. On injunctions, see 17 U.S.C. §502(a); Cadence Design Sys, Inc. v. Avant! Corp., 125 F.3d 824, 827 n.4 (9th Cir. 1997) (noting that injunctions are presumptive remedy for infringing use); cert. denied 523 U.S. 1118 (1998).

6. Professor Benkler (2002) was the first to use this metaphor, in his very thoughtful analysis of open source practices.

7. GPL ¶0; ¶1.

8. GPL ¶2(b).

9. GPL ¶2.

10. GPL ¶6; ¶4.

11. GPL ¶5.

12. For example, ProCD, Inc. v. Zeidenberg, 86 F.3d 1447 (7th Cir. 1996) (shrinkwrap license); I.Lan, Inc. v. NetScout Serv. Level Corp., 183 F. Supp. 2d 328 (D. MA 2002) (click-through license).

13. See Midway Mfg Co. v. Artic Int'l, Inc., 704 F.2d 1009 (7th Cir.), cert. denied, 464 U.S. 823 (1983), and also Hogle (2001) discussing contributory infringement argument.

14. See Free Software Foundation, Frequently Asked Questions About the GNU GPL, available at http://www.gnu.org/licenses/gpl-faq.html.

15. See Lawrence Rosen, The Unreasonable Fear of Infection, available at http://www.rosenlaw.com/html/GPL.PDF.

16. *Cf* 17 U.S.C. §103(a) ("protection for a work employing preexisting material in which copyright subsists does not extend to any part of the work in which such material has been used unlawfully").

17. 17 U.S.C. §103(b) ("The copyright in a compilation or derivative work extends only to the material contributed by the author of such work, as distinguished from the preexisting material employed in the work"); Stewart v. Abend, 495 U.S. 207, 223 (1990) ("The aspects of a derivative work added by the derivative author are that author's property, but the element drawn from pre-existing work remains on grant from the owner of the pre-existing work"). The GPL does not vest ownership

of the derivative work in the licensor, so a court presumably would consider the author of the new code to hold its rights.

18. B could release her own code, standing alone, on any terms she chose, as long as standing alone that code did not infringe A's right to make works based on A's program.

19. LGPL, preamble.

20. LGPL ¶0 ("work based on a library"); ¶5 ("work that uses a library"); ¶2 (restrictions on distribution).

21. Id. ¶¶5–6.

22. Cf. Restatement of Property §512, comment (a) ("In a broad sense, the word 'license' is used to describe any permitted unusual freedom of action").

23. For example, Restatement of Property §342.

24. See Cal. Civ. Code §1714(a) (creating general duty of care); Louis v. Louis, 636 N.W. 2d 314 (Minn. 2001) (landowner owes duty of care to all persons invited onto land).

25. GPL §§11–12.

26. For example, Uniform Commercial Code §2–719; Uniform Computer Information Transactions Act §406 ("disclaimer or modification of warranty"); M.A. Mortenson, Inc. v. Timberline Software Co., 140 Wash. 2d 568 (2000); I.Lan, Inc. v. NetScout Service Level Corp., 183 F. Supp. 2d 328 (D. MA 2002).

27. UCC §2–204(1); Uniform Computer Information Transactions Act §112(a)(2) (assent may be shown by conduct); §202(a) (contract may be formed in any manner sufficient to show agreement).

28. For example, Forrest v. Verizon Comms, Inc., 805 A.2d 1007 (D.C. App. 2002) (click-through agreement; enforcing forum selection clause); I. Lan, Inc. v. NetScout Service Level Corp., 183 F. Supp. 2d 328 (D. MA 2002) (click-through agreement; enforcing damages limitation); Moore v. Microsoft, 741 N.Y.S. 2d 91 (2002) (click-through agreement enforceable; warranty disclaimer valid); M.A. Mortenson, Inc. v. Timberline Software Co., 140 Wash. 2d 568 (2000) (shrinkwraps); Rinaldi v. Iomega Corp., 41 UCC Rep Serv 2d 1143 (Del. 1999) (enforcing shrinkwrap disclaimer of warranty); Brower v. Gateway 200, Inc., 676 N.Y.S. 2d 569 (1998) (shrinkwrap; enforcing arbitration clause but not choice of arbitrators); Hill v. Gateway 2000, Inc., 105 F.3d 1147 (7th Cir.) (shrinkwrap), cert. denied 522 U.S. 808 (1997); Micro Star v. FormGen, Inc., 942 F. Supp. 1312 (C.D. Cal. 1996), affirmed in part, reversed in part on other grounds 154 F.3d 1107 (9th Cir. 1998); ProCD, Inc. v. Zeidenberg, 86 F.3d 1447 (7th Cir. 1996) (shrinkwrap license). The leading case criticizing the shrinkwrap method is Step-Saver Data Systems, Inc. v. Wyse Technology, 939 F.2d 91 (3rd Cir. 1991). For a critique of *Step-Saver*, see McGowan (2002).

29. Karl N. Llewellyn, *The Common Law Tradition: Deciding Appeals 370* (1960).

30. Restatement (Second) Contracts, §211(3).

31. Restatement (Second) Contracts, §2(c).

32. Persons who redistribute the author's code are bound by the notice provisions, and their failure to place an adequate copyright notice on each copy of the code technically would constitute a breach of their GPL obligations, thus terminating their GPL rights (GPL ¶4). Depending on the circumstance, persons who received code from such breaching parties still might have enough notice to satisfy the formation requirements of contract law.

33. Specht v. Netscape Communications Corp., 306 F.3d 17 (2d Cir. 2002).

34. Robert Merges, *"The End of Friction? Property Rights and Contract in the Newtonian World of On-Line Commerce"*, 12 *Berkeley Tech. L.J.* 115, 128–129 (1997) ("what is most significant about the [GPL] is that it purports to restrict subsequent transferees who receive software from a licensee, presumably even if the licensee fails to attach a copy of the agreement. As this new transferee is not in privity with the original copyleft licensor, the stipulation seems unenforceable").

35. Figuring out which state that is would be a significant problem where code is floating around on the Net. I leave that issue for another time.

36. Korman v. HBC Florida, Inc., 182 F.3d 1291 (11th Cir. 1999); Walthal v. Rusk, 172 F.3d 481 (7th Cir. 1999).

37. Rano v. Sipa Express, Inc., 987 F.2d 580 (9th Cir. 1993).

38. 17 U.S.C. §203(a)(3).

39. The Free Software Foundation's GPL FAQ disagrees with the conclusion I reach here. The FAQ asks rhetorically "can a developer of a program who distributed it under the GPL later license it to another party for exclusive use?" and answers "No, because the public already has the right to use the program under the GPL, and this right cannot be withdrawn." http://www.gnu.org/licenses/gpl-faq.html. I am not aware of the basis for this statement.

40. Stewart v. Abend, 495 U.S. 207, 223 (1990); 17 U.S.C.

§103(b).

41. See Declaration of Eben Moglen In Support of Defendant's Motion for Preliminary Injunction on Its Counterclaims, ¶23, Progress Software Corp. v. MySQL AB, No. 01-CV 11031 (D. MA 2002), available at http://www.gnu.org/press/mysql-affidavit.html.

42. Microsystems Software v. Scandinavia Online, A.B., 226 F.3d 35 (1st Cir. 2000).

43. Copy on file with author.

44. The restraining order eventually became a stipulated permanent injunction. Microsystems Software v. Scandinavia Online, A.B., 98 F. Supp. 2d 74 (D. Ma. 2000).

45. See Lawrence Lessig, "Battling Censorware," *Industry Standard*, April 3, 2000 (quoting Professor Moglen as saying that "GPL is software that cannot be revoked").

46. I say "might" here because this is a case in which a court that construed the GPL as simply a permission to use might find that users had no rights to enforce against the author, while a court that construed the GPL as a bargain might reach the opposite conclusion.

47. Professor Benkler suggests that open source production relies on copyright only to defend itself from copyright, and that "a complete absence of property in the software domain would be at least as congenial to free software development as the condition where property exists, but copyright permits free software projects to use licensing to defend themselves from defection." Benkler, supra note 11, at 446. Perhaps open source production would be better off if Congress revoked copyright protection for software; we would have to see. I do not think that is likely to happen, however, so I see no prospect of open source development freeing itself from copyright.

48. 17 U.S.C. §101.

49. Litchfield v. Spielberg, 736 F.2d 1352, 1357 (9th Cir. 1984), cert. denied 470 U.S. 1052 (1985); see also H. R. Rep. No. 94–1476 (94th Cong., 2d Sess. (1976)) ("to constitute a violation of section 106(2), the infringing work must incorporate a portion of the copyrighted work in some form").

50. 736 F.2d at 1357.

51. Lewis Galoob Toys, Inc., v. Nintendo of Am., Inc., 964 F.2d 965, 968 (9th Cir. 1992) (derivative work need not be fixed to infringe author's rights), cert. denied, 507 U.S. 985 (1993); see also H. R. Rep. No. 94–1476 (94th Cong., 2d Sess. (1976)) ("reproduction requires fixation in copies or phonorecords, whereas the preparation of a derivative work, such as a ballet, pantomime, or improvised performance, may be an infringement even though nothing is ever fixed in tangible form"). Fixation is not a stringent requirement, however. See MAI Sys Corp. v. Peak Computer, Inc., 991 F.2d 511 (9th Cir. 1993) (RAM copies sufficiently fixed to support infringement action); cert. dismissed, 510 U.S. 1033 (1994). The DMCA partially reversed the holding in this case. 17 U.S.C. §117.

52. 17 U.S.C. §103(a); Dun and Bradstreet Software Servs., Inc. v. Grace Consulting, Inc., 307 F.3d 197, 210 (3d Cir. 2002).

53. See Free Software Foundation, Frequently Asked Questions About the GNU GPL, available at http://www.gnu.org/licenses/gpl-faq.html. Professor Eben Moglen, who also serves as general counsel to the FSF, made the point succinctly in a message posted on Slashdot in February 2003 in response to a developer's question:

The language or programming paradigm in use doesn't determine the rules of compliance, nor does whether the GPL'd code has been modified. The situation is no different than the one where your code depends on static or dynamic linking of a GPL'd library, say GNU readline. Your code, in order to operate, must be combined with the GPL'd code, forming a new combined work, which under GPL section 2(b) must be distributed under the terms of the GPL and only the GPL. If the author of the other code had chosen to release his JAR under the Lesser GPL, your contribution to the combined work could be released under any license of your choosing, but by releasing under GPL he or she chose to invoke the principle of "share and share alike."

Available at http://interviews.slashdot.org/interviews/03/02/20/1544245.shtml?tid=117andtid=123. The Free Software Foundation has said that when a program employs communication mechanisms normally used to communicate between separate programs, then the modules of code connected are likely to be separate programs under the GPL. It qualifies this conclusion, however, by saying that a different conclusion might be warranted on the facts of particular cases. http://www.gnu.org/licenses/gpl-faq.html.

54. Progress Software Corp. v. MySQL AB, 195 F. Supp. 2d 328, 329 (D. MA 2002). The court did say in dicta that the GPL licensor "seems to have the better argument here," but concluded that "the matter is one of fair dispute." Id.

55. John Locke, *The Second Treatise of Government* 288 (Peter Laslett, ed. 1988). For discussions of this theory in the context of intellectual property, see Wendy J. Gordon, "A Property Right in Self-Expression: Equality and Individualism in the Natural Law of Intellectual Property," 102 *Yale L. J.* 1533 (1993); Jeremy Waldron, "From Authors to Copiers: Individual Rights and Social Values in Intellectual Property," 68 *Chi.-Kent L. Rev.* 841, 849–50 (1993); Justin Hughes, "The Philosophy of Intellectual Property," 77 *Geo. L.J.* 287, 288 (1988). Because consumption of information is nonrivalrous, a developer's use of information in writing the commons would not deplete the store of information, thus satisfying Locke's proviso.

56. 123 S.Ct. 769, 780 (2003).

57. Sony Corp. v. Universal City Studios, Inc., 464 U.S. 417, 429 (1984) ("the limited grant is a means by which an important public purpose may be achieved. It is intended to motivate the creative activity of authors and inventors by the provision of a special reward, and to allow the public access to the products of their genius after the limited period of exclusive control has expired"); Fox Film Corp. v. Doyal, 286 U.S. 123, 127 (1932) (government interests in copyright grant "lie in the general benefits derived by the public from the labors of authors."); Yochai Benkler, "Siren Songs and Amish Children: Information, Autonomy and Law," 76 N.Y.U. L. Rev. 23, 59 (2001) ("the basic ideological commitment of American intellectual property is actually heavily utilitarian, not Lockean or Hegelian").

58. Micro Star v. FormGen, Inc., 942 F. Supp. 1312 (S.D. Cal. 1996), affirmed in part, reversed in part on other grounds 154 F.3d 1107 (9th Cir. 1998). The description of the 29 game levels is at 942 F Supp. at 1314. The build editor referred users to a file

containing a license that granted back to FormGen all rights in games created by the players. Id. at 1315. Micro Star argued the license was not binding because players were not given adequate notice of its terms before writing their levels. It used this premise to argue that FormGen had waived the right to enforce any rights it might have had in the player levels. The district court avoided this question by finding that Micro Star knew of the restrictions in the license agreement, and that this knowledge was enough to defeat its waiver argument. Id. at 1318.

59. 154 F.3d at 1109–1110.

60. Lewis Galoob Toys, Inc., v. Nintendo of Am., Inc., 964 F.2d 965, 967 (9th Cir. 1992), cert. denied, 507 U.S. 985 (1993). The court distinguished between protection as a derivative work, which required fixation, and infringement of the derivative right, which did not.

61. 154 F.3d at 1111–12 (emphasis added).

62. Id. (quoting United States v. Taxe, 540 F.2d 961, 965 n.2 (9th Cir. 1976).

63. Id. at n.5.

64. See Sony Corp. v. Universal City Studios, Inc., 464 U.S. 417, 442 (1984).

65. *Galoob*, 964 F.2d at 967.

66. 307 F.3d 197 (3d Cir. 2002), cert. denied, 538 U.S. 1032 (2003).

67. The case involved a successor to Dun and Bradstreet Software Service, called Geac, and a consulting firm called Grace. At one point, citing *Micro Star*, the court said "[u]nless authorized by Geac, its right to create derivative works has been usurped by Grace, whose product instructs the computer to incorporate Geac copyrighted material with its W-2 program." Id. at 210. The court later said "Grace's W-2 program using Copy and Call commands copies Geac's computer copyrighted code. Thus, it is a derivative work; the inclusion of the Copy and Call commands makes Grace's W-2 programs infringing, derivative works of Geac's copyrighted software." Id. at 212. The court later rejected Grace's arguments (i) that its "Copy command does not modify the code"; (ii) that "industry practice uses the commands 'to interoperate two systems;'" and (iii) that "the Copy command does not insert text from one program into another; their program remains separate in memory." Id. at 213. The court said "Grace admitted that the installation, testing, compiling and link editing of its W-2 programs required copying Geac's software and link editing the Geac code. Geac therefore argues that these trial admissions compel the conclusion that, 'as a matter of Law,' Grace's W-2 programs are infringing because they contain copies of Geac's copyright code and are derivative works of Millennium. We agree." Id. These statements are the strongest support of which I am aware for the FSF's position on derivative works.

68. See 17 U.S.C. §101; Ty, Inc. v. Publications Int'l, Ltd., 292 F.3d 512, 520 (7th Cir. 2002) ("A derivative work thus must either be in one of the forms named or be

'recast, transformed, or adapted'"); Castle Rock Ent., Inc., v. Carol Pub. Group, Inc., 150 F.3d 132, 143 (2d Cir. 1998) ("derivative works that are subject to the author's copyright transform an original work into a new mode of presentation").

69. Lawrence Rosen, "The Unreasonable Fear of Infection," available at http://www.rosenlaw.com/html/GPL.PDF.

70. GPL ¶2(b).

71. See Lewis Galoob Toys, Inc., v. Nintendo of Am., Inc., 964 F.2d 965, 970 (9th Cir. 1992), cert. denied, 507 U.S. 985 (1993) (discussing possible fair use defense by users of utility that modified output from game console; rejecting claim that defendant could be liable for contributory infringement even if consumers did not infringe; 3 Melville B. Nimmer and David Nimmer, *Nimmer on Copyright*, §12.04(3)(a)(2003).

72. Sony Corp. v. Universal City Studios, Inc., 464 U.S. 417, 442 (1984). It may seem odd that authors of *other* GPL'd programs could frustrate the claims of an author who objected to interaction, but the contributory infringement standard compels this result. Sony provides an example of this point. In discussing why the video cassette recorders at issue in that case had substantial noninfringing uses, the court pointed out that many rightsholders, such as the producers of public television programs (Mr. Rogers) or the National Football League, were happy to have their works recorded. 464 U.S. at 445–46. As the Court put it, "in an action for *contributory* infringement against the seller of copying equipment, the copyright holder may not prevail unless the relief that he seeks affects only his programs, or unless he speaks for virtually all copyright holders with an interest in the outcome." Id. at 446.

73. Cf. Lee v. A.R.T. Co., 125 F.3d 580 (7th Cir. 1997) (Easterbrook, J.) ("Because the artist could capture the value of her art's contribution to the finished product as part of the price for the original transaction, the economic rationale for protecting an adaptation as 'derivative' is absent.").

74. For example, Sony Computer Entertainment, Inc. v. Connextix Corp., 203 F.3d 596 (9th Cir.), cert. denied 531 U.S. 871 (2000); Sega Enters.s, Ltd. v. Accolade, Inc., 977 F.2d 1510 (9th Cir. 1992).

75. *Sega*, 977 F.2d at 1523.

76. See Joseph Farrell and Michael L. Katz, "The Effects of Antitrust and Intellectual Property Law on Compatibility and Innovation," 43 *Antitrust Bull.* 609 (1998); David McGowan, Innovation, Uncertainty, and Stability in Antitrust Law, 16 *Berkeley Tech. L. J.* 729, 807–08 (2001).

77. "Some Questions Every Business Should Ask About the GNU General Public License (GPL)," question 3 ("How does your use of GPL software affect your intellectual property rights?"). As of this writing, Microsoft seems to have taken down the FAQ. A copy is on file with the author.

78. 17 U.S.C. §504.

79. See Sony Corp. v. Universal City Studios, Inc., 464 U.S. 417, 442 (1984).

80. I am not aware of a case that deals with this question. Section 103(a) of the Copyright Act provides some support for the position taken in the text, however. It states that protection for works "employing preexisting material in which copyright subsists does not extend to any part of the work in which such material has been used unlawfully." 17 U.S.C. §103(a). If the derivative work at issue is the *combination* of a firm's program and GPL'd code, then Section 103(a) would deny the firm rights *in that combination*. In the hypothetical case at issue here, the original program would not itself employ preexisting GPL'd material, so Section 103 would not deny it copyright protection. (My thanks to Mark Lemley for this suggestion.)

81. As far as I know, however, there is no evidence to support the FAQ's ungenerous implication that open source developers will knowingly distribute infringing code, counting on the GPL to protect them. See "Some Questions Every Business Should Ask About the GNU General Public License (GPL)" §11 ("You should also ask yourself if GPL developers may conclude that this disclaimer makes it okay to distribute code under the GPL when they *know* they don't have the rights required to do so").

82. See Uniform Computer Information Transactions Act §401(d) (allowing disclaimer of warranty of noninfringement).

Nonprofit Foundations and Their Role in
Community-Firm Software Collaboration

Siobhán O'Mahony

Contributors to community-managed projects have created nonprofit
foundations, despite the fact that such formal structures are an anathema
to the hacker ethos of technical autonomy and meritocratic decision
making. The technical organizations that emerged since the federal government privatized the Internet may have partially influenced the design
of these foundations, but some features are the unique product of managing community software in a commodity world. One thing that stands
out from either the early Internet working groups or the typical corporate
standard-setting bodies of the past is the role of nonprofit software foundations in enabling collaboration between a community of individuals and
corporate actors.

Many people may be surprised by the emergence of open source software
foundations, because incorporation requires a degree of formality that may
seem inconsistent with the portrayal of open source contributors as guided
only by their own desires (e.g., Raymond 2001). As many who contribute to
such projects know, most open source projects manage their efforts through
normative control on discussion mailing lists and instant message channels. Minimal constraints define programming formats and protocols, but
not the technical direction of the project. Despite collectively determined
code format and check-in and -out procedures, the technical direction of
most community projects is typically the product of negotiation among a
small group of core developers. How these forms of control shape the
architecture and evolution of software is still not well understood. What we
do know is that the combination of peer-based normative control and
collectively determined procedural standards have been effective enough to
permit commercial-grade software to be developed without the efficiency
benefits typically equated with bureaucratic controls.

Many programmers who contribute to community-managed projects identify with the hacker community. As readers of this book do not need to be told, the hacker community is not one that embraces centralized modes of governance. The hacker ethos, as articulated by those who know it best (Levy 1994; Raymond 2001; Pavlicek 2000; Himanen 2001), values the intrinsic satisfaction from solving technical challenges, as well as truth, independence, and individual autonomy. "A happy programmer is one who is neither under-utilized nor weighed down with ill-formulated goals and stressful process friction" (Raymond 2001, 74). This is particularly true for projects that rely on volunteer contributors, for volunteers are more likely to be motivated by intrinsic reasons and thus less likely to welcome formal organizing mechanisms (Lakhani and Wolf 2003; Chap 1, this volume; Butler et al. 2002). Indeed, these studies show that many volunteer contributors to software projects do so in order to learn, hone their skills, solve a technical challenge, "make their mark," or improve their careers (Lakhani and Wolf 2003; Chap 1, this volume; Lerner and Tirole 2002; Hann et al. 2002).

The literature on the hacker ethos is not inconsistent with research on the motivations, preferences, and occupational identities shared by engineers and other technical workers. Organizations have long struggled with how to manage people who are more likely to be motivated by the work itself, less likely to want to leave their work for management positions, and less likely to respect authority that is not rooted in technical competence (Ritti 1971, 1998; Whalley 1986; Whalley and Barley 1997). The concept of a dual career ladder was essentially an attempt to integrate the ethos of the engineer within an organizational framework (Allen and Katz 1986). While there is variance in the motivations of contributors to free and open source software, underlying this divergence is a shared belief in the value of challenging work, technical autonomy, self-management, and freedom from a positional basis of power. Thus, even programmers that do not explicitly identify with the hacker community or the ideals of the open source and free software movements may hold beliefs about the forms of organization they prefer. This is important, because as the open source and free software community becomes more diverse in attitude and affiliation, fewer elements of the hacker ethos may be as widely shared. The occupational identity that is common to programmers who prefer the community development model may provide a source of organizational resiliency that extends beyond individual motivations or political affiliations (Van Mannen and Barley 1984).

The Organizational and Legal Dilemma

Given these preferences, why would community-managed projects create nonprofit foundations? What role, if any, do these foundations have in fostering collaboration between communities and firms? The commoditization of open source and free software created new opportunities for many projects, but also created new dilemmas. Managing community software in a commodity world brought new challenges such as how to treat corporate contributions of code, how to communicate to the press the difference between a project and a company, and how to enforce a community's terms for software modification and distribution within a user and developer population that was growing not only larger but also more diverse in its attitudes toward commercial software. With growth in market share and enhanced media and industry attention came a degree of exposure that even the most mature projects had not heretofore experienced. Greater public exposure elicited new areas of vulnerability. With more users of the software, there was greater probability that liability issues could arise and, as an unincorporated entity, fewer protections to prevent volunteers from individual liability.

This is because communities are not legal actors. Community-managed software projects are open source or free software projects initiated and managed by a distributed group of individuals who do not share a common employer.[1] Contributors may be associated with the free software or open source social movements, unaffiliated or sponsored by a firm. Most importantly, contributors are not employees of the project and project relations are independent of employment relations.[2] Community mailing lists are well-bounded: membership is clear and members share distinct norms that guide list behaviors and programming protocols. Yet they have few legal rights.

The lack of legal rights granted to online communities became a real problem when several leaders within the community realized that they might have difficulty protecting the "Linux" and "open source" terms and concepts. After the open source term was created in early 1998, firms and members of the press sometimes used the term "open source" in ways that extended beyond what creators of the term had intended. Companies were not just downloading free software for their own use, they were bundling it with other software and selling it in combination with hardware and services. While long-term contributors to free and open source software were delighted to see their work proliferate, firms developing Linux and other open source products and services sometimes created confusion as to what these terms represented, and as to where community work stopped and corporate work began.

In 1999, the small group of community leaders who created the open source term found the concept too common to earn trademark rights. The leaders announced, "We have discovered that there is virtually no chance that the U.S. Patent and Trademark Office would register the mark 'open source'; the mark is too descriptive. Ironically, we were partly a victim of our own success in bringing the 'open source' concept into the mainstream. So 'Open Source' is not and cannot become a trademark" (OSI Announcement, June 16, 1999).

These leaders created a nonprofit organization, the Open Source Initiative (OSI), to ensure that the open source concept would not be misrepresented as the concept grew in commercial popularity.[3] Without legal rights, community-managed projects not only had trouble defending their concepts and code, but also were unable to form contracts and legal agreements as a single entity. One Fortune 100 executive faced with structuring a formal relationship with the Apache Project in the late 1990s, noted this unusual state by asking: "How do I make a deal with a Web page?" Collaboration between a firm and a community-managed project was a relatively foreign idea and there was little precedent to help make it happen.

Organizing Options and Models

What organizational options are available for open source and free software programmers who want to move beyond the status of "a Web page" and at the same time avoid forming a firm? Cooperatives are one legal form with communal norms and values. Producer cooperatives pay their members a set price for their contributions and apportion dividends pro rata to their members yearly. Consumer cooperatives pay earnings to members based on the amounts that members spend, as opposed to the amounts they sell (Hansmann 1996: 13–14). Both of these forms redistribute profits to their members, which is incompatible with the goals of community-managed software projects. What unites software communities is the goal of producing open source and free software (Williams 2002; Pavlicek 2000; Raymond 2001) and perhaps a shared culture and occupational identity (van Mannen and Barley 1984). What does not bind the community is the desire to earn a profit as a direct product of their collective work.[4]

Other organizing possibilities include forming a consortium, alliance, or task force, as technical communities critical to the development of the

Internet have done. Indeed, the open source and free software communities are not the first technical communities to wrestle with the problem of creating a form that can exist independent of any one person. The U.S. government's privatization of the Internet led to the creation of professional working groups and technical societies that were familiar to leaders of community-managed software projects. Internet standards work that was once the responsibility of Defense Advanced Research Projects Agency (DARPA) has, since 1986, been delegated to the Internet Engineering Task Force (IETF). The IETF calls itself a "loosely self-organized group of people [volunteers] who contribute to the engineering and evolution of Internet technologies" ("The Tao of IETF" 2001). The IETF differs from corporate-led standard-setting bodies in that it maintains no specific membership or dues requirements. Any interested individual can attend a meeting, join a working group mailing list, or contribute to a project. Members do not represent their affiliated organizations, but act on their own capacity.

On the other hand, the World Wide Web Consortium (W3C) is a consortium of organizations: individuals cannot become members.[5] Three universities on different continents host the W3C.[6] This design was explicitly intended to preserve pluralism and prevent the emergence of a United States–centric World Wide Web (WWW) (Berners-Lee, Fishetti, and Dertouzous 2000). A third organization responsible for ensuring that all Internet domain names will be universally resolvable, the Internet Corporation for Assigned Names and Numbers (ICANN), has not been able to successfully integrate individual and organizational representation.[7] ICANN has declared that its structure is incomplete, its funds inadequate, and is currently pursuing major reform efforts. It is an unlikely organizational model.[8] Neither the W3C nor the IETF are incorporated, but both have incorporated hosts. The Internet Society (ISOC), a nonprofit professional membership association that allows both individuals and organizations to be members, hosts the IETF. Many of the technical working groups under the ISOC charter have well-established processes for receiving, reviewing, and integrating comments on technical standards that stem from early government-sponsored efforts. These processes, as well as IETF's focus on individuals as members, may have influenced the type of form leaders in the open source software that community leaders wanted to create.

The first foundation for community-managed software, the Free Software Foundation (FSF), was created even before the IETF, ISOC, W3C, or ICANN organizations existed. Table 20.1 shows when organizations representing

Table 20.1
Institutions founded to represent technical communities

Date	Organization founded	Mission
1979	*ICCB-DARPA*	Develop TCP/IP Protocal Suite
1983	*Internet Architecture Board*	Provide oversight of archictecture of Internet, integrate working group activities
1985	Free Software Foundation (FSF)	Dedicated to promoting computer users' right to use, study, copy, modify, and redistribute computer programs (instiutional host for GNU project and steward of the GNU GPL)
1986	*Internet Engineering Task Force (IETF)*	Concerned with the evolution of the Internet architecture and the smooth operation of the Internet
1991	*IANA*	Dedicated to preserving the central coordinating functions of the global Internet for the public good
1992	*Internet Professional Society (ISOC)*	Provides leadership in addressing issues that confront the future of the Internet and is the organization home for the groups responsible for Internet infrastructure standards
1994	*W3C (World Wide Web Consortium)*	Develops interoperable technologies (specifications, guidelines, software, and tools) to lead the Web to its full potential
1997	**Software in the Public Interest**	**Helps organizations develop and distribute open hardware and software (institutional host for Debian)**
1998	Open Source Initiative	Dedicated to managing the promoting the Open Source Definition
1998	*ICANN*	Responsible for global DNS management
1999	**Apache Software Foundation**	**Provides support for the Apache community of open source software projects**
1999	Linux Professional Institute	To design and deliver a standardized, multinational, and respected program to certify levels of individual expertise in Linux

Table 20.1

(continued)

Date	Organization founded	Mission
2000	Perl Foundation	Dedicated to the advancement of the Perl programming language through open discussion, collaboration, design, and code
2000	FreeBSD Foundation	Dedicated to supporting the FreeBSD operating system
2000	Free Standards Group	Dedicated to accelerating the use and acceptance of open source technologies through the development, application, and promotion of standards
2000	**GNOME Foundation**	**Provide a user-friendly suite of applications and an easy-to-use desktop; to create an entirely free desktop environment for free systems**
2000	KDE League	Promote the use of the advanced Open Source desktop alternative by enterprises and individuals and to promote the development of KDE software by third-party developers
2000	Linux International	To work with corporations and others to promote the growth of the Linux operating system and the Linux community
2001	Python Foundation	Advancing open source technology related to Python programming language
2001	Jabber Foundation	Provides organizational and technical assistance to projects and organizations within the Jabber community
2002	Open Source Application Foundation	To create and gain wide adoption for software applications of uncompromising quality using open-source methods

Key:

Internet Governance Organizations

Free Software/Open Source Organizations

Organizations in bold studied in greater detail.

technical communities were founded. However, until 2002, the FSF was not a membership organization. FSF leadership viewed a democratic governance structure as potentially detrimental to its mission, stating, "We don't invite all the people who work on GNU to vote on what our goals should be, because a lot of people contribute to GNU programs without sharing our ultimate ideals about why are we working on this" (FSF founder, April 26, 2001).

The trade-off that the FSF made to ensure commitment to its political goals was to sacrifice democratic goals.[9] Thus, while its influence technically, legally, and conceptually is immeasurable, its influence as an organizational model for community-managed projects was limited. Without members, the FSF functioned as a corporate shell for the GNU project and as a political organization devoted to changing the social, economic, and legal arrangements that guide software development.

Since Fortune 500 firms were first challenged with the idea of "collaborating with a Web page," Apache, Debian, Gnu, Gnome, FreeBSD, Jabber, Perl, Python, KDE, BIND, Samba, the Linux kernel, Linux Standards Base, Mozilla, and Chandler have designed private nonprofit foundations to "host" their projects. The institutional hosting concept may be borrowed from the IETF and W3C models, but these projects have adopted it in different ways. This chapter compares the foundations created by the Debian, Apache, and GNOME projects and concludes by examining the role of nonprofit foundations in community-firm software collaboration.

Research Methods

Between April 2000 and April 2001, I interviewed 70 contributors to community-managed projects[10] to find out how the commercialization of Linux was affecting the free software community and the peer-managed development style that had emerged over the late 1980s and 1990s. I was curious as to how commercial attention and participation on open source and free software projects would affect the hacker culture and loose decision-making structure. Two-thirds of my informants were corporate-sponsored and the rest were volunteers. Most of the sponsored contributors had initially been volunteers and now worked in firms supporting the development of open source software. To assess how specific projects were affected, I focused on the structuring activities of three of them: Debian, GNOME, and Apache. Observations at project meetings, conferences, "hackathons," and other events, coupled with online project documentation such as project discussions, charters, bylaws, and meeting minutes,

helped provide triangulation of the data. This data was coded and analyzed, with a focus on the emergence of common themes that held across
variance in perspectives.

Comparing the Emergence of Three Foundations

After the FSF was established in 1985, few foundations emerged until the
Debian project created one (Software in the Public Interest) in 1997. The
Apache httpd server group founded the first membership-based foundation in 1999. During the course of this research, the GNOME project began
crafting their foundation. Each of these projects varied in their stance
toward commercial relations, but they all shared a large, mature user and
developer base and had attracted commercial attention. Comparison of
their approaches shows how different project ecologies approached the
task of building a foundation at different points in time.

Debian
Debian, the most popular noncommercial distribution of Linux, has been
operating for almost 10 years under the guidance of six different leaders.
Over 1,000 members of Debian contribute to the 7,000 packages that constitute the Debian operating system.[11] Debian is viewed, even by long-time
members in the community, as a serious hacker's distribution. Thus, it is
of no surprise that although Debian was one of the earliest projects to
create a nonprofit foundation, Software in the Public Interest (SPI), it did
so with some ambivalence. Members of Debian were more resistant to
the idea of incorporation and had greater fear of losing control over the
technical direction of their project than members on the other projects.
However, some leaders were concerned enough about individual liability
to want to pursue incorporation and encouraged resisters to adapt the idea
in its most minimal form.

Of the three foundations studied, SPI is the least active: it does little more
than hold Debian's assets. Members of Debian revised their bylaws to stipulate that SPI's role is to merely serve the project as a legal steward. Debian,
like the FSF, has struggled with how to become a membership organization. All potential contributors must pass a very formalized five-step
process to become an official Debian member. However, membership in
Debian does not trigger membership in SPI. Project members preferred an
"opt-in" approach, as opposed to equating Debian membership with SPI
membership. Membership in SPI has thus been slow to activate, which has
led to some concern about how an appointed board can represent the

project. As a board member commented, "SPI without a membership is just a legal framework for Debian, but with a membership it becomes an organization that can attempt to move on issues that are key to the development of the Net. This is also why the membership is important: SPI without a membership (and just a board of directors) may not always reflect the concerns of the community. With a membership, SPI becomes a representation of the community, and can involve itself in issues that decide the future of that very community" (SPI Board Member Posting, October 26, 2001).

SPI is not structured to ensure representation of project members. However, the Debian Constitution outlines a sophisticated process whereby project members elect leaders for a one-year term. Member representation thus rests within the project as opposed to the foundation. While the other two foundations created a role for firms to provide a voice into their organization, SPI did not.[12] Debian was also the only project of the three to have an internal project leader initiate incorporation. The other two projects all received legal assistance in drafting their charters and thinking through governance issues from two different Fortune 500 companies.

Apache
The primary reason for incorporation proffered by informants on all three projects was to obtain protection from individual liability. The ability to accept donations, hold assets, host additional projects, and represent the project as one legal entity to the public were also concerns. Apache was the only project to explicitly mention the welfare of its customers as an additional reason to incorporate.[13] As one founding member explained, "It is a valuable project. Most of us will stay involved in it forever. Also our customers need stability. Apache had to be seen as an ongoing group and I think that making a legal entity was the way to do it" (Founding Member #1, Apache Project, September 28, 2000).

This is evidence of the distinctness of the Apache group culture. First, the founding eight members of this project licensed their httpd server software under a license that allows proprietary extensions of their work (the Apache License, a variant of the BSD License). Second, many of the early contributors worked in enterprises that were building Web sites and using the software for commercial purposes. The Apache group was also one of the earliest projects to be approached by a Fortune 500 firm to collaborate and the first project to create a membership-based foundation that integrated project governance. This is most likely why informants from projects that incorporated later often cited the Apache Software Foundation (ASF) as an influential model.

The code contributing population of Apache is smaller than Debian and more centralized. Over 400 individuals contributed code to the httpd server project between February 1995 and May 1999, but the top 15 developers contributed over 80 percent of code changes (Mockus, Fielding, and Herbsleb 2000). Code contributions are a necessary but insufficient condition for membership. ASF membership additionally requires nomination by a current member, a written application and a majority vote. There are currently 109 members of the ASF, of which 34 percent are independent or have no organizational affiliation. The ASF has maintained that only individuals can become members, but that companies may be represented by individuals. The ASF has not implemented any formal approaches to ensure pluralistic representation as of yet, although it has been discussed. Sponsored contributors are from organizations that are diverse enough that no majority or controlling interest from a single organization has yet to emerge.

The ASF's governance structure is akin to a federalist model. Since its founding in 1999, the ASF has grown to host 20 projects in addition to the httpd server. Each project has a Project Management Committee (PMC) with a chairman who also serves as an officer of the corporation. PMC chairs report project status to ASF members and the board, but technical direction of the projects remains the purview of those on the project. ASF members meet annually to elect their board of directors. Directors do not typically interfere with the discretion of PMC leaders, but can decide whether to charter, consolidate, or terminate PMCs. The ASF also organizes conferences and annual face-to-face meetings. Neither the ASF nor SPI employ people to manage administration, largely because members on both projects did not want to engage in the business of "managing people." Members on both projects worried that engaging in employment relations might distract them from what they best enjoyed about participating in their respective projects.

According to volunteer and industry informants, ways to formalize the "core" Apache group had been the subject of discussion for some time prior to incorporation, but corporate interest in collaborating was a catalyst to begin drafting the ASF bylaws. "With [a Fortune 500 company] getting involved and wanting to figure out what the structure was, we realized that we needed to kind of solidify our processes a bit and put some formalism to it" (Founding Member #2, Sponsored Contributor, Apache, September 28, 2000).

The ASF did not create an explicit role for firms other than through sponsored individual contributors. However, the ASF has engaged in several formal transactions to accept intellectual property contributions from Fortune 500 companies, most recently brokering an intellectual property agreement on an open source implementation of Java with Sun Microsystems.[14] Like SPI, the ASF holds assets in trust for the Apache project and the other projects it hosts. This includes the Apache trademark, donated hardware and equipment, and intellectual property donated by firms as well as by members. The ASF asks volunteer contributors to sign an agreement that ensures the software they donate rightfully belongs to them and assigns a nonexclusive copyright license to the ASF. The ASF was more vigilant in seeking copyright assignment than the other two projects.[15]

GNOME

More than 500 developers contribute to the GNU Object Model Environment (GNOME) project, 20 percent of whom are reportedly full-time paid developers. GNOME is a complete, graphical user interface (GUI) desktop application designed to run on Linux-based operating systems, BSD, and a variety of other Unix and Unix-like operating systems.[16] The GNOME Foundation membership is larger than the other projects with over 300 members, and new members do not require a vote by the majority. Candidates who feel that they have made nontrivial contributions are welcomed to apply for membership, but the exact criteria are not well articulated at this stage. Foundation members have the right to elect a Board of Directors and have held three successful elections thus far. GNOME has hired an executive director to oversee fundraising and the development and growth of the foundation.

More corporations directly participated in the creation of the GNOME Foundation than on the other projects. Similar to Apache, a different Fortune 500 firm donated their legal expertise to help a steering committee draft the GNOME charter and file the necessary paperwork. While firms that wanted to collaborate with the Apache project were primarily interested in seeing the group formalize to make transactions more viable and secure, firms working with the GNOME project wanted to influence the foundation to gain a greater voice in decision making.[17] As one contributor working on the bylaws put it, "with [Fortune 500 firm #2] coming to the front, all these issues of control and governance became so much more urgent, because look at [firm #2]—it's a very competitive, very aggressive culture there. And the way they started their conversations with GNOME reflected that" (Sponsored Contributor, GNOME, February 8, 2001).

The GNOME foundation resisted this type of direct pressure by granting firms a role on an Advisory Board that provides a venue for firms to articulate their concerns and ideas, but does not offer technical decision-making rights.

The GNOME project was the only project of the three that allowed their foundation to assume control over release coordination. If there was one role assumed by foundations that was most controversial in the eyes of informants, it was release coordination. Release coordination includes setting a schedule, choosing the modules that will define a release, and marketing.[18] One informant felt that granting the foundation release coordination authority could effectively blur the boundaries between organizational and technical decision making and threaten members' control over the technical domain. "The reality is that, in my opinion, the foundation is going to end up running GNOME. And people don't want to say that because it just runs counter to the democratic values of the thing, but [. . .] if you look at release coordination alone, it gives you so much control, that you're effectively running the thing. Because what you end up saying when you do a release is deciding what is a part of it and what is not a part of it, right?" (Sponsored Contributor, GNOME, February 8, 2001).

How this authority is enacted with the developers directly responsible for modules within GNOME is still evolving. The GNOME Foundation has greater project representation within its foundation, but also has centralized more power than the other two projects.

Evidence from informants and project documentation indicates that GNOME faced greater pressures from commercial sources to coordinate in ways that were atypical to the hacker ethos than did the other two projects. These pressures were manifested in project members' resistance to expressed commercial preferences for a more predictable and stable development environment. Centralized release coordination authority enhances a firm's ability to more reliably predict components and deadlines associated with a release and thus better manage its own product development activities.

GNOME's experience may have differed because its foundation worked with more firms in more formalized and explicit roles than did the other two projects or because application development by its nature demands more commercial collaboration than software development at the operating system and Web server level. Pressure to coordinate may also be a function of commercial interest in the advancement of open source desktop applications or a function of the later stage at which the GNOME foundation was developed. (The GNOME foundation was created much later than either the ASF (1999) or SPI (1997), at a time when commercial entities had become more aware of open source software.) Regardless of the weight attributed to these reasons, the GNOME project experienced more commercial pressure when creating their foundation than either Apache or Debian. Their resulting foundation exhibits greater centralized authority over software development.

Other Foundations

Nonprofit foundations help programmers retain the normative order they prefer while creating a legal entity that can protect their work in commercial markets. In addition to these three foundations, there are now at least a dozen foundations that support the development of free and open source software, five of them founded in 2000 alone. All but two of the foundations listed in Table 20.1 are 501(c)(3) nonprofit organizations.[19] The precise structure of each foundation reflects challenges specific to each project's ecology, but there are also patterns developing that will likely change with challenges from commercial markets. This is an evolving model that has yet to reach settlement. One of the most well-known open source projects, the Linux kernel project, initially resisted the need to create a foundation:

For a long time, there has been some talk about having more structure associated with the kernel. The arguments have not been that strong. People just expect the structure to be there. So they want to build structure because they think it is wrong to not do it. That seems to be the strongest argument, even though it is never said that way. But there have been for example, commercial companies who wanted to transfer intellectual property rights and there is nothing to transfer to, which makes their legal people scratch their heads, right? (Project leader, Linux kernel, March 12, 2001)

The community's and industry's faith in the leadership of this project and the leader's disinterest in institution building enabled the Linux kernel project to manage legal ambiguity for a long time without undue pressure to incorporate. With the creation of http://kernel.org, the Linux kernel project now has a shell foundation in place but trademark rights remain individually held.

Foundation Efficacy

It is too early to determine how successful project foundations have been at fulfilling their mission. Project leaders recognized that any structure that was too formal or burdensome would conflict with the hacker ethos and lead to potential mutiny. A successful organizational design was, in the eyes of one informant, one that "members could live with"; an organization that infringed minimally upon the hacker ethos of technical autonomy and self-determination: "[A]s far as I can tell, we have created an organization that can live with the community and the community can live with it and work together towards maintaining our software over a long period" (Volunteer contributor, Apache Project, July 19, 2000).

Informants indicated that there were early signs that their foundations helped facilitate communication between communities and firms and helped to avoid, or at least diffuse, potential problems. If this were true, these effects would be more difficult to detect.

Another test of the efficacy of a foundation is its ability to maintain mutually beneficial relations between firms and communities. Informant explanations of mutualism often focused on the different types of competencies and resources that communities and firms could contribute to technical problems:

I think our main contribution is that we are using Debian and we are looking at Debian from a commercial point of view. And making improvements to make it more attractive to companies as an alternative to the commercial systems. So we are doing work that a nonprofit group is not necessarily interested in doing and looking at Debian from a different point of view. So our hope is that by doing that, we are going to be able to help Debian improve and expand its audience beyond where it is now. (Former leader, Debian, open source firm founder, February 16, 2001)

As this informant explains, the customer-oriented commercial lens that firms brought to development work could provide a different, but complementary, focus to the more foundational concerns of hackers. Complementary as opposed to competing foci fostered symbiotic working relations between community-managed projects and firms. To the degree that firms and community projects share the same goals and interests (for example, to expand their market share) despite divergent motivations, and to the degree that each type of actor maintains different foci, informants felt that symbiotic relations were possible. Maintaining this balance was understood however to require social structures that reinforced pluralism and the balancing of community and firm interests.

Facilitating Community-Corporate Collaboration: A New Actor in the Supply Chain

The foundations that emerged in this study are incorporated and organized by and for individual members. They produce benefits for the public, but do not redistribute profits to their members. What is unique about these foundations, in relation to technical communities of the past, is that these foundations also own assets that are sold by third parties in commercial markets and may in fact compete with other commercial offerings. Firms that use free and open source software have, in effect, allowed community-managed projects that grew out of a politically motivated social movement to become a part of their supply chain. This interdependence has fostered a new set of working relations among community projects, their foundations, and firms. Figure 20.1 outlines the role of nonprofit foundations in this new collaboration model. Foundations hold the assets and property rights of technical communities that produce software, but do not pay their developers or redistribute profits to their members. Community members retain the ability to set their own technical direction and manage the culture, norms, and governance of their own projects. In return for assigning their intellectual property to a foundation, they are granted protection from individual liability and a means to legally represent the project.

Firms can sell and distribute the community's work at a profit by creating complementary software, hardware, and services that reflect their conception of market needs. They can modify the work of the community as long as they respect the terms of community licenses and contribute improvements back to the code base where required. In return, firms offer sponsorship and support to both individuals and foundations. Individual volunteers that are working on components of critical interest to firms may be hired to continue their efforts as sponsored contributors. Proprietary code, financial resources, hardware, and equipment that firms wish to donate to the project are entrusted to the foundation. In return, some foundations offer firms advisory or sponsor roles: mechanisms that can provide them with a voice on the project. On a day-to-day basis, commercial support of community-managed projects is enacted through the sponsored contributors that work on those projects. On a legal basis, the foundations play an important mediating role. In figure 20.1, release coordination is depicted with a question mark sitting between the authority of projects and their foundation. The strength and role that foundations play when collaborating with firms may well depend on the degree to which the authority of the foundation touches the technical core of the project.

In this model, the ownership and maintenance of code is decoupled from its sale and distribution. Without some means to retain their rights, it is unlikely that community-managed projects would have had the base of power necessary to engage with firms and create this model (O'Mahony

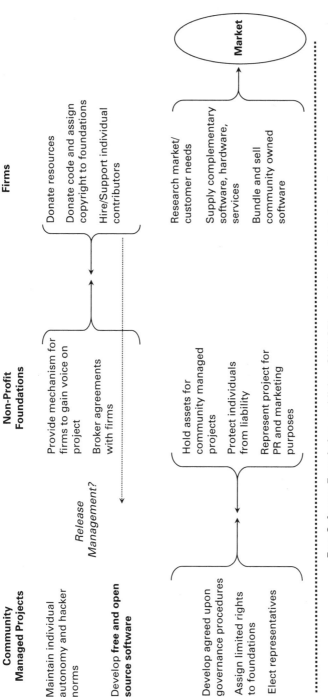

Figure 20.1
The role of nonprofit foundations

2003). Firms, for example, could have legally used community-developed software without necessarily collaborating with them. Community-managed projects held two bases of power that helped firms consider them a credible partner for collaboration: the market share and user base that derived from a project's technical excellence and the legal and normative controls that encouraged users to "give back" to the project. These two bases of power offset technical communities' lack of economic and political power and helped establish them as a viable commercial actor with which firms could partner.[20]

Granted, this analysis provides a rather static view of the legal and organizational structures that underlie a larger and more complex network of social relationships that flow in and out of these different forms. For example, a volunteer contributor could become sponsored by a firm and then be elected to a board position in a nonprofit foundation. Individuals who were once volunteers and have since founded firms may be active in shaping the nonprofit foundations that represent their project. Informants often stressed that they wished to perceive each other as individual contributors without regard to organizational affiliation. And yet, many informants that occupied two or more roles acknowledged that they often experienced role conflict when their activities touched multiple interests.

An implicit but unarticulated tenet of the hacker ethos is the desire to maintain pluralism. This belief takes two forms. First, there is pluralism in voice and process. Raymond has argued that with "more eyes, more bugs are shallow" (2001). An unstated condition is that diverse eyes are necessary for this lay maxim to hold. The more programmers from diverse cultures and backgrounds run various applications in different computing environments, the more likely it is that each user will detect problems unique to them. This allows code to be tested and contributions designed at a level that would require more permutations than are possible at most software firms. Diversity matters as much as volume. The second form of pluralism is required to make multilateral contributions possible: pluralism in the computing infrastructure itself. Software that is created independent of any one vendor's terms, is portable to different types of operating systems, and is interoperable with other applications allows pluralistic contributions to continue. The principle of pluralism depends upon shared standards and protocols, but I would argue that it also depends upon a form of organization that prevents dominant interests from forming.

Herein lies a source of conflict. Individuals contributing to community projects want to recognize each other as individuals, retain their individual autonomy, and remain as free from their employment affiliations as possible. On the other hand, without recognition of organizational affiliation, preserving pluralism will be more difficult. Project responses to potential conflict of interest problems have varied, but one feature that works in their favor is public disclosure. The organizational affiliation of project leaders is typically publicly available. When the relationship of one's activities to one's organizational affiliation becomes suspect, other community members are likely to be vocal about their concerns. For contributors who adopt project-based e-mail addresses, affiliation is less public. Over time, this could lead to further blurring of these different roles. The governance structure foundations provide may become one way to help preserve pluralism.

The evolution of a symbiotic relationship between community-managed projects and firms required adaptation from both actors, and some of these changes are manifested in the roles that nonprofit foundations fulfill, but not all. An understanding of how community-managed projects and firms maintain this relationship at the level of code contribution requires much more explication than has been discussed here. This structural examination of the community-firm collaboration model distributes a very different set of power, ownership, and rights than has been fully appreciated. From an economic perspective, one might ask whether community-managed projects outsourced their distribution costs, or whether firms outsourced their development costs. Arguments could be made to support both lines of thought, which is in itself perhaps a test of mutualism. A more sociological perspective might question whether community-managed projects that are both politically and pragmatically motivated have successfully resisted cooptation by powerful market dominants. Legally, nonprofit foundations play a critical role in preventing this from happening, but this role reinforces mutual relations that are normatively maintained. Equally significant implications are likely to stem from the intellectual and innovative contributions that can result from collaboration with a new type of actor in the software industry.

Notes

The research in this chapter was supported by a grant from the Social Science Research Council, with funds provided by the Alfred P. Sloan Foundation, as well as by funds from Stanford University's Center for Work, Technology, and Organization and the Stanford Technology Ventures Program. This research benefited from the helpful comments of the editors as well as Steve Barley, Bob Sutton, Mark

Granovetter, Jason Owen-Smith, Woody Powell, Neil Fligstein, Doug Guthrie, Rachel Campagna, Fabrizio Ferraro, and Victor Seidel. All errors are mine. I also thank my informants, who generously contributed their time.

1. A few community-managed projects allow organizations to participate as contributors; most only allow individuals to participate as contributing members.

2. I use *community-managed software project* to distinguish from *open source* and *free software* projects that can be sponsored and managed by firms, because firms can also start and manage open source projects.

3. The definition of *open source software*, which is based on the Debian Free Software Guidelines, is located at http://www.opensource.org. Without a trademark, the OSI, in consultation with their attorneys, designed an "open source" certification program that helps ensure that corporate software licenses that claim to be open source do indeed meet the criteria for open source as defined by the community.

4. This does not exclude the possibility of earning a profit from modifications, extensions of products, hardware, and services to collectively produced efforts.

5. There are more than 450 members who pay dues to the consortia and nearly 70 full-time staff around the world who contribute to W3C specifications.

6. The Massachusetts Institute of Technology (MIT) in the United States, the European Research Consortium for Informatics and Mathematics (ERCIM) in Europe, and Keio University in Japan host the W3C (http://www.w3.org).

7. ICANN was created in 1998 after a Department of Commerce white paper recommended that this federal function mission be privatized. For more information, see http://www.icann.org/general/white-paper-05jun98.htm.

8. For more information see "President's Report: ICANN—The Case for Reform," February 24, 2002, located at http://www.icann.org/general/lynn-reform-proposal-24feb02.htm. The privatization of ICANN may have been a more challenging task than that of the IETF, because global DNS management requires the active participation of governments and because it had less time to grow a community to support it before Internet access became ubiquitous.

9. In 2002, the FSF developed an associate membership plan, but it offers members limited decision-making rights.

10. I interviewed seven more contributors to community-managed projects in 2002–2003, for a total of 77.

11. The FSF supported Debian in its early years (1994–1995).

12. However, Debian does acknowledge the 143 vendors in 39 countries that sell Debian distribution and its other corporate supporters with a Partners Program.

13. http://www.apache.org/foundation/press/pr_1999_06_30.html

14. "Apache Software Foundation Reaches Agreement with Sun Microsystems To Allow Open Source Java Implementation," March 25, 2002, located at: http//jakarta.apache.org/site/jspa_agreement.html

15. The FSF is also vigilant in asking software contributors to assign their copyright. For more information on a comparison of copyright assignment practices across different projects, see O'Mahony 2003.

16. http://foundation.gnome.org/press/pr-gnome20.html.

17. Although a Fortune 500 firm helped catalyze the creation of the ASF, I did not find primary or secondary evidence of direct pressure from firms in the design of their foundation.

18. Gnome Project Charter, October 23, 2000.

19. The Free Standards Group and Linux International are incorporated as a 501(c)(6) organization. This class of nonprofits is reserved for business leagues and groups such as chambers of commerce. One distinction is that 501(c)(3) organizations provide public benefits, while 501(c)(6) organizations provide mutual benefits to a designated group. In order to earn a 501(c)(3) exemption from taxation from the IRS, an organization must be primarily devoted to charitable, religious, educational, scientific, literary, or public safety endeavors. The IRS has interpreted the development of free and open source software as furthering education or scientific goals.

20. Two other factors may have been important in enabling this collaborative model to unfold: the presence of a monopoly in the software market and digital technology. If cooperatives are partial, as opposed to identical suppliers of the same good, incumbent nonmonopoly firms are more likely to cooperate with a community form. Thus open source software's weakness in some areas of the consumer market coupled with the presence of a monopoly might have provided an opportunity structure favorable to cooperation with nonmonopoly firms. A second enabling factor is the material attributes of digital intellectual property itself. The ability to decouple development, modification, ownership, and distribution of rights helped grant organizing flexibility.

21   Free Science

Christopher Kelty

What is the *value* of science? In speculating about the success of open source/free software (OS/FS), users and advocates often suggest that it is "like science." It has characteristics of peer review, open data subject to validation and replication, and a culture of academic freedom, credit, civility, and reputation. The point of this comparison is that these characteristics directly contribute to producing (morally or technologically) better software, just as science is improved by them. This begs the question: what exactly is the value of either endeavor—financial, personal, aesthetic, moral, or all of these? How can we specify it?

This chapter investigates the value of science from the perspective of its social constitution; in particular, the importance of law, informal norms, and technology. It poses two related questions: "Is science like open source/free software?" and "Can you do science without open source/free software?"

Two Economies of Science

In studies of OS/FS, the question of motivation inevitably arises, and is usually answered in terms of reputation. Reputation, it is asserted, is like money, and governs how people make choices about what software they use or to which projects they contribute. A similar issue infuses the social and historical study of science: here the question of motivation concerns what might be called the "remunerative structure of science"; that is, the difference between cash payment for knowledge and ideas, and the distribution of reputation, trust, or credit for knowledge and ideas. On the one hand, many people (Merton 1973; Polanyi 1969; Mirowski 2001; Mirowski and Sent 2002) suggest that it is the latter that keeps science on the right track towards truth and objectivity. Much like the claim in OS/FS that openness and freedom lead to better software, the structure of remuneration through credit and public acknowledgment in science is said to ensure that the truest truths, and neither the cheapest or the most expensive ones emerge from the cauldron of scientific investigation.

On the other hand, the political economy of science is also deeply embedded in the health and progress of nations and societies. Science (like software) simply must be paid for somehow, and most scientists know this, even if they like to ignore it. What's more, if it is to be paid for—by governments, rich people, or corporations—it is probably required to contribute to their agenda somehow. In a representative democratic society, this means that the funding of science is done on condition that it contributes to "progress." It is only through science and technology (or so many economists have concluded) that growth, progress, and increasing prosperity are even possible. Scarce resources must be effectively distributed or the value of the whole enterprise collapses. Markets and money are one very effective way of achieving such allocation, and science, perhaps, should not be an exception.

The tension between these two demands can be summed up in two different questions concerning "value": (1) What is the best way to achieve efficient allocation of scarce resources? and (2) What is the proper way to organize a secular scientific and technological society so that it can contribute to the improvement of question 1? Needless to say, these questions must be kept separate to be meaningful. Where OS/FS appears, it is often in response to the subordination of question 2 to question 1. Free software licenses, the open collaborative ethic of OS/FS hackers, and the advocacy of lawyers and economists are all ways of reminding people that question 1 is not the only one on the table. This issue strikes science and technology at its heart—especially in its European and American forms in the universities and research labs. It is left to scientists, engineers, and managers in these places to insist on a continual separation of these two questions. In a practical sense, this separation means maintaining and improving systems of remuneration based on the principles of peer review, open access, experimental verification and the reduction of conflicts of interest. Without these, science is bought and sold by the highest bidder.

Doing Science

Is science like open source/free software? Yes, but not necessarily so. There are far too many examples in science of secrecy, meanness, Machiavellian plotting, and downright thievery for us to believe the prettied-up claim that science is inherently characterized by openness and freedom. Curiously, this claim is becoming increasingly accurate. From the sixteenth century on, norms and forms of openness have improved and evolved alongside the material successes of science and technology. The creation of institutions that safeguard openness, peer review, trust, and reputation is coincident with the rise and dominance of scientific and technical expertise today. The myth of a scientific genius toiling away in an isolated lab, discovering the truths of nature, bears little resemblance to the historically situated and fundamentally social scene of Robert Boyle demonstrating his air pump before the assembled Royal Society. Though it is easy to show how political, how contextual, or how "socially constructed" science is, this is not the point I am making (for some canonical references in this field, see Bloor 1976; Barnes 1977; Collins 1985; Pickering 1984; Latour 1986; Haraway 1997). Rather, the point is that the creation and maintenance of the institutions of science over the last 400 years has been a long, tortured, and occasionally successful attempt to give science the character of truth, openness, and objectivity that it promises. However, we are not there yet, and no scientists are free from the obligation of continuing this pursuit.

One compelling study of how science has become analogous to the OS/FS movements is the work of Robert K. Merton, the American sociologist who first attempted to think through what he called the "normative structure of science"—a sociological account of scientific action that focused on the reward system and the ethos of science (Merton 1973). The ethos of science (not unlike the famous "Hacker Ethic," Himanen 2001) is that set of norms and forms of life that structure the activity of scientists across nations, disciplines, organizations, or cultures. Merton identified four norms: universalism, communism (Merton's word), disinterestedness, and organized skepticism.

These norms are informal, which is to say that they are only communicated to you by your becoming part of the scientific establishment—they are not written down, and are neither legally nor technically binding (along the same lines as "You are a hacker when another hacker calls you a hacker"). However, despite the informal character of these norms, the institutions of science as we know them are formally structured around them. For example, communism requires a communication structure that allows the communally owned property—ideas, formulae, data, or results —to be disseminated: journals, letters, libraries, university postal systems, standards, protocols, and some more or less explicit notion of a public domain.

Or, another example. The norm, disinterestedness, is not an issue of egoism or altruism, but an institutional design issue. For disinterestedness to function at all, science must be closed off and separate from other parts of society, so that accountability is first and primarily to peers, not to managers, funders, or the public—even if this norm is continually under assault both from within and without. Similarly, organized skepticism is not simply methodological (whether Cartesian doubt or acceptable "p" values), but institutional as well—meaning that the norms of the institution of science must be such that they explicitly, if not exactly legally, promote the ability to maintain dissent even in the face of political power. Otherwise, truth is quickly compromised.

To take a historical example, consider Robert Boyle, as told by Steven Shapin and Simon Schaffer (1985) in *Leviathan and the Air Pump*. Boyle's genius lay not only in his formulation of laws concerning the relation of temperature, pressure and volume (a significant achievement in itself), according to Shapin and Schaffer, Boyle's activities also transformed the rules of modern experimentalism, of "witnessing" and of the means for establishing modern facts. Boyle's experimental air pump was seventeenth-century "big science." It required Boyle's significant fortune (he was, after all, the son of the Earl of Cork), access to master glass blowers and craftsmen, a network of aristocratic gentlemen interested in questions of natural philosophy, metaphysics, and physics. Perhaps most importantly, it required the Royal Society—a place where members gathered to observe, test, and "debug" (if you will) the claims of its members. It was a space by no means open to everyone (not truly public—and this is part of the famous dispute with Thomas Hobbes, which Shapin and Schaffer address in this book), because only certain people could be assumed to share the same language of understanding and conventions of assessment. This is a shortcoming that OS/FS shares with Boyle's age, especially regarding the relative absence of women; the importance of gender in Boyle's case is documented in (Potter 2001); there is much speculation, but little scholarship to explain it in the case of OS/FS.

To draw a parallel with OS/FS here, the Royal Society is in some ways the analog of the CVS repository: demonstrations (software builds), regular meetings of members (participation in mailing list discussion), and independent testing and verification are important structural characteristics they have in common. They both require a common language (or several), both natural and artificial.

Hackers often like to insist that the best software is obvious, simply because "it works." While it is true that incorrectly written software simply will not compile, such an insistence inevitably glosses over the negotiation, disputation, and rhetorical maneuvering that go into convincing people, for instance, that there is only one true editor (emacs).

A similar claim exists that scientific truth is "obvious" and requires no discussion (that is, it is independent of "our" criteria); however, this claim is both sociologically and scientifically simplistic. It ignores the obvious material fact that scientists, like programmers, organize themselves in collectivities, dispute with each other, silence each other, and engage in both grand and petty politics. Boyle is seen to have "won" his dispute with Hobbes, because Hobbes science was "wrong." This is convenient shorthand for a necessary collective process of evaluation without which no one would be right. It is only after the fact (literally, after the experiment becomes "a fact") that Boyle's laws come to belong to Boyle: what Merton called "intellectual property." A science without this process would reduce simply to authority and power. He with the most money pronounces the Law of the Gases. The absurdity of this possibility is not that the law of the gases is independent of human affairs (it is) but that human affairs go on deliberately misunderstanding them, until the pressure, so to speak, is too great.

Merton and others who study science and technology like to point out just how widespread and extensive this system of disputation, credit, and reward is: it includes eponomy (the naming of constants, laws, and planets), paternity (X, father of Y), honors, festschrifts, and other forms of social recognition, prizes like the Fields medal or the Nobel, induction into royal societies, and ultimately being written into the history books. These mechanisms are functional only in hindsight; it is perhaps possible to say that science would still proceed without all these supports, but it would have neither collective existence in nor discernible effect on the historical consciousness and vocational identity of practicing scientists. That is to say, the question of motivation is meaningless when considered in isolation. It is only when considered as a question of institutional evolution and collective interaction that motivation seems to have a role to play. In the end, it is equally meaningless to imagine that people have a "natural" desire to pursue science as it is to suggest that we are somehow programmed to desire money. Curiosity and greed may be inevitabilities (this hangs on your view of human nature), but the particular forms they take are not self-determining.

Funding Science

Of course, such informal norms are all well and good, but science costs money. On this point, there is no dispute. In Boyle's day, air pumps were like linear accelerators: expensive and temperamental. Even books could be quite dear, costing as much as the air pump itself (Johns 1998). For Boyle, money was no object; he had it, and other people around him did too. If they didn't, then a rich friend, a nobleman, a patron could be found. The patronage structures of science permeated its institutional, and perhaps even its cognitive, characteristics (Biagioli 1993). By contrast, twentieth-century science looks very different—first, because of massive philanthropy (Carnegie, Rockefeller, and others); second, because of massive military and government investment (Mirowski 2002; Mirowski and Sent 2002); and third, because of massive "soft money," research and development and contract investment (this most recent and rapid form of the commercialization of science differs from field to field, but can be said, in general, to have begun around 1980). The machines and spaces of science were never cheap, and have gotten only less so. The problem that this raises is essentially one of the dispensation of credit and return on investment.

Sociologists of science have attempted to finesse this difficulty in many of the same ways as observers of OS/FS: through notions of "reputation." Gift economies, in particular, were the study of a short article by Warren Hagstrom. He attempted to explain how the contributions to scientific research—such as giving a paper or crediting others—made the circulation of value an issue of reciprocity that approximated the gift-exchange systems explored by Marcel Mauss and Bronislaw Malinowski (Hagstrom 1982). Bruno Latour and Steve Woolgar also explore the metaphors of non-monetary exchange in science, in the course of their work on the construction of facts in laboratories. They suggested that there is a "cycle of credit" that includes both real money from granting agencies, governments, and firms and the recognition (in the form of published articles) that leads full circle to the garnering of grant money, and so on ad infinitum. In this cycle, both real money and the currency of reputation or credit work together to allow the scientist to continue to do research (Latour and Woolgar 1979). Here, the scientist wears two masks: one as the expert witness of nature, the other as the fund-seeking politician who promises what needs to be promised. Most scientists see the latter as a necessary evil in order to continue the former (see Latour 1986 for an alternate account). There is a similarity here with OS/FS programmers, most of whom, it is said, keep their day jobs, but spend their evenings and weekends working on OS/FS projects (Raymond 2001).

In these studies to date, the focus has been on the remuneration of the scientists, not the return on investment for the funders. In the cases of early modern patronage systems, the return to the patron was not strictly financial (though it could be), but was often also laden with credit in a more circumscribed and political sense (for example, the status of a monarchy or of a nation's science; see Biagioli 1993). In a similar sense, philanthropists build for themselves a reputation and a place in history. Government and military funding expects returns in specific areas: principally war, but also health, eradication of disease, and economic growth. Soft money, venture capital, and research and development, on the other hand, are primarily interested in a strictly calculated return on investment (though here too, it would be disingenuous to suggest that this were the only reward—venture capitalists and corporations seek also to be associated with important advances in science or technology and often gain more in intangible benefits than real money). The problem of funding science is never so clean as to simply be an allocation of scarce resources. It includes also the allocation of intangible and often indescribable social goods. Strangely, Robert Merton called these goods "intellectual property" (Garfield 1979).

It is important to distinguish, however, the metaphorical from the literal use of intellectual property: in the case of the scientist, reputation is inalienable. No one can usurp a reputation earned; it cannot be sold; it cannot be given away. It may perhaps be shared by association; it may also be unjustly acquired—but it is not an alienable possession. Intellectual property granted by a national government, on the other hand, exists precisely to generate wealth from its alienability: inventors, artists, writers, composers, and yes, scientists, can sell the products of their intellectual labor and transfer the rights to commercialize it, in part or in whole, by signing a contract. The reputation of the creator is assumed to be separate from the legal right to profit from that creativity. This legal right—intellectual property as a limited monopoly on an invention or writing—is often confused with the protection of reputation as an inalienable right to one's name; this is not guaranteed by intellectual property law (on this confusion throughout history, see Johns 1998).

This confusion of the metaphorical and the literal uses of intellectual property goes both ways. Today it is virtually impossible to step foot in a lab without signing a licensing agreement for something, be it a machine, a tool, a process, a reagent, a genetic sequence, or a mouse. Many of the things biologists or engineers once traded with each other (cell lines, testing data, images, charts, and graphs) are now equally expected to generate revenue as well as results. The race to publish is now also a race to patent. It might even be fair to say that many scientists now associate success in science with return on investment, or see the "free" exchange of ideas as more suspicious than a quid pro quo based on monetary exchange (see Campbell et al. 2002). This metaphorical confusion necessitates a closer look at these practices.

Valuing Science

The metaphors of currency and property in science meet in a peculiar place: the Science Citation Index. Citation indices give one a very prominent, if not always precise, indicator of value. It is a funny kind of value, though. Even though citation is quantifiable, not all reputation depends on citations (though some tenure committees and granting agencies beg to differ on this point). Qualitative evaluation of citing practices is an essential part of their usefulness. Even though work that isn't included in such databases is at a rather serious disadvantage, reputationally speaking, science citation indices do not simply measure something objective (called reputation). Rather, they give people a tool for comparative measure of success in achieving recognition.

Robert Merton clearly understood the power of citation indexing—both as currency and as a kind of registration of intellectual property for the purposes of establishing priority. In the preface to Eugene Garfield's 1979 book *Citation Indexing*, Merton says, "[Citations in their moral aspect] are designed to repay intellectual debts in the only form in which this can be done: through open acknowledgment of them" (Garfield 1979, viii). He thus makes citations the currency of repayment. But he goes even further, explaining scientific intellectual property in a manner that directly parallels the claims made for OS/FS's success as a reputation economy:

We can begin with one aspect of the latent social and cultural structure of science presupposed by the historically evolving systematic use of references and citations in the scientific paper and book. That aspect is the seemingly paradoxical character of property in the scientific enterprise: the circumstance that the more widely scientists make their intellectual property available to others, the more securely it becomes identified as their property. For science is public, not private knowledge. Only by publishing their work can scientists make their contribution (as the telling word has it) and only when it thus becomes part of the public domain of science can they truly lay claim to it as theirs. For the claim resides only in the recognition of the source of the contribution by peers. (Garfield 1979, vii–viii)

This claim is remarkable, but not dissimilar to that remarkable claim of OS/FS (particularly open source) advocates—that openness results in the creation of better software. Merton here claims as much for science. The incentive to produce science depends on the public recognition of priority. The systems involved in making this property stick to its owner are reliable publishing, evaluation, transmission, dissemination, and ultimately, the archiving of scientific papers, equations, technologies, and data. As stated previously, this priority is inalienable: when it enters this system of registration, it is there for good, dislodged only in the case of undiscovered priority or hidden fraud. It is not alienable intellectual property, but constant; irretrievably and forever after granted. Only long after the fact can diligent historians dislodge it.

Who grants this property? The key is in Merton's paradox: "the more widely scientists make their intellectual property available to others, the more securely it becomes identified as their property" (Garfield 1979, vii). That is, no one (or everyone) grants it. The wider the network of people who know that Boyle is responsible for demonstrating that under a constant temperature gas will compress as pressure is increased, the more impossible it becomes to usurp. Only by having a public science in this sense is that kind of lasting property possible. A privatized science, on the other hand, must eternally defend its property with the threat of force, or worse, of litigation. While a public science tends toward ever greater circulation of information in order to assure compensation in reputation, a private science must develop ever more elaborate rules and technologies for defining information and circumscribing its use. Not only is a private science inefficient; it also sacrifices the one thing that a public science promises: progress.

Nonetheless, a public science is only possible through publication. The publication and circulation of results is a sine qua non that up until the advent of the Internet was possible only through academic publishers, university presses, and informal networks of colleagues and peers. Reputation was effectively registered through the small size and manifest fragility of the publication network. It has been successful enough and widespread enough that most people now associate the quality of a result with the publication it appears in. We have a well-functioning system, however imperfect, that allows a widely distributed network of scientists to coevaluate the work of their peers.

From an institutional standpoint, this is a very good thing. As I said earlier, science has not always been open or free, but it has become more and more so over the last 400 years. The functions of openness that have developed in science exist only because publishers, universities, and academic presses—along with scientists—believe in them and continue to propagate them.

To some extent, this system of reputational remuneration has lived in strained but peaceful coexistence with the monetary structure of funding. It is only of late, with the expansion of intellectual property law and the decreasing vigilance of anti–trust policing, that the legal and institutional framework of the U.S. economic system has actually become hostile to science.

Consider the situation scientists face today. Most scientists are forced to explicitly consider the trade-off between the ownership of data, information, or results and the legal availability of them. In designing an experiment, it is no longer simply a process of finding and using the relevant data, but of either licensing or purchasing it, and of hiring a lawyer to make sure its uses are properly circumscribed. In economic terms, the transaction costs of experiment have skyrocketed, specifically as a result of the increased scope of intellectual property and more generally due to the ever increasing dangers of attendant litigation. In scientific terms, it means that lawyers, consultants, and public relations agents are increasingly stationed in the lab itself, and they increasingly contribute to the very design of experiments.

The result is a transformation of science, in which the activity of using an idea and giving credit is confused with the activity of buying a tool and using it. Science becomes no longer public knowledge, but publically visible, privately owned knowledge.

The skeptic might ask: why not let intellectual property law govern all aspects of knowledge? What exactly is the difference between using an idea and buying one? If the copyright system is an effective way of governing who owns what, why can't it also be an effective way of giving credit where credit is due? Such a proposition is possible in the context of U.S. law, and less so in European intellectual property law, which makes an attempt (however feeble) to differentiate the two activities. In German law, for instance, the "moral right of the author" is presumed to be inalienable, and therefore a separate right from that of commercial exploitation. While U.S. law doesn't make this distinction, most U.S. citizens do. Even the firm believer in copyright law wants to protect his reputation; no one, it seems, wants to give up (metaphorical) ownership of their ideas. Unfortunately, these are issues of fraud, plagiarism, and misappropriation—not of commercial exploitation. And these are fears that have grown enormously in an era of easy online publication. What it points to is not a need for stronger intellectual property law, but the need for an alternative system of protecting reputation from abuse.

The need to somehow register priority and (metaphorical) ownership of ideas is a problem that cannot be solved through the simple expansion of existing intellectual property law. It will require alternative solutions. These solutions might be technical (such as the evolution of the science citation index—for example, cite-seer and LANL) and they might also be legal (devices like the Creative Commons licenses, which require attribution, but permit circulation). In either case, science and technology are both at a point similar to the one Robert Boyle faced in the seventeenth century. A new way of "witnessing" experimental knowledge is necessary. A new debate over the "public" nature of science is necessary.

Many people in OS/FS circles are aware of this relationship between informal reputation and calculable monetary value. Even Eric Raymond's highly fantastic metaphorical treatment of reputation reports an important fact: the list of contributors to a project should never be modified by subsequent users (that is, contribution is inalienable). To do so is tantamount to stealing. Similarly, Rishab Ayer Ghosh and Vipul Ved Prakash (2000) also recognize this nonlegal convention; they combined it with the formal availability of free software packages and created a tool much like the Science Citation Index: it adds up all contributions of individuals by grepping (using a Unix text search command) packages for e-mail addresses and copyrights. We might call what they find "greputation," since it bears the same relation to reputation that money supposedly does to value. That is, it is the material and comparable marker of something presumed to be more complex—the reputation of a scientist—just as money is an arbitrary technology for representing value.

In order to understand why reputation is at stake in science, we might take this analogy a bit further and ask what exactly is the relationship between money and value. Economic dogma has it that money is a standard of value. It is a numerical measure that is used to compare two or more items via a third, objectively fixed measure. This is an unobjectionable view, unless one wants to ask what it is that people are doing when they are valuing something—especially when that something is an idea.

However, from the perspective of Georg Simmel, the early twentieth-century German sociologist whose magnum opus is devoted to the subject (Simmel 1978), considering money as something that simply facilitates a natural human tendency (to value things according to cardinal ranking) is a sociologically and anthropologically illegitimate assumption. Humans are not born with such an objective capacity vis-à-vis the world around them. Rather, since money is a living set of institutions that calibrate value and a set of technologies (cash, check, credit, and so on) that allow it to circulate or accumulate, then humans are caught within a net that both allows and teaches them how to reckon with money—how to count with it, as well as on it. Even if staunch neoclassicists agree that the rational actor of economic models does not exist, that by no means suggests he cannot be brought into existence by the institutions of economic life. To borrow David Woodruff's willful anachronism: "Humans are endowed only with an ordinal sense of utility; they attain something like a cardinal sense of utility ("value") only through the habit of making calculations in money" (Woodruff 1999).

If we consider this insight with respect to the currency of reputation, as well as that of money, we can say the following: the standard of value (money, or the citation) serves only to stabilize the network of obligations thus created: in the case of money economies, a single cardinal value; in the case of citations, a widely recognized, though sometimes disputed reputation. The vast interconnected set of legal obligations that money represents can be universally accounted by a single standard—a cardinal value. But if we reckoned the world of obligations using a different standard—a nonnumerical one, for instance—then humans could also learn to express utility and value in that system. Money, it should be very clear, simply isn't natural.

Therefore, a similar approach to scientific citations would have to focus on something other than their cardinality. And in fact, this is exactly what happens. Citations are simply not fungible. Some are good (representing work built upon or extended), some are bad (representing work that is disputed or dismissed), some are indifferent (merely helpful for the reader), and some are explicit repayments (returning a citation, even when it is not necessarily appropriate). Often the things that are most well known are so well known that they are no longer cited (F = ma, or natural selection), but this could hardly diminish the reputation of their progenitors. It requires skill to read the language and subtleties of citations and to express gratitude and repay intellectual debt in similarly standardized, though not simply quantitative ways. There are whole stories in citations.

This description is equally accurate in open source and free software. Although some might like to suggest that good software is obvious because "it works," most programmers have deep, abiding criteria for both efficiency and beauty. Leaf through Donald Knuth's *The Art of Computer Programming* for a brief taste of such criteria and the interpretive complexity they entail (Knuth 1997). The scientist who does not cite, or acknowledge, incurs irreconcilable debts—debts that cannot be reckoned in the subtle currency of citations. The more legitimate the information infrastructure of scientific publications, databases, and history books becomes, the more essential it is to play by those rules, or find increasingly creative ways to break them. In money, as in science, to refuse the game is to disappear from the account.

Today, we face a novel problem. The institutions we've inherited to manage the economy of citation and reputation (publishing houses, journals, societies and associations, universities and colleges) used to be the only route to publicity, and so they became the most convenient route to verification. Today we are faced with a situation where publication has become trivial, but verification and the management of an economy of citation and reputation has not yet followed. In the next section, I conclude with two cases where it will very soon be necessary to consider these issues as part of the scientific endeavor itself.

A Free (as in Speech) Computational Science

In 1999, at the height of the dot-com boom, there was an insistent question: "But how do you *make money* with free software?" I must admit that at the time this question seemed urgent and the potential answers seductive. In 2003, however, it seems singularly misdirected. From the perspective of science and technology, where software can be as essential a tool as any other on the lab bench, the desire to make free software profitable seems like wanting a linear accelerator to produce crispier french fries. You *could* do that, but it is a rather profound misunderstanding of its function.

I propose a different, arguably more important, question: "Can you do science without free software?"

By way of conclusion, I want to offer two compelling examples of computational science as it is developing today. The promise of this field is evident to everyone in it, and these examples should be viewed as evidence of early success, but also as early warnings. What they share is a very precarious position with respect to traditional scientific experiment, and—in terms Robert Boyle would understand—traditional scientific "witnessing." It is impossible to think about either of these endeavors without considering the importance of software (both free and proprietary), hardware, networks and network protocols, standards for hardware and software, and, perhaps most importantly, software development methodologies. It is in the need to explicitly address the constitution, verification, and reliability of the knowledge produced by such endeavors that something like OS/FS must be an essential part of the discussion.

Bioelectric Field Mapping

Chris Johnson is the director of the Scientific Computing Institute (SCI) at the University of Utah. SCI is a truly stunning example of the kind of multidisciplinary computational "big science" that relies equally on the best science, the best software programming, and of course, the best hardware money can buy. Dr. Johnson's bioelectric field mapping project (http://www.sci.utah.edu) extends the possibilities of understanding, simulating, and visualizing the brain's electrical field. It makes EEGs look positively prehistoric.

The project makes sophisticated use of established mathematical and computational methods (methods that have been researched, reviewed, and published in standard science and engineering publications); neuroanatomical theories of the brain (which are similarly reviewed results); mathematical modeling software (for instance, MatLAB, Mathematica); graphics-rendering hardware; and a wonderful array of open and closed, free and non-free software. It is a testament both to the ethos of scientific ethos and to the best in management of large-scale scientific projects.

What makes Dr. Johnson's project most interesting is the combination of traditional scientific peer-review and his plea for more effective large-scale software management methodology in science. Here is a chance for the best of science and the best of business to collaborate in producing truly exceptional results. But it is here that Dr. Johnson's project is also a subject of concern. In a recent talk, amidst a swirl of Poisson equations, Mesh generation schemes, and finite element models, Johnson pointed out the difficulty of *converting file formats*. Dr. Johnson's admirable attempt to create a computational science that weaves mathematical models, computational simulations, and graphical visualization has encountered the same problem every PC user in the world laments daily: incompatible file formats.

Part of this problem is no doubt the uncoordinated and constant reinvention of the wheel that scientists undertake (often in order to garner more credit for their work). The other part, however, concerns the legal and political context where such decisions are made—and they are usually not made in labs or institutes. This second and more serious problem concerns whether the circumvention of particular file formats in scientific research is affected by the institutional changes in intellectual property or antitrust law. Even if it isn't, knowing requires the intervention of lawyers aplenty to find out—and the unfortunate alternative is to do nothing. These issues must be addressed, whether through licenses and contracts or through the courts, in order to ensure that the ordinary activity of scientists continues—and does not fall afoul of the law.

The best science, in this case, depends on an analogy with the principles and practices of free software and open source: not only are source code and documentation resources that Dr. Johnson would like to see shared, but so are data (digital images and data from high-end medical scanners) as well as geometric and computational models that are used in the computational pipeline. Only by sharing all of these creations will it be possible for science as a distributed peer-reviewed activity to reach even tentative consensus on the bioelectric fields of human brains.

An Internet Telescope

In order to avoid any suggestion that a large Redmond-based corporation is at fault in any of this, take a second example. Jim Gray, research scientist at Microsoft, has been working on an "Internet telescope," which federates astronomical data from telescopes around the world (http://research.microsoft.com/~Gray). His manifest skill in database engineering (he is a Turing Award winner) and his extraordinary creativity have resulted in a set of database tools that can be used to answer astronomical questions no single observatory could answer—simply by querying a database.

Dr. Gray's project is a triumph of organizational and technical skill, another example of excellent project management combined with the best of traditional scientific research. Dr. Gray is assisted considerably by the fact that astronomical data is effectively worthless—meaning that, unlike genetic sequence data, it is neither patented nor sold. It is, though, hoarded and often unusable without considerable effort invested into *converting file formats*. Gray will ultimately be more successful than most university researchers and amateur database builders, because of the resources and the networks at his command, but the problem remains the same for all scientists: the social and normative structure of science needs to be kept institutionally and legally open for anything remotely like peer-reviewed and reliable knowledge to be possible. All of this data, and especially the programming languages, web services, databases, and Internet protocols that are used in the creation of the telescope, need to remain open to inspection, and remain ultimately legally modifiable without the permission of their owners. If they are not, then scientific knowledge is not "witnessed" in the traditional sense, but decided in advance by lawyers and corporate public relations departments (Dr. Gray gets around this problem because of his skill in achieving informal and formal participation from each participant individually—but this is probably a solution only Microsoft can afford, and one that does not scale).

Can these sciences exist without free software, or something like it? George Santayana famously quipped: "Those who cannot remember the past are condemned to repeat it." Now might be a time to both remember the past, and to *insist* upon repeating it. Science, as an open process of investigation and discovery, validation, and verification, is not a guaranteed inheritance, but something that had to be created and has yet to be perfected. Openness can not be assumed; it must be asserted in order to be assured.

High Noon at OS Corral: Duels and Shoot-Outs in Open Source Discourse

Anna Maria Szczepanska, Magnus Bergquist, and Jan Ljungberg

The open source software (OSS) movement can be related to the societal changes that started in the late 1960s: the rise of a network society supported by new information and communication technologies and the rise of new forms of collective actions, which also have been referred to as "new social movements" (see Touraine 1981; Melucci 1996; Thörn 1997). The emergence of these movements has been explained by changes in the relations between the economic, political, and cultural powers and institutions that have supported a transition from a modern to a late modern or postindustrial society and lately been linked to an understanding of the importance of the rise of a global network society and new forms of communication (Castells 1996; Giddens 1990). The emergence of a network society, or information society, has involved new conflicts regarding the control over information, knowledge, symbolic capital, and social relationships. These are conflicts closely connected to unequal or transformed power relations between different social positions in the new global society. According to both Thörn (1997) and Melucci (1996), it is in this social climate of opposition, ambivalence, and conflict that new forms of collective actions have emerged.

American contemporary movements of the 1960s gave rise, as Castells (1996) has shown, to an intellectual climate that contributed to and inspired the march of technical innovations and the "culture of IT". However, the rise of information technology also gave birth to conflicting ideas about how the tools to create and bring forth information should be developed, and what they should look like. When large hardware and software companies—such as IBM and later, Microsoft—slowly gained dominance over the growing IT market, this had serious consequences for how the power relations between different actors in the field of software development were organized. A resistance to this development has been growing around different advocates of open source and free software, raising questions on the freedom of speech and information. Advocates of open source and free software have also in recent years been noticeable in the discussions on how to bridge the "digital divide," thus trying to offer an alternative IT infrastructure that avoids expensive licensing structures. In order to achieve a position in the world of systems development as a counter-movement to proprietary software actors, the members of the open source movement have to be able to create a shared identity. As Thörn (1997) points out, collective identity is one of the most important traits of any social movement. Collective identity is created by, or related to, a movement culture comprised of a relatively autonomous network of interactions between different individuals, institutions, and organizations. In order to be effective, movements have to be goal-oriented, and act as strategic collectives that always strive toward social change. Collective identity is a powerful force that has to be fully recognized when understanding how social movements are assembled and constituted. Collective identity provides an important context for the creation of meaning, social integration, and action. The symbolic dimension of collective action is to manifest, and thereby constitute, the unity of the group. This is done through a multidimensional process of communication—that is, rituals and demonstrations—or with the help of texts. Collective identity thereby incorporates different forms of narrative that create an overall meaning for the individual, for his or her everyday practices, and for the symbolic manifestations that are communicated by members. Accordingly, the production and use of texts give new social movements a discursive form (Thörn 1997).

Viewing Open Source from a Discourse Perspective

The concept of discourse builds on a social constructionist perspective where language is seen as constitutive of social reality; this means that an important access to reality is through language and its manifestation in discourses. A discourse can be understood as a group of statements that produce and define objects of knowledge, but also inform us in how to conduct our social and cultural practices (Foucault 1972). Discourse is tied to practice, and is articulated not only through text, but also through metaphors, symbols, cultural codes, stories, pictures, and other forms of representation.

Discourse constructs the subject and present reality in a certain way, thus creating limits between true and false, relevance and irrelevance, right and wrong. It also limits other ways in which a topic can be defined (Hall 1992).

Discourses thereby create webs of meaning that cluster around certain topics. However, a discourse is not a closed entity, but is continuously reconstructed in contact and struggle with other discourses. Different discourses that represent certain ways of speaking about the world then struggle for domination. This struggle concerns taking command in defining the world from a certain point of view; that is, to become the normative discourse defining social order and making sense of the world according to that view. Discourses possess different powers, which in some sense make us more secure, feeling safer in a world that is somewhat predictable, but they also operate in disciplinary and authoritarian ways.

Analyzing discourses in the open source movement is not about reducing the movement to texts. It is, rather, a way to understand how collective identity is created, communicated, and managed in the form of "webs of meanings." Understanding discursive practices becomes especially important because of the movement's decentralized and networked character. In this chapter, we will analyze different discourses taking place both within and outside the open source movement. First we present discourses that are related to how a sense of "us" is created within the movement. Then we discuss how authority and leadership is created, or how discourses are "managed." We then elaborate on how the enemy is constructed, and how the enemy's discourse fights back. Finally we address internal dynamics between different actors in the open source community.

Constructing the Hacker

Developing discourses is vital for providing the members of the movement with a meaningful context that enables creative software development activities across organizational and geographical boundaries. People feel a bond with others not because they share the same interest, but because they need that bond in order to make sense of what they are doing. Discourses in the form of texts and symbols enable members of a community to affirm themselves as subjects of their action and parts of a collective action. Actors in the open source movement handle a specific set of discursive practices. They gain status as they learn to master the rhetoric of the community.

This process of socialization often starts with being a "newbie" and ends with achieving the status of being a "hacker" (Bergquist and Ljungberg 2001). In order to be able to socialize new members into the community, symbolic representations of the core values in the community must be created and communicated. This is done in several ways: through virtual objects, symbols, strings of statements and messages, and with the help of certain ways of associating with symbolic tokens that sometimes, from an objective point of view, are only vaguely related to the core business of open source. In this section, some examples will be given on how the relationship between discourse, practice, and identity is constructed and communicated in the open source movement.

One way to understand the collectiveness within the open source community is through the concept "hacker." Even if there seems to be no unambiguous definition of the concept, certain characteristics like creativity and a genuine interest for troubleshooting most commonly describes the work of a hacker (see for example, http://wikipedia.org). The online document "The New Hackers Dictionary" including the Jargon File (Jargon File 4.3.1), which is well known within the hacker community, gives a comprehensive insight in the tradition, folklore, and humor of the hacker community. The Jargon File includes the Jargon Lexicon a compilation of the specific vocabulary used by hackers. The Jargon File is one instantiation of a discourse that is continuously replicated in different forms in the community. Implicitly the documentation contains general social and cultural aspects of what it means to be a hacker, what they do, what their preferences are, and, in that sense, what defines them as a collective.

The Jargon File is a continuing work-in-progress. The earliest version of the Jargon File was created in university milieus, especially the MIT AI Lab and the Stanford AI Lab and other communities that grew out of the cultures around ARPANET, LISP, and PDP-10 in the 1970s. It was also in these technical milieus that the concept of *hacker* came into use. Eric Raymond, one of the leading figures within the community, has done the main work, with the latest version updated and presented with the characteristic version numbers: 4.3.1, 29 June 2001. It has been revised so that it complements the cultures that have emerged due to new programming languages, hardware and software applications: most prominently the C language and Unix communities, but also, for example, IBM PC programmers and Amiga fans. The fact that Raymond has updated the original Jargon File to include different hacker cultures indicates the importance of defining the hacker community so that it represents different understandings of what it means to be a hacker.

Eric Raymond divided the content in the Jargon Lexicon into three categories: (1) slang, or informal language from mainstream English or nontechnical subcultures; (2) jargon, "slangy" language peculiar to or predominantly found among hackers, and finally, (3) techspeak, the formal technical vocabulary of programming, computer science, electronics, and other fields connected to hacking. The understanding of hacker culture thus must be seen as a multidimensional process of communication between different cultural manifestations deriving from both a social (real-life) and a technical (virtual) level. The hacker culture takes inspiration from and merges different cultural expressions. It also expresses different distinct fields that stand in opposition to each other. In this process, we can see several discourses take form. These involve hackers as a distinct field that excludes other fields as nonhackers, but also "internal" fields constituted by different hacker cultures as defined by their interests in and use of different technologies.

Looking up the word *hacker* in the Jargon File, the affinity toward the "intellectual challenge of creatively overcoming or circumventing limitations" is considered the primary characteristic, but a hacker is also defined as connoting "membership in the global community defined by the Net" and as "a person capable of appreciating hack value" and one possessing "hacker ethics." Since the hacker community is described as a meritocracy based on ability, it is also stated that hackers consider themselves something of an elite (Jargon File 4.3.1). The problem-solving aspects of participation in the open source movement—to be able to fix a bug right away and participate in rapid software development through knowledge sharing—are characteristics commonly associated with the strengths of the movement, and the skills of the programmers.

However, a common characteristic of movements is internal conflicting relations between different groups of actors. In the open source movement, some conflicts are due to different hacker cultures and traditions. In an enclosure to the *New Hackers Dictionary*, Eric Raymond has incorporated a section called "Updating JARGONG.TXT Is Not Bogus: An Apologia" (Jargon File 4.3.1). In this text, Raymond responds to criticism from hackers representing the PDP-10 culture. The criticism pointed out that the Jargon File was Unix-centric, that Raymond lacked insider knowledge of their culture, and that blending Unix and PDP-10 cultures distorted the original jargon file. This illustrates an example of the importance of experiences and meaning connected to a certain field of interest and practices with its own historical process. It also points to the significance of being accepted as a separate collective with its own cultural identity. In Raymond's answers to the criticism, he verified the fact that the Unix and the PDP-10 community did have their own identities but that they also belong together as being hackers. The "us" is thereby expanded to include various groups and networks creating an even greater potential developer and user base. The tension between different (groups of) actors within the open source movement, and between the open source movement and the free software movement, is an interesting topic leading to a deeper understanding of how collective identity is created and managed in the open source movement. This topic is elaborated upon later in this chapter.

Managing the Production of Discourses—The Leaders

Eric Raymond has become a leading figure within the open source movement, and he is the president of the movement's formal body, the Open Source Initiative. He attained this position as a recognized contributor to the Linux project, and as the author of a much-cited anthropological analysis of the open source movement (Raymond 2001). He has also drawn considerable attention to the open source community with, for example, the publication of the "Halloween documents," a set of confidential Microsoft memos that discussed the potential threat from open source software to Microsoft products. These memos were important for the open source movement, in the sense that their competitors acknowledged the potential of the movement.

Through these different types of contributions and through widespread reputation, Raymond has become a key person in the open source movement. Such leaders or "movement intellectuals" are interesting, because they possess great power through the advantage of interpreting the orientation, goal, and work of the movement. They have the power to formulate and set standards of what should be done, how it should be done, and why it should be done. They also have the power to define and manipulate texts and symbols and arrange them within the discursive context. As in the example of the Jargon File, we can see how Raymond tries to formulate a "true hacker nature" as a strong symbol for a collective identity throughout his vivid descriptions of how hackers are, and how they think and code.

In the sense that movement intellectuals play a central role for identifying the collective, they enjoy the ability to include and exclude (Thörn 1997). They create cultural forms that set the agenda for the movement, but also create new forms of cultural and social understanding of the community. This can be exemplified by the rhetoric of different movement intellectuals, as with the polemic between Eric Raymond and Richard Stallman, founder and leader of the free software movement from which open source grew.

Stallman, a hacker formerly at MIT, has positioned himself as one of the most prominent activist within the programming community, with large contributions to free software, his GNU/Linux project, for example, and as the founder of the Free Software Foundation (FSF). Stallman always adopted a more ideological line in his work with free software, promoting the freedom of hacking and information, than that found in the open source movement. Taking a look at his personal website, his political interest in different "freedom of speech"—and in the civil rights movements—are evident. However, Raymond has a more pragmatic outlook, which maybe is best explained via a well-known dispute between Raymond and Stallman, initiated by a posting from Stallman to an Internet bulletin board:

People have been speaking of me in the context of the Open Source movement. That's misleading, because I am not a member of it. I belong to the Free Software movement. In this movement we talk about freedom, about principle, about the rights that computer users are entitled to. The Open Source movement avoids talking about those issues, and that is why I am not joining it. The two movements can work together on software. . . . But we disagree on the basic issues. (Stallman 1999b)

Raymond responded with an essay where he stated that he could agree on Stallman's ideas about freedom and rights, but that it was ineffective and bad tactics for the free software community to engage in those issues:

OSI's tactics work [. . .] FSF's tactics don't work, and never did. [. . .] RMS's [Richard Matthew Stallman] best propaganda has always been his hacking. So it is for all of us; to the rest of the world outside our little tribe, the excellence of our software is a far more persuasive argument for openness and freedom than any amount of high-falutin appeal to abstract principles. So the next time RMS, or anybody else, urges you to "talk about freedom," I urge you to reply "Shut up and show them the code." (Raymond 1999b)

Though the open source and free software movements share an ambition to create free software of high quality, and share mutual cultural expressions through the hacker community, this is an example of a power struggle where the leaders take different roles as symbolic organizers. It is a battle that originates from different perspectives on how work should be done and what the strategies are to be. Most importantly, this inspires members to act on different forces and purposes when contributing to the movement.

Last but not least, Linus Torvalds should be mentioned, as he is considered an icon of the open source movement. Because of his extraordinary contribution in leading the development of the Linux kernel and his further work making decisions about contributions to the Linux kernel project, he is considered one of the father figures of the open source movement. Torvalds seldom comments on political issues concerning the work of the movement. Torvalds keeps a low profile, which can be seen as a symbolic incarnation of the hacker ethic. At the same time he is seen as the charismatic leader of the movement. The charismatic leader is recognized as being such by virtue of the extraordinary qualities that ensure him/her a mass following (Melucci 1996). In this case, Torvalds has become a symbol for the movement as such; he stands for the kind of values and practices that are associated with the hacker. It might seem contradictory to define a person who keeps low profile as charismatic, but then it is considered good manners amongst hackers not to brag about the exploits made. A movement leader receives his/her position as a leader of the community if he/she is publicly acknowledged by the collective. In the hacker context, this is therefore mainly a matter of exceptional contributions and reputation. This is clearly expressed in the Jargon File by the definition of *demigod*:

demigod *n.* A hacker with years of experience, a world-wide reputation, and a major role in the development of at least one design, tool, or game used by or known to more than half of the hacker community. To qualify as a genuine demigod, the person must recognizably identify with the hacker community and have helped shape it. Major demigods include Ken Thompson and Dennis Ritchie (co-inventors of Unix and C), Richard M. Stallman (inventor of emacs), Larry Wall (inventor of Perl), Linus Torvalds (inventor of Linux), and most recently James Gosling (inventor of Java, NeWS, and GOSMACS) and Guido van Rossum (inventor of Python). In their hearts of hearts, most hackers dream of someday becoming demigods themselves, and more than one major software project has been driven to completion by the author's veiled hopes of apotheosis. See also **net.god**, **true-hacker**. (Jargon File 4.3.1)

Us and Them—Constructing the Enemy

In order to be able to construct an "us" that can be successfully communicated within the movement, a "them" also has to be constructed in order to sharpen the edges and help the movement build their collective identity. A "them" is a part of all movements. It has the function of strengthening the movement as well as legitimating its norms, values, and actions. The following examples taken from the Jargon Dictionary show how hackers define themselves when articulating what they are not. In the humorous example of *suit*, a certain "hackish" lifestyle is expressed by an ironic description of lifestyle tokens that belong to the other:

suit 1. Ugly and uncomfortable "business clothing" often worn by nonhackers. Invariably worn with a "tie," a strangulation device that partially cuts off the blood supply to the brain. It is thought that this explains much about the behavior of suit-wearers. (Jargon File 4.3.1)

The open source movement seems to have created a notion of open source software being superior to proprietary software. A movement needs an "enemy" to strengthen the community from the inside. In the open source movement the enemy part is played by the proprietary software industry, most often represented by Microsoft, which has played an important role as the "evil empire," as in this example taken from the Jargon File:

Evil Empire [from Ronald Reagan's famous characterization of the communist Soviet Union] Formerly IBM, now Microsoft. Functionally, the company most hackers love to hate at any given time. Hackers like to see themselves as romantic rebels against the Evil Empire, and frequently adopt this role to the point of ascribing rather more power and malice to the Empire than it actually has. (Jargon File 4.3.1)

The world of proprietary software is not only the evil enemy; it is also portrayed as a world of less intelligence. In an example of "adbusting" (figure 22.1), found at the "Micro$oft HatePage," a certain "collective excellence" constituting the open source movement is implicitly stated in contrast to what are considered the weaknesses of the "enemies."

The argument is that even though the enemy has resources in the form of people and money, the software developed is of low quality. The open source movement has a superior organization, smarter developers, and a culture that enables the movement to create software of higher quality in less time. Open source software is based on real needs, addressing real problems and developed in a fashion that secures the best quality compared to proprietary software development, which is driven only by the desire to make money and protect its intellectual property rights. The "Evil Empire" and "Borgs" symbolize this oppression by monopolistic software companies that try to limit the freedom of using and modifying software.

Borg [. . .] In *Star Trek: The Next Generation*, the Borg is a species of cyborg that ruthlessly seeks to incorporate all sentient life into itself; their slogan is "You will be assimilated. Resistance is futile." In hacker parlance, the Borg is usually Microsoft, which is thought to be trying just as ruthlessly to assimilate all computers and the

Figure 22.1
An example of "adbusting"

entire Internet to itself (there is a widely circulated image of Bill Gates as a Borg). Being forced to use Windows or NT is often referred to as being "Borged."

An important part of constructing the enemy is the enemies' own construction of open source. First Microsoft appeared to ignore open source as irrelevant and not a real threat. When the "Halloween documents" were leaked to Eric Raymond, it became obvious that Microsoft saw it as a threat and took it seriously. By annotating the memorandum with explanations and ironic comments and releasing it to the national press, Raymond made the memorandum part of the open source movement's strategy of constructing the proprietary software industry as an enemy. From being an internal Microsoft affair, the Halloween documents developed into an important story in open source folklore, embodying both the evilness and clumsiness of the enemy. The Halloween documents confirmed Microsoft's status as enemy; Raymond even felt obliged to thank the original authors:

This page originally continued with an anti-Microsoft jeremiad. On reflection, however, I think I'd prefer to finish by thanking the principal authors, Vinod Valloppillil and Josh Cohen, for authoring such remarkable and effective testimonials to the excellence of Linux and open-source software in general. I suspect that historians may someday regard the Halloween memoranda as your finest hour, and the Internet community certainly owes you a vote of thanks. (Raymond 2003a)

When the "enemies" get back at open source in the media, they attack aspects of the software like quality and security, but also (mostly) its core values, such as the free distribution of software code, particularly through the GPL. The arguments draw on metaphors from cancer to communism, and the GPL has even been likened to Pac-Man, the little monster eating all in its way. It all serves to deconstruct the distribution model, arguing that it will stifle innovation and eat the healthy part of the software industry: According to Microsoft executive Jim Allchin, "Open-source is an intellectual property destroyer. I can't imagine something that could be worse than this for the software business and the intellectual property business (cited on CNET News.com Feb. 14, 2001). And Steve Ballmer, CEO of Microsoft, added, "Linux is a cancer that attaches itself in an intellectual property sense to everything it touches", (cited in *The Register*, June 2, 2001).

From the open source movement's point of view, these attacks are characterized as FUD (Fear, Uncertainty, and Doubt), spread with the purpose of maintaining Microsoft's monopoly. FUD is defined as a marketing technique used when a competitor launches a product that is both better and costs less than yours; that is, when your product is no longer competitive. Unable to respond with hard facts, scaremongering is used via "gossip channels" to cast a shadow of doubt over the competitors' offerings and make people think twice before using it. FUD has been alleged to have been first used on a large scale by IBM in 1970s, and the technique is now argued to have been applied by Microsoft.

Another part of this discourse attacks the free distribution model by accusing it of being unAmerican: "I am an American; I believe in the American Way, I worry if the government encourages open source, and I don't think we've done enough education of policymakers to understand the threat" (Jim Allchin, of Microsoft, cited on CNET News.com, Feb. 14, 2001).

Microsoft's rhetoric of the American way and of open source being unAmerican is used by open source supporters, to associate Microsoft with the McCarthy era and another way of being unAmerican. "If this continues I may one day be sitting in front of the House of Un-American Activities Committee with a modern McCarthy asking: Are you or have you ever been an advocate of open source software" (Reed 2001).

Both proponents and opponents of free software and open source software use the discourse about the "true American Way" to support their claims. Discourses attached to open source thereby become related to webs of meaning that are of profound significance to the people who make the claims—in this case, Americans—regardless of whether they are for or against the movements. Microsoft refers to the software industry as the American Way, because it is an expression of the free market and civil rights. Free software and open source advocacy groups use the idea of the American Way to argue that the "freedom" in free software and the "openness" in open source connote American core values from the pioneering era and the constitution. Symbolic objects can be found that support the idea that the movements are an incarnation of the American Way; for example, when Richard Stallman puts the American flag on his home page together with the text "America Means Civil Liberties, Patriotism Is Protecting Them."

By citing Gandhi's famous words, this author describes the state of the process in the open source versus Microsoft combat: "'First they ignore you, then they laugh at you, then they fight you, then you win' (Gandhi). This is the exact path Microsoft has taken with open source software. When I first got involved with Linux eight years ago, we were in the ignore stage. We are definitely in the fighting stage now" (Reed 2001).

Dynamics within the Open Source Community

We have pointed out the persistent voices of proponents claiming the superiority of the social production of technological achievements presented by the open source movement. Openness is regarded as the key to technological excellence, profit making, different freedoms, and might even be the way to world domination or a new sociotechnical order. This discourse of supremacy, pride and self-assurance must be understood in relation to the meritocracy of hacker culture proposing that ideas, innovation, and problem solving form the fundamental basis of openness and freedom. The hacker culture, with its roots in academia and science, expresses a "belief in the inherent good of scientific and technological development as a key component in the progress of humankind" (Castells 2001, 39). Linked to this discourse is also the rhetoric about the different models used for the "success" of open source: the bazaar approach, the principles of gift culture and the peer-review process. Even if these aspects refer to what might seem uncontested and coherent communitarian subcultural hacker values, as well as the work for common good, these models include more or less institutionalized discursive practices that involve specific rules, authorities, competencies (in other words, powers). These powers manage and coordinate and therefore control the social organization of open source communities and work, but also define the relevance and rank the individual performances of the contributors. As highlighted by an open source developer, "If you look closely, there really isn't a bazaar. At the top, it's always a one-person cathedral. It's either Linus, Stallman, or someone else. That is, the myth of a bazaar as a wide-open, free-for-all of competition isn't exactly true. Sure, everyone can download the source code, diddle with it, and make suggestions, but at the end of the day it matters what Torvalds, Stallman, or someone else says" (Wayner 2000, 115).

Due to the transnational feature and Internet-based networking aspects of the extensive open source movement, the best strategy for a person willing to contribute to the movement is either to join a project group or start a project on his/her own. The keystones of the development process within the project group are the open communication, cooperation, and sharing of resources (ideas, knowledge, and information). The peer review system is a way to ensure the quality of the development processes within different projects. Yet, as suggested in the previous quote, the openness of the development process is not always in the end the common cause of the community, but rather determined by the hacker elite. Raymond (2001) has characterized the sharing of personal assets as a gift culture. There is often no monetary compensation to be expected for efforts conducted, which is in line with the informal hacker ethic not to use common resources for personal benefit. Contributions to the movement therefore have to be explained in terms other than being based on the traditional cost-benefit rationality (Bergquist and Ljungberg 2001). Rather, the benefits are those of being part of and learning from the community, and the inner satisfaction of being able to contribute and being acknowledged for the efforts made, as well as the impact the community has on the surrounding world. Reputation and status due to intellectual and technological skills as a driving force is of course comparable with the aspirations within the academic tradition, as noted by Castells, for example, who also reminds us that the Internet was born out of academic circles where the academic values and habits—such as academic excellence, peer review, openness in research findings, credit to the authors of discovery, as well as academic ranks—"diffused into the hacker culture" (Castells 2001, 40).

It is evident that open source software development can be understood as some kind of gift culture. However, exchanging gifts does not automatically create a society without borders, driven only by individuals' inner satisfaction, where everyone steps back for the sake of the common good. An important dimension is also how power structures the exchange of gifts. This element in gift giving has been analyzed by the anthropologist Marcel Mauss in *The Gift* (1950/1990). Mauss understands gift giving as the transaction of objects coordinated by a system of rules. The rules are in fact symbolic translations of the social structure in a society or a group of community members. He argues that giving a gift brings forth a demand for returning a gift, either another object or, in a more symbolic fashion, forces of power connected to the objects. Gift giving therefore creates social interdependencies and becomes a web upon which the social structure is organized. To give away something is to express an advantageous position in relation to the recipient.

Gifts therefore express, but also create, power relations between people. A gift culture, in this sense, has the power to discipline loosely coupled networks of individuals with no organizational forces in terms of economy or management that can otherwise force individuals to behave in a certain way. The gift culture in the open source setting is thus often, in contrast to traditional gift giving between two persons, rather an exchange between a contributor and the whole community of developers and users. Therefore, the obligation of returning a "favor" lies more, as already suggested, in the symbolic powers of acknowledgment, status and gratitude (Bergquist and Ljungberg 2001). Bergquist and Ljungberg (2001) have pointed out several aspects of how power and social stratification are expressed within the open source gift culture. For example knowing how and when to show respect and appreciation is a commonsense "netiquette" within the OS community. The norms and values though are not obvious for a first time visitor or a "newbie" who has to be socialized into the outspoken as well as the nonverbal practices of the community. Even if a common trait of the open source discursive rhetoric is the warm welcome of an expansion and growing strength of the movement, a more unspoken discursive practice built upon a memory from the tribal days of the techno-elite and a strong meritocracy where talent and advanced skills are all that matter, are quite evident. The frequency of FAQs for beginners to learn the most basic issues—from the "flamewars" against bad contribution or behavior and, as Bergquist and Ljungberg have pointed out, the humiliation of oneself before a more advanced community as a survival strategy of a newbie—are some aspects that point to elitism and a strong meritocracy. Norms and values are not always accepted without protest, though, and countermovements are being developed. In the following example from a newsgroup posting, the practice of flaming is questioned:

More than once I have had the urge to begin contributing to the community. I have written code, documented it, and gained authorization for its release. But at the last minute I always hesitate and then stop. Why? I think I fear the fangs of the community. At this point, everywhere I turn, it's a big flamefest and getting quite tiresome. Its gotten to the point where it seems one has to be some sort of Jedi Master–level coder to contribute. On more then a few mailing lists, I have seen contributors flamed for their contributions! Flaming someone for *giving* something away. It's incredible. (In Bergquist and Ljungberg 2001, 315)

As the posting reveals, the practice of flaming is due not only to inappropriate behavior and the overruling of core communitarian values, but might also be used by the inner circle of a project team as a means to reject contributions. The system of peer review might in this way be a powerful tool to manifest authority and maintain the hierarchy of "excellence." The open source peer review model has no objective criteria for what counts as relevant or impressive contributions. On the other hand, project leaders try to be reasonable when making their selections. But what seems reasonable for one person is not always reasonable for another. Peer review is thus a social mechanism, through which a discipline's experts or the core members of a community maintain control over new knowledge entering the field (Merton and Zuckerman 1973; Chubin and Hackett 1990). Peer review can thus be seen as a way of organizing power relationships within a given community, but as we have also seen, in relation to other fields of social practices.

Conclusion

A discourse perspective gives important access to an understanding of how networked movements like open source are organized and managed. It also brings insight to the power struggles going on between different actors. One interesting point is that the values created within the movement's discourses are now spreading to larger circles outside the movement, expanding its territory. Thus, it can be concluded that the force of open source discourses is very powerful.

First, we illustrated the internal discourses forming open source identity. Then we described the struggle between open source and proprietary software (particularly Microsoft) discourses. The discourses about "the American Way" is an example of how both the open source movement and the proprietary software industry try to legitimate activities by relating to an external discourse about "good" American society.

In conclusion, we note that external actors in public sector and governments, representing a particular user category, have also linked to several open source discourses in order to change their policies and practices regarding information systems. These new discourses have the potential enormous for an impact. Governments exist in every country and represent large user groups. The public sector discourse relates to several of the themes originating in open source discourses, some of them previously discussed in this chapter. Concepts like "freedom" and "openness" easily relate to democratic values, and in some countries (for example, Sweden) it is a constitutional right to have access to large parts of governmental information. Thus some would ask: Why should the source code of public sector information systems therefore be excluded from this openness? Because governments invest in information technology using taxpayers' money, there is a related demand to increase the value for money." For these reasons, it seems likely that the next major shoot-out will take place in the governmental and public sector arena.

23 Libre Software Policies at the European Level

Philippe Aigrain

Initial Drivers and Motivations

Until the last months of 1998, there was only a limited awareness of free software/open source software ("libre software" for the rest of this chapter) in the various European institutions.[1] There was a libre software section in the portal of the Information Society Project Office, but it was considered a marginal activity. A few staff members were also actively involved as developers in projects or as users. When the libre software achievements became more visible, including, in business circles, through the efforts of the Open Source Initiative campaign, a variety of factors led to a series of libre software initiatives. This did not happen through an overall policy impulse, as there was not—and to my knowledge still is not—an overall policy on these issues. Instead, as is often the case, a number of people driven by a variety of motivations were each able to build a sufficient case to convince their decision-making hierarchy that it was worth "giving it a try." This mostly occurred in the European Commission, which, due to its policy proposal role, is open to experimental actions. It is interesting to recall the motivations of these initiatives.

Within the research funding programs, the initial impetus arose from:

- The growing frustration with the poor dissemination, usage, and commercial exploitation record of European software research results licensed under proprietary terms[2]
- A positive vision of an information society based on open creation and exchanges of information, knowledge, and contents

In policy and regulatory units, as well as in the European Parliament, security and privacy concerns were an additional driver. Within units dealing with European administrations data interchange (closely connected with National Member States IT for administration offices), the fear of excessive dependency upon supplier(s) and the search for long-term control of costs were the initial drivers.

At the same time, there was a growing criticism by libre software groups of the European Commission regulatory initiatives; in particular, in the field of software patentability. This led a few software technology-aware persons (including myself) to try to better understand and interface with these initiatives. Little did we realize at the time that it would become a heavy challenge, and one that we would end up perceiving as engaging the full future of human rights and intellectual exchanges in our civilisation.

From the start, the individuals involved in exploring potential libre software related actions chose to coordinate their efforts. Coordination between technology research actions and policy units was encouraged by higher management. Furthermore, open, informal horizontal cooperation is quite common in the European Commission administration, at least when no significant budget spending or regulatory initiative is at stake. An initial step was the creation of an informal group of external experts (chosen because they came from different countries and different libre software backgrounds, such as community NGOs, companies, and technical projects). These experts were asked to draft an issues paper,[3] which was finalized in November 1999 and presented at the IST'99 Conference in Helsinki and publicly debated until a workshop concluded this debate in March 2000. This report made a number of recommendations in various domains, including research and development policy, standardisation, rejection of software patentability, education, and usage in administrations. It received significant attention.[4] Parallel initiatives were developed in European countries, such as the KBST report[5] in Germany and the Bouquet du Libre Prime Minister agency action[6] and the National Software Research Network (RNTL) report[7] in France. Together with recommendations given by the official Advisory Group of the IST Programme (ISTAG),[8] these helped to create a favorable environment for implementing some of the proposed actions.

Research and Technology Development: From Experimental Actions to Mainstream Scheme?

The European Working Group on Libre Software and the IST advisory group suggested some specific domains or modes of support for libre software innovation. ISTAG pointed to platform and infrastructural software, meaning software on top of which many applications or services can be built. The Working Group on Libre Software recommended that support particularly target libre software whose development called for an initial investment going beyond what normal individual or community projects can afford before the "first threshold of usefulness" can be reached, the idea being that it is only when such a threshold of usefulness is reached that a community development process can take over. But there were some challenges to address beyond these orientations. For example, how did one get the innovative libre software developers involved in types of programs that they generally ignored, or perceived as being reserved for large corporations or their established academic partners? And how could one make sure that despite all the inherent management constraints to European-level funding (calls for proposals and related delays between proposing a project and actual start of funding, and financial viability requirements for participants, for instance), the participants would still find the game worthwhile, and that practical results would truly emerge? How could one ensure the quality of the peer evaluation process used for the selection of project funding, and guarantee that moving the selection of projects at an earlier stage compared to the community-based developments would not bias the overall development ecosystem?[9]

The approach taken was pragmatic. A first call was published calling for the adoption of libre software platforms in embedded systems. This domain had been chosen because there were strong European activities in the field, and because there were indications of the great potential value of libre software platforms, but also because there was some reluctance to make the initial steps in that direction. European funding often acts as a mechanism for "unlocking" such situations. A limited number of projects were selected in 2000, mostly in the areas of embedded telecom (gateways, routers) and industrial systems (controllers, real-time systems). These projects have been technically successful, demonstrating the performance and reliability of libre software platforms in these demanding application spaces. Even more significantly, though it was not required, these projects have actually released new libre software. The release has ranged from release of tools developed (or adapted) in the project, to the release of the full software.[10]

Although initiatives supporting the adoption of libre software platforms were having some impact, the main aim of research and development actions was to make possible the *development* of innovative libre software in areas where it would not exist without EC funding. After a limited experimentation in 2000, a specific call for proposals[11] was organised in 2001 under the heading "Free Software Development: Towards Critical Mass." Seven projects were selected for a total budget of a little more than €5 million, which represents only 0.16 percent of the overall IST program funding for research in the 1999–2002 period. Five software developments projects were driven by user organizations and software suppliers (including a limited number of academic research labs), all wanting to adopt libre software strategies. They targeted next-generation components for some essential information society applications, such as large-scale public key infrastructures and their applications, reference implementation for standards, and agent-based workflow tools for administrations. Two projects are trying to address specific needs of the libre software development process. The AMOS project is providing indexing and searching technology for libre software packages and components, and the AGNULA project is developing and disseminating specialized audio/music libre software distributions (including innovative software from music research centres) and is providing advanced hardware detection and configuration facilities.

These actions remained limited in scope. In parallel, libre software projects emerged at the initiative of external participants in other domains of the IST programme (IT for health, education, mathematical software or libraries). However, overall the share of libre software in all software having received IST program funding remained arguably below 1.5 percent. Is it possible to make libre software a mainstream or default choice for publicly funded research software, as the author,[12] the UK government policy paper,[13] and grassroots petitions[14] have all proposed? Progress in this direction within the European research programs would call for a deep rethinking of the intellectual property rules built into these programs. The European research actions are predominantly giving partial (shared) funding to cooperative efforts between industry and research partners from various countries. As a result, the funding contracts have built-in rules granting participants the property of results, and pushing them to use "adequate and effective protection" for these results. Many experts have argued that use of libre software and open contents licensing is indeed an adequate and effective means to reach some essential objectives of the research policy.[15] However, the inertia in interpreting the intellectual property rules plays in favor of restrictive licensing approaches and extensive usage of patent mechanisms that create heavy transaction costs in the dissemination path for results, or even inhibit some development models.

A Libre Software Technology Strategy?

Will it be enough for libre software to be under a libre software license to achieve the goals that motivate its promoters? One can doubt that it was ever enough. Without the sound peer-to-peer architecture of the Internet, without some nice modular properties of UNIX systems that could be further elaborated in GNU/Linux (despite other limitations), libre software would have achieved much less towards the values that motivate it. In the keynote speech he delivered at the Georgetown University Open Source Summit in October 2002, Tim O'Reilly stressed the need for libre software developers to become more aware of the link between what they try to achieve through licensing regimes and the nature of the information society infrastructure they are developing. One particularly difficult challenge is that this must today be achieved at all three "layers" identi- fied by Yochai Benkler:[16] the physical computing and network infrastruc- ture layer, the logical software layer, and the information and contents layer.

At the physical computing and network layer, we are faced with some risks for the peer-to-peer structure of the Internet and its end-to-end prop- erties, and even stronger risks for the end-user control on computing. Can new forms of networks such as ubiquitous mesh wireless networks repre- sent an alternative to the "re-broadcastising"[17] of the Internet? One can hope so, even if in some national contexts, the regulatory context for open wireless networks is not favorable. Meanwhile, it will also be necessary to preserve the structure of the classical Internet.

Furthermore, the introduction of trusted computing platforms—in par- ticular, in the context of Digital Rights Management systems—is the most visible symptom of a general attack against end-user control on comput- ing platforms, an attack that could simply ruin the promise of informa- tion technology for culture and for democracy. These threats arise from the Palladium[18] or similar products. They likewise arise from trends towards creating information devices (for instance consumer electronics devices or e-books) that are supposedly open platforms, but which are quite limited in practice. Often, users cannot physically control which software is running, nor install new software, or can install only software that is "approved" by some central supplier. This situation will make clear for everyone that libre software alone is not enough: a libre software imple- mentation of a totally closed system such as Palladium-based DRM will just work against the open cooperation platform that libre software advocates have created and are expanding. As with standards, an end-to-end analy- sis of openness is required: it is not enough for one component to be open, it is the full chain of components necessary to a realistic usage situation that must be analyzed to understand whether it is under user control or open.

At the software logical layer, similar risks arise from the monopolization of some critical functions of interaction between people and software components: authentication, identity management, security management. The libre software communities have identified these risks, and there are alternatives in development, but it is unclear whether they carry the sufficient momentum.

Finally, the information, media and contents layer will have critical cultural and societal impact. Open information and contents, creative commons, open science publishing, and other forms of cooperative knowledge production from distributed genome annotation to Wikipedia and alternative networked media are among the most exciting achievements of our times. Their continued development calls both for the protection of the open infrastructure that enables them, and for new innovative functionality to enable more people to contribute to their increased quality. This includes ability to criticize centralized media (broadcast in particular) and to publish the results of this criticism according to quotation and other fair use types of rights.

On these issues, the European institutions have not defined policies, nor even minimal requirements, and probably no other government has either. But in the absence of such requirements, large integrated media industries and a few dominant players in information or communication technology will simply roll out technology and obtain legislation to stop what they fail to understand, or what they see as a danger to their established businesses.

Information Technology for Administrations

Around 1998, use of libre software became an issue on the government/administration agendas of most European countries. In September 1998, Roberto di Cosmo, a researcher, and Dominique Nora, a journalist, published "Un hold-up planétaire, la face cachée de Microsoft."[19] In addition to criticizing Microsoft's approach to technology, business, and competition, it drew the attention of the general public to the risks of having one company controlling the essential tools of information technology. The authors called for national and European governments to support usage of what they saw as the only practical alternative: libre software systems. In parallel, some civil servants in IT central agencies and in local government started being able to build cases for a more voluntary approach to the introduction of libre software solutions. Finally the European Parliament Science and Technology Office of Assessment produced a report on the Echelon system of universal surveillance of communications. This led the Parliament to adopt a resolution in 1999,[20] in which the Parliament urged:

the Commission and Member States to devise appropriate measures to promote, develop, and manufacture European encryption technology and software and above all to support projects aimed at developing user-friendly open-source encryption software; calls on the Commission and Member States to promote software projects whose source text is made public (open-source software), as this is the only way of guaranteeing that no backdoors are built into programmes.

Even if this text was somewhat ambiguous on the definition of open source software, and even though such resolutions are not truly binding for the European Commission, it was a clear political signal.

Four years later, explicit policies are in place in several countries, implemented in general through central government information technology or e-government agencies. This is the case, for instance, in Germany (KBST, BMWi-Sicherheit-im-Internet), France (ATICA, now renamed ADAE), the UK (Office of the e-Envoy), the Netherlands, and Italy (AIPA). Other countries are doing preliminary studies or implementing pilot experiments. Regions and local governments are also very active. Those countries implementing direct policies use a variety of instruments:

• Guidelines for, and exchanges of experiences between administrations that wish to develop usage of libre software
• Emphasis on standards for which libre software implementations exist
• Tendering of libre software components for some layers (cryptography and secure e-mail or groupware in Germany)

In terms of usage rates, there is a wide diversity. The FLOSS survey sponsored by the European Commission[21] found that in 2002, the current and directly planned use in German public sector ranged from 44 percent for small establishments to 69 percent in large establishments, while the comparable figures were 16 to 23 percent only in Sweden. These figures follow closely the figures for the private sector usage. One should be cautious when interpreting them: they do not represent the share of libre software compared to proprietary software, but only the percentage of establishments consciously using libre software in parts of their IT infrastructure. As much as 12 percent of German establishments (companies and public sector) have libre software on the desktop.

In the practical implementation of libre software usage in administration policy, the key motivation for governments lies in supplier independence, and greater control over the evolution of their infrastructure. In the already mentioned FLOSS study, 56 percent of those companies and public sector entities using libre software quoted it as an important factor, making it clearly the most important single motivation.

Except in Germany, where a voluntary policy was conducted, the very slow progress towards actual introduction of libre software solutions in administrations has led to an increased pressure for legislation in Europe, as in most areas in the world. Laws or regulation pushing a more proactive approach to the introduction of libre software solutions in administrations have been adopted in Andalucia and Catalonia, or were proposed at several levels of the Belgium administration.

The European institutions had a timid approach to introduction of libre software in their own administration, limiting it to some server-side software and more recently a limited pilot of introducing it on desktops in the European Commission. This shyness is not surprising: for years, the IT departments have been asked to build an infrastructure that would be as integrated as possible, supporting as few different "products" as possible. The recruitments were conducted at insufficient level, favoring, at least at operational level, the presence of staff with know-how centred on to the configuration and management of solutions from a given provider. In some cases, there are high operational challenges: the European Parliament, for instance, manages one of most multilingual large-scale public Web sites. Of course libre software solutions could support all these operations, but there is strong inertia working against change. There is growing consciousness that this supposed cost limitation in the short term actually works against cost and functionality control in the long run, but it is far from being yet translated in concrete action.

The European Commission programs have nonetheless played an important role in favoring pooling and exchange of libre software experiences between administrations in Europe. This was mostly achieved through the IDA program[22] of Interchange of Data between Administrations, and, to a lesser extent, in the e-Europe action plans. IDA first conducted a survey of libre software for use in the public sector, then initiated actions for pooling libre software produced by the administrations themselves, and also conducted a study on migration towards libre software in a German regional government.

Information Technology for Development and Social Inclusion

The great potential of libre software for development and social inclusion has long been emphasized. The cost aspect of it, though it might act as a driver, is only one limited aspect of the benefits of libre software in developing countries, deprived regions, or urban areas. The empowerment of persons and groups to not only use technology, but understand it, at the level and rhythm that fits them, with the resulting ability to become active contributors and to innovate are the essence of libre software. Of course libre software can play this role only if some basic infrastructure and services are in place: from power supply to telecommunication, education, and health. But experience in even poorest countries has shown that these two areas (basic infrastructure and libre software empowerment) can be worked out in parallel and contribute to one another.

It is thus not surprising that every development-minded organization, from UNESCO to UNDP, UNCTAD, and the World Bank InfoDev program, has given a more or less explicit role to libre software. The developing countries' national and local governments have developed policy that is often more explicit and more voluntarist. The breadth of these actions is reflected, for instance, in the series of EGOVOS conferences.[23] Two examples can be taken from the European Commission development actions. The @LIS programme[24] of cooperation between Europe and Latin America in the field of information society has included libre software as one of its objectives (in association with open standards). In Vietnam, the European Commission delegation has provided technical support to the ongoing actions there, which have been analyzed in an interesting paper by Jordi Carrasco-Munoz.[25]

The social inclusion contribution of libre software is not limited in any sense to developing countries. Several European regions or local governments have actually centred their regeneration or development programmes on libre software, including the Junta de Extremadura LINEX programme[26] in Spain, the libre software technopolis in the French city of Soissons,[27] and the UK region of West Midlands.[28]

A Software and Information Commons Perspective on the Crisis of Intellectual Rights

The interface between libre software and the information commons, on one side, and the ongoing regulatory or legislative efforts on the other is difficult, to say the least. Regulatory efforts have often focused on widening the scope, the duration, the intensity, and the enforcement of restrictive intellectual property instruments. The scope of this chapter does not allow for discussing this issue in depth, but it is worth stressing a few important perspectives.

The tension is evident in crisis mode when a regulatory or legislative initiative is challenged for its possible harm to libre software, information commons and open contents, or more recently, simply for harming fundamental human rights by setting extreme enforcement mechanisms.[29] But neither the community players, nor those people who understand these matters in administrations, can afford to do case-by-case battles on each of these texts. In addition to limiting damage from some critical texts, one must work out why all this is happening, and set new foundations for approaches that would consider common goods not as limited exceptions but as a realm in its own rights.

Worldwide, a few contributors to intellectual debates[30] have tried to set these new foundations. The key idea is that informational commons, from software to contents, scientific information and publishing, and cooperative media are to be considered in their own rights, and not as tolerated anomalies. Of course, one can only be happy when the existence of these commons proves to be extremely favorable to the development of markets, as is often the case. But in arguing it, one should never forget that the first contribution of informational commons, the one we can see as the cornerstone of a new civilization, lies simply in their existence, and in the exchanges that human beings can build on its basis.

Notes

Views presented in this chapter are the author's and do not necessarily represent the official view of the European Commission. At the time of the drafting of this chapter, the author was head of sector "Software Technologies" in the Information Society Technologies Programme of the European Commission. He left that position in May 2003. He is today the CEO of Sopinspace, Society for Public Information Spaces, a company developing free software tools and providing services for public debate on complex technical issues.

1. Key political institutions at the European level are: the European Commission, which has policy proposal and policy implementation roles; the European Council, representing the Union member states, which has policy decision and legislative roles; and the European Parliament, which has legislative and budgetary power.

2. It is ironic that some proprietary software companies today attack libre software policies as hostile to commercialization of research results, as it is precisely the failure of proprietary licensing to put results in practical usage that motivated some of these policies. In other terms, it might well be that commercialization (in the proprietary licensing meaning) defeats commerce (in the human and economic sense).

3. Report from the European Working Group on Libre Software: "Free Software/ Open Source, Opportunities for Europe?" is available at http://eu.conecta.it/ paper.pdf.

4. Notably thanks to its Slashdotting at http://slashdot.org/article.pl?sid=99/12/ 15/0943212.

5. An English version of the original report from Egon Troles is accessible at http://www.kbst.bund.de/Anlage302856/KBSt-Brief+-+English+Version.pdf. General information on KBST open source software actions is at http://linux.kbst.bund.de.

6. Now at http://www.adae.pm.gouv.fr.

7. Accessible at http://www.industrie.gouv.fr/rntl/.

8. Known as ISTAG, this advisory group brings together high-level information and communication technology industry experts, academic research experts, and some national and regional government experts. See ftp://ftp.cordis.lu/pub/ ist/docs/istag_kk4402472encfull.pdf for a recent report giving libre software recommendations.

9. In community-based software development, the initial investment (often by a single individual) is followed by a selection phase during which many initiated project fall out. This step is thought by some to be a waste, but one can also see it as a guarantee of exploring sufficiently diverse paths. To keep the process as open as possible, we invested a lot in inciting experts of all flavors of libre software communities and related industries and researchers to register in the expert databases.

10. For an example of full distribution, see the project OPENROUTER at http://www.inaccessnetworks.com/projects/openrouter/project/software/distribu tion_html.

11. See http://www.cordis.lu/ist/ka4/tesss/impl_free.htm#historical for a record of specific RTD actions targetting libre software, and http://www.cordis.lu/ist/ka4/tesss/ impl_free.htm#running for a list of all libre software projects selected during the fifth framework program.

12. Philippe Aigrain, "Open Source Software for Research," Proceedings of the Global Research Village Conference on Access to Publicly Funded Research, OECD, Amsterdam, December 2000.

13. http://e-government.cabinetoffice.gov.uk/assetRoot/04/00/28/41/04002841. pdf.

14. http://www.openinformatics.org/petition.html.

15. For example, the development of basic scientific and technical infrastructure, the creation of standards, and the creation of new markets by initiation of innovative usage. See, for example, the report of the Adaptation and Usage of IPR for

ICT-Based Collaborative Research working group of European Commission, 2003, http://europa.eu.int/comm/research/era/pdf/ipr.ict.report.pdf.

16. Yochai Benkler, "Property, Commons, and the First Amendment: Towards a Core Common Infrastructure" (White Paper for the Brennan Center for Justice, March, 2001). Available at http://www.benkler.org/WhitePaper.pdf.

17. For example, the introduction of differentiated quality of service levels or the development of IP over something else, where the something else is under the control of broadcasters or operators, both technically and with regard to terms of usage, or the deployment of asymetric bandwidth.

18. Palladium is Microsoft's hardware-based implementation of the Trusted Computing Platform Alliance specification. Microsoft now claims that it is not specifically targeting Digital Rights Management applications and that it is compatible with user control of software running on a computer, but there is some evidence that it will be used mostly for DRM, and could lead to users completely losing control, unless they accept to live in a ghetto, severed from any access to "protected" contents.

19. Calmann-Lévy, Paris.

20. http://www2.europarl.eu.int/omk/sipade2?PUBREF=-//EP//TEXT+TA+P5-TA-2001-0441+0+DOC+XML+V0//EN&L=EN&LEVEL=3&NAV=S&LSTDOC=Y.

21. http://www.infonomics.nl/FLOSS.

22. http://europa.eu.int/ISPO/ida/jsps/index.jsp?fuseAction= showChapterandchapterID=134andpreChapterID=0-17.

23. http://www.egovos.org.

24. http://europa.eu.int/comm/europeaid/projects/alis/index_en.htm.

25. Jordi Carrasco-Munoz, "The case for free, open source software as an official development aid tool, ASI@ITC News, 17.

26. http://www.linex.org.

27. Soissons Informatique Libre, http://www.sil-cetril.org/.

28. http://telematics.cs.bham.ac.uk/seminars/linux/.

29. See the recent directive on Intellectual Property Enforcement, initially designed to fight counterfeiting and piracy of physical goods, but extended in scope so that it could lead to extreme measures on alleged infringers of property rights for intangibles, those providing infringes software means, or even those accused of inciting infringement.

30. In addition to the well-known works of Lawrence Lessig, see in particular the works of David Bollier, accessible at: http://www.bollier.org; for instance, his

"Why open source software is fundamental to a robust democratic culture" address to the Georgetown University Open Source software in October 2002, http://www.bollier.org/pdf/Georgetown_remarks_%20Oct2002.pdf. See also Yochai Benkler's "Coase's Penguin, or Linux and the Nature of the Firm," Yale Law Journal, 112, 2002, http://www.benkler.org/CoasesPenguin.html, and the contribution of the author of this chapter: "Positive intellectual rights and information exchanges," http://opensource.mit.edu/papers/aigrain.pdf, expanded in a book to appear in early 2005 at Editions Fayard.

Tim O'Reilly

In 1962, Thomas Kuhn published a groundbreaking book entitled *The Structure of Scientific Revolutions*. In it, he argued that the progress of science is not gradual, but (much as we now think of biological evolution) a kind of punctuated equilibrium, with moments of epochal change. When Copernicus explained the movements of the planets by postulating that they moved around the sun rather than the earth, or when Darwin introduced his ideas about the origin of species, they were doing more than just building on past discoveries, or explaining new experimental data. A truly profound scientific breakthrough, Kuhn (1996, 7) notes, "is seldom or never just an increment to what is already known. Its assimilation requires the reconstruction of prior theory and the re-evaluation of prior fact, an intrinsically revolutionary process that is seldom completed by a single man and never overnight."

Kuhn referred to these revolutionary processes in science as "paradigm shifts," a term that has now entered the language to describe any profound change in our frame of reference.

Paradigm shifts occur from time to time in business as well as in science. And as with scientific revolutions, they are often hard fought, and the ideas underlying them not widely accepted until long after they were first introduced. What's more, they often have implications that go far beyond the insights of their creators.

One such paradigm shift occurred with the introduction of the standardized architecture of the IBM personal computer in 1981. In a huge departure from previous industry practice, IBM chose to build its computer from off-the-shelf components, and to open up its design for cloning by other manufacturers. As a result, the IBM personal computer architecture became the standard, over time displacing not only other personal computer designs, but, over the next two decades, also minicomputers and mainframes.

However, the executives at IBM failed to understand the full consequences of their decision. At the time, IBM's market share in computers far exceeded Microsoft's dominance of the desktop operating system market today. Software was a small part of the computer industry, a necessary part of an integrated computer, often bundled rather than sold separately. What independent software companies did exist were clearly satellite to their chosen hardware platform. So when it came time to provide an operating system for the new machine, IBM decided to license it from a small company called Microsoft, giving away the right to resell the software to the small part of the market that IBM did not control. As cloned personal computers were built by thousands of manufacturers large and small, IBM lost its leadership in the new market. Software became the new sun that the industry revolved around; Microsoft, not IBM, became the most important company in the computer industry.

But that's not the only lesson from this story. In the initial competition for leadership of the personal computer market, companies vied to "enhance" the personal computer standard, adding support for new peripherals, faster buses, and other proprietary technical innovations. Their executives, trained in the previous, hardware-dominated computer industry, acted on the lessons of the old paradigm.

The most intransigent, such as Digital's Ken Olson, derided the PC as a toy, and refused to enter the market until too late. But even pioneers like Compaq, whose initial success was driven by the introduction of "luggable" computers, the ancestor of today's laptop, were ultimately misled by old lessons that no longer applied in the new paradigm. It took an outsider, Michael Dell, who began his company selling mail order PCs from a college dorm room, to realize that a standardized PC was a commodity, and that marketplace advantage came not from building a better PC, but from building one that was good enough, lowering the cost of production by embracing standards, and seeking advantage in areas such as marketing, distribution, and logistics. In the end, it was Dell, not IBM or Compaq, that became the largest PC hardware vendor.

Meanwhile, Intel, another company that made a bold bet on the new commodity platform, abandoned its memory chip business and made a commitment to be the more complex brains of the new design. The fact that most of the PCs built today bear an "Intel Inside" logo reminds us that even within commodity architectures, there are opportunities for proprietary advantage.

What does all this have to do with open source software? you might ask.

My premise is that free and open source developers are in much the same position today that IBM was in 1981 when it changed the rules of the computer industry, but failed to understand the consequences of the change, allowing others to reap the benefits. Most existing proprietary software vendors are no better off, playing by the old rules while the new rules are reshaping the industry around them.

I have a simple test that I use in my talks to see whether my audience of computer industry professionals is thinking with the old paradigm or the new. "How many of you use Linux?" I ask. Depending on the venue, 20 to 80 percent of the audience might raise their hands. "How many of you use Google?" Every hand in the room goes up. And the light begins to dawn. Every one of them uses Google's massive complex of 100,000 Linux servers, but they were blinded to the answer by a mindset in which "the software you use" is defined as the software running on the computer in front of you. Most of the "killer apps" of the Internet—applications used by hundreds of millions of people—run on Linux or FreeBSD. But the operating system, as formerly defined, is to these applications only a component of a larger system. Their true platform is the Internet.

It is in studying these next-generation applications that we can begin to understand the true long-term significance of the open source paradigm shift.

If open source pioneers are to benefit from the revolution we've unleashed, we must look through the foreground elements of the free and open source movements, and understand more deeply both the causes and consequences of the revolution.

Artificial intelligence pioneer Ray Kurzweil[1] once said, "I'm an inventor. I became interested in long-term trends because an invention has to make sense in the world in which it is finished, not the world in which it is started."

I find it useful to see open source as an expression of three deep, long-term trends:

- The *commoditization* of software
- Network-enabled *collaboration*
- Software *customizability* (software as a service)

Long-term trends like these "three Cs," rather than the Free Software Manifesto or the Open Source Definition, should be the lens through which we understand the changes that are being unleashed.

Software as Commodity

In his essay "Some Implications of Software Commodification," Dave Stutz writes:

The word *commodity* is used today to represent fodder for industrial processes: things or substances that are found to be valuable as basic building blocks for many different purposes. Because of their very general value, they are typically used in large quantities and in many different ways. Commodities are always sourced by more than one producer, and consumers may substitute one producer's product for another's with impunity. Because commodities are fungible in this way, they are defined by uniform quality standards to which they must conform. These quality standards help to avoid adulteration, and also facilitate quick and easy valuation, which in turn fosters productivity gains. (Stutz 2004b)

Software commoditization has been driven by standards, and in particular by the rise of communications-oriented systems such as the Internet, which depend on shared protocols, and define the interfaces and datatypes shared between cooperating components rather than the internals of those components. Such systems necessarily consist of replaceable parts. A Web server such as Apache or Microsoft's IIS, or browsers such as Internet Explorer, Netscape Navigator, or Mozilla, are all easily swappable, because in order to function, they must implement the HTTP protocol and the HTML data format. Sendmail can be replaced by Exim or Postfix or Microsoft Exchange, because all must support e-mail exchange protocols such as SMTP, POP, and IMAP. Microsoft Outlook can easily be replaced by Eudora, or pine, or Mozilla mail, or a Web mail client such as Yahoo! Mail for the same reason.

(In this regard, it's worth noting that Unix, the system on which Linux is based, also has a communications-centric architecture. In *The Unix Programming Environment*, Kernighan and Pike (1984) eloquently describe how Unix programs should be written as small pieces designed to cooperate in "pipelines," reading and writing ASCII files rather than proprietary data formats. Eric Raymond (2003b) gives a contemporary expression of this theme in his book *The Art of Unix Programming*.)

Note that in a communications-centric environment with standard protocols, both proprietary and open source software become commodities. Microsoft's Internet Explorer Web browser is just as much a commodity as the open source Apache Web server, because both are constrained by the open standards of the Web. (If Microsoft had managed to gain dominant market share at both ends of the protocol pipeline between Web browser and server, it would be another matter![2] This example makes clear one of the important roles that open source does play in "keeping standards honest." This role is being recognized by organizations like the W3C, which are increasingly reluctant to endorse standards that have only proprietary or patent-encumbered implementations.

What's more, even software that starts out proprietary eventually becomes standardized and ultimately commodified. Dave Stutz eloquently describes this process:

It occurs through a hardening of the external shell presented by the platform over time. As a platform succeeds in the marketplace, its APIs, UI, feature-set, file formats, and customization interfaces ossify and become more and more difficult to change. (They may, in fact, ossify so far as to literally harden into hardware appliances!) The process of ossification makes successful platforms easy targets for cloners, and cloning is what spells the beginning of the end for platform profit margins. (Stutz 2004a)

Consistent with this view, the cloning of Microsoft's Windows and Office franchises has been a major objective of the free and open source communities. In the past, Microsoft has been successful at rebuffing cloning attempts by continually revising APIs and file formats, but the writing is on the wall. Ubiquity drives standardization, and gratuitous innovation in defense of monopoly is rejected by users.

What are some of the implications of software commoditization? One might be tempted to see only the devaluation of something that was once a locus of enormous value. Thus, Red Hat founder Bob Young once remarked, "My goal is to shrink the size of the operating system market." (Red Hat however aimed to own a large part of that smaller market!) Defenders of the status quo, such as Microsoft VP Jim Allchin, have made statements that open source is an intellectual property destroyer, and paint a bleak picture in which a great industry is destroyed, with nothing to take its place.

On the surface, Allchin appears to be right. Linux now generates tens of billions of dollars in server hardware–related revenue, with the software revenues merely a rounding error. Despite Linux's emerging dominance in the server market, Red Hat, the largest Linux distribution company, has annual revenues of only $126 million, versus Microsoft's $32 billion. A huge amount of software value appears to have vaporized.

But is it value or overhead? Open source advocates like to say they're not destroying actual value, but rather squeezing inefficiencies out of the system. When competition drives down prices, efficiency and average wealth levels go up. Firms unable to adapt to the new price levels undergo what the economist E.F. Schumpeter called "creative destruction," but what was "lost" returns manyfold as higher productivity and new opportunities.

Microsoft benefited, along with consumers, from the last round of creative destruction as PC hardware was commoditized. This time around, Microsoft sees the commoditization of operating systems, databases, Web servers and browsers, and related software as destructive to its core business. But that destruction has created the opportunity for the killer applications of the Internet era. Yahoo!, Google, Amazon, eBay—to mention only a few—are the beneficiaries.

And so I prefer to take the view of Clayton Christensen,[3] the author of *The Innovator's Dilemma* and *The Innovator's Solution*. In a recent article, he articulates "the law of conservation of attractive profits" as follows: "When attractive profits disappear at one stage in the value chain because a product becomes modular and commoditized, the opportunity to earn attractive profits with proprietary products will usually emerge at an adjacent stage" (Christensen 2004, 17).

We see Christensen's thesis clearly at work in the paradigm shifts I'm discussing here. Just as IBM's commoditization of the basic design of the personal computer led to opportunities for attractive profits "up the stack" in software, new fortunes are being made up the stack from the commodity open source software that underlies the internet, in a new class of proprietary applications that I have elsewhere referred to as "infoware."[4]

Sites such as Google, Amazon, and Salesforce.com provide the most serious challenge to the traditional understanding of free and open source software. Here are applications built on top of Linux, but they are fiercely proprietary. What's more, even when using and modifying software distributed under the most restrictive of free software licenses, the GPL, these sites are not constrained by any of its provisions, all of which are conditioned on the old paradigm. The GPL's protections are triggered by the act of software distribution, yet Web-based application vendors never distribute any software: it is simply performed on the Internet's global stage, delivered as a service rather than as a packaged software application.

But even more importantly, even if these sites gave out their source code, users would not easily be able to create a full copy of the running application! The application is a dynamically updated database whose utility comes from its completeness and concurrency, and in many cases, from the network effect of its participating users.[5]

And the opportunities are not merely up the stack. There are huge proprietary opportunities hidden inside the system. Christensen notes: "Attractive profits . . . move elsewhere in the value chain, often to subsystems from which the modular product is assembled. This is because it is improvements in the subsystems, rather than the modular product's architecture, that drives the assembler's ability to move upmarket towards more attractive profit margins. Hence, the subsystems become decommoditized and attractively profitable." (Christensen 2004, 17).

We saw this pattern in the PC market with most PCs now bearing the brand "Intel Inside"; the Internet could just as easily be branded "Cisco Inside." But these "Intel Inside" business opportunities are not always obvious, nor are they necessarily in proprietary hardware or software. The open source BIND (Berkeley Internet Name Daemon) package used to run the Domain Name System (DNS) provides an important demonstration.

The business model for most of the Internet's commodity software turned out to be not selling that software (despite shrinkwrapped offerings from vendors such as NetManage and Spry, now long gone), but services based on that software. Most of those businesses—the Internet Service Providers (ISPs), who essentially resell access to the TCP/IP protocol suite and to e-mail and Web servers—turned out to be low-margin businesses. There was one notable exception.

BIND is probably the single most mission-critical program on the Internet, yet its maintainer has scraped by for the past two decades on donations and consulting fees. But meanwhile, domain name registration—an information service based on the software—became a business generating hundreds of millions of dollars a year, a virtual monopoly for Network Solutions, which was handed the business on government contract before anyone realized just how valuable it would be. The Intel Inside opportunity of the DNS was not a software opportunity at all, but the service of managing the namespace used by the software. By a historical accident, the business model became separated from the software.

That services based on software would be a dominant business model for open source software was recognized in *The Cathedral and the Bazaar*, Eric Raymond's (2001) seminal work on the movement. But in practice, most early open source entrepreneurs focused on services associated with the maintenance and support of the software, rather than true software as a service. (That is to say, software as a service is not service in support of software, but software in support of user-facing services!)

Dell gives us a final lesson for today's software industry. Much as the commoditization of PC hardware drove down IBM's outsize margins but vastly increased the size of the market, creating enormous value for users, and vast opportunities for a new ecosystem of computer manufacturers for whom the lower margins of the PC still made business sense, the commoditization of software will actually expand the software market. And as Christensen (2004, 17) notes, in this type of market, the drivers of success "become speed to market and the ability responsively and conveniently to give customers exactly what they need, when they need it."

Following this logic, I believe that the process of building custom distributions will emerge as one of the key competitive differentiators among Linux vendors. Much as a Dell must be an arbitrageur of the various contract manufacturers vying to produce fungible components at the lowest price, a Linux vendor will need to manage the ever-changing constellation of software suppliers whose asynchronous product releases provide the raw materials for Linux distributions. Companies like Debian founder Ian Murdock's Progeny Systems already see this as the heart of their business, but even old-line Linux vendors like SuSe and new entrants like Sun tout their release engineering expertise as a competitive advantage.[6]

But even the most successful of these Linux distribution vendors will never achieve the revenues or profitability of today's software giants like Microsoft or Oracle, unless they leverage some of the other lessons of history. As demonstrated by both the PC hardware market and the ISP industry (which as noted previously is a service business built on the commodity protocols and applications of the Internet), commodity businesses are low-margin for most of the players. Unless companies find value up the stack or through an "Intel Inside" opportunity, they must compete only through speed and responsiveness, and that's a challenging way to maintain a pricing advantage in a commodity market.

Early observers of the commodity nature of Linux, such as Red Hat's founder Bob Young, believed that advantage was to be found in building a strong brand.[7] That's certainly necessary, but it's not sufficient. It's even possible that contract manufacturers such as Flextronix, which work behind the scenes as industry suppliers rather than branded customer-facing entities, may provide a better analogy than Dell for some Linux vendors.

In conclusion, software itself is no longer the primary locus of value in the computer industry. The commoditization of software drives value to services enabled by that software. New business models are required.

Network-Enabled Collaboration

To understand the nature of competitive advantage in the new paradigm, we should look not to Linux, but to the Internet, which has already shown signs of how the open source story will play out.

The most common version of the history of free software begins with Richard Stallman's ethically motivated 1984 revolt against proprietary software. It is an appealing story centered on a charismatic figure, and leads straight into a narrative in which the license he wrote—the GPL—is the centerpiece. But like most open source advocates, who tell a broader story about building better software through transparency and code sharing, I prefer to start the history with the style of software development that was normal in the early computer industry and academia. Because software was not seen as the primary source of value, source code was freely shared throughout the early computer industry.

The Unix software tradition provides a good example. Unix was developed at Bell Labs, and was shared freely with university software researchers, who contributed many of the utilities and features we take for granted today. The fact that Unix was provided under a license that later allowed ATT to shut down the party when it decided it wanted to commecialize Unix, leading ultimately to the rise of BSD Unix and Linux as free alternatives, should not blind us to the fact that the early, collaborative development preceded the adoption of an open source licensing model. Open source licensing began as an attempt to preserve a culture of sharing, and only later led to an expanded awareness of the value of that sharing.

For the roots of open source in the Unix community, you can look to the research orientation of many of the original participants. As Bill Joy noted in his keynote at the O'Reilly Open Source Convention in 1999, in science, you share your data so other people can reproduce your results. And at Berkeley, he said, we thought of ourselves as computer scientists.[8]

But perhaps even more important was the fragmented nature of the early Unix hardware market. With hundreds of competing computer architectures, the only way to distribute software was as source! No one had access to all the machines to produce the necessary binaries. (This demonstrates the aptness of another of Christensen's "laws," the law of conservation of modularity. Because PC hardware was standardized and modular, it was possible to concentrate value and uniqueness in software. But because Unix hardware was unique and proprietary, software had to be made more open and modular.)

This software source code exchange culture grew from its research beginnings, but it became the hallmark of a large segment of the software industry because of the rise of computer networking.

Much of the role of open source in the development of the Internet is well known: the most widely used TCP/IP protocol implementation was developed as part of Berkeley networking; BIND runs the DNS, without which none of the Web sites we depend on would be reachable; sendmail is the heart of the Internet e-mail backbone; Apache is the dominant Web server; Perl is the dominant language for creating dynamic sites, and so on.

Less often considered is the role of Usenet in mothering the Net we now know. Much of what drove public adoption of the Internet was in fact Usenet, that vast distributed bulletin board. You "signed up" for Usenet by finding a neighbor willing to give you a newsfeed. This was a true collaborative network, where mail and news were relayed from one cooperating site to another, often taking days to travel from one end of the Net to another. Hub sites formed an ad hoc backbone, but everything was voluntary.

Rick Adams, who created UUnet, the first major commercial ISP, was a free software author (though he never subscribed to any of the free software ideals—it was simply an expedient way to distribute software he wanted to use). He was the author of B News (at the time the dominant Usenet news server) as well as SLIP (Serial Line IP), the first implementation of TCP/IP for dialup lines. But more importantly for the history of the Net, Rick was also the hostmaster of the world's largest Usenet hub. He realized that the voluntary Usenet was becoming unworkable, and that people would pay for reliable, well-connected access. UUnet started out as a nonprofit, and for several years, much more of its business was based on the earlier UUCP (Unix-Unix Copy Protocol) dialup network than on TCP/IP. As the Internet caught on, UUnet and others liked it helped bring the Internet to the masses. But at the end of the day, the commercial Internet industry started out of a need to provide infrastructure for the completely collaborative UUCPnet and Usenet.

The UUCPnet and Usenet were used for e-mail (the first killer app of the Internet), but also for software distribution and collaborative tech support. When Larry Wall (later famous as the author of Perl) introduced the patch program in 1984, the ponderous process of sending around nine track tapes of source code was replaced by the transmission of "patches"—editing scripts that update existing source files. Add in Richard Stallman's GNU C compiler (gcc), and early source code control systems like RCS (eventually replaced by CVS and now Subversion), and you had a situation where anyone could share and update free software. Early Usenet was as much a "Napster" for shared software as it was a place for conversation.

The mechanisms that the early developers used to spread and support their work became the basis for a cultural phenomenon that reached far beyond the tech sector. The heart of that phenomenon was the use of wide-area networking technology to connect people around interests, rather than through geographical location or company affiliation. This was the beginning of a massive cultural shift that we're still seeing today. This cultural shift may have had its first flowering with open source software, but it is not intrinsically tied to the use of free and open source licenses and philosophies.

In 1999, together with with Brian Behlendorf of the Apache project, O'Reilly founded a company called Collab.Net to commercialize not the Apache product but the Apache process. Unlike many other OSS projects, Apache wasn't founded by a single visionary developer but by a group of users who'd been abandoned by their original "vendor" (NCSA) and who agreed to work together to maintain a tool they depended on. Apache gives us lessons about intentional wide-area collaborative software development that can be applied even by companies that haven't fully embraced open source licensing practices. For example, it is possible to apply open source collaborative principles inside a large company, even without the intention to release the resulting software to the outside world.

While Collab.Net is best known for hosting high-profile corporate-sponsored open source projects like OpenOffice.Org, its largest customer is actually HP's printer division, where Collab's SourceCast platform is used to help more than 3,000 internal developers share their code within the corporate firewall. Other customers use open source–inspired development practices to share code with their customers or business partners, or to manage distributed worldwide development teams.

But an even more compelling story comes from that archetype of proprietary software, Microsoft. Far too few people know the story of the origin of ASP.Net. As told to me by its creators, Mark Anders and Scott Guthrie, the two of them wanted to re-engineer Microsoft's ASP product to make it XML-aware. They were told that doing so would break backward compatibility, and the decision was made to stick with the old architecture. But when Anders and Guthrie had a month between projects, they hacked up their vision anyway, just to see where it would go. Others within Microsoft heard about their work, found it useful, and adopted pieces of it. Some six or nine months later, they had a call from Bill Gates: "I'd like to see your project."

In short, one of Microsoft's flagship products was born as an internal "code fork," the result of two developers "scratching their own itch," and spread within Microsoft in much the same way as open source projects spread on the open Internet. It appears that open source is the "natural language" of a networked community. Given enough developers and a network to connect them, open source–style development behavior emerges.

If you take the position that open source licensing is a means of encouraging Internet-enabled collaboration, and focus on the end rather than the means, you'll open a much larger tent. You'll see the threads that tie together not just traditional open source projects, but also collaborative "computing grid" projects like SETI@home, user reviews on Amazon.com, technologies like collaborative filtering, new ideas about marketing such as those expressed in the Cluetrain Manifesto, weblogs, and the way that Internet message boards can now move the stock market. What started out as a software development methodology is increasingly becoming a facet of every field, as network-enabled conversations become a principal carrier of new ideas.

I'm particularly struck by how collaboration is central to the success and differentiation of the leading Internet applications. eBay is an obvious example, almost the definition of a "network effects" business, in which competitive advantage is gained from the critical mass of buyers and sellers. New entrants into the auction business have a hard time competing, because there is no reason for either buyers or sellers to go to a second-tier player.

Amazon.com is perhaps even more interesting. Unlike eBay, whose constellation of products is provided by its users, and changes dynamically day to day, products identical to those Amazon sells are available from other vendors. Yet Amazon seems to enjoy an order-of-magnitude advantage over those other vendors. Why? Perhaps it is merely better execution, better pricing, better service, better branding. But one clear differentiator is the superior way that Amazon has leveraged its user community.

In my talks, I give a simple demonstration. I do a search for products in one of my publishing areas, JavaScript. On Amazon, the search produces a complex page with four main areas. On the top is a block showing the three most popular products. Down below is a longer search listing that allows the customer to list products by criteria such as bestselling, highest-rated, price, or alphabetically. On the right and the left are user-generated "Listmania" lists. (These lists allow customers to share their own recommendations for other items related to a chosen subject.)

The section labeled "most popular" might not jump out at first. But as a vendor who sells to Amazon.com, I know that it is the result of a complex, proprietary algorithm that combines not just sales but also the number and quality of user reviews, user recommendations for alternative products, links from Listmania lists, "also bought" associations, and all the other things that Amazon.com refers to as the "flow" around products.

The particular search that I like to demonstrate is usually topped by my own *JavaScript: The Definitive Guide*. As of this writing, the book has 196 reviews, averaging 4½ stars. Those reviews are among the more than ten million user reviews contributed by Amazon.com customers.

Now contrast the #2 player in online books, barnesandnoble.com. The top result is a book published by Barnes & Noble itself, and there is no evidence of user-supplied content. *JavaScript: The Definitive Guide* has only 18 comments, the order-of-magnitude difference in user participation closely mirroring the order-of-magnitude difference in sales.

Amazon.com doesn't have a natural network-effect advantage like eBay, but they've built one by designing their site for user participation. Everything from user reviews, alternative product recommendations, Listmania, and the Associates program (which allows users to earn commissions for recommending books) encourages users to collaborate in enhancing the site. Amazon Web Services, introduced in 2001, take the story even further, allowing users to build alternate interfaces and specialized shopping experiences (as well as other unexpected applications), using Amazon's data and commerce engine as a back end.

Amazon's distance from competitors, and the security it enjoys as a market leader, is driven by the value added by its users. If, as Eric Raymond (2001) said, one of the secrets of open source is "treating your users as co-developers," Amazon has learned this secret. But note that it's completely independent of open source licensing practices! We start to see that what has been presented as a rigidly constrained model for open source may consist of a bundle of competencies, not all of which will always be found together.

Google makes a more subtle case for the network effect story. Google's initial innovation was the PageRank algorithm, which leverages the collective preferences of Web users, expressed by their hyperlinks to sites, to produce better search results. In Google's case, the user participation is extrinsic to the company and its product, and so can be copied by competitors. If this analysis is correct, Google's long-term success will depend on finding additional ways to leverage user-created value as a key part of their offering. Services such as Orkut and Gmail suggest that this lesson is not lost on them.

Now consider a counter-example. MapQuest is another pioneer who created an innovative type of Web application that almost every Internet user relies on. Yet the market is shared fairly evenly between MapQuest (now owned by AOL), maps.yahoo.com, and maps.msn.com (powered by MapPoint). All three provide a commodity business powered by standardized software and databases. None of them have made a concerted effort to leverage user-supplied content, or engage their users in building out the application. (Note also that all three are enabling an "Intel Inside"–style opportunity for data suppliers such as Navteq, now planning a multibillion-dollar IPO!)

The Architecture of Participation

I've come to use the term "the architecture of participation" to describe the nature of systems that are designed for user contribution. Larry Lessig's (2000) book *Code and Other Laws of Cyberspace*, which he characterizes as an extended meditation on Mitch Kapor's maxim that "architecture is politics," made the case that we need to pay attention to the architecture of systems if we want to understand their effects.

I immediately thought of Kernighan and Pike's (1984) description of the Unix software tools philosophy. I also recalled an unpublished portion of the interview we did with Linus Torvalds to create his essay for the book *Open Sources* (DiBona et al. 1999). Linus too expressed a sense that architecture may be important than source code. "I couldn't do what I did with Linux for Windows, even if I had the source code. The architecture just wouldn't support it." Too much of the Windows source code consists of interdependent, tightly coupled layers for a single developer to drop in a replacement module.

And of course the Internet and the World Wide Web have this participatory architecture in spades. As outlined earlier in the section on software commoditization, any system designed around communications protocols is intrinsically designed for participation. Anyone can create a participating, first-class component.

In addition, the IETF, the Internet standards body has a great many similarities with an open source software project. The only substantial difference is that the IETF's output is a standards document rather than a code module. Especially in the early years, anyone could participate, simply by joining a mailing list and having something to say, or by showing up to one of the three annual face-to-face meetings. Standards were decided on by participating individuals, irrespective of their company affiliations. The very name for proposed Internet standards, RFCs (Request for Comments) reflects the participatory design of the Net. Though commercial participation was welcomed and encouraged, companies (like individuals) were expected to compete on the basis of their ideas and implementations, not their money or disproportional representation. The IETF approach is where open source and open standards meet.

And while there are successful open source projects like Sendmail that are largely the creation of a single individual, and have a monolithic architecture, those that have built large development communities have done so because they have a modular architecture that allows easy participation by independent or loosely coordinated developers. The use of Perl, for example, exploded along with CPAN, the Comprehensive Perl Archive Network, and Perl's module system, which allowed anyone to enhance the language with specialized functions and make them available to other users.

The Web, however, took the idea of participation to a new level, because it opened that participation not just to software developers but to all users of the system.

It has always baffled and disappointed me that the open source community has not embraced the Web as one of its greatest success stories. Tim Berners-Lee's original Web implementation was not just open source, it was public domain. NCSA's Web server and Mosaic browser were not technically open source, but their source was freely available. While the move of the NCSA team to Netscape sought to take key parts of the Web infrastructure to the proprietary side, and the Microsoft-Netscape battles made it appear that the Web was primarily a proprietary software battleground, we should know better. Apache, the phoenix that grew from the NCSA server, kept the open vision alive, keeping the standards honest, and not succumbing to proprietary embrace and extend strategies.

But even more significantly, HTML, the language of Web pages, opened participation to ordinary users, not just software developers. The "View source" menu item migrated from Tim Berners-Lee's original browser, to Mosaic, and then on to Netscape Navigator and even Microsoft's Internet Explorer. Though no one thinks of HTML as an open source technology, its openness was absolutely key to the explosive spread of the Web. Barriers to entry for "amateurs" were low, because anyone could look "over the shoulder" of anyone else producing a Web page. Dynamic content created with interpreted languages continued the trend toward transparency.

And more germane to my argument here, the fundamental architecture of hyperlinking ensures that the value of the Web is created by its users. In this context, it's worth noting an observation originally made by Clay Shirky (2001) in a talk at my 2001 P2P and Web Services Conference (now renamed the Emerging Technology Conference), entitled "Listening to Napster." There are three ways to build a large database, said Clay. The first, demonstrated by Yahoo!, is to pay people to do it. The second, inspired by lessons from the open source community, is to get volunteers to perform the same task. The Open Directory Project, an open source Yahoo! competitor is the result. (Wikipedia provides another example.) But Napster demonstrates a third way. Because Napster set its defaults to automatically share any music that was downloaded, every user automatically helped to build the value of the shared database.

This architectural insight may actually be more central to the success of open source than the more frequently cited appeal to volunteerism. The architecture of Linux, the Internet, and the World Wide Web are such that users pursuing their own "selfish" interests build collective value as an automatic byproduct. In other words, these technologies demonstrate some of the same network effect as eBay and Napster, simply through the way that they have been designed.

These projects can be seen to have a natural architecture of participation. But as Amazon demonstrates, by consistent effort (as well as economic incentives such as the Associates program), it is possible to overlay such an architecture on a system that would not normally seem to possess it.

Customizability and Software as Service

The last of my three Cs, customizability, is an essential concomitant of software as a service. It's especially important to highlight this aspect because it illustrates just why dynamically typed languages like Perl, Python, and PHP, so often denigrated by old-paradigm software developers as mere "scripting languages," are so important on today's software scene.

As I wrote in my essay "Hardware, Software and Infoware" (O'Reilly 1997, 192–193):

If you look at a large web site like Yahoo!, you'll see that behind the scenes, an army of administrators and programmers are continually rebuilding the product. Dynamic content isn't just automatically generated, it is also often hand-tailored, typically using an array of quick and dirty scripting tools.

"We don't create content at Yahoo! We aggregate it," says Jeffrey Friedl, author of the book *Mastering Regular Expressions* and a full-time Perl programmer at Yahoo. "We have feeds from thousands of sources, each with its own format. We do massive amounts of 'feed processing' to clean this stuff up or to find out where to put it on Yahoo!." For example, to link appropriate news stories to tickers at finance.yahoo.com, Friedl needed to write a "name recognition" program able to search for more than 15,000 company names. Perl's ability to analyze free-form text with powerful regular expressions was what made that possible.

Perl has been referred to as the "duct tape of the Internet," and like duct tape, dynamic languages like Perl are important to Web sites like Yahoo!

and Amazon for the same reason that duct tape is important not just to heating system repairmen but to anyone who wants to hold together a rapidly changing installation. Go to any lecture or stage play, and you'll see microphone cords and other wiring held down by duct tape.

We're used to thinking of software as an artifact rather than a process. And to be sure, even in the new paradigm, there are software artifacts, programs, and commodity components that must be engineered to exacting specifications because they will be used again and again. But it is in the area of software that is not commoditized, the glue that ties together components, the scripts for managing data and machines, and all the areas that need frequent change or rapid prototyping, that dynamic languages shine.

Sites like Google, Amazon, or eBay—especially those reflecting the dynamic of user participation—are not just products, they are processes. I like to tell people the story of the Mechanical Turk, a 1770 hoax that pretended to be a mechanical chess-playing machine. The secret, of course, was that a man was hidden inside. The Turk actually played a small role in the history of computing. When Charles Babbage played against the Turk in 1820 (and lost), he saw through the hoax, but was moved to wonder whether a true computing machine would be possible.

Now, in an ironic circle, applications once more have people hidden inside them. Take a copy of Microsoft Word and a compatible computer, and it will still run ten years from now. But without the constant crawls to keep the search engine fresh, the constant product updates at an Amazon or eBay, the administrators who keep it all running, the editors and designers who integrate vendor- and user-supplied content into the interface, and in the case of some sites, even the warehouse staff who deliver the products, the Internet-era application no longer performs its function.

This is truly not the software business as it was even a decade ago. Of course, there have always been enterprise software businesses with this characteristic. (American Airlines' Sabre reservations system is an obvious example.) But only now have they become the dominant paradigm for new computer-related businesses.

The first generation of any new technology is typically seen as an extension to the previous generations. And so, through the 1990's, most people experienced the Internet as an extension or add-on to the personal computer. E-mail and Web browsing were powerful add-ons, to be sure, and they gave added impetus to a personal computer industry that was running out of steam.

(Open source advocates can take ironic note of the fact that many of the most important features of Microsoft's new operating system releases since Windows 95 have been designed to emulate Internet functionality originally created by open source developers.)

But now, we're starting to see the shape of a very different future. Napster brought us peer-to-peer file sharing, SETI@home introduced millions of people to the idea of distributed computation, and now Web services are starting to make even huge database-backed sites like Amazon or Google appear to act like components of an even larger system. Vendors such as IBM and HP bandy about terms like "computing on demand" and "pervasive computing."

The boundaries between cell phones, wirelessly connected laptops, and even consumer devices like the iPod or TiVO, are all blurring. Each now gets a large part of its value from software that resides elsewhere. Dave Stutz (2003) characterizes this as "software above the level of a single device" (http://www.synthesist.net/writing/onleavingms.html).[9]

Building the Internet Operating System

I like to say that we're entering the stage where we are going to treat the Internet as if it were a single virtual computer. To do that, we'll need to create an Internet operating system.

The large question before us is this: what kind of operating system is it going to be? The lesson of Microsoft is that if you leverage insight into a new paradigm, you will find the secret that will give you control over the industry, the "one ring to rule them all," so to speak. Contender after contender has set out to dethrone Microsoft and take that ring from them, only to fail. But the lesson of open source and the Internet is that we can build an operating system that is designed from the ground up as "small pieces loosely joined," with an architecture that makes it easy for anyone to participate in building the value of the system.

The values of the free and open source community are an important part of its paradigm. Just as the Copernican revolution was part of a broader social revolution that turned society away from hierarchy and received knowledge, and instead sparked a spirit of inquiry and knowledge sharing, open source is part of a communications revolution designed to maximize the free sharing of ideas expressed in code.

But free software advocates go too far when they eschew any limits on sharing and define the movement by adherence to a restrictive set of software licensing practices. The open source movement has made a concerted effort to be more inclusive. Eric Raymond[10] describes the Open Source Definition as a "provocation to thought," a "social contract . . . and an invitation to join the network of those who adhere to it." But even though the open source movement is much more business-friendly and supports the right of developers to choose nonfree licenses, it still uses the presence of software licenses that enforce sharing as its litmus test.

But the lessons of previous paradigm shifts show us a more subtle and powerful story than one that merely pits a gift culture against a monetary culture, and a community of sharers versus those who choose not to participate. Instead, we see a dynamic migration of value, in which things that were once kept for private advantage are now shared freely, and things that were once thought incidental become the locus of enormous value. It's easy for free and open source advocates to see this dynamic as a fall from grace, a hoarding of value that should be shared with all. But a historical view tells us that the commoditization of older technologies and the crystallization of value in new technologies is part of a process that advances the industry and creates more value for all. What is essential is to find a balance, in which we as an industry create more value than we capture as individual participants, enriching the commons that allows for further development by others.

I cannot say where things are going to end. But as Alan Kay[11] once said, "The best way to predict the future is to invent it." Where we go next is up to all of us.

Conclusion

The Open Source Definition and works such as *The Cathedral and the Bazaar* (Raymond 2001) tried to codify the fundamental principles of open source. But as Kuhn notes, speaking of scientific pioneers who opened new fields of study, "Their achievement was sufficiently unprecedented to attract an enduring group of adherents away from competing modes of scientific activity. Simultaneously, it was sufficiently open-ended to leave all sorts of problems for the redefined group of practitioners to resolve. Achievements that share these two characteristics, I shall refer to as 'paradigms'" (Kuhn 1996, 10).

In short, if it is sufficiently robust an innovation to qualify as a new paradigm, the open source story is far from over, and its lessons far from completely understood. Rather than thinking of open source only as a set of software licenses and associated software development practices, we do better to think of it as a field of scientific and economic inquiry, one with many historical precedents, and part of a broader social and economic story. We must understand the impact of such factors as standards and their effect on commoditization, system architecture and network effects, and the development practices associated with software as a service. We must study these factors when they appear in proprietary software as well as when they appear in traditional open source projects. We must understand how the means by which software is deployed changes the way in which it is created and used. We must also see how the same principles that led to early source code sharing may affect other fields of collaborative activity. Only when we stop measuring open source by what activities are excluded from the definition and begin to study its fellow travelers on the road to the future will we understand its true impact and be fully prepared to embrace the new paradigm.

Notes

1. Speech at the Foresight Senior Associates Gathering, April 2002.

2. See http://salon.com/tech/feature/1999/11/16/microsoft_servers/print.html for my discussion of that subject.

3. I have been talking and writing about the paradigm shift for years, but until I heard Christensen speak at the Open Source Business Conference in March 2004, I hadn't heard his eloquent generalization of the economic principles at work in what I'd been calling business paradigm shifts. I am indebted to Christensen and to Dave Stutz, whose recent writings on software commoditization have enriched my own views on the subject.

4. http://www.oreilly.com/catalog/opensources/book/tim.html.

5. To be sure, there would be many benefits to users were some of Google's algorithms public rather than secret, or Amazon's One-Click available to all, but the point remains: an instance of all of Google's source code would not give you Google, unless you were also able to build the capability to crawl and mirror the entire Web in the same way that Google does.

6. Private communications, SuSe CTO Juergen Geck and Sun CTO Greg Papadopoulos.

7. http://www.oreilly.com/catalog/opensources/book/young.html.

8. I like to say that software enables speech between humans and computers. It is also the best way to talk about certain aspects of computer science, just as equations are the best ways to talk about problems in physics. If you follow this line of reasoning, you realize that many of the arguments for free speech apply to open source

as well. How else do you tell someone how to talk with their computer other than by sharing the code you used to do so? The benefits of open source are analogous to the benefits brought by the free flow of ideas through other forms of information dissemination.

9. Dave Stutz notes (in a private e-mail, 4/29/04, in response to an early draft of this chapter), this software "includes not only what I call 'collective software' that is aware of groups and individuals, but also software that is customized to its location on the network, and also software that is customized to a device or a virtualized hosting environment. These additional types of customization lead away from shrinkwrap software that runs on a single PC or PDA/smartphone and towards personalized software that runs 'on the network' and is delivered via many devices simultaneously."

10. Private e-mail, 4/28/04, in a response to an earlier draft of this chapter.

11. Spoken in a 1971 internal Xerox planning meeting, as quoted in http://www.lisarein.com/alankay/tour.html.

Epilogue: Open Source outside the Domain of Software

Clay Shirky

The unenviable burden of providing an epilogue to *Perspectives on Free and Open Source Software* is made a bit lighter by the obvious impossibility of easy summation. The breadth and excellence of the work contained here makes the most important point—the patterns implicit in the production of Open Source software are more broadly applicable than many of us believed even five years ago. Even Robert Glass, the most determined Open Source naysayer represented here, reluctantly concludes that "[T]here is no sign of the movement's collapse because it is impractical."

So the publication of this book is a marker—we have gotten to a point where we can now take at least the basic success of the Open Source method for granted. This is in itself a big step, since much of the early literature concerned whether it could work at all. Since even many of its critics now admit its practicality, one obvious set of questions is how to make it work better, so that code produced in this way is more useful, more easily integrated into existing systems, more user-friendly, more secure.

These are all critical questions, of course. There are many people working on them, and many thousands of programmers and millions of users whose lives will be affected for the better whenever there is improvement in those methods.

There is however a second and more abstract set of questions implicit in the themes of this book that may be of equal importance in the long term. Human intelligence relies on analogy (indeed, Douglas Hofstadter, a researcher into human cognition and the author of *Gödel, Escher, Bach: An Eternal Golden Braid* suggests that intelligence is the ability to analogize). Now that we have identified Open Source as a pattern, and armed with the analytical work appearing here and elsewhere, we can start asking ourselves where that pattern might be applied outside its original domain.

I first came to this question in a roundabout way, while I was researching a seemingly unrelated issue: why it is so hard for online groups to make decisions? The answer turns out to be multivariate, including, among other things, a lack of perceived time pressure for groups in asynchronous communication, a preference in online groups for conversation over action; a lack of constitutional structures that make users feel bound by their decisions, and a lack of the urgency and communal sensibility derived from face-to-face contact. There is much more work to be done on understanding both these issues and their resolution.

I noticed, though, in pursuing this question, that Open Source projects seemed to violate the thesis. Open Source projects often have far-flung members who are still able, despite the divisions of space and time, to make quite effective decisions that have real-world effects.

I assumed that it would be possible to simply document and emulate these patterns. After all, I thought, it can't be that Open Source projects are so different from other kinds of collaborative efforts, so I began looking at other efforts that styled themselves on Open Source, but weren't about creating code.

One of the key observations in Eric Raymond's seminal *The Cathedral and the Bazaar* (2001) was that the Internet changed the way software was written because it enabled many users to collaborate asynchronously and over great distance. Soon after that essay moved awareness of the Open Source pattern into the mainstream, we started to see experiments in applying that pattern to other endeavors where a distributed set of users was invited to contribute.

Outside software production, the discipline that has probably seen the largest number of these experiments is collaborative writing. The incredible cultural coalescence stimulated by *The Cathedral and the Bazaar* led to many announcements of Open Source textbooks, Open Source fiction, and other attempts to apply the pattern to any sort of writing, on the theory that writing code is a subset of writing, and of creative production generally.

Sadly, my initial optimism about simple application of Open Source methods to other endeavors turned out to be wildly overoptimistic. Efforts to create "Open Source" writing have been characterized mainly by failure. Many of the best-known experiments have gotten attention at launch, when the Open Source aspect served as a novelty, rather than at completion, where the test is whether readers enjoy the resulting work. (Compare the development of Apache or Linux, whose fame comes not from the method of their construction but from their resulting value.)

The first lesson from these experiments is that writing code is different in important ways from writing generally, and more broadly, that tools that support one kind of creativity do not necessarily translate directly to others. Merely announcing that a piece of writing is Open Source does little, because the incentives of having a piece of writing available for manipulation are different from the incentives of having a piece of useful code available.

A good piece of writing will typically be read only once, while good code will be reused endlessly. Good writing, at least of fiction, includes many surprises for the reader, while good code produces few surprises for the user. The ability to read code is much closer, as a skill, to the ability to write code than the ability to read well is to the ability to write well.

While every writer will tell you they write for themselves, this is more a statement of principle than an actual description of process—a piece of writing, whether a textbook or a novel, needs an audience to succeed. A programmer who claims to writes code for him or herself, on the other hand, is often telling the literal truth: "This tool is for me to use. Additional users are nice, but not necessary."

The list of differences goes on, and has turned out to be enough to upend most attempts at Open Source production of written material. Writing code is both a creative enterprise and a form of intellectual manufacturing. That second characteristic alone is enough to make writing code different from writing textbooks.

This is the flipside of Open Source software being written to scratch a developer's particular itch; Open Source methods work less well for the kinds of things that people wouldn't make for themselves. Things like GUIs, documentation, and usability testing are historical weaknesses in Open Source projects, and these weaknesses help explain why Open Source methods aren't applicable to creative works considered as a general problem. Even when these weaknesses are overcome, the solutions typically involve a level of organization, and sometimes of funding, that takes them out of the realm of casual production.

Open Source projects are special for several reasons. Members of the community can communicate their intentions in the relatively unambiguous language of code. The group as a whole can see the results of a proposed change in short cycles. Version control allows the group to reverse decisions, and to test both forks of a branching decision. And, perhaps most importantly, such groups have a nonhuman member of their community, the compiler, who has to be consulted but who can't be reasoned with—proposed changes to the code either compile or don't compile, and when compiled can be tested. This requirement provides a degree of visible arbitration absent from the problem of writing.

These advantages allow software developers to experience the future, or at least the short-term future, rather than merely trying to predict it. This ability in turn allows them to build a culture made on modeling multiple futures and selecting among them, rather than arguing over some theoretical "best" version.

Furthermore, the overall value built up in having a collection of files that can be compiled together into a single program creates significant value, value that is hard to preserve outside the social context of a group of programmers. Thus the code base itself creates value in compromise.

Where the general case of applying Open Source methods to other forms of writing has failed, though, there have been some key successes, and there is much to learn from the why and how of such projects. Particularly instructive in this regard is the Wikipedia project (http://wikipedia.org), which brings many of the advantages of modeling culture into a creative enterprise that does not rely on code.

The Wikipedia is an open encyclopedia hosted on a *wiki*, a collaborative Web site that allows anyone to create and link to new pages, and to edit existing pages. The site now hosts over 200,000 articles in various states of completion, and many of them are good enough as reference materials to be on the first page of a Google search for a particular topic.

There are a number of interesting particularities about the Wikipedia project. First, any given piece of writing is part of a larger whole—the cross-linked encyclopedia itself. Next, the wiki format provides a history of all previous edited versions. Every entry also provides a single spot of contention—there can't be two wikipedia entries for Islam or Microsoft, so alternate points of view have to be reflected without forking into multiple entries. Finally, both the individual entries and the project as a whole is tipped toward utility rather than literary value—since opposing sides of any ideological divide will delete or alter one another's work, only material that both sides can agree on survives.

As a reference work, the Wikipedia creates many of the same values of compromise created by a large code base, and the history mechanism works as a version control system for software does, as well as forming a defense against trivial vandalism (anyone whom comes in and deletes or defaces a Wikipedia entry will find their vandalism undone and the previous page restored within minutes).

Open Source methods can't be trivially applied to all areas of creative production, but as the Wikipedia shows, when a creative endeavor takes on some of the structural elements of software production, Open Source methods can create tremendous value.

This example suggests a possible reversal of the initial question. Instead of asking "How can we apply Open Source methods to the rest of the world?" we can ask "How much of the rest of the world be made to work like a software project?" This is, to me, the most interesting question, in part because it is the most open-ended. Open Source is not pixie dust, to be sprinkled at random, but if we concentrate on giving other sorts of work the characteristics of software production, Open Source methods are apt to be a much better fit.

A key element here is the introduction of a recipe, broadly conceived; which is to say a separation between the informational and actual aspects of production, exactly the separation that the split between source code and compilers or interpreters achieves. For example, there are two ways to get Anthony Bourdain's steak au poivre—go to Bourdain's restaurant, or get his recipe and make it yourself. The recipe is a way of decoupling Bourdain's expertise from Bourdain himself. Linus Torvalds's operating system works on the same principle—you don't need to know Torvalds to get Linux. So close is the analogy between software and recipes, in fact, that many introductory software texts use the recipe analogy to introduce the very idea of a program.

One surprise in the modern world is the degree to which production of all sorts is being recipe-ized. Musicians can now trade patches and plug-ins without sharing instruments or rehearsing together, and music lovers can trade playlists without trading songs. CAD/CAM programs and 3D printers allow users to alter and share models of objects without having to share the objects themselves. Eric von Hippel, who wrote the chapter in this book on user innovation networks, is elsewhere documenting the way these networks work outside the domain of software. He has found a number of places where the emergence of the recipe pattern is affecting everything from modeling kite sails in virtual wind tunnels to specifying fragrance design by formula.

Every time some pursuit or profession gets computerized, data begins to build up in digital form, and every time the computers holding that data are networked, that data can be traded, rated, and collated. The Open Source pattern, part collaborative creativity, part organizational style, and part manufacturing process, can take hold in these environments whenever users can read and contribute to the recipes on their own.

This way of working—making shared production for projects ranging from encyclopedia contributions to kite wing design take on the characteristics of software production—is one way to extend the benefits of Open Source to other endeavors. The work Creative Commons is doing is another. A Creative Commons license is a way of creating a legal framework around a document that increases communal rights, rather than decreasing them, as typical copyrights do.

This is an almost exact analogy to the use of the GPL and other Open Source licensing schemes, but with terms form-fit to writing text, rather than to code. The most commonly used Creative Commons license, for instance, allows licensed work to be excerpted but not altered, and requires attribution for its creator. These terms would be disastrous for software, but work well for many forms of writing, from articles and essays to stories and poems. As with the recipe-ization of production, the Creative Commons work has found a way to alter existing practices of creation to take advantage of the work of the Open Source movement.

Of all the themes and areas of inquiry represented in *Perspectives on Free and Open Source Software*, this is the one that I believe will have the greatest effect outside the domain of software production itself. Open Source methods can create tremendous value, but those methods are not pixie dust to be sprinkled on random processes. Instead of assuming that Open Source methods are broadly applicable to the rest of the world, we can instead assume that that they are narrowly applicable, but so valuable that it is worth transforming other kinds of work, in order to take advantage of the tools and techniques pioneered here. The nature and breadth of those transformations are going to be a big part of the next five years.

References

Adams, E. N. 1984. Optimising preventive maintenance of software products. *IBM Journal of Research & Development* 28 (1): 2–14.

Aghion, P., and J. Tirole. 1997. Formal and real authority in organizations. *Journal of Political Economy* 105: 1–29.

Allen, R. C. 1983. Collective invention. *Journal of Economic Behavior and Organization* 4 (1): 1–24.

Allen, T. J., and R. Katz. 1986. The dual ladder: Motivational solution or managerial delusion? *R&D Management.* 185–197.

Amabile, T. M. 1996. *Creativity in context.* Boulder, CO: Westview Press.

Anderson, R. J. 2001a. Security engineering—*A guide to building dependable distributed systems.* New York: Wiley.

Anderson, R. J. 2001b. Why information security is hard—An economic perspective. Proceedings of the Seventeenth Computer Security Applications Conference. IEEE Computer Society Press. 358–365. Available from: http://www.cl.cam.ac.uk/ftp/users/rja14/econ.pdf.

Anderson, R. J. 2002. Security in open versus closed systems—The dance of Boltzmann, Coase, and Moore. Proceedings of the Open Source Software: Economics, Law, and Policy Confocuce, June 20–21, 2002, Toulouse, France. Available from: http://www.ftp.cl.cam.ac.uk/ftp/users/rja14/toulouse.pdf.

Anderson, R. J., and S. J. Beduidenhoudt. 1996. On the reliability of electronic payment systems. *IEEE Transactions on Software Engineering* 22 (5): 294–301. Also available from: http://citeseer.ist.psu.edu/cache/papers/cs/623/http:zSzzSzwww.cl.cam.ac.ukzSzftpzSzuserszSzrja14zSzmeters.pdf/anderson96reliability.pdf.

Anderson, R. J., and M. Bond. 2003. Protocol analysis, composability, and computation. *Computer Systems: Papers for Roger Needham.* Microsoft Research. Available from: *http://cryptome.org/pacc.htm.*

Ang, M., and B. Eich. 2000. A look at the Mozilla technology and architecture. 2000 O'Reilly Open Source Convention. Available from: http://mozilla.org/docs/ora-oss2000/arch-overview/intro.html.

Apache Group. 2004. Available from: http://dev.apache.org/guidelines.html.

Arora, A., R. Telang, and H. Xu. 2004. Timing Disclosure of Software Vulnerability for Optimal Social Welfare. Workshop on Economics and Information Security, May 13–15, 2004, Minneapolis. Available from: http://www.dtc.umn.edu/weis2004/agenda.html.

Baker, F. 1972. Chief programmer team management of production programming. *IBM Systems Journal* 11 (1): 56–73.

Baker, M. 2000. *The Mozilla project and mozilla.org.* Available from: http://www.mozilla.org/editorials/mozilla-overview.html.

Barbrook, R. 1998. The hi-tech gift economy. *First Monday* 3 (12). Available from: http://www.firstmonday.org/issues/issue3_12/barbrook/.

Barnes, B. 1977. *Interests and the growth of knowledge.* London and Boston: Routledge and K. Paul.

Basili V. R., and D. M. Weiss. 1984. A methodology for collecting valid software engineering data. *IEEE Transactions on Software Engineering* 10:728–738.

Baskerville, R., J. Travis, and D. Truex. 1992. Systems without method: The impact of new technologies on information systems development projects. In *IFIP Transactions A8, The Impact of Computer Supported Technologies on Information Systems Development*, ed. K. Kendall, K. Lyytinen, and J. DeGross, 241–269. Amsterdam: North-Holland Publishing Co.

Bauer, F. L. 1972. Software engineering. *Information Processing 71.* Amsterdam: North-Holland Publishing Co., p. 530.

Beck, K. 2000. *Extreme Programming Explained: Embrace Change*, 2nd ed. Reading, MA: Addison-Wesley.

Benkler, Y. 2002. Coase's penguin, or Linux and the nature of the Firm. 112 Yale Law Journal.

Bergquist, M., and J. Ljungberg. 2001. The power of gifts: Organising social relationships in open source communities. *Information Systems Journal* 11 (4): 305–320.

Berners-Lee, T., M. Fishetti, and M. L. Dertouzous. 2000. *Weaving the Web: The original design and ultimate destiny of the World Wide Web.* New York: HarperBusiness.

Bessen, J. 2001. *Open source software: Free provision of complex public goods.* Research on Innovation paper. Available from: http://www.researchoninnovation.org/opensrc.pdf.

Biagioli, M. 1993. Galileo, courtier: The practice of science in the culture of absolutism. Chicago: University of Chicago Press.

Bishop, P., and R. Bloomfield. 1996. A conservative theory for long-term reliability-growth prediction. *IEEE Transactions on Reliability* 45 (4): 550–560.

Bishop, P. G. 2001. Rescaling reliability bounds for a new operational profile. Preseuted at the International Symposium on Software Testing and Analysis (ISSTA 2002), July 22–24, 2001, Rome, Italy.

Bloor, D. 1976. *Knowledge and social imagery*. London and Boston: Routledge & K. Paul.

Bohm, N., I. Brown, and B. Gladman. 2000. Electronic commerce: Who carries the risk of fraud? *Journal of Information Law and Technology* 3. Available from: http://elj.warwick.ac.uk/jilt/00-3/bohm.html.

Bollier, D. 1999. The Power of Openness: Why Citizens, Education, Government and Business Should Care About the Coming Revolution in Open Source Code Software. Available from: *http://h20project.law.harvard.edu/opencode/h20/*.

Bollinger, T., R. Nelson, K. M. Self, and S. J. Turnbull. 1999. Open-source methods: Peering through the clutter. *IEEE Software* (July 1999): 8–11.

Bond, M., and P. Zielinski. 2003. *Decimalisation table attacks for PIN cracking*. Cambridge University Computer Laboratory Technical Report, no. 560. Available from: http://www.cl.cam.ac.uk/TechReports/UCAM-CL-TR-560.pdf.

Boston Consulting Group (BCG). 2002. *Survey of free software/open source developers*. Available from: http://www.osdn.com/bcg/.

Bovet, D. P., and M. Cesati. 2000. *Understanding the Linux Kernel*, 1st ed. Sebastopol, CA: O'Reilly & Associates.

Brady, R. M., R. J. Anderson, and R. C. Ball. 1999. *Murphy's law, the fitness of evolving species, and the limits of software reliability*. Cambridge University Computer Laboratory Technical Report, no. 471. Available from: http://www.cl.cam.ac.uk/ftp/users/rja14/babtr.pdf.

Boooks, F. 1975. The mythical man month. Reading, MA: Addison-Wesley.

Brooks, F. 1987. No silver bullet: Essence and accidents of software engineering. *IEEE Computer*, April: 10–19.

Brooks, F. P. 1995. *The mythical man-month: Essays on software engineering*, 2nd, 20th anniversary ed. Reading, MA: Addison-Wesley.

Brown, K. 2002. *Opening the open source debate*. Alexis de Toqueville Institution. Available from: http://www.adti.net/opensource.pdf.

Browne, C. B. 1999. Linux and decentralized development. *First Monday* 3 (3). Available from: http://www.firstmonday.dk/issues/issue3_3/browne/index.html.

Butler, B., L. Sproull, S. Kiesler, and R. Kraut. 2002. *Community effort in online groups: Who does the work and why?* (Unpublished Work.)

Butler, R. W., and G. B. Finelli. 1991. The infeasibility of experimental quantification of life-critical software reliability. ACM Symposium on Software for Critical Systems, December 1991, New Orleans. 66–76.

Caminer, D., J. Aris, P. Hermon, and F. Land. 1996. *User-driven innovation: The world's first business computer.* New York: McGraw-Hill.

Campbell, E. G., B. R. Clarridge, M. Gokhale, L. Birenbaum, S. Hilgartner, N. A. Holtzman, and D. Blumenthal. 2002. Data withholding in academic genetics: Evidence from a national survey. *JAMA* 287 (4): 23–30.

Capiluppi, A., P. Lago, and M. Morisio. 2003. Evidences in the evolution of OS projects through changelog analyses. In *Proceedings of the 3rd Workshop on Open Source Software Engineering, ICSE2003, Portland, Oregon,* J. Feller, B. Fitzgerald, S. Hissam, and K. Lakhani, eds. Available from: http://opensource.ucc.ie/icse2003.

Carayol, N., and J.-M. Dalle. 2000. Science wells: Modelling the "problem of problem choice" within scientific communities. Presented at the 5th WEHIA Conference, June 2001, Marseille.

Carleton, A. D., R. E. Park, W. B. Goethert, W. A. Florac, E. K. Bailey, and S. L. Pfleeger. 1992. *Software measurement for DoD systems: Recommendations for initial core measures.* Tech. Rep. CMU/SEI-92-TR-19 (September). Software Engineering Institute, Carnegie Mellon University, Pittsburgh.

Cassiman, B. 1998. *The organization of research corporations and researcher ability.* (Unpublished working paper, University Pompeu Fabra.)

Castells, M. 1996. *The rise of the network society.* Malden, MA: Blackwell.

Castells, M. 2001. *The Internet galaxy.* Oxford: Oxford University Press.

Christensen, C. 2004. The law of conservation of attractive profits. *Harvard Business Review* 82 (2): 17–18.

Chubin, D. E, and E. J. Hackett. 1990. *Peerless science: Peer Review and U.S. Science Policy.* Albany: State University of New York Press.

Claymon, D. 1999. Apple in tiff with programmers over signature work. *San Jose Mercury News,* December 2.

CNET News.com. 2001. Microsoft executive says Linux threatens innovation (Update 1) [accessed February 14, 2001]. Archive closed. Authors retain paper copy. Available on request.

Cockburn, I., R. Henderson, and S. Stern. 1999. *Balancing incentives: The tension between basic and applied research.* Working Paper 6882. National Bureau of Economic Research.

Collar-Kotelly, J. 2002. *United States of America vs Microsoft, Inc.* U.S. District Court, District of Columbia, Civil Action No. 98-1232(CKK), Final Judgment (12 November 2002). Available from: http://www.usdoj.gov/atr/cases/f200400/200457.htm.

Collins, H. M. 1985. *Changing order: Replication and induction in scientific practice.* London and Beverly Hills, CA: Sage.

Comer, D. E. 2000. Internetworking with TCP/IP: Principles, protocols, and architecture. Upper Saddle River, NJ: Prentice Hall.

Cox, A. Cathedrals, Bazaars and the Town Council." Available from: http://slashdot.org/features/98/10/13/1423253.shtml, October 1998.

Csikszentmihalyi, M. 1975. Beyond boredom and anxiety: The experience of play in work and games. San Francisco: Jossey-Bass, Inc.

Csikszentmihalyi, M. 1990. *Flow: The psychology of optimal experience.* New York: Harper and Row.

Csikszentmihalyi, M. 1996. Creativity: Flow and the Psychology of Discovery and Invention. New York: HarperCollins.

Curtis, B., H. Krasner, and N. Iscoe. 1988. A field study of the software design process for large systems. *Communications of the ACM* 31: 1268–1287.

Cusumano, M. A. 1991. *Japan's software factories: A challenge to U.S. management.* New York: Oxford University Press.

Cusumano, M. A., and R. W. Selby. 1995. *Microsoft secrets: How the world's most powerful software company creates technology, shapes markets, and manages people.* New York: Free Press.

Dalle, J.-M., and N. Jullien. 2000. NT vs. Linux, or some explorations into the economics of free software. In *Application of simulation to social sciences*, G. Ballot and G. Weisbuch, eds., 399–416. Paris: Hermès.

Dalle, J.-M., and N. Jullien. 2003. "Libre" software: Turning fads into institutions? *Research Policy* 32 (1): 1–11.

Dasgupta, P., and P. David. 1994. Towards a new economics of science. *Research Policy* 23: 487–521.

David, P. A. 1998a. Reputation and agency in the historical emergence of the institutions of "open science." Center for Economic Policy Research, Publication No. 261. Stanford University, revised March 1994; further revised; December 1994.

David, P. A. 1998b. Common agency contracting and the emergence of "open science" institutions. *American Economic Review* 88(2), May.

David, P. A. 1998c. Communication norms and the collective cognitive performance of "invisible colleges." In *Creation and the transfer of knowledge: Institutions and incentives*, G. Barba Navaretti, P. Dasgupta, K.-G. Maler, and D. Siniscako, eds. Berlin, Heidelberg, New York: Springer-Verlag.

David, P. A. 2001a. Path dependence, its critics, and the quest for "historical economics." In *Evolution and Path Dependence in Economic Ideas: Past and Present*, P. Garrouste and S. Ioannidies, eds. Cheltenham, England: Edward Elgar.

David, P. A. 2001b. The political economy of public science. In *The Regulation of Science and Technology*, Helen Lawton Smith, ed. London: Palgrave.

David, P. A., S. Arora, and W. E. Steinmueller. 2001. Economic organization and viability of open source software: A proposal to the National Science Foundation. SIEPR, Stanford University, 22 January.

Davis, G., and M. Olson. 1985. *Management information systems: Conceptual foundations, structure, and development*, 2nd ed. New York: McGraw-Hill.

Deci, E. L, and R. M. Ryan. 1985. *Intrinsic motivation and self-determination in human behavior*. New York: Plenum Press.

Deci, E. L., R. Koestner, and R. M. Ryan. 1999. A meta-analytic review of experiments examining the effects of extrinsic rewards on intrinsic motivation. *Psychological Bulletin* 125:627–688.

Dempsey, B. J., D. Weiss, P. Jones, and J. Greenberg. 1999. A quantitative profile of a community of open source Linux developers. (Unpublished working paper, School of Information and Library Science, University of North Carolina at Chapel Hill.) Available from: http://metalab.unc.edu/osrt/develpro.html [accessed 01 November 1999].

Dempsey, B. J., D. Weiss, P. Jones, and J. Greenberg. 2002. *Who is an open source software developer?* Communications of the ACM, April, 2002. Available from: http://www.ibiblio.org/osrt/develpro.html.

Dessein, W. 1999. *Authority and communication in organizations*. (Unpublished working paper, Université Libre de Bruxelles.)

DiBona, C., S. Ockman, and M. Stone, eds. 1999. *Open sources: Voices from the open source revolution*. Sebastopol, CA: O'Reilly.

Eich, B. 2001. Mozilla development roadmap. Available from: http://www.mozilla.org/roadmap.html.

Elliott, M. 2003. The virtual organizational culture of a free software development community. In *Proceedings of 3rd Workshop on Open Source Software Engineering, ICSE2003, Portland Oregon*, J. Feller, B. Fitzgerald, S. Hissam, and K. Lakhani. Available from: http://opensource.ucc.ie/icse2003.

Enos, J. L. 1962. *Petroleum progress and profits: A history of process innovation*. Cambridge, MA: MIT Press.

Farrell, J., and N. Gallini. 1988. Second sourcing as a commitment: Monopoly incentives to attract competition. *Quarterly Journal of Economics* 103:673–694.

Farrell, J., and M. L. Katz. 2000. Innovation, rent extraction, and integration in systems markets. *Journal of Industrial Economics* 48:413–432.

Feller, J., and B. Fitzgerald. 2000. A framework analysis of the open-source software development paradigm. Proceedings of the 21st International Conference on Information System: 58–69.

Feller, J., and B. Fitzgerald. 2002. *Understanding open source software development*. London: Addison-Wesley.

Fenton, N. 1994. Software measurement: A necessary scientific basis. *IEEE Transactions on Software Engineering* 20:199–206.

Fenton, N. E., and M. Neil. 1999. A critique of software defect prediction models. *IEEE Transactions on Software Engineering* 25 (5): 675–689. Available from: http://www.dcs.qmul.ac.uk/~norman/papers/defects_prediction_preprint105579.pdf.

Fielding, R. T. 1999. Shared leadership in the apache project. *Commun. ACM* 42:42–43.

Fisher, D. 2003. *OIS tackles vulnerability reporting.* Eweek.com (accessed 20 March 2003). Available from: http://www.eweek.com.

Fitzgerald, B., and T. Kenny, 2003. Open source software in the trenches: Lessons from a large-scale implementation. Proceedings of the 24th International Conference on Information Systems (ICIS), Seattle, December 2003.

Forrester, J. E., and B. P. Miller. 2000. An empirical study of the robustness of Windows NT applications using random testing. Available from: ftp://ftp.cs.wisc.edu/paradyn/technical_papers/fuzz-nt.pdf.

Foucault, M. 1972. *The archaeology of knowledge and the discourse on language.* New York: Pantheon.

Franke, N., and E. von Hippel. 2002. *Satisfying heterogeneous user needs via innovation toolkits: The case of Apache security software.* MIT Sloan School of Management Working Paper No. 4341-02, January.

Franke, N., and S. Shah. 2003. How communities support innovative activities: An exploration of assistance and sharing among end-users. *Research Policy* 32:157–178.

FreeBSD. 2003a. Documentation project: Committer's guide. Available from: http://www.freebsd.org/doc/en_US.ISO8859-1/articles/committers-guide/.

FreeBSD. 2003b. Documentation Project: FreeBSD Handbook. Available from: http://www.freebsd.org/doc/en_US.ISO8859=1/books/handbook/.

FreeBSD Release Engineering Team. 2003. The roadmap for 5-STABLE. Available from: http://www.freebsd.org/doc/en/articles/5-roadmap/article.html.

Freeman, C. 1968. Chemical process plant: Innovation and the world market. *National Institute Economic Review* 45:2957.

Frey, B. 1997. *Not just for the money: An economic theory of personal motivation.* Brookfield, VT: Edward Elgar.

Gal-Or, E., and A. Ghose. 2003 The economic consequences of sharing security information. Second Annual Workshop on Economics and Information Security, May 29–30, 2003, University of Maryland.

Gambardella, A. 1995. *Science and innovation: The U.S. pharmaceutical industry during the 1980s.* Cambridge, UK: Cambridge University Press.

Garfield, E. 1979. *Citation indexing: Its theory and application in science, technlogy, and humanities.* New York: Wiley.

German, D. M. 2002. The evolution of the GNOME Project. Proceedings of the 2nd Workshop on Open Source Software Engineering, May 2002.

German, D. M. 2003. GNOME, a case of open source global software development. Proceedings of the International Workshop on Global Software Development, May 2003.

German, D. M., and A. Mockus. 2003. Automating the measurement of open source projects. Proceedings of the 3rd Workshop on Open Source Software Engineering, May 2003.

Ghosh, R. A. 1994. The rise of an information barter economy. *Electric Dreams* 37 [accessed 21 November 1994]. Available from: http://dxm.org/dreams/dreams37.html.

Ghosh, R. A. 1995. Implicit transactions need money you can give away. *Electric Dreams* 70 [accessed 21 August 1995). Available from: http://dxm.org/dreams/dreams70.html.

Ghosh, R. A. 1996. Informal law and equal-opportunity enforcement in cyberspace. (Unpublished manuscript.)

Ghosh, R. A. 1998a. Cooking pot markets: an economic model for the trade in free goods and services on the Internet. *First Monday* 3 (3). Available from: http://www.firstmonday.org/issues/issue3_3/ghosh/index.html.

Ghosh, R. A. 1998b. What motivates free software developers: Interview with Linus Torvalds. *First Monday* 3 (3). Available from: http://www.firstmonday.dk/issues/issue3_3/torvalds/index.html.

Ghosh, R. A. 2002. *Clustering and dependencies in free/open source software development: Methodology and tools.* SIEPR-Project NOSTRA Working Paper. Draft available from: http://dxm.org/papers/toulouse2/.

Ghosh, R. A. 2005. Cooking-pot markets and balanced value flows. In *Collaboration and ownership in the digital economy*, R. Ghosh, ed. Cambridge, MA: MIT Press.

Ghosh, R. A., and P. David. 2003. *The nature and composition of the Linux kernel developer community: a dynamic analysis.* SIEPR-Project NOSTRA Working Paper. Draft available at http://dxm.org/papers/licks1/.

Ghosh, R. A., and V. Ved Prakash. 2000. The Orbiten free software survey. *First Monday* 5 (7). Available from: http://firstmonday.org/issues/issue5_7/ghosh/.

Ghosh, R. A., R. Glott, B. Kreiger, and G. Robles-Martinez. 2002. The free/libre and open source software developers survey and study—FLOSS final report. June. Available from: http://www.infonomics.nl/FLOSS/report_Final4.pdf.

Ghosh, R. A., R. Glott, B. Krieger, and G. Robles-Martinez. 2003. *Community above profits: Characteristics and motivations of open source and free software developers.* MERIT/Infonomics Working Paper. Draft available from: http://flossproject.org/papers.htm.

Gibbons, R. 1997. Incentives and careers in organizations. In *Advances in economic theory and econometrics*, D. Kreps and K. Wallis, eds., vol. 2. Cambridge, England: Cambridge University Press.

Gibbons, R., and M. Waldman. 1999. Careers in organizations: theory and evidence. In *Handbook of Labor Economics*, O. Ashenfelter and D. Card, eds., vol. 3B. North Holland, New York: Elsevier.

Giddens, A. 1990. *The consequences of modernity*. Cambridge: Polity.

Glass, R. L. 1999. The realities of software technology payoffs. *Communications of the ACM*, February.

Glass, R. L. 2002a. Holes found in open source code. *The Software Practitioner*. September. Article available from author.

Glass, R. L. 2002b. Open source: It's getting ugly (and political) out there! *The Software Practitioner*. September. Article available from author.

Glass, R. L. 2003a. Security-related software defects: A top-five list. *The Software Practitioner*. January. Article available from author.

Glass, R. L. 2003b. Software security: Which is better, open source or proprietary? *The Software Practitioner*. January. Article available from author.

The GNOME Foundation. 2000. GNOME Foundation Charter Draft 0.61. Available from: http://foundation.gnome.org/charter.html.

Godden, F. 2000. *How do Linux and Windows NT measure up in real life?* Available from: http://gnet.dhs.org/stories/bloor.php3.

Gomulkiewicz, R. W. 1999. How copyleft uses license rights to succeed in the open source software revolution and the implications for article 2B. *Houston Law Review* 36:179–194.

Gorman, M. 2003. A design, implementation, and algorithm analysis of a virtual memory system for Linux. (Unpublished PhD thesis proposal.)

Greene, W. H. 2000. *Econometric analysis*. Upper Saddle River, NJ: Prentice-Hall.

Grinter, R. E., J. D. Herbsleb, and D. E. Perry. 1999. The geography of coordination: Dealing with distance in r&d work. In *GROUP '99*, 306–315. Phoenix, AZ.

Gwynne, T. 2003. GNOME FAQ. Available from: http://www.linux.org.uk/~telsa/GDP/gnome-faq/.

Hagstrom, W. 1982. Gift giving as an organizing principle in science. In *Science in Context: Readings in the Sociology of Science*, B. Barnes and D. Edge, eds. Cambridge, MA: MIT Press.

Haitzler, C. 1999. Rasterman leaves RedHat. Slashdot. Available from: http://slashdot.org/articles/99/05/31/1917240_F.shtml.

Hall, S. 1992. The West and the rest: Discourse and power. In *Formations of Modernity*, S. Hall and B. Gieben, eds. Cambridge, MA: Polity Press.

Hammerly, J., T. Paquin, and S. Walton. 1999. Freeing the source: The story of Mozilla. In *Open sources: Voices from the open source revolution*, C. DiBona, S. Ockman, and M. Stone, eds. Sebastopol, CA: O'Reilly.

Hann, I-H., J. Roberts, S. Slaughter, and R. T. Fielding. Economic incentives for participation in open source software projects? In *Proceedings of the 23rd International Conference on Information Systems (ICIS 2002)*, Barcelona, Spain, December 2002.

Hansmann, H. 1996. *The ownership of enterprise*. Cambridge, MA: The Belknap Press of Harvard University Press.

Haraway, D. J. 1997. *Modest-Witness@Second-Millennium.FemaleMan-Meets-OncoMouse: feminism and technoscience*. New York: Routledge.

Harhoff, D., J. Henkel, and E. von Hippel. 2003. Profiting from voluntary information spillovers: How users benefit from freely revealing their innovations. Available from: http://opensource.mit.edu/papers/evhippel-voluntaryinfospillover.pdf.

Hars, A., and S. Ou. 2002. Working for free? Motivations for participating in open-source projects. *International Journal of Electronic Commerce* 6 (3): 25–39.

Healy, K., and A. Schussman. 2003. *The ecology of open-source software development*. (Unpublished manuscript, January 29, 2003. University of Arizona.)

Hecker, F. 1999. Mozilla at one: A look back and ahead. Available from: http://www.mozilla.org/mozilla-at-one.html.

Henderson, R., and I. Cockburn. 1994. Measuring competence? Exploring firm effects in pharmaceutical research. *Strategic Management Journal* 15:63–84.

Herbsleb, J. D., and R. E. Grinter. 1999. Splitting the organization and integrating the code: Conway's law revisited. Proceedings from the International Conference on Software Engineering (ICSE '99), 85–95.

Herstatt, C., and E. von Hippel. 1992. From experience: Developing new product concepts via the lead user method: A case study in a "low-Tech" field. *Journal of Product Innovation Management* 9:213–221.

Hertel, G., S. Niedner, and S. Herrmann. 2003. Motivation of software developers in open source projects: an Internet-based survey of contributors to the Linux kernel. *Research Policy*. 32 (7): 1159–1177.

Himanen, P. 2001. *The hacker ethic and the spirit of the information age*. New York: Random House.

Hissam, S., D. Carney, and D. Plakosh. 1998. *SEI monograph series: DoD security needs and COTS-based systems* (monograph). Pittsburgh, PA: Software Engineering Institute, Carnegie Mellon University.

Hissam, S., D. Plakosh, and C. Weinstock. 2002. Trust and vulnerability in open source software. *IEE Proceedings-Software* (149), February 2002. 47–51.

Hissam, S., C. B. Weinstock, D. Plakosh, and J. Asundi. 2001. *Perspectives on open-source software*. Technical Report CMU/SEI-2001-TR-019. Software Engineering Institute, Carnegie Mellon University.

Hogle, S. 2001. Unauthorized derivative source code 18, no. 5, Computer and Internet Law 1: 6.

Holmström, B. 1999. Managerial incentive problems: A dynamic perspective. *Review of Economic Studies* 66:169–182.

Honeypot Project. 2002. Know your enemy: Revealing the security tools, tactics, and motives of the blackhat community. Reading, MA: Addison-Wesley.

Howard, D. 2000. Source code directories overview. Available from: http://mozilla.org/docs/source-directories-overview.html.

Howard, M., and D. LeBlanc. 2002. *Writing secure code*. Redmond, WA: Microsoft Press.

Iacono, S. and R. Kling 1996. Computerization movements and tales of technological utopianism. In *Computerization and Controversy*, 2nd ed., R. Kling, ed., San Diego: Academic Press.

IEEE Computer Society. 1990. *Standard computer dictionary: A compilation of IEEE standard computer glossaries* (610-1990), IEEE Std 610.12-1990. New York: IEEE Publishing.

Iivari, J. 1996. Why are CASE tools not used? *Communications of the ACM* 30 (10): 94–103.

Jacobson, I., G. Booch, and J. Rumbaugh. 1999. *The unified software development process*. Reading, MA: Addison-Wesley.

Jargon File 4.3.1 [online], [accessed 18 February 2002]. This version is now archived. It can be viewed at: http://www.elsewhere.org/jargon.

Johns, A. 1998. *The nature of the book*. Chicago: University of Chicago Press.

Johnson, J. P. 1999. *Economics of open-source software*. (Unpublished working paper. Massachusetts Institute of Technology.)

Jones, P. 2002. Brooks' law and open source: The more the merrier? Does the open source development method defy the adage about cooks in the kitchen? *IBM developerWorks*, August 20.

Kelty, C. M. 2001. Free software/free science. *First Monday* 6 (12), December. Available from: http://www.firstmonday.org/issues/issue6_12/kelty/index.html.

Kerckhoffs, A. 1883. La cryptographie militaire. *Journal des Sciences Militaires* (5): 38. Available from: http://www.petitcolas.net/fabien/kerckhoffs/crypto_militaire_1.pdf.

Kernighan, B. W. and R. Pike. 1984. *The Unix programming environment*. Upper Saddle River, NJ: Prentice-Hall.

Klemperer, P. 1999. Auction theory: A guide to the literature. *Journal of Economic Surveys* 13 (3): 227–286. Available from: http://www.paulklemperer.org.

Klemperer, P. 2002. *Using and abusing economic theory—lessons from auction design.* Alfred Marshall lecture to the European Economic Association. Available from: *http://www.paulklemperer.org.*

Knight, K. E. 1963. *A study of technological innovation: The evolution of digital computers.* (Unpublished PhD dissertation, Carnegie Institute of Technology, Pittsburgh, PA.)

Knuth, D. 1997. *The art of computer programming.* 3rd ed. 3 vols. Reading, MA: Addison Wesley.

Kogut, B., and A. Metiu. 2001. Open-source software development and distributed innovation. *Oxford Review of Economic Policy* 17 (2): 248–264.

Kollock, P. 1999. The economies of online cooperation: Gifts and public goods in cyberspace. In *Communities in cyberspace*, M. A. Smith and P. Kollock, eds. London: Routledge.

Krishnamurthy, S. 2002. Cave or community? An empirical examination of 100 mature open source projects. University of Washington, Bothell. Available from: http://faculty.washington.edu/sandeep.

Krochmal, M. 1999. Linux interest expanding. TechWeb.com. Available from: http://www.techweb.com/wire/story/TWB19990521S0021.

Kuan, J. 2001. Open source software as consumer integration into production. Available from: http://papers.ssrn.com/paper.taf?abstract_id=259648.

Kuhn, T. 1962. The structure of scientific revolutions. Chicago: University of Chicago Press.

Kuhn, T. 1996. *The structure of scientific revolutions*, 3rd ed. Chicago: University of Chicago Press.

Lakhani, K. R., and E. von Hippel. 2003. How open source software works: "free" user-to-user assistance. *Research Policy* 32:923–943.

Lakhani, K. R., and R. Wolf. 2001. Does free software mean free labor? Characteristics of participants in free and open source communities. *BCG Survey Report.* Boston, MA: Boston Consulting Group Report. Available from: http://www.ostg.com/bcg/.

Lakhani, K. R., B. Wolf, J. Bates, and C. DiBona. 2003. The Boston Consulting Group hacker survey (in cooperation with OSDN). Available from: http://www.osdn.com/bcg/bcg-0.73/BCGHackerSurveyv0-73.html.

Latour, B. 1986. *Science in action.* Cambridge, MA: Harvard University Press.

Latour, B., and S. Woolgar. 1979. *Laboratory life: The social construction of scientific facts.* Beverly Hills, CA: Sage.

Lerner, J., and J. Tirole. 2000. *The simple economics of open source.* National Bureau of Economic Research (NBER) Working Paper 7600 (March). Available from: http://www.nber.org/papers/w7600.

Lerner, J., and J. Tirole. 2002. Some simple economics of open source. *Journal of Industrial Economics* 50 (2): 197–234.

Lessig, L. 2000. *Code: And other laws of cyberspace.* New York: Basic Books.

Leung, K. S. 2002. Diverging economic incentives caused by innovation for security updates on an information network. Available from: http://www.sims.berkeley.edu/resources/affiliates/workshops/econsecurity/econws/19.pdf

Levy, S. 1994. *Hackers: Heroes of the computer revolution.* New York: Penguin Books.

Lim, K. 2000. The many faces of absorbtive capacity: Spillovers of copper interconnect technology for semiconductor chips. (MIT Sloan School of Management working paper #4110.)

Lindenberg, S. 2001. Intrinsic motivation in a new light. *Kyklos* 54 (2/3): 317–342.

Lipner, S. B. 2000. Security and source code access: Issues and realities. Proceedings of the 2000 Symposium on Security and Privacy, May 2000, Oakland, CA. IEEE Computer Society, 124–125.

Ljungberg, J. 2000. Open source movements as a model for organising. *European Journal of Information Systems* 9 (4): 208–216.

Lüthje, C. 2003. Characteristics of innovating users in a consumer goods field. MIT Sloan School of Management working paper #4331-02, *Technovation* 23 (forthcoming).

Lüthje, C., C. Herstatt, and E. von Hippel. 2002. The dominant role of "local" information in user innovation: The case of mountain biking. MIT Sloan School of Management working paper (July). Available from: http://userinnovation.mit.edu.

Malone, T. W., and K. Crowston. 1994. The interdisciplinary study of coordination. *ACM Computing Surveys* 26 (1): 87–119.

Markus, L., B. Manville, and C. Agres. 2000. What makes a virtual organization work? *Sloan Management Review* 42 (1): 13–26.

Marwell, G., and P. Oliver. 1993. *The critical mass in collective action: A micro-social theory.* Cambridge, England: Cambridge University Press.

Mateos-Garcia, J., and W. E. Steinmueller. 2003. *The open source way of working: A new paradigm for the division of labour in software development?* INK Open Source Research working paper No. 1, SPRU-University of Sussex, Brighton, England.

Mauss, M. 1950/1990. *The gift: The form and reason for exchange in archaic societies.* London: Routledge.

McConnell, S. 1996. *Rapid development.* Redmond, WA: Microsoft Press.

McConnell, S. 1999. Open-source methodology: Ready for prime time? *IEEE Software* (July/August): 6–8.

McGowan, D. 2002. Recognizing usages of trade: A case study from electronic commerce, *Wash. U. J. Law and Policy* 8 (167): 188–193.

McGraw, G. 2000. Will openish source really improve security? Proceedings of the 2000 Symposium on Security and Privacy, May 2000, Oakland, CA. IEEE Computer Society, 128–129.

McKusick, M. K., K. Bostic, M. J. Karels, and J. Quarterman. 1996. *The design and implementation of the 4.4BSD operating system*. Reading, MA: Addison-Wesley.

McLuhan, M. 1994. *Understanding media*. Cambridge, MA: MIT Press.

Melucci, A. 1996. *Challenging codes: Collective action in the information age*. Cambridge: Cambridge University Press.

Merton, R. 1973. *The sociology of science: Theoretical and empirical investigations*. Edited and with an introduction by Norman W. Storer. Chicago: University of Chicago Press.

Merton, R. K., and H. Zuckerman. 1973. Institutionalized patterns of evaluation in science. In *The Sociology of Science*, N. W. Storer, ed. Chicago: University of Chicago Press.

Michlymayr, M., and B. Hill. 2003. Quality and the reliance on individuals in free software projects. In Proceedings of 3rd Workshop on Open Source Software Engineering, ICSE2003, Portland Oregon, J. Feller, B. Fitzgerald, S. Hissam, and K. Lakhani, eds. Available from: http://opensource.ucc.ie/icse2003.

Midha, K. 1997. Software configuration management for the 21st century. *Bell Labs Tech. J.* 2:154–155.

Milgrom, P., and R. Weber. 1982. A theory of auctions and competitive bidding. *Econometrica* 50 (5): 1089–1122.

Miller, B. P., L. Fredriksen, and B. So. 1990. An empirical study of the reliability of UNIX utilities. Available from: ftp://ftp.cs.wisc.edu/paradyn/technical_papers/fuzz.pdf.

Miller, B. P., D. Koski, C. P. Lee, V. Maganty, R. Murthy, A. Natarajan, and J. Steidl. 1995. Fuzz revisited: A re-examination of the reliability of UNIX utilities and services. Available from: ftp://ftp.cs.wisc.edu/paradyn/technical_papers/fuzz-revisited.pdf.

Mintzberg, H. 1979. *The structuring of organizations*. Upper Saddle River, NJ: Prentice Hall.

Mirowski, P. 2001. Re-engineering scientific credit in the era of the globalized information economy. *First Monday* 6 (12). Available from: http://firstmonday.org/issues/issue6_12/mirowski/index.html.

Mirowski, P. 2002. *Machine dreams: Economics becomes a cyborg science*. New York: Cambridge University Press.

Mirowski, P., and E. Sent. 2002. *Science bought and sold: Essays in the economics of science*. Chicago: University of Chicago Press.

Mockus, A., and D. M. Weiss. 2001. Globalization by chunking: A quantitative approach. *IEEE Soft.* 18 (2): 30–37.

Mockus, A., R. Fielding, and J. Herbsleb. 2000. A case study of open source software development: The Apache server. Proceedings of the International Conference on Software Engineering, June 5–7, 2000, Limerick, Ireland.

Moody, G. 2001. Rebel code: Inside Linux and the open source revolution. New York: Perseus Press.

Moon, J. Y., and L. Sproull. 2000. Essence of distributed work: The case of the Linux kernel. *First Monday* 5 (11). Available from: http://firstmonday.org/issues/issue5_11/moon/index.html.

Morisio, M., A. Capiluppi, and P. Lago. 2003. How the open source projects evolve: First drafts of models analyzing changelogs. In Proceedings of Workshop: How to Make F/OSS Work Better, XP2003, Genoa, Italy, B. Fitzgerald and D. L. Parnas, eds.

Morrison, P. D., J. H. Roberts, and E. von Hippel. 2000. Determinants of user innovation and innovation sharing in a local market. *Management Science* 46 (12): 1513–1527.

Mozilla Project. Bugzilla. Available from: http://bugzilla.mozilla.org.

Mozilla Project. Module Owners. Available from: http://www.mozilla.org/owners.html.

Mozilla Project. Quality Assurance page. Available from: http://www.mozilla.org/quality/.

Mozilla Project. Source Code via CVS. Available from: http://www.mozilla.org/cvs.html.

Mueth, D., and H. Pennington. 2002. GNOME Foundation FAQ. Available from: http://mail.gnome.org/archives/foundation-list/2002-August/msg00208.html.

Nadeau, T. 1999. *Learning from Linux* [accessed 12 November 1999]. Available from: http://www.os2hq.com/archives/linmemo1.htm.

Nakakoji, K., and Y. Yamamoto. 2001. Taxonomy of open-source software development. Making sense of the bazaar: Proceedings of the 1st workshop on open source software engineering. IEEE Computer Society: 41–42.

Nakamura, J., and M. Csikszentmihalyi. 2003. The construction of meaning through vital engagement. In *Flourishing: Positive psychology and the life well-lived*, C. L. Keyes and J. Haidt, eds. Washington, DC: American Psychological Association.

Narduzzo, A., and A. Rossi. 2003. Modularity in action: GNU/Linux and free/open source software development model unleashed. Available from: http://opensource.mit.edu/papers/narduzzorossi.pdf.

Naur, P., and B. Randall, eds. 1969. *Software engineering: A report on a conference*. Sponsored by the NATO Science Committee, Brussels: The Scientific Affairs Committee, NATO.

Neumann, P. G. 1995. *Computer-related risks*. New York: ACM Press and Reading, MA: Addison-Wesley.

Neumann, P. G. 1999. Robust open-source software. *Communications of the ACM* 42 (2): 128–129.

Neumann, P. G. 2000. Robust nonproprietary software. Proceedings of the 2000 Symposium on Security and Privacy, May 2000, Oakland, CA. IEEE Computer Society: 122–123. Available from: http://www.csl.sri.com/neumann/ieee00.pdf.

Neumann, P. G. 2003a. Achieving principled assuredly trustworthy composable systems and networks. Proceedings of DISCEX3, April 2003, volume 2. DARPA and IEEE Computer Society.

Neumann, P. G. 2003b. *Illustrative risks to the public in the use of computer systems and related technology, index to RISKS cases*. Technical report, Computer Science Laboratory, SRI International, Menlo Park, CA. Available from: http://www.csl.sri.com/neumann/illustrative.html.

Neumann, P. G. 2004. *Principled assuredly trustworthy composable architectures*. Technical report, Computer Science Laboratory, SRI International, Menlo Park, CA. Final report, SRI Project 11459. Available from: http://www.csl.sri.com/neumann/chats4.html.

Nichols, D. M., and M. B. Twidale. 2003. The usability of open source software. *First Monday* 8 (1). Available from: http://firstmonday.org/issues/issue8_1/nichols/index.html.

Niedner, S., G. Hertel, and S. Hermann. 2000. *Motivation in free and open source projects*. Available from: http://www.psychologie.uni-kiel.de/linux-study/.

Oberndorf, P., and J. Foreman. 1999. Lessons learned from adventures in COTS-land. Track 8 on CD-ROM. Proceedings of the 11th Annual Software Technology Conference, Utah State University, May 2–6, 1999, Salt Lake City, UT. Hill AFB, UT: Utah State University-Extension in cooperation with the Software Technology Support Center.

Oeschger, I., and D. Boswell. 2000. Getting your work into Mozilla. Available from: http://www.oreillynet.com/pub/a/mozilla/2000/09/29/keys.html.

Ogawa, S. 1997. Does sticky information affect the locus of innovation? Evidence from the Japanese convenience-store industry. *Research Policy* 26:777–790.

O'Mahony, S. 2002. Community-managed software projects: The emergence of a new commercial actor. (Doctoral dissertation, Stanford University.)

O'Mahony, S. 2003. Guarding the commons: How community-managed software projects protect their work. *Research Policy* 1615:1–20.

O'Mahony, S. Forthcoming. Managing community software in a commodity world. In *Frontiers of capital: Ethnographic reflections on the new economy*, G. Downey and M. Fisher, eds. (Duke University Press, forthcoming.)

Open Source Initiative. 1999. *Open source definition* [accessed 14 November 1999]. Available from: http://www.opensource.org/osd.html.

O'Reilly, T. 1999. Ten myths about open source software. Available from: http://opensource.oreilly.com/news/myths_1199.html.

O'Reilly, T. 2000. Open source: The model for collaboration in the age of the Internet. *Wide Open News*. Available from: http://www.oreillynet.com/pub/a/network/2000/04/13/CFPkeynote.html.

Ortega, J. 2000. *Power in the firm and managerial career concerns*. (Unpublished working paper, Universidad Carlos III de Madrid.)

Paquin, T., and L. Tabb. 1998. Mozilla.org: Open-Source Software. Available at http://www.mozilla.org.

Parnas, D. L. 1972. On the criteria used in decomposing systems into modules. *Communications of the ACM* 15 (12): 1053–1058.

Parnas D. L. 1979. Designing software for ease of extension and contraction. *IEEE Transactions on Software Engineering* (March): 128–138.

Parnas, D. L. 1994a. Inspection of safety critical software using function tables. Proceedings of IFIP World Congress, August 1994, Volume III. 270–277.

Parnas, D. L. 1994b. Software aging. Proceedings of the 16th International Conference on Software Engineering, May 16–21, 1994, Sorento, Italy. IEEE Press: 279–287.

Parnas, D. L., G. J. K. Asmis, and J. Madey. 1991. Assessment of safety-critical software in nuclear power plants. *Nuclear Safety* 32 (2): 189–198. (special issue on the 7th International Conference on Software Engineering).

Parnas, D. L., P. C. Clements, and D. M. Weiss. 1985. The modular structure of complex systems. *IEEE Transactions on Software Engineering* 11 (3): 259–266.

Pavlicek, R. 2000. *Embracing insanity: Open source software development*. Indianapolis: SAMS Publishing.

Pavlicek, R. 2002. Buggy whips for India. *Infoworld* [accessed 22 November 2002]. Available from: http://www.infoworld.com/article/02/11/22/021125opsource_1.html (requires free website registration).

Peirce, C. S. 1879. Note on the theory of the economy of research. *United States Coast Survey* for the fiscal year ending June 1876. Washington, D.C.: U.S. Government Printing Office, 1879. Reprint. *The collected papers of Charles Sanders Peirce*, vol. 7, A. Burkes, ed. Cambridge, MA: Harvard University Press, 1958.

Perazzoli, E. 2001. Ximian evolution: The GNOME groupware suite. Available from: http://developer.ximian.com/articles/whitepapers/evolution/.

Perens, B. 1998. Why KDE is still a bad idea. Slashdot.com. Available from: http://slashdot.org/features/older/9807150935248.shtml.

Perens, B. 1999. The open source definition. In *Open sources: voices from the open source revolution*, C. DiBona, S. Ockman, and M. Stone, eds. Sebastopol, CA: O'Reilly.

Pickering, A. 1984. *Constructing quarks: A sociological history of particle physics.* Chicago: University of Chicago Press.

Polanyi, M. 1969. The republic of science: Its political and economic theory. *Minerva* 1:54–73.

Potter, E. 2001. *Gender and Boyle's law of gases.* Bloomington: Indiana University Press.

President's Information Technology Advisory Committee (PITAC). 2000. Panel on open-source software for high-end computing, L. Smarr, L., and S. Graham, co-chairs. *Developing open-source software to advance high-end computing* [accessed 11 September 2000]. Available from: http://www.itrd.gov/pubs/pitac/pres-oss-11sep00.pdf.

Pressman, R. S. 2000. *Software Engineering.* London: McGraw-Hill.

Rain Forest Puppy. 2003. *Issue disclosure policy v1.1.* Available from: http://www.wiretrip.net/rfp/policy.html.

Raymond, E. 1996. *The New Hacker's Dictionary*, 3rd ed. Cambridge, MA: MIT Press.

Raymond, E. S. 1999a. A response to Nikolai Bezroukov. *First Monday* 4 (11). Available from: http://firstmonday.org/issues/issue4_11/raymond/index.html.

Raymond, E. S. 1999b. *Shut up and show them the code* [accessed 18 August 2002]. Available from: http://www.tuxedo.org/~esr/writings/shut-up-and-show-them.html.

Raymond, E. S. 2001. The cathedral and the bazaar: Musings on Linux and open source by an accidental revolutionary. Sebastopol, CA: O'Reilly.

Raymond, E. S. 2003a. Introduction to The Halloween Documents [accessed 10 February 2003]. Available from: http://www.opensource.ac.uk/mirrors/www.opensource.org/halloween/.

Raymond, E. S. 2003b. *The art of Unix programming.* Reading, MA: Addison-Wesley.

Reed, T. 2001. An "un-American" essay [accessed 10 February 2003]. Available from: http://lwn.net/2001/0222/a/tr-unamerican.php3.

The Register. 2001. Ballmer: Linux is a cancer. *The Register* [accessed 6 February 2001]. This version is now archived. It can be viewed at: http://www.theregister.co.uk/2001/06/02/ballmer_linux_is_a_cancer/.

Rescorla, E. 2004. Is finding security holes a good idea. Workshop on Economics and Information Security, May 13–15, 2004, Minneapolis. Available from: http://www.rtfm.com/bugrate.html.

Rice, J. R., and S. Rosen. 2002. *History of the department of computer sciences at Purdue University*. Available from: http://www.cs.purdue.edu/history/history.html.

Riggs, W., and E. von Hippel. 1994. Incentives to innovate and the sources of innovation: The case of scientific instruments. *Research Policy* 23 (4): 459–469.

Ritti, R. R. 1971. *The engineer in the industrial corporation*. New York: Columbia University Press.

Ritti, R. R. 1998. Between craft and science technical work in U.S. settings. *Administrative Science Quarterly* 43 (9): 724–726.

Robles-Martínez, G., H. Scheider, I. Tretkowski, and N. Weber. 2001. *WIDI: Who is doing it?*. Technical University of Berlin. Available from: http://widi.berlios.de/paper/study.html.

Rochkind, M. J. 1975. The source code control system. *IEEE Trans. Softw. Eng.* 1:364–370.

Ronde, T. 1999. *Trade secrets and information* sharing. (Unpublished working paper, University of Mannheim.)

Rosenberg, N. 1976a. *Perspectives on technology*. Cambridge: Cambridge University Press.

Rosenberg, N. 1976b. Technological change in the machine tool industry, 1840–1910. In *Perspectives on technology*. Cambridge. See also: Uncertainty and technological change. In *The Mosaic of Economic Growth*, Landau, Taylor and Wright, Stanford 1996, esp. 345–347.

Rosenbloom, R. S., and W. J. Spencer, eds. 1996. *Engines of innovation: U.S. industrial research at the end of an era*. Boston: Harvard Business School Press.

Roy, A. 2003. Microsoft vs. Linux: Gaining traction. *Chartered Financial Analyst* 9 (5): 36–39.

Ryan, R. M., and E. L. Deci. 2000. Intrinsic and extrinsic motivations: Classic definitions and new directions. *Contemporary Educational Psychology* 25:54–67.

Sanders, J. 1998. Linux, open source, and software's future. *IEEE Software* 15 (September/October): 88–91.

Santayana, G. 1906. *The Life of Reason, or The Phases of Human Progress*. New York: Scribner's Sons.

Scacchi, W. 2002. Understanding the requirements for developing open source software systems. *IEEE Software* 149 (1): 24–39.

Schach, S., B. Jin, and D. Wright. 2002. Maintainability of the Linux kernel. In Proceedings of 2nd Workshop on Open Source Software Engineering, ICSE2002, Orlando, FL, J. Feller, B. Fitzgerald, S. Hissam, and K. Lakhani, eds. Available from: http://opensource.ucc.ie/icse2002.

Schaefer, M. 2001. Panel comments at the 2001 IEEE Symposium on Security and Privacy, Oakland, CA, May 13–16, 2001.

Schneider, F. B. 2000. Open source in security: Visiting the bizarre. In Proceedings of the 2000 Symposium on Security and Privacy, May 2000, Oakland, CA. IEEE Computer Society: 126–127.

Shah, S. 2000. Sources and patterns of innovation in a consumer products field: Innovations in sporting equipment. Sloan Working Paper #4105 (May).

Shankland, S. 2002. Tiemann steers course for open source. *ZDNet* [accessed 4 December 2002]. Available from: http://news.zdnet.com/2100-3513 22-975996. html.

Shapin, S., and S. Schaffer. 1985. *Leviathan and the air pump: Hobbes, Boyle, and the experimental life*. Princeton, NJ: Princeton University Press.

Shaw, B. 1985. The role of the interaction between the user and the manufacturer in medical equipment innovation. *R&D Management* 15 (4): 283–292.

Shaw, M. 1996. Truth vs. knowledge: The difference between what a component does and what we know it does. Proceedings of the 8th International Workshop on Software Specification and Design, March 22–23, Schloss Velen, Germany. Los Alamitos, CA. IEEE Computer Society: 181–185.

Shepard, A. 1987. Licensing to enhance demand for new technologies. *RAND Journal of Economics* 18:360–368.

Shirky, C. 2001. The great re-wiring. Presented at Inventing the Post-Web World: The O'Reilly Peer-to-Peer and Web Services Conference. Washington, D.C., November 5–8, 2001.

Simmel, G. 1978. *The philosophy of money*. Translated by Tom Bottomore and David Frisby. London, Boston: Routledge & Kegan Paul.

Smith, M. and P. Kollock, eds. 1999. *Communities in cyberspace*. London: Routledge.

Software Engineering Institute. 2003. *What is software engineering?* Available from: http://www.sei.cmu.edu/about/overview/whatis.html.

Sommerville, I. 2001. *Software engineering*, 6th ed. Hanlow: Pearson.

Stallman, R. M. 1999a. The GNU operating system and the free software movement. In *Open sources: Voices from the open source revolution*, C. DiBona, S. Ockman, and M. Stone, eds. Sebastopol, CA: O'Reilly.

Stallman, R. M. 1999b. RMS responds [accessed 18 February 2002]. Available from: http://slashdot.org/ articles/99/06/28/1311232.shtml.

Stamelos, I., L. Angelis, and A. Oykonomou. 2001. Code quality analysis in open-source software development. *Information Systems Journal* 11 (4): 261–274.

Steven, W. R. 1994. *TCP/IP Illustrated: The Protocols (APC)*. Reading, MA: Addison-Wesley.

Stutz, D. 2003. Advice to Microsoft regarding commodity software. Available from: http://www.synthesist.net/writing/onleavingms.html.

Stutz, D. 2004a. The natural history of software platforms. Available from: http://www.synthesist.net/writing/software_platforms.html.

Stutz, D. 2004b. Some implications of software commodification. Available from: http://www.synthesist.net/writing/commodity_software.html.

Taschek, J. 1999. Vendor seeks salvation by giving away technology [accessed 17 December 1999]. Available from: http://www.zdnet.com/pcweek/stories/news/ 0,4153,404867,00.html (no longer on line).

Taschek, J. 2002. Can the LSB resist industry pressure? *eWeek.com.* Available from: http://www.eweek.com/article2/0,3959,485538,00.asp.

The Tao of IETF. 2001. A novice's guide to the Internet Engineering Task Force. RFC 3160. August. Available from: http//www.faqs.org/rfcs/rfc3160.html.

Thompson, K. 1999. Unix and beyond: An interview with Ken Thompson. *IEEE Computer* (5): 58–64.

Thörn, Håkan. 1997. *Modernitet, sociologi och sociala rörelser.* (Monograph from the Department of Sociology, Göteborg University (62).)

Torvalds, L., and Diamond, D. 2001. *Just for fun: The story of an accidental revolutionary.* New York: Harper Collins.

Touraine, A. 1981. *The voice and the eye: An analysis of social movements.* Cambridge: Cambridge University Press.

U.S. Department of Commerce, U.S. government working group on electronic commerce. 2001. "Leadership for the new millennium: Delivering on digital progress and prosperity."

Urban, G. L., and E. von Hippel. 1988. Lead user analyses for the development of new industrial products. *Management Science* 34 (5): 569–582.

U.S. Department of Labor, Bureau of Labor Statistics. 2000. *Occupational outlook handbook: 2000–2001 edition.* Washington: Government Printing Office.

Valloppillil, V. 1998. *Open source software: A (new?) development methodology* [also referred to as *The Halloween Document*] [accessed 9 November 1999]. (Unpublished working paper, Microsoft Corporation.) Available from: http://www.opensource.org/ halloween/halloween1.html.

van Maanen, J., and S. R. Barley. 1984. Occupational communities: Culture and control in organizations. *Research in Organizational Behavior* 6:287–365.

Varian, H. 2002. System reliability and free riding. Available from: http:// www.sims.berkeley.edu/resources/affiliates/workshops/econsecurity/econws/49.pdf.

Vitalari, N., and G. Dickson. 1983. Problem solving for effective systems analysis: An experimental exploration. *Communications of the ACM* 11:948–956.

Vixie, P. 1999. Software engineering. In *Open sources: Voices from the open source revolution*, C. Dibona, S. Ockman, and M. Stone, eds. Sebastopol, CA: O'Reilly.

von Hippel, E. 1986. Lead users: A source of novel product concepts. *Management Science* 32 (7): 791–805.

von Hippel, E. 1988. *The sources of innovation*. New York: Oxford University Press.

von Hippel, E. 1994. Sticky information and the locus of problem solving: Implications for innovation. *Management Science* 40 (4): 429–439.

von Hippel, E. 2001a. Innovation by user communities: Learning from open source software. *Sloan Management Review* 42 (4): 82–86.

von Hippel, E. 2001b. Perspective: User toolkits for innovation. *Journal of Product Innovation Management* 18:247–257.

von Hippel, E. 2002. Horizontal innovation networks—by and for users. MIT Sloan School of Management (April). Available from: http://opensource.mit.edu/papers/vonhippel3.pdf.

von Hippel, E. 2005. *Democratizing innovation*. Cambridge, MA: MIT Press.

von Hippel, E., and S. N. Finkelstein. 1979. Analysis of innovation in automated clinical chemistry analyzers. *Science & Public Policy* 6 (1): 24–37.

von Hippel, E., and G. von Krogh. 2003. Open source software and the private-collective innovation model: Issues for organization science. *Organization Science* March–April 14 (2): 209–223.

von Krogh, G., S. Spaeth, and K. R. Lakhani. 2003. Community, joining, and specialization in open source software innovation: A case study. *Research Policy* 32:1217–1241.

Wall, L. 1999. The origin of the camel lot in the breakdown of the bilingual Unix. *Communications of the ACM* 42 (4): 40–41.

Wayner, P. 2000. *Free for all: How Linux and the free software movement undercut the high-tech titans*. New York: HarperBusiness.

Weber, M. 1946. Science as vocation. In *From Max Weber: Essays in sociology*. Translated, edited, and with an introduction by H. H. Gerth and C. Wright Mills. New York: Oxford University Press.

Weber, S. 2000. *The political economy of open source software*. BRIE Working Paper 140, E-conomy Project Working Paper 15 (June). Available from: http://economy.berkeley.edu/publications/wp/wp140.pdf.

Wellman, B., J. Boase, and W. Chen. 2002. *The networked nature of community on and off the Internet*. (Working paper, Centre for Urban & Community Studies, University of Toronto, May.)

Whalley, P. 1986. Markets, managers, and technical autonomy. *Theory and Society* 15: 223–247.

Whalley, P., and S. R. Barley. 1997. Technical work in the division of labor: Stalking the wily anomaly. In *Between craft and science: Technical work in U.S. settings*, S. R. Barley and Julian E. Orr, eds. Ithaca, NY: Cornell University Press.

Wiegers, K. 2002. *Peer reviews in software: A practical guide.* Boston, MA: Addison-Wesley.

Wikipedia. 2003. *The free encyclopedia* [accessed 17 February 2003]. Available from: http://www.wikipedia.com/wiki/Hacker.

Williams, S. 2000. Learning the ways of Mozilla. Upside Today. Available from: http://www.upside.com/texis/mvm/story?id=39e360180 (no longer published).

Williams, S. 2002. *Free as in freedom: Richard Stallman's crusade for free software.* Sebastopol, CA: O'Reilly.

Winton, D., G. P. Zachary, J. Halperin, and PBS Home Video. 2000. *Code rush.* Winton/duPont Films: distributed by PBS Home Video. San Jose, CA. Available from: http://scolar.vsc.edu:8004/VSCCAT/ACZ-6594.

Witten, B., C. Landwehr, and M. Caloyannides. 2000. Will open source really improve security? 2000 Symposium on Security and Privacy (oral presentation only), May 2000, Oakland, CA. IEEE Computer Society. Available from: http://www.csl.sri.com/neumann/witten.pdf.

Woodruff, D. 1999. *Money unmade: Barter and the fate of Russian capitalism.* Ithaca, NY: Cornell University Press.

Yeh, C. 1999. Mozilla tree verification process. Available from: http://www.mozilla. org/build/verification.html.

Zawinski, J. 1999. Resignation and postmortem. Available from: http://www.jwz.org/ gruntle/nomo.html.

Zhao, L., and S. Elbaum. 2000. A survey of quality-related activities in open source. *Software Engineering Notes.* May, 54–57.

Zoebelein, H. U. 1999. The Internet Operating System Counter. Available from http://www.leb.net/hzo/ioscount/.

List of Contributors

About the Editors

Joseph Feller   PhD is a Senior Lecturer in Business Information Systems at University College Cork, Ireland. He has chaired the annual international Open Source Software Engineering workshop series since it was established at ICSE in 2001. He is the coauthor, with Brain Fitzgerald, of *Understanding Open Source Software Development* (Addison-Wesley, 2002). His research on free/open source software has been presented in international journals and conference proceedings, and he has served as guest editor (again with Fitzgerald) for F/OSS special issues of *Information Systems Journal, IEE Proceedings–Software* (with Andre van der Hoek), and *Systèmes d'Information et Management* (with Frederic Adam). Joseph received his PhD from UCC, and a BA from American University.

Brian Fitzgerald   holds the endowed Frederick A. Krehbiel II Chair in Innovation in Global Business and Technology, at the University of Limerick, Ireland, where he is also a research fellow and a Science Foundation Ireland investigator. He has a PhD from the University of London and has held positions at University College Cork, Ireland, Northern Illinois University, U.S., the University of Gothenburg, Sweden, and Northumbria University, UK. His publications include seven books and more than 60 papers published in leading international conferences and journals. Having worked in the industry prior to taking up an academic position, he has more than 20 years experience in the IS field.

Scott A. Hissam   is a senior member of the technical staff for the Software Engineering Institute at Carnegie Mellon University, where he conducts research on component-based software engineering and open source software. He is also an adjunct faculty member of the University of Pittsburgh. His previous publications include one book, papers published in international journals including *IEEE Internet Computer* and the *Journal of Software Maintenance*, and numerous technical reports published by CMU. Prior to his position at the SEI, Hissam held positions at Lockheed Martin, Bell Altantic, and the U.S. Department of Defense. He has a bachelor of science degree in computer science from West Virginia University.

Karim R. Lakhani is a doctoral candidate in management at the MIT Sloan School of Management and a strategy consultant with the Boston Consulting Group. He is a cofounder of the MIT Open Source Research Project and runs the MIT-based Open Source Research Community Web portal. His research at MIT is focused on the management of technological innovation with a specific focus on coordination and innovation in open source communities and firms. His work at BCG is at the intersection of emerging technologies, intellectual property and new organization forms. He has a bachelor's degree in electrical engineering and management from McMaster University, Canada, and a masters in technology and policy from MIT. Previously he worked at GE Medical Systems.

About the Contributors

Philippe Aigrain is the founder and CEO of the Society for Public Information Spaces (www.sopinspace.com), a venture specializing in free software tools and services for Internet-based public debate on policy issues. Prior to that, he worked for the Information Society DG of the European Commission where he coordinated actions related to F/OSS until April 2003. He was trained as a mathematician and computer scientist, and has researched subjects such as compilers, interaction with audiovisual media, and the sociology of information exchanges.

Ross Anderson was one of the founders of the study of information security economics and chairs the Foundation for Information Policy Research. A fellow of the IEE, he was also one of the pioneers of peer-to-peer systems, of API attacks on cryptographic processors, and of the study of hardware tamper-resistance. He was one of the inventors of Serpent, a finalist in the competition to find an advanced encryption standard. He is Professor of Security Engineering at the Computer Laboratory, Cambridge University, and wrote the standard textbook *Security Engineering—A Guide to Building Dependable Distributed Systems* (Wiley).

Magnus Bergquist is associate professor in cultural anthropology, Göteborg University. He was written several papers and book chapters on open source and free software communities with special focus on the social, cultural, and symbolic issues in F/OSS communities related to organization, identity, power, knowledge sharing, gift giving, and cooperation.

Michael A. Cusumano is the Sloan Management Review Distinguished Professor at the MIT's Sloan School of Management. He specializes in strategy, product development, and entrepreneurship in the computer software industry, as well as automobiles and consumer electronics. Professor Cusumano received a BA degree from Princeton in 1976 and a PhD from Harvard in 1984. He completed a postdoctoral fellowship in production and operations management at the Harvard Business School during 1984–1986. Professor Cusumano is the author or coauthor of eight books. His most recent book, *The Business of Software*, was published in spring 2004.

Jean-Michel Dalle is an adjunct professor with the University Pierre-et-Marie-Curie and a researcher with IMRI-Dauphine, both in Paris. He specializes in the economics of innovation, and since 1998 he has been studying open source software. In this respect, his contributions have focused on competitive changes in software markets, open source business models and the current evolutions of the software industry, and the dynamics of open source communities. Most of these research activities have been realized in the context of collaborative projects sponsored by the Réseau National des Technologies Logicielles (RNTL, France), the Sixth Framework Programme (FP6, EU) and the National Science Foundation (NSF, United States).

Paul A. David is known internationally for his contributions to economic history, economic and historical demograhy, and the economics of science and technology. A pioneering practitioner of the so-called new economic history, his research has illuminated the phenomenon of path dependence in economic processes. Two lines in David's research—one on the ways that "history matters" in the evolution of network technology standards, and the other on the organization of scientific research communities (including the impacts of IPR policies upon "open science")—recently have coalesced in his undertaking of an extensive international collaborative program of research on free/libre and open source software development. During the past decade David has divided his time between Stanford University, where he is professor of economics and a senior fellow of the Stanford Institute for Economic Policy Research (SIEPR), and the University of Oxford, where he is a senior fellow of the Oxford Internet Institute and an emeritus fellow of All Souls College.

Roy T. Fielding is chief scientist at Day Software and a member, cofounder, and former chairman of The Apache Software Foundation. He is best known for his work in developing and defining the modern World Wide Web infrastructure by authoring the Internet standards for HTTP and URI, defining the REST architectural style, and founding several open source software projects related to the Web. Dr. Fielding received his PhD degree in information and computer science from the University of California, Irvine, and serves as an elected member of the W3C Technical Architecture Group.

Rishab Aiyer Ghosh is founding international and managing editor of *First Monday*, the most widely read peer-reviewed on-line journal of the Internet. He is programme leader at MERIT/International Institute of Infonomics at the University of Maastricht, Netherlands, and has published over a million words on the socioeconomics, law, and technology of the Internet for newsletters, journals, and magazines around the world. He speaks frequently at conferences on the socioeconomics of the Internet and free/open source software, most recently at the UNCTAD Commission, Geneva, and the Business Council for the UN, New York. He published one of the first surveys of open source code authorship based on an automated source code scan (the Orbiten Free Software Survey, 1999–2000), a major source code survey of 25,000 open source projects as part of the FLOSS Project in 2002, and the Linux: Chronology of Kernel Sources (LICKS) project together with Stanford University. He continues to collaborate on joint research related to open source metrics and productivity with Stanford University supported by the U.S. National Science Foundation.

Daniel M. German is assistant professor at the University of Victoria, Canada. His areas of research are the design of hypermedia applications, the formal specification of hypermedia and software systems, and the evolution of open source software. He obtained his PhD from the University of Waterloo in 2000.

Robert L. Glass is president of Computing Trends, publishers of *The Software Practitioner*. He has been active in the field of computing and software for over 45 years, largely in industry (1954–1982 and 1988–present), but also as an academic (1982–1988). He is the author of 25 books and over 90 papers on computing subjects, editor of *The Software Practitioner,* editor emeritus of Elsevier's *Journal of Systems and Software,* and a columnist for several periodicals including *Communications of the ACM* (the "Practical

Programmer" column) and *IEEE software* ("The Loyal Opposition"). He was for 15 years a lecturer for the ACM, and was named a fellow of the ACM in 1998. He received an honorary PhD from Linkoping University in Sweden in 1995. He describes himself by saying "my head is in the academic area of computing, but my heart is in its practice."

James Herbsleb is associate professor of computer science at Carnegie Mellon University. His research focuses primarily on communication and coordination in large software projects, including geographically distributed commercial and open source developments. He has a PhD in psychology from the University of Nebraska, and completed an MS in computer science and a postdoctoral research fellowship at the University of Michigan. His research includes both empirical studies and the design and deployment of collaboration technologies.

Niels Jørgensen is associate professor at Roskilde University, Denmark. He is interested in open source (of course) and in technologies for data security, such as encryption, and how they are shaped by scientific, technical, and social processes. He has studied cultural sociology and mathematics and earned a PhD in computer science in 1992.

Christopher Kelty is an assistant professor in the Department of Anthropology at Rice University. His undergraduate degree is from the University of California, Santa Cruz, and his PhD in the history and social study of science and technology is from MIT. Kelty has studied telemedicine professionals and the political economy of information in healthcare; the free software and open source movements; cultural aspects of intellectual property law; and the ethics and politics of research in computer science and in nanotechnology. He is a core participant in the Connexions project (an open content educational commons).

Sandeep Krishnamurthy is associated professor of e-commerce and marketing at the University of Washington, Bothell. He obtained his PhD from the University of Arizona in marketing and economics. He has developed and taught several innovative courses related to e-commerce to both MBA and undergraduate students and has written extensively about e-commerce. Most recently, he has published a 450-page MBA textbook titled *E-Commerce Management: Text and Cases*. His scholarly work on e-commerce has appeared in journals such as the *Journal of Consumer Affairs*, the *Journal of Computer-Mediated Communication*, the *Quarterly Journal of E-Commerce*, *Marketing Management*, *First Monday*, the *Journal of Marketing Research*, and the *Journal of Service Marketing*. His writings in the business press have appeared on Clickz.com, Digitrends.net, and Marketingprofs.com. His comments have been featured in press articles in outlets such as *Marketing Computers, Direct Magazine, Wired.com, Medialifemagazine.com,* Oracle's *Profit Magazine,* and the *Washington Post.* Sandeep also works in the areas of generic advertising and nonprofit marketing.

Mark Lawford is an assistant professor with the Department of Computing And Software, MacMaster University. He was awarded the PhD by the University of Toronto. Formerly, he was a contractor at Ontario Hydro performing formal verification of the Darlington Nuclear Generating Station Shutdown System Trip Computer Software, during which time he was a corecipient of an Ontario Hydro New Technology award. His research interests fall under the general heading of control of discrete event systems (DES) and in particular formal methods for real-time systems (synthesis, verification, and model reduction), supervisory control of both nondeterministic and probabilistic DES, and hybrid systems. Mark is a licensed professional engineering in the province of Ontario.

Josh Lerner is the Jacob H. Schiff Professor of Investment Banking at Harvard Business School, with a joint appointment in the finance and the entrepreneurial management units. He graduated from Yale with a special divisional major that combined physics with the history of technology. He worked for several years on issues concerning technological innovation and public policy at the Brookings Institution, for a public-private task force in Chicago, and on Capitol Hill. He then undertook his graduate study at Harvard's Economics Department. His research focuses on the structure of venture capital organizations and the impact of intellectual property protection, particularly patents, on the competitive strategies of firms in high-technology industries. He is a research associate in the National Bureau of Economic Research's Corporate Finance and Productivity Programs and serves as coorganizer of the Innovation Policy and the Economy Group, coeditor of their publication *Innovation Policy and the Economy,* organizer of the Entrepreneurship Working Group, as well as serving a variety of administrative roles at Harvard.

Lawrence Lessig is a professor of law at Stanford Law School and founder of the school's Center for Internet and Society. Prior to joining the Stanford faculty, he was the Berkman Professor of Law at Harvard Law School. Lessig was also a fellow at the Wissenschaftskolleg zu Berlin, and a professor at the University of Chicago Law School. He clerked for Judge Richard Posner on the 7th Circuit Court of Appeals and Justice Antonin

Scalia on the United Sates Supreme Court. More recently, Professor Lessig represented Web site operator Eric Eldred in the groundbreaking case Eldred v. Ashcroft, a challenge to the 1998 Sonny Bono Copyright Term Extension Act. Lessig was named one of *Scientific American's* Top 50 Visionaries, for arguing "against interpretations of copyright that could stifle innovation and discourse online." He is the author of *The Future of Ideas* and *Code and Other Laws of Cyberspace*. He also chairs the Creative Commons project. Professor Lessig is a board member of the Electronic Frontier Foundation, a board member of the Center for the Public Domain, and a commission member of the Penn National Commission on Society, Culture, and Community at the University of Pennsylvania. Professor Lessig earned a BA in economics and a BS in management from the University of Pennsylvania, an MA in philosophy from Cambridge, and a JD from Yale.

Jan Ljungberg is associate professor in informatics, School of Economics and Commercial Law, Göteborg University. He is also leader of the knowledge management group at the Viktoria Institute. Ljungberg has written several papers on free and open source software communities and is mainly concerned with organizational and social aspects of F/OSS as well as the impact of F/OSS movements on commercial and public organizations and the network society at large.

Jason Matusow is manager of the Shared Source Initiative at Micro-soft Corp. The Shared Source Initiative has established the companywide policy and framework regarding the sharing of Microsoft's most valuable intellectual property assets including Windows®, Windows CE.NET®, and .NET® technologies. Matusow also consults with governments, corporations, academics, and analysts globally on the business implications of software intellectual property issues.

David McGowan is an associate professor of law and Julius E. Davis Professor of Law (2003–2004) at the University of Minnesota Law School. He studies and writes about the legal regulation of technology. In addition to the legal and economic aspects of open source development, he has written on topics such as the regulation of expressive uses of code, optimal rules for governing Website access, the foundations of copyright policy, and the role of competition policy in network markets. Before joining the UMLS faculty, he practiced law in San Francisco.

Audris Mockus conducts research of complex dynamic systems by designing data mining methods to summarize and augment the system evolution data, interactive visualization techniques to inspect, present, and control the systems, and statistical models and optimization techniques to understand the systems. He received BS and MS in applied mathematics from Moscow Institute of Physics and Technology in 1988 and in 1994, he received PhD in statistics from Carnegie Mellon University. He works at the Software Technology Research Department of Avaya Labs. Previously, he worked at the Software Production Research Department of Bell Labs.

Peter G. Neumann has doctorates from Harvard and Darmstadt. After 10 years at Bell Labs in Murray Hill, New Jersey in the 1960s, he has been in SRI's computer science lab since September 1971. He is concerned with computer systems and networks, trustworthiness/dependability, high assurance, security, reliability, survivability, safety, and many risks-related issues such as voting-system integrity, crypto policy, social implications, and human needs including privacy. Neumann moderates the Association for Computing Machinery (ACM) Risks Forum, edits *Communication of the ACM's* monthly Inside Risks column, chairs the ACM Committee on Computers and Public Policy, and chairs the National Committee for Voting Integrity (http://www.epic.org/privacy/voting). He cofounded People For Internet Responsibility (PFIR, http://www.PFIR.org) and cofounded the Union for Representative International Internet Cooperation and Analysis (URIICA, http://www.URIICA.org). His book, *Computer-Related Risks*, is in its fifth printing. He is fellow of the ACM, IEEE, and AAAS, and is also an SRI Fellow. The 2002 recipient of the National Computer System Security Award, he is a member of the U.S. General Accounting Office Executive Council on Information Management and Technology, and the California Office of Privacy Protection advisory council. He has taught at Stanford, University of California, Berkeley, and the University of Maryland.

Siobhán O'Mahony is assistant professor at the Harvard Business School. She holds a PhD from Stanford University in management science and engineering, specializing in organizational studies. Her research, based on interviews and observations of more than 80 leaders in the free software and open source software movements, examined how community-managed software projects designed governance structures while negotiating new rules for collaboration with firms. O'Mahony's future research will examine how firms manage their collaboration with community-managed projects and how, when contributing to shared platforms, firms articulate what will be shared and what will be unique to the firm.

Tim O'Reilly is founder and CEO of O'Reilly Media, thought by many to the best computer book publisher in the world. In addition to publishing pioneering books like Ed Krol's *The Whole Internet User's Guide and Catalog* (selected by the New York Public Library as one of the most significant books of the twentieth century), O'Reilly has also been a pioneer in the popularization of the Internet. O'Reilly's Global Network Navigator site (GNN, which was sold to America Online in September 1995) was the first Web portal and the first true commercial site on the World Wide Web. O'Reilly continues to pioneer new content development on the Web via its O'Reilly Network affiliate, which also manages sites such as Perl.com and XML.com. O'Reilly's conference arm hosts the popular Perl Conference, the Open Source Software Convention, and the O'Reilly Emerging Technology Conference. Tim has been an activist for Internet standards and for open source software. He has led successful public relations campaigns on behalf of key Internet technologies, helping to block Microsoft's 1996 limits on TCP/IP in NT Workstation, organizing the "summit" of key free software leaders where the term "open source" was first widely agreed upon, and, most recently, organizing a series of protests against frivolous software patents. Tim received Infoworld's Industry Achievement Award in 1998 for his advocacy on behalf of the open source community.

David Lorge Parnas   is professor of software engineering, SFI fellow and director of the Software Quality Research Laboratory at the University of Limerick and on leave from McMaster University in Canada. He received his BS MS and PhD degrees in electrical engineering from Carnegie Mellon University and honorary doctorates from the ETH is Zurich and the Catholic University of Louvain. Dr. Parnas has been contributing to software engineering literature for more than 30 years. He is a fellow of the Royal Society of Canada, the Canadian Academy of Engineering, and the Association for Computing Machinery (ACM) and is licensed as a professional engineer in Ontario.

Jason Robbins   founded the GEF and ArgoUML open source projects as part of his research on the usability and adoption of software engineering tools. From 1999 until 2003, he played a key role in the development of Collab-Net's SourceCast$^{(tm)}$ collaborative development environment. Dr. Robbins is currently a lecturer at the School of Information and Computer Science at the University of California, Irvine, and a leader in the Tigris.org software development community. His latest project is ReadySET, an open source set of ready-to-use templates for software engineering project documents.

Srdjan Rusovan   was born in Belgrade in 1968. He graduated from the Faculty of Electrical Engineering, University of Belgrade, and worked with Alcatel Telecom Yugoslavia as an electrical engineer for the past several years. Srdjan holds an MSc in Computer Science from McMaster University, Ontario. His master's thesis was *Software Inspection of the Linux*

Implementation of TCP/IP Networking Protocols (Address Resolution Protocol, Point to Point Protocol) Using Advanced Software Inspection Techniques. Srdjan is employed as a software analyst in Alcatel Transport Automation Solutions in Toronto.

Clay Shirky divides his time between consulting, teaching, and writing on the social and economic effects of Internet technologies. He is an adjunct professor in NYU's graduate interactive telecommunications program (ITP). Prior to his appointment at NYU, Mr. Shirky was a partner at the international investment firm The Accelerator Group in 1999–2001. The Accelerator Group was focused on early stage firms, and Mr. Shirky's role was technological due diligence and product strategy. He was the original professor of new media in the media studies department at Hunter College, where he created the department's first undergraduate and graduate offerings in new media and helped design the current MFA in integrated media arts program. Mr. Shirky has written extensively about the Internet since 1996. Over the years, he has had regular columns in *Business 2.0 FEED, OpenP2P.com* and *ACM Net Worker*, and his writings have appeared in the *New York Times*, the *Wall Street Journal*, the *Harvard Business Review, Wired, Release 1.0, Computerworld*, and *IEEE Computer*. He has been interviewed by *Slashdot, Red Herring, Media Life*, and the *Economist's* Ebusiness Forum. He has written about biotechnology in his "After Darwin" column in *FEED* magazine and serves as a technical reviewer for O'Reilly's bioinformatics series. He helps program the "Biological Models of Computation" track for O'Reilly's emerging technology conferences. Mr. Shirky frequently speaks on emerging technologies at a variety of forums and organizations, including PC Forum, the Internet Society, the Department of Defense, the BBC, the American Museum of the Moving Image, the Highlands Forum, the Economist Group, Storewidth, the World Technology Network, and several O'Reilly conferences on peer-to-peer, open source, and emerging technology.

Anna Maria Szczepanska is a PhD student in sociology at Göteborg University and part of the knowledge management group at the Viktoria Institute. She has written several papers that focus on aspects within the open source and free software movement such as cultural politics and collective identity. Her forthcoming thesis deals with questions on how to understand the open source/free software phenomenon from a social movement perspective.

Jean Tirole is scientific director of the Institut d'Economie Industrielle, University of Social Sciences, Toulouse. He is also affiliated with CERAS,

Paris, and MIT, where he holds a visiting position. Before moving to Toulouse in 1991, he was professor of economics at MIT. In 1998, he was president of the Econometric Society, whose executive committee he has served on since 1993. He is president-elect of the European Economic Association. Tirole received a Doctorate Honoris Causa from the Free University in Brussels in 1989, the Yrjö Jahnsson prize of the European Economic Association in 1993, and the Public Utility Research Center Distinguished Service Award (University of Florida) in 1997. He is a foreign honorary member of the American Academy of Arts and Sciences (1993) and of the American Economic Association (1993). He has also been a Sloan Fellow (1985) and a Guggenheim Fellow (1988). Tirole has published over a hundred professional articles in economics and finance, as well as six books. He received his PhD in economics from MIT in 1981, engineering degrees from Ecole Polytechnique, Paris (1976) and from Ecole Nationale des Ponts et Chaussées, Paris (1978) and a "Doctorat de 3ème cycle" in decision mathematics from the University Paris IX (1978).

Eric von Hippel is professor and head of the Innovation and Entrepreneurship Group at the MIT Sloan School of Management. His research examines the sources and economics of innovation, with a particular focus on the significant role played by users in the innovation development process. His most recent work explores how innovating users collaborate in voluntary innovation development groups as in the case of open source software development projects.

Charles B. Weinstock is a senior member of the technical staff at the Software Engineering Institute in Pittsburgh in the Performance Critical Systems initiative. He has a PhD in computer science, an MBA, and a BS in mathematics, all from Carnegie Mellon University. Dr. Weinstock's current interests are in the area of dependable computing.

Robert G. Wolf is a consultant with The Boston Consulting Group, where he is part of the Strategy practice initiative and currently leads BCG's networks practice. Since joining BCG in 1985, Wolf has led many projects focused on innovation, including emerging technologies, knowledge management, multimedia training, collaborative learning, intellectual property, and motivation. In his consulting practice, he has applied his thinking to businesses in many industries. He has a BA in economics and history from Duke University and PhD in economics from the University of Pennsylvania. Prior to joining BCG, he held faculty positions at Boston University and Tufts University.

Index

Academic development, 335–336
Acrobat Reader, 334
Adams, Rick, 470
Adbusting, 439
Address Resolution Protocol (ARP), 113–120
Adhocracy, 229
Adobe Systems, 334
Agent-based modeling, 297, 304, 323
Agnostos, 293
AGNULA project, 450
Allchin, Jim, 441, 465
AllCommerce, 145, 147
Allman, Eric, 62
Allocating resources, 297–323
  agent-based modeling, 297, 304, 323
  C-mode/I-mode production, 306
  commercial software, 306–307, 322
  effort endowments, 310–312, 321
  microbehaviors, 320
  modularity, 308–309, 311
  motivation, 304–305
  problem choice, 309
  release policies, 314, 316–318, 320–321
  reputational rewards, 306–309, 314, 322
  simulation, 309–315
  social utility measurements, 315–317
  user needs, 321–322
Alpha testing, 132
Altruism, 48

Alumni effect, 59
Amazon.com, 293, 466, 472–473, 476
American Airlines, 477
AMOS project, 450
Anders, Mark, 471
Anderson theorem, 128
Ant, 257–258
Apache Group (AG), 171–172
Apache server, 99, 171–188, 293, 469, 475
  code ownership, 181–182, 186–187
  and commercial projects, 179–181, 183–184
  Concurrent Version Control Archive (CVS), 167–168, 175
  coordination mechanisms, 204
  core developers, 55, 149, 172, 177–179, 186–187, 206
  defects, 182–184, 187–188
  developer contributions, 145, 147, 155–156, 176–181, 403
  development process, 171–176
  distribution, 164
  and IBM, 333
  leadership, 65, 157
  licensing, 367, 402
  mailing list, 167, 172–173
  and Mozilla, 192, 195–200, 207–208
  Problem Reporting Database (BUGDB), 168, 172–173, 176, 181, 184, 204

Apache server (cont.)
 releases, 175
 reputational benefits, 61–62
 resolution interval, 184–185
 robustness, 288
 testing, 174, 187–188
 Usenet newsgroups, 173
 as user innovation network, 267–268
Apache Software Foundation, 398, 402–404
Apple Computer, 333
ArgoUML, 259
ARP cache, 113–114
ARP packet, 113–115
Art of Computer Programming, The, 426
ASP.Net, 471
AT&T, 51, 469
@LIS programme, 455
ATMs, 135
Auction equivalence, 128–130
Autoconf, 257
Automake, 257
Aviation industry, 335–336

B News, 470
Babbage, Charles, 477
Backward compatibility, 70
Baker, Mitchell, 189, 209
Ballmer, Steve, 441
Barnesandnoble.com, 473
"Bazaar" metaphor, 86–87, 94–95, 303, 317, 442–443
BCG/OSDN survey, 25, 31
Behlendoft, Brian, 61–62, 69, 471
Benkler, Yochai, 451
Berkeley Conundrum, 101
Berkeley Internet Name Daemon (BIND), 467, 469
Berkeley System Distribution (BSD), 230, 280, 367. *See also* FreeBSD
Berners-Lee, Tim, 475
Beta testing, 132, 134, 138
BIND, 467, 469

Bioelectric field mapping, 428–429
Black box, F/OSS as, 151–153
Blackboard, 295
Bloaty code, 182–183
Bostic, Keith, 62
Boston Consulting Group, 25
Bouquet du Libre Prime Minister agency action, 448
Boyle, Robert, 418–420
Brooks, Fred, 109–110, 120, 235
Brooks Law, 95, 109–110
BSD, 230, 280, 367. *See also* FreeBSD
Bug. *See* Debugging
Bugzilla, 168–169, 190–191, 202, 254
Build systems, 237, 257–259
Burney, Derek, 92
Business models, OSS, 157, 279–296
 advantages/disadvantages, 287–289
 community as producer, 280–282
 competition, 294–295
 costs and performance, 293
 distributors, 282–283
 GPL, 284
 marketing, 295
 non-GPL, 283
 profit potential, 289–295
 third-party service provider, 285–286

C language, 215
Cache, ARP, 113–114
Caldera/SCO, 279, 282, 294
Career concern incentive, 58
Carrasco-Munoz, Jordi, 455
CASE tools, 245–246
Castor, 259
"Cathedral and bazaar" metaphor, 86–87, 94–95, 303, 317, 442–443
Cathedral and Bazaar, The, 317, 484
Checkstyle, 261
Chief Programmer Team (CPT), 96
Christensen, Clayton, 466–467, 469
Cisco, 467
Citation indexing, 422, 426–427

Citibank, 127
Closed source software (CSS), 358. *See also* Commercial software
Code. *See* Source code
Code and Other Laws of Cyberspace, 474
Code generation tools, 259–260
Code sharing, 336–338, 469, 478–479
  commercial software, 66–69, 336–337
  history, 50–51
  licensing, 342
  network-enabled collaboration, 469
  Shared Source Initiative, 329–331, 338–344
  user innovation networks, 273–274
Codestriker, 261
Collab.Net, 69, 96, 333, 471
Collaborative development environment (CDE), 248, 262–264
Collaborative writing, 484–485
Collective identity, 432
Commercial software, 331–335
  allocating resources, 306–307, 322
  and Apache server, 179–181, 183–184
  code escrow, 154
  code review, 252
  code sharing, 66–69, 336–337
  and commoditization, 466–467
  competition, 295
  coordination mechanisms, 203–204
  derived product, 283
  development process, 157, 170–171
  in Europe, 447
  and F/OSS, 66–69, 104, 123–124, 127–140, 146, 150–156, 331–335
  functionality, 250–251
  LGPL, 366–367
  motivation, 59–61, 66–69, 248
  and Mozilla browser, 196, 198
  releases, 251
  requirements, 123–124, 149, 247
  reuse, 250
  service, 285–286
  standardization, 249, 465
  testing, 132, 136, 149, 156
  upgrades, 152
Commoditization, software, 463–468
Commons, 352–353, 356, 358–359, 456
Community-based intrinsic motivation, 5–6, 13–14, 16, 41–42
Compaq, 462
Compatibility, 70, 99–100
Compiler, 485–486
Component acquisition, 150–151
Computational science, 427–430
Computer-Aided Software Engineering (CASE) tools, 245–246
Concurrent Versions System (CVS), 252–253
  Apache server, 167–168, 175
  GNOME project, 214–215
Conectiva, 294
Connectivity, 27
Contract law, 367–373
Contributor distribution, 54–56
Cooperatives, 396
Copyleft, 362
Copyright, 351–352, 372–373. *See also* Intellectual property; Licensing
  Apache Software Foundation, 404
  default rule, 367–368
  derivative works, 374–382
  Digital Millennium Copyright Act, 354–355
  GPL, 362–363
  and science, 424
  television, 356–357
Core developers, 149, 172, 177–179, 186–187, 200–201, 203
COTS software. *See* Commercial software
CPAN (Comprehensive Perl Archive Network), 475
"Cracker," 85
Creative Commons, 488

Creativity
  and effort, 16–17
  and flow, 4–5, 11–12
  intrinsic motivation, 5
  and payment, 17–18
CruiseControl, 258
CSS algorithm, 355
Culture, F/OSS, 104–106
Customer applicability, 289–293
Customer support, 185, 188, 203,
  283
Customizability, software, 476–478
CVS. *See* Concurrent Versions System
  (CVS)
CyberPatrol, 372–373
Cyberspace, 354

DARPA CHATS program, 125
Debian Free Software Guidelines, 52
Debian project, 105–106, 401–402
Debugging, 84. *See also* Security
  correlated bugs, 135
  defect density, 182–184, 197–198,
  202, 205–206
  Evolution mailer, 221
  integration, 237–238
  Linux, 111
  parallel, 240–241
  proprietary vs. F/OSS, 140
  reliability growth theory, 130–131
  shared code, 341–342
  time-to-market issues, 133–134,
  136–137
  vendor response, 136–138
deCSS, 355
Defense Advanced Research Projects
  Agency (DARPA), 125, 397–398
de Icaza, Miguel, 218, 219, 221
Dell, Michael, 462
Delta, 170
Demigod, 438
Demographics, developer, 8–9, 24–25,
  30–32

Dependency analysis, 230–231
Derivative works, 283, 364–365,
  374–382
*Design and Implementation of the 4.4BSD
  Operating System, The*, 230
Design process
  commercial, 170–171
  OSS, 147–148
  tools, 259
Deutsch, L. Peter, 62
Development model, commercial,
  170–171
Development model, OSS, 148–150,
  155–158, 163–164
Dia, 259
di Cosmo, Roberto, 452
Digital, 462
Digital Millennium Copyright Act,
  354–355
Discourse analysis, 432–446
  collective identity, 432
  gift culture, 443–444
  hacker community, 433–436
  leadership, 436–438
  role of enemy, 439–442
Documentation, 116–120, 153, 343
Domain name registration, 467, 469
Domain-specific reuse, 150
Doxygen, 260
Driver development kit (DDK), 334
Duke Nukem, 376–378
Dun and Bradstreet, 378
DVDs, 355
Dynamic languages, 476–477

Eazel, 217
eBay, 472
Economic motivation. *See* Extrinsic
  motivation
Economic perspectives, FOSS, 48–73
  commercial software companies,
  66–69, 71–72
  communist/utopian, 85–87

compatibility/upgrades, 70
competition, 70
free-rider problem, 67
licensing, 51–54, 69, 71
opportunity cost, 57–58
research and development, 49–50
short-term/delayed rewards, 59–62
signaling incentive, 58–61
user groups, 48–49
Ego gratification incentive, 58
EGOVOS conferences, 455
Enhydra, 145–146
Enjoyment-based intrinsic motivation,
4–5, 12–13, 18
ERP systems, 102
European Commission, 447–448,
454
development initiatives, 455
EU resolution of 1999, 453
intellectual property rules, 450
IST program, 448–450
European Working Group on Libre
Software, 448–449
Evaluation. *See also* Security; Testing
bazaar model, 95
business strategies, 101
code review, 84, 89, 97, 146, 236,
251–252, 263, 445
design and documentation, 116–120
developer talent and leadership,
96–97, 105
forking, 88, 99–100
legal issues, 103
Linux, 107–121
modularity, 95–96, 98–99, 109–110
programmer performance, 60, 83
project initiation, 97–98
reliability and security, 84–85, 116,
130–131, 134
secondary development tasks, 99
user-friendliness, 103–104
vertical domains, 102
Evolution mailer, 218, 220–224

Extended Change Management System
(ECMS), 169–170
Extrinsic motivation, 6–7, 12–14, 16

FAQ-O-Matic, 256
FAQs, 256
Feature creep, 134, 250
Female developers, 31
Fermat, Pierre de, 350–351
File formats, 428–429
Flaming, 444–445
Flawfinder, 261
Flextronix, 468
FLOSS developer survey, 23–43
behavior, 27–28
demographics, 24–25, 30–32
monetary measures, 23–24
motivation, 26–27, 32–35, 38–42
organizational structure, 27–28, 35–37
sampling, 29–30
surveys, 24–26
FLOSS source code scan, 42
Flow state, 4–5, 11–12
Forking, 53, 58, 65, 88, 99–100
FormGen, 376–378
FreeBSD, 227–243, 463
coding, 235–236
development releases, 239–240
integration activities, 231–232,
234–235
maintainers, 232
motivation, 233–234
organization, 228–230
production releases, 241–242
reviewing, 236–237
SMP project, 234
stabilization, 241–242
FreeBSD Foundation, 399
Free Desktop group, 100
Free software, 89–90, 101, 110–111,
437
GNOME, 218
licensing, 478–479

Free Software Foundation (FSF), 51, 362, 372, 375, 397–400, 437
Free speech, 357
Free Standards Group, 100, 399
Freshmeat.net, 96–97
Friedl, Jeffrey, 476
FUD, 441
Fuzz Papers, 84

General Public License (GPL), 51–54, 71, 108, 362–366
and contracts, 367–373
copyright issues, 362–366
criticisms of, 381–383
derivative works, 282, 374–382
and intellectual property rights, 373–381, 441
LGPL, 366–367, 379
and non-GPL licenses, 284
and Web-based application vendors, 466
Gift culture, 103, 443–444
Gift-exchange systems, 420
GIMP, 148
Glass, Robert, 483
GNOME Foundation, 219–220, 399, 404–406
GNOME project, 103, 211–224
architecture, 213–214
and commercial companies, 212, 217
committees, 220
CVS repository, 214–215
Evolution mailer, 218, 220–224
internationalization, 217
modules, 214–217
programmers, 215
release coordination, 405
requirements analysis, 217–219
GNU C compiler (gcc), 470
GNUe project, 102
GNU software, 51. *See also* General Public License (GPL); Linux
Google, 293, 463, 466

Gosling, James, 318, 438
GotDotNet, 343
Government development, 335–336
Government off-the-shelf (GOTS) software, 150, 154–155
GPL. *See* General Public License (GPL)
Grace Consulting, 378
Gray, Jim, 429–430
Grepping, 425
Gump, 258
Guthrie, Scott, 471

Hacker community, 6, 14, 393–394, 410
cathedral and bazaar metaphor, 442–443
gift culture, 443–444
Jargon File, 434–436
leadership, 436–438
and Microsoft, 439–442
socialization, 433–434
Halloween documents, 436, 440
Helix, 334
Helixcode, 219, 221
Hewlett-Packard, 68–69
Hibernate, 259
Hierarchy, F/OSS, 87–89
High-profile nichers, 293
History of F/OSS, 50–54, 90–92
Hobbes, Thomas, 418–419
Hobbes measure, 41
Hofstadter, Douglas, 483
"Hold-up planétaire, un," 452
"Homesteading the Noosphere," 307
Honscheid, Jurgen, 268
Horgan, Mike, 268
HOWTOs, 256
HTML, 475

IANA, 398
IBM, 90, 441
and Apache, 333
debugging, 133
introduction of PCs, 461–462

ICCB-DARPA, 398
iCraveTV, 356–357
IDA program, 454
Ideas, nature of, 353–354
Identity, 5–6, 14, 432
IEEE Symposium on Security and
    Privacy, 125
Incentive. *See* Motivation
Incorporation, 393
Information society, 431
Information technology (IT), 431–432
Infoware, 466
Innovator's Dilemma, The, 466
Integration, software, 27, 227–228,
    230–231. *See also* FreeBSD
    incremental, 234–235
    testing, 230, 237–238, 240–241
Intel, 462, 467
Intellectual property, 336–337, 344,
    351, 373–381. *See also* Copyright;
    Licensing
    and commons, 356
    and cyberspace, 354–355
    Europe, 450, 455–456
    GPL, 373–381, 441
    and nonprofit foundations, 404, 408
    and science, 419, 421–425
Interchange of Data between
    Administrations (IDA) program, 454
Interdependency error, 230
Interface, module, 109–110, 116
Internationalization, 217, 254
Internet, 451, 463, 469, 475
    collaboration, 468–476
    TCP/IP, 112
    Usenet, 470
Internet Corporation for Assigned
    Names and Numbers (ICANN),
    397–398
Internet Engineering Task Force (IETF),
    397–398, 474
Internet operating system, 478–479
Internet Service Providers (ISPs), 467

Internet Society (ISOC), 397–398
Internet telescope, 429–430
Interoperability, 410
    copyright issues, 378–382
    Linux versions, 99–100
Intrinsic motivation, 4–6
    and creativity, 5
    enjoyment-related, 4–5, 12–13, 18
    obligation/community-based, 5–6,
        13–14, 16, 41–42
IP address, 112
Issue-tracking tools, 249, 254
IST advisory group (ISTAG), 448
IT market, 431–432

Jabber Foundation, 399
Jannson, Eddy L. O., 372–373
Jargon File, 434–436
Jargon Lexicon, 434–435
Java, 404
JavaScript: The Definitive Guide, 472–473
JCSC, 261
JDepend, 261
Jefferson, Thomas, 353–354, 356
Johnson, Chris, 428–429
Joy, William, 62, 469
JUnit, 260–261
JUnitDoclet, 260

Kapor, Mitch, 474
Kasichainula, Manoj, 209
Kay, Alan, 479
KBST report, 448
KDE League, 399
KLOCA, 182
Knuth, Donald, 426
KOffice, 280
Kolmogorov-Smirnov test, 178
Kuhn, Thomas, 461, 479
Kurzweil, Ray, 463

Languages, dynamic, 476–477
LClint, 261

Leadership, 52, 59, 63–65, 105, 157
  Apache, 65, 157
  and community support, 294
  "movement intellectuals," 436–438
Lesser General Public License (LGPL),
  366–367, 379
Lessig, Larry, 474
Leviathan and the Air Pump, 418
LGPL, 366–367, 379
Liability, 368–369, 377, 379. *See also*
  Licensing
  Apache, 402
  Debian, 401
  and nonprofit foundations, 395–396,
  408
Libre software, 447–459
  development and social inclusion,
  454–455
  end-user control, 451–452
  and European Commission, 447–448,
  454
  government policies, 453
  intellectual property, 450, 455–456
  IST program funding, 448–450
  licensing, 450–451
  and proprietary monopoly, 452–453
  security, 452
  usage, 453–454
Licensing, 154, 361–367, 469. *See also*
  Copyright; General Public License
  (GPL)
  Apache, 367, 402
  BSD, 367
  commercial/noncommercial software,
  332–335
  and contract law, 367–373
  copyleft, 362
  Creative Commons, 488
  Debian Free Software Guidelines, 52
  derivative works, 364–365, 374–382
  hijacking, 71
  intellectual property, 373–381
  international, 340

LGPL, 366–367, 379
liability, 368–369, 377, 379, 401–402
library material, 366–367
libre software, 450–451
Microsoft, 338, 342
MIT, 367
Netscape/Mozilla, 69
non-GPL, 283–284
Open Source Definition, 52–53, 61,
  361–362, 367, 479
  shared code, 342
LICKS project, 42
Lifespan, F/OSS, 70–71
Lint command, 261
Linux, 47, 63–64, 68, 107–121, 164
  ARP module, 115–120
  code quality, 97
  custom distributions, 468
  design and documentation, 116–120
  distribution, 282, 294
  foundations, 406
  and Google, 293, 463, 466
  history of, 108
  inception, 156
  and Microsoft, 147, 295
  Net initiative, 280
  and Red Hat, 333, 465, 468
  reliability/robustness, 136, 288
  and SCO Group, 103
  stable/development kernel, 111–112
  support, 288
  and Unix, 108
  version proliferation, 99–100,
  288–289
  VM subproject, 98
  and Web-based application vendors,
  466
Linux Desktop Consortium, 100
Linux International, 399
Linux Professional Institute, 398
Linux Standard Base and United Linux,
  100
Local area network, 112

Locke, John, 375
Low-profile nichers, 292

McConnell, Steve, 227
McCool, Rob, 171, 267–268
MacCVS, 252
Mailing lists, 255
Make command, 257
Makefile, 257
MapQuest, 473–474
Maps.msn.com, 473–474
Maps.yahoo.com, 473–474
Mastering Regular Expressions, 476
Mauss, Marcel, 443
Maven, 258
Mechanical Turk, 477
Merges, Robert, 370
Merton, Robert, 417, 422–423
Micro Star, 376–378
Microsoft, 478
 ASP.Net, 471
 and BSD, 280, 283
 code delivery, 343
 criticisms of OSS, 441
 DDK, 334
 debugging, 137
 and Europe, 452
 and GPL, 382–383
 and hacker community, 439–442
 Halloween documents, 436, 440
 and IBM, 462
 Internet telescope, 429–430
 licensing policy, 338, 342
 and Linux, 147, 295
 MVP initiative, 101
 and Netscape, 475
 Open Value policy, 101
 security, 127
 Shared Source Initiative, 329–331,
  338–344
 and standardization, 464–465, 477
 Windows, 136, 333, 336
Microsystems, Inc., 372–373

MIT license, 367
Modeling, agent-based, 297
Modification request (MR), 167, 170,
 214–215
Modularity, 27, 62–63, 95–96, 469
 difficulties of, 98–99
 GNOME project, 214–217
 interfaces, 109–110, 116
 and motivation, 308–309, 311
 Mozilla browser, 205
 and participation, 475
Money, 425–426
Motivation, 3–7, 12–16, 248, 443.
 See also Reputational rewards
 allocating resources, 304–305
 assumed, 26–27
 career/monetary, 39–42, 58
 commercial software, 59–61, 66–69,
  248
 determinants of effort, 16–18
 economic theory, 56–59
 extrinsic, 6–7, 12–14, 16
 FLOSS developer survey, 26–27, 32–35,
  38–42
 FreeBSD, 233–234
 and income, 6, 9–11, 15–17, 39–40
 innovation, 305–306
 intrinsic, 4–6, 12–14, 16, 18, 41–42
 and science, 415–416, 419
 short-term/delayed rewards, 59–62
 signaling incentive, 58–61, 66, 306
 social/community, 41–42
 technical professions, 394
 user needs, 6–7, 12, 16, 270–273
Movement culture, 432
Mozilla browser, 68–69, 148, 188–203
 and Apache, 192, 195–200, 207–208
 Bugzilla, 168–169, 190–191, 202,
  254
 code ownership, 196–197, 201
 and commercial projects, 196, 198
 coordination mechanisms, 204–205
 data sources, 168–169

Mozilla browser (cont.)
 defect density, 197–198, 202–203,
  205–206
 developer contributions, 192–196, 202
 development process, 189–192
 modularity, 205
 problem reporting, 190–191, 195–196
 resolution interval, 198–200
 roles and responsibilities, 190–191
 testing, 191–192
Mozilla.org toolset, 248
MSDN Code Center Premium, 343
MSN, 473–474
Murdock, Ian, 468
Mythical Man Month, The, 109, 235

NAIS, 146
Napster, 475–476, 478
National Software Research Network
 (RNTL) report, 448
NCSA, 475
Net initiative, 280
Net-negative producer (NNP), 97
Netscape, 68–69, 148, 188–189, 475.
 See also Mozilla browser
Network society, 431
Network Solutions, 467
Network-enabled collaboration,
 468–476
 code sharing, 469
 Internet, 469–470, 472–475
 system architecture, 474–476
New Hackers Dictionary, The, 434
Noncommercial software, 332
Nonprofit foundations, 393–411
 Apache Software Foundation (ASF),
  398, 402–404
 and commercial companies, 401–407
 community-corporate collaboration,
  407–411
 efficacy, 406–407
 Free Software Foundation (FSF),
  397–400

GNOME Foundation, 399, 404–406
 hosting concept, 397, 400
 and intellectual property, 404, 408
 Internet Society (ISOC), 397
 and liability, 395–396, 408
 models for, 396–400
 Open Source Initiative (OSI), 396
 and pluralism, 410–411
 Software in the Public Interest,
  401–402
Nora, Dominique, 452
Novell, 334
NUnit, 260

Object Constraint Language (OCL),
 259
Obligation/community-based intrinsic
 motivation, 5–6, 13–14, 16
Olson, Ken, 462
Online groups, 484
Open Directory Project, 475
Open science, 299–301
Open society, 349, 349–360, 360
Open Source Application Foundation,
 399
Open Source Definition, 52–53, 61,
 361–362, 367, 479
Open Source Initiative (OSI), 361, 396,
 398, 436
OpenCourse, 295
OpenOffice, 279, 295
Opportunity cost, 57–58
ORBit, 213–214
Orbiten Survey, 42
Orbitz, 293
O'Reilly, Tim, 451, 471
Organizational structure, 27–28, 35–37,
 62–67

PageRank algorithm, 473
Palladium, 451
Paradigm shift, 461–463, 479–480
Patch program, 470

PDP-10, 435
Peer review, 84, 89, 97, 146, 251–252
  FreeBSD, 236
  OSS tools, 263
  as social mechanism, 445
Perens, Bruce, 211, 361
Perl, 61, 293, 469, 475–477
Perl Foundation, 399
PHP, 476
PHPUnit, 260
Pierce, Charles, 309
PINs, 135
Power of Peonage, 82
President's Information Technology
  Advisory Committee (PITAC), 153
Privity of contract, 370–371
Producer/consumer dependency, 231
Professionalism, scientific, 299
Progeny Systems, 468
Programming skills
  evaluation of, 83
  and extrinsic motivation, 7
  and intrinsic motivation, 16
Property. *See also* Intellectual property
  and commons, 352–353
  Locke's theory of, 375
  protection of, 349, 356–357, 360
Proprietary software. *See* Commercial
  software
Proxy ARP, 115
Public domain, 352–353
Public-domain software, 52
PyCheck, 261
Python Foundation, 399
Python language, 476
PyUnit, 260

Quality assurance, 260–261

Rapid Development, 227
RapidSVN, 253
Rasterman, Carsten Haitzler, 219
RATS, 261

Raymond, Eric, 307, 317–318, 434–437,
  440, 467, 473
RealNetworks, 333–334
Recipes, 487
Red Hat, 67, 104, 217
  competition, 294
  and Linux, 333, 468
  revenues, 279
  software commoditization, 465
Regression, 257
Relative product importance, 289–293
Release policies, 67–69
  allocating resources, 314, 316–318,
  320–321
  Apache, 175
  commercial software, 251
  FreeBSD, 241–242
  GNOME, 405
  tools, 251–263
Reliability growth theory, 130–131, 134
Reputational rewards, 306–309, 314,
  322. *See also* Motivation
  Apache, 61–62
  citation indexing, 422, 426
  grepping, 425
  science, 415–416, 420–421
Requirements analysis, 102
  commercial software, 149, 247
  GNOME project, 217–219
  tools, 262
Research and development, 49–50
Resolution interval, 184–185
Resource allocation. *See* Allocating
  resources
Reuse, 150, 249–250, 260, 263–264
Revenue equivalence theorem, 129
Ritchie, Dennis, 438
Robustness, 287–288
Rocket-and-wire technique, 158

Sabre reservation system, 477
Salesforce.com, 466
Scarab, 254

Schumpeter, E. F., 465
Science, 415–430
bioelectric field mapping, 428–429
citations, 422, 426–427
and free software, 427
funding, 420–422
intellectual property, 419, 421–425
Internet telescope, 429–430
motivation, 415–416, 419
norms of, 417–418
paradigm shifts, 461
political economy of, 416
public/private, 422–423
value of, 415
Science Citation Index, 422
Scientific Computing Institute (SCI), 428
SCO Group, 103
Scripting languages, 476
Security. *See also* Debugging
code, 84–85, 125–126
industry structure, 137
libre software, 452
patches, 134
proprietary vs. F/OSS, 127–141, 146
stack overflow, 135
Sendmail, 53–54, 279, 474
Serial Line IP (SLIP), 470
Service providers, 285–286
SETI@home, 478
Shared Source Initiative, 329–331, 338–344
Shareware, 51–52
Shelfware, 246
Shirky, Clay, 475
Signaling, 55–56, 58–61
allocating resources, 306
closed source development, 66
Simmel, Georg, 425
Skala, Matthew, 372–373
Sky-TV, 136
SLIP (Serial Line IP), 470
Smoke test, 240

Software commoditization, 463–468
Software customizability, 476–478
Software development kit (SDK), 334
Software engineering, 149
Software Engineering Institute (SEI), 143
Software in the Public Interest, 398, 401–402
Source code. *See also* Code sharing; Licensing
authorship, 35, 42, 181–182, 186–187, 196–197, 201
comments, 341
commercial/noncommercial software, 332–335
compiling, 485–486
defect density, 182–184
generation tools, 259–260
modularity, 27, 62–63, 95–96, 109–110
open/closed, 358
quality, 97, 135
release, 67–69
reuse, 150
review, 84, 89, 97, 146, 236, 251–252, 263, 445
security, 84–85, 125–126
Source Code Control System (SCCS), 169–170
SourceCast, 262
SourceForge, 7, 148, 262
SourceXchange service, 96
Spectrum Object Model, 68
Splint, 261
SquirrelMail, 293
Stack overflow, 135
Stallman, Richard M., 51, 61, 318, 352, 436–438, 442, 468, 470
Standardization, 100
and commercial software, 249, 465
and commodities, 464–465
IETF, 474
Microsoft, 464–465, 477
tools, 248–249

Stanley, Larry, 268
Structure of Scientific Revolutions, The,
461
Stutz, David, 463, 465, 478
Subversion, 253
SubWiki, 256–257
Sun Microsystems, 217, 404, 468
Support services, 185, 188, 203
 distributors, 283
 documentation, 343
 Linux, 288
Surveys, 24–26
SuSe, 282, 294, 468
Symmetric Multiprocessing (SMP), 234

TCP/IP, 112, 336, 469–470
Teardrop, 146
Testing, 131–133, 141–142. *See also*
 Debugging; Evaluation
 alpha/beta, 132, 134, 138
 Apache server, 174, 187–188
 commercial software, 132, 136, 149,
 156
 hostile, 136
 integration, 230, 237–238, 240–241
 Mozilla, 191–192
 operational profile, 138
 tools, 262
Thau, Robert, 171
Thompson, Ken, 97, 438
Tiemann, Michael, 62
Tigris.org, 246–247
Tinderbox, 192, 258
Tools, OSS, 148, 245–264
 access to project artifacts, 247
 build systems, 257–259
 CDEs, 248, 248–249, 262
 design and code generation, 259–260
 functionality, 250–251
 HOWTOs, FAQs, and Wikis, 256–257
 issue-tracking, 249, 254
 mailing lists and Web sites, 255–256
 quality assurance, 260–261

releases, 251, 263
reuse, 249–250
Subversion, 253
version control, 252–253
Torque, 259
TortoiseCVS, 252
TortoiseSVN, 253
Torvalds, Linus, 62–64, 87, 98, 105, 108,
 120, 156, 288, 294, 318, 437–438, 474
TouchGraph, 293
Trade secret law, 337
Transaction costs, 134
Transient effects, 133–134
Trusted system, 354
TurboLinux, 294
Turing, Alan, 128
TWiki, 256–257

UML, 259
UnitedLinux, 294
Unix, 51, 88, 257, 435
 architecture, 464
 code sharing, 469
 and Linux, 108
Unix-Unix Copy Protocol (UUCP), 470
Upgrades, 70, 152, 283
Usability, 289
Usenet, 173, 470
User groups, 48–49
User innovation network, 267–276
 Apache server, 267–268
 conditions favoring, 270
 diffusion, 274–275
 free revealing, 273–274
 lead users, 271–273
 and manufacturers, 269–270, 276
 motivation, 270–273
 windsurfing, 268–269
User needs, 6–7, 12, 16
 customer applicability and support,
 185, 188, 203, 283, 289–293
 developers as users, 157–158
 high-end, 53–54, 60

User needs (cont.)
  libre software, 451–452
  motivation, 6–7, 12, 16, 230–233
  and participation, 475, 477
  resource allocation model, 321–322
  user-friendliness, 103–104
UUCP (Unix-Unix Copy Protocol), 470
UUnet, 470

Value, 425–426
van Rossom, Guido, 438
vDoclet, 260
Version control, 252–253
  Apache server, 167–168, 175
  GNOME project, 214–215
Version proliferation, 99–100, 288–289
Vertical domains, 102
Vietnam, 455
ViewCVS, 252
Vixie, Paul, 62
von Hippel, Eric, 487

Wall, Larry, 62, 64, 438, 470
Waugh, Jeff, 220
Web sites, OSS, 255–256
WebCT, 295
WebSphere, 333
Whine feature, 254
White box, F/OSS as, 153
WIDI survey, 30
Wiki, 256–257
Wikipedia, 475, 486
Wiles, Andrew, 350–351
WinCVS, 252
Windows, 136, 333, 336
Windsurfing, 268–269
Wings3D, 292
World Wide Web Consortium (W3C),
  397–398
Writing, collaborative, 484–485

X11, 213
XDoclet, 260

Xemacs project, 71
XenoFarm, 258
Ximian, 217, 219, 221, 280
XML, 258

Yahoo, 293, 473, 475–476
Young, Bob, 465, 468